POLITICS AND PEOPLE

The Ordeal of Self-Government in America

POLITICS AND PEOPLE

The Ordeal of Self-Government in America

THE ORIGINS
OF NATIVISM
IN THE
UNITED STATES
1800 - 1844

by

Ray Allen Billington

ARNO PRESS

A New York Times Company

New York — 1974

Reprint Edition 1974 by Arno Press Inc.

Copyright © 1974, by Ray Allen Billington
Reprinted by permission of Ray Allen Billington

POLITICS AND PEOPLE: The Ordeal
of Self-Government in America
ISBN for complete set: 0-405-05850-0
See last pages of this volume for titles.

Manufactured in the United States of America

Library of Congress Cataloging in Publication Data

Billington, Ray Allen, 1903-
    The origins of nativism in the United States, 1800-
1844.

    (Politics and people: the ordeal of self-government
in America)
    Reprint of the 1933 ed. which was originally presented
as the author's thesis, Harvard.
    1. Catholics in the United States--History.
2. Nativism. 3. American Party. 4. United States--
Politics and government--19th century. I. Title.
II. Series.
E184.C3B54   301.45'28'2073   73-19129
ISBN 0-405-05854-3

The Origins of Nativism

in

The United States

1800-1844

by

Ray Allen Billington

A Thesis
submitted in partial fulfilment
of the requirements for the degree of
Doctor of Philosophy
at
Harvard University

Cambridge
1933

CONTENTS

Preface i

I The Roots of Anti-Catholic Prejudice 1

II The No-Popery Cry is Raised, 1820-1829 49

III The First Convent is Burned, 1830-1834 111

IV The Flames Spread, 1835-1840 177

V Saving the West from the Pope, 1835-1840 246

VI Saving the Children for Protestantism,

1840-1844 325

VII The Protestant Organization is Strengthened,

1840-1844 385

VIII The Propaganda of Anti-Catholicism,

1834-1844 457

IX No-Popery Enters National Politics, 1840-1844 533

X The Philadelphia Riots of 1844 575

Appendix A 613

Appendix B 622

Bibliography 630

ILLUSTRATIONS

Facing
Page

Typical Page from the Downfall of Babylon 203

Typical Page from the Protestant Vindicator 209

Maria Monk 226
      (from the Further Disclosures of the Hotel
      Dieu Convent)

Nunnery in the Wilderness 233
      (from Smith, Samuel B., Decisive Confirma-
      tion of the Awful Disclosures of Maria
      Monk)

The Flight of Popery 287
      (from Smith, Samuel B., The Flight of
      Popery from Rome to the West)

Mother Abbess Strangling an Infant 475
      (from Hogan, William, Synopsis of Popery
      as it Was and as it Is)

Catholic Persecution 482
      (from the National Protestant, May, 1845)

Philadelphia in 1844 581
      (from The New Englander, 1844)

PREFACE

Historians who have dealt with the rise and progress of nativistic political parties before the Civil War have patterned their observations closely upon the conclusions drawn by Hermann von Holst. Von Holst, explaining all political events of the period in terms of slavery, ascribed to this factor sole credit for the creation of these peculiar political organizations. People unable to decide where to turn on the great question of slavery, he says, cast their lot with the Know Nothing party or the others which preceded it, so that they rose "like a deus ex machina" on the American scene.[1] This explanation has been the commonly accepted one since Von Holst published his findings,[2] although many of his views on other political and economic events of that time have been disputed.

It is the purpose of this study to show that the Know Nothing party and its nativistic predecessor,

1 - Von Holst, Hermann, Political and Constitutional History of the United States, (Chicago, 1885), vol. v, p. 379.
2 - Channing, Edward, History of the United States (New York, 1905), vol. vi, pp. 129-137; Rhodes, James Ford, History of the United States from the Compromise of 1850 (New York, 1920), vol. ii, pp. 7-15; Smith, Theodore C., Parties and Slavery (The American Nation Series, Albert Bushnell Hart, editor, New York, 1906), pp. 115-116.

the American Republican Party, enjoyed their phenomenal growth not because of slavery, but incidental to
it. These parties were based on opposition to the
Catholic and immigrant, and were pledged to protect
America from their influence. Hatred of foreigner
and Papist was no new thing in the 1840's and 1850's;
prejudice against them had been bred throughout the
years of America's existence as a colony and Republic.
This study attempts to trace the growth of that prejudice from its beginnings in colonial America through
the formation of the American Republican party in 1844.
It attempts to show that hatred had been bred by pulpit
and press and propaganda influencing thousands of people
and sending them into the ranks of these parties to express an honest nativistic conviction. It attempts to
prove that the American Republican party would have risen
had the question of slavery never existed, and that but
for the rise of slavery, a graver issue, just at the time
when the American Republicans were launched on the road
to success, that party might have gone ahead to continued
political triumphs.

Research has been concentrated largely in the
American Antiquarian Society, the Harvard University
Library and the Boston Public Library. Use has also

been made of the Brown University Library, the Yale
University Library, the Massachusetts Historical So-
ciety, the Burton Historical Collection and the
Worcester Historical Society.

THE ROOTS OF ANTI-CATHOLIC PREJUDICE

The stern men who shook the soil of seventeenth century England from their boots to settle the bleak coast of Massachusetts Bay were Puritans, driven from their homes in search of economic betterment, as well as religious freedom. The fact that some materialistic motive underlay the new colony made them no less Puritans. They were zealous dissenters, sharing little in common with their hearty countrymen who were already turning the wilderness that was Virginia into fertile fields of tobacco.

And these fellow Englishmen along the prospering southern coast were staunch supporters of the hated Church of England which, having failed by decree to force the Puritans to worship in a way they would not, had turned them free in a chaos of pine and granite and savage to work out their own salvation. Secure in the approved church of mother country and king, the southern colonists regarded with cold eye their solemn New England neighbors.

These two groups, disapproving of each other as they were, had a background of religious bigotry and intolerance in common. The Puritan hated most in his life

Prelacy and Popery; the Virginian hated with equal
vigor the Dissenter and the Papist.

Nor was it by mere accident that these two
isolated and struggling groups should share this hatred
of Popery and of all things connected with the name of
Rome. The England that had spawned them forth had been
an England steeped in anti-Catholic prejudice. It had
been an England not long emerged from worship before the
throne of Saint Peter and his successors, and like most
converts to a cause, it was enthusiastic about the new
and bitter against the old.

The grandfathers of the Massachusetts Bay Puritans and the Anglicans of Virginia were alive when Henry
VIII led the nation away from Rome by usurping her power
and parceling her vast lands and treasures among the
people. Their fathers had seen their country plunged
into war with Catholic France, and had shuddered at rumors of invasion and conquest to restore the hated Pope
to his former supremacy. They had trembled for their
very lives when Bloody Mary had ascended the throne and
threatened not only to return the whole land to the Catholic fold, but, by alliances with both Spain and France,
to undermine England as the power for which Prince Hal
had striven.

These settlers themselves had been cradled in

an England that felt deeply against the Pope; more
deeply than any generation before or since. They had
seen Elizabeth come to her throne to check Mary's
reign of blood, and to hail as martyrs those who had
died in the flames for their Protestant God. They
had seen, too, a rising onslaught against their queen -
an onslaught that could only be directed by the Pope
and his henchmen. There had been the uprising of the
Irish at Kerry. There had been the threatened attack
by Spanish armies headed by the Duke of Lenox from
Scotland. There had been the blows struck near at
home by the Jesuits, Champion and Parsons. There
had been the failure of the plot of 1583 to restore
Mary to the throne, and the assassination of William
the Silent only a year later. There had been the menacing Armada sent out by Catholic Spain. If any doubt
remained in the minds of these Puritans and Anglicans
that an insidious Popish plot was being carried on to
return their country to Rome, it had been dispelled
not long before they had sailed by the Gunpowder Plot
and the net of Jesuitical manipulation that surrounded
it.

By this reign of intrigue and counterplot, the
conviction had been firmly established in the minds of
the good Protestant subjects of Queen Bess that Catholi-

cism was thoroughly anti-national. Popery was feared,
not so much as a religion alone, but as an instrument
through which England itself was to be overthrown. The
continued aggressions of Catholic France and Spain upon
their country had shown them that. Catholicism was a
thing to be feared as well as hated. No sane Englishman
of the seventeenth century doubted that.

But the fear that clung to these subjects of
Queen Elizabeth and King James was a deeper one than
could be caused by attacks on English nationality alone.
People can be stirred to a frenzy of hatred when their
country is attacked, but the utter bigotry that swept
over England in these years was more subtle in its origins; more outspoken in its effects. It was an intolerance brought about by the semi-historical propaganda
that had insinuated itself into the very lives of the
people since the Reformation.

This influence that was to play such a part in
the creation of English and American anti-Catholic prejudice, had its origin in the first battle of the pens
wielded in the controversy over the Reformation. Luther's
disciples realized that profound theological arguments
over points of dogma had little appeal to the popular
mind. They realized too that upon the friendship of the
mass of the people the success of their movement must depend. The appeal that they made to the masses was the

appeal of history; to prove that the old ecclesiastical order had broken down and was steeped in corruption and inefficiency would be in itself a justification of the new.

Luther himself was heartily in favor of such a form of propaganda. He summed up his opinion in a preface to a History of the Popes from the pen of Robert Barnes in 1536: "I have been constrained by sorrow of heart, and also by legitimate rage, to pour out all this in order that I might inspire other pious and Christian souls to investigate, as much as they can be investigated, the popish tyranny and the Pope's Church. For without doubt all those who have the spirit of Christ know well that they can bring no higher or more acceptable praise offering to God than all they can say or write against this blood-thirsty, unclean, blasphemic, whore of the devil. I for my part, unversed and ill informed as I was at first with regard to history, attacked the papacy, a priori, as they say, that is, out of the Holy Scriptures. And now it is a wonderful delight to me to find that others are doing the same thing a posteriori, that is, from history - and it gives me the greatest joy and satisfaction to see, as I do most clearly, that history and Scripture entirely coincide in this respect."[1]

1 - Hay, M. V., The Chain of Error in Scottish History (New York, 1927), pp. 3-4.

So fully did Luther realize the value of
historical propaganda that he formulated the plan
for a cooperative historical work to give it weight
and circulation. This scheme was accomplished by
the organization of the scholars at Magdelburg, who,
under the direction of Falacuis Illyricus, produced
a collaborative history of the Christian Church,
which was published at Basel in 1559. A work of
considerable historical merit, the Magdelburg history nevertheless performed well the task that Luther
assigned it. It was bristling with misrepresentations
designed to discredit the Catholic church; in it appeared for the first time the legend of Popess Joan and
the story of the six thousand children's heads found
in the nunnery fish pond in the days of Gregory. I.[2]

Catholic historians were quick to refute these
errors of the Magdelburg group, but their notable work
of protest had little influence on England in the seventeenth century. The English monarchs, staunch in their
defense of Protestantism, had by this time erected an
effective barrier around the country to prohibit the
introduction of any publication which upheld the Catholic church. Under a series of laws passed during the

2 - Ibid., p. 4.

reign of Elizabeth it became a penal offense to possess
histories of the church not based on the work of the
Centuriators of Magdelburg.[3]

English colonists, as well, found their intellectual nourishment limited to this propaganda of
prejudice. During the seventeenth and eighteenth centuries several hundred historical works appeared by
English writers, all based upon the Magdelburg writings.[4]
Swept away by Catholic attacks upon the nationalism of
their country, they gave to their efforts a bitterness
and prejudice that surpassed even the inspired efforts
of Luther's disciples. By 1757 a history of the Popes,
deemed mild in its denunciation, described Popery: "I
have no interest to praise or blame the See of Rome.
Avarice, ambition, sacrilege, perjury, an absolute contempt of everything sacred, the most amazing dissolute-
ness, every species of debauchery in excess, a total depravity and corruption of doctrine and morals, character-
ize the history of the Popes."[5]

In a country so influenced, it was inevitable

3 - Ibid., p. 13.
4 - Hay has collected a list of several hundred titles
    of such works published during the seventeenth and
    eighteenth centuries.
    Ibid., p. 14. An interesting study of this anti-
    Catholic historical writing by a Catholic is in,
    Thurston, Herbert, No Popery: Chapters on Anti-
    Papal Prejudice (New York, 1930)
5 - Hay, Chain of Error in Scottish History, p. 15

that the lot of the sincere Roman Catholic should be
an unpleasant one. Legislation against worshippers
at the shrine of Rome began with the Acts of Supremacy
and Uniformity in 1559 and grew more violent as England
bore the brunt of attack by Catholic powers. In 1563
Catholics were excluded from the legal profession, from
teaching and from the universities; in 1571 it was decreed that anyone denouncing the queen as a heretic or
a schismatic was to suffer the penalty of treason. As
war with Spain drew near, priests were required to leave
the land under penalty of death on their return, and in
1593 this penalty was extended to all of their religion
who did not possess goods to a considerable amount. Even
these well-to-do Catholics were ordered to retire to their
estates and not go above five miles from them, and to attend the services of the Church of England or pay twenty
pounds each month should they refuse.[6]

     The severity of these Elizabethan laws was made
even more unbearable by a Parliament spurred to new fear
by the Gunpowder Plot. Three new laws were placed on the
statute books in 1606 and 1610 dealing with the Roman
Catholics. By these laws the fines levied against any
follower of the Pope who failed to attend services at

6 - Channing, Edward, History of the United States (New
    York, 1905), vol. i, pp. 246-247.

the Established Church regularly were increased and
it was provided in addition that much of his property
should be confiscated by the king. Catholics were
forced to take a new oath of allegiance in which they
publicly declared that the Pope had no power to depose
the English monarch or discharge any subject from allegiance to his king. Professions open to Catholics
were still further narrowed by these laws and even home
life was violated by an act requiring that "all married
recusants" should be placed in prison and kept there
until their husbands purchased their freedom by paying
fines of ten pounds each month.[7]

Had these laws been rigorously enforced, all
Catholics would have been driven from England. The tolerance of James I saved the harsh persecution that might
have come, but even with this benevolent influence the
records of one county show eleven hundred indictments
against followers of Rome in the ten years preceding
1619. In this same county an unlucky priest was captured and sentenced to the picturesque death that the
seventeenth century provided for those guilty of treason.[8]

It was from this England that the Puritans of
Massachusetts Bay and the yeomen of Virginia had come;

7 - Ibid., vol. i, pp. 247-248.
8 - Ibid., vol. i, pp. 248-250. Professor Channing has
    drawn this analysis from the records of Middlesex
    county.

an England steeped in anti-Catholic propaganda, an
England threatened constantly by Popish plots and aggressions, an England filled with sturdy Protestant
souls who hunted down priests, jailed women, seized
property, and shouted against Romanism with sincerity
and with conviction. It was this background of bigotry
and hatred that was transferred from the old world to
the new.

Once in America, these convictions were not
allowed to dim. Catholic colonists were few in numbers,
but the fact that the enemy was lacking did not lessen
the intolerance in the hearts of their Protestant neighbors. Rather did American conditions increase those convictions. In New England the long winters gave ample
time for reflection on the harm caused their native England by Romanism; in the south sparse settlement was con-
ducive to introspection on matters of religious aggression. These local factors quickened the hatred of Popery,
but especially important in keeping alive the flames of
prejudice was the distance of the colonies from the mother
country.

The colonists who came to America during the
seventeenth century were soon isolated from the intellectual streams that flowed in England and in Europe. As
time went on England sublimated her religious fervor in

her economic forays and adopted the more liberalistic
attitude of continental Europe. But Americans were out
of touch with these new currents. Their ministers were
still steeped in the prejudice against Popery that had
been the mental and emotional background of early seventeenth century England. New Englander and Virginian
listened each Sabbath to ideas that had been carried
from the mother country when the first settlers came,
and that had been handed down from father to son; from
retiring clergyman to incoming clergyman. An able study
has shown that the colonial pulpit, removed as it was
from the new liberalism, inculcated the doctrines of
the seventeenth century Puritan revolt into its listeners and sent them forth to fight a greater revolution of their own.[9] A similar study would undoubtedly
show that to these same clergymen may be attributed the
still vigorous intolerance of all that pertained to
Popery.

At the same time, the only literature available
in both the northern and southern colonies was tinged
deeply with the propaganda of No-Popery which had its
beginnings a century earlier in the Magdelburg school.
Their prejudices were deepened as they read. Bishop

9 - Baldwin, Alice M. The New England Clergy and the
    American Revolution (Durham, N. C., 1928)

England, many years later, penned an excellent description of the state of mind engendered in the people by
reading matter typical of this period: "The Pope was
an old rogue, who had a respectable pair of horns; the
city of Rome was a great big lady of pleasure, patched
and painted and drunk and dressed in scarlet. The people
of Spain were perpetually burning heretics; the French
wore wooden shoes, which were one day to serve them as
canoes, in which they were to be conveyed across the
straits of Dover, for the purpose of eating up the King
of England and the Archbishop of Canterbury."[10]

The hatred of Catholics which was continually
kindled by pulpit and propaganda was destined to conflagration. A whole series of acts were passed during the
seventeenth century against all papal adherents. Designed to restrict their personal liberty, to check them
in the practice of their religion, and to limit their
power as freemen, the statutes that found their way
through colonial legislatures had their inception in the
first days of Virginia's settlement. The charter which
was granted to the Virginia Company in 1606, together
with the charters of 1609 and 1612, stated that the colonists should be considered as Englishmen, and "obliged

10 - Catholic Miscellany, July 4, 1822. Quoted in Guil-
     day, Peter, The Life and Times of John England,
     First Bishop of Charleston, 1786-1842 (New York,
     1927), vol. ii, pp. 424-425.

to the duties attached to that character," which included conformity to the established church.[11] Not
many years later the House of Burgesses, in 1642,
moved to save themselves from the threat of Popery
by disfranchising all Catholics and threatening any
priest with expulsion within five days who dared
tread the sacred soil of Virginia.[12]

Behind this action of Virginia was genuine
fear of the Catholic colony that had been set up at
its very doors, Maryland. The charter that had been
granted to Sir George Calvert, Lord Baltimore in 1632,
had provided that he should be a patron of all churches
to be established within his grant, a provision that was
generally understood to mean that Catholics could find
toleration there, since he himself was one. Beyond this
broad statement the crown dared not go; a direct statement of the Catholic nature of Maryland might have aroused
Massachusetts and Virginia against the founding of the
colony.[13] Vague as the charter was it brought down a
storm of criticism; Protestants in England and America
shouted of Lord Baltimore's design to establish Romanism

11 - Williams, Michael, The Shadow of the Pope (New York)
     1932) p.23.
12 - Cobb, Sanford H., The Rise of Religious Liberty in
     America (New York, 1902), p. 85; Williams, Shadow
     of the Pope, p. 24.
13 - Cobb, Rise of Religious Liberty, pp. 363-365.

in America; Catholics with almost equal vigor denounced his intended toleration of heretic Protestants.[14]

Despite the protest of friend and foe, Lord Baltimore and his son after him were firm in their determination to establish a colony where members of their faith could have freedom. The first settlers sent out from England numbered 220; of these 128 were Protestants.[15] The Protestant majority steadily increased, due to a considerable migration from Virginia.[16] That the project never attracted Catholics may have been due to their objection to the toleration granted Protestants.[17]

Even with this preponderance of Protestants, the Catholic nature of the colony plunged it into controversy and trouble almost as soon as its first settlers had set foot on the new land. The trouble arose when William Clayborne, secretary of Virginia, laid claim to Kent Island, lying within the grant made to Lord Baltimore. Sailing to the island in a ship named "The Reformation,"[18] Clayborne established himself and refused to

14 - Ibid., p. 368.
15 - Ibid., p. 368.
16 - Fiske, John, Old Virginia and Her Neighbors (Boston 1899) vol. i, p. 312. Fiske estimated that about 1,000 settlers from Virginia had established themselves in Maryland by 1649, many of them driven from the home colony by the harshness of Governor Berkley.
17 - Cobb, Rise of Religious Liberty, p. 347.
18 - Maury, Reuben, The Wars of the Godly(New York 1928) p. 19.

leave, despite the indignant demands of Baltimore. This
seemingly willful antagonism was due largely to Clayborne's hatred of Romanism and he found many who were
willing to support him on the same grounds.[19] The dis-
putes and bickering which grew from these conflicting
claims were to cause the Baltimore family to lose its
patent years later.[20]

While Baltimore was busy defending his rights
against the aggressions of Clayborne and his followers,
troubles were brewing in Maryland itself. The Protestant
majority there was steadily increasing, and the settlers
were growing more and more resentful of the authority of
office given to Catholics by the proprietor. It was evident to Baltimore that Protestants must soon be allowed
control of the colonial assembly; by 1648 he had decided
to remodel the government to effect this.[21] Knowing Protestant intolerance, he secured the passage of the Maryland
Toleration act of 1649 before turning over the assembly to
them - a premeditated move to prevent the incoming Protestant majority from dealing too harshly with the Catholics for whom the colony had been founded.[22]

19 - Cobb, Rise of Religious Liberty, p. 369.
20 - Ibid., p. 370.
21 - Ibid., pp. 375-376.
22 - Mereness, N. D. Maryland As A Proprietary Province
     (New York, 1901) pp. 430-433.

The fears for his people which were harbored
by the founder of Maryland were justified. Protestant
control of the colonial assembly came just at the time
of the Puritan Revolution. Encouraged thus in the colony and stimulated by the successful uprising in England,
Protestants of Maryland hastened to wield their new got
legislative cudgel against the ancient bogey, Catholicism.
One of the first blows was the banishment of Baltimore
from his own colony. In 1654 the Toleration act was repealed and in its stead the law enacted that "none who
profess to exercise the Popish religion, commonly known
by the name of the Roman Catholic religion, can be protected in this province."[23] Fortunately the act did not
receive Cromwell's approval, but the spirit of the Protestants was manifest.

On the death of the second Lord Baltimore in
1675, the colony was left to his son, Charles. This was
the signal for a new outburst of complaints, most of them
centering about the Romish religion of the proprietor. No
Protestant had suffered in the colony, but the complaints
received sympathetic ear in England where Titus Oates was
stirring up the old cry against the Pope. Soon after the
third Lord Baltimore took over the administration of his
heritage, the English ministry acceded to the demands of
the colonists, and issued order that offices in Maryland

23 - Osgood, H. L. The American Colonies in the Seventeenth
     Century (New York, 1907) vol. iii, pp. 130-131.

should be entrusted only to Protestants.[24]

The third Lord Baltimore was to have the pleasure of governing his colony for only a short time. When the bloodless revolution of 1689 established William and Mary on the throne, the Protestants of Maryland seized upon the affair as an excuse to rise in force against the political appointees of Baltimore. Headed by John Coode, the rebellion was built almost entirely upon the cry of No-Popery. Stories were circulated of a Popish plot to kill all Protestants, and although they were utterly without foundation, they were so widely believed that an "Association in Arms for the Defense of the Protestant Religion and Assisting the Rights of King William and Queen Mary" was formed. Baltimore's officials gave way before this demonstration and Coode took possession of the government, making his first act the issuing of a proclamation against Popery. The assembly that he called to govern the colony neglected civil affairs for two years while it devoted its time to the sending of petitions to the crown, praying that Protestants be relieved from persecution by Romanists.[25]

William and Mary, new to the throne and not well acquainted with colonial affairs, naturally took

24 - Bancroft, George, History of the United States of America, (Boston, 1876) vol. ii, p. 242; Mereness, Maryland As A Proprietary Province, p.38
25 - Osgood, American Colonies in the Seventeenth Century, vol. iii, pp. 491-506; Mereness, Maryland As A Proprietary Province, pp. 38-42.

these petitions far more seriously than actual conditions warranted. Carried away by these persistent
accusations, William voided the Maryland charter, de-
posed Baltimore, and took over the colony as a royal
province. To sympathizers of the Catholic cause, the
only cheerful note in this otherwise disgraceful series
of events was that the royal government established by
the crown immediately set up the Anglican church in Maryland, depriving Puritans of the influence which they
sought.[26]

While Virginia and Maryland were marshalling
their forces against the inroads of Popery, Catholics
in the northern colonies were meeting with even greater
hostility. The Puritanism of the settlers of Massachusetts Bay made them intolerant of any dissent; they alone,
they believed, understood the manner in which God wished
His people to live and His name to be worshipped. Tolerance was a word removed from the Puritan vocabulary;
the erring children of Adam must either be converted by
force or removed so that their false doctrines might not

26 - Osgood, H. L. The American Colonies in the Eighteenth
     Century (New York, 1924) vol. i, pp. 353-354. The
     lot of Catholics in Maryland remained so difficult
     and disagreeable that Charles Carroll, father of
     the first American Bishop, petitioned France for
     the right to remove members of his sect to Louisi-
     ana. The petition was denied by the French govern-
     ment. Channing, History of the United States, vol.
     ii, p. 427.

contaminate others. John Cotton had declared that
"it was toleration that made the world anti-Christian,"[27] and when Sir Richard Saltonstall had re-
monstrated against the persecutions carried on by
the clergy of Boston, Cotton and White had joined
in answering: "Better be hypocrites than profane
persons! There is a great difference between God's
inventions and man's inventions. We compell none
to man's inventions."[28]

The lot of the Catholic in such an atmosphere was certain to be an unpleasant one. Hardly
had the colonists established themselves at Massachusetts Bay before they had opportunity to vent their
antipathy for Rome. In 1631 Sir Christopher Gardiner
was expelled from the colony on the mere suspicion
that he was one of the Pope's subjects,[29] and in the
same year the General Court forced the removal of an
elder in Watertown who had the audacity to state that
he believed the Church of Rome was a true church because the reformed churches had not re-baptized those
who had come over from Rome.[30]

27 - Cobb, Rise of Religious Liberty, p. 86
28 - Ibid., p. 62.
29 - Adams, James T. The Founding of New England (Bos-
     ton 1927) pp. 149-150, Maury, Wars of the Godly,
     p. 24.
30 - Cobb, Rise of Religious Liberty, pp. 173-174.

The general law of Massachusetts Bay forbade Roman Catholics to settle, and in 1647 the Jesuits in particular were singled out by a provision that if one were bold enough to enter he should be banished immediately and on his return executed.[31] Twelve years later the General Court concerned itself with a law forbidding the celebration of that hated Popish festival, Christmas, a law made necessary by the disgraceful tendency of some of the younger members to flaunt the plain will of God by making merry on the Birthday of His Son.[32]

Secure in their isolation, the good Puritans of Massachusetts celebrated the Cromwellian revolt, and trembled with fear at the Restoration lest it should mean the return of Popery to their colony. New England divines waxed loud against the proclamation of religious liberty by James II in 1687[33] and breathed a unanimous sigh of relief when William and Mary were placed on the throne. Their delight was only slightly dimmed when the Charter of New England was granted by the new sovereigns, declaring "that forever hereafter shall there be a liberty of con-

31 - Ibid., p. 177.
32 - Ibid., p. 209.
33 - Ibid., pp. 232-233.

science allowed in the worship of God to all Christians (except Papists) inhabiting or which shall inhabit or be resident within our said province or territory."[34] The true Puritan, even in 1691, hated the general tolerance that this charter granted, but even it had saved him from the greatest danger: Popery from within.

James II had been able to do nothing more startling than alarm New England Puritans with his leanings toward Catholicism, but in New York his sympathies created a revolution of sorts. Thomas Dongan, sent out by James as governor of the province, was a Catholic, and immediately the worst fears swept over the colony. Rumors spread of the creation of a Popish stronghold in New York, and the population grew increasingly uneasy. Actually the rumors were without foundation. Dongan would not countenance intolerance to members of his faith and the steady influx of Catholics eager to find haven in the new world served to increase the general feeling of apprehension, especially when three Jesuits were found to be numbered among them. Such a mental and emotional state among the settlers was certain to lead to trouble; the fall of James II set spark to the agitation. Uniting against Catholicism, the people

34 - Channing, History of the United States, vol. ii, p. 423 note.

placed Jacob Leisler in power and he immediately called
together an assembly which agreed "to suspend all Roman
Catholics from Command and Places of Trust."[35] In addition Leisler ordered the arrest of all "reputed Papists"
and denied the franchise to all excepting Protestant
freemen.[36]

Leisler held office only until Governor Sloughter,
sent out by the new monarchs, arrived. But Sloughter made
little attempt to return the toleration that Catholics had
enjoyed under Dongan. He began a rigid campaign for the
enforcement of the Test Oath upon all office holders, requiring them to sign a declaration against the Roman doctrine of transubstantiation and to take the sacrament according to the rites of the church of England.[37] The campaign against Catholicism was made even more violent under
the Earl of Bellomont, governor between 1698 and 1701, who
saw the enactment of "An Act against Jesuits and Popish
Priests." Under this gentle piece of legislation, any
priests coming into New York was faced with life imprisonment, and any one harboring such a priest was to be fined

35 - Cobb, Rise of Religious Liberty, p. 336.
36 - "Leisler's No Popery Revolt in New York," American
        Catholic Historical Researches, vol. xiv (July,
        1897) pp. 123-125; Cobb, Rise of Religious Liberty,
        p. 337; Osgood, American Colonies in the Seventeenth
        Century, vol. iii, pp. 458-459.
37 - Cobb, Rise of Religious Liberty, p. 337.

two hundred and fifty pounds and spend three days in
the pillory.[38]   In the following year the franchise
was taken from Catholics in the colony.[39]

Other colonies, numbering almost no Catholics
among their people, constantly indulged their fears in
harsh legislation lest the followers of Rome overrun
their lands and restore the dreaded Papal power. The
first provincial assembly of New Hampshire bestowed the
franchise on "all Englishmen, being Protestants" who
conformed to qualifications of age and property.[40] A
year later, in 1681, the annual fast day proclamation
called upon the people to urge divine favor against
"the popish party throughout the world,"[41] even though
Catholics were lacking in the colony itself. Again in
1696 when the conspiracy against William and Mary
aroused Protestant prejudice, the New Hampshire legislature required all inhabitants to repeat an oath containing a declaration against the Pope and all peculiar
doctrines of the Roman Catholic religion.[42]

In North Carolina an act of the same year extended toleration to "all Christians (Papists only being

38 - Flynn, Joseph M., The Catholic Church in New Jersey
        (Morristown, 1904), p. 8.
39 - Ibid., p. 8.
40 - Cobb, Rise of Religious Liberty, p. 294.
41 - Ibid., p. 294.
42 - Ibid., p. 299.

excepted),[43] and while the New Haven colony persecuted only Quakers, there is no reason to assume that Catholics would have been served more generous fare had any of them attempted to enter the colony.[44]

Only in Rhode Island and Pennsylvania did the antagonism against Popery fail to draw blood. Attempts have been made to show that even in tolerant Rhode Island Catholic persecution was proposed,[45] but careful study has shown that these claims are without foundation and that here at least members of the Roman church were given impartial treatment.[46] In Pennsylvania the liberal Quaker

43 - Raper, Charles L., North Carolina: A Study in English Colonial Government (New York, 1904) p. 31.
44 - Cobb, Rise of Religious Liberty, p. 227.
45 - Williams, Shadow of the Pope, p. 27, accepts as true the alleged Rhode Island law of 1664 declaring: "That all men professing Christianity and of competent estates and of civil conversation who acknowledge and are obedient to the civil magistrate, though of different judgment in religious affairs (Roman Catholics only excepted) shall be admitted freemen, and shall have liberty to choose and be chosen officers in this colony, both military and civil."
46 - Bancroft, History of the United States, vol. ii,p.65, has demonstrated that the act of 1664, was never actually passed, but that the committee of revisal, preparing the statutes of the colony for printing in 1744 interpolated this law because of the condition of English politics at that time. Lack of knowledge of the date of passage of the law certainly supports this view, as the revisers would probably have known the date of enactment if it had been passed. Bancroft's conclusions have been generally accepted by later historians. See Channing, History of the United States, vol. ii, pp. 426-427; and Rider, S.S., "Inquiry Concerning the Origin of the Clause Disfranchising Roman Catholics," Rhode Island Historical Tracts, Second Series, No. 1. Roger Williams had no love for Catholics, despite this, and shared in the universal fear of their influence. This is shown in: "Letters of Roger Williams Referring to 'Romanists' and the 'Popish Leviathan,'" American Catholic Historical Researches, n. s., vol. v, (January, 1909), pp. 3-4.

assembly in 1682 offered franchise and office to all
believing Christ to be the Savior of the world, thus
allowing Catholics equal rights with members of other
sects. Eleven years later, however, the English government under William and Mary ordered Pennsylvania
to impose an oath on its office holders in which they
specifically abjured the doctrine of transubstantiation,
the adoration of Mary and saints; and the sacrifice of
the mass.[47] When the order met with objections in the
Pennsylvania legislature the Quakers only found their
troubles increased by the accusation that they were
really Jesuits in disguise.[48] They were forced to obey,
and the order, repeated in 1701 and 1703, barred Catholics from office in that colony.[49]

By the close of the seventeenth century nearly
every colony had given proof of its inbred fear of Popery.
Stirred to zealous bigotry by pulpit and penned propaganda, the collective will of the people felt no shame -
saw no injustice. Only in Rhode Island in 1700 could a
Catholic find complete equality under the law, and even
here it is doubtful what the interpretation of the liberal statutes might have been. The bete noir of Romanism

47 - Shea, John Gilmary, History of the Catholic Church
     in the United States (New York, 1886-1892), vol. I,
     p. 365.
48 - Cobb, Rise of Religious Liberty, p. 445.
49 - Ibid., p. 444.

might here be given a politely evasive welcome on the
statute books but to the early colonists it remained
always the wolf at the door.

This antagonism which permeated the earliest
years of the colonies did not subside when the settlements became more secure and their population more
dense. The seventeenth century battle cries against
the Pope were intensified with the new enthusiasm characteristic of eighteenth century America. Until this
time the anti-Catholic prejudice of the colonists had
to a large extent been influenced by their English upbringing; there were few Catholics among them and these
few were entirely harmless. But with the beginning of
the eighteenth century the colonies found themselves
plunged into a series of wars with Catholic France and
Spain which threatened their very existence. Every
Catholic became a potential enemy, a person to be viewed
with constant suspicion and a hated ally of the powers
that were attacking colonial borders and driving Indians
against their outposts. America for the first time saw
its institutions menaced and its people in immediate
danger.

The first manifestation of this overwhelming
dread of Papal agression was a stiffening of legislation
against Romanists. New Jersey, where laws against Catholics had been absent before, proposed in 1701 that only

Protestants in the colony should be exempt from penal laws relating to religion.[50] Delaware, on its separation from Pennsylvania, provided that only Protestant churches and societies could receive and hold real estate.[51] In Massachusetts hysterical rumors had it that a nearby foothold had been taken by the hated Catholics. An expedition set out for the Kennebec river in Maine where a crude church built by a lowly priest was found and burned to the ground.[52] The laws under which Maryland had become a royal colony, depriving Catholics of religious and civil rights, were enforced with renewed vigor. In addition the Maryland assembly in 1704 passed an "Act to Prevent the Growth of Popery," forbidding any "popish priest or bishop" to exercise his duties in the colony under threat of a fifty pound fine and six months' imprisonment. The same act levied a tax of twenty shillings on every Irish servant imported into the colony "to prevent the entrance of papists."[53] In 1715 the assembly

50 - Ibid., pp. 404-406.
51 - Ibid., p. 452.
52 - Maury, Wars of the Godly, p. 25.
53 - Osgood, American Colonies in the Eighteenth Century vol. ii, p. 199; 204. South Carolina also moved to protect itself in 1716 when an act of the General Assembly to encourage the importation of white servants provided against the introduction of any "native Irish or persons of known scandalous characters or Roman Catholics." McCrady, Edward, The History of South Carolina Under the Proprietary Government 1670-1719 (New York, 1901) pp. 556-557.

of this same colony provided that Children of a
Catholic mother and a Protestant father should,
on the death of the father, be taken from the sur-
viving parent. Three years later the franchise
was denied Catholic worshippers who refused conversion.[54]

Connecticut took its first action against
the menace to Popery in 1743 by granting complete
toleration of Protestants and at the same time denying it to Catholics, thus making it impossible for a
Catholic Church to exist there.[55] In the same year
the colony took a step to protect itself from a new
evil. An "Act Providing Relief from the Evil and
Dangerous Designs of Foreigners and Suspected Persons" was passed, directed against a colony of Moravians engaged in the laudable work of teaching nearby
Indians. Rumors had been spread about Connecticut
that these Moravians were actually French Jesuits in
disguise, who were working in the interests of the
Canadian Romanists by influencing the Indians against
the English.[56] With the colony in such a distrustful
state of mind against Catholics, such a rumor was sufficient justification for increasingly harsh legisla-

54 - Ibid., vol. iii, p. 11; Channing, History of the
      United States, vol. ii, pp. 424-425.
55 - Cobb, Rise of Religious Liberty, pp. 276-277.
56 - Ibid., p. 277.

tion.

Whisperings similar to those directed
against the harmless Moravians flew thick and fast
throughout the colonies as the wars with France and
Spain progressed. Georgia, prejudiced with a charter that denied toleration to Catholics,[57] and ever
fearful of her Catholic neighbor, Florida, lent a
willing ear to Dame Rumor. James Oglethorpe, while
warring against Spain in Florida, was responsible for
more anti-Catholic misgivings when in 1740 he wrote to
the other colonies warning them against Spanish spies
and stating that they would usually be Romish priests.
His letter had a disastrous effect in New York, for it
arrived just after an Anglican chapel there had been
burned. The people alarmed at once by Oglethorpe's
lotter, decided that this must be the work of a priestly
spy. They seized upon a poor non-juring Church of England clergyman, there being no priests available, and
after accusing him of being a Catholic and a church
burner, hanged him.[58]

57 - McCain, James R., Georgia As A Proprietary Province
     (Boston 1917) p. 309. The Georgia charter, issued
     in 1732 by George II, stated: "That forever here-
     after there shall be a liberty of conscience al-
     lowed in the worship of God to all persons within
     our said province, and that all such persons, ex-
     cept Papists, shall have a free exercise of re-
     ligion."
58 - Maury, Wars of the Godly, pp. 28-29.

Many of the colonies and towns exposed to
attack from the French or Spanish forces took special
action to protect themselves. Often this action consisted of acts providing that all Papists in the colony should be disarmed, Pennsylvania[59] and Virginia[60]
carrying out provisions of this sort. The Virginia
act contained in addition a curious specification that
no Papist could keep a horse worth more than five pounds,
a ruling evidently designed only to annoy. A Boston town
meeting in 1746 named a committee to "take care and prevent any danger the town may be in from Roman Catholics
residing here," however Catholics there were not actually
harmed.[61] The New Hampshire legislature was so impressed

---

59 - Cobb, Rise of Religious Liberty, p. 450. The act was
     passed during the Seven Years War, when the fear of
     Catholicism reached its height. Also indicative of
     feeling in Pennsylvania were laws passed by the col-
     ony limiting Irish immigration because of its Catho-
     lic nature. See: "Objections to Irish Immigration
     to Pennsylvania, 1736," Pennsylvania Magazine of
     History and Biography, vol. xxi, (Philadelphia,1897);
     and "Projected Settlement West of Pennsylvania from
     which the Church of Rome would have to be Excluded,"
     American Catholic Historical Researches, n.s.vol. v,
     (January, 1909), pp. 5-7. An excellent brief account
     of the activity of the Pennsylvania press and pulpit
     against Catholicism at this time is in, "Fear of
     Catholicism in Colonial Pennsylvania, 1755-1766,"
     American Catholic Historical Researches, vol. xvii
     (April 1900) pp. 74-77.
60 - Cobb, Rise of Religious Liberty, p. 108, Act of 1756
     Channing, History of the United States, vol. ii,p.425.
61 - Maury, Wars of the Godly, p. 29. Acts were passed
     in both Massachusetts and New York ordering all Cath-
     olic priests to depart the colonies. Channing, His-
     tory of the United States, vol. ii, p. 426.

with the dangers about them that all of its members
joined in an oath renouncing Rome in 1752, although
they did not attempt to enforce the oath on the people.[62]
Behind this series of acts and resolutions, typical of
those passed in all the colonies, lay a deep seated and
universally felt fear of Popery.

The peace that came in 1763 did not lessen the
menace in the eyes of the colonists. Although French Canada no longer loomed as a constant danger, the Catholic settlers there were regarded with suspicion and hatred. How
intense was this hatred can be realized by the objections
raised at the passage of the Quebec Act in 1774. An able
act, designed to provide a government for the much abused
Catholics of Quebec and to extend the boundaries of their
province into the Ohio country, it was in the eyes of the
American colonists a Rome-manipulated coup of aggression.
A bitter press pointed to the colonies as surrounded on
all sides by enemies and drew a picture of the fate that
would befall the land. "We may live," one such account
began, "to see our churches converted into mass houses
and our lands plundered by tythes for the support of the
Popish clergy. The Inquisition may erect her standard
in Pennsylvania, and the city of Philadelphia may yet experience the carnage of St. Bartholomew's Day."[63] A pam-

62 - Cobb, Rise of Religious Liberty, pp. 299-300.
63 - Quoted in Shea, History of the Catholic Church, vol.
     ii, pp. 136-137.

phlet that was widely read throughout the colonies
decried the toleration granted Catholics by this act
in extraordinarily bad verse:

> If gallic Papists have a right
> To worship their own way,
> Then farewell to the liberties,
> Of poor America.[64]

The excitement caused by the passage of the
Quebec act led to the persecution of a group of Scotch
Irish settled in the Mohawk valley and the oppression
continued until they were forced to leave the country
for Canada.[65] Colonial radicals, plunging their country
daily nearer revolution, seized upon the act to stir up
further discontent and shouted through the colonies that
England had succumbed to the will of the Pope. When the
Continental Congress came together it expressed this discontent in a petition to the king deploring the encouraging
of Romanism on the borders of America.[66]

It was this same furor against so-called Catholic
aggression that led to the establishment of one of the great
festival days of colonial America. Pope Day, celebrated especially in New England on November 5 of each year, was the
American counterpart of the English Guy Fawkes Day. The

---

64 - "The Anti-Catholic Spirit of the Revolution," American
     Catholic Historical Researches, vol. vi,
65 - Williams, The Shadow of the Pope, p. 34.
66 - Maury, Wars of the Godly, p. 33.

Puritans found it difficult to celebrate the delivery
of James I from assassination when they had themselves
been responsible for the execution of his son, but they
could shout against the Catholic creators of the Gunpowder Plot.[67] Especially in Boston did this annual
celebration assume a position of importance. Rival
popes were produced each year in the north and south
end of Boston, the Avignon and Rome of the city, and
carried through the streets by enthusiastic mobs of
followers. The day ended with supporters of each pope
trying to get control of that carried by the rival fac-
tion to burn it in effigy. The Governor of Massachusetts
made efforts to end the practice of 1775, but the people
of Boston were too enthusiastic about this one day when
they had opportunity to vent their spleen against Rome
and refused to relinquish it readily.[68]

Something of the spirit of the day in Boston
can be gathered from a broadside printed in that city
and widely distributed:

67 - Williams, Shadow of the Pope, p. 36.
68 - "Catholic Recollections of Samuel Breck," American
Catholic Historical Researches, vol. xii (October
1895), p. 146. In addition to the excellent personal description of the day given by Breck, a
good account of the practice is to be found in:
Shea, John Gilmary, "Pope Day in the Colonies,"
United States Catholic Historical Magazine, vol.
ii,(January, 1888) pp. 1-8

Huzza, brave boys, behold the Pope,
Pretender and Old Nick,
How they together lay their heads,
To plot a poison trick.

To blow up King and Parliament
To flitters rent and torn,
Oh blundering poet, since the plot
Was this Pretender born.[69]

The celebration of Pope Day nearly plunged the colonies into serious trouble. With the revolution begun, soldiers from New England in the continental armies planned to stage a giant celebration of the event, just at the time when the struggling colonies were trying to get aid from Canada.[70] Washington heard of the plans in time, and issued immediate orders against them, deploring the "ridiculous and childish custom of burning the effigy of the Pope" and expressing his surprise that there should be men and officers in the army "so void of common sense as not to see the unpropriety of such a step at this juncture."[71] Thus Pope Day came to an end with Washington's orders. The Colonists were too busy to parade the streets of Boston with the effigy of their imaginary enemy while in the harbor were anchored the warships of an immediate and real menace. With political upheaval was born the spirit of freedom and equal-

69 - "Pope Day in the Colonies," American Catholic Historical Researches, n. s., vol. iii (April, 1907),p.132
70 - Maury, Wars of the Godly, pp. 34-35; Williams, pp. 34-35; Williams, Shadow of the Pope, pp. 36-37.
71 - Washington, George, The Writings of George Washington edited by Worthington C. Ford (New York, 1889), vol. iii, pp. 200-201.

ity and brotherhood. The revolution had to be won;
Catholic and Protestant found a new cause in which
their zealotry might for a little while find sublima-
tion.

Anti-Catholicism had run its course in colonial
America. It had played its part in providing one of the
many minor forces working toward the start of the revolution. Colonists, steeped in prejudice against Rome, were
more willing to vision the danger of an Anglican episcopate in America, more willing to go to arms to prevent the
establishment of dread prelacy. But when they had taken
up their arms and started this war which was to lead to
the independence of the colonies, their religious prejudice died within them. Catholic France, no longer an
enemy, had actually come to their aid by the Alliance of
1778.[72] Staunch enemies of Catholicism had an opportunity to see French officers and French soldiers, and to
realize that if they had horns at all, they were well
concealed. Moreover a spirit of toleration had been
bred in the people by the Declaration of Independence;
religious persecution of the fellowman who had been proclaimed equal by that document was not easy in the midst

72 - Bacon, L. W. A History of American Christianity
(New York, 1897), p. 185; "Change in the Sentiments of the Revolutionists toward 'Popery' after
the French Alliance," American Catholic Historical
Researches, n.s. vol. v, (January, 1909), pp.57-60.

of the liberal doctrines which it spread.

The period of the revolution, then, was a period of liberalism unmarked by anti-Catholic outbreaks. Leading Catholics of the colonies expressed frequent amazement at the kind treatment suddenly accorded them. Bishop Carroll, visiting Boston where the No-Popery cry had been raised with such vigor in the past, commented with joy on the change. "It is wonderful to tell," he wrote, "what great civilities have been done to me in this town, where a few years ago a parish priest was thought to be the greatest monster in creation. Many here, even of their principal people, have acknowledged to me that they would have crossed to the opposite side of the street rather than meet a Roman Catholic some time ago. The horror that they associated with the idea of the papist was incredible; and the scandalous misrepresentations by the ministers increased this horror every Sunday."[73]

But Americans, long bred and reared in a spirit of anti-Catholicism, were not ready to surrender complete equality to the hated Papists without a struggle.[74] They might be willing to admit that the 30,000 Catholics who were in the country at the time of the revolution[75] could

73 - O'Gorman, Thomas, History of the Roman Catholic Church in the United States (New York, 1895) p. 277.
74 - "The Anti-Catholic Spirit of the Revolution," American Catholic Historical Researches, vol. vi, (October, 1889), pp. 146-178.
75 - Carroll, H. K., The Religious Forces in the United States (New York, 1895), p.68. More than half of this number were in Maryland.

do them little harm, but there was the future to consider, and the future might bring Catholic immigration
and so endanger their Protestant institutions. The
state constitutions adopted while the war was being
fought reflect this caution. The New Jersey constitution of 1776 contained a safeguarding clause that
no Protestant could be denied enjoyment of civil rights
because of his religion, and closed offices of the state
or legislature to Catholics.[76] The North Carolina con-
sitution put into operation the same year contained a
similar provision in respect to office holders,[77] as
did that of Georgia.[78] In Connecticut the colonial
charter was retained with its restrictions on Catholics.[79] Vermont required an oath from office holders
in which they owned "and professed the Protestant Religion" in its constitution drafted in 1777.[80] The
New York constitution of the same year attempted to
limit the franchise to Protestants by requiring that
all persons naturalized in the state must swear to

76 - Cornelison, Isaac A., The Relation of Religion to
     Civil Government in the United States of America
     (New York, 1895), p. 99.
77 - Ibid., p. 101.
78 - Cobb, Rise of Religious Liberty, p. 507.
79 - Ibid., p. 500.
80 - Dohan, James H., "Our State Constitutions and Relig-
     ious Liberty," American Catholic Quarterly Review,
     vol. xi, (April 1915) p. 295.

give up allegiance to any foreign power or potentate
in civil or ecclesiastical matters.[81] A year later
South Carolina definitely established Protestantism
as the state religion.[82]

New Hampshire adopted a series of constitutions in 1779, 1781 and 1784, all of them bitter against
Catholicism.[83] The Massachusetts Body of Laws of 1780,
justly famed for the liberalism that surrounded its
drafting and adoption, empowered townships to lay taxes
"for the institution of the public worship of God, and
for the support and maintenance of public Protestant
teachers of piety, religion and morality, in all cases
where such provision shall not be made voluntarily."[84]
This provision of the Massachusetts constitution was
carried into effect by the legislature in 1800.[85]

81 - Ibid., p. 290. A good account of the drafting of
     this constitution is in, Williams, The Shadow of
     the Pope, pp. 43-44; Channing, History of the
     United States, v. iii, p. 564.
82 - Cornelison, Isaac, op. cit., pp. 101-103;
     Cobb, Rise of Religious Liberty, p. 506.
83 - Dohan, op. cit., p. 288.
84 - Shea, History of the Catholic Church, vol. i, p. 161.
     The Massachusetts constitution also provided that
     all office holders must be Protestants, as did the
     constitutions of New Hampshire, North Carolina,
     South Carolina and Georgia.
     Channing, History of the United States, vol. iii,
     p. 565.
85 - Cornelison, op. cit., pp. 105-107.

So by the end of the revolution, seven
states, Massachusetts, New Hampshire, New Jersey,
Connecticut, North Carolina, South Carolina and
Georgia insisted on Protestant office holders and
other states inflicted additional liabilities on
Catholics in their constitutions. The gesture of
generosity and liberalism evinced in the Declaration of Independence had offered some relief to
Catholics, but time alone could heal such a heritage of hatred.[86]

Despite an undercurrent of antipathy, the
constitutional convention drafting the instrument of
government for the United States, remained aloof from
this old controversy. North Carolina was the only state
voting against the clause by which Congress was forbidden to impose any religious test for federal office holders.[87] Later, when the state legislatures were propos-
ing the amendments that were to emerge as the Bill of
Rights, there was more dissension. The New Hampshire
legislature submitted an amendment designed to restrict
Catholic power,[88] and a member of the Massachusetts
governing body wrote that he "shuddered at the idea

---

86 - The struggles of a priest in upholding his religion
     against typical attacks by Americans as told in:
     Walsh, James S. "Some Religious Discussions in Phil-
     adelphia Just After the Revolution," Records of the
     American Catholic Historical Society of Philadel-
     phia, v. xvii March 1906, pp. 33-43.
87 - Article vi - Williams, Shadow of the Pope, p. 49.
88 - Ibid., p. 50.

that Roman Catholics, Papists and Pagans might be introduced into office and that Popery and the Inquisition may be established in America."[89]

Despite these objections, the Constitution
went into effect, together with the first ten amendments that portrayed a new liberalism. The principles
of religious freedom so vividly expressed in the First
Amendment had a profound effect upon the people. It
was difficult to shout against Popery when that amendment had stated that congress could "make no law respecting an establishment of religion, or prohibiting
the free exercise thereof." Especially was this so
in the first few decades after the instrument of government with its Bill of Rights had been adopted. Americans were proud of their constitution. They saw it as
an immortal document fitting the glorious country that
they had established by force of arms. American pride
was at the basis of American religious freedom in those
days.

At the same time other factors tended to discredit the harsh intolerance of the colonists. Immigration was almost at a standstill in the years just after
the adoption of the constitution and the menace of the
foreigner and the Catholic seemed a thing of the past.

89 - Cobb, Rise of Religious Liberty, p. 508.

Americans were kept well employed building a civilization in their new country; they had no time to reflect
on the dread danger of Popery during the period of
prosperity that ushered the constitution into being.
Prices were high, new farms could be supported, and
population marched into the west to supply them. With
this westward expansion, the old home colonies were
being depleted of population. New England especially
felt the effect of these changes; New England wondered
why her sons should leave in such vast numbers to take
up their homes in the wilderness. Thus reflecting, that
section engaged in a bit of Puritan self scrutiny. It
admitted one expelling factor lay in the harsh religious
laws inflicted on its people, and it set about to reform
them.[90] This process was made easier by the activity of
prominent reformers such as Thomas Jefferson and James
Madison, who through their efforts to establish religious
freedom and equality in Virginia, set a pattern of toleration that other states could follow.[91]

Thus people throughout the eastern states began
recasting their constitutions and their laws to instill

90 - Purcell, Richard J., Connecticut in Transition,
      1775-1818 (Washington, 1918) pp. 414-418.
91 - Nevins, Allan, The American States During and
      After the Revolution 1775-1789 (New York, 1927)
      pp. 420-441.

into them this new spirit of liberalism. Between the
times of the drafting of the federal constitution and
the 1820's this change was going on. Vermont dropped
the clause inflicting liabilities on Catholics in
1786;[92] South Carolina followed in 1790 and New Hampshire attempted a similar change in 1792[93] although
public opinion was still too strong to allow it to be
carried out. Delaware decided to enfranchise every
free white male who lived in the state regardless of
his creed, and Georgia did away with the religious
test for civil office before the turn of the century.[94]
Connecticut abolished her established Congregationalism
in 1818.[95] Four years later New York removed her objectionable oath against Catholics.[96] Massachusetts
had already abolished the religious test,[97] and in 1833
effected the complete separation of church and state.[98]
So at least in law, liberalism triumphed.

But beneath this seeming religious tranquillity
still brewed the elements of misgiving and fear of Popery.

92 - Dohan, "Our State Constitutions and Religious Lib-
     erty," p. 295.
93 - Cornelison, The Relation of Religion to Civil Gov-
     ernment, pp. 103-104. Dohan, op. cit., p. 228.
94 - McMaster, John Bach, A History of the People of
     the United States, (New York, 1907) vol. v, p. 397
95 - Purcell, op. cit., p. 418.
96 - Dohan, op. cit., p. 292.
97 - Purcell, op. cit., p. 419.
98 - Ibid., p. 420.

Throughout the Revolution the Tory press had hammered constantly at the age old danger of Romish invasion. The Royal Gazette of New York had frowned upon the French Alliance of 1778 and drawn a dismal picture of America as a Catholic country ten years hence.[99] When members of Congress attended masses in honor of French and Spanish officials in 1779 and 1780 another Loyalist paper expressed the grave fear that Congress "might go over to Rome in a body,"[100] and Benedict Arnold was able to point to this danger in imploring his countrymen to join him against the struggling colonists.[101] Doggerel quoted in Tory papers at the time expressed the apprehension of this small group at least:

> O Brother, things are at a terrible pass.
> Brother, we sinned in going to the mass;
> The Lord, who taught our fingers how to fight
> For this denied to curb the tempest's might.[102]

This conservative heritage of fear was to find expression when the Federalists, the nativistic party of their day, secured control of the government in the dying years of the eighteenth century. They gave early evidence of their distrust and hatred of foreigners and Catholicism by extending the period of residence necessary for naturalization from two to five years, and the debate on the measure

99 - Issue of March 17, 1779. Quoted in Williams, Shadow of the Pope, pp. 38-39.
100- Ibid., p. 40.
101- Ibid., p. 41.
102- Ibid., p. 39.

in Congress bristled with anti-Catholic sentiment.[103]
This revival of intolerance reached its culmination
with the passage of the Alien and Sedition acts in
1798. Behind the passage of these acts lay hysterical
fear of France and the French revolution. Behind them
too lay Federalist alarm at the accession to Republican
ranks of the thin stream of political refugees and immigrants from that country and Ireland,[104] refugees who
made up for their lack of numbers with their enthusiastic championing of the Republican cause.[105] It was bad
enough, in the minds of the followers of John Adams, to
admit radical French refugees into the country; it was
worse to allow them to attack Federalist principles
through the press. But almost as vital in causing the
passage of the acts in 1798 was danger from Ireland
and the Irish.

Fears of this island and its Popish population
came with the Irish insurrections in the 1790's. The
insurrectionists sought sympathy in the United States,
and in order to secure it formed the American Society
of United Irishmen, a group including such notable American Irishmen as Mathew Carey and William Duane. In the

103 - Bowers, Claude G., Jefferson and Hamilton (Boston,
        1925), p. 264.
104 - McMaster, John Bach, With the Fathers (New York,
        1896), p. 88.
105 - Ibid., p. 89.

face of Federalist opposition to these discordant elements
on the American scene, the _Aurora,_ mouthpiece of Jefferson,
published a series of articles encouraging their activity.[106] If the Federalists were alarmed at this Catholic
interposition the English government was even more stirred
up. Sir Robert Lister, minister to the United States,
sought out President Adams and persuaded him that the
presence of such Irish enthusiasts was a menace to American institutions and American liberty. In 1798, the
year of the actual rebellion in Ireland, Adams secured
the passage of the Alien and Sedition acts.[107]

It was no accident, then, that Mathew Lyon, good
Irish Catholic that he was, was first to suffer under these
two Federalist acts.[108] Nor was it an accident that the
Alien Riots in Philadelphia were staged just outside a
Catholic church.[109] Thus early in the history of the coun-
try the distinction was beginning to be made between the
Catholic foreigner and the Protestant foreigner, a distinc-
tion that was to be clearly marked throughout the early na-

---

106 - Condon, Edward J., "Irish Immigration to the United
      States since 1790" Journal of the American Irish
      Historical Society, vol. iv (Boston, 1904) p.89.
107 - Ibid., p. 89.
108 - Foik, Paul J., "Anti-Catholic Parties in American
      Politics, 1776-1860," Records of the American
      Catholic Historical Society of Philadelphia, vol.
      xxxvi (March, 1925), p. 45.
109 - Williams, Shadow of the Pope, p. 54.

tivistic struggles.

The Alien and Sedition acts passed from existence when Jefferson became president, but even this advocate of religious freedom was not above suspicion of
foreigners. He himself suggested an amendment to the
constitution that would bar any man from citizenship
who took a title or gift from European powers, an amendment that needed the vote of only one more state to be
adopted.[110] But it was in New England, steeped in Puritan tradition, that real objection to the immigrant and
the Catholic lay. This objection was to find expression
when economic disaster goaded New Englanders into calling the Hartford convention, a convention that wrote into its records a proposed amendment to the federal constitution debarring naturalized citizens from civil office in the United States Government.[111] Behind this
proposal was the disappointment of the New England Federalists that naturalized citizens were flocking into
the opposition party and aiding their opponents in the
war with England that was ruining their trade. Behind

110 - McMaster, With the Fathers, pp. 89-92.
111 - The proposed amendment read: "No persons who shall
      hereafter be naturalized, shall be eligible as a
      member of the senate or house of representatives
      of the United States, nor capable of holding any
      civil office under the authority of the United
      States." In Macdonald, William, Select Douments
      Illustrative of the History of the United States,
      1776-1861 (New York, 1898), p. 207.

it too was the enthusiasm with which the Irish who had
poured into New England welcomed the war as a means of
revenge upon the England that they hated.[112] To strike
a blow at the existing government was to strike a blow
at these Irish, and such an opportunity was relished by
New England Federalists.

The nativistic manifestation of the Hartford
Convention was only a ripple on the prevailing sea of
calm. For the most part the people of the United States
were willing to let well enough alone in the period between the adoption of the constitution and 1820 - at
least in legislation. During these years, however, an
undercurrent of feeling continued the warfare in America that had been waged since the reformation in Europe
a struggle of individual Protestants against the great
error and gigantic corruption of the Roman hierarchy.
It was not the handful of Catholics among them that pro-
voked their opposition;[113] it was more the remembrance of
a dreadful power than the instruments of that power. Not

112 - Desmond, Humphrey J., The Know Nothing Party
      (Washington, 1904) p. 12.
113 - Bishop Carroll estimated that there were 35,000
      Catholics in the United States in 1790 of a total
      population of about 3,000,000. The acquisition
      of Louisiana added a large number, but it was
      not until the influx of immigrants set in after
      1820 that their influence was clearly felt.
      Guilday, Life and Times of John England, vol. i,
      p. 7.

until the first substantial wave of Catholic immigration swept over the country, however, did the religious strife develop a means of expression characteris-
tically American - a strife of organized groups against
an evil no more understood than sympathzied with.

II

THE NO-POPERY CRY IS RAISED, 1820-1829.

The tide of immigration which surged upon the American shore in the years before the Civil war provided the necessary stimulation to nativistic sentiment that later was to culminate in the Know Nothing Party. During the period of the Revolution and that immediately following, the reservoirs of Europe had drained their excessive population only slowly into the fertile fields of America. Europe, engaged in almost constant warfare was slow to release her man power, during the early years of the American republic and it was not until 1815 when the Napoleonic menace had been checked that she was ready to open the gates and release a human deluge which was destined to mount to flood proportions in the next decades.[1]

1 - Estimates of the amount of yearly immigration vary greatly for the period before 1820. One careful student has placed the total number of arrivals between 1790 and 1820 as 250,000. With a population of 4,000,000 in 1790 and 9,000,000 in 1820 this would mean an annual average immigration of only one tenth or one twentieth of the total population. Farrand, Max., "Immigration in the Light of History," The New Republic, December 23, 1916, p. 209. Another student has estimated that between 1784 and 1810 345,000 immigrants reached the United States. Fairchild, Henry P., Immigration, A World Movement and its American Significance (New York, 1926),pp.57-58. Regardless of the correctness of these figures it is obvious that up to 1815 immigration created no serious problem with only about 10,000 arrivals yearly.

This surplus population which had found employment during the inflation of war years now hung as a menace over England and the continental powers. It was a population released from productive sources by the introduction of machine methods that in turn had been spurred onward by the war. To add to the fears of officials, the Malthusian theory was enunciated at this time, with all its grim suggestion.[2] It was inevitable, as a result, that Europe should encourage emigration.

The people themselves were ready to leave bare homes and seek new prosperity in America. Many of them were faced with economic ruin as prices tumbled in the usual post-war depression. Machine methods in manufacture, introduced all over Europe but particularly in England, meant a decline in wages as the productivity of each workman increased. In 1826 an observer estimated that the machines of England alone were doing the work of two hundred million men.[3] Wages in the principal industries in England declined from one half to one third between 1810 and 1820.[4] In Ireland bad conditions were made

2 - Hutchins, Fred D., The Colonial Land and Immigration Commission (Philadelphia, 1931), p. 2
3 - Carey, Mathew, Reflections on the Subject of Emigration from Europe with a View to Settlement in the United States (3d. edition, Philadelphia, 1826) p.vii.
4 - Ibid., p. viii. Spinners received 42 s 6 p. each week in 1810; 32 s. in 1820. Pickers wages dropped from 11 s. 6 p. in 1810 to 9 s. in 1820. Other wages declined in proportion.

worse by the constant drain of wealth from the country
under the absentee system, a drain amounting to
$13,500,000 yearly.[5]   The increase in poverty through-
out Great Britain is reflected in the mounting expendi-
tures for poor relief, growing from Ł700,000 in 1749,
not long before Arkwright's machine went into operation,
to Ł7,329,594 in 1820.[6]

With poverty thus stalking throughout the land,
the English government, soon after the close of the continental wars, gave its attention to the problem of surplus
population.   Particularly alarming was the Irish situation,
and it was to this that England first turned.   Crown officials were not anxious to send the Irish to the United
States; they were jealous of the growth of the new country,
particularly after the War of 1812, and had no desire to
increase its population strength.[7]   They did move to send
poverty stricken Irish peasants to Canada, several grants
being made to aid this emigration between 1823 and 1827.[8]
In addition to active aid, land in Canada was granted free

5 - Ibid., p. iv.
6 - Ibid., pp. v-vi.
7 - Condon, "Irish Immigration to the United States since
       1790," p. 91.
8 - Hutchins, Colonial Land and Immigration Commission,
       p. 4.   Parliament voted 15,000 pounds in 1823, 30,000
       pounds in 1825, and 20,000 pounds in 1827.   The first
       two grants were to be used to encourage emigration
       from the south of Ireland, the last grant was to be
       used over the entire United Kingdom.

to Irish settlers and local societies and organizations
played a large part in encouraging them to emigrate.[9]

In encouraging Irish emigration, England was
releasing the first great stream from that island into
the United States. The Irish, congenial by nature,
found sparsely settled lands of Canada little to their
liking and nearly all of them thus deposited at government expense ultimately made their way to the more settled regions of the United States.[10]

While the British government was thus unwitting-
ly aiding the growth of American immigration a still larger
stream of Irish settlers was making its way to the new
world without governmental assistance. The lumber trade
which had developed between Ireland and New Brunswick with
the beginning of the Irish cooperage industry offered an
easy and convenient route between the two countries for
the starving Irish peasants. Nearly every sea port along
the southern and western coasts of Ireland annually sent
out its vessels to return laden with the products of the
Canadian forests. The captains of these vessels were
eager to take passengers as ballast; they formed a convenient freight, loading and unloading themselves, shifting themselves in heavy weather, and willing to take a

9 - Condon, op. cit., p. 91.
10-Ibid., p. 92.

turn at the pumps during a storm. Once in Canada, the
Irish could earn the few dollars necessary to take them
to the United States in the gypsum vessels plying to
New England ports by loading the lumber ships, or they
could make the long trek overland to the settled communities that they sought.[11]

As early as 1804 a group of peasants who had
arrived in New Brunswick on lumber ships were reported
making their way to New England over land,[12] and indica-
tions in the years following show an ever increasing
stream flowing in the same direction.[13] As the trade
increased in volume, ship captains offered passage from
Ireland to Canada for as low as fifteen shillings.[14] Thousands of peasants, eager to escape famine in their native
land, took advantage of this opportunity, and a constant
flow of settlers found their way into New England through
Canada, an influx which was neglected entirely in the immigration statistics of the time.[15]

Even with this constant flow neglected, the

11 - The effect of this lumber trade in encouraging Irish
     emigration is well described in Hansen, Marcus L.,
     "The Second Colonization of New England," New England
     Quarterly, vol. ii, (October, 1929) pp. 544-546. The
     trade and its effects are discussed in House Docu-
     ments, 25th Congress, Session No. 1040, pp. 20 ff.;
     and in Page, Thomas W., "The Transportation of Immi-
     grants and the Reception Arrangements in the Nine-
     teenth Century," Journal of Political Economy, vol.
     xix (November, 1911), p. 734.
12 - Condon, op. cit., p. 88.
13 - Niles Register, August 30, 1823; July 29, 1826.
14 - Hansen, op. cit., p. 546.
15 - Condon, op. cit., p. 88.

immigration statistics that were collected after 1820[16]
were sufficient to cause alarm in the hearts of nativistically inclined Americans. From the 8,383 recorded arrivals on American shore in 1820, the number had leaped to
27,382 in 1828,[17] of whom more than 17,000 were Irish.[18]
By 1830 a slight decline had set in, but the 23,322 settlers who arrived in that year stood in marked contrast
to the few who had come to America a decade before.[19]

To the sober minded American citizen of the
1820's there was little cause for alarm in this growth,
great as it was. The country was well able to absorb
the flow; there were more than ten and a half million
people scattered over the eastern part of the nation,[20]
and the few thousand immigrants that arrived each year
were negligible in comparison.[21] Moreover the immi-

16 - No statistics on immigration were compiled by the
    Federal government before 1820. By a law of March
    2, 1819, collectors of customs were required to is-
    sue quarterly reports on the number of passengers
    arriving at their port, listing the age, occupation,
    sex and place of birth of each arrival. These re-
    ports form the basis of census statistics and of other
    compilations consulted for this and subsequent chap-
    ters. The most useful of these compilations is, Brom-
    well, M. J., History of Immigration to the United States
    (New York, 1856) Bromwell was a clerk in the state de-
    partment and had full access to all of the reports.
17 - Kennedy, Joseph C. G., Preliminary Report on the
    Eighth Census, 1860 (Washington, 1862), p. 13.
18 - Bromwell, History of Immigration, p. 176.
19 - Kennedy, Preliminary Report on the Eighth Census, p.13.
20 - DeBow, J.D.B., Statistical View of the United States,
    Embracing its Territory, Population - White, Colored
    and Slave - Moral and Social Condition, Industry,
    Property and Revenue; the Detailed Statistics of Cit-
    ies, Towns and Counties; Being a Compendium of the
    Seventh Census (Washington, 1854), p. 49. Hereafter
    referred to as DeBow's Compendium.
21 - In 1830 the total number of recorded arrivals amounted
    to only a little more than two tenths of one per cent
    of the population of the United States.

grants were needed; the manufacturing fostered by the War of 1812 was in a period of rapid growth; turnpikes were spreading their network over the eastern half of the country and the Irish were willing and able to build them.[22] Even though the immigrants were grouping themselves in cities and showing a decided lack of interest in the governmental problems of their adopted home,[23] there was little actual cause for alarm; rather a cause for welcome.

But while the feeling of actual danger from immigration in the decade of the 1820's was negligible, there were forces constantly breeding hostility and opposition toward the immigrant. The population streams from Europe were flowing almost entirely into the northern and eastern states of the Union; Philadelphia re-

22 - Fairchild, Immigration, p. 63. During the decade 1820-1830 the number of spindles used in mills more than quadrupled and the factory looms increased tenfold. Faulkner, H. U., American Economic History (New York, 1924) pp. 275-276.
23 - This lack of interest is shown by the large number of aliens in 1830 who had failed to make efforts at naturalization. There were in 1830 more than 107,000 unnaturalized alliances in the country, of the total of 128,502 immigrants who had arrived during the decade before. Compendium of the Enumeration of the Inhabitants and Statistics of the United States as Obtained at the Department of State, from the Returns of the Sixth Census, (Washington, 1849) p. 371. Hereafter referred to as Compendium of the Sixth Census. Most of these unnaturalized aliens were concentrated in the eastern states. There were 52,488 in New York, 15,376 in Pennsylvania and 8,788 in Massachusetts, these states having the largest number.

mained the chief port of entry until 1818 when it
was outstripped by New York.[24]   Boston also shared
largely in the quota, while the southern states received almost no immigration at all.   New Orleans
was to become a popular port of entry only when the
cotton trade of the west gave the Germans an easy access to that region.   Its neglect was due to the
voyage being two or three weeks longer and proportionately more expensive than to the eastern ports.
Too, New Orleans was shunned by the immigrants who
feared the yellow fever there.[25]   Although a few German settlements had been founded along the Mississippi
River[26] it was not until later that they proved an
attraction to others of their countrymen.   As a result, the south, expanding rapidly into the western
cotton lands, looked with envy upon the labor available in the north, and took steps to turn the immigrant
streams to their shores.[27]   When these steps availed

24 - Niles Register, XIII, p. 314; 360.
25 - Page, "Transportation of Immigrants," p. 736.
26 - The John Law Colony founded on the Mississippi in
     1718, had endured, together with another colony
     just above New Orleans established in 1750.
     Faust, Albert B., The German Element in the
     United States (Boston, 1909), vol. ii, chap. XIV.
27 - McGill, Caroline E., "Economic History, 1607-
     1865," The South in the Building of the Nation
     (Richmond, 1909), vol. v, pp. 596-600.   The
     southern states kept agents in Europe to en-
     courage immigration at this time, and in addition
     offered special inducements.   Thus Mississippi in
     1816 offered land rent free for three years to
     immigrants.

nothing, southern envy turned to resentment; a resentment that took its form in intense nativism.

The northern states had seeming cause for
their cold welcome to the strangers at their door.
Young America, a land of boundless opportunity, had
known no pauper problem until these famished and
destitute souls arrived. With their coming the
eastern cities saw their tax rates ever mounting to
care for a horde of emigrants turned away from Europe's
lean board. Many of them were not inherent paupers;
but they had exhausted their slender resources in
reaching America and needed help until they could re-
establish themselves. Charitable organizations formed
by their own countrymen aided them in moving to the
west where they could secure cheap land,[28] but the
activities of such societies had limitations soon
reached, and they also despaired the problem of coping
with such numbers.

28 - Typical societies of this nature were the Hibernian
Society of Baltimore and the Irish Emmigrant Association of New York. Similar societies existed in
Boston and Philadelphia. These societies were active in seeking land grants in the west from Congress, one such petition in 1818 for land in Illinois arousing the nativistic sentiments of Congress before it was refused. McMaster, History
of the People of the United States, vol. iv, pp.
392-392. For a fuller account of the activities
of one of these societies see: Meehan, Thomas F.,
"New York's First Irish Emigrant Society," United
States Catholic Historical Society Records and
Studies, vol. vi (New York, 1913), pp. 202-211.

There was a growing belief in the minds of
Americans at the time that all these impoverished aliens
were not able to care for themselves and never had been;
that America was being used as a dumping ground for destitute Europeans. Evidence shows that European national
governments were not responsible for the shifting of
the burden of pauper support to shoulders of Americans
but there is no doubt that many parishes in Ireland and
England were paying the passage of their poor to the new
world to be freed from the expense of their support. As
early as 1818 the editor of Niles Register had occasion
to report the arrival of a ship load of such immigrants,[29]
a few years later he was again referring to the arrival
of more of these "precious cargoes."[30] There were repeated accounts of parish-sent paupers in later issues
of the paper,[31] and with each account the editor grew
more bitter against them.[32] There was some justification
for alarm when in 1824 it was estimated that there was
one pauper for every 68 persons in Massachusetts, one
for every 150 persons in Connecticut, and one for every

29 - Niles Register, vol. xiii, p. 378.
30 - Ibid., April 26, 1823.
31 - Ibid., August 23, 1823; July 21, 1823; August 14,
     1830; August 21, 1830.
32 - Compare his statements in Ibid., July 3, 1830,
     with his more tolerant attitude in Ibid., July
     21, 1823, only seven years before.

100 persons in New Hampshire,[33] a percentage far in
excess of the numbers a decade before.

Most of the states along the seaboard receiving the brunt of this poor immigrant problem had
passed laws designed to protect themselves from Europe's unwanted soon after they began their independent
existence. New York law against the landing of persons
likely to become public charges had gone into effect in
1788[34] and Massachusetts had followed with a similar
measure in 1794.[35] South Carolina and Pennsylvania
had in addition protected themselves against the landing of foreign convicts.[36] But these acts were poorly
enforced and brought little relief. As the rising tide
of immigration swept over eastern states a growing sentiment developed for laws that would stop the influx of
dependent persons. The demand was met by a Massachusetts
law in 1820, increasing the bond required of captains to
$500;[37] in New York an act of 1824 provided for a $300.
bond to be forfeited if the immigrant became a public

33 - Ibid., June 26, 1824.
34 - Law of March 7, 1788. This act provided that the
master of a vessel landing a person likely to become a public charge had to either carry that person back to his native country, or post bond of
$100. that the community would not be liable for
his support. Printed in Abbott, Edith, Immigration,
Select Documents and Case Records (Chicago, 1924),
pp. 104-105.
35 - Law of February 26, 1794. Ibid., pp. 105-106.
36 - The South Carolina act was passed in 1788. Ibid.,
pp. 103-104. The Pennsylvania act followed in 1789.
Ibid., p. 102.
37 - Ibid., p. 108.

charge within two years.[38]

The ineffectiveness of these laws was demonstrated from the time in which they went into operation. Professional bondsmen immediately took over the work of supplying the bonds, and the passengers were charged for them. So inefficiently was the whole administration handled that by 1830 the price had fallen as low as two dollars for bonds for a whole ship load.[39] The state legislatures had failed in their attempt to protect Americans from the duty of supporting foreign paupers. Here was just cause for objection to the immigrant. The nativists seized this sound economic argument upon which to rest their claims against all aliens.

But even with this pauper menace, the immigrant stream that flowed at this time would normally have been welcomed with open arms by a country on the verge of industrial development and greatly in need of additional man power. That it was not so welcomed was in a measure due to the joint denunciation of press and pulpit. They saw in these immigrants no ordinary people; they were Papists, and the coming of the alien gave rise anew to all the deep seated dread of Romanism so long dormant in the breasts of Americans.

38 - Kapp, Freidrich, Immigration and the Commissioners of Emigration of the State of New York (New York, 1870), pp. 44-45.
39 - Ibid, pp. 45-48.

The average American of that day, with suspicions of Catholics which had been inherited from colonial times, saw only in this immigration stream a new menace of Popery.   Nearly all of the immigrants were Catholics; a majority of them were Irish[40] for the great German migration of the next decades had not set in.   The Protestant inhabitants of America saw for the first time actual danger to their institutions; the traditional horror of Romanism for the first time took on new and terrifying meaning.

To the nativistically inclined Americans of that generation there was every reason for alarm.   The Catholic Church, long a weak and struggling outcast among them, took on new life with this flow of worshippers to its shrines.   So small had the church been in the early years of American independence that Bishop Carroll had been able to handle all the affairs for the entire country without undue labor.   In 1808, when, at his request, the original See of Baltimore was divided and the Sees of New York, Philadelphia, Boston and Bards-

40 - Bromwell, History of Immigration, p. 176. In a
      typical year, 1828, while only 1,806 recorded
      immigrants arrived from Germany, 17,840 were
      landing from Ireland and England. In addition
      many hundreds of Irish not recorded in immigra-
      tion statistics were making their way into New
      England from Canada.

town erected, there were only 70 priests and 80 churches
in the entire country, with a total Catholic population
of about 70,000.[41] In the years following the church
grew but slowly, in 1818 there were only four priests
in the entire upper Mississippi valley.[42]

But with the growth of immigration, rapid expansion was necessary. In 1820 two new Sees, those of
Richmond and Charleston, were erected;[43] so amazing was
the spread that three more had to be created in the following decade.[44] By 1830 there were 14,000 Catholics,
with 16 churches, in New England alone.[45] In Ohio where
not a single church had existed fourteen years before,
there were twenty-four priests and twenty-two churches,
in addition to several congregations that had no churches,
a college, a seminary and a religious newspaper.[46] At the
time of the opening of the First Provincial Council in
Baltimore in 1829, when the church could look back upon
its record of progress, the hierarchy of the United States

41 - O'Gorman, History of the Roman Catholic Church,
     pp. 291-293.
42 - O'Hanlon, John, Life and Scenery in Missouri
     (Dublin, 1890), p. 77.
43 - O'Gorman, op. cit., pp. 300-301.
44 - Salzbacher, J., Meine Reise nach Nord-Amerika in
     Jahre 1842 (Vienna, 1845), Tables of statistics
     on growth of Catholic church in the United States
     at end of volume.
45 - Shea, History of the Catholic Church in the United
     States, vol. ii, p. 159.
46 - O'Daniel, V. F. The Right Rev. Edward Dominic
     Fenwick, O. P. Founder of the Dominicans in the
     United States (Washington, 1920), p. 402.

consisted of the Province of Baltimore, containing
seven Sees, while outside the province were three
more Sees having no center in the United States but
depending directly upon the Propaganda in Rome -
those of New Orleans and St. Louis, and the vicariate
of Alabama and Florida. According to the address of
this council to the Pope, there were at the time six
seminaries, nine colleges, thirty-three monasteries
and houses of religious women, and many schools and
hospitals scattered over the land.[47] Here indeed was
cause for alarm in the minds of Protestants. Their
mythical molehill was taking on mountainous proportions.

Not only was the Catholic church growing by
rapid strides in the United States, but events were
occurring within the church itself that called this
growth to the attention of the Americans. The Papal
Jubilee of Leo XII in 1827 was a signal for great activity and renewed interest in Catholicism the world
over; priests throughout the country were inspired in
their efforts to win converts.[48] Coming as it did when
the church was expanding in America, this activity was
viewed by Protestant natives as part of a general attack
upon all that was dear to their religious souls. But the

47 - O'Gorman, op. cit., pp. 336-338.
48 - O'Daniel, op. cit., pp. 320-335.

Papal Jubilee was celebrated in Rome. The thing that
brought the growth of Catholicism to the attention of
natives in the United States was the First Provincial
Council of Catholicity in America that met in Baltimore
on October 1, 1829.

The calling of this Provincial Council had
been due to the efforts of the Bishop of Charleston,
John England, and had been inspired by the growing sentiment of anti-Catholicism. He realized that much of the
objection to the church was due to its foreign nature,
and his efforts to secure the council were caused by a
desire to bring about a more independent American church
with native rather than foreign bishops.[49] But the council, rather than allaying the cry of No-Popery, served
only to encourage it. The assembling of the American
hierarchy in all its glory was a sight to cause concern
among simplicity loving Americans. Still more alarming
were the thirty-eight decrees issued by the bishops, decrees warning Catholics against "corrupt translations of
the bible," urging parishes to build Catholic schools to
save children from "perversion," dealing with proper school
books for the youth of the land, and lauding the baptism
of non-Catholic children when there was a prospect of
their being brought up in the Catholic faith.[50] When news

49 - Guilday, The Life and Times of John England, vol. ii,
       pp. 68-110.
50 - Guilday, Peter, A History of the Provincial Councils
       of Baltimore (New York, 1932) pp. 89-95.

of these decrees was spread about the land, Americans
saw justification for their fears of Romanism and Roman
aggression. The Papal serfs were actually bold enough
to attack their schools and their school books and, worst
of all, their sacred Bible! What next but their inviolate
freedom so recently won?

More powerful than even these events in centering attention on Catholicism was a controversy that broke
forth among the Catholics of Philadelphia and threatened
for a time to lead to a serious schism in the ranks of
American Catholics. The controversy was over a subject
which was to plague the church throughout its early history in the United States, the question of trusteeism.

The conflict over trusteeism, centering about
the question of whether the church should be controlled
and the clergy appointed by a group of trustees representing the congregation or by the bishop of the diocese,
was not new when it rocked the very foundations of the
church in Philadelphia. The diocese of Baltimore had seen
such a struggle on the death of Bishop Carroll in 1815;[51]
in the same year the Bishop of New Orleans was forced to
move from his own Cathedral to St. Louis to escape control
by the congregation.[52] When Bishop England took over the
See of Charleston in 1820 he was faced with a rebellious

---

51 - O'Gorman, History of the Roman Catholic Church,
     pp. 299-300.
52 - Ibid., pp. 329-33.

church, and only prompt action on his part through the
cooperation of the state legislatures in North Carolina,
Georgia and South Carolina checked serious disorders.[53]
But these conflicts had been mild, and had attracted
little attention outside of the community affected. It
remained for the Philadelphia fracas to bring trusteeism
and the Catholic church to the immediate attention of
the American people.

The roots of the Philadelphia struggle reach
back to the creation of the diocese in 1808. When the
Reverend Michael Egan became bishop at that time he found
that the trustees of Saint Mary's Cathedral were well or-
ganzied and willing to oppose him. When he refused to remove one of the two assistant priests of the Cathedral to
satisfy their demands for economy, a war was precipitated
which was to last for more than two decades. Egan died in
its midst, in 1814, and it was not until 1820 that his
place was taken by the bishop who was to bear the brunt
of the struggle, Reverend Henry Conwell. Bishop Conwell
was too old and too mild a man to meet the years that
opened before him, for under his rule the Philadelphia
church faced its great crisis.

Bishop Conwell however made the first move in the
controversy with the still rebellious trustees. He withdrew the faculties of the cathedral from one of the priests,

53 - Ibid., p. 308.

the Reverend William Hogan, charging that Hogan had
openly ridiculed him from the pulpit. Hogan retaliated
by insisting that he was being removed because he had
distributed the Bible among the people.[54] The trustees
announced their intention of supporting him and defying
the Bishop. There was only one course open to Bishop
Conwell if he was to retain his authority. He informed
Hogan that unless he resigned he would be excommunicated.

Hogan was alarmed at this threat, and was ready
to give up the struggle.[55] But the trustees had gone too
far to withdraw, and forced him to continue as priest and
accept the excommunication that was pronounced in May,
1822. They were aware that to continue in this defiance
of the bishop would require support of other Catholics,
and in order to secure this, issued a proclamation to the
people of the country: "Owing to the arbitrary and unjust-
ifiable conduct of certain foreigners," they declared,
"We are imperiously called upon to adopt some measures
by which a uniform system may be established for the
future regulation of our churches and the propagation
of our holy faith by the nomination and selection of proper pastors from our own citizens, from whom alone ought

54 - Hogan, William, Synopsis of Popery As It Was and As
It Is (Hartford, 1854), p. 113.
55 - Shea, History of the Catholic Church in the United
States, vol. iii, p. 232.

to be chosen our bishops, without our being compelled
to depend upon persons sent to us from abroad, who have
uniformly shown themselves hostile to our institutions."[56]

This bold statement met with little favorable
response from the Catholics of the country and Hogan,
disgusted with the whole struggle and alarmed by a brief
against the trustees issued by Pius VII, finally resigned
in 1824. The trustees appointed in his place the Reverend
A. Inglesi, a priest with a shady reputation. Before
coming to Philadelphia he had appeared in Quebec, announced that he was a sub-deacon, set up a theater in
which he gave pantomines, and carried on a thriving business as a wine merchant on the side. While there he had
been married to a Catholic woman by a Presbyterian minister, and, growing tired of her, attempted to marry again.
When his plans failed he had left Quebec, leaving an unpaid boarding bill behind him, and sought to reap new
profits from the Philadelphia controversy.[57]

Such a scoundrel could not remain long in the

56 - O'Gorman, History of the Roman Catholic Church in
the United States, p. 320.
57 - Bishop Plessis of Quebec to Bishop Conwell, Sept.
15, 1823. "Correspondence between Bishop Conwell
of Philadelphia and Bishop Plessis of Quebec,
1821-1825, relating Principally to the Hogan Schism,"
Records of the American Catholic Society of Philadelphia, vol. xxii (Philadelphia, 1911) pp. 277-279.

favor of even the St. Mary's trustees, and his place
was taken a short time later by the Reverend Thaddeus
J. O'Meally, who officiated as priest over the congregation for nearly a year without permission from the
Bishop of the diocese. This poor leadership proved
disastrous. In 1826 the trustees, seeing that their
cause was losing popularity, agreed to a compromise in
which they were to have equal power with the bishop in
appointing priests. The Pope refused to allow any such
arrangement, and the struggle dragged on, sending Bishop
Conwell into retirement with the disgrace of failure upon
his shoulders.

It was not until a new and more vigorous bishop,
the Reverend Patrick Kenrick, took charge of the diocese
in 1830 that affairs could be settled. He immediately announced his intention of assuming pastoral charge of the
rebellious Saint Mary's and when the trustees objected,
placed an interdict upon the church. Worshippers there
went quietly to other churches, the trustees, left with
no financial aid, were forced to submit. Bishop Kenrick,
his control undisputed, opened the Cathedral and the long
struggle was at an end.[58]

58 - This account of the Philadelphia controversy is drawn
from the following standard works: O'Gorman, History
of the Roman Catholic Church in the United States,
vol. iii, pp. 229-257; England, John, The Works of
the Right Reverend John England, First Bishop of
Charleston (Cleveland, 1908), vol. vi, pp. 389-486,
a series of letters from Bishop England to Bishop
Conwell telling of the controversy in some detail;
Hassard, J. R. G., The Life of the Most Reverend
John Hughes (New York, 1866) pp. 50-115.

Although terminating in triumph for the church and its hierarchy, the Philadelphia controversy did the cause of Catholcism in America untold harm. For ten years the trustees and bishops had been deadlocked and the eyes of all the country had been fastened upon them. American Protestants, understanding little of the true nature of the Catholic church, had listened to charges hurled by the trustees in their accusations against the bishops. Americans had heard of foreigners controlling the church, they had been told that those foreigners wanted to rule the people of their congregations as despots rule their subjects, they had been told that the very name of democracy was flaunted by this great engine of Popery. The Bishops of the country meeting in the Baltimore Provincial Council in 1829, had done little to aid the popularity of their cause when they had condemned lay trusteeship and decreed that no church should be erected in the future without being legally assigned to the Bishop.[59] The press characterized this stand as a "singular specimen of papal authority exercised over the people of a free country,"[60] and a petition was immediately presented to the Pennsylvania legislature by a group of citizens praying that char-

59 - Guilday, Life and Times of John England, vol. ii, pp. 125-126.
60 - The Philadelphian, quoted in New York Observer, June 28, 1829.

ters in the future be denied to churches not having lay
trustees. The petition was aimed specifically at the
declaration of the Baltimore Council. "It is against
such tyrannical and unchristian acts," it said, "so
repugnant to our republican institutions, that your
petitioners humbly solicit your Honorable body to grant
legislative aid."[61] And it drew a lengthy picture of
the actual danger that faced the United States if bishops were allowed to control church property.

The feelings stirred by the controversy loosed
a whole flood of propaganda upon the country, none of it
flattering to the Catholic church. William Hogan contributed much, circulating widely printed statements charging
Catholicism with deserting the true purity of the Gospel,[62]
while he was yet ministering to his congregation. Upon his
resignation he married and devoted his life to attacking
Catholicism, becoming one of the great propaganda writers
of the decades to come.[63] No less than thirty-seven books
and pamphlets varying from eight to 280 pages in length
were published between 1812 and 1825 upon the Philadelphia
controversy, a flood of anti-Catholic literature that was

61 - Petition printed in American Catholic Historical Re-
     searches, vol. xi (July 1894) pp. 129-132.
62 - Typical is a communication in the New York Observer
     August 14, 1824.
63 - Hassard, Life of John Hughes, p. 53. For the part
     played by Hogan in the coming controversy over Cath-
     olicism see supra., pp. 457-521.

telling in its effects.[64]

Protestant Americans, suddenly aware that a
powerful Catholic church was growing in their midst,
were more than ready to believe all the propaganda inspired by the Hogan schism. Not only was the whole
heritage of their thought bred in such tales, but conditions in the 1820's were peculiarly ripe for a manifestation of anti-Catholic feeling. The country was
wrapt in its burst of excitement over Masonry that culminated in the failure of the presidential candidate of
the Anti-Masonic party, William Wirt, in 1832. Conservative farmers, reading of the dread oaths and black
secrets of the Masons, were more ready to accept such
stories about the other great secret organization of
which they were beginning to hear, the Catholic Church.
The feeling was heightened because Andrew Jackson was the
only politician who openly favored the Masons and the
latter flocked into his party, as did the Catholics and

64 - Baltimore Literary and Religious Magazine, February
    1839, p. 71. The editor of this nativistic magazine
    states that he purchased a bundle of books and pam-
    phlets concerning the Hogan controversy "at a pretty
    high price, after strong competition, by a priest
    who stood nearby." While this particular bundle
    contained the thirty-seven books and pamphlets it
    must be supposed that there were others published
    at the time that were not included.

the foreigners.[65] So Masonry and Catholicism, dread
oaths and the inquisition, became linked in the minds
of the people.

More important in preparing the American mind
for the onslaught against Catholicism that was to come
were new tendencies becoming apparent in religion. About
1826 the term "New Measures" began to come into use to
designate new means being employed by the churches. The
New Measures represented a swing away from the liberalism
that had followed the revolution with its Deistic tendencies; and that had given birth to Unitarianism and Univer-
salism; a swing toward a rigid fundamentalism that rivaled
the stern religion of the Puritans of colonial New England.
Preaching throughout the land became bolder and more de-
nounciatory, the practice of praying for individuals by
name was begun, converts were pleaded with and led to the
anxious seat when they had accepted the truth, females
were encouraged to speak and pray in public meetings. This
new revivalism was introduced into the country by the Reverend Charles G. Finney, a lawyer of western New York, and
the enthusiasm with which it was accepted in that region

65 - McCarthy, Charles, The Anti-Masonic Party: A study
of Political Anti-Masonry in the United States
1823-1840 (Washington, 1903) p. 539. Jackson
alone of the prominent political leaders of the
day openly favored the Masons during the attacks
upon them and thus won their support.

formed the background for the eccentric religions
that were to begin there in the next decades.[66]

Throughout the country the New Measures
were accepted by a widening group during the 1820's.
The Presbyterians were most active in proclaiming
this new way to their God;[67] it was no accident that
this church was to be the one most prominent in denouncing Popery in the coming years. Revivals were
held throughout the land, the New York Observer and
other religious papers devoted at least a column each
week to describing these manifestations of the new
spirit. The whole country was under the influence of
a wave of religious excitement. The people were ready
to shout against any attack upon their religion or
their beliefs; were eager to denounce with zealous
glee the anti-Christ that was Romanism.

This new burst of interest in religion inspired the founding and operation of a number of societies that were to add their voices to the cry against
Popery in the coming years. Several state tract societies had been in operation from 1807 to the organization

66 - Sweet, W. W., The Story of Religions in America
     (New York, 1930) pp. 396-397; 409-411; Davis,
     Emerson, The Half Century; or, a History of Changes
     that have taken Place and Events that have Trans-
     pired, Chiefly in the United States, between 1800
     and 1850. (Boston, 1851) p. 355-356.
67 - Davis, The Half Century, p. 356.

of the New England Tract Society in 1814. In 1823 this
organization changed its name to the American Tract Society and two years later another tract society formed
in New York was merged with it to make a great national
organization.[68] Swayed by clergy who had drunk too
eagerly of the Hogan controversy propaganda, local
branches of the society immediately began using the
organization as a means of attack on Popery.[69] Added
to the force of the American Tract Society were a series of Bible societies, inspired by the success of the
Philadelphia Bible Society that had been formed in 1808
to supply destitute families with the Scriptures.[70] The
many similar organizations founded in various states and
communities immediately afterward were banded together
into the American Bible Society at a meeting in New York
in 1816,[71] a society that from the time of its organization turned much of its attention against the Catholics.

The conflict between the American Bible Society
and the Catholic church was inevitable. The first article

68 - Sweet, The Story of Religions in America, p. 366.
69 - Thus in Pennsylvania Nicholas Murray, then a student at the Princeton Theological Seminary, helped
organize the local society and insisted that one
of its first publications should be The History
of Andrew Dunn, an anti-Catholic work that had
been circulated in Ireland. Murray, Nicholas,
Memoirs (New York, 1862), p. 99.
70 - Sweet, The Story of Religions in America, p. 366.
71 - Dwight, Henry O., The Centennial History of the
American Bible Society (New York, 1916), vol. 1,
p. 24.

of the constitution adopted by the society declared
that its "sole object shall be to encourage a wider
circulation of the Holy Scripture without note or
comment. The only copies in the English language
to be circulated by the Society shall be of the version now in common use."[72] Such activities of the
Society immediately threw it into conflict with the
Catholic church. This church, believing as it did
that it was the "divinely appointed custodian and interpreter of the Holy Writ,"[73] could not approve of
the policy of the society in distributing the Scriptures "without note or comment." With approval of a
bishop necessary for editions of the Bible read by
Catholics,[74] opposition developed as soon as the American Bible Society began spreading the Protestant version of the Gospel among Catholics; a conflict which
culminated in Papal letters denouncing the society.[75]
Members of the society, incensed at this treatment and
seeing in the Catholic attitude an attack upon the
Bible rather than one version of the Bible, added their
enthusiastic voices to the chorus of complaint against
Popery which was rising throughout the land.[76]

72 - Ibid., p. 25.
73 - The Catholic Encyclopedia (New York, 1908) vol. ii,
     p. 544.
74 - Ibid., vol. ii, p. 544.
75 - Ibid., vol. ii, p. 545.
76 - See communication of Bible Society in the Boston
     Recorder, April 26, 1834.

Equally influential in the swelling tide of
No-Popery were the Home Missionary societies which were
formed throughout New England and the eastern states to
carry religion to the frontier. A whole series of these
societies were organized after 1801 when the New Hampshire Society began its successful existence, resulting
in the formation of the American Home Missionary Society
in 1826.[77] From the time of its inception it too waged
a merciless war on Romanism.

National organizations were thus focusing their
attention upon Catholicism and it was the pre-ordained
prejudice of such scrutiny that was to bring a new meaning to nativism within the next few years. The clergy
under the influence of so vast a system of propaganda
and inspired by the revivalistic tendencies of the New
Measures, began in the 1820's to inquire more closely
into the life of the Catholic Church.

This inquiry resulted in large measure from
the activity of Catholics against the Bible societies.
Ministers were warned that the Bible was everywhere
being attacked by Catholics and that the Bible societies would be driven from existence if the Pope and

---

77 - Sweet, The Story of Religions in America, pp. 361-
363. For an account of the founding and activities
of the American Home Missionary Society see:Goody-
koontz, Colin B., The Home Missionary Movement and
the West, 1798-1861. (Unpublished doctoral disser-
tation, Harvard University, 1920)

Jesuits could have their way,[78] they were told that
a great contest was to be fought in America between
Popery and Protestantism and that they must prepare
themselves for the struggle if theirs was to be the
victory.[79] Preachers began turning their attention
to sermons chiefly anti-Catholic in feeling in an
effort to stimulate righteous indignation and outright
intolerance in the minds of their flocks.[80] A convention of the Protestant Episcopal Church in 1826 listened to a lengthy sermon on Romanism[81] and three years
later the bishops of that same church issued a pastoral
letter on the perils of Popery, so violently did they
feel on the subject.[82] Throughout the land the churches
rallied round the standard of fear which was to give so
much support to the No-Popery epoch to come.

The popular interest in religion which followed
in the wake of the New Measures brought into existence a
vast number of religious newspapers. These raised their
voices in universal lamentation against the evils of
Rome. The first religious newspaper in the country,
the Boston Recorder, was founded in 1818 to spread the

78 - The New York Observer, April 16, 1825.
79 - Ibid., January 23, 1829.
80 - England, The Works of John England, vol. iii,
     pp. 452-518, prints one of these sermons preached
     at Washington and Bishop England's answer to it.
81 - Ibid., vol. ii, pp. 171-209.
82 - Guilday, Life and Times of John England, vol. ii,
     p. 451.

doctrines of Presbyterianism.[83]   Others followed all
over the country, although New York city remained without such a paper until 1823.   The New York Observer,
founded at that time, more than made up for the delay
by its widespread influence.   In its first issue it
spoke of the great need for a journalistic shepherd to
guide public opinion to Gospel views;[84] in future years
the Observer became that Keeper of thousands of American
minds.

The founders of the New York Observer were
Sidney E. Morse, who had established the Boston Recorder,
and his brother, Richard Morse.   They were sons of that
staunch defender of Congregationalism, the Reverend
Jedidiah Morse of Charlestown,[85] and brothers of Samuel
F. B. Morse, who was to gain fame in the coming years
not only as inventor of the telegraph but as wielder of
one of the most vitriolic and influential pens among anti-Catholic propagandists.   The Morse heritage of Catholic hatred was well embodied in the Observer.   Its policy as to Rome was announced in an early issue.   "Many
Protestants," the editors wrote, "begin to think that
Popery has of late assumed a mild form.   It is no doubt

83 - New York Observer, December 15, 1827.
84 - Ibid., May 17, 1823.
85 - Mott, Frank L., A History of American Magazines,
      1741-1850 (New York, 1930), p. 373.

true that the Papal church has lost her power, and
therefore cannot play the tyrant as heretofore. But
Protestants ought to remember that it is Papal policy to be mild until they have power to be severe."[86]
A few years later the Catholic church was being branded
as a real menace to the freedom of the United States
and a great insidious machine sending its emigrants to
this country to stamp out liberty and democracy.[87] From
that time on the Observer gave much of its space[88] to
the crusade against Rome that was embraced with such
enthusiasm by the Morse family.

The campaign carried on by the Observer was
not a narrow one. The editors flayed every feature of
the Catholic church within their knowledge, and some
features of which their understanding was most question-
able. Many of the barbs were directed against the "image worship" of Catholicism, its "lying and supersiti-
tion and its rites of almost blasphemous folly."[89] Other
articles described the ceremony of the transit of the
Virgin with outspoken ridicule,[90] denounced the blessing of animals[91] and bells[92] in Rome, and condemned
the miracle of the melting blood of Saint Januarius in

86 - New York Observer, November 13, 1824.
87 - Ibid., December 19, 1829.
88 - During the first years of its existence, the New
     York Observer averaged more than one lengthy arti-
     cle on Romanism each issue.
89 - Ibid., March 22, 1828.
90 - Ibid., December 16, 1826; October 11, 1828.
91 - Ibid., November 12, 1825; March 22, 1828.
92 - Ibid., November 21, 1829.

Naples.[93] How, the editors asked, can people be "so
duped and so enslaved in superstitious belief?"[94]
Classed with these miracles in the minds of the readers
of the Observer were the penances that Irish Catholics
performed[95] and the presence of a Purgatorian Society
that existed in that land.[96] These two things represented only papal ignorance and delusion, they were,
the Observer insisted, dreadful relics of the dark
ages.

Miracles and superstition were not alone in
contaminating the Romish religion, not, at least, if
the Observer of these years can be believed. The
boasted unity of the Catholic church was attacked as
mere "authority substituted for faith and uniformity
of ignorance preferred to the investigation of truth."[97]
Age old tales of the temporal power of the Pope were
revived, and one correspondent made boast of how he
had forced a priest to acknowledge that the church still
claimed such power.[98] The morals of the clergy were considered too indecent to flaunt before the readers of a
good Presbyterian journal, but ponderous articles told

93 - Ibid., November 4, 1826.
94 - Ibid., January 29, 1825.
95 - Ibid., March 19, 1825.
96 - Ibid., February 5, 1825.
97 - Ibid., June 20, 1829.
98 - Ibid., November 13, 1824.

of South American laws passed to keep priests from
the streets at night as the only means of protecting
the women of that land[99] and of how Cuban priests kept
mistresses openly under the name of housekeepers.[100]
An absurd story told of a French priest who donned a
mask and robbed an aged widow of money of which she
had told him in confession.[101] Readers put down the
journal with no high respect for the moral character
of Rome.

The Inquisition was not unknown in America,
and the Observer saw to it that its readers were not
allowed to forget this Popish cruelty.[102] Furthermore
the Inquisition was proved to be still a thriving institution in Spain,[103] and it was boldly asserted that
the same thing would be true of the United States if
Romanism continued to thrive.[104] Catholics were hailed
as breakers of that honorable Puritan institution, the
Sabbath[105] not only by the Observer but by less violent
papers as well.[106] Anecdotes sworn to be valid were
used as propaganda. One of the most amusing concerned
a Protestant wife and a Catholic husband. His efforts

99 - Ibid., September 23, 1826.
100- Ibid., March 14, 1829.
101- Ibid., April 28, 1827.
102- Ibid., October 5, 1829.
103- Ibid., December 16, 1826.
104- Ibid., September 26, 1829.
105- Ibid., September 23, 1826.
106- Massachusetts Yeoman, August 8, 1829.

to secure her conversion finally resulted in her consent with the stipulation that she should bake the wafer
to be used as the host. After the priest had announced
that the wafer had been changed into the body of Christ
she asked him to eat it, saying that she had mixed ar-
senic with the flour, but that there could be no harm
left now as there was nothing of the original substance
remaining. The readers of the Observer must have chuckled
over the way in which the priest cursed and left the room,
and especially how the husband, seeing the error of his
ways, became a good Presbyterian immediately.[107]

The close association of the Observer with the
church that gave it its support meant that both Catholic
attacks on Protestants and Protestant victories over
Catholics would make exceptionally able reading. Accounts from Peru[108] and Ireland[109] told of how priests
had burned the Holy Scriptures, and forbidden their circulation. Articles from European countries recounted
with pious joy the conversion of Papists to true Christianity[110] as did other articles with their scenes laid
in America.[111] Resolute Presbyterians could also read
with horror of how Protestants were kept from missionary

107 - New York Observer, August 26, 1826.
108 - Ibid., April 15, 1826.
109 - Ibid., October 27, 1827.
110 - Ibid., June 26, 1824; April 16, 1825; August 16, 1828.
111 - Ibid., April 25, 1829.

work among the heathen Japanese and Chinese by the
Jesuits[112] and how the good Anglicans of the British
Army were forced into Popish worship in Malta.[113] So
the New York Observer with the Morse brothers at its
helm went about its work of spreading propaganda against
the Catholicism which it honestly hated.

But the Observer was not the only paper in the
field. The success of the Boston Recorder and of the
Observer brought numerous other religious papers into
existence. By the middle of the 1820's every denomination had several newspapers sending out a weekly stream
of information to the members of its congregations. In
1827 there were thirty religious newspapers in the country, which weekly invaded between fifty and sixty thousand homes and boasted an annual circulation of about
three million sheets.[114] All of this vast array gave
more or less attention to the menace of Catholicism.
Bishop England, of Charleston, complained most of the
Gospel Advocate,[115] the Christian Advocate,[116] and the
Mount Zion Missionary[117] and devoted much of his life to

112 - Ibid., April 6, 1825.
113 - Ibid., July 25, 1829.
114 - Ibid., December 15, 1827.
115 - England, The Works of the Right Reverend John
England, vol. iii, pp. 385-423, prints replies
made by Bishop England to attacks by this paper.
116 - Ibid., vol. iii, pp. 329-384.
117 - Ibid., vol. iii, pp. 223-326.

replying to their barbed attacks. The Baptist Recorder was so bitter in its bigotry that it became involved in controversies with the president of a Catholic college.[118] Almost as prolific in propaganda was the Theological Repertory,[119] and the Southern Religious Telegraph.[120] Nor were the religious newspapers alone in the field. Secular papers of a more popular sort took every occasion to poke ridicule at Catholicism, the North American Review,[121] the American Daily Advertiser[122] and the Massachusetts Yeoman[123] being active among others.

This marshaling of the forces of the press against Catholicism was justly resented by the Church itself. Attacked on all sides, the leaders of the Church in America were faced with the problem of how to meet this clamor. Some favored answering the attacks as they were made,[124] but more sedate councils prevailed. The whole matter of the adverse Protestant press was taken up by the Baltimore Provincial Council

118 - New York Observer, May 26, 1827.
119 - England, op. cit., vol. iii, pp. 104-222. Consists of attacks by Bishop England on statements made by this paper.
120 - Williams, Shadow of the Pope, p. 60.
121 - Ibid., p. 60.
122 - American Daily Advertiser, July 26, 1817.
123 - Massachusetts Yeoman, November 17, 1827.
124 - Bishop England is a prominent example of this type of churchman. He devoted much of his life to answering Protestant attacks on the Church that he loved; his Works in their most recent edition are more than half given over to such defenses.

in 1829 and considered in a pastoral letter issued
to the clergy and people of the Church. "Not only,"
the letter read, "do they assail us and our institutions in a style of vituperation and offense, misrep-
resent our tenets, vilify our practices, repeat the
hundred times refused calumnies of the days of angry
and bitter contention in other lands, but they have
even denounced you and us as enemies to the liberties
of the republic, and have openly proclaimed the fanatical necessity of obstructing our progress, and of using
their best efforts to extirpate our religion. It is
neither our principle nor our practice to render evil
for evil, or railing for railing, and we exhort you
rather to the contrary, to render blessing."125

Despite this commendable attitude on the part
of the Catholic church the growth of propaganda continued
in the religious periodicals which thrived throughout the
1820's and later decades. Serious results must necessarily follow any such concentrated and widely circulated
agitation. But anti-Catholic feeling in the United States,
fostered by this steady stream of reading matter, was
suddenly stirred by an influence from abroad. The passage of the English Catholic Emancipation Bill in 1829 and
the long period of controversy that preceded its passage,

125 - O'Gorman, History of the Roman Catholic Church,
        pp. 342-343.

gave new weight to the cry of No Popery in America.

The passage of the Catholic Emancipation Bill itself[126] aroused resentment and heated comment from the Protestant Press in America. The Church Register, prominent Philadelphia paper, warned "we shall be sorry for this measure, if the revival and dissemination of the trumperies and delusions of Popery are to be the result of it.[127] But this manifestation of feeling came only as an anti-climax. The principal effect of the Emancipation Bill upon America was due to the propaganda spread over England in the years before and just after its passage.

As soon as a need became manifest for a measure that would grant civil rights to Catholics in England, the antipathy of English Protestants inherited from the time of the Reformation flamed anew. Stories that had been told at the time of the Gunpowder Plot and the Gordon Riots were revived and spread wholesale over the land. Propaganda writers whose numbers were legion be-

126 - Shea, History of the Catholic Church in the United States, vol. iii, p. 420, remarks on the effect this bill must have had on the American anti-Catholic movement without analyzing the manner of this effect. His remarks are copied by Desmond, The Know Nothing Party, p. 14, and Maury, Wars of the Godly, pp. 52-53.

127 - Quoted in Hassard, Life of John Hughes, pp. 92-93. Hughes replied to the statement in a series of letters in the United States Gazette, July 14 - August 9, 1829.

sieged the English people with books and pamphlets
warning them of the dire consequences if the hated
Papists were given power. For a time this agitation
remained unorganized, but in 1827 new strength was
given to the whole movement by the formation of a
powerful nativistic society, the British Society
for the Promotion of the Principles of the Protestant Reformation, formed at London on May 21.[128] Societies for the conversion of Irish Catholics to Protestantism had existed earlier, such as the London Hibernian Society, the Irish Evangelical Society, and the
Baptist Irish Society,[129] but this new organization was
the first group formed with the definite purpose of attacking Catholicism.

News of this concentrated effort against the
Church spread rapidly in America. The speeches at the
annual meetings of the British Society for the Promotion
of the Principles of the Protestant Reformation were reported in full in American papers,[130] and the growing
financial success of the organization was hailed with
enthusiasm.[131] When the success of the society had been

128 - New York Observer, July 28, 1827.
129 - Ibid., March 12, 1825.
130 - Reports of the first meeting of the society are
        in the New York Observer, July 28, 1827; and
        September 6, 1828; of the second meeting in Ibid.,
        July 18, 1829.
131 - Receipts of the society in its first year were
        1,889 pounds. Ibid., September 6, 1828. In
        the second year of its existence receipts leaped
        to 2,662 pounds. Ibid., July 18, 1829.

great enough to force the Irish Catholics to form a
rival organization, the Roman Catholic Book Society
of Dublin, the American press expressed frank admira-
tion.[132]

The British Reformation Society, as it was
commonly called, carried on an active and long continued career. It sent agents through the land to lecture against the claims of Rome, it published tracts
that it distributed free for the asking, and it issued
books tearing Popery to fine shreds.[133] American anti-
Catholic societies which were to be founded in the next
decade gave evidence of this British influence by following in name and method the mother country organization
of intolerance.

Any literary effort against Catholicism was
given encouragement, and the work of the British Reformation Society there meant that England teemed with
these works. They were bitter bigotry in the extreme,
and directed an attack on the Church from every angle.
Many of these books found their way to America or were
reprinted in the United States. American authors, aware
of the favorable reception that such works received from
a people always ready to believe the worst about Catholi-

132 - Ibid., July 11, 1829.
133 - Ibid., July 18, 1829.

cism, saw a fertile field for their talents in propaganda. Thus, inspired by the success of Protestant pens in the controversy over the Emancipation Bill, American propagandists deluged their readers with a flood of paper and ink which was to create new intolerance and proclaim nativism the power to be.

The English works reprinted or circulated in the United States varied in effectiveness. Some of them were nearly entirely English in their appeal.[134]. Others, while written largely to combat the Emancipation Bill, were broad enough in their challenge or outspoken enough in their attacks upon Catholicism that they attracted wide attention in America. In this class may be placed the books of J. Blanco White, Letters from Spain,[135] appearing in 1822, and Practical and Internal Evidence against Catholicism,[136] published four years later. J. Blanco White was one of the first to advertise himself as "late a Popish priest." Born in Spain, he had spent

134 - In this group may be classed: Richardson, James. The Roman Catholic Convicted upon his Own Evidence of Hostility to the Protestant Churches of Britain (New York, 1823); Connelly, Pierce, Domestic Emancipation from Roman Rule, a Petition to the Honourable House of Commons (London, 1829); Connelly, Pierce, The Coming Struggle with Rome not Religious but Political; or, words of Warning to the English People (London, 1830)
135 - White, J. Blanco, Letters from Spain (London 1822)
136 - White, J. Blanco, Practical and Internal Evidence against Catholicism with Occasional Strictures on Mr. Butler's Book of the Roman Catholic Church; in Six Letters Addressed to the Impartial among the Roman Catholics of Great Britain and Ireland (London, 1826)

ten years as a priest there before renouncing Catholicism and moving to England in 1800, there to join the Anglican church.[137] Letters from Spain described the harmful effects of Catholicism and the Inquisition on that country, but Practical and Internal Evidence against Catholicism was a barb directly aimed at the Catholic Emancipation Bill. White argued that, if Catholics were ever admitted to Parliament, they would be compelled by the nature of their allegiance to Rome to destroy Protestantism in the British Isles.[138]

Here was a fetching argument as far as the United States was concerned. It implied that if Catholics were given any political power they would be obliged to obey the Pope no matter what he commanded them to do, even to the overthrow of the cherished republic. Readers of the book were instructed never to trust a Catholic in office. Here was a practical suggestion, and readers of J. Blanco White gave it enthusiastic reception in America. A group of Protestant ministers numbered among many denominations recommended the book to their flocks as a "temperate and able exposition of the errors of Popery."[139] Its popularity only was increased when Catholics in Baltimore brought pressure to keep the book from being dis-

137 - Guilday, Life and Times of John England, vol. ii, pp. 435.
138 - White, Practical and Internal Evidence, pp. 4-6.
139 - Guilday, Life and Times of John England, vol. ii, p. 436.

played by book sellers there, a move that thousands of Protestants accepted as proof of Catholic guilt and intolerance.[140]

More important even than the volumes of Blanco White was the work of another converted "Popish priest," Anthony Gavin. Gavin's Master Key to Popery was not inspired by the Emancipation Bill, it had been written during the eighteenth century and had attained wide circulation even then.[141] But the renewed attack on Catholicism in England brought it to the fore once more. New editions were published in England, and it was reprinted in America as early as 1812.[142] With the publication of the work in America, a great piece of propaganda was launched which was to reappear under different titles and in different forms all through the period of nativistic excitement lasting down to the Civil war.[143]

The Master Key to Popery was well executed to

140 - New York Observer, December 19, 1829.
141 - Gavin, Anthony, A Master Key to Popery (3rd edition, London, 1773)
142 - Gavin, Anthony, A Master Key to Popery, Giving a Full Account of all the Customs of the Priests and Friars and the Rites and Ceremonies of the Popish Religion.(New York, 1812)
143 - Among the many editions were: Gavin, Anthony, The Master Key to Popery: Customs of Priests and Friars, and Rites and Ceremonies of the Popish Religion, Inquisition, etc. (Cincinnati, 1834); Gavin, Anthony, The Great Red Dragon, or the Master Key to Popery (Boston, 1854). It was also reprinted in part in several anti-Catholic books by other authors.

hold the interested Americans. Stern religious life
in the new country frowned upon literature that smacked
of the obscene, but in Anthony Gavin's opus they could
read stories not unlike those of Bocaccio to their
heart's content and console their consciences with
the thought that here was truth about hated Romanism.
The reading of obscenity was made a religious duty by
Gavin.

        The book plunges immediately into the murky
depths of Romish rites. In treating the confessional,
Gavin admits that priests below forty years of age are
not allowed to hear confessions of women, but points
out frequent cases from his own experiences as a priest
when the rule was neglected. He declares that it is sel-
dom lived up to.[144] The situation that resulted from
this open violation of the rule made the confessional
nothing more than a bawdy meeting between attractive
priests and beautiful ladies. At least so Gavin im-
plies. In fact he admits that priests serve as pro-
curers in many countries, being employed by colorful
filles de joie to lure innocent damsels into the path
of sin.[145] Many of the priests do this only uncon-

---

144 - Gavin, Master Key to Popery, pp. 11-12. The edi-
       tion published in New York in 1812 is referred to
       in this and the following notes.
145 - Ibid., pp. 80-83.

sciously, however, and simply instruct innocent virgins through the lewd questions put to them in confession.   Perhaps, he says, young women going to confession "do not know what simple fornication is? What
voluntary or involuntary pollution? What impure desire? By the confessor's indiscreet questions, the
penitents learn things of which they had never dreamed
before; and when they come to that tribunal with a sincere innocent heart, to receive advice and instruction,
they go home with light knowledge and an idea of sins
unknown to them before."[146]   Gavin even gives an example
of this insidious practice; he tells of seeing a little
girl ten years old come from a cathedral in Spain and
tell her mother that the priest had asked her if she
were deflowered or not.[147]   When the mother explained
that the priest meant only if she liked to smell flowers
or not Gavin felt that such a definition was bound to
lead the child sooner or later into troublesome paths.

Having given his readers ample warning of the
pornography to follow, Gavin turns to tales told at confession by young ladies; stories which equalled those of
Rabelais in all save literary merit. A typical confession concerns a young lady named Mary who, according

146 - Ibid., p. 15.
147 - Ibid., p. 79.

to her confession, had been living in sin for two
years. She had lived out of wedlock with a young
neighbor who came to her bed each night through a
secret passage way connecting the houses. More than
this, he brought his servant, and the servant had seduced Mary's maid. She had escaped the usual consequences of her sin, she says, because a cousin of hers,
a friar, had also approached her, and she had consented
to receive him into her already well occupied bed if he
would provide her with medicine with which she might
keep her innocence unblemished on the surface, at least.
But this friar was not satisfied. He made her submit to
the lust of several of his friends of the cloth, and he
insisted on using the maid for the same purpose.[148] The
priest hearing this remarkable confession was a young
and attractive man, and how, Gavin asks, could he keep
his purity with such stories, whispered into his ears?
Gavin obviously does not believe in the impossible.

With such bawdy stories he denounced the confessional before turning his attention to other things.
He skips through an account of the gambling proclivities
of the clergy,[149] of their poor treatment of poverty-
stricken Catholics who have little money to give them,[150]

148 - Ibid., pp. 22-32. Similar accounts, pp. 32 ff.
149 - Ibid., p. 160.
150 - Ibid., p. 59.

of the mass as an institution "with greater power and virtue than the lodestone, as the lodestone only draws iron, but the mass allures silver, gold and precious stones."[151] He tells of nuns taking money from people with the promise that it will be used to have masses said for them, of the nuns keeping the money and giving their bodies as payment for the masses to the priests instead.[152] He even dwells upon the immorality of so-called image worship by insisting that barren women become fruitful before the image of the Virgin at Sara-gossa only because of the attractive priests in atten-dance.[153]

Gavin gives a lurid description of the Inquisi-tion in Spain with its bloody instruments[154] and its use by Rome in order to carry out the great aim of Catholi-cism - the extermination of all Protestants.[155] Such a prosaic subject might seem to give him little opportunity to play upon the lascivious side of his reader's natures. But such an author as Gavin would let no obstacle stand in his way. He found a means of appealing to his readers by telling of the part that women played in the Inquisi-tion! One lady tells of her experiences; how she was

151 - Ibid., p. 146.
152 - Ibid., p. 163.
153 - Ibid., pp. 277-278.
154 - Ibid., p. 228.
155 - Ibid., p. 113.

lured into the Inquisition at Sarogossa, how she was
given a maid and a luxurious establishment, and how
she was threatened with death by slow roasting unless
she submit to the passions of the priest in charge.
"I had not the liberty to make any excuse," she writes,
"So by extinguishing the fire of his passion, I was
free from the gradual fire and dry pan."[156] Considering the moral tone of the general reading matter peculiar to this religious generation there is little reason
to wonder that Gavin's work passed through many editions.

  With other English books brought into America
during the decade of the 1820's, less important than the
works of White and Gavin, but adding their part to the
influence,[157] it was inevitable that American authors
should begin to imitate them, thereby conveying some of
of the profits of nativism to their own pockets. Two

156 - Ibid., pp. 220-235.
157 - A typical publication was the novel long popular
      in England, The Conversion and Edifying Death of
      Andrew Dunn (Philadelphia, 182_) Others dealt with
      Catholic persecution as: An Awful Warning; or, the
      Massacre of St. Bartholomew (London, 1812). The
      great majority of the English works poured into the
      country after 1830 when the demand for them had
      been well demonstrated. Others that were not pub-
      lished in America were well known here because of
      complete articles describing them and recommending
      them to readers in church periodicals. A typical
      review of Faber's Difficulties of Romanism, is in
      the Biblical Repertory, 1829.

books that mark the real beginning of American nativistic literature were published in 1821. Jeremiah
Odel, a native of Vermont, spun a long and dull attack
upon the priesthood,[158] labeling them as the "very
sink of corruption, calamity and cruelty to mankind.[159]
John Coustos set forth his adventures with the Inquisition in Spain.[160] It was a somewhat gruesome account
of the tortures endured by him[161] when he refused to
give up his membership in the order of the Free Masons,[162]
and attempting to convert the Catholic Inquisitors to
Protestantism by means of long Biblical arguments.[163]
American authorship during this period fell below the
standard set by Gavin.

Nor did the books that immediately followed
these first two pioneers reach a very high level of

158 - Odel, Jeremiah, Popery Unveiled; to which is Annexed a Short Recital of the Origin, Doctrines,
Precepts and Examples of the Great Church Militant and Triumphant. (Bennington, Vt., 1821)
An earlier American publication with a strictly
religious appeal was, Wharton, C. H. Concise
View of the Principal Points of Controversy between the Protestant and Romish Churches. (New
York, 1817)
159 - Odel, Popery Unveiled, pp. 124-125.
160 - Coustos, John, The Mysteries of Popery Unveiled
in the Unparalleled Sufferings of John Coustos,
at the Inquisition of Lisbon, to which is added,
the Origin of the Inquisition and its Establishment in Various Countries; and the Master Key to
Popery by Anthony Gavin (Hartford, 1821)
161 - Ibid., pp. 45-54.
162 - Ibid., pp. 9-25.
163 - Ibid., pp. 26-37.

interest. A learned monograph entitled <u>Five Discourses</u>
<u>against Popery</u>[164] dealt in technical terms with the
Catholic faith, attempting to prove that the Bible
alone should be the basis of all faith as opposed to
the Catholic doctrines,[165] that worship of the Virgin
Mary,[166] the doctrine of transubstantiation,[167] and
the confession[168] were earthly concepts having no place
in the Divine will. A popular work in the south, <u>The</u>
<u>Protestant Catechism, Showing the Principal Errors of</u>
<u>the Church of Rome</u>;[169] had greater appeal, for it ex-
plained the theological attack upon Rome in words that
every layman could understand.[170] Probably the most
widely circulated work was an anonymous book, <u>Father</u>
<u>Clement, a Roman Catholic story</u>.[171] This was the first

---

164 - Secker, T., <u>Five Discourses Against Popery</u> (Windsor,
　　　Vt., 1827) A second edition appeared in Columbus,
　　　Ohio, in 1835.
165 - Ibid., pp. 5-28.
166 - Ibid., pp. 32-38.
167 - Ibid., pp. 46-50.
168 - Ibid., pp. 57-63.
169 - <u>The Protestant Catechism, Showing the Principal</u>
　　　<u>Errors of the Church of Rome</u> (Charleston, 1828)
170 - A typical extract from the <u>Protestant Catechism</u>:
　　　"Q. Why are the Scriptures kept from the people?
　　　A. The professed reason is the incompetency of
　　　the mass of the people to the right understand-
　　　ing of the scriptures. The effect is, their
　　　not discovering how contrary their religion is
　　　to the word of God."
171- <u>Father Clement, a Roman Catholic Story</u> (Boston,
　　　1827)

of a long line of anti-Catholic novels to flow from the
pens of American authors.

Father Clement could hardly be described as
gripping fiction. It sets forth the adventures of two
families of eighteenth century England, the Clarenhams
and the Montagues, Catholic and Presbyterian respectively.
The Clarenhams have a Jesuit confessor, Father Clement,
and the Montagues have a studious son, named, of course,
Ernest. Much of the work is devoted to long Biblical arguments between these two, aided occasionally by members
of the families to which they belong.[172] There is a
story, of course, a tale of the Catholic son of the
Clarenhams who falls into the hands of the Inquisition
when he is betrayed by Father Clement and is only res-
cued after violent activity on the part of sturdy
Ernest, culminating in a hand to hand battle with a
group of priests.[173] All ends happily, there are mar-
riages to be celebrated, and Father Clement dies repent-
ant, admitting that Romanism is wrong and that he has
found the true salvation in Presbyterianism.[174]

Circulation of these works, and others that

172 - Ibid., pp. 18-38; 58-81; 110-117.
173 - Ibid., pp. 169-205.
174 - Ibid., pp. 205-252.

were to follow,[175] naturally caused the Catholics of
the country considerable alarm. Their church was being
attacked on every side, it was natural that they should
take steps to defend it. Bishop England described the
condition of affairs in a later publication: "I found
that it was by no means considered a want of liberality,
on the part of the Protestants, to vilify the Catholic
religion, and to use the harshest and most offensive
terms when designating its practices. The newspapers
were generally stuffed with extracts and articles which
gave offense to Catholics."[176]

Few Catholics with spirit could see this condition continue without some effort to remedy it. The
Protestants were assailing them with newspapers and
books; it would only follow that retaliation should be
in kind. Newspapers should be founded and books written

175 - Other books published at the time: Narrative of
Van Halen's Don Juan; Imprisonment in the Dungeons
of the Inquisition at Madrid, and his Escape in
1817 and 1818; to which are added his Journey to
Russia, his Campaign with the Army of the Cauco-
sus, and his Return to Spain in 1821 (New York
1828); Waddell, Thomas, Letters to the Editors
of the Catholic Miscellany: Illustrating the
Papal Doctrine of Intention! The Opus Operatum,
Roman Infallibility, and the Knavery of Popish
Writers (New York, 1830); and An Exposition of
the Principles of the Roman Catholic Religion
with Remarks on its Influence in the United
States (Hartford, 1830)
176 - England, Works of Right Reverend John England,
vol. ii, p. 213.

to uphold the Catholic cause. At this time there were
a number of Irish newspapers in the country, the Sham-
rock (1810) and the Globe and Emerald (1824) being the
most prominent.[177] But it was not until 1822 that a
newspaper was founded with the avowed purpose of defending the church from thrusts of Protestant fanatics.
This first Catholic newspaper was the United States
Catholic Miscellany published in Charleston between
1822 and 1832 by Bishop John England.[178]

Bishop England was an able man, and he threw
his whole energy into this problem of combatting Protestant falsification through the columns of his paper. For
two years he contributed weekly articles attacking the
stand taken by J. Blanco White,[179] and his journal was
rarely without some defense or attack upon misstatement[180]
The Truth Teller, established in New York in 1825 attempted to carry on this same work in the northern states.[181]
It was aided after 1829 by The Jesuit, published in Boston

177 - Guilday, Life and Times of John England, vol. ii,
      p. 7.
178 - Mott, History of American Magazines, p. 136.
179 - Published between 1826 and 1828. Articles re-
      printed in England, Works of the Right Reverend
      John England, vol. ii, pp. 213-562, vol. iii,
      pp. 9-103.
180 - For accounts of these controversies see Ibid., vol.
      iii, pp. 104-122; 230-326; 329-384; 385-423; vol.
      iv, pp. 385-425. Guilday, Life and Times of John
      England, vol. ii, p. 426.
181 - Foik, Anti-Catholic Parties, p. 46.

under the authority of Bishop E. D. Fenwick.[182]

Leaders of the Catholic Church expended their energy in the task of answering the books that had appeared against them, as well as the newspapers. Reverend John Hughes, destined to be elevated to the center of the controversy as Bishop of New York in future years, established a Catholic Tract Society in 1827 [183] for the sole purpose of defending Catholicism and attacking Protestantism. One of its first publications was a book by Hughes attacking the English anti-Catholic story that had just been published in Philadelphia, The Conversion and Edifying Death of Andrew Dunn. Hughes book was published under the same title, and the principal differences between the two had to do with the conversion of one hero to Protestantism and the other to Catholicism.[184] An attempt was also made to bring the true nature of the Catholic church before the people of the United States, with the belief that only when the truth were known could attacks be stopped.[185]

182 - Mott, History of American Magazines, p. 373.
183 - Hassard, Life of John Hughes, pp. 77-78.
184 - Hughes' Conversion and Edifying Death of Andrew was published in Philadelphia in 1828. For an account of the origins and operation of this society see: "An Early Philadelphia Catholic Truth Society," Records of the American Catholic Historical Society of Philadelphia, vol. xxxviii (March 1927) pp. 8-14.
185 - Baxter, John, The Most Important Tenents of the Roman Catholic Church Fully Explained (Washington 1820) The author expresses the hope that it will be widely read by Protestants in order that they may understand the true nature of the Catholic church. Ibid., p. 1.

In all probability this armor that the Catholic church was girding about itself did little good and much harm. The labored defense of Catholicism penned by Bishop England, able as it was, was read only by Catholics, for no good Protestant would read a Catholic paper. So it was with all Catholic publications that they were ineffective in all save arousing Protestant ire. Americans objected to the manifestation of the power of the Church - a power that allowed it to establish and control great newspapers. They objected to the tone of the papers published; especially to the articles appearing in the Jesuit. The mere title of this paper was enough to arouse alarm in the breasts of most Protestants. Too late the name was changed to the Boston Pilot,[186] and only after members of the Catholic clergy had voiced objections.[187] Nativistic feelings increased like wild fire with every gust of Catholic objection. Nor would calm have diminished its spread.

The most important result of the establishment of a Catholic press was that it led to the founding of the first avowedly anti-Catholic newspaper in America. Protestants who were stern in their faith began to ask themselves why Catholics could support three newspapers

---

186 - Mott, History of American Magazines, p. 373.
187 - O'Daniel, The Right Rev. Edward Dominic Fenwick, p. 379.

when they had not one devoted wholly to the cause of Protestantism. And from these queries, the first No-Popery newspaper of the country, The Protestant, was born.

Behind the publication of The Protestant was the first of the nativistic societies of the United States, the New York Protestant Association, probably established in 1829.[188] It carried on an active part in the local crusade against Popery from the first, sending out individuals to engage Catholics in public arguments about their religion, and subsidizing lecturers to attack Rome and Romanism.[189] In carrying on this work, the leaders of the Association felt that the power of the press was necessary; through it would come strength. In order to secure this power they established a weekly news-paper, published in New York and proclaiming its true na-ture in its title, The Protestant. The first issue ap-peared January 2, 1830.

The Protestant left no doubt in regard to the stand on Romanism. A prospectus sent out before the es-tablishment of the paper stated its platform simply. "The sole objects of this publication," it read, "are, to in-culcate Gospel doctrines against Romish corruptions - to

188 - There is no evidence of the existence of the society before the Protestant was established. The
American Protestant Vindicator, January 6, 1836,
speaks of its formation about five years before.
189 - American Protestant Vindicator, January 6, 1836.

maintain the purity and the sufficiency of the Holy
Scriptures against Monkish traditions - to exemplify
the watchful care of Immanuel over 'the Church of God
which he has purchased with his own blood,' and to defend that revealed truth which Luther and Zwingli, Calvin and Arminius, Whitefield and Wesley, and all their
different followers ex anima and una voca have approved,
against the creed of Pope Pius IV and the Canons of the
Council of Trent, and no article will be admitted into
The Protestant which does not contribute to these desired
results."190

Another prospectus went into more detail as to
the type of material that The Protestant would print.
Its columns would, it announced, be given over to "narratives displaying the rise and progress of the Papacy; its
spirit and character in former periods; its modern pretensions; and its present enterprising efforts to recover and
extend its unholy dominion, especially on the western continent. Biographical notices of Martyrs, Reformers and
Popish Persecutors. Essays describing the doctrines, dis-
cipline and ceremonies of the Romish hierarchy; and its
desolating influence upon individual advancement, domestic
comfort and national prosperity. Illustrations of Sacred
Prophecy relative to the Mystical Babylon. A faithful ex-

190 - Massachusetts Yeoman, December 19, 1829.

pose of the moral and religious conditions of lower
Canada, as debased by the prevalence of the Roman supremacy."[191] All in all The Protestant outlined a
rather broad task for itself, and no sympathetic nativist could criticize its narrowness.

The new paper was launched with encouraging
comments by the religious press. The New York Observer
contributed a long editorial wishing it success and
warning the country of the dangers of Romanism. It
took this occasion to review the growth of Catholicism
in the country, the erection of new churches and newspapers, and the activity of the hated Jesuits in gaining
converts even among Protestants.[192] Despite this praise
The Protestant was forced to voice pleas now and then for
more support, using the danger of Popery and the necessity
of combating it for the need of subscribers. "What may be
the ultimate effect," it told its readers, "of the efforts
made by the adherents of Rome to propagate its tenets,
aided by the apathy of the half apostate party, it must
be difficult to affirm; certainly there never was a period
when the members of the Papal community were so active and
enterprising, and the greatest number of Protestants so
torpid and indifferent."[193]

191 - New York Observer, November 14, 1829.
192 - Ibid., November 14, 1829.
193 - The Protestant, December 18, 1830.

But dearth of subscribers was not the only worry of editors of this first nativistic journal. The Reverend John Hughes, a playful young priest at the time, wrote a series of letters to the paper under the signature of "Cranmer," telling outrageous lies about the growth and practice of the Catholic Church. The Protestant published them all and ended by writing a fitting eulogy of this unknown writer who penned such able attacks on Rome.[194] Hughes ended the farce by confessing in a public letter in the Truth Teller, and though the editors of The Protestant fumed and refused to believe anything that he said, their cause was not helped.[195]

Despite this episode, the new paper continued to thrive well into the next decade when it was merged with other nativistic papers. By the end of the 1820's the forces of anti-Catholicism were training their guns against Popery. Books were being published, and the New York Protestant Association had set the precedent of a series of anti-Catholic lectures as additional means of attack.[196] A newspaper had been established, and all available inroads were made against the dread foe, Romanism.

194 - Ibid., March 13, 1830.
195 - Hassard, Life of John Hughes, pp. 105-108.
196 - The New York Observer, October 17, 1829, carried
       the advertisement of a lecture against Popery to
       be delivered by the Reverend E. M. Ellis, a re-
       cent missionary in the Illinois country, who was
       to tell of the great efforts Catholics were making
       to secure control of the west.

In such a situation, where popular opinion was being fired to white hot heat by rampant propagandists trouble was inevitable. Unruly Protestants, carried away by their enthusiasm, began to mutter openly against Catholicism, and physical violence often superseded that of the printed page. A monument in a Catholic emetery at Lansingburgh, New York, erected by a convert in memory of his wife, was broken to pieces by a mob.[197] When a new church was being erected in Cincinnati the Bishop decided that the feeling was so great that he dared not build it within the city, and it was constructed just outside to quiet the growing discontent and to check mob fury.[198] A missionary working among the Indians in Maine was forced to face the jeers of lumber jacks[199] and another in the west reported that priests were universally looked down upon as "vile and ignorant men."[200]

By such violence, the stage had been set on which the great struggle against Catholicism in the United States was to take place. The pen, which had fostered the early growth of this American drama, was

197 - Shea, History of the Catholic Church, vol. iii, p. 497.
198 - O'Daniel, The Right Reverend Edward Dominic Fenwick, pp. 216-217.
199 - Shea, op. cit., vol. ii, p. 150.
200 - "Letters Concerning some Missions to the Mississippi Valley 1818-1827," American Catholic Historical Society of Philadelphia Records, vol. xiv (March 1903) p. 216.

to be put aside.   The curtain was to rise upon a mob
scene where men moved by bitter bigotry were to inter-
pret their inalienable right to freedom in one-sided
terms of fagot and tar and firebrand.

III

THE FIRST CONVENT IS BURNED, 1830-1834.

On the night of August 11, 1834, the sky
above Charlestown, Massachusetts, glowed red with
flame. Beneath it a shouting mob stormed and milled.
Nuns, hastily clothed in their somber garb, huddled
panic-stricken children into safety. The Ursuline
Convent was ablaze. A blow had been struck at Romanism.
No-Popery had taken its first toll.

Behind the torches that touched off the great
convent building on Mount Benedict were years of persistent propaganda and prejudice. A mob of a thousand
men had been plunged to such inhuman depths that they
were willing to attack the home of a score of defenseless nuns and a handful of children. Thousands more
had been willing to stand quietly by and watch the convent burn, taking no active part, but giving silent
assent. Anti-Catholic feeling was at its height in
Boston; in other cities and rural hamlets throughout
the land feeling was only slightly less violent. The
flames that licked the walls of the Ursuline home had
been nourished in the years before. Propaganda had
borne a fiery fruit.

That this propaganda had thrived throughout

the early years of the 1830's was due to the success
which followed in the wake of the writers of a decade
before. The pioneers in prejudice had found willing
ears and loose purse strings. The situation was a
simple one of insatiable demand and abundant supply.
It was evident that America should be flooded in the
coming years with an increasing number of anti-Catholic
books and pamphlets.

The authors of these works, however, professed
only the most unselfish of motives. They insisted that
their books were necessary. The alarming growth of
Popery in the past ten years together with the arrogant attitude taken by Catholics in striving for power
had made such an antidote necessary.[1] Books were needed,
they said, not to rail and denounce Romanism, but to demonstrate its true nature so that Americans might be
warned.[2] Wild and exaggerated statements convinced every
true Protestant as he read that the enemy in his midst
was a dangerous enemy - and that salvation for his country and soul could only come when Catholicism was stamped
from existence.

1 - A History of Popery, Including its Origin, Progress,
    Doctrines, Practice, Institutions and Fruits to the
    Commencement of the Nineteenth Century (New York,
    1834), pp. 3-4.
2 - New York Observer, March 1, 1834.

Many of these works were imported from
England, or reprinted from English books created
by the excitement over the Catholic Emancipation
bill.[3] Others were products of American soil.[4]
While a decade before there had been a noticeable
difference between the quality of American and English books, this difference now suddenly disappeared.
Americans had learned that the true way to profit was
to produce exaggerated exposes and the Yankee loved
profit above all things.

3 - Typical titles of such English works: Ricci, Scipio
de, Secrets of Nunneries Disclosed (New York, 1834)
McGavin, William, The Protestant; Essays on the
Principal Points of Controversy between the Church
of Rome and the Reformed (2nd American edition from
9th London edition, Hartford, 1833); Secret Instructions to the Jesuits (Princeton, 1831); Ellmer Castle
(Boston, 1833); Gavin, Anthony, The Master Key to
Popery: Customs of Priests and Friars, and Rites and
Ceremonies of the Popish Religion, Inquisition, etc.,
(Cincinnati, 1834)
4 - Some American books published during this brief period
from 1830 to 1834: Bassiere, Peter, Conversion of
Peter Bassiere from the Romish Religion to the Protestant Faith, in a Letter to his Children (New York,
1833); Cramp, J. M., The Text Book of Popery (New
York, 1832); Baxter, Richard, Jesuit Juggling; Forty Popish Frauds Detected and Disclosed (New York,
1834); Horne, Thomas F., Romanism Contradictory to
the Bible (New York, 1833); Howitt, William, History
of Priestcraft in all Ages and Nations (New York,
1833); Stratton, Thomas, The Book of the Priesthood:
an Argument in Three Parts (New York, 1831); Lorette,
History of Louise, Daughter of a Canadian Nun (New
York, 1834); Smith, Samuel B., Renunciation of Popery
(6th edition, Philadelphia, 1833).

Excerpts from the type of literature flooding
the market show that no part of the Church escaped the
deluge. Catholicism was branded a "carcass of pretences,
forms, shows, epithets and every holy thing that can be
put into language or represented by grimace; but inwardly
it is all rottenness; and practically it is the very smoke
of the bottomless pit."[5] Indulgences were attacked as
causing crime,[6] and the confessional as causing sin because pardons could be obtained by paying a little money.[7]
"What idea of sin can men have," readers were asked, "when
they are taught that the most abandoned of all the human
race, if they are only in possession of holy orders, are
clothed with the power of pardoning it."[8]

The practice of confession did not escape with
but these mild attacks upon it. Charges of its immorality
were brought to the surface and flaunted with increasing
violence. It was openly claimed that in Ireland all priests
heard the confessions of women in their own bedrooms, and
that the same condition existed to a lesser extent in the
United States.[9] Not only has such an institution no biblical basis,[10] writers insisted, but it led to untold sin

5 - A History of Popery, p. 413.
6 - Ibid., pp. 193-200.
7 - McGavin, The Protestant, vol. i, p. 143.
8 - New York Observer, January 8, 1831.
9 - McGavin, The Protestant, vol. i, pp. 192-193.
10- Ibid., vol. ii, pp. 602-666.

and corruption. Books listed the questions put to
girls by priests,[11] and stressed the lessons in sin
thus given innocent youth. "The confessional," one
author claimed, "is truly a school of vice and defile-
ment, whose catechumens are trained up for the service
of Satan."[12]

The discussion of such sin naturally led to
a consideration of the moral life of the clergy. In
enforced celibacy the writers found a vital point.
They shouted that such celibacy had no sanction in
the Bible,[13] that it alone had caused the reformation,[14]
and that immorality was bound to follow in its wake.
One writer told of laws passed in Switzerland forcing
priests to keep concubines so that innocent women would
be safe from their lust and gave this same reason to explain why the Pope had encouraged houses of ill-fame in
Rome.[15] The old story of the six thousand children's
heads found in the convent fish pond during the days of
Gregory was revived, and clerical celibacy was placed
at the bottom of the whole incident.[16]

Proof of this state of affairs was advanced

11 - History of Popery, pp. 180-183
12 - Ibid., pp. 183-184.
13 - McGavin, The Protestant, vol. ii, pp. 67-94.
14 - Ibid., vol. ii, pp. 81-87.
15 - Ibid., vol. ii, pp. 79-80.
16 - Ibid., vol. ii, p. 80.

in a book that was claimed to have been written by
Catholics themselves, The Secret Instructions to the
Jesuits,[17] laying bare the crimes of that order in
moral as well as in other fields.[18]

But if the whole institution of the confe-
sional suffered from these attacks, convents and monastic institutions suffered even more. Brought to bear
upon them was an English book reprinted in America in
1834. Scippio de Ricci's Secrets of Nunneries Disclosed, a pornographic volume that rivaled in erotic
appeal even Anthony Gavin's Master Key to Popery.
Ricci did not live to see the profits of his enterprise. He had been a reforming priest in Tuscany in
the middle of the eighteenth century, and had had occasion to keep a record of much of the corruption against
which he directed his efforts. The English No-Popery
excitement had caused a translation and republication
of some of these revelations in 1829,[19] and a few years
later an American publisher, seeing their possibilities,
gave them to American readers.

17 - This ancient attack upon Catholicism had had a long
history in England; a third edition was published
in London in 1773. Produced as an anti-Catholic
work at that time, it was accepted as gospel by
most of the nativistic writers of America and reprinted several times before the Civil war.
18 - New York Observer, October 29, 1831, hails the publication with joy and recommends it to ministers as
showing the true nature of Popery.
19 - Ricci, Secrets of Nunneries, pp. i-ii.

Despite the lurid title of Ricci's book, the introduction added by an anonymous American author was the most exciting part of the volume. The writer of the introduction attacks monastic institutions with all the force of a vitriolic pen. Convents are branded as "the prolific source of the most horrid uncleanliness."[20] They are cursed as breeding a contempt for all religion, for "would you look for evangelical missionaries in those dens of ignorance, sloth and corruption?"[21] Monks and nuns are pictured as wallowing in a sloth of ignorance and vice and even satirized in verse:

> In shirt of hair and weeds of canvass dressed,
> Girt with a bell rope that the Pope has blessed;
> Wearing out life in his perbicious whim,
> Till his mischievous whimsy wears out him.[22]

The actual book itself is rather disappointing after the lurid promises given in the introduction. Ricci describes his attempted reforms among the nuns and convents of Tuscany, he quotes letters from nuns telling of their seduction by Jesuit confessors;[23] of their gay revels with the priests,[24] of secret passage ways connecting convents with the homes of their confessors.[25] He tells of plays performed by pious sisters better than in the theaters of the city,[26] and of one rascally confessor who made the

20 - Ibid., p. xii.
21 - Ibid., p. xviii.
22 - Ibid., p. xiv.
23 - Ibid., pp. 57-60.
24 - Ibid., pp. 80-81.
25 - Ibid., p. 94.
26 - Ibid., pp. 92;97.

sisters that he confessed lift up their clothes before
him, telling them that they were performing an act of
virtue because they overcame a natural repugnance.[27]
But most of the book is taken up with a description of
the persecution that Ricci was forced to endure as a
result of his reforms[28] and of similar reforms that
he attempted on the ritual of the church; matters hardly
in keeping with the promises of the title.

The other books available to Americans in these
years were less libidinous. Several of them told of the
conversion of individuals from Catholicism to Protestantism and were thickly sprinkled with Biblical passages to
explain their acts.[29] A few stories were circulated of
misunderstood girls who are cast into convents by their
parents and made to suffer there until they could convince their cruel fathers that Popery was wrong and convents more so.[30] Samuel B. Smith appeared on the scene
with the first of his books, bearing the endorsement of

27 - Ibid., p. 101.
28 - Ibid., p. 115; 177-237.
29 - Reeves, James, Popery Renounced (New York, 1829);
     Bassiere, Peter, Conversion of Peter Bassiere from
     the Romish Church to the Protestant Faith in a Let-
     ter to his Children (New York, 1833) The New York
     Observer, January 2, 1830, recommends James Reeves
     book highly, especially to Catholics. Any conver-
     sion of a Catholic was cause for rejoicing by the
     Protestant Press. See New York Observer, March 20,
     1830.
30 - Reflections and Tales (Philadelphia, 1830) pp.76-108.

nine ministers of Philadelphia,[31] and describing how
he had left the Catholic priesthood to embrace the
Protestant cause.[32] While the capture of a former
priest must have warmed the heart of many an enthusiastic religionist, Samuel Smith's first work was
far below the standard that he was to set for himself in coming years.[33]

The renewed activity of these writers was
destined not to go unanswered by Catholics. Catholic
newspapers were founded over the entire country in an
unprecedented burst of activity. In the four years
between 1829 and 1833 no less than thirteen papers
were established devoted to the defense of Catholicism
against the attacks of its enemies.[34] Most of them were

31 - Smith, Samuel B., Renunciation of Popery (6th edi-
     tion, Philadelphia, 1833), p. 2.
32 - Ibid., pp. 20-64.
33 - Samuel B. Smith was one of the most prolific writers
     in the anti-Catholic cause in the decade of the
     1830's, producing such books as The Wonderful Ad-
     ventures of a Lady of the French Nobility, and the
     Intrigues of a Romish Priest, her Confessor, to
     Seduce and Murder Her (New York, 1836); and Synop-
     sis of the Moral Theology of the Church of Rome,
     from the Works of St. Ligori (New York, 1836); in
     addition to many pamphlets and lesser publications.
     He also edited one of the leading anti-Catholic
     Newspapers, The Downfall of Babylon. See above,
     pp. 203-207.
34 - A list of the papers started is in Guilday, Life
     and Times of John England, vol. ii, pp. 218-220.

published in cities along the eastern seaboard where
the rising tide of European immigration had deposited
many Catholic readers, The Shepherd of the Valley at
St. Louis and the Catholic Telegraph[35] at Cincinnati,
were destined to become two of the most influential
papers in the country however.

All these newspapers threw themselves into
the defense of Catholicism with admirable vigor. Until
1832 Bishop John England of Charleston through the agency
of his United States Catholic Miscellany served as their
leader, hurling back arguments against Protestant attacks[36]
and producing such prolific works that his biographer has
been able to state that "Generally speaking, all of Dr.
England's writings during the twenty-two years of his
episcopate belong to the literature created by the anti-
Catholic movements of this epoch."[37]

35 - Bishop Fenwick of Cincinnati stated that the Catholic
     Telegraph was founded purely as a means of combating
     attacks on Catholics that were surging from the Prot-
     estant press and pulpit. O'Daniel, The Right Rev.
     Edward Dominic Fenwick, p. 384; 394.
36 - England, Works of John England, vol. i, pp. 301-348
     and vol. iv, pp. 415-510, contain typical answers of
     Bishop England to attacks by Protestant writers. For
     Bishop England's earlier defense of Catholicism
     against such attacks see above, pp.
37 - Guilday, Life and Times of John England, vol. ii,
     p. 425.

Sporadic arguments of this nature were not looked upon with too great favor by either the Catholic or Protestant factions. It was felt by both parties that organized debate would be far more effective in voicing claims. So it was that when a leading Presbyterian minister, the Reverend John Breckinridge of Philadelphia, issued a challenge to public debate on Catholicism it was readily accepted and the first of the great controversies that were to mark the next few years was begun.

Pastor of a church in Philadelphia and secretary of the Board of Education of the Presbyterian church, he issued his challenge in a letter written to the Christian Advocate in the fall of 1832.[38] He was, he said, prepared to meet any champion that the opposition could produce "on the broad field of this important and vital discussion," over the question "Is the Protestant Religion the Religion of Christ."[39] A Catholic champion responded immediately: the Reverend John Hughes, then just emerging from the obscurity of a priesthood in Philadelphia. For three months he and Breckinridge engaged in a series of

38 - Hassard, Life of John Hughes, p. 134.
39 - Hughes, John and John Breckinridge, Controversy Between Rev. Messrs. Hughes and Breckinridge on the Subject, "Is the Protestant Religion the Religion of Christ?" (Philadelphia, 1833), Introduction.

conferences to decide how the controversy was to be
carried on, it being finally agreed that each party
should write and publish articles alternately in a
weekly paper The Presbyterian, and in a Catholic
weekly paper yet to be established. It was further
agreed that each letter should be confined to four
columns length and the controversy end in six months.[40]

Reverend Hughes, with money supplied by interested friends, established the Catholic Herald in
Philadelphia to serve as the medium for his letters,
and on January 21, 1833, published the first letter
on the subject of the Rule of Faith. The debate was
hailed with enthusiasm from the start.[41] Breckinridge's
answer to his opponent's first thrust was acclaimed by
the religious papers that supported him, and four of
them immediately began reprinting the controversy
either in full or in abridged form.[42]

The rules of the controversy drawn up by the
two debaters had required the dispute to be "conducted
in a language of decorum and in a spirit of Christian

40 - Hassard, Life of John Hughes, pp. 135-142.
41 - Protestant Episcopalian and Church Register,
     February, 1833. New York Observer, March 9, 1833.
42 - Hassard, Life of John Hughes, p. 142. See also
     The Protestant Magazine, September, 1833; and the
     Protestant Episcopalian and Church Register,
     March 1833 and ff.

politeness."[43] The first letters followed these instructions well. Hughes argued pointedly that Protestantism could not be the religion of Christ because
its rule of faith was in the Bible alone, which Christ
could not have established as the guide for his church
since it was not completed until fifty years after his
death. Breckinridge answered with equal politeness and
with ponderous Biblical arguments.[44] But after letters
had flown back and forth for a month or so the contestants grew impatient and resorted to emotional appeals that had little place in such a contest. "In a
word," Breckinridge wrote: "A new era has come to our
country. The American people will promptly see who the
serpent is (to use your own illusion) that stings the
bosom that warms it. They will henceforth know where
to send their children for education, and when to contribute in generous and abused confidence, to build the
schools and convents and chapels that are to train our
children to call their parents heretics; and are rising
to re-establish a religion which never did, never will,
and never can, permit a free government or religious toleration."[45] Here was language that his anti-Catholic

43 - Maury, Wars of the Godly, p. 68.
44 - Controversy between Rev. Messrs. Hughes and Breck-
     inridge, pp. 10 ff.
45 - Ibid., p. 252.

readers could understand, but not language fitted to
sober debate.

As the contestants increased in their bitterness, the enthusiasm with which the contest had opened
began to lessen. The debate moved with surprising slow-
ness. Five months after it began they were still arguing
over the original question, and correspondents who had
reported its progress in full threw up their hands and
prophesied that unless progress were made the contestants
would be going on for decades.[46] The original period of
six months was extended to October to allow at least two
subjects to be debated.[47] Finally, on October 3, Hughes
wrote his last letter and Breckinridge replied to it in
a burst of enthusiasm and defiance. "I thank God," he
wrote, "that the time is not yet come when the threat
of a Roman priest can make me tremble for my reputation,
my liberty, or my hopes of heaven. Even the Bulls of
your master become very harmless animals when sent to
pasture on our happy soil. Your arrogant and impotent
threats only show what you would do if you could."[48]
When it was all over Hughes issued a postscript, in the
Catholic Herald, claiming he had won the debate, by re-

46 - Protestant Episcopalian and Church Register, May, 1833.
47 - Hassard, Life of John Hughes, p. 142.
48 - Controversy between Rev. Messrs. Hughes and Breckin-
     ridge, p. 470.

calling the original question and asserting that Breckinridge had not even shown what the Protestant religion
was. Breckinridge challenged Hughes to public oral debate, probably suffering from writer's cramp after his
nine months and the two hundred and fifty thousand words
which he had produced, but Hughes declined. There the
matter rested for the time being because Breckinridge
was called away from the city.[49]

Meanwhile a new controversy had arisen in New
York city which was to attract almost as much attention.
This contest found one lone Protestant, the Reverend
William Craig Brownlee of the Dutch Reformed Church
arrayed against three priests, the Reverends John Powers,
Thomas C. Levins, and Felix Varela.[50] No such elaborate
rules surrounded this debate as the one between Hughes
and Breckinridge. The contestants agreed to publish letters in the Truth Teller, a New York Catholic paper, and
in the Protestant. No time limit was set and there seems
to have been no definite subject to be discussed.[51]

Dr. Brownlee threw himself into the contest with
great enthusiasm. He attacked the boasted unity of the
Catholic church in his first letter, mocking the various
schisms that had marked its course,[52] but by the second

49 - Maury, Wars of the Godly, p. 71.
50 - New York Observer, March 9, 1833.
51 - Ibid., March 9, 1833.
52 - Ibid., March 9, 1833.

letter he had settled down to the usual argument concerning the Rule of Faith.[53]   As in the Hughes-Breckinridge controversy the Rule of Faith proved the stumbling block and for several weeks the contestants wrote lengthy arguments[54] upholding their own views.[55]   By the middle of June, however, this subject had been left behind, and Dr. Brownlee was attacking idolatry and saint worship[56] and "Romish superstition"[57] with all his vigor, while the three priests vainly tried to answer his rabid arguments with sober facts.

Such a debate could not go on forever. The Catholic Truth Teller objected to having to spread such abuse before its readers. The priests, as a result, in July issued a new challenge to Dr. Brownlee, asking him to debate the question, "What articles of faith found

53 - Ibid., March 16, 1833.
54 - The New York Observer and several other religious papers gave a great amount of space to the controversy, reprinting the letters of all contestants in full. On March 23 the New York Observer devoted seven full columns to letters from Dr. Brownlee and the three priests, a greater part of the paper. On March 30 five full columns were printed. In the following numbers throughout the debate a similar amount of space was devoted to it.
55 - Ibid., March 16, 1833; March 30, 1833.
56 - Ibid., June 15, 1833.
57 - Ibid., July 20, 1833.

in the Scriptures, in express terms, must be believed
in order to be saved?"[58] Dr. Brownlee howled his objections immediately. Here was another Popish plot,
he said, designed to keep him from exposing all the
deformities of the Catholic church as he had been doing.
He would answer their new challenge in one paragraph,
and he does so to his own satisfaction by quoting a
number of verses from the Bible showing that a belief
in Christ is necessary for salvation. But then he will
go on exposing the Old Harlot, the Mother of Babylon,
just as he has before. And he challenges the priest
to reply to his arguments.[59]

Dr. Brownlee's opponents recognized the fact
that they could only reply to abuse by more abuse. The
letters they wrote from that time on teemed with invective against their adversary. They charged him with
"ribald phrase, recklessness of truth, foul vituperation
and untenable assertion."[60] They insisted that he should
take part in the next Feast of Asses that he had ridiculed and provided a little poem to illustrate the ceremony:

> The preacher was born and bred with long ears,
> Heigh Ho, my assy --
> And still the preacher of asses appears
> Bray preacher ass, and you shall get grass,
> And straw and hay too, in plenty.[61]

58 - Ibid., July 27, 1833.
59 - Ibid., July 27, 1833.
60 - Ibid., August 3, 1833.
61 - Ibid., August 3, 1833.

After this final outburst, the priests withdrew from the debate. They announced that the controversy was ended as Dr. Brownlee had failed to stick to any argument but simply attacked the Catholic church. "To continue polemic discussion with you," they wrote, "cannot add to reputation, for your substitutes for argument are foul falsehood, ribald words, gross invective, disgusting calumny and the recommendation of an obscene tale. These have been your weapons from your first to your last puerile letter."[62] With his opponents withdrawn, Dr. Brownlee went ahead with a free rein. He continued to attack the Catholic church in a series of letters running over several months, widely printed in The Protestant and in the other newspapers devoted to its cause.[63]

The Brownlee controversy, widely printed as it was, aroused a great deal of interest in the cause of anti-Catholicism. The Protestant papers proclaimed loudly that their champion had emerged a victor since

62 - Ibid., August 17, 1833.
63 - Ibid., September 7, 1833, and ff. The letters were printed in the Christian Intelligencer, the Protestant, and the New York Observer. The Truth Teller stopped printing the letters as soon as the priests withdrew from the controversy. Ibid., July 19, 1831. The letters were also printed in The Protestant Magazine, October 1833.

the priests had withdrawn;[64] and their claims were
widely believed. But such controversies on the whole,
did the anti-Catholic cause little good. Thinking
Protestants who had been bred in hatred of the Catholic church realized for the first time that the Catholics did have an argument and a sound one. They realized that many of the charges hurled at Popery by
writers and speakers were equally repudiated by the
Church itself. Where before they had refused to admit
any justice for Catholicism, now Catholic writers had
demonstrated that there was much to be said for it.[65]
Protestant writers themselves realized this danger.
They shouted loudly that controversies were unfair because priests were trained in sin and corruption and
under pledge to keep no faith with heretics; they could
refuse to tell the truth while Protestant orators and
writers were forced to make only simple and correct
statements under the pledge of their religion.[66] But
behind these shouts was the grim realization that their
champions had not achieved the devastating victories
that had been expected.

64 - New York Observer, July 19, 1834.
65 - Guilday, Life and Times of John England, vol. ii,
      p. 378; Shea, History of the Catholic Church,
      vol. iii, p. 555.
66 - History of Popery, p. 16.

As a consequence, there occured a renewal
of activity in the ranks of the rapidly growing group
devoting themselves to the cause of anti-Catholicism.
The New York Observer began a series of continued articles, a correspondent from France contributing a dismal
picture of the effects of Popery on that country which
occupied much space through the first part of 1832.[67]
In the fall of 1833 a new series started, taking up distinctive features of the Catholic church one by one and
riddling them with venomous barbs.[68] Published later
in book form, these articles were to become a powerful
instrument in the crusade against the Pope.[69] Another
series of "Letters on Popery" pictured affairs in Malta
as viewed by a Protestant missionary.[70] In addition to
these continued articles, the Observer printed an ever
increasing list of writings attacking Catholicism, av-
eraging two or more to every issue, from November, 1833
on. At this time, at least three columns of the front
page of each number were devoted to flings against the
Church, and it was not unusual to give up nearly the entire front page to this cause.

67 - New York Observer, March 20, 1832 ff.
68 - Ibid., October 26, 1833 and ff. The series lasted
     for more than a year.
69 - The author of these articles was William Nevins, a
     Baltimore pastor. They were published in book form
     under the title, Thoughts on Popery (New York 1836)
70 - New York Observer, December 18, 1830 and ff.

Meanwhile, the entire anti-Catholic press
was going through a process of rejuvenation that was
to fit it for the battles ahead. This renewed activity
was only spurred by the bitter charges made by the newly
founded Catholic press against the one purely anti-Catholic paper then published, The Protestant. The Jesuit
and the Catholic Sentinel branded it as "a paper from
whose profligacy of expression, satanic baseness, anti-
Christian spirit, the sensible, respectable and virtuous
Protestants of New York and the Union at large shrink
with honest Christian indignation."[71] The editors of
the Metropolitan of Baltimore wrote in just as indignant
terms: "Without a solitary sentiment of that charity
which is characteristic of a follower of Christ, without a particle of that sincerity which is the noblest
attribute of a man of honor; without an iota of the decorum which is the ornament of human character, you have
risen in fierce and unprovoked resentment against us, and
with the desperation of an assassin, attempt to plunge
your dagger into the reeking heart of Catholicism."[72]

Such bitter reproach only inspired The Protestant to greater efforts. The editorship, held by Reverend

71 - Quoted in Foik, Anti-Catholic Parties in American
     Politics, p. 47.
72 - Issue of April, 1830. Quoted in Guilday, Life and
     Times of John England, vol. ii, pp. 452-453.

George Bourne, was taken over by the Reverend William
Craig Brownlee, who was later to distinguish himself
in the controversy with the Catholic priests, and,
aided by the public support of seventy-three ministers
of New York, it continued its vituperative assault with
renewed vigor.[73] Articles, violent in tone, told of a
dark plot to convert America by forcing Catholic girls
in the United States to marry Protestant men,[74] laid
claim that Papists had no respect for the Bible,[75] and
reported with unfeigned egotism how anti-Catholic sentiment in different parts of the country had been stirred
to new heights because of their own activities.[76] The
appointment of Roger Brooks Taney as attorney general by
President Andrew Jackson stirred Editor Brownlee and his
assistants to clamor against a "bigoted Papist" in office,
and to insist that this was all simply part of a great
scheme to take over the Union for the Pope.[77]

The rabid nature of these attacks on Catholicism
lost The Protestant much of the support with which it had
started. The clergy who were principally instrumental in

73 - Foik, Anti-Catholic Parties on American Politics,
       p. 47. The change of editorship and its results
       is discussed in The Protestant Magazine, August 1834.
74 - The Protestant, December 18, 1830.
75 - Ibid., December 18, 1830.
76 - Ibid., December 18, 1830.
77 - Quoted in Guilday, Life and Times of John England,
       vol. ii, p. 221.

its founding began to grow alarmed at its excesses, and
to drop away from the list of those who recommended it
and gave it patronage. Finally in 1832 Dr. Brownlee resigned as editor,[78] the name of the publication was
changed to The Reformation Advocate[79] and the subscription list began to mount again. But this new paper fared
little better than its predecessor. The bigoted attack
upon Catholicism that had characterized The Protestant
was continued, and it soon became apparent that another
change was necessary. In September, 1833, The Reformation Advocate was sold, and the new publisher promptly
changed it from a weekly newspaper to a monthly magazine
entitled The Protestant Magazine.[80]

The change from a weekly to a monthly publication was explained by the editor in the first issue of
the new magazine. "The important cause in which we are
engaged," he wrote, "in consequence of the almost total
silence of religious papers formerly, rendered a weekly

78 - The Protestant Magazine, August, 1834. This issue
     contains a history of the New York anti-Catholic
     press up to that time which is of the greatest
     value.
79 - The New York Observer, November 23, 1833. When Dr.
     Brownlee gave up the editorship the paper was turned
     over to its publishers, the firm of Gibson and Ir-
     vine. One of the members of the firm, James Irvine,
     took over the duties of editorship.
80 - The Protestant Magazine, August, 1834. The change
     from a weekly to a monthly magazine was affected by
     a new publisher who purchased The Reformation Advo-
     cate in September, 1833, C.C.P. Crosley. The new
     publisher retained James Irvine as editor.

publication necessary. But happily a great change has of
late taken place: articles against popery are now appearing weekly in almost every part of our country...But to
embody for dissemination and preservation all the valuable
articles which may be written against popery; and especially to elicit from the pens of ready and able writers,
well digested, well prepared papers against the great
enemy of truth, a monthly magazine is thought by many
discerning men to be necessary."[81]

But the editor took pains to insist that the
change did not mean a lessening of the attack upon this
great enemy. Popery, he said, still continues the great
scourge of mankind. "Deeply convinced of the dangerous
tendency of this anti-Christian system; of its soul-
corrupting and soul-destroying influence; dreading the
dangers to which our country, if indifferent to its increase in political influence, is exposed, and influenced
by a love of country, and by an ardent desire to promote
the interests of immortal souls, we have entered upon this
work, resolved, as far as in us lies, to defend the great
truths of the Gospel opposed by popery, and to exhibit
those doctrines and practices of Roman Catholics which
are contrary to the interests of mankind."[82]

81 - Ibid., September,1833.
82 - Ibid., September,1833.

In one of the early issues, The Protestant
Magazine replied to a prospectus of a new Catholic
paper which was to contain a department devoted to
answering attacks on Catholicism, "We can promise the
writers for this department a full amount of exercise.[83]"
The threat was well fulfilled. For more than a year
The Protestant Magazine issued twenty-four pages each
month crammed with invective and abuse against the Catholic church. A typical issue contained the following
articles: "A Candid examination of the Doctrines and
Usages of Roman Catholics;" "Popish Principles Tend to
Subvert Civil Liberty;" "Letter of Dr. Miller on Popish
Education of Children;" "Extract from Milton on Popery
and the Reformation;" "Letters on the Religious State
of France;" "Catholic Priests Hate the Savior;" "Letter
of Dr. Breckinridge addressed to Rev. Hughes;" and "The
Village Churchyard."[84]

Despite the lurid titles, most of the articles
in The Protestant Magazine were a little dull; the stress
was upon the theological argument rather than the emotional
appeal that Dr. Brownlee had applied in The Protestant.
But The Protestant Magazine prospered, and as its sub-

83 - Ibid., October, 1833. The Catholic paper was The
     New York Weekly Register and Catholic Diary.
84 - Ibid., September, 1833.

scription list grew, rivals began to appear. When news
of a new anti-Catholic publication to be started in New
York in the summer of 1834 reached the ears of the publishers of The Protestant Magazine, they sought out the
backers of this new publication intending to offer their
subscription list for sale. To their chagrin, however,
they found that the backer of the proposed new publication was the Reverend George Bourne, whose rabid statements as the first editor of The Protestant had started
it on its downward path. So instead of selling their
subscription list, they moved hurriedly to keep the
Reverend Bourne from the profitable field that they
then monopolized. Continuing the issue of their monthly magazine, they founded a new weekly paper, The Anti-
Romanist, in August, 1834,[85] The fate of both this new
weekly publication and of the Protestant Magazine itself
is unknown, although it is fairly certain that both of
them ceased publication only a short time later. Certainly
no copies of either published after August 1834 remain,
and mention of them in other anti-Catholic publications
is lacking.

Aiding The Protestant Magazine and the Anti-
Romanist in their crusade were other papers, established
to attack priesthood in all its forms, but especially as

85 - Ibid., August, 1834.

exemplified in the Catholic church. The first of these
papers was entitled Priestcraft Unmasked, and the first
number issued on January 1, 1830, set forth its aims.
Priests, it said, were ruining America. They must be
driven out, and the first to go must be the clergy of
the hated Romanists. "Friends of America," the editor
wrote, "Friends of intellectual emancipation! The tree
of liberty was planted upon your soil amid the whirl-
wind and the storm! It has been watered with tears and
blood! And now when its towering branches have well
nigh reached the heavens, will ye see it felled to the
earth, without a single effort to prevent its destruction? We say no! God forbid!"[86]

Priestcraft Unmasked devoted itself to seeing
that God was aided in forbidding any such thing. It was
a small, semi-monthly paper, containing articles on how
priests have ruined every country and now seemed on the
way to repeating the ghastly process in the United States.[87]
But its work was unappreciated. It died a quiet death on
November 15, 1830 after twenty-two issues.

A few years later, in 1834, its place was taken
by another paper devoted to the same cause and entitled
Priestcraft Exposed. Like its predecessor it directed

86 - Priestcraft Unmasked, January 1, 1830.
87 - Ibid., January 1, 1830.

its shafts against the Catholic clergy who were "covering their hypocrisy with the cloak of <u>religion</u>, and
with more than the serpent's guile, warming themselves
into the confidence and affections of their unsuspect-
ing victims."[88] A bi-monthly publication, issued from
the hills of Concord, New Hampshire, it survived through
most of the year in which publication began.

With the religious press devoting itself as it
was to the cause of anti-Catholicism, it was inevitable
that many of the secular papers should feel the same influence and give more and more of their space to attacks
upon Rome. The <u>New York Journal of Commerce</u> was particularly susceptible to the influence, and took every opportunity to poke fun and hurl invective at the Catholic
church and its members.[89] The <u>Massachusetts Yeoman</u> gave
its columns to a series of articles attacking popery,[90]
and claimed that other papers did not follow suit because
controlled by gold from Rome.[91] The <u>Vermont Patriot</u>
painted a dismal picture of Catholicism in the United
States, and warned its readers that "if you suffer the

88 - <u>Priestcraft Exposed</u>, April 1, 1834.
89 - <u>The Protestant Magazine</u>, November, 1830, prints
     an article from this paper typical of its atti-
     tude. The article states that a week ago the
     <u>Journal of Commerce</u> made a mistake in the date,
     publishing the Saturday date line on Friday. It
     apologizes, and offers to grant absolution to
     any Catholics who ate meat on that day due to
     this faulty information.
90 - <u>Massachusetts Yeoman</u>, December 25, 1830 and ff.
91 - <u>Ibid.</u>, December 25, 1830.

priest by law to ride on your back, you will soon have
to carry a king behind him."[92]

Such a widespread interest on the part of the
press led naturally to an increase in the organizations
designed to combat and destroy the Catholic church. Gen-
tler souls who disliked trouble yet looked upon Popery as
an enemy to be put down found means of carrying on their
work in the great religious societies that had been formed
in the 1820's: the American Tract Society and the American
Bible Society.[93] Especially was the interest of sympathizers with the anti-Catholic crusade aroused when the
American Bible society resolved in 1829 to supply every
destitute family in the United States with a copy of the
Holy Scriptures in the Protestant version.[94] Catholic
protest[95] only stirred them to greater efforts, and the
members of the society actually resolved to supply every
family in the world with a copy and would have undertaken
the task had they not been convinced that the task was

92 - Quoted in Boston Courier, March 17, 1831.
93 - The Christian Watchman expressed the belief that a
     percentage of those joining these two societies did
     so because they felt it was their duty to enlighten
     those men who "for ages and ages have slept in the
     darkness of Popery, blindfolded by ignorant and
     blinded priests, hardly desiring to see the heaven-
     ly light which was ready to burst upon them." Quoted
     in Massachusetts Yeoman, April 20, 1825.
94 - Sweet, The Story of Religions, p. 366.
95 - The Jesuit, January 12, 1833, prints an objection to
     this attempt of the Bible Society written by Bishop
     Fenwick.

too large.[96] At the same time the American Tract Society
was making a bid for support from the anti-Catholic sympathizers by beginning the publication of tracts against
Popery, the first appearing in 1832.[97] The cause was
aided when the General Conference of the Methodist Episcopal Church gave it their approval in 1832 the same
year.[98]

While the more peaceful elements were seeking
outlet against Catholicism in the Tract and Bible societies, more violent and outspoken members of society were
beginning to demand an anti-Catholic society that would
be a fitting background for their efforts. The British
Reformation Society, established a decade before, was
enjoying immense success. American religious magazines
and papers kept their readers well informed of its progress.[99] Beginning in 1832 The Protestant began to campaign
for a national society in America formed along the same
lines,[100] but it was not until the No Popery cry had been
fanned to new intensity by the burning of the Ursuline

96 - Davis, The Half Century, p. 326.
97 - American Tract Society, Annual Report for 1832. The
     first tract printed was Horne, T. H., Romanism Con-
     tradictory to the Bible, (New York, 1832). In the
     following year The Conversion of Peter Bassiere ap-
     peared. New York Observer, April 6, 1833.
98 - Journals of the General Conference of the Methodist
     Episcopal Church, 1796-1856 (New York, 1856), vol. 1,
     p. 410.
99 - Accounts of meetings of the British society were pub-
     lished in the Christian Spectator, June, 1835; in the
     New York Observer, November 20, 1830; July 16, 1831;
     and June 28, 1834, as well as in other religious news-
     papers and magazines.
100- Quoted in Guilday, Life and Times of John England,
     vol. ii, p. 221.

convent that these demands were to be answered.

Until that time zealous Protestants had to be content with the New York Protestant Association which had been formed in the closing years of the last decade and which had attained a new record in importance with the growing tide of nativism. The activity of this pioneering organization was centered principally in holding public meetings and lectures in which Romanism was attacked by speakers and debaters. One such meeting devoted itself to a discussion of the subject: "Is Popery that 'Babylon the Great' which John had described in the Apocalypse?";[101] another grew excited over the question: "Are Cruelty and Persecution for Conscience Sake Inseparable from Popery?"[102] It may safely be assumed that the groups which crowded themselves into New York churches to hear these discussions came away with a firm answer in the affirmative stamped upon their minds. Such would be expected with Reverend W. C. Brownlee as president of the association.

One of these speeches against Catholicism nearly ended in disaster for the speaker. Samuel B. Smith, already rising to fame as an advocate of No Popery, journeyed to Baltimore from his Philadelphia home in March, 1834, to

101 - The Protestant, March 31, 1832.
102 - Ibid., March 31, 1832.

address a Baptist church meeting. Scarcely had the
speech been started when a group of Irish in the audience rose in righteous anger and stormed the speaker,
forcing him to flee for his life.[103] There was an immediate burst of contumely in the Protestant press. The
New York Observer printed an account of the affair entitled "Popish Intolerance,"[104] and Samuel Smith capitalized the incident by writing an article for the Protestant
Magazine in which he demanded indignantly, "must I be
mobbed as I was in Baltimore because I use the liberty
guaranteed me by my country: the liberty of free speech?"[105]
By this single incident the attention of the Protestant
public was focused upon Catholicism and the anti-Catholic
movement received a great influx of supporters.

Despite the increase of adherents, the anti-Catholic cause suffered under a great weakness. Its disciples
being drawn from the ranks of many denominations, their
strength was dissipated in a lack of common organization.
More, they were opposing a great church that stood as a
unit. No-Popery leaders throughout the land realized that
their greatest hope for success came in organizing the various Protestant denominations and in forcing them to for-

103 - The Protestant Magazine, March, 1834.
104 - New York Observer, March 22, 1834.
105 - The Protestant Magazine, April, 1834.

get their differences in uniting against this common
enemy. It was with this in mind that they turned their
attention to securing the support of the various church
units throughout the land.

Leading in this enterprise was The Protestant
and the members of the New York Protestant Association
that backed it. In January, 1830, soon after the paper
was established, it issued a prospectus to the clergymen of the nation, calling on them to unite to prevent
"the fearful increase of Popery in the United States."
"If there were a staunch united phalanx of Protestants,"
it said, "in opposition to Papal encroachments, and a
corresponding energy and combination on the part of
those who abjure Rome, then might we hope for a successful resistance. But mark the bodeful converse! There
is apathy and disunion among Protestants! What a deplorable contrast to the zeal, artifices and union of
papists! ... Thus cause exists for intense alarm at the
present crisis for there is danger that the principles
of Popery will be rapidly diffused, and gain an ascendancy, from the apathy and time-serving spirit of Protestants. Be it remembered that if we participate in
Romish guilt, we shall consequently be involved in the
destruction of idolatrous Rome."106

106 - Quoted in Guilday, Life and Times of John England,
       vol. ii, pp. 451-452.

The pleas of <u>The Protestant</u> met with a ready response. If churches did not forget their differences and unite throughout the country there was at least a marked increase of interest in Catholicism and its errors on the part of the Protestant clergy. In every large city ministers mounted their pulpit to deliver invective and abuse against Popery and all that it stood for.[107] An extract from a typical sermon shows the enthusiasm with which the clergy had embraced this new clause: "The coffers of Europe pour out their treasures upon the lap of this mother of <u>Harlots!</u> Oh! My dear fellow Christians, as you love virtue and hate vice - as you prize morality beyond crime - as you prefer the sacred spring that flows from the Bible, and gushes forth in such pure streams from the founts of our holy churches, in preference to the muddy waters and defrauding mummeries of a monstrous system of idolatry and superstition - come forth now in your strength and put down these erroneous doctrines forever."[108]

Such isolated sermons, important as they were in shaping public opinion against the Catholic church,

---

107 - Bishop Fenwick complained in 1830 that every pulpit in Boston was given over to attacks on Catholicism. O'Daniel, <u>The Right Reverend Edward Dominic Fenwick</u>, p. 384.
108 - Quoted in Guilday, <u>Life and Times of John England</u>, vol. ii, pp. 454-455.

failed to satisfy the leaders. They wanted organized
support and they turned their attention to the various
denominations to secure their sanction. In the Presbyterian church they found a group with ready ears. As
early as 1830 the General Assembly of the Presbyterian
church looked into the matter of Catholicism, and had
passed a resolution expressing resentment at Catholic
persecution of Protestants in Switzerland.[109] Two years
later sentiment in the General Assembly was so strong
against admitting the validity of Roman Catholic Baptism
that a committee bringing in a report upholding the validity was discharged and a new committee named. The debate
over the measure teemed with arguments against Romanism.[110]

While the General Assembly was thus expressing
itself, individual synods of the Presbyterian church were
giving vent to more outspoken feelings. In 1832 the Synod
of Indiana named a committee to investigate Popery in the
state. Reporting a year later, the committee deplored the
rapid increase of Catholicism and urged a united effort by
the clergy to keep it from gaining too much headway.[111]
The Synod of Philadelphia in October, 1833, adopted a series

109 - New York Observer, June 5, 1830. The New York Ob-
       server, a Presbyterian paper, printed full accounts
       of each meeting of the General Assembly.
110 - Ibid., June 1, 1833.
111 - The Protestant Magazine, June, 1834.

of fiery resolutions, urging the ministers to make a
special study of Catholicism, to preach on it frequently, to bring pressure on their flocks to prevent
Presbyterian children from attending Popish schools,
and to encourage the printing of tracts and books
against Catholicism in all its forms.[112]

But the activity of the Presbyterians did not
stop with these sporadic attacks. The General Assembly
that met in Philadelphia in July, 1834, saw the first
instance of an attempt to unite the clergy of that church
against Catholicism. The attempt came in a speech delivered by the Reverend Philo F. Phelps, designed to provide the clergy who listened to his words with material
for many a No Popery sermon. The Reverend Phelps spared
no invective in dealing with his subject. He told his
clerical audience that conflict between Popery and Protestantism was inevitable in this country, and that Protestants must prepare themselves for the struggle. He
stressed the fact that the Catholic church longed to
wipe out the Republican United States, for only by abolishing republican institutions could her own despotism
continue. He warned his listeners that politicians were
giving the Papists aid in return for their votes, and
that these politicians would make the struggle a dif-

112 - Ibid., January, 1834.

ficult one. But what was difficulty compared with the
result - a Protestant nation or one steeped in the idolatry of Rome.[113] Reverend Phelps not only sent his
audience away firmly convinced that their sermons on
Popery during the coming year should aid in that struggle; in addition he gave to Presbyterianism the impulse
that was to make it the leading church in the crusade
against Catholicism in coming years.

Other denominations, while not embracing the
cause with the enthusiasm of the Presbyterians, showed
considerable interest. The General Association of Congregational Churches of Massachusetts, meeting in June,
1834, adopted a series of resolutions calling on the
clergy to labor "in all suitable ways to save our country from the degrading influence of Popery, and bring
our fellow citizens into the glorious liberty of the
Gospel." The Association did not consider it expedient
to form an anti-Catholic society at that time but it
did name a committee in each district to study the
growth of Romanism and keep the clergy informed.[114]

The Protestant Episcopal church found cause
for alarm in the Catholic ideas of the Rule of Faith

113 - New York Observer, July 12, 1834. The speech
      is also summarized in The Protestant Magazine,
      July, 1834.
114 - Ibid., July 5, 1834.

set forth by Reverend John Hughes in his lengthy controversy with Reverend John Breckinridge, and when the clergy assembled for their annual convention they listened to
a profound attack upon Hughes' stand which was delivered
by Bishop Henry V. Onderdonk.[115] The attitude taken by
Onderdonk was violently opposed to Catholicism in every
form and was heartily applauded by every Episcopalian
paper in the country.[116] When Hughes attempted to answer it, he was flayed in reviews.[117] While members of
other denominations took no direct action, the Methodist
and Baptist clergymen were almost as active as others in
denouncing Catholicism in individual sermons from their
pulpits.

Thus had the forces of anti-Catholicism been
mustered in the years between 1830 and 1834. Writers of
books and pamphlets were pouring out a steadily increasing
stream of volumes, new activity had been instilled into
the anti-Catholic press and the anti-Catholic societies,
the churches had taken an interest in the cause and min-

---

115 - Onderdonk, Henry V., The Rule of Faith; a Charge
to the Clergy of the Protestant Episcopal Church
in the Commonwealth of Pennsylvania, delivered
in St. James Church, Philadelphia, May 22, 1833,
at the opening of the Convention. (Philadelphia,
1833)
116 - Protestant Episcopalian and Church Register, July,
1833.
117 - Ibid., August, 1833. The answer was published
under the title, Hughes, John, The Review of the
Charge Delivered May 22, 1833 by the Right Reverend Bishop Onderdonk, on the Rule of Faith.
(Philadelphia, 1833)

isters the country over were pouring forth abuse from their pulpits. Such a torrent of propaganda must have some vent. The culmination of this wave of bigotry took place the night of August 11, 1834, in the burning of the Ursuline convent in Charlestown.

Much of the tirade against Catholicism from pulpit and pen was aimed specifically at American convents and the part which they were playing in the education of the youth of the land. Propagandist writers saw in the presence of these convents a grave menace to Protestant institutions. They demanded to know why it was that these convent schools educated only Protestant children and allowed the children of Catholics to grow up in ignorance and sloth.[118] To the minds of these writers there was only one answer to their question. Convent schools were maintained simply as a means of gaining converts to Catholicism.[119] "The sole object of all the monastic institutions in America," one author stated dogmatically, "is merely to proselyte youth of the influential classes of society, and especially females; as the Roman priests are conscious that by this means they shall silently but effectually attain the control of pub-

[118] - Ricci, Secrets of Nunneries, p. xxi; New York Observer, June 18, 1831; August 16, 1834.
[119] - Protestant Magazine, September, 1833; History of Popery, p. 412; New York Observer, December 19, 1829.

lic affairs."[120]

Proof of such a design on the part of the Catholic church was said to be everywhere apparent. School books used in the convent schools were denounced as tending to win Protestant children away from their faith.[121] The low tuition rates charged by Catholic schools seemed additional proof; how could they afford to give education at a loss if it were not to win converts?[122] Catholic schools seemed simply a part of a great plot to convert and conquer America. And especially active in this plot, according to the writers, were the two Catholic orders, the Jesuits and the Ursulines. "These Roman ecclesiastics," it was declared, "the Jesuits, and their Ursuline sisters, have been uniformly the most loathsome examples of unnatural licentiousness, whose vitiosity is recorded in the annals of mankind."[123] Parents were urged not to put their children in the care of such monsters. The Presbyterian Synod of Indiana became so alarmed by the charges that they warned their followers against Catholic schools.[124] Similar apprehension throughout the country resulted in a large number of withdrawals from convent schools.[125]

120 - Ricci, Secrets of Nunneries, p. xxii.
121 - The Protestant, December 18, 1830.
122 - Smith, Renunciation of Popery, p. 10; History of Popery, pp. 9-10.
123 - Ricci, Secrets of Nunneries, pp. xxii-xxiii.
124 - An Account of the Conflagration of the Ursuline Convent, (Boston, 1834), pp. 17-18.
125 - Williams, The Shadow of the Pope, pp. 60-61. The attendance at a school established by Bishop England in Charleston fell from 130 pupils to only 30 pupils in 1832.

There was one convent school, however, that went ahead steadily and quietly in the work that it was doing, the Ursuline convent, in Charlestown. This convent, established in Boston first in 1818, had been moved to Charlestown in 1826 to provide a more healthful atmosphere for the nuns.[126] Living first in a farm house at the foot of Mount Benedict, the sisterhood had braved the mild antipathy which greeted their advent,[127] and had grown steadily in wealth and influence. A few years after their establishment in Charlestown they had been able to build an imposing brick structure on the crest of Mount Benedict.[128] Like other members of the order, the Charlestown Ursulines engaged themselves in conducting a school that attracted the daughters of the wealthier families of Boston and neighbouring towns. More liberal members of the Boston population who were beginning to rebel against the stern Congregationalism of the public school system, found in the Ursuline school an ideal place where their daughters could receive culture without embracing the bigotry and narrowness typical of the usual education in the commonwealth.[129]

126 - Vogel, E. V., "The Ursuline Nuns in America," Records of the American Catholic Historical Society, xxx, vol. i, (MARCH, 1919), pp. 214-222.

127 - Spafford, Harriet, E. P., New England Legends, (Boston, 1871), p. 9.

128 - Tucker, Ephraim, "The Burning of the Ursuline Convent," Worcester Society of Antiqiuity Collections, vol.ix,p. 41.

129 - Whitney, Louisa, The Burning of the Convent; A Narrative of the Destruction by a Mob, of the Ursuline School in Mount Benedict, Charlestown, as Remembered by one of the Pupils, (Boston, 1877), pp. 3-4.

The presence of this school in the center of Puritanical Boston was resented from the time of its inception. Good Congregationalists who heard their minister shout from the pulpit against Romanism saw in the presence of the handful of nuns a menace to their liberty and religion. The fact that most of the pupils were children of Unitarians did not increase its popularity in those days of intense religious strife.[130] "Atheists and infidels," cried the good Congregationalists, "will always be ready to sympathize with Catholics, to unite with them in crushing Protestantism preparatory to the subversion of Christianity."[131]

This latent discontent against Catholicism and the convent was fanned to open hostility by the Reverend Lyman Beecher, who was pastor of the Park Street Congregationalist church and a prominent revivalist.[132] He had long been interested in Popery, just as were other ministers of his faith. In 1831 he gave vent to his feelings in a series of sermons delivered from his pulpit and widely circulated throughout New England. In his first address Reverend Beecher laid down his text, "He that is first in his own cause seemeth just, but his neighbor cometh and

130 - Tucker, The Burning of the Ursuline Convent, p. 43.
131 - Massachusetts Yeoman, January 15, 1831.
132 - Beecher, Lyman, Autobiography and Correspondence
       (New York, 1865) vol. i, p. 183.

searcheth him."[133] For many Sundays he played the part
of the neighbor and searched the religion of the Catholics, flaying it with all the intolerance of which his
Puritan soul was capable.

The initial sermon struck immediately at the
center of the Catholic problem as Dr. Beecher saw it.
Catholicism and Republicanism could not exist side by
side, he said. Catholicism had definitely sided with
despotism; the Church recently had aided the monarchs
in their battles with freedom loving people in Europe.
Catholics were naturally in alliance with despotism, then,
and this alliance was increased by the allegiance they
owed the Pope who was a foreign despot. Thus the United
States was in grave danger - it was being peopled by
Catholics who were only the allies of kings opposed to
our liberties.[134]

In the remaining lectures, Dr. Beecher ridiculed the Catholic church for its sacraments, its saint
worship and its penances.[135] He attacked the supremacy
and infallibility of the Pope,[136] and indulged in the

133 - New York Observer, January 29, 1831.
134 - Ibid., January 29, 1831. The sermons were printed
in the New York Observer, the Boston Recorder, the
Massachusetts Yeoman and other religious papers.
They are also in Beecher, Lyman, The Works of the
Reverend Lyman Beecher (Boston, 1852), vol. i.
135 - Ibid., January 29, 1831.
136 - Ibid., February 5, 1831.

usual intolerance so common to anti-Catholic writers and speakers. Widely circulated as they were, the sermons immediately became the principal topic of conversation in Boston. People there were ready to believe Dr. Beecher's fabulous tales. A revival under the leadership of the Reverend Charles G. Finney was in progress.[137] Popular enthusiasm about Protestantism was at its height. Bishop Fenwick and a priest of the diocese, Reverend O'Flaherty, alternated in replying to Dr. Beecher's attacks,[138] but while their audience was plentifully sprinkled with Protestants, the lower elements most affected by anti-Catholic tales were not present.[139] Religious papers took up the Catholic replies and ridiculed them. One of Bishop Fenwick's sermons was branded as "boastful and boisterous, and assumptive and wholly devoid of Christian meekness," by the Boston Christian Herald.[140] Feeling among the lower classes ran so high that handbills were widely distributed, one reading:

TO THE PUBLIC

> Be it known unto you far and near, that all Catholics and all persons in favor of the Catholic church, are a set of vile imposters, liars, villians and cowardly cut-throats. (Be-

137 - Rourke, Constance, M., Trumpets of Jubilee (New York, 1927), pp. 44-45.
138 - Boston Courier, February 10, 1831.
139 - Shea, History of the Catholic Church, vol. iii, p. 467.
140 - Copied in New York Observer, January 29, 1831.

ware of false doctrines) I bid defiance to
that villian - THE POPE.

A True American.[141]

With public feeling running high, it was natural that suspicious glances should be cast in the direction of the Ursuline convent, situated high above the
houses of Charlestown. Popery seemed to have insinuated
itself into the very cradle of Republicanism. What power
and wealth and intrigue lay behind those towering walls?
Here was food for feasts of conjecture. And so tales began to fly among the lower classes of Boston. Stories of
barbarities practiced on the nuns; a sick child sent away
in the last stages of scarlet fever; a dying nun cruelly
treated.[142] Parents considering enrolling their daughters
in the convent school were subjected to pressure and plied
with stories of the horrors of convent life.[143] A novel
appearing just at this time, The Nun by Miss S. Sherwood,
and widely read by the upper classes, seemed to confirm
their worst fears.[144]

At first this growing apprehension had its outlet only in mild persecution and petty outbreaks of trouble.

141 - The Catholic Press, January 22, 1831. Quoted in
      Dowling, History of the Catholic Church in New
      England, vol. ii, p. 27.
142 - Spafford, New England Legends, p. 10.
143 - Whitney, The Burning of the Convent, p. 18. Miss
      Whitney tells of repeated visits that her father
      received from friends and well wishers after he
      had resolved to send her to the convent school.
144 - Ibid., pp. 28-29.

In 1829 a group of Americans, keyed to a high pitch by
the exhortations of a revivalistic preacher, attacked
the homes of Irish Catholics on Broad street and stoned
them for three days in succession.[145] A year later the
selectmen of Charlestown raised vigorous objections when
Bishop Fenwick purchased three acres of land on Bunker
Hill to use as a Catholic cemetery. These objections
were only intensified when the bishop's right to the
purchase was upheld in the courts.[146] In 1833 a monument to Father Role erected in Norridgewock was destroyed by a mob.[147] Later in the same year a group of
drunken Irishmen attacked a native American citizen and
beat him to death on the streets of Charlestown. The
next night five hundred natives formed themselves into
a mob and marched on the Irish section. Troops were
called out but stood helplessly by while Irish homes
were torn down, although their presence averted actual
bloodshed.[148]

These early acts of violence were only a prelude. While the people of Boston were still stirred by

145 - Leahy, William, The Catholic Church in New England
(Boston, 1899), vol. i, p. 53.
146 - Shea, History of the Catholic Church, vol. iii, pp.
462-463. This early controversy between Bishop
Fenwick and the Charlestown Selectmen explains in
some degree the attitude of the Selectmen toward
the burning of the convent.
147 - Guilday, Life and Times of John England, vol. ii,
p. 232.
148 - New York Observer, December 7, 1833.

the rioting between Irish and natives in Charlestown
a series of events occurred that centered all of their
attention upon the Ursulines and their school. For
suddenly there appeared in their midst an escaped nun.
Moreover she was a nun who had escaped from the Ursuline
convent. Rebecca Theresa Reed was her name, and the
fact that she had been known before as a commonplace
chit of a girl about Charlestown made little difference
to those that listened to the stories she told. Neither
did it matter that she had not been a nun at all, that
she had insisted on being taken into the convent for a
six months' period of probation to prove her worth, and
had been dismissed two months before her period was up.[149]
Rebecca's own tales were far more fascinating than that.
She told of dread things that went on within the walls
of that somber building on Mount Benedict; she told of
how she had heard the Mother Superior and Bishop Fenwick
plotting to kidnap her and send her to Canada, she told
of how she had escaped in the dead of night to defeat
their evil plans.[150] This was the sort of thing the
people wanted, and stories that Rebecca Reed told flew

---

149 - The Mother Superior of the convent so testified
      at the trial of the rioters. Trial of John R.
      Buzzell, the Leader of the Convent Rioters, for
      Arson and Burglary Committed on the Night of the
      11th of August, 1834, by the Destruction of the
      Convent on Mount Benedict in Charlestown, Mass-
      achusetts. (Boston, 1834), p. 7.
150 - Report of the Committee Relating to the Destruc-
      tion of the Charlestown Convent (Boston, 1834)
      pp. 7-8.

thick and fast over Boston.

      While these tales were still being told another nun escaped. This time it was a real nun, Elizabeth Harrison, who had been a member of the Ursuline order since 1824. Miss Harrison had taught music in the convent school, and in the early months of 1834 had been very much overworked, giving lessons ten or twelve hours each day.[151] Long feeble in health, her mind gradually broke down under this continual strain. The other sisters noticed her peculiar behavior; how she insisted on having all doors open in the convent and acted strangely in other ways.[152] On July 28, 1834, came the most violent act of all. That night she rushed from the convent, ran across fields to the home of a neighboring brick manufacturer, Edward Cutter, and burst into his house, demanding refuge from persecutions she was forced to endure on Mount Benedict. Mr. Cutter complied with her request to take her to the home of her brother, Thomas Harrison, in Cambridge.[153] There reason returned, Miss Harrison realized what she had done, and immediately asked that Bishop Fenwick be sent

151 - Ibid., p. 8.
152 - According to the testimony of the Mother Superior at the trial of the rioters. Trail of John R. Buzzell, the Leader of the Convent Rioters, p. 8.
153 - Mr. Cutter wrote an account of the affairs of that night of July 28, published a little later. See New York Observer, August 16, 1834. Letter printed also in The Charlestown Convent; its Destruction by a Mob on the Night of August 11, 1834; with a History of the Excitement before the Burning, and the Strange and Exaggerated Reports Relating Thereto, the Feeling of Regret and Indignation Afterwards; the Proceedings of Meetings, and Expressions of the Contemporary Press. (Boston, 1870), p. 9.

for. He visited her the next day, she told him of her mental disorder, and asked that she be taken back to the convent, a request that was readily granted.[154]

But the mischief had been done. By the end of the day after she had fled the convent all Boston had heard the story, and as it flew from lip to lip it grew in proportions. Rumors circulated that the escaped nun had been taken back by coercion, that she had been forced to flee in the first place because of the ill treatment she had received, that now she was in a deep dungeon in the cellars of the convent building.[155] It remained for a later generation of writers to assert that she had left the convent to bear a child;[156] but the stories at the time approached even that later tale in their fantastic nature.

The spread of such misstatements was given impetus when one of the Boston papers, the Mercantile Journal, published an article headed "Mysterious," on the morning of August 8. "We understand," the paper stated, "that a great excitement at present exists in Charlestown, in consequence of the mysterious disappearance of a young

154 - New York Observer, August 16, 1834. Letter of Mr.
       Cutter.
155 - American Quarterly Review, vol. xvii (March, 1835)
       p. 216; Report of Committee Relating to the Destruc-
       tion of the Ursuline Convent, p. 9.
156 - Hogan, William, Synopsis of Popery, as it Was and
       as It is. (Hartford, 1854) p. 77.

lady at the Nunnery in that place. The circumstances, as far as we can learn, are as follows: The young lady was sent to the place in question to complete her education, and became so pleased with the place and its inmates, that she was induced to seclude herself from the world and take the black veil. After some time spent in the nunnery, she became dissatisfied and made her escape from the institution, but was afterwards persuaded to return, being told that if she would continue but three weeks longer, she would be dismissed with honor. At the end of that time, a few days since, her friends called for her, but she was not to be found, and much alarm is excited in consequence."[157]

The inflammatory article was copied by the Morning Post, and the Boston Commercial Gazette and immediately caused a flurry of excitement among the sensation loving populace.[158] Placards were posted all over the city which called on the selectmen of Charlestown to investigate and threatened mob violence against the convent unless Miss Harrison were found.[159] Other placards designed to stir up public

157 - Quoted in An Account of the Conflagration of the Ursuline Convent, p. 8.
158 - The Charlestown Convent; its Destruction by a Mob, p. 7.
159 - Ibid., p. 70.

feeling were widely circulated. One read:

> Go ahead! To Arms! To Arms!! Ye
> brave and free the avenging sword unshield!!.
> Leave not one stone upon another of that
> curst Nunnery that prostitutes female vir-
> tue and liberty under the garb of Holy Re-
> ligion. When Bonapart opened the Nunneries
> of Europe he found cords of infants skulls.!![160]

With public feeling at such a pitch, the clergy
was quick to sense an opportunity to deliver a blow at
their old enemy, Catholicism. Sermons berating the Catholic church and pointing out its evils were preached in
a number of Boston pulpits, particularly at the Baptist
church in Hanover street.[161] In the midst of this excitement Doctor Lyman Beecher returned to town.

Two years before, in 1832, Dr. Beecher had accepted the presidency of the Lane Theological Seminary
at Cincinnati.[162] Like so many schools of its kind, Dr.
Beecher's Seminary was sadly in need of funds, and in
the summer of 1834 he launched a speaking tour through
the east to add money to its coffers.[163] He reached
Boston during the week of August 3, when public sentiment
against Catholicism was rising rapidly. Realizing the
possibilities of a situation which would permit him to

160 - Ibid., p. 70.
161 - The Jesuit, August 16, 1834.
162 - Beecher, Autobiography and Correspondence, vol. ii,
p. 243.
163 - Ibid., vol. ii, p. 333.

deal another thrust at the Catholic church and at the
same time secure the money which he was seeking, Dr.
Beecher chose for his Boston sermon his famous Plea for
the West, one of the most bitter attacks on Catholicism
ever produced. He told three audiences that overflowed
from three separate churches, including his old Park
Street church on "Brimstone corner,"[164] that they must
give money to save the west from the dread menace of
Popery. He painted a dismal picture of a growing priesthood in the Mississippi Valley, and he warned that unless
Protestant activity were renewed there the great western
lands would be taken over bodily by the Pope.[165] This
rabid attack on Catholicism was delivered on the night
of August 10 and met with such success that he was able
to collect $4,000 from the congregation of one church
alone.[166] Only a few hours later a mob swept down upon
the Ursuline convent with torch and faggot.

Dr. Beecher maintained afterward that his sermons had nothing to do with the burning of the convent.

164 - Nicholas, Thomas, Forty Years of American Life
(London, 1864), vol. ii, p. 89. Nicholas states
that the Park Street church was known as Brimstone Corner because of the activities of Dr.
Beecher there.
165 - Beecher, Lyman, A Plea for the West (Cincinnati,
1835) pp. 11 ff.
166 - Beecher, Autobiography and Correspondence, vol.ii,
p. 334.

He admitted that they had much to do with developing
an anti-Catholic sentiment that found expression in
the next few years,[167] but he pointed out that his
audience could scarcely have rushed directly from his
sermons to the scene of the mob violence several miles
away.[168] In this contention Dr. Beecher is probably
correct, despite the blame that has been placed on his
shoulders by the Catholic historians.[169] There seems
to be little doubt, however, that an organized conspiracy was under way to attack the convent, backed
by the well organized truckmen of Boston and Charlestown,[170] and receiving the tacit consent of the lower
classes of the population who knew of its existence.
The official committee which investigated the whole
affair believed that the conspirators were goaded in
their attack by the appearance of the article entitled
"Mysterious,"[171] and similar testimony was given in the
trial of the rioters by one of them who turned state's

---

167 - Ibid., vol. ii, p. 335.
168 - Ibid., vol. ii, p. 462.
169 - Shea, History of the Catholic Church, vol. iii,
       pp. 473-480; Desmond, The Know Nothing Party,
       pp. 15-16.
170 - Whitney, The Burning of the Convent, p. 29.
171 - Report of the Committee Relating to the Destruction
       of the Ursuline Convent, p. 9.

evidence.[172] One of the girls in the convent school
stated afterward that several times men offered to
aid her companions in escaping the clutches of the
convent as they were playing in the yard of the convent grounds.[173]

Even with so much misunderstanding, the
selectmen of Charlestown could have done much to quell
the growing feeling and perhaps could have saved the
convent from the hands of the mob. They were prevented
from taking such action by a mild controversy that was
raging at that time which served to embitter them against
Bishop Fenwick. Bishop Fenwick had purchased three acres
of land on Bunker Hill to use as a Catholic cemetery, and
had applied to the Charlestown selectmen for permission
to bury two children there just as sentiment was reaching
its height. The selectmen had replied that the health
regulations of the town prevented the burial of any Roman

172 - Trial of John R. Buzzell, the Leader of the Convent Rioters, pp. 11-12. This conspirator was
Henry Buck, who told of frequent meetings for
several weeks before the burning in which each
move was carefully planned. The attack of defense counsel on Buck's character, however, makes
his testimony of doubtful value.
173 - Thaxter, Lucy, An Account of Life in the Convent
at Mount Benedict, Charlestown. Manuscript account in Treasure Room of Widener Library, Harvard, written by one of the pupils shortly after
the burning.

Catholics there![174] Bishop Fenwick buried the children
in the cemetery despite this opposition, and the selectmen brought suit against him as a result.[175] This suit
was still pending when excitement over the convent reached
its height, and this controversy must be borne in mind
when the negligent attitude of the selectmen is considered.[176]

The increasing chorus of threats against the convent finally drove the selectmen to some action, however.
On Saturday, August 9, they visited the convent building
in a body, and asked to be allowed to make an inspection,
but the Mother Superior, taking the attitude that they
were responsible for all of the rumors, refused them ad-
mittance.[177] Edward Cutter, who had sheltered Elizabeth
Harrison during her mental derangement, met a better response. He was admitted, talked to Miss Harrison, and
was assured by that lady that she was well treated, in
good health and that stories told of her being cast into
darkened dungeons were pure fabrication.[178] The selectmen

174 - The Jesuit, November 1, 1834.
175 - Ibid., November 1, 1834.
176 - The case was finally tried before the Supreme Ju-
      dicial Court at the Middlesex session on October
      18, 1834, and the town by-laws forbidding burial
      of Catholics declared invalid since the only pur-
      pose of such laws should be to regulate public
      health, not for discriminatory legislation. The
      Jesuit, November 1, 1834.
177 - Whitney, The Burning of the Convent, pp. 71-75.
178 - His account was printed in the Boston Morning Post,
      August 11, 1835. Reprinted in the New York Ob-
      server, August 16, 1834. Also in The Charlestown
      Convent, its Destruction by a Mob, p. 8.

tried their luck again on Monday, August 11, and this
time were allowed to make an inspection. They prepared
a report that appeared in the Boston papers on the next
morning, together with a report by Cutter,[179] expressing themselves as certain that Miss Harrison was "entirely satisfied with her situation, it being that of
her own choice, and that she has no desire or wish to
alter it."[180] When the Boston papers published those
reports on Tuesday morning it was too late. The convent was a mass of smouldering ruins.

The mob began to gather outside its doors
about nine o'clock Monday night, carrying banners and
shouting "No Popery" and "Down with the Cross."[181] One
of the Charlestown selectmen was present, and the others
were notified, but they insisted that there was no danger
and refused to take any action.[182] After milling about

179 - The Boston Transcript, August 11, 1834, stated that
      it had intended to print a refutation of the charges
      by Bishop Fenwick, but that he had heard of the
      proposed refutation by Cutter, and would allow that
      to appear first. An Account of the Conflagration
      of the Ursuline Convent, p. 5.
180 - Their report was printed in the Boston Morning Post,
      August 11, 1834. Reprinted in the New York Observer,
      August 16, 1834; Report of Committee Relating to the
      Destruction of the Charlestown Convent, p. 9.
181 - Thie, Joseph A., "German Catholic Activity in the
      United States Seventy Years Ago" Records of the
      American Catholic Historical Society of Philadelphia,
      vol. xx (June, 1909) p. 97. The statement is made in
      a letter published at the time in the Wahrheitsfreund,
      a German Catholic newspaper, published at Cincinnati.
182 - Report of the Committee Relating to the Destruction
      of the Charlestown Convent, p. 10.

before the doors for an hour, forty or fifty men,
evidently well organized and with their faces painted
to disguise them, approached the building and demanded
that they be shown the nun who was secreted there.[183]
They were told to return the next day when the children
would not be awakened and they withdrew for a short time.
But at eleven o'clock a pile of tar barrels which had
been assembled in a neighboring field was lighted; evidently a prearranged signal.[184] Fire bells were set
ringing, and crowds of people began pouring into Charlestown. Fire companies appeared, but realizing the futility of stemming mob enthusiasm, stood helplessly by while
the rioters began their attack.[185] The Mother Superior
stood on a balcony of her home and made efforts to appeal to the milling throng - first by pleading, then by
threatening that "the Bishop had twenty thousand Irishmen at his command in Boston," a statement that only
fired the rioters to greater violence.[186]

183 - New York Observer, August 16, 1834. The account
      is reprinted from the Boston Daily Advertiser,
      August 12, 1834.
184 - Report of the Committee Relating to the Destruc-
      tion of the Ursuline Convent, p. 10.
185 - The Board of Engineers of the Boston Fire Depart-
      ment published a report on August 13, 1834, ex-
      onerating members of the companies from any blame
      for the burning. The report shows that only two
      companies reached the scene of the fire, and both
      of those promptly withdrew to a point several hun-
      dred yards away where they watched the whole af-
      fair. Report printed in, An Account of the Con-
      flagration of the Ursuline Convent, pp. 22-24.
186 - Whitney, The Burning of the Convent, p. 113.

At a little after eleven o'clock the attack came. Led by the forty or fifty men who had made the first advance, they burst open the doors and entered the convent building.[187] There were at that time twelve nuns and about sixty children in the building. Hurriedly assembled under the care of the frantic sisters, they were bundled through a back door and managed to escape from the grounds, taking refuge in the home of Edward Cutter, who figured so prominently in the whole affair.[188] They had left the convent none too soon. The torch was applied a little after midnight, and in a few moments the whole building was in flames.[189] A farmhouse belonging to the Ursuline order adjoining the main building met a similar fate, but there seems to be little evidence that the convent vault was desecrated as it was charged later.[190]

---

187 - New York Observer, August 16, 1834.
188 - Accounts of the escape of the nuns and their pupils written a little later by two of those pupils vary only in details: Whitney, The Burning of the Convent, pp. 145-160; and Thaxter, An Account of Life in the Convent at Mount Benedict.
189 - New York Observer, August 16, 1834; Report of the Committee Relating to the Destruction of the Ursuline Convent, p.11; An Account of the Conflagration of the Ursuline Convent, p. 6. The burning is well described, although in a prejudiced tone, in Shea, History of the Catholic Church, vol. iii, pp. 473-485. Niles Register, October 11, 1834, also has an excellent description.
190 - American Quarterly Review, March, 1835; Thie, German Catholic Activity, p. 97. The Report of the Committee Relating to the Destruction of the Ursuline Convent, fails to mention such an outrage, a thing that it would certainly have done for the members of the committee showed little sympathy with the mob. The story has been accepted by most Catholic historians, however, as Shea, op. cit., vol. iii, pp. 480-485.

The whole city of Boston was plunged into
a furor of excitement by the burning. Rumors spread
abroad that organized bodies of Irishmen were march-
ing on the city from the neighboring railroad camps
to inflict retaliation,[191] and Bishop Fenwick hurriedly
dispatched six priests in different directions to meet
them and stop their onslaught.[192] The Bishop himself
held a meeting of Boston Catholics in which he urged
them to remain quiet. "Turn not a finger in your defense," he said, "There are those around you who will
see justice done you."[193] Soothing statements such as
these did not calm the fears of the people, however;
the militia was called out,[194] Harvard students appointed
regular patrols to protect the Yard from Catholic van-
dals,[195] "I have never witnessed such a scene of excitement through the whole mass of the phlegmatic and peaceful population of Boston," a correspondent wrote.[196]

On the night after the burning a band of armed

191 - New York Observer, August 16, 1834.
192 - The Jesuit, August 16, 1834.
193 - American Quarterly Review, March, 1835.
194 - Monroe, James B., The New England Conscience (Boston,
      1915) p. 138. The Charlestown Convent, its Destruc-
      tion by a Mob, pp. 24-25.
195 - Darling, Arthur B., Political Changes in Massachu-
      setts, 1824-1848 (New Haven, 1925), p. 165.
196 - Boston Correspondent of the New York Journal of Com-
      merce. Quoted in New York Observer, August 23, 1834.

men and boys marched to Mount Benedict, pulled down the trees on the convent grounds, burned the fences and did other damage while troops guarding the home of Edward Cutter stood quietly by and watched. The troops did prevent them from attacking a nearby church.[197] The next night a crowd of more than a thousand men roamed the streets of Boston, alarmed by rumor that Irish laborers were descending on the city.[198] On Friday, August 15, a group of rioters burned a shanty in Charlestown occupied by thirty-five Irish laborers, but further damage was averted when the drawbridge was raised to prevent the Boston mob that quickly formed from reaching the scene of the blaze.[199]

There were sober elements of the population that shuddered at such violent action, however. Many of the communities held meetings in which resolutions were adopted denouncing the mob action,[200] although the Charlestown meeting did little good when it placed the blame on a "Boston mob" and nearly caused an armed attack by citizens of that city, whose name was thus sullied.[201] The largest meeting,

197 - New York Observer, August 23, 1834. Quoting Boston Transcript, August 13, 1834.
198 - Ibid., August 23, 1834. Quoting the Boston Gazette, August 14, 1834.
199 - Ibid., August 23, 1834.
200 - The Jesuit, August 16, 1834.
201 - The Charlestown Convent, its Destruction by a Mob, p.22

held in Faneuil Hall in Boston, with Harrison Gray Otis
presiding, passed a series of resolutions declaring "that
the destruction of property and danger of life caused
thereby, calls loudly on all good citizens to express,
individually and collectively, the abhorrence they feel,
of this high handed violation of the laws."[202]   A committee was named to investigate the causes of the burning, and the mayor of Boston was authorized to offer a
reward for the apprehension of the ring leaders of the
mob.[203]

      After fourteen days of investigation the Boston
committee reported its findings. It found as the cause
for the burning the wide spread dislike of the Catholic
faith, fomented to hatred by misrepresentations spread
by Rebecca Reed and growing from the "elopment" of Elizabeth Harrison.[204] The committee recommended several
changes in the laws, to make magistrates more responsible for checking such outrages, and recommended especially
that the members of the Ursuline order be reimbursed for
their loss by the state legislature.[205] The Governor hesi-

202 - Report of the Committee Relating to the Destruction
of the Charlestown Convent, p. 2. Also in Niles
Register, October 11, 1834.
203 - Report of the Committee Relating to the Destruction
of the Charlestown Convent, p. 2. New York Observer,
August 16, 1834.
204 - Report of the Committee Relating to the Destruction
of the Charlestown Convent, p. 4.
205 - Ibid., pp. 13-15.

tated to take this step, however, because of the personal unpopularity that would result. More drastic riot laws were passed,[206] and reports were introduced by special committees of the General Court favoring reparation, but the members refused to vote the money asked.[207] Repeated efforts over a span of years were made in this direction, a committee in 1842 urging reparation upon the General Court[208] and an inadequate sum being voted in 1846 that was refused.[209] Again in 1853 a bill granting the Ursuline Order proper compensation was rejected by the legislature.[210] It was obvious that while legislative leaders might talk of religious liberty and justice, the great mass of the voters were glad that the convent had been burned, and were unwilling to do anything toward restoring it. The ruins of the convent stood for half a century, authorities of the Catholic Church allowing them to remain as a perpetual monument to the injustice shown the Catholic faith in Massachusetts.[211]

---

206 - "Bill more effectively to suppress Riots," Commonwealth of Massachusetts, Legislative Documents No. 17 (1835), pp. 1-5.
207 - "Report on Convent of Mt. Benedict," Commonwealth of Massachusetts, Legislative Documents, No. 37, (1835) pp. 1-24.
208 - Documents Relating to the Ursuline Convent in Charlestown (Boston, 1842), pp. 21-32.
209 - American Protestant Magazine, June, 1846.
210 - The American Union, April 23, 1853.
211 - Whitney, The Burning of the Convent, pp. 4-5. The ruins were still standing when this account was written, in 1877.

The tacit approval of such mob violence was
given even more outspoken emphasis in the trial of
rioters accused of leading the attack. While excitement over the burning was still high, the mayor of
Boston offered a reward of $500. for the capture of
the leaders[212] and within two weeks thirteen men had
been arrested.[213] Eight held for the capital offence
of arson were arraigned before the Supreme Judicial
Court of Massachusetts on October 10, 1834, and trial
was set for December 1. The early date of the trial
was protested by the attorney general who charged that
the high state of public feeling on the part of the
people of Boston and their general approval of the
mob's action, would make it impossible to get witnesses for the prosecution. All the witnesses that
he had approached had received threats, he said, and
he himself had received threatening letters, and had
been hanged in effigy.[214]

The court refused to be moved by these protests and the trial of the first of the rioters, John

212 - The proclamation is printed in the New York Observer, October 23, 1834.
213 - Report of the Committee Relating to the Destruction of the Ursuline Convent, pp. 3-4.
214 - The Charlestown Convent, its Destruction by a Mob,
pp. 29-30.

R. Buzzell, began on December 2. The anti-Catholic
nature of the proceedings was made evident from the
first. Questions by the attorney general to the
jurors as to whether they were prejudiced against
Catholicism were not allowed.[215] The defense attorney, in his opening address, laid down the broad
lines that the defense would take; he said he would
prove that the Ursuline convent did not have charity
for its object, that the Lady Superior and nuns had
been brought into court to make a good impression, and
that all female witnesses were pretending to have a cold
caught on the night of the burning. "The prisoner at
the bar cannot be convicted without Catholic testimony,"
he told the jury, "we will endeavor to show what that
testimony is worth."[216]

The opening speech set the pattern for the
whole trial. Rebecca Reed was placed on the stand,
and testified as to the horrors of convent life.[217]
The cross examination of Bishop Fenwick and the Mother

215 - Ibid., pp. 30-31.
216 - The Trial of John R. Buzzell, the Leader of the
Convent Rioters, pp. 15-16. For other accounts
of the trial see, Trial of John R. Buzzell Before
the Supreme Judicial Court of Massachusetts for
Arson and Burglary in the Ursuline Convent at
Charlestown (Boston, 1834); The Trial of Persons
Charged with Burning the Convent in the Town of
Charlestown (Mass.) before the Supreme Judicial
Court Holden at East Cambridge on Tuesday, December 2, 1834 (Boston, 1834); The Trial of the Convent Rioters (Cambridge, 1834). These accounts
giving the anti-Catholic testimony in full, served
as powerful propaganda in furthering attacks upon
the church.
217 - Ibid., p. 17.

Superior of the convent turned only about the immorality
of convent life and had nothing to do with the matter at
issue.[218] Testimony of the two principal witnesses of
the prosecution was branded as "imported foreign testimony," and the jurors urged to ignore it.[219] When the
jury retired its decision was a foregone conclusion. But
even more pressure was brought to bear. Handbills were
circulated reading:

> Liberty or Death!
> Suppressed Evidence!
> Sons of Freedom! Can you Live in a
> Free Country and Bear the Yoke of Priest-
> hood, Veiled in the Habit of a Profligate
> Court?[220]

The verdict of acquittal, brought in by the jury
after twenty hours of deliberation, was received with thun-
derous applause by the crowded courtroom.[221] Immediately
upon his release, Buzzell was congratulated by thousands
of citizens and showered with gifts; such a manifestation
of approval that he felt called upon to place a card of
thanks in the Boston newspapers.[222] He was reported to
have signed a death bed confession a few years later[223]
but he was alive enough to write in 1887 of a plot to re-

218 - Ibid.,pp. 1-11; The Charlestown Convent, its Destruction by a Mob, p. 35.
219 - The Charlestown Convent, its Destruction by a Mob,p.40.
220 - Ibid., p. 58.
221 - The Trial of John R. Buzzell, the Leader of the Convent Rioters, p. 55.
222 - The Jesuit, December 18, 1834.
223 - New York Observer, July 29, 1837.

lease him from jail if he had been convicted.[224]

After this first acquittal, the trial of the remaining rioters was a mere matter of form. They were released with only one exception, a youth who was sentenced to a life of hard labor.[225] He was pardoned only a few months later, however, after the Catholic citizens of Boston bidding for popular favor had presented a petition asking for his release.[226]

Thus the first great burst of anti-Catholic sentiment in America ended in grim tragedy, in profligate destruction and in acquittal that was a mockery of justice. Well might a Catholic poet write a year later:

> Now shout, ye monsters! Feast your bigot eyes,
> As fiercely ye behold those flames arise -
> But first dispatch a herald who may haste,
> To tell good Beecher of your goodly waste;
> His pious heart will leap from joy to know
> His words, like genial seeds which farmers grow,
> Have fruitful proved: and think your deed divine
> If arson makes the Popish cause decline.[227]

224 - Boston Globe, December 24, 1887.
225 - American Quarterly Review, March, 1835.
226 - Ibid., March, 1835.
227 - Scank, Philemon, A Few Chapters to Brother Jonathan Concerning Infallibility etc.; or, Stricture's on Nathan L. Rice's Defense of Protestantism. (Louisville, 1835) p. 34.

IV

THE FLAMES SPREAD, 1835-1840.

The torches that turned a peaceful Ursuline convent into a mass of flame kindled more than mere walls. Sparks from this anti-Catholic outburst were to cause bitter conflagration in hearts and minds throughout the land before they could be quenched. The burning of the convent brought the attention of all America to the crusade against Popery. Men might not approve of mob violence and such wanton destruction of property, but throughout the country there grew a comfortable feeling of a good deed well done; riot might be a poor way to achieve an end, but for the most part the people were in accord with the end achieved. A convent had been destroyed. A blow had been struck at Romanism. Catholics had been warned in decisive fashion.

As soon as news of the Boston riot swept over the country, a storm of protest arose. Editors hurled invective against mob violence and lawlessness. The burning of the convent was deplored as "Fanaticism" aroused by a concentrated effort of anti-Catholic agitators."[1] "The expressions of indignation and abhorrence,"

1 - An Account of the Conflagration of the Ursuline Convent, p. 1.

said the Christian Examiner, "with which the perpetra-
tors of that crime must feel themselves blasted....
cannot do away with the fact that they, and wretches
like them, exist in the bosom of our community."[2] Yet
the editors insisted in the same editorial that Catholicism was wrong, and urged united Protestant effort
to combat it.

This same sentiment was expressed from pulpits throughout the land. "Do you wish to introduce
a Protestant Inquisition?" one minister asked his flock,
"to establish a religion by law, crush out all dissenters from the legal faith, and bring back the age
of persecution for opinion? If this is your wish, then
let public sentiment speak out....Let the sword, the
rack, the flames, again be made the patent arguments
for Christian truth!"[3] A few years later another minister deplored the continued spirit of intolerance that
kept the Ursuline order from being granted compensation
due them and expressed his disgust with a community so
anti-Catholic in spirit that justice could not be done.[4]

2 - Christian Examiner, September, 1834.
3 - Stetson, Caleb, A Discourse on the Duty of Sustain-
    ing the Laws, Occasioned by the Burning of the Ursu-
    line Convent (Boston, 1834), p. 14. A sermon preached
    at the First Church in Medford, August 23, 1834.
4 - Curtis, George T., The Rights of Conscience and of
    Property; or, the True Issue of the Convent Question
    (Boston, 1842), pp. 20-21.

Even Reverend Lyman Beecher whose bitter antipathy
toward Romanism had done so much to lead to the burning of the convent, spoke from his pulpit in Boston
the Sunday following the attack regretting such mob
violence. Catholics should be treated with kindness
and affection, he told his listeners, but this should
not mean that our own rights of freedom should be
taken away. We should be free to tell the truth about
Popery to show its errors, and persecutions, to tell
of a plan now being formed by the Pope to capture the
United States. But mob attack was a poor weapon to
use in combating this great enemy.[5]

Meanwhile the Catholic press was not inactive
in its criticism of such violence. The Jesuit spoke of
the Bunker Hill Monument, then under construction. "Under its very brow", it said, "are the dark, the gloomy
proofs, that there are those among the descendants of
the heroes of '76, who are craven enough to war upon
women; and sufficiently bigoted and ignorant to think
they do God service by sacrilege, arson, and desecration of the grave."[6] A Catholic poet leaped to the cry,
and painted a picture of:

5 - New York Observer, August 30, 1834; Protestant
    Magazine, August, 1834.
6 - Quoted in Foik, "Anti-Catholic Parties in American
    Politics," p. 54.

Devouring flames; insulting rabble near;
A band of Holy Virgins pale with fear,
Retiring from their consecrated cells
Pursued by curses worse than savage yells.[7]

A Pastoral Letter issued by the Catholic Bishops assembled at the Third Provincial Council in Baltimore in 1837, spoke with equal frankness of the shame upon Massachusetts in not making compensation to the Ursulines.[8]

These attacks by Catholics were not to go unchallenged. Religious newspapers began commenting on the bitter tone of Catholic editors, and found in this bitterness an excuse not to believe anything that Catholic writers asserted.[9] They complained that aliens in this country were using the riot as excuse to make the people of Boston ashamed of their Puritan ancestry.[10] Statements made by Catholic editors were taken up and refuted; St. Bartholomew's Day and the Spanish Inquisition were flung at those who called the burning of the convent the worst outrage in history.[11] The remark attributed to the Mother Superior during the excitement of the attack,

7 - Scank, A Few Chapters to Brother Jonathan, p. 7.
8 - Guilday, History of the Councils of Baltimore, p. 118.
9 - Boston Observer and Religious Intelligencer,
April 23, 1835.
10- Supplement to Six Months in a Convent, Confirming
the Narrative of Rebecca Theresa Reed, by the Testimony of more than 100 Witnesses. (Boston, 1835)
pp. 21-22.
11--Ibid., pp. 22-23.

that the Bishop had ten thousand Irishmen at his
command, was taken up and magnified and made the
basis for many an editorial comment.[12] "Has it
come to this," Reverend Lyman Beecher thundered,
"that the capital of New England has been thrown
into consternation by the threats of a Catholic mob,
and that her temples and mansions stand only through
the forbearance of a Catholic bishop?"[13]

The work of the Boston Investigating Committee was flayed with almost equal vigor. The Boston
Christian Watchman, the leading Baptist paper of New
England, told its readers that the report of the committee could be understood only when it was realized
that all priests in Boston were Jesuits, and that the
watchword of that order was expediency, which meant
falsehoods in any testimony.[14] It was complained too
that the committee passed over the real cause of the
burning in their attempt to lay the blame on Dr.
Beecher's shoulders, and that the real cause was the

12 - New York Observer, December 27, 1834.
13 - Beecher, Autobiography and Correspondence, vol.ii,
     p. 335. For a similar sentiment see Stevens,
     R.V.A., An Alarm to American Patriots, A Sermon
     on the Political Tendencies of Popery, considered
     in respect to the Institutions in the United
     States, in the Church Street Church, Boston,
     November 27, 1824. (Boston, 1834)
14 - Quoted in New York Observer, October 25, 1834.

elopment of Elizabeth Harrison and her forced return.[15] The whole report, it was stated, was based on Catholic authorities, hence utterly worthless.[16]

Some of the Boston papers went so far as almost to praise the actual destruction of the convent. The Boston Recorder, a Presbyterian paper, stated it had little sympathy with mob violence but that it had a "deep conviction that convents have been, are now, and while continued ever will be, highly injurious to the great interests of the community."[17] This attitude just after the burning meant that the acquittal of the rioters by the courts would be taken as a signal for actual rejoicing by the religious press. The Concord Freeman, scourged the attorney general for defending the hated Papists and insisted that his office should be abolished.[18] The Boston Observer and Religious Intelligencer steadfastly upheld the acquittal of so many of the rioters against criticism,[19] and the New York Observer defended the burning in subsequent years.[20] Zion's Herald, another Boston paper,

15 - Supplement to Six Months in a Convent, pp. 68-69.
16 - Ibid., pp. 62-63.
17 - Quoted in An Account of the Conflagration of the Ursuline Convent, p. 18.
18 - Quoted in the Downfall of Babylon, June 20, 1835.
19 - Boston Observer and Religious Intelligencer, January 15, 1835.
20 - New York Observer, June 23, 1838.

grew frantic in its efforts to prevent the state from
giving funds to rebuild the convent.[21]   Throughout
the land similar comments began to pour from the pens
of editors already steeped in the anti-Catholic cause
and a mass of propaganda which was larger in volume
than any attained before, saw light of day.

While this torrent of words was growing,
Bishop Fenwick tried to establish the homeless Ursuline nuns where they could carry on their work of education and mercy. They were placed in a house in Rox-
bury first, but inflammatory handbills again appeared
and a mob formed intent on burning this new convent, a
design that was only frustrated by troops who were
hurriedly called out.[22] Churches that were threatened
at the same time were only saved from destruction by
the presence of large numbers of Catholics gathered to
guard them.[23] It was not until a year later that sentiment had died down sufficiently for the Ursuline sisters
to be established in Boston, but pupils now refused to
attend their school and in 1838 the Mother Superior and
her followers, abandoning the project, left for Canada.[24]

21 - Quoted in New York Observer, November 29, 1834.
22 - New York Observer, December 27, 1834.
23 - O'Gorman, History of the Roman Catholic Church,p.383.
24 - Shea, History of the Catholic Church, vol. iii,p.489.

So great was the feeling throughout the land that Bishop
England hesitated to establish in Charleston an order of
Ursulines with whom he had just returned from Europe,[25]
and when he did so was roundly flayed by the editor of
the Charleston Observer.[26]

These belated attacks on the Ursulines were
not confined to Boston. Mob spirit against Catholics
and their institutions flared throughout the United
States. Perhaps the power of suggestion played its
part; certainly the ease with which the Boston rioters
secured acquittal must have encouraged others. An epidemic of disorder swept over the country, with the
Catholic church as the victim.

The first burning of a Catholic church in New
York had occurred as early as 1831,[27] but the year 1834
marked a new outburst against Catholics and foreigners.
The charter election of that year was a scene of bloody
feuds fought openly between natives and aliens,[28] with
blame for them placed upon the aliens because of their

25 - England, The Works of John England, vol. vii,
pp. 44-55.
26 - Guilday, Life and Times of John England, vol. ii,
pp. 143-144.
27 - Shea, History of the Catholic Church, vol. iii,
pp. 489-499. St. Mary's Church was robbed and
burned by a mob after the church bell had been
removed to prevent an alarm.
28 - New York Observer, April 19, 1834. The election
riots are best described in: Headley, Joseph T.,
The Great Riots of New York, 1712 to 1873, (New
York, 1873), pp. 66-78.

religion.[29]   When the Five Point Riots of the next year
led to further open warfare between foreigners and Americans,[30] it was even hinted that priests stirred up
trouble so that they could use their influence to stop
it and thus increase their power.[31]   At the same time
Catholic property in Mobile, Alabama, was destroyed,[32]
and a Catholic church in Sault Ste. Marie, Michigan,
burned to the ground.[33]

　　　　This tendency toward violence was especially
marked in Boston where the citizens had had a taste of
rioting.   Two new Catholic churches there were threatened
in 1835, and it became necessary for men of the parish to
take turns at guarding them day and night.   This fear was
also reflected in the insurance companies which refused
to place a policy upon one of them until its wooden frame-
work had been sheated in brick.[34]   In Lowell, at this
same time, a mob tore the crosses from tombs in a Catholic graveyard.[35]

29 - Protestant Magazine, May, 1834.
30 - Headley, The Great Riots of New York, p. 95.
31 - Morse, Samuel F. B., A Foreign Conspiracy Against
　　　the Liberties of the United States, (New York,
　　　1841, pp. 90-92.
32 - Whipple, Leon, The Story of Civil Liberty in the
　　　United States, (New York, 1927), p. 61.
33 - Shea, History of the Catholic Church, vol. iii,
　　　p. 635.
34 - Leahy, William, The Catholic Church in New England,
　　　(Boston, 1899), vol. i, p. 63.
35 - Ibid., vol. i, p. 63.

A year after the Charlestown burning another
great mob gathered at the scene of the destruction to
celebrate the first anniversary of the event. The
rioters had intended to march through the town and
fire at a target on which was painted a caricature
of the Mother Superior, but the Charlestown selectmen refused them the right to parade as a military
company and ordered their arms taken from them. A
scuffle followed in which one of the selectmen was
assaulted, but the authorities were successful and
the demonstration was broken up.[36] This was followed
in 1836 by the revival of "Pope Day" by the Washington
Artillery and by a successful celebration of the anniversary of the Convent burning during which an effigy
of Bishop Fenwick was set up and used as a target.[37]
At the same time a riotous group of young men organized themselves as the "Convent Boys," and began
a systematic marauding of Catholic property.[38]

A year later, in 1837, Boston was again
plunged into the center of the nativistic controversy

36 - Niles Register, August 22, 1835.
37 - Leahy, The Catholic Church in New England, vol. i,
     p. 63.
38 - "Anti-Catholic Movements in the United States,"
     Catholic World, vol. xxii (March, 1876), p. 84.

when the Broad Street riot occurred. On June 11 of
that year a group of Irish, waiting for a funeral
procession to form, clashed with a fire company. Members of the company, worsted in the struggle, sent in
an alarm to secure aid. Fire companies rushing to their
rescue clashed with the funeral procession just after it
got under way, clubs were secured, and within a few moments, the fighting forces filled Broad Street.[39] The
Irish were soon defeated, but the natives continued a
systematic sacking of the Irish quarter, with looting
going on until the militia was called out to break up
the mob.[40] Authorities moved slowly to punish those
guilty in this outburst; eventually four natives and
fourteen Irishmen were indicted, although the majority
of them were set free with only a small fine.[41]

In September another display against Irish
Catholics sent a flurry through Boston. When an Irish
military company, the Montgomery Guards, appeared on
Boston common for the annual militia day ceremonies,
the nine other companies, composed of native Americans,
marched from the field to the tune of Yankee Doodle.[42]

39 - Niles Register, June 24, 1834..
40 - Massachusetts Spy, June 14, 1837.
41 - Ibid., July 12, 1837.
42 - Cullen, James B., The Story of the Irish in Boston
       (Boston, 1889), pp. 72-73.

The Montgomery Guards, left alone, returned to their
quarters, but were followed through the streets of Boston by a mob that pelted them with stones and brickbats.[43]
A year later a Catholic church in Burlington, Vermont,
was burned to the ground by a group of shopkeepers and
college students.[44]

While these manifestations against Catholicism
were growing in violence, there was emerging from them a
new and more important nativistic literature than the
country had before known. Based upon the burning of
the Ursuline convent, and dependent upon the popular
interest aroused by that event, this propaganda led
directly to the first political outburst of anti-Catholicism in the United States.

The ruins of the Ursuline Convent had scarcely
cooled when shrewd minded men began to turn their attention toward exploiting the interest excited by the burning. It was natural that they should hit upon the young
girl, Rebecca Theresa Reed, whose stories had been so instrumental in leading to the rioting. Less than a year
after that fatal day in August, 1834, the newspapers
throughout the land were announcing that a true revela-

43 - Ibid., p. 73.
44 - Shea, History of the Catholic Church, vol. iii, p. 488;
     Thie, German Catholic Activity Seventy Years Ago,
     p. 119.

tion of life within the Ursuline Convent was to appear.[45] Finally, in April, 1835, the book made its
bow; Rebecca Reed's Six Months in a Convent began
its phenomenal career as a best seller.

There is considerable doubt as to the authorship of this volume. It was sponsored by a "Committee
of Publication," who kept their identities modestly in
the background. It was stated at the time, however,
that the author of the lengthy "Preliminary Remarks"
with which the book opened was the editor of the Boston
Advocate, for it was common knowledge that he was the
"General Grand High King of the Anti-Catholic Fraterni-
ty."[46] Probably this gentleman and his associates had
much to do with writing the book as well; certainly
Rebecca Reed seems incapable of it.

Regardless of the authorship, Six Months in a
Convent was hailed as a success as soon as it appeared.
The Boston newspapers joined in praising it highly, and
no doubt or criticism of its contents appeared in their
columns.[47] Only one newspaper, the Catholic Sentinel,

45 - Boston Traveler, quoted in New York Observer,
     March 21, 1835; Downfall of Babylon, March 14, 1845.
46 - "The Press and the Convent Question," New England
     Magazine, vol. viii, (June, 1835), p. 454.
47 - Ibid., p. 452.

spoke against it, and the harsh language used only
added strength to the cause of the anti-Catholics.[48]
The excitement over its publication was transmitted
to New York where the first supply of several thousand
copies sent was exhausted within two hours. When the
New York Star dared attack it, it found itself subjected
to a storm of criticism from the Commercial Gazette,
the New York Observer, and other papers.[49] Within the
first week of the publication of Six Months in a Convent, ten thousand copies were sold. Thirty men were
employed day and night in printing the book to keep up
with the demand. It was conservatively estimated that
two hundred thousand copies would be sold within the
first month of publication.[50]

Actually, Rebecca Reed's book deserved little
of the popularity it received. It was a harmless little
volume, telling of the author's early life, of her conversion to Catholicism, and of her final entrance into
the convent on Mount Benedict, after the Bishop of the
Diocese and the Mother Superior had both pleaded with her
to get her to join.[51] Much of the book is devoted to a
detailed description of life in the convent, telling of

48 - Ibid., p. 452.
49 - New York Observer, April 18, 1835.
50 - Downfall of Babylon, April 11, 1835.
51 - Reed, Rebecca Theresa, Six Months in a Convent,
     (Boston, 1835) pp. 49-72.

how the nuns were forced to kiss the floor repeatedly,[52] how they wore hair cloth and girdles and walked with pebbles in the shoes,[53] how they were forced to perform penances by making the sign of the cross on the floor with their tongues.[54] Interwoven with these interesting details is the story of a nun who is dissatisfied and is thought insane by the Mother Superior, an obvious attempt to portray the famous Elizabeth Harrison.[55] Interwoven too, is the tale of how Rebecca Reed herself grew more and more dissatisfied, until finally, over-hearing the Bishop and Mother Superior plotting to kidnap her and send her to a Canadian convent,[56] she decided to escape. The book ends with an account of that escape, a rather easy one all in all,[57] and of the author's return to Protestantism, a pattern to be followed by many "escaped nuns" in writing their memoirs in the future.

Mild as it was, such an onslaught against the Catholic religion could not go unanswered. A champion for the Ursulines appeared in no less a person than the Mother Superior of the Convent on Mount Benedict, Mary

52 - Ibid., p. 75.
53 - Ibid., pp. 78-79.
54 - Ibid., p. 93.
55 - Ibid., pp. 98-110.
56 - Ibid., pp. 162-163.
57 - Ibid., pp. 172-176.

Edmund Saint George. Her <u>An Answer to Six Months in a</u> <u>Convent Exposing its Falsehoods and Manifold Absurdities</u>[58] appeared only a few months after Rebecca Reed's book. After a lengthy introduction attacking Rebecca Reed's character,[59] the Mother Superior devoted most of her publication to a minute attack upon <u>Six Months in a Convent</u>, taking it up page by page, and refuting its statements in a thorough if rather dull manner.[60] Leaders of the No-Popery forces announced immediately that the book was not to be believed, "for it was written by a Popish nun, and when Popery is at stake, truth takes wings."[61]

But such refutation was felt to be insufficient, and an anonymous pamphlet <u>A Review of the Lady Superior's</u> <u>Reply to Six Months in a Convent, being a Vindication of</u> <u>Miss Reed</u>[62] was hurried from the press. In this latest

---

58 - Saint George, Mary Edmund, <u>An Answer to Six Months</u> <u>in a Convent Exposing its Falsehoods and Manifold</u> <u>Absurdities</u>, (Boston, 1835)
59 - <u>Ibid</u>., pp. 1-35.
60 - Typical of the style is the following extract: "(page 7) our prices for education were at the <u>lowest</u>, not the <u>highest</u>, rate. Should a young lady, 'crossed in love, or disappointed in securing a fashionable establishment in marriage,' apply to become a nun, <u>she could not be admitted</u>; nor can 'wealthy parents, who have more daughters than they can portion' ... find it convenient or practical to persuade the least beautiful to take the veil." <u>Ibid</u>., p. 4.
61 - <u>Downfall of Babylon</u>, April 25, 1835.
62 - <u>A Review of the Lady Superior's Reply to Six Months</u> <u>in a Convent, being a Vindication of Miss Reed</u> (Boston, 1835).

publication Rebecca Reed's book was completely upheld.
Her statements, it said, were "those of a school girl,
telling what happened in her presence and do not appear
like the 'fabrications of an artful and designing person'
as she is represented."[63] Having thus vindicated the
central figure of the controversy, the author spreads
most of his ink vigorously attacking the Catholic church,
flaying the whole convent system,[64] insisting that Bishop
Fenwick was only a tool of foreign despots,[65] and warning
that unless Catholic aggression was stopped America "would
feel the chill of rayless and perpetual winter - under
the icy grasp of Catholic oppression."[66]

Such a refutation of the Mother Superior's book
was not enough to satisfy the champions of anti-Catholicism-
or incidentally to reap a proper share of the gold beginning
to shower upon the writers of such books. Of this the Committee of Publication that had sponsored Six Months in a
Convent undoubtedly was aware. Consequently another small
volume was hurried from the press, entitled A Supplement
to Six Months in a Convent, Confirming the Narrative of
Rebecca Theresa Reed, by the Testimony of more than 100
Witnesses.[67] They felt constrained to apologize for the

63 - Ibid., pp. 5-6.
64 - Ibid., p. 50.
65 - Ibid., pp. 25-26.
66 - Ibid., pp. 50-51.
67 - Supplement to Six Months in a Convent (Boston, 1835)

delay in publication, saying that they were waiting
for the promised second volume from the Mother Superior.[68] Having thus satisfied their readers, the
anonymous authors launch into a complete story of
events leading to the burning of the Ursuline convent, telling of the tortures inflicted upon Elizabeth
Harrison and of her escape,[69] of her forced return and
how the Popish priests taught her to plead insanity to
hush up the clamor that was being raised.[70] Rebecca
Reed's story was accepted completely, and vindicated
by a curious piece of logic. The story must be correct,
said the authors, because the Mother Superior denies
everything she says. She would surely have made some
correct statements, and when the Catholics deny everything it shows that they are lying.[71] Thus was the authenticity established beyond reasonable doubt, in the
minds of the Protestants at least.

The flare of periodical rebuttal and of book
and counterbook was not without its national effects.
"The brands from that burning," wrote a Catholic at the
time, "have set fires throughout the country, that seem

68 - Ibid., p. iii.
69 - Ibid., pp. 73-123.
70 - Ibid., pp. 124-145.
71 - Ibid., pp. 146-185..

already to have consumed all the Christian virtues
and to threaten that religion itself will not escape
unscathed."[72]

The effect of this new importance upon the
leaders of the crusade against popery was significant.
Much of the publicity that descended upon them was un-
favorable; the mob violence against the Ursuline dwell-
ing was attacked by the press throughout the land. New
defenses against those attacks were necessary, if the
cause was to enjoy any success. And while the majority
of the newspapers and magazines frowned upon the violence,
there was a feeling of general satisfaction among the
common people. A silent factor before, this great mass
began to give their support to the anti-Catholic movement the nation over. In both of these things, then,
the leading agitators found encouragement and incentive
for further effort. It was inevitable that anti-Catholicism should show increasing vigor in the years just
after that fatal night in August, 1834.

With this popular appeal, a steady demand rose
throughout the nation for some form of national organization, one of which could give unity and direction to the
new found friends of the movement. Suggestions for such

[72] - St. George, An Answer to Six Months in a Convent,
     pp. 36-37.

an organization began to be made soon after the burning
of the convent, by the press[73] and by individual writers.[74]
While the American Tract Society[75] and the American Bible
Society[76] were aiding the cause, it was generally agreed
that some organization on a national scale directed wholly
against the Catholic church would give the movement added
strength.

The agitation for such a society was given weight
by the continued success of the one local society that was
in operation, the New York Protestant Association, which
had been formed in 1829. Although the Association had
been forced to abandon its official publication, The Protestant in 1832 in the face of competition from other anti-
Catholic publications, a new and active form of bigotry
had been found in sponsoring lectures in New York City[77]

73 - Cincinnati Journal, quoted in New York Observer,
     February 28, 1835. The society suggested by the
     Cincinnati Journal was to have as its object the
     conversion of foreigners in the United States from
     Catholicism to Protestantism.
74 - Morse, Samuel F. B., Foreign Conspiracy Against the
     Liberties of the United States (5th Edition, New York,
     1841) pp. 116-119. Morse suggested that a society
     called the "Anti-Popery Union" should be formed.
75 - American Tract Society, Annual Reports, 1835-1839.
     The Annual reports list the following publications
     of the society against Catholicism: Andrew Dunn(1835),
     A. Nevins, Thoughts on Popery (1836); Tracts on Roman-
     ism (1836); Roman Catholic Female Schools (1837); On
     Purgatory and Infallibility (1839)
76 - New York Observer, May 25, 1839.
77 - Protestant Vindicator, December 16, 1835.

and neighboring towns.[78] The lecturers, usually ministers who had embraced the cause of the society, were
bitter in their abuse. A typical course given in 1835
included such subjects as: "Nunneries Unconstitutional,"
"Jesuit Seminaries and Convents Dangerous to the United
States," "Foreign Romish Governments are Conspirators
Against the Existence of the United States," and "Popish
Penance and Auricular Confession are a System of Priestcraft and Robbery."[79]

On March 13, 1835, one of the lectures of the
Association on the subject, "Is Popery Compatible with
Civil Liberty?", was given in Broadway Hall in New York
City. In the midst of the proceedings a crowd forced
their way into the hall shouting "Huzza! Burn the heretics! Down with the Protestants!"[80] A free for all
fight followed, with the presiding clergy fleeing for
their lives.[81] The intruders were Irish Catholics, and
while Bishop John Hughes hastened to disavow their actions
in a flamboyant proclamation[82] and the Catholics who had

---

78 - New York Observer, December 27, 1834. An account of
     a series of lectures on Popery given in Philadelphia
     by Reverend Robert Breckinridge. He was interrupted
     by a priest during the first lecture and public in-
     terest became so great that subsequent lectures had
     to be held in a larger hall.
79 - Protestant Vindicator, December 16, 1835.
80 - Downfall of Babylon, March 28, 1835.
81 - New York Observer, March 21, 1835.
82 - New York Catholic Diary, quoted in Ibid., April 18,
     1835.

intruded issued an apology in which they stated that
they were goaded into their action by anti-Catholic
street preachers such as Reverend George Bourne,[83] the
mischief was already done. The directors of the New
York Protestant Association issued a statement in which
they insisted that the sole object of their organization
was to "spread the knowledge of Gospel truth, and to show
wherein it is inconsistent with the tenets and dogmas of
Popery." Any discussions, they said, were "merely of
theological questions."[84] The anti-Catholic press took
up the cry, pointing out that the meeting, before the
interruption was devoting itself to the question of whether or not Catholicism was compatible with civil liberty
and proclaimed now that Catholics themselves had shown
that it was not.[85] The dangers to the country from such
Irish immigrants were stressed[86] and one editor moaned
the fact that "clergymen have to fly from their churches
to save themselves from the cudgels and brickbats of Popish mobs."[87] Much of the invective heaped upon Protestants for their attack upon the Ursuline Convent was turned

83 - Supplement to Six Months in a Convent, p. 31.
84 - New York Observer, March 21, 1835.
85 - Downfall of Babylon, March 28, 1835; Boston Observer
     and Religious Intelligencer, March 26, 1835.
86 - New York Observer, April 18, 1835.
87 - Downfall of Babylon, March 28, 1835.

now upon their Catholic adversaries.

This manifestation, attracted nation wide attention to a need for an anti-Catholic society and served to
increase the growing demand for a national organization
along similar lines. The first such society was formed
only a month after the attack, "The Society for the Diffusion of Christian Knowledge," founded in New York City
by Reverend W. C. Brownlee who was chosen its first
president. The avowed purpose of this new society was
to recommend the Bible to mankind and to assist the principles of the Protestant Reformation. The chief method
by which this task was to be carried on was through the
press. The society planned to send to each member a weekly
publication of 24 pages, setting forth some of the distinctive errors of Popery. Its first publication, An Apology
for the Bible by Reverend R. Watson, was typical of those
which were to follow.[88]

A month later another group of New York citizens
met and formed a new society, with political leanings, known
as the North American Democratic Association. Resolutions
adopted at the first meeting stated that the purpose of the
society was to prevent the government from falling into the
hands of Catholic foreigners, and the members pledged them-

[88] - Downfall of Babylon, April 11, 1835.

selves to oppose the appointment or election of such
foreigners to office. A committee was named to carry
out a ward organization for this purpose in New York
City, and thus another anti-Catholic society was launched.[89]

Of a more directly anti-Catholic nature was a
third society, formed in July, 1835. This society, the
Canadian Benevolent Association of New York, was organized through the exertions of Reverend W. K. Hoyt, long
active in missionary work in Canada. The efforts of this
new society were directed toward the Canadian field; the
members were pledged to combat the ravages of popery among
the Canadians and to convert them to the true religion of
the Bible. Reverend W. C. Brownlee, rapidly rising to
leadership among the forces gathering against Romanism,
was named vice president at the first meeting, with Hoyt
as president.[90] A short time later a Society for the Diffusion of Light on the Subject of Romanism was formed at
Reading, Massachusetts[91] as was another society at Shelburne,
Vermont.[92] An attempt by American Catholics to form a simi-

89 - Ibid., June 20, 1835.
90 - Ibid., July 11, 1835.
91 - Ibid., October 15, 1836. The society began its existence with 50 members who immediately began distributing anti-Catholic propaganda about the community.
92 - Ibid., May 14, 1836.

lar society to spread the principles of their religion was hailed by nativistic editors as "the embryo of the American Inquisition."[93]

The rapid formation of these anti-Catholic societies in the period just after the Charlestown affair shows the universal demand that was felt for such organizations. There still existed a place for a society that would devote itself to general attacks upon the Catholic church, organized along national lines. It was inevitable that such a society should grow from the demand.[94] In 1836, there was formed at New York the "American Society for Promoting the Principles of the Protestant Reformation."[95] The preamble of its constitution stated the aims and desires of its members: "Whereas," it read, "the principles of the Court of Rome are totally irreconcilable with the Gospel of Christ; liberty of conscience, the rights of man; and with the Constitution and Laws of the United States of America,- and whereas, the influence of Romanism is rapidly extending

93 - Ibid., December 20, 1834.
94 - Continued activities of foreign anti-Catholic societies, widely reported in the American press, also served as an incentive to the formation of an American society. For such reports see: the New York Observer July 4, 1835; August 8, 1835.
95 - Circular Issued by the American Protestant Society, December, 1847 (New York, 1847), pp. 3-4. The circular contains a history of the American Protestant Reformation Society and its descendant, the American Protestant Society.

throughout this Republic; endangering the peace and freedom of our country - therefore, being anxious to preserve the ascendancy of 'pure religion and undedefiled' and to maintain and perpetuate the genuine truths of Protestantism unadulterated; with devout confidence in the sanction of the Great Head of the Church to aid our efforts in withstanding the 'power and great authority of the Beast, and the strong delusion of the False Prophet;'"they agreed to form themselves into a national organization.[96]

The constitution[97] set forth, too, the method of operation to be followed by the society. It was, it stated, to be a home missionary society, distributing information on Popery, arousing Protestants to a proper sense of their duties toward Romanism, and laboring to "convert the Papists to Christianity" by means of lectures and tracts and standard books.[98] A board of twenty directors was named to carry out these duties, in addition to the regular officers, and it was provided that local societies with the same ends could affiliate with this main organization. A small yearly fee was charged to

96 - The constitution of the society is printed in the Protestant Vindicator, June 24, 1840.
97 - The complete constitution of this and other anti-Catholic societies is in Appendix A.
98 - Protestant Vindicator, June 24, 1840.

THE DOWNFALL OF BABYLON.

BY SAMUEL B. SMITH, a Popish Priest.

NEW-YORK, SATURDAY, APRIL 30, 1836.

VOL. II. NO 17.

☞ The annexed cut represents three scenes in the Hotel Dieu Nunnery at Montreal, as represented in the "*Awful Disclosures*" of Maria Monk.

In one part of the piece, we see a Nun throwing a murdered infant into a deep pit in the cellar of the Nunnery. At a little distance from her, a Priest is seen rising up through a trap-door, from the subterranean passage that leads from the Seminary of the Priests to the Hotel Dieu Nunnery. Against the wall are two solitary cells, in which are confined two Nuns. It appears that the rest of the wretched inmates of this fiend-like place, did not positively know for what reason these poor creatures were confined in those dark and loathsome cells. One of the Nuns, St. Xavier, of whom

Maria Monk made some inquiries respecting those who were confined in the cells, told her that they were punished for refusing to obey the Superior, Bishops, and Priests. Others, however, conjectured that they were thus confined in punishment, because they were heiresses, whose property was desired for the Convent, and who would not consent to sign deeds of it.

The white substance which appears about the mouth of the pit, is lime, which is thrown upon the bodies when they are cast into the pit, in order to consume them, and prevent noxious exhalations.

Poor, helpless, inoffensive babes—how shocking is the sight!—Born but to breathe a few short pangs, then to be strangled by fiends in human shape, called Nuns and Priests!

TERMS.

The "Downfall of Babylon, or the Triumph of Truth over Popery," is published semi-monthly, at $1 per annum, payable in advance.

To subscribers living in the city of New York or Philadelphia, the Paper will be delivered, at their doors, at $1 per annum for the Paper, and twenty-five cents per annum for delivering it.

All letters enclosing money, post paid, may be sent at the risk of the proprietor, SAMUEL B. SMITH.

Publication office in Clinton Hall, No. 131 Nassau St. New York.

BOOK I.

ON THE MORAL CORRUPTION OF THE POPISH HIERARCHY, MONKS, NUNS, AND PEOPLE.

CHAPTER 3.

SECTION LXI.

ON THE ROMISH HIERARCHY.

[NARRATIVE OF ROSAMOND, or the female who was captured under the Popish Priests, in the island of Cuba.]

CHAPTER III.

"Fear God!" the thunders said; "Fear God!" the waves;
"Fear God!" the lightning of the storm replied;
"Fear God!" deep loudly answered ock to deep.
POLLOK.

We left New Orleans for Matanzas, there being no vessel direct for Havanna, and had a rough and dangerous passage of ten days. Once we were in a severe storm, and every one on board expected to perish. This was the first time I ever was afraid to die. Oh! I well remember what my feelings were at the time; when I thought, if I died, I should go to everlasting torments. Now I reflected on my cruel treatment to my dear mother, and what I had done while at Nashville, which I had never thought or felt the wickedness of till then. I prayed, and said, if God would spare my life, and let me get on land again, I would go home to my dear parents. One of the sailors was washed over board, and lost in the storm. When we got to Ma-

tanzas, I soon forgot the serious promise I had made; and how could I expect to prosper! We remained here but a few days, and then went to Havanna.

Here I found myself in another world, as I thought, in a Spanish country; I did not understand their language, nor they mine. The people are more easy and free in their manners, than in New Orleans; but, as to character, it does not make much difference who, or what stranger you are, so long as you dress, and make a good appearance. Several American ladies were living on the island, who were all wealthy, and appeared happy in their private relations. I had been there but a few days, before I became acquainted, through one of my female friends, with a Spanish Priest, named Manuel Canto, and commonly called Father Canto, who belonged to St. Francisco Convent. Through an interpreter, he made me an offer to take me under his protection; and I consented to live with him, not knowing, at the time, that he was a Priest. He immediately hired a house for me, at three *ounces*, or fifty dollars a month, and he furnished me five hundred dollars to commence with, and I put myself under his protection wholly. Then it was too late to reconsider the step; for if once you put yourself under their protection, it is dangerous to leave a Roman Catholic Priest in that country. I remained with him there on the island about five years. In that time I was put in the way to learn and see a great deal of their wickedness, and the way they lead their people in darkness. At the time I went first to live with him, I could not understand one word of his language, nor he of mine.

He was always desirous to learn the English; but he preferred that I should learn to speak and read the *Champara* language, which is a sort of Creole Spanish, half Spanish and half African. In this language he always conversed and corresponded with me; and in it I shall write the names and Spanish words found here.

He got me a teacher, and I soon learned his language; and when I left him he could write and un-

derstand my own language. During that five years I lived a gloomy and a wretched life with him. I suffered every thing but death, in body and in mind; I was as ignorant as any heathen in the right view of eternity, although I was born here in America; but I was young when I first went to live in those countries. I still knew and felt that their religion was not right.

When I had learned sufficient of the language to understand what he said, I soon forgot my past troubles, the value of a character, and the promises I had made while crossing the ocean.

I had lived here but a short time with him, before I took the creole, or stranger's fever, which they call the black vomit. I laid very sick three weeks, and was not expected to recover by any one even by the doctor, who belonged to one of the Convents. I was visited by several of Manuel's friends, and treated kindly by all. I was again afraid to die, and they wanted me to be christened, and said I was a Protestant, and if I died I must go to hell. I never can forget, when I lay very low one day, my Priest came to my bed, and told me he was afraid I was going to die, and it was his desire I should be christened, as I was a Protestant. I did not know what he meant by a Protestant, as I had been always brought up in darkness. I cannot help saying, Lord! why was I kept so long in darkness, without knowing I had such a kind and merciful God? Yes, dear Saviour, I can never do too much to serve thee here, should I live ten thousand years; for I now know, and can see, what a merciful and forgiving God I have! When I knew thee not, I used to think, in trouble, what an unjust God! but I adore the righteous God, and pray, O Lord! that from this very day, this very hour, I am writing this, I may serve thee henceforth with sincerity, since thou hast opened my blind eyes!

They soon after lighted up candles in my room, and a Capuchin Priest came, with three or four Priests in habits, and death-candles were lighted. I asked Manuel what the candles were burning for. He said, to get me through Purgatory. I did no

---

Typical Page from the Downfall of Babylon

members, and any person contributing twenty dollars
in one sum could be made a life member.[99]

From that time on the American Protestant
Reformation Society, as it was commonly called, centered the activity against Catholicism. It sent out
lecturers, published a newsapaper, and issued tracts
denouncing Romanism. Anti-Catholicism now had unity,
and violence increased with new strength.

The same burst of anti-Catholic feeling which
gave birth to the American Protestant Reformation Society
carried over into the field of the press. Concurrent
with the firing of the Ursuline convent was the founding
of two powerful American newspapers which were devoted
entirely to exposing the errors and sins of Popery.

The first paper in the field was a weekly entitled The Downfall of Babylon, or the Triumph of Truth
over Popery. Edited by Samuel B. Smith, who proclaimed
himself as "late as Popish priest," and who had already
attained some fame as an author of anti-Catholic works,
this new publication early established itself as one of
the most violent agencies of invective in that age of
intolerance. Smith did not hesitate to use his former
association with the Catholic church to his own advan-

99 - Ibid., June 24, 1840.

tage. In a Prospectus circulated about the country before his paper appeared, he promised to tell the people
the truth about Romanism as he knew it. He would, he
said, expose the great plot to take over the United States
and lay it at the feet of Rome. Such intrigue was already
under way, he continued, and was being carried on through
the Catholic immigrants who were flocking to the new land.
In a short time the Pope would command them to strike.
"When that time arrives," he proclaimed, "we shall have
a popish president, popish representatives, and popish
officers in every department. Then the heretics will
hear the thunder of anathema rolling and the vengeance
of the pope bursting upon them like streams of lightning."
All of these things would be exposed, Smith promised.
"A tale I have to tell," he said, "that will shake the
mighty Babylon in her center; at which the darkest night
will blush, and nature shrink with horror."[100]

      The first number of the Downfall of Babylon ap-
peared on August 14, 1834. The leading editorial summed
up the policy to be followed throughout. Its name, the
editor stated, was chosen not because the publication itself would bring about the downfall of the Babylon of
Popery, but because it would aid in that great work.
"I consider the prevelance of Romanism in a country the

100 - The Protestant Magazine, July, 1834.

greatest of scourges," Smith wrote "I shall spare no
pains to render this paper an antidote against it."[101]

   Most of the first issue was taken up with the
first installment of a long account of the "Moral Corruption of the Popish Hierarchy, Monks, Nuns and People."[102]
This account is drawn largely from Editor Smith's own
experience in which he tells of going to a western convent to officiate over the nuns, of their immoral life
and his condemnation of their actions, of the attempt
of one of them to kill him when he refused her absolu-
tion for her sins,[103] of how convents are designed to
facilitate criminal love affairs between priests and
nuns,[104] and of the harships that nuns have to endure
as a result.[105] One fantastic tale is told of a nun
in this western convent who called for him when she
was in the pangs of childbirth, of his shocked horror,
and how the Mother Superior explained that she was suffering from wind colic and nothing more.[106] Even the
method of the nuns in disposing of their babies by burying them in nearby graves is expounded.[107] After several

101 - Downfall of Babylon, August 14, 1834.
102 - Ibid., August 14, 1834.
103 - Ibid., August 14, 1834.
104 - Ibid., October 30, 1834; November 29, 1834.
105 - Ibid., December 6, 1834.
106 - Ibid., October 30, 1834.
107 - Ibid., October 30, 1834.

months of such publication the editor explains that he
has told them to arouse sympathy with those who destroyed the Ursuline convent by exposing the true character of nunneries, and attributed their subsequent acquittal to his journalistic efforts.[108]

These sensational accounts seem to have won
popular favor, for the Downfall of Babylon prospered.
The first few numbers proved so much in demand that
the supply was exhausted and 30,000 additional copies
printed.[109] Samuel Smith found it necessary to move
from Philadelphia to the greater hunting grounds of
New York City.[110] By the end of the first year more
than seven thousand copies were circulating each week,[111]
and Editor Smith was thinking up more lurid ways in
which to appeal to the reading public. Starting in
April, 1836, a number of pictures showing the immoral
practices of nuns were reproduced,[112] and at about the
same time the size of the paper was doubled. This boon
was offset by bi-monthly publication and was a scheme
designed to save postage for the subscribers.[113] Ministers were loud in praising its work,[114] and the Downfall

108 - Ibid., January 3, 1835.
109 - Ibid., May 30, 1835.
110 - Ibid., November 29, 1834.
111 - Ibid., December 12, 1835.
112 - Ibid., April 2, 1836 and ff.
113 - Ibid., January 23, 1836.
114 - Ibid., December 12, 1835.

of Babylon seemed destined to success and prosperity.
Its publication ceased in 1837 however, for by this
time competition had developed which was to prove disastrous for any anti-Catholic newspaper.

The rivalry was provided by a second paper,
founded only a week after the Downfall of Babylon, and
bearing the even more imposing name of The American
Protestant Vindicator and Defender of Civil and Religious Liberty against the Inroads of Popery. The Protestant Vindicator, as its semi-monthly issues were entitled, had no such advantage as a late popish priest
as editor, but it did have sanction in the No Popery
circles of the nation. It was founded as the official
organ of the American Protestant Reformation Society,
and edited throughout its long existence by the president
of that society, Reverend W. C. Brownlee. An eight page
paper in diminished newspaper size, it carried on a vigorous campaign against Catholicism from the time that its
first number was hurried from the presses on August 20,
1834, until it ceased publication in 1842 because of a
change in the nature of the society that sponsored it
and the death of its editor.

Its religious influence was typified by the
choice of Dr. Brownlee as editor, and its first number
listed twelve clergymen in New York City as regular con-

tributors.[115] Any hope that Christian mildness would
be exemplified in its publication was dispelled in the
first issue. The leading article was entitled "Romanism,"
and had been "transmitted by a Christian brother, whose
elegant lucubrations we hope often to insert." Following
this was another article on the "Grasping Character of
the Romish Priesthood," another on "The Contrast between
Protestantism and Popery," and a third on "Popish Female
Seminaries."[116] The contents of this first issue were
typical of the many that were to follow.

A reader of the various articles in the columns
of this vituperative sheet could have no doubt of its
stand, and the editors repeatedly stressed the justice
of their cause and swore to carry it through to fruition.
Little sympathy was expressed for men who flinched from
religious controversies. "We would affectionately ask
those over delicate Christians," wrote the editor, "whether they would tamely stand by and see their houses robbed
and their children carried off? Would they stand by with
folded arms and see the Jesuit priest enter their domo-
cile, and use infinite pains to corrupt the minds of their
children by papal idolatry, and pollute their hearts by
the obscenities and shocking vices of the confessional?"[117]

115 - Protestant Vindicator, August 20, 1834.
116 - Ibid., August 20, 1834.
117 - Ibid., June 24, 1840.

THE PROTESTANT VINDICATOR.

IN DEFENCE OF CIVIL AND RELIGIOUS LIBERTY AGAINST THE INROADS OF POPERY

The Engraving represents four Protestant Reformers standing on the Rock of Truth.—1. Luther bearing the German Bible. 2. Calvin holding a manuscript roll of the Institutes. 3. Cranmer with the English Bible. 4. Knox exhibiting the New Testament, and preaching "Peace by Jesus Christ."

No. 20—Vol. 3—New Series.   NEW YORK, WEDNESDAY, MARCH 17, 1841.   *Editor.*—Dr. BROWNLE

Published semi-monthly by the American Society for promoting the principles of the Protestant Reformation.

OFFICE, 142 NASSAU STREET,
Over the New York Observer.

☞ Our Patrons and Subscribers are respectfully requested to address their Letters (post paid) to "the Agent of the Protestant Vindicator," at the office, as above.

TERMS:
ONE DOLLAR per annum,
☞ To be invariably paid in advance.
Five Dollars will be received as payment for six copies.
☞ All letters intimating change of residence, and stoppage of paper, must be post-paid, otherwise they will not be taken from the office.
Advertisements inserted on the usual terms.

MISSIONARY AGENTS
For presenting the claims of the Amer. Protestant Reformation Society, are

Rev. Charles Sparry. | Rev. N. W. Smith.
" Alonzo Welton. | " Rufus Pomeroy.
" C. Shumway. | " Epaphras Goodman.
" Hervy Smith. | " Thomas Beachem.

From the Achill Missionary Herald.

LATE CONVERSION OF AN ITALIAN PRIEST.

We have read with much interest the published correspondence of the Rev. John Baptist Di Menna with two Roman Catholic priests.

Dr. Di Menna, we learn from this publication, was formerly priest, confessor, and preacher of the order of Capuchins, Lecturer in philosophy, and Divinity at Pescara and Tocco in Italy, and apostolic Missionary of the Propaganda Fide of Rome, at Tunis in Barbary, but is now an humble follower of Christ, and a member of the Church of England.

From a brief sketch of the life of this interesting person, prefixed to the correspondence, we learn that he is a native of Agnone in the Kingdom of Naples, where three of his brothers and sisters, who are married, still reside and occupy a respectable rank in society, his father is dead, his mother, towards whom Di Menna cherishes the warmest feelings of filial affection, is still alive, but the government of Naples, being under the influence of Rome, has interdicted all communication between Di Menna and his family.

The change in Di Menna's views of religion which terminated in his separation from the Romish church was very gradual, and was produced by the diligent perusal of the Holy Scriptures without the aid of any Protestant instructor. When it was known at Rome that Di Menna had abandoned the

Romish faith, a communication was privately made to him from the Propaganda, to the effect, that if he would depart from Malta, where his conversion created a considerable stir, and engage never to publish, *with his name*, any thing to the injury of the papacy, he should regularly receive from Rome an annuity sufficient to provide for all his temporal wants, a proposal which Di Menna rejected with just indignation. The individual who had been authorized by the Propaganda to make this communication to him, enjoined him secrecy, observing that the matter was well known, but that the injunction to secrecy was necessary to prevent it from reaching the ears of the common people.

In consequence of Di Menna's determined opposition to the papacy, he was subjected to severe persecution at Malta, and having with his abandonment of popery forfeited his means of support, he is now seeking to earn an honorable maintenance by teaching the Italian language. Although we have not the pleasure of being personally acquainted with Dr. Di Menna, yet sympathizing with him as a witness for the truth as it is in Jesus, against the abominations of the papal antichrist, we take the liberty of testifying the interest which we feel in his welfare by transferring his advertisement to our columns. He has claims which need only be known to ensure the sympathy and support of faithful Protestants.

THE CONFESSION.

Nay, holy father, come not near,
The secrets of my heart to hear;
For not to mortal ear I tell
The griefs that in this bosom swell,
The thoughts, the wishes, wild and vain,
That wander through this burning brain.
Frail fellow being! why should I
Before thee kneel imploringly?
'Twere worse than madness to believe
Man can his brother worm forgive,
Or yield unto the contrite one
That peace which comes from heaven alone.
No! let me spend my vesper hour
In commune with a Higher Power:
The world shut out, I'll lowly bend
To my Almighty Father Friend!
To him for mercy I'll appeal—
To him my inmost soul reveal;
He knows the heart that he has made,
By each alternate passion swayed,
And can forgive it; for he knows
Its wants, its weakness, and its woes:
By his protecting pardon blest,
How sweetly might I sink to rest,
And sleep his sheltering wing beneath;
Though 'twere the last dark sleep of death:

THE ROMISH PRIESTS OF IRELAND.
CONCLUDED FROM OUR LAST.

Most of the Irish people,—except in rem native Irish districts, where the liberalizing in ence which was at work, was comparatively fee in itself, and was counteracted by the excessive slavement of the people's condition—became, consequence, considerably independant of priest's power on all secular topics, and began look upon it with less awe than before, in questi of ' ghostly' superintendence and instruction.

In such districts as Ennis, Achill,* and Cum mara, the decrease of priestly domination is as hardly, if at all perceptible. The poor ser peasants of these and similar districts, conti sack-clothed in a mental abasement; and enchai in a moral slavery scarcely inferior to those of worst part of Europe during the middle ages. men, as beings capable of rational thought, t have no freedom; and so thoroughly imbued they with superstition, that a priest's threat to c vert them instantaneously into stones or bro sticks, would, in many instances, be understood literally as a threat to denounce them from altar, and would effectually reclaim them from disposition they might show to become restive der the weight of their chains. Even in dome matters, they submit, in a very abject manner, priestly interference. And as to any political me ment, they may still, on the eve of a day for turning members to parliament in a contested e tion, be occasionally seen in large companies b ing along the highway in advance of a pr exceedingly in the style of a mass of cattle mov along before a drover to market! In districts e in a very small degree under Anglo-Irish, or S tish-Irish influence, the spirit of incipient free among the Romish people, has for several ye been quite apparent,—and apparent not only in cular matters, but also in affairs connected religion.

In one place where, for a considerable pe after the formation of the Bible Society, one tence from a priest would have prevented a tributer of Bibles from obtaining a welcome single cottage, and might even have roused a rude opposition as would have rendered any atte to hold any public Bible Association meeting a tive, efforts so successful were, after a time m that public demonstrations on behalf of the B were achieved, some twenty voluntary canva for its diffusion were set encouragingly at wo and knots of Roman catholics openly avowing right to possess and read it were formed, in the of a whole posse of priests, doing their utmo prevent change and innovation. In another p when a Calvinistic missionary visited it in

Sprinkled among such ponderous attacks on Catholicism as this were articles exposing numerous vices. Others were attempts at humor: a man who jokingly said to an Irishman who was digging a ditch in New York, "Why, Pat, that pit will soon be deep enough for one of the dungeons of the Spanish Inquisition." To which Pat, of course, replies, "Faith, an' that's where we'll be puttin' some a' th' heretics one o' these days."[118] Despite such brilliant sallies, the Protestant Vindicator was forced to admit at the end of the first year of its publication that it had failed to realize a great financial profit, and to urge its readers to enlist more subscribers in the cause.[119] That subscribers came is indicated by the fact that it continued to expand as it did.

Thus the Protestant Vindicator and the Downfall of Babylon maintained undisputed lead among those publications devoted to attacking Catholicism through the 1830's. But they were not alone in the field. In the south the Watchman of the South was founded in 1837,[120] and while it was designed as a regular Presybterian paper, it early

118 - Ibid., September 3, 1834.
119 - Ibid., December 30, 1835.
120 - New York Observer, September 9, 1837. Publication of the Watchman of the South was begun in October, 1837. It was edited by Reverend W. S. Plumer.

began a series of vigorous attacks on Catholicism,
printing a weekly column entitled "Selections on
Popery."[121]   In the west the Pittsburg Times devoted
much space to the errors of Romanism,[122] but it was
supplanted in popular favor by the Western Protestant
published at Bardstown, Kentucky, and founded in 1836
by the Reverend Nathan L. Rice. Although Rice became
involved in a libel suit when he charged a priest with
immorality with nuns of the Loretto order of which he
was superior, his paper flourished until his death.[123]

New York supported both the Downfall of Babylon
and the Protestant Vindicator but enthusiastic publishers
who feared for the safety of their country and looked to
the lining of their pockets believed that still another
journal could be used. In 1835 they founded a daily newspaper entitled with patriotic zeal, The Spirit of '76.[124]
Each day the leading editorial of this newest publication
showered abuse on Catholics and foreigners,[125] and in addition serial articles attacking the Catholic church were
given prominent display.[126]

---

121 - Watchman of the South, August 15, 1839 and ff.
122 - Downfall of Babylon, August 27, 1835.
123 - Webb, Benjamin J., The Centenary of Catholicism in
       Kentucky (Louisville, 1884), p. 244.
124 - Spirit of '76, July 29, 1835.
125 - A typical editorial is in Ibid., September 23, 1835.
126 - Ibid., August 4, 1835 and ff.

No anti-Catholic newspapers were attempted
in Baltimore at this early date, but the deficiency
was more than made up for by a monthly magazine founded
in 1835. This <u>Baltimore Literary and Religious Magazine</u>
carried on a vigorous campaign against Romanism for almost a decade. Its editors, the Reverend Robert J.
Breckinridge and the Reverend Andrew B. Cross, both
prominent clergymen in the national councils of the
Presbyterian church,[127] filled more than half the for-
ty-eight pages of each issue with bitter attacks on
every phase of Catholicism.[128] Despite the wide circulation that the magazine attained, it was not a financial success, but this did not discourage the editors.
After five years of publication they wrote that they
were perfectly satisfied, that they had found true success in "that we have demonstrated the capability of a
thorough Protestant's Journal being published under the
very frown of the archbishop, the united opposition of
his priests, and the threats and persecution of his
people."[129]

The Reverend Breckinridge's complaint of persecution was to find justification, in his own eyes

127 - <u>Baltimore Literary and Religious Magazine</u>, January,
        1838.
128 - <u>Ibid</u>., January 1838 and following numbers.
129 - <u>Ibid</u>., January, 1839.

at least, the very next year. The Baltimore Literary
and Religious Magazine contained an article charging
the keeper of the Baltimore almshouse with having
denied Protestant instruction to an inmate under his
charge and calling the almshouse under his jurisdiction a "papal prison."[130] The keeper referred to, James
L. Maguire, promptly brought suit for libel, the resulting case attracting nation wide attention.[131] Anti-
Catholic papers shouted loudly that this was a great new
Catholic plot to still their voices and point to similar
libel cases in England.[132] This case certainly did not
dampen the journalistic ardor of the Baltimore Literary
and Religious Magazine. Even the court was noticeably
favorable to Breckinridge, and he was released when the
jury failed to agree.[133] Breckinridge immediately boasted
that the Papists had failed in their ambition to establish
the purity of the Catholic church before the bar of law,
and insisted that purity which in itself did not exist,
could never be established.[134]

This group of anti-Catholic periodicals, circulating thousands of copies each week, played a large

130 - Ibid., November, 1839.
131 - Ibid., June, 1840. The entire issue of this number
       of the magazine is filled with the report of the
       trial, filling more than two hundred pages.
132 - Protestant Vindicator, November 11, 1840.
133 - Baltimore Literary and Religious Magazine, June, 1840
134 - Ibid., January, 1840. The trial is described briefly
       in Shea, History of the Catholic Church, vol. iii,
       p. 451.

part in stirring up feeling against Catholics throughout the country. Each of them kept a large number of
agents scattered throughout the nation employed to
solicit subscribers and win them over to the side which
they championed. The Downfall of Babylon employed sixty-
three such agents in August, 1835,[135] less than a year
later their forces had been increased to one hundred and
fifteen[136] and by October, 1836, to one hundred and sev-
enty-four.[137] In October, 1835, Samuel B. Smith, editor
of this paper, hit upon a new scheme for encouraging subscriptions which was to have important consequences. At
that time the Reverend C. Sparry was named lecturing
agent for the Downfall of Babylon and started upon a
career of touring the country for the new cause. He
was commissioned to travel through every state in the
Union, stopping at each city and town to give a lecture
or a course of lectures against Popery, and at the same
time to solicit subscriptions for the paper which he
represented.[138]

The editors of the Protestant Vindicator were
quick to see the advantages of such an arrangement, and
a month after Sparry's appointment, announced that Rev-

135 - Downfall of Babylon, August 1, 1835.
136 - Ibid., March 5, 1836.
137 - Ibid., October 15, 1836.
138 - Ibid., October 24, 1835.

erend T. Book had been appointed lecturing agent for
their paper with duties similar to the agent of the
Donwfall of Babylon.[139] These rival agents seem to
have developed conflicts, at least Samuel Smith complained early in 1836 that the Protestant Vindicator's
agent was defaming his character unjustly,[140] but the
system was demonstrated as successful despite this
bickering. A second agent was added to the lecturing
staff of the Downfall of Babylon in the spring of 1836,[141]
and the wide territory covered by these agents in their
lecture tours is testified to by testimonials printed in
the columns of the paper supporting them.[142] By 1840 the
Protestant Vindicator had six agents scouring the country
delivering speeches, and had even captured Reverend C.
Sparry from their rival.[143]

139 - Protestant Vindicator, November 18, 1835.
140 - Donwfall of Babylon, July 9, 1836. Smith devotes
much of this issue of his paper to testimonials presented by leading ministers upholding his high character in refutation of these charges.
141 - Ibid., May 28, 1836. The agent appointed was Reverend David R. Gillmer. He was assigned to work in
the New England states. Sparry covering the rest
of the country.
142 - Ibid., November 12, 1836. The testimonials printed
show that one of the lecturing agents delivered addresses at Providence, Bristol, and Pawtucket, Rhode
Island, Fall River, Taunton, South Reading, West Reading, Reading, Stoneham, and Woburn all in the space
of a week.
143 - Protestant Vindicator, June 24, 1640. Agents for the
paper at this time were: Rev. C. Sparry, Rev. C. Shum-
way, Rev. Rufus Pomeroy, Rev. Henry Smith, Rev. Samuel
F. Bunnell and Rev. Epaphros Goodman.

Samuel Smith, as editor of the <u>Downfall of</u>
<u>Babylon,</u> showed his true ingenuity in propaganda and
finance by inaugurating a second new policy in the
summer of 1836. He announced through the columns of
his paper that he would be pleased to receive contributions from readers to publish tracts on Popery that
could be distributed free of charge.[144] By November
sufficient donations had been received and the first
tract published, one entitled <u>On Nunneries, and Colonel</u>
<u>Stone's Visit to Montreal</u>,[145] seven thousand copies being
printed for gratuitous circulation.[146] From that time on
a constant stream of such tracts poured from Smith's
press to aid in the conversion of Protestants to anti-
Catholics.

Inspired by the lecturing agents of the two
leading periodicals, independent clergymen leapt to the
stump to aid in the spread of anti-Catholic doctrines.
The Reverend George Bourne, former editor of <u>The Prot-</u>
<u>estant</u>, gave a series of twelve lectures against Popery
in New York in 1835.[147] The Reverend W. C. Bronwlee and
the Reverend Robert J. Breckinridge collaborated in a

144 - <u>Downfall of Babylon</u>, June 25, 1836.
145 - For an account of Colonel Stone see above, pp. 238-241.
146 - <u>Downfall of Babylon</u>, November 12, 1836.
147 - <u>Protestant Vindicator</u>, November 4, 1835.

similar series in Philadelphia the same year.[148] They
separated their efforts after this, the Reverend Breckinridge conducting meetings in Richmond, Virginia, where
nearly every adult citizen heard his speeches. The effect upon the community was so great that a committee
of ministers from the Richmond Protestant churches expressed the pious belief that the city was saved from
Popery.[149] Brownlee, transferring his efforts to New
York, gave a series of fifteen lectures there in 1839
and 1840.[150]

This renewed activity by Protestant speakers
arousing natural resentment, some effort was made in
Catholic circles to combat it, an effort that resulted
in a new epidemic of religious controversy over all the
land. The Reverend John Hughes, having gained fame as
a defender of Catholicism in his earlier debate with
the Reverend John Breckinridge, emerged as the central
character in another religious quarrel in 1836. Hughes
was plunged into this latest argument when he was invited to preside over a debating society in Philadelphia
during a discussion of the well worn question of the re-

148 - Downfall of Babylon, February 28, 1835.
149 - Watchman of the South, September 5, 1839; Baltimore
      Literary and Religious Magazine, September, 1839.
150 - Protestant Vindicator, June 24, 1840.

lation of Catholicism to civil and religious liberty.
Hughes in declining, cautioned members of the society,
composed of both Catholics and Protestants, that similar debates were being held over the entire country,
and that all were sponsored by the New York Protestant
Association.[151]

Members of the debating society accepted his
answer, but asked him to speak before them a short time
later. When he appeared to make this address, Hughes
found an agent representing the Reverend Breckinridge
already there, and was forced to debate with him rather
than allow Protestant papers to charge that he had been
afraid. But this was only a preliminary affair. Hughes
was required to meet Breckinridge in a series of twelve
debates before the matter was dropped. Each discussion
was carried on before an audience that packed the Philadelphia hall, and in each the listeners showed marked
enthusiasm for Breckinridge's charges.[152] The speeches
were published subsequently and only added more fuel to
the flames.[153]

151 - Hughes' letter is printed in Hassard, Life of John
      Hughes, p. 154.
152 - Ibid., pp. 153-160.
153 - New York Observer, November 12, 1836, explained that
      the delay in publication was caused by Hughes, who
      took much time to revise his speeches to make them
      appear better in the light of Breckinridge's logic.
      The controversy was finally published under the title:
      A Discussion of the Question, Is the Roman Catholic
      religion, in any or in all its Principles or Doctrines
      Inimicable to Civil or Religious Liberty?(Philadelphia,
      1836)

A short time after this debate, another controversy that attracted even more attention was developing in Ohio. The Ohio College of Teachers, meeting at Cincinnati in 1836, were addressed by a Baptist clergyman, the Reverend A. Campbell, of Bethany., Virginia.[154] Campbell gave his address to a thorough attack upon Catholicism, and his remarks were objected to by Bishop Purcell of Cincinnati, who was in the audience.[155] Campbell challenged Bishop Purcell to public debate as a result, and a series of seven meetings was arranged, seven subjects being chosen, with one to be debated each day.[156] Accounts of this latest struggle were widely printed in the west and, when it was over, a public meeting of the citizens of Cincinnati expressed complacent satisfaction with the manner in which Campbell had devastated arguments advanced by the Bishop.[157]

The prevalence of similar oral jousts in the east was attested, when, in the same year, 1837, the Bishop of New York warned Catholics to stay away from debating societies where their religion was being dis-

154 - Shea erroneously states that Campbell was Alexander Campbell, founder of the Campbellites. History of the Catholic Church, vol. iii, pp. 625-6256.
155 - American Baptist, quoted in New York Observer, November 12, 1836.
156 - Cincinnati Whig, quoted in Ibid., January 28, 1837.
157 - New York Journal of Commerce, February 3, 1837.

cussed.[158] This order was in itself the cause of a
lengthy controversy carried on through the columns of
the New York Journal of Commerce.[159]

In 1839 Bishop England, long versed in arguments with over-enthusiastic advocates of Protestantism,
was plunged into another dispute in Charleston. A local
temperance society there had issued a petition comparing
the state's system of licensing liquor selling to the
practice of the Catholic church of selling the privilege
to sin before sin was committed.[160] Bishop England, quick
to resent such a statement, refused to allow such defama-
tion to go unchallenged. The Reverend R. Fuller, a Baptist, took up the cudgels for Protestantism.[161] The
principal point in controversy was over the authenticity
of a book, Taxe de la Chancellerie Romaine, ou Boutique
du Pope, published at Lyons in 1564 upon which Fuller

158 - New York Observer, January 28, 1837.
159 - New York Journal of Commerce, January 4, 1837;
      January 14, 1837; January 25, 1837, and ff. The
      controversy was opened by a Protestant author
      who signed himself Obsta Principis, charging
      that this order from the Bishop was typical of
      efforts of the church to stop free discussion.
      He was answered by a Catholic under the signature
      of Catholicus. The discussion lasted through the
      early months of 1837.
160 - Guilday, Life and Times of John England, vol. ii,
      pp. 472-473.
161 - Maury, Wars of the Godly, p. 71.

based most of his arguments regarding the sale of indulgences,[162] Bishop England claiming that the book was
a forgery. But technical arguments over these matters
soon gave way to general attacks upon Catholicism and
Protestantism by the writers, until they finally ended
with a discussion of Ireland in the nineteenth century
and the effects of Catholicism upon it.[163] The only
sufferer from this wordy debate was the Charleston
Courier in whose columns the letters of both contestants appeared. Half way through the exchange of thrusts
the editors announced that if the contestants wished to
continue they would have to pay for space at advertising
rates.[164] Despite this threat, and an offer of the Baltimore Literary and Religious Magazine to take over the controversy rather than allow the claims of Bishop England to
go unanswered[165] the contestants continued in the Courier
until both were more or less winded.

The great burst of activity among anti-Catholic
agencies which gave rise to these lectures and controversies created a vast amount of popular interest in their
cause. It was obvious to all concerned that the excite-

162 - Baltimore Literary and Religious Magazine, November,
       1839.
163 - England, Works of John England, vol. iv, pp. 28-194.
164 - Maury, Wars of the Godly, pp. 71-73.
165 - Guilday, Life and Times of John England, vol. ii,
       pp. 475-476.

ment about Catholicism gradually spreading over the
nation had stimulated the reading public to greater
anxiety in regard to Rome. Mercenary minded authors
saw in this a new opportunity to line their pockets
with gold. It was this situation that gave birth to
the greatest of the propaganda works aimed at the Catholic church, Maria Monk's <u>Awful Disclosures of the Hotel</u>
<u>Dieu Convent of Montreal, or the Secrets of Black Nunnery</u>
<u>Revealed</u>.[166] Published in 1836, this monumental little
volume was to be reprinted frequently in coming years,
and earn for itself undisputed claim to the title of
the "Uncle Tom's Cabin of Know Nothingism."

The story of the author's life is as uncertain
and as varied as her own autobiographical accounts. The
tale that Maria Monk told of her birth and girlhood is
contained in the <u>Awful Disclosures</u>, and what it lacks in
truth is more than made up by the color and glamour of
the adventures that she describes. She was, she relates,
born of Protestant parents in Montreal, but being sent to
a nunnery school for her education, soon embraced Cath-

---

166 - Monk, Maria, <u>Awful Disclosures of the Hotel Dieu</u>
<u>Convent of Montreal, or the Secrets of Black Nun-</u>
<u>nery Revealed</u> (New York, 1836). Another edition
published in 1836 bears the title of: <u>Awful Dis-</u>
<u>closures by Maria Monk of the Hotel Dieu Nunnery</u>
<u>of Montreal</u> (New York, 1836)

olicism and resolved to become a nun.[167] Plans of
a glorious religious life did not seem to be fulfilled
during her two years as a novice in the Black Nunnery,
and so, not waiting to complete her period of probation,
she left, went to a neighboring town, and there got
married.[168] However, life as Bride of the Lamb seemed
preferable to cohabitation with the husband of her own
selection and after a short time she returned, reen-
tered, and this time completed her training and received
the veil.[169]

As soon as Maria had taken this fateful step,
she was called aside by the Mother Superior and initiated
into the secrets of convent life. She was told that "one
of my great duties was to obey the priests in all things;
and this I soon learnt, to my utter astonishment and horror,
was to live in the practice of criminal intercourse with
them."[170] When Maria objected the Superior explained that
this was a glorious duty; for the priests could not marry
and the nuns could not be forgiven of sins without them;
hence it was only fair that the nuns should do as the
priests demanded to set matters right.[171] But poor del-

167 - Monk, Awful Disclosures, pp. 11-19.
168 - Ibid., pp. 19-41.
169 - Ibid., pp. 42-44.
170 - Ibid., p. 47.
171 - Ibid., pp. 47-48.

icate Maria was destined to have her feelings shocked
still more. For the Mother Superior went on to tell
her that infants were sometimes born in the convent,
but that they were always baptized and strangled immediately. "This secured their everlasting happiness,"
the Superior explained, "for the baptism purified them
from all sinfulness, and being sent out of the world
before they had time to do anything wrong, they were
at once admitted into heaven. How happy, she exclaimed,
are those who secure immortal happiness to such little
things. Their little souls would thank those who kill
their bodies if they had it in their power."[172]

After this conversation Maria felt that she knew
the worst. But as new events unfolded she was horrified
beyond even this. One day she was sent to an upper room,
and then witnessed the execution of a nun who had refused
to obey a priest, the extreme penalty being administered
by a number of priests and nuns who cast the condemned
sister on a bed, placed a mattress on her, and then jumped
up and down upon the mattress until she was dead.[173] Such
revelations are interrupted while Maria gives a detailed
description of the convent, of the daily life of its inmates,[174] and of one sister named Jane Ray who leaned

172 - Ibid., pp. 48-49.
173 - Ibid., pp. 97-105.
174 - Ibid., pp. 54-96.

toward pranks and practical jokes.[175] She returns, however, to the morbid again and again, describing with
gruesome fascination the execution of two babies[176] and
telling how she accidentally discovered a large hole in
the basement of the convent, around which a white powder was sprinkled. This, she concluded, must be the place
where the dead babies were cast after they had been strangled, the white material being lime to destroy their bodies.[177] While in the basement, too, she tells of finding
the entrance of a secret passage connecting the convent
with a neighboring priests' home, a passage designed to
keep the priests from the elements and the eyes of the
community whenever they felt the need of a nun.[178]

There appeared throughout Maria's story a repeated return to the subject of the babies, how they were
born and strangled. At last she explains her great interest in this subject. She found, she said, that she
was going to have a baby herself - that one Father Phelan
was to become a father. Maria felt the urge of mother-
hood so strongly that she could not bear the thought of
having the baby strangled. There was only one way to

175 - Ibid., pp. 106-135.
176 - Ibid., pp. 155-157.
177 - Ibid., pp. 81-82.
178 - Ibid., pp. 127-128.

avoid this, and that was to escape. The escape itself
proved unusually easy. Carrying an order to the director of the convent hospital, she burst past a guard as
though on an important mission and was free.[179]

The first edition of Maria Monk's narrative
ended rather abruptly at that point. Her readers must
have been curious as to the fate of an obviously pregnant young nun wandering the streets of Montreal in the
dead of night. This curiosity was satiated in a second
edition which followed the first almost immediately
after its popular reception. It contained a lengthy
Sequel to the original tale.[180] In this Sequel the
story of Maria's life is carried forward to the time
of the publication of her book. She was, she confessed,
a little puzzled at her own predicament as soon as she
had found herself free. But she sought out an old friend,
traded her nun's outfit for one more befitting a traveler,
and shipped for Quebec, a city that she seemed to believe
was a center of Protestantism in contrast to Catholic
Montreal.[181] Before she reached there the captain of the
boat recognized her and carried her back to Montreal.[182]
This was too much for poor Maria, life seemed sad, and she

179 - Ibid., pp. 197-200.
180 - The Sequel is bound with all regular editions of the
    Awful Disclosures.
181 - Monk, Awful Disclosures, pp. 257-262.
182 - Ibid., pp. 262-264.

decided to end it all. To carry out this intention
she cast herself into the Lachine Canal (sic) but
two workmen fished her out, emptied her, and carried
her to the office of a nearby doctor.[183]

        This lucky rescue and her continued ability
to avoid the priests that must have been scouring the
countryside for her convinced Maria that she had been
destined by God to tell the world of her experiences,
and strike another blow at Popery. To do this, she believed, she must reach the United States where a recep-
tive audience waited. And she hit upon one man who might
aid her project. Her husband, she believed, would be
glad enough to get rid of her to pay her way. Her belief was justified, the money was provided, a traveling
companion selected, and the journey started.[184] But the
traveling companion deserted poor Maria as soon as they
reached New York City. Again death seemed the only alternative; this time she sought a deserted spot planning to
starve herself to death. Again fate intervened. Four
hunters found her, and carried her to a charity hospital.
There, expecting her baby at any time and afraid of the
death that might result, she asked for a Protestant minis-

183 - Ibid., pp. 265-268.
184 - Ibid., pp. 269-281.

ter to whom she could tell her whole story. One responded, the tale was deemed worthy of publication, and
Maria, who lived through the birth of her child, set
about the telling of her life story.[185] Thus the Awful
Disclosures came into being.

   This was the story that Maria told in her book.
Immediately other versions were put forward; versions that
lacked the fine imagination of Maria's, but that probably
were more truthful. Her mother, a Protestant lady living
in Montreal, testified that she had never been in the
Hotel Dieu Convent, that she had run a slate pencil into
her head as a young girl and had been queer ever since.
Maria, she testified, had been a wild young girl, and
had been confined to a Catholic Magdalen asylum in
Montreal. This, her mother believed, provided the basis
for her convent stories. Moreover, she insisted that
Maria had gotten into trouble even in the home, and been
forced to escape, aided by a former lover who had been
responsible for the child born in New York.[186]

   There seems little doubt that this is the correct
story. There seems little doubt, too, that the former

185 - Ibid., pp. 282-296.
186 - Stone, William L., Maria Monk and the Nunnery of
        the Hotel Dieu; Being an Account of a Visit to
        the Convents of Montreal and a Refutation of
        the Awful Disclosures. (New York, 1836) pp. 46-48.
        The mother's affidavit, is printed in Awful Dis-
        closures, pp. 215-220.

lover was the Reverend William H. Hoyt, long active
against Canadian Catholics and responsible for the Canadian Benevolent Association. Hoyt saw in Maria a
chance to strike a telling blow and at the same time
enrich himself. In all probability he took her to
New York, arranging that there she should meet other
members of the clergy who should be active in forward-
ing her publication.[187] One of these was the Reverend
J. J. Slocum, who testified later that Maria Monk and
Hoyt had called upon him in October, 1835, and requested
him to write the story of Maria's life. He had done so,
he said, but he insisted that the story had been Maria's
own, as told from her own lips.[188] Other affidavits sworn
by another of the ministers involved, the Reverend Arthur
Tappin, insisted that Maria did not know Hoyt until after
she was in New York,[189] and the four hunters who had found
her came forward to testify to the truth of that part of
her story.[190] Subsequent events, however, served only to
cast doubts upon these statements. Certainly it was with

187 - Stone, Maria Monk and the Nunnery of the Hotel
      Dieu, pp. 46-48.
188 - Slocum, J. J., Reply to the Priests Book, Denomi-
      nated "Awful Exposure of an Atrocious Plot formed
      by Certain Individuals Against the Clergy and Nuns
      of Lower Canada, Through the Intervention of Maria
      Monk (New York, 1837) pp. 103-112.
189 - Ibid., pp. 101-102.
190 - Ibid., pp. 97-99.

Hoyt that Maria visited Montreal in September, 1835,
in an effort to bring legal proceedings against the
priest she alleged was the father of her child.[191] Nor
is there much doubt that while there she lived with Hoyt
in a way that allowed the Montreal paper to state that
"des liaisons plus intimes" existed between them.[192]

Regardless of the truth of this storm of affidavits and counter affidavits, Maria Monk's book was
written, probably by the Reverend J. J. Slocum, assisted
by Theodore Dwight.[193] The editors of the Protestant
Vindicator, also engaged in the plot, began a program
of publicity just before the Awful Disclosures appeared.
A marked increase in the number of articles upon the
immorality of convents and nuns appeared[194] and in addition there were veiled references to an escaped nun
in the city soon to write her memoirs.[195]

But difficulties of publication still stood in
the way. The manuscript of the book was offered to Harper
Brothers, but Harper's while lured by the prospect of profits, considered the book a little too immoral and outspoken
for so dignified a firm. While they hesitated, a device

191 - Monk, Awful Disclosures, pp. 297-323.
192 - From L'Ami du Peuple, printed in Protestant Vindi-
      cator, November 18, 1835.
193 - Stone, Maria Monk and the Nunnery of the Hotel Dieu,
      pp. 48-49.
194 - Protestant Vindicator, October 14, 1835; October 21,
      1835.
195 - Ibid., October 14, 1835.

was hit upon that allowed them to keep their fair name
and also share in the receipts. A dummy publishing firm,
Howe and Bates, was set up, Howe and Bates being two
employees of Harper's. Under their name the book appeared, and the world was given its Awful Disclosures
in January, 1836.[196]

The reception of this startling volume by the
press varied with the enthusiasm of the editors for the
anti-Catholic cause. The Protestant Vindicator and the
Downfall of Babylon proclaimed the book a remarkable exposition of the truth about nunneries[197] and immediately
began reprinting it in serial form.[198] The New York Observer, more cautious, gave notice of its publication and
stated that while the truth of this particular account
could not be attested, conditions which it described were
typical of most convents.[199] A few months later the Observer printed a thorough analysis of the evidence for and
against the truth of Maria Monk's book, expressing its conviction that every statement in it was true.[200] This attitude was maintained and insisted upon when the second edition appeared in July.[201]

196 - O'Gorman, History of the Roman Catholic Church in the
      United States, p. 366.
197 - Downfall of Babylon, February 6, 1836.
198 - Ibid., February 6, 1836.
199 - New York Observer, January 23, 1836.
200 - Ibid., May 7, 1836; May 21, 1836.
201 - Ibid., July 9, 1836.

The furor over Maria Monk's book loosed a
whole storm of controversial literature upon the country. While the clergy and officials of the Hotel Dieu
convent maintained a stony silence, defenders of the
Catholic church rushed a volume from the press entitled:
Awful Exposure of the Atrocious Plot formed by Certain
Individuals against the Clergy and Nuns of Lower Canada,
through the Intervention of Maria Monk.[202]   Divided between unsupported denials of statements in the Awful Disclosures[203] and a whole series of affidavits from all
people who could possibly be concerned,[204] the Awful Exposure proved an effective instrument.   It was so effective that Reverend J. J. Slocum himself was called upon
to answer it, and did so in a: Reply to the Priests Book,
Denominatod, "Awful Exposure of an Atrocious Plot formed
by Certain Individuals Against the Clergy and Nuns of
Lower Canada through the Intervention of Maria Monk."[205]
The Reply consisted for the most part of more affidavits,

202 - Awful Exposure of an Atrocious Plot formed by
      Certain Individuals against the Clergy and Nuns
      of Lower Canada through the Intervention of Maria
      Monk. (New York, 1836)
203 - Ibid., pp. 3-71.
204 - Ibid., pp. 75-129.
205 - Slocum, J. S., Reply to the Priests Book, Demoni-
      nated, an Awful Exposure of an Atrocious Plot
      formed by Certain Individuals against the Clergy
      and Nuns of Lower Canada through the Intervention
      of Maria Monk. (New York, 1837)

forming a detailed refutation of everything stated in
the Awful Exposure,[206] but ending with a general account
of the immorality of all convents, drawn from the writings of Scippio di Ricci, Da Costa and other famous exposers of Popery.[207]

While Slocum was thus struggling to uphold
Protestant supremacy, aid came from an unexpected quarter. Although the editors of the Protestant Vindicator
seem to have capitalized most upon the Maria Monk episode, Samuel B. Smith, editor of the rival publication,
the Downfall of Babylon, was not one to allow such a
scoop to stand in the way of a little honest money making.
So he came forward now, publishing a flaming pamphlet under the title: Decisive Confirmation of the Awful Disclosures of Maria Monk, Proving her Residence in the
Hotel Dieu Nunnery, and the Existence of the Subterranean Passages.[208] In his Decisive Confirmation Smith
presents a few more of the usual affidavits from persons
who had seen the subterranean passage connecting the convent and the priests' home, as Maria had charged.[209] But

206 - Ibid., pp. 15-159.
207 - Ibid., pp. 160-176.
208 - Smith, Samuel B., Decisive Confirmation of the Aw-
       ful Disclosures of Maria Monk, Proving Her Resi-
       dence in the Hotel Dieu Nunnery, and the Existence
       of the Subterranean Passages. (New York, 1836)
209 - Ibid., pp. 3-5.

Nunnery in the Wilderness

Samuel Smith was unable to forget that he was a priest
himself at one time and so the story grew to autobiographical proportions. The greater part of this latest
publication was concerned with his own experiences. He
told of a Popish belief that priests could not sin because the devil entered into their bodies and sinned
for them,[210] of how priests always confessed nuns in
their own bedrooms[211] and how babies were born in convents over all the United States.[212] They were usually
not cast into a hole in the basement, as in the Hotel
Dieu, he says, but were "buried by night in the recess
of some lonely mountain, or under the bog of some marshy
fen."[213] In fact, Smith finds in Maria's story of the
basement pit for babies the greatest evidence of the
truth of her account. That story is so improbable, he
writes, that no one could have invented it; it must be
true.[314] While the Decisive Confirmation was replied
to by another writer[215] its popularity was only increased by such attacks, and the publishers were unable to keep up with the public demand for the work.[216]

210 - Ibid., pp. 15-16.
211 - Ibid., p. 29.
212 - Ibid., pp. 19-26.
213 - Ibid., p. 19.
214 - Ibid., p. 10.
215 - Vale, G. Review of the Awful Disclosures of Maria
      Monk (New York, 1836)
216 - Downfall of Babylon, April 16, 1836.

Such accusations, shouted back and forth,
meant nothing, however. There was a growing feeling
that the only way to find out the truth of Maria's
statements was to make a search of the interior of
the Hotel Dieu and thus either confirm or deny all
that the Awful Exposures had exposed. The New York
Protestant Association, quick to seize the opportunity,
offered to send a committee to Montreal with Maria
Monk as a member to make a thorough inspection.[217]
Needless to say the offer was declined, as were similar offers made by Maria herself.[218] Finally a committee of Protestant ministers, being allowed to make the
inspection, reported all of Maria's accusations false
and that the building of the Hotel Dieu did not re-
semble the one which she had described.[219] Maria's
supporters immediately charged that the Catholics had
hired masons and carpenters to completely remodel the
interior to fool the Protestants,[220] and more affidavits were produced from architects to show that this
could have been done easily.[221] But the editors of the

217 - Protestant Vindicator, November 25, 1835.
218 - New York Observer, August 6, 1836.
219 - Catholic Diary, quoted in Ibid., August 6, 1836.
220 - Downfall of Babylon, July 23, 1836; Protestant
       Vindicator, November 25, 1835.
221 - Slocum, Reply to the Priest's Book, pp. 65-88.

Protestant Vindicator were alarmed and gave increased
emphasis to their attacks on the Hotel Dieu, printing
stories from Montreal of workmen who had seen nuns
burying a dead baby in the convent yard[222] and of an
excavation near there where the bones of murdered infants were found.[223]

A public meeting of citizens of New York,
held in the rooms of the American Tract Society, passed
resolutions upholding Maria Monk and stating that they
were satisfied, despite the report of the investigating
committee.[224] They even named a new committee to go
with Maria to Montreal for another investigation, a
committee containing such well known nativists as the
Reverend J. J. Slocum and Samuel F. B. Morse.[225]

While affairs were in this condition, with
neutral observers not knowing what statements to believe, a new escaped nun appeared in New York city.
She was, she announced, Saint Francis Patrick. She

222 - Protestant Vindicator, November 4, 1835.
223 - Ibid., December 2, 1835.
224 - Downfall of Babylon, August 20, 1836.
225 - New York Observer, August 20, 1836. The meeting
      decided to send copies of their resolutions up-
      holding Maria Monk to the Governor of Canada, the
      Secretary of the Colonial Department, the "Romish
      Bishop of Montreal," to King William IV and to
      every paper in New York.

said she had been in the Hotel Dieu while Maria was
there, that they had known each other well, and that
she was willing to confirm everything Maria had said.[226]
Samuel Smith rushed out a pamphlet: The Escape of St.
Francis Patrick, another Nun from the Hotel Dieu Nunnery of Montreal.[227] He became so enthusiastic that
he burst into verse to describe his emotions:

> Down from the north a torrent comes;
> A moral deluge sweeps out shores;
> Two captives driven from their homes,
> Come to lament, to weep, deplore
> Their mis-spent days.
>
> Their homes, we say? Such homes as these,
> The reptiles of the earth would scorn;
> Hot beds of every vice that grows,
> And sinks where virtue droops forlorn,
> To rise no more.
>
> One tale is told, and horror shrieks;
> We stand aghast, appalled with fear,
> And listening now, the echo speaks,
> Strikes to the heart, excites the fear;
> Alas, - how true.[228]

St. Francis Patrick made some interesting revelations that Maria had neglected. She told, for one
thing, how the whole interior of the building had been
remodeled before the investigating committee arrived,
and how the nuns had gone around giggling behind their

226 - New York Observer, September 3, 1836; Downfall of
      Babylon, September 17, 1836.
227 - Smith, Samuel B., The Escape of St. Francis Patrick,
      another Nun from the Hotel Dieu Nunnery of Montreal
      (New York, 1836)
228 - Ibid., Introduction.

hands at the way the stupid Protestants were being fooled.[229] Why, she said, at the time the investigation was made two murdered babies were in a closet, but of course the investigators never looked in there.[230] She also added one interesting sidelight as to life in the convent. She displayed four tiny marks on her left arm and announced that it was her brand - that each priest branded his own nuns, and, while they were not his exclusively, from that time on he had a prior right to them in case of dispute.[231]

Maria Monk and this newest of the fence climbing group of nuns were brought together at a public meeting and there, tearfully embracing each other, talked over the days they had spent together in the Hotel Dieu.[232] This in itself should have been enough to brand Maria Monk as an impostor, for only the most gullible could believe St. Francis Patrick and she was exposed, as a fraud, within a short time. But Maria had been made the toast of New York and Boston, she was entertained lavishly and clergymen fought for her company. Another blast was needed before faith in her story began to weaken. This

229 - Ibid., p. 7.
230 - Ibid., p. 7.
231 - Ibid., pp. 5-6.
232 - Interview of Maria Monk with her Opponents, the Authors of the Reply to her Awful Disclosures, now in Press, held in This City on Wednesday, August 17 (New York, 1836); Stone, Maria Monk and the Nunnery of the Hotel Dieu, p. 45.

blast came from a new investigation, one conducted by
Colonel William L. Stone, editor of the New York Com-
merical Advertiser. A Protestant who had interested
himself mildly in the anti-Catholic crusade in the
past, Colonel Stone, happened to be in Montreal in
1836 and sought for and secured permission to make a
thorough investigation. He made the examination with
Maria's book in his hand, poking into every closet,[233]
climbing to a high window to see into one unopened room,[234]
and smelling a row of jars in the basement which might
have contained lime to dissolve strangled babies.[235] He
came away completely satisfied, and published an account
which[236] ended with the pronouncement, "I most solemnly
believe that the priests and nuns are innocent in this
matter."[237] But despite his findings, he said, he was
still opposed to Catholicism and still believed that
nunneries caused immorality the world over.[238]

233 - Stone, Maria Monk and the Nunnery of the Hotel
      Dieu, pp. 23-24.
234 - Ibid., p. 25.
235 - Ibid., pp. 26-29.
236 - Stone, Maria Monk and the Nunnery of the Hotel
      Dieu; being an Account of a Visit to the Con-
      vents of Montreal and a Refutation of the Awful
      Disclosures (New York, 1836). The report was
      also published in Stone's paper, the Commercial
      Advertiser. New York Observer, October 15, 1836.
237 - Stone, Maria Monk and the Nunnery of the Hotel
      Dieu, p. 33.
238 - Ibid., pp. 54-55.

Here was a serious charge for Maria's friends to answer. A pamphlet was rushed from the press entitled Evidence Demonstrating the Falsehoods of William L. Stone.[239] Dr. Brownlee issued a long statement in which he insisted that Stone could not have examined the whole building in three hours as he claimed.[240] Aid came to Dr. Brownlee from an unexpected quarter when an anonymous poem appeared, aimed at Colonel Stone and his investigation. The Vision of Rubeta; an Epic Story of the Island of Manhattan,[241] filling more than four hundred pages, formed a criticism of Colonel Stone and his visit to the convent that must have aroused many a merry laugh among the literati of New York. Modeled on Butler's Hudibras, with "Illustrations done on Stone," and with profound footnotes in a humorous vein, the Vision deserves far more credit from students of American humor than it has received.

The whole visit that Colonel Stone made is lambasted. He pictures Stone, as Rubeta, going to the convent and announcing to the Superior:

A new gold finder in your sinks of shame,
I come! Prepare! Dead babe hope not to hide,
Nor friars sandal, where this wand is guide!
Aided by which, shall pierce your very stones
My eagle eyes, and find those little bones.[242]

239 - Evidence Demonstrating the Falsehoods of William L. Stone (New York, 1836)
240 - New York Observer, October 15, 1836.
241 - The Vision of Rubeta; an Epic Story of the Island of Manhattan (Boston, 1838)
242 - Ibid., p. 43.

Thus the search starts, with Rubeta marshalling all
the nuns and telling them:

> Resolved I am, to search you through and through;
> From vault to chimney top; each door undo.
> Lift every trap, explore each secret nook,
> Inspect your closet, in your night pans look,
> Walls, vessels, urinals, chests, cupboards, sound,
> And thread your pleasure garden underground.[243]

The search is unsuccessful until Rubeta and the nuns come
upon a locked door. They refuse him the key, but he
climbs up to look inside, and while standing there the
nuns steal the stool he is standing on. Struggling, his
braces give way, and he hears one nun remark:

> The nasty beast, to wear a shirt so short.[244]

Hanging there, Rubeta grew discouraged:

> For I, whose planet promised fame and riches,
> Now see all slipped with those confounded breeches.[245]

But Rubeta gets down, aided by the nuns, and his braces
are replaced with several pages of description of this
event. And the search goes on. He finds the same jars
that Colonel Stone found in the basement, and feels in
them, to his great discomfort, although the contents are
only implied.[246]

  Finally the last of the convent has been in-

243 - Ibid., pp. 91-92.
244 - Ibid., p. 108.
245 - Ibid., p. 207.
246 - Ibid., pp. 119-122.

spected, and Rubeta announces:

> Ladies, the charm has worked; the trial's o'er!
> Virgins ye are, and pure as ever before.[247]

The nuns carry him away in triumph singing his praises,
and the author brings his volume to a reluctant close.

No sooner had this monumental poem appeared than
it was answered, this time by a play, a one act drama,
The Critique of the Vision of Rubeta: a Dramatic Sketch
in One Act,[248] by one who signed himself "Autodicus." It
was not really a criticism at all. It devoted itself to
high praise of the Vision of Rubeta, and especially to
insisting that the poem was not immoral as charged.[249]
While it may be doubted if the Critique was ever performed, it did add vastly to the amusement of the enlightened few who had been able to enjoy the Vision.

While this literary war was growing from Colonel
Stone's visit, the backers of Maria Monk went ahead to
capitalize upon the stir of interest that had been created.
An artist was pressed into service to supply a series of
pictures depicting the various scenes in the Awful Disclosures, and they were rushed from the press.[250] A kidnap-

247 - Ibid., p. 165.
248 - "Autodicus," A Critique of the Vision of Rubeta:
  a Dramatic Sketch in One Act (Philadelphia, 1838)
249 - Ibid., pp. 1-32.
250 - Dreadful Scenes in the Awful Disclosures of Maria
  Monk (New York, 1836)

ping feat was hatched to attract[251] public interest,
and with excitement high, Maria herself was persuaded
to take up her pen again, and this time emerged with
a volume entitled Further Disclosures of Maria Monk,
Concerning the Hotel Dieu Nunnery of Montreal; and
also Her Visit to Nun's Island and Disclosures Concerning that Secret Retreat.[252] The standard of this
new work was below that set in the Awful Disclosures.
Maria added some new facts to her account, she told
how the priests sometimes allowed other men to come
into the Hotel Dieu to get at the nuns in return for
a good fee,[253] how the nuns themselves sometimes dressed
in men's clothes and were taken to the priests' home,[254]
and how Jane Ray continued her practical jokes.[255] The
revelations promised about Nun's Island were rather disappointing; Nun's Island, Maria explained, was simply an
island near Montreal where nuns from the United States
came to have babies after they had been seduced by
priests.[256]

251 - Downfall of Babylon, June 25, 1836; New York Observer,
      June 11, 1836; Slocum, Reply to the Priests Book, p.
      147. An earlier kidnapping feat had received some
      publicity just before the Awful Disclosures appeared.
      Protestant Vindicator November 18, 1835; December
      23, 1835.
252 - Monk, Maria, Further Disclosures of Maria Monk, Con-
      Cerning the Hotel Dieu Nunnery of Montreal; and also
      her Visit to Nun's Island and Disclosures Concerning
      that Secret Retreat (New York, 1837)
253 - Ibid., p. 135.
254 - Ibid., pp. 102-112.
255 - Ibid., pp. 72-76.
256 - Ibid., pp. 144-174.

Regardless of its merits, the Further Disclosures was the last book about Maria Monk to appear.
Shortly after its publication a story was circulated
that Maria Monk had confessed to Colonel William L.
Stone that she was an impostor and that all that she
knew of the Hotel Dieu convent had been told her by the
Reverend George Bourne.[257] The editors of the Protestant
Vindicator refused to believe this,[258] and Colonel Stone
himself issued a statement saying the story was without
foundation.[259]   But regardless of this one rumor, Maria's
star was on the wane. She had been cheated of most of
her profits by her backers and a series of law suits
failed to restore them.[260] Any faith that her supporters
might have in her was dispelled early in 1838 when she
again gave birth to a fatherless child[261] and made no

257 - New York Observer, August 5, 1837.
258 - Ibid., September 16, 1837.
259 - Ibid., September 30, 1837.
260 - Maria Monk and Rev. J. J. Slocum were jointly sued
      by William K. Hoyt for a share of the profits in
      1836. New York Observer, November 26, 1836. In
      a second suit brought by Maria Monk through her
      next friend, John Slocum against Harper Brothers
      and others, it was disclosed that the copyright
      on Awful Disclosures had been taken out by Rev-
      erend George Bourne and employed by him with the
      aid of Harpers Brothers, with the authoress rec-
      ceiving no share in the profits. The court re-
      fused to grant her any relief. I Edward's Chanc.
      Rep. 109. (May 16, 1837)
261 - New York Observer, October 6, 1838; Niles Register,
      October 20, 1838.

pretence by naming it after a priest, as she had the
first.[262] At about the same time Saint Francis Patrick
added to her already fading popularity by bringing a
child into the world.[263] Despite this, the editor of
the Protestant Vindicator continued to believe Maria
Monk's story, maintaining, however, that she had written
the book ironically and insisting that her second preg-
nancy had been arranged by the Jesuits to discredit her.[264]

  If a book published by a woman who claimed to
be Maria Monk's daughter thirty years later[265] can be believed, her downfall from that time on was rapid. She
married a man named St. John, lived with him in a New
York tenement, and dissipated his earnings in drink and
riotous living. Finally, when she had gone so far as
to sell the family furniture to obtain money for gin,
the father and children left her. Her daughter's last
glimpse of Maria Monk came as they passed the corner

262 - Niles Register, October 20, 1838.
263 - New York Observer, October 6, 1838.
264 - Statement of Brownlee quoted in New York Observer,
  November 3, 1838. In 1841, when accused of writing
  Maria Monk's book for her, Dr. Brownlee steadfastly
  maintained his innocence and stated that the story
  had been dictated by Maria to a Presbyterian clergyman just as it appeared. Protestant Vindicator,
  April 28, 1841. St. Francis Patrick, he insisted
  at the same time, was a Jesuit in disguise sent by
  the convent priests to discredit Maria Monk. Ibid.,
  June 9, 1841. Yet when rumor spread that another
  nun had escaped from the Hotel Dieu Brownlee expressed the belief that she would write her memoirs.
  Ibid., September 30, 1840.
265 - Eckel, L. St. John, Maria Monk's Daughter; an Autobiography (New York, 1874) The daughter tells of
  her conversion to Catholicism, and nearly all of the
  book is devoted to a vigorous defense of the Catholic
  faith.

saloon and saw her swaying drunkenly inside.[266] In
1849 she was arrested for picking the pocket of her
paramour of the moment in a Five Points den, and died
in prison a short time later.[267]

Despite the sordid ending of the author, Maria's
book lived on. Discredited as she was, her revelations
of convent life continued to sell, more than three hundred thousand copies being circulated up to the time of
the Civil war,[268] and editions have appeared since that
time.[269] Maria Monk had played her part.[270] She had
demonstrated the profit that could come from anti-Catholic propaganda, especially if it smacked of the pornographic. Much of the credit for the wave of nativism
which followed can be attributed to the widely read and
accepted Awful Disclosures.

266 - Ibid., pp. 1-15.
267 - Dalman's Register, October 20, 1849. Quoted in Walsh,
      J. J., "Keeping up the Protestant Tradition,"Catholic
      World,vol. ci (June, 1915), p. 330.
268 - Wright, Richardson, Forgotten Ladies (Philadelphia,
      1928), pp. 142-143.
269 - Typical of such reprints is Monk, Maria, The Mysteries
      of a Convent and the Awful Disclosures of Maria Monk.
      (_____, 1874)
270 - The literature on Maria Monk is vast, but most of it
      is superficial and filled with repeated mistakes.
      Nearly all authors who have touched upon her career
      have based their remarks upon those in Shea, History
      of the Catholic Church, vol. iii, pp. 209-512, that
      are not only prejudiced, but also inaccurate. Typical
      of such accounts: "The True Story of Maria Monk",
      Catholic Truth Society Publications, vol. xix (Lon-
      don, 1894); and "The Truth about Maria Monk," Watson's
      Magazine, May, 1816. A popular account of her life
      based upon the better known works concerning her is
      in Wright, Forgotten Ladies, pp. 121-155.

V

SAVING THE WEST FROM THE POPE, 1835-1840.

While Maria Monk and her followers were hawk-
ing their wares of invective against nuns and the immorality of Catholicism, a new group of venders of
prejudice was rising throughout the land bent on exposing another vulnerable spot in the Catholic structure. Headed by that eminent inventor, artist and
nativist, Samuel F. B. Morse, these later members of
the anti-Catholic cohorts placed before the people of
the United States grave evidence of a great Popish
plot already in operation. Romanism was dying out in
Europe, they averred. Romanism had sucked dry the car-
rion carcasses of despotic Italy and France and Spain.
Romanism sought a new victim as host. Romanism had
selected the United States for that new life, and the
Pope had chosen the Mississippi Valley for his next
home. This was the cry of Morse and his disciples,
and the legion of No-Popery advocates whose ranks had
been swelled recently by the tales of Maria Monk.

The popularity of Maria Monk and her kind
had been limited in its appeal to the enthusiastic
native who was ready to believe the worst of Cathol-

icism and not unready to delve into pornographic
tales in the guise of church literature. Morse and
his later day propagandists knew no such limitation.
They preached the unbounded news of a glorious contest soon to be fought in the Mississippi Valley, a
struggle to the death between Catholicism and Protestantism. Never before had the world had an opportunity to test the strength of these two great religious
systems. They had met and fought in Europe at the time
of the Reformation, but there the contest was not purely
religious, it was political as well. Catholics and
Protestants alike had been supported by the sword and
their own strength remained untested. The great interior valley of the United States offered a vast
sparcely occupied stretch of territory where these
ancient opponents could match their powers. Here was
a battleground royal, and both of the opposing factions
took full advantage of it.

But the struggle for the Mississippi Valley
was more than a mere quarrel between two great religious
systems. Throughout the land, Americans were firm in
the conviction that they had flung down the gauntlet at
the feet of despotic Europe by creating a glorious republicanism, and the flush of pride was still on them
whenever they considered their prowess. They believed

they had created a perfect state, the example of which
had spread to Europe, where downtrodden serfs were beginning to rock the thrones that ground them down. Nativistic propagandists seized quickly upon Europe's unrest and assured all willing ears that the despots of
the continent, recognizing the danger of overthrow
through the inculcating of the "life, liberty and pursuit of happiness" in the minds of their peasants, were
eager to stamp out the seeds of republicanism. Especially in the new world did the despots take cognizance
of the wide-spread tendency toward revolt and they determined to dam the stream of liberty at its fountain
head. The belief was general that these monarchs would
strike first at the Mississippi Valley. If they could
control that fertile garden spot they could swing their
strength against the eastern states and drive freedom
from the face of the earth. The Mississippi Valley must
be protected, not only for Protestantism, alone, but for
civil liberty.

Warnings of this grave danger to the United
States began to be sounded not long after the crusade
against the immigrant and the Catholic got under way.
At first these warnings ignored the question of Catholicism and pointed only to the manner in which Europe
looked upon this country, viewing it as a conflagration

of republicanism which had to be stamped out.[1]   By 1827,
however, religious papers were beginning to sound the
new warning - that Protestants had been neglecting the
West and that unless they turned their attention to
sending missionaries and Bibles to the Mississippi Valley, Rome would occupy the ground and "build up a system
of ignorance, priestcraft and superstition, such as now
casts a blight over some of the fairest portions of
Europe."[2]

From that time on the Protestant press expressed
sincere alarm at the danger. Stories of the growth of the
Catholic church in the West[3] and of the erection of new
chapels and schools[4] were printed with earnest warnings
to readers. Statistics were mustered showing that Protestants were outnumbered in many western cities[5] and this
was considered sufficient ground for the charge that already "in our western wilds a superstitious and corrupt
church" was being established.[6] Sabbath school teachers

1 - New York Observer, August 14, 1824. The warning was
    voiced in an article entitled "The Holy Alliance vs.
    the United States of America."
2 - Ibid., October 20, 1827.
3 - Ibid., December 19, 1829; February 13, 1830.
4 - Ibid., May 2, 1829.
5 - Ibid., December 19, 1829.
6 - Church Register, June 6, 1829. Quoted in Hassard,
    Life of John Hughes, pp. 92-93.

of Boston were warned that unless they contributed
to the American Union of Sunday Schools to send missionaries to the interior valley, that region would
fall before the sway of Popery.[7]

These sporadic attempts to arouse the Protestant population to action against Popery were given
new strength by the revolution that swept over France
in 1830. News of the disestablishment of Catholicism
as the state religion of France was hurried to America.
Immediately the cry was raised that Catholicism was
being driven from Europe; that the people of the old
world were rising in their wrath to free themselves
from Papal tyranny.[8] There was only one place for it
to turn now - and that was to the United States. Popish
designs on the Mississippi Valley took on new meaning.

That such propaganda was given credence is
attested by the burst of activity in the Protestant
press immediately after the revolution. The Connecticut Observer reminded its readers that "so long as the
example of the United States is held out before the
world, the subjects of monarchical Europe will have
a hankering after the liberty enjoyed by republicans,"

7- Massachusetts Yeoman, March 31, 1829.
8- New York Observer, October 9, 1830; July 28, 1832;
January 28, 1835.

and expressed its belief that the monarchs were attempting to stamp out republicanism by introducing Catholicism into the United States.[9]   The New York Observer, taking up the cry, stated it baldly as a fact that the Pope wanted to get control of the west, citing as proof the Catholic schools and colleges being established there. "If the Jesuits send out swarms of teachers and missionaries," it cried, "we must send out from our northern hive larger swarms of better teachers and more devoted missionaries."[10]   The Protestant Episcopalian and Church Register pictured the "Romish community" as "on the tiptoe of expectation, indulging the most sanguine hopes... of soon recovering all that it has lost."[11]   The Protestant Magazine shouted that "Protestants of this land of Protestantism" must awaken or lose all.[12]

Especially did these newspapers and magazines warn their readers not to be deceived by the character of American Catholics, who obviously appeared too passive to be considered unduly dangerous. This, it was pointed out, was only part of the plot; Catholics were trained to assume a mask of meekness until they had won over the

9 - Quoted in Ibid., January 16, 1830.
10- Ibid., March 6, 1830.
11- Protestant Episcopalian and Church Register,
    January, 1831.
12- Protestant Magazine, December, 1833.

country, then they would burst forth like the dragon and destroy.[13] They could never be trusted. They had been taught to keep no faith with heretics[14] and they even boasted of this by telling of how their principles never changed.[15] "Popery," said the editors of The Protestant, "imperceptibly makes its way through the land, polluting the moral atmosphere as it advances, and death and hell are in its train...The disposition of the Pope's forces shows that he has taken the dimensions of his antagonists accurately. He does not come openly to it, nor create alarms: but with good words and fair speeches; and his hatred is more deadly if possible, and tenfold more to be dreaded."[16]

Such a clamor by the religious press was certain to come to the attention of the societies formed to spread Protestantism throughout the land. The American Bible Society, quick to see the threat of Catholic domination in the Mississippi Valley, issued a circular in 1830 warning that the Pope was doing his best to make Romanism supreme in that section, and would succeed unless Protestants forgot their differences and united against their

13 - New York Observer, September 4, 1830; March 12, 1831.
14 - McGavin, The Protestant, vol. i, pp. 199-231.
15 - Protestant Episcopalian and Church Register, January, 1831.
16 - The Protestant, December 18, 1830.

common enemy.[17] Two years later an agent of that society
was expressing the public belief that "the Mississippi
Valley has been mapped as well as surveyed by emissaries
from the Vatican; and Cardinals are exulting in the hope
of enriching the Papal See by accessions from the United
States."[18] The American Education Society, through its
publication, the Quarterly Register, expressed the great
need for schools in the West to combat Romanism and urged
all Protestant churches to unite against this "foreign
enemy."[19] Similar warnings from the British Reformation
Society were broadcast in America[20] and Dr. Lyman Beecher
found opportunity to express the same ideas in speaking
before the Boston Sunday School Union.[21] Even the churches
felt this urgent need. Presbyterian clergymen gathered
for the General Assembly of that denomination in 1834
heard the Reverend Philo F. Phelps describe a great Popish plot to subjugate the country and wipe out republicanism.[22] Episcopalian ministers were meanwhile warned that
without their efforts the Mississippi Valley within a

17 - Massachusetts Yeoman, April 17, 1830.
18 - New York Observer, July 21, 1832.
19 - Quarterly Register, quoted in New York Observer,
     March 6, 1830.
20 - New York Observer, August 14, 1830; July 16, 1831.
21 - Ibid., December 3, 1831. Beecher, Autobiography,
     vol. ii, p. 219.
22 - Protestant Magazine, July, 1834; New York Observer,
     July 12, 1834.

short time would be "shared between infidelity, popery
and impiety."[23]

Enthusiastic as these denunications were, they
lacked a tangible basis. Fears existed, but they were
nebulous and lost some of their force as a result. By
1834, however, the propagandists had found a definite
cause for alarm. In January of that year there appeared
in the New York Observer a great clamor regarding the
Leopold Foundation, which was branded a Romish organization formed with the express purpose of sending Catholics
to the United States in order to subdue the country and
stamp out the fair name of liberty.[24] The Protestant
Magazine was quick to sense the importance of this revelation. It took up the original cry[25] and enlarged it
until by July its readers were being informed that every
Catholic immigrant was sent to the West and told to settle
in a definite strategic spot by the directors of the Foundation in Vienna.[26]

The Leopold Foundation, about which Americans
grew excited in 1834, actually deserved little of the concern given it by Protestant periodicals. It was a mission-

23 - Protestant Episcopalian and Church Register, October,
     1833.
24 - New York Observer, January 18, 1834; January 25,
     1834, and ff.
25 - Protestant Magazine, February, 1834; March, 1834.
26 - Ibid., July, 1834.

ary society, formed in Vienna in 1829, to aid Catholic
missions in North America. Need for such a society
had long been felt by a number of the American hierarchy, and in 1828 Bishop Edward Fenwick of Cincinnati,
whose diocese contained many German Catholics, had sent
one of his priests, Father Rese, to Europe to recruit
financial aid and to take steps toward the formation
of a permanent society for this purpose.[27] At Munich
Father Rese appealed to King Louis I for aid, and the
ready reception which he received resulted in the formation of the Ludwigmissionsverein, a minor missionary
society that sent regular contributions to America for
many years thereafter.[28] It was at Vienna however, that
the real fruits of the trip were reaped. There Father
Rese's pleas came to the attention of the Archbishop
who brought the matter before the Austrian royal family.
Father Rese was granted an audience with the Emperor,
and together they agreed on the terms upon which the
new missionary society was to be launched, with the
emperor's brother, Archduke Rudolph, assuming the role
of patron.[29]

27- Catholic Encyclopedia, vol. xvi, p. 52.
28- Guilday, Life and Times of John England, vol. ii,
    pp. 182-183; O'Daniel, The Right Reverend Edward
    Dominic Fenwick, p. 265.
29- Catholic Encyclopedia, vol. xvi, p. 52.

Under the terms of this agreement, to which
the Pope gave his approval in April, 1829, the society
was to be known as the Leopold Association, in honor
of the deceased Empress of Brazil, Leopoldina, daughter
of Francis I and wife of Pedro I. Its chief source of
income was to be weekly contributions from its members,
who were limited to residents of Austria-Hungary. Each
member was pledged to offer daily prayers for the success
of the undertaking and to contribute five kreutzers, or
about two cents, each week, toward its support. A careful organization was perfected to collect the offerings,
the members being grouped into units of ten each, with
an appointed collector who received the gifts and turned
them over to the parish priest. The money then passed
through the many stages of the hierarchy until it reached
the central office in Vienna. By authority of Leo XII
certain indulgences were allowed members of the association in return for their gifts and their prayers.[30]

From the time of its inception the Leopold Association played an active part in the affairs of the American Catholic church. At first its contributions were
sent to Cincinnati, but within a short time all of the

[30] - The constitution of the Association is printed in
the American Catholic Historical Researches, n.s.,
vol. i, (October, 1905) pp. 314-316. See also
O'Daniel, The Right Rev. Edward Cominic Fenwick,
pp. 360-361.

bishoprics in the country were receiving its support.
Its contributions, however, were never large. In 1830,
34,000 florins were sent to the United States, from that
time to the Civil War the contributions ranged from
30,000 florins to 50,000 florins annually. Between 1829
and 1846 about 677,000 florins, or $330,000 were sent to
America through its efforts.[31]

Far more active and influential than the Leopold
Association, although strangely neglected by nativistic
writers, was a similar organization operating in France,
the Association de la Propagation de la Foi. This Association,formed in 1822 at Lyons, through the efforts of
the Bishop of New Orleans, directed its missionary efforts not to the United States alone, but to all heathen
and Protestant countries.[32] Its organization was similar
to the one adopted by the Leopold Association,[33] but from

31 - Payne, Raymond, "Annals of the Leopoldine Association,"
     Catholic Historical Review, vol. i, pp. 52-57. The
     yearly contributions of the society are listed in:
     Verwyst, P. C., Life and Labors of the Right Reverend
     Frederick Baroga (Milwaukee, 1900), pp. 454-456.
32 - Freri, Joseph, The Society for the Propagation of the
     Faith and Catholic Missions, 1822-1900 (Baltimore,
     1902), p. 58.
33 - Annales de l'Association de la Propagation de la Foi,
     recueil Periodiquedes lettres des eueques et des
     missionaries des missions des deux mondes, et de
     tous les documens relatifs aux missions et l'Asso-
     ciation de la Propagation de la Foi (Paris et Lyons,
     1827 ____), vol. i, p. 31. Contains the plan of
     organization and operation of the society.

the first it displayed greater activity in aiding
Catholicism in America. Receipts collected the
first year amounted to $4,000, two-thirds of which
was sent to the United States[34] and from that time
on they mounted rapidly. By 1831 the Catholic church
in the United States was receiving about $25,000 an-
nually from this source; in 1840 the sum had leaped
to $125,000.[35]

American Catholicism undoubtedly benefitted
greatly through the efforts of these societies. But
while the flow of wealth across the Atlantic stimulated
the building of new churches and missions, it also
heightened the antagonism that was fast mounting against
Catholicism. Americans leaped upon the published reports of bishops and priests in which they appealed for
money from one or the other of the associations, and
believed they found in them ample cause for alarm.[36]

34 - Ibid., vol. i, pp. 28-29.
35 - Freri, The Society for the Propagation of the Faith,
     pp. 27-28. Annual amounts sent to the United States
     by the society are listed in Guilday, Life and Times
     of John England, vol. ii, pp. 211-212.
36 - Reports of the Leopold Association and the Lyons'
     Propaganda were widely printed in American news-
     papers and made the basis for lengthy editorial
     comment. See: Protestant Magazine, February,1834;
     New York Observer, January 18, 1834; April 15,1837;
     November 25, 1837; December 2, 1837; Downfall of
     Babylon, August 29, 1835.

The Archbishop of Baltimore reported that he found a
praiseworthy curiosity about Catholicism on the part
of Protestants, and that with more priests he could
win many converts.[37] Bishop England stressed the need
of funds to prevent a rapid drifting of members away
from the Catholic church, pointing out in 1836 that
the Catholic population of the country was only
1,200,000 whereas the immigrants and children of immigrants should have amounted to 4,000,000.[38] The Bishop
of Baltimore pleaded for money to offset Protestant
fanaticism,[39] a cry that Bishop England echoed when he
wrote that so much harm had been done by the societies
in stimulating Protestant activity that unless Catholic
contributions were increased, the cause would be hurt
rather than strengthened.[40] Both associations appealed

37 - Annales de l'Association de la Propaganda de la Foi,
     vol. x, p. 494; Payne, Annals of the Leopoldine
     Association, p. 52.
38 - England, Works of John England, (1849 edition),
     vol. iii, p. 227. The feeling that the Catholic
     church was losing much by immigration to America
     was prevalent at the time, Bishop Reynolds of
     Charleston telling an Irish priest that he could
     do his greatest good for religion by preventing
     the Irish from coming to America. Dorchester,
     Christianity in the United States, (New York,
     1889), p. 618. Recent scholarship has questioned
     the accuracy of the estimates of losses of that
     time however. See American Catholic Historical
     Researches, n.s., vol. viii, p. 28.
39 - Annales de l'Association de la Propagation de la
     Foi, vol. x, p. 494.
40 - Bishop England to Central Council for the Propagation
     of the Faith at Lyons, September 1836, in England,
     Works of John England, (1849 edition), vol.iii, p.245.

for funds in Europe by reporting the chaos of American Protestantism[41] and by stressing the ignorance of the American Protestant clergymen.[42]

Appeals such as these, spread wholesale before American newspaper readers, were hardly destined to foster a spirit of kindly toleration toward Catholicism. Especially were antagonisms heightened by the realization that the work of these societies was effective. Catholicism appeared to outsiders, at least, as a flourishing and vigorous organization showing more strength than Protestantism. Harriet Martineau attributed the "prodigious increase" in the number of Catholics to the fact that they dispensed a mild, indulgent gospel in contrast to the harshness of the ascetic Protestant sects.[43] Captain Marryat thought that the Protestant cause was being weakened daily by the disunion and indifference of the churches, while Catholicism was "silently but surely advancing."[44]

---

41 - Annales de l'Association de la Propagation de la Foi, vol. iv, p. 655; vol. iii, p. 211, ff.
42 - Ibid., vol. i, p. 654. One writer said of American clergymen: "En Europe, un homme qui, quoique sans instruction, a cependant de la faconde, du verbiage, se fait charlaton; en Amerique, il se fait predicant."
43 - Martineau, Harriet, Society in America (London, 1837) vol. iii, p. 236.
44 - Marryat, F., A Diary in America (London, 1839), vol. iii, p. 157.

Here was a fanning breeze for the spark of intolerance in the breasts of nearly all American Protestants. The Catholics were making steady inroads through their great societies in Europe. A champion was needed to expose these societies, and show America their true purpose.

Protestants found that champion in Samuel F. B. Morse, who entered the ranks of the nativistic propagandists with a heritage that fitted him well for the work that he was to do. Son of the Reverend Jedediah Morse of Charlestown, famed Congregationalist divine and publisher of the Panapolist, Morse was descended from a distinguished line of educators and clergymen.[45] His father had experienced a flare of nativistic sentiment when the Bavarian Illuminati scare circulated throughout the country, and he had preached a sermon against such a menace in May, 1798.[46] Samuel Morse himself had been brought up with no more antipathy toward Catholicism and the immigrant than was usual for the son of a Congregationalist clergymen of the time, and through his early years as an inventor and artist had displayed no

45 - Trowbirdge, John, Samuel Finley Breese Morse (Boston, 1901), pp. 2-5.
46 - Stauffer, V., New England and the Bavarian Illuminati Columbia University Studies in History Economics and Public Law vol. 82, (New York, 1918) p. 279.

marked bigotry.[47] But in 1829 he sailed for Europe
to pursue his artistic inclinations, and in February,
1830, entered Rome in the midst of the celebrations
and ceremonies of a Holy Year.[48] It was this visit
to Rome that was to change Morse's entire point of
view and make him one of the most powerful of the
propaganda writers of the period.

At first Morse did not display this prejudice
that was to become so prominent a little later. His
Journals of his early months in Rome are filled with
glowing praise of the color and pageantry of the festi-
vals of the Holy Year which he was privileged to see.
He went from mass to procession and recorded his enthusiastic impressions in the discerning terms of an artist.[49] But in June, 1830, when he was watching a papal
procession, an event occurred which changed Morse's
rosy viewpoint. "I was standing," he wrote in his
Journal, "close to the side of the house when, in an
instant, without the slightest notice, my hat was struck
off to the distance of several yards by a soldier, or
rather by a patron in a soldier's costume, and this

47 - Trowbridge, Samuel Finley Breese Morse, pp. ix-xiv.
48 - Morse, Edward L. (editor) Samuel F. B. Morse, His
       Life and Journals (Boston, 1914), vol. 1, p. 339.
49 - Ibid., vol. 1, pp. 339 ff.

courteous manoeuvre was performed with his gun and
bayonet, accompanied with curses and taunts and the
expression of a demon on his countenance. In cases
like this there is no redress. The soldier received
his orders to see that all hats are off in this religion of force, and the manner is left to his discretion....The blame lies after all, not so much with the
pitiful wretch who perpetrates the outrage, as it does
with those who give him such base and indiscriminate
orders."[50]

When Morse picked up his hat from the dust
of the Roman street, he did so as an enthusiastic nativist and a bitter enemy of Catholicism. He continued
to visit masses and processions, but where before he
had admired with the eye of an esthete, now he scoffed
with the soul of a bigot.[51] It was with bitter antipathy
toward Rome that Morse turned his steps to the United
States in 1832. Just before he accepted a professor-
ship at New York University, this new found prejudice
was voiced. Morse penned a series of letters entitled
"A Foreign Conspiracy Against the Liberties of the
United States," published in the New York Observer

50 - Ibid., vol. i, p. 353.
51 - Compare the descriptions of processions before this
     incident in Ibid., pp. 339 ff. to the descriptions
     written afterwards.

over the signature of "Brutus." All his enthusiasm
against Rome was herein set forth.[52] Meeting with
an enthusiastic reception, they were published in
book form in the same year, and added one more vitriolic volume in the series of propaganda studies.

In writing his Foreign Conspiracy Morse
probably came under the influence of exposures of
the Leopold Foundation which had been made in the
New York Observer just at this time.[53] His own disclosures were centered about this organization, and
gave considerable weight to the vague fears which were
being felt by American nativists in connection with
foreign missionary societies. In the operations of
this foundation, Morse saw a great conspiracy against
the United States. He pointed out that an agent of
the Austrian government, Frederick Schlegel, had given
a series of lectures in Vienna in 1828 in which he showed
how monarchy and Catholicism were interdependent and how
both were opposed to the republicanism[54] which had its

52 - New York Observer, August 30, 1834 and ff. The
     last letter of the series appeared on November 22,
     1834; twelve being published in all. The editor
     recommended the letters to his readers as a start-
     ling disclosure of true facts.
53 - See above, pp. 254-255.
54 - Morse, Samuel F. B., Foreign Conspiracy Against the
     Liberties of the United States (5th edition, New
     York, 1841), pp. 15-19.

origins in North America.[55] In the very next year,
the Leopold Foundation, centered in Vienna, was formed.
This was no mere coincidence, in Morse's eyes. It was
all part of an insidious plot to wipe out republicanism
in America by means of Rome's bloody gold.

The *Foreign Conspiracy* demonstrated just why
such a plot should be launched. The beacon light of
liberty shed upon the old countries of Europe, and
especially upon despotic Austria, forced those countries either to stamp out the United States or to face
rebellion among their own people.[56] "How can it be
otherwise," Morse asked. "Will one born to think a
dungeon his natural home, learn through his grated
bars that man may be free, and not struggle to obtain
his liberty?"[57] Thus the only hope of the monarchies
of Europe was to crush the bloom of liberty of the
United States. These despotic countries had formed
a league for their own protection, the Holy Alliance,
and heading that league was Austria.[58] But Austria
could do nothing against the United States by itself,
so it had enlisted as ally that other great foe of

55 - Schlegel, F., The Philosophy of History Translated
     by J. G. Robertson, (London, 1835), vol. ii, p. 298.
56 - Morse, Foreign Conspiracy, p. 38.
57 - Ibid., p. 38.
58 - Ibid., pp. 43-46; 55-56.

liberty and republicanism, the Catholic church. Through
the Leopold Foundation, the doctrines of Popery were to
be spread over the United States until the freedom of
that country had bowed before the tyranny of Rome.[59]
That the Leopold Society was engaged in missionary efforts alone brought great scorn from Morse. "Is it
credible," he asked, "that the manufacturers of chains
for binding liberty in Europe, have suddenly become
benevolently concerned only for the religious welfare
of this Republican people? If this society be solely
for the propagation of the Catholic faith, one would
think that Rome, and not Vienna should be its headquarters, that the Pope, not the Emperor of Austria, should
be its grand patron!"[60]

Having outlined this nefarious plot, Morse went
ahead to instruct the people in methods which might be
used in thwarting the designs of Popish despots. He
urged Protestants to drop their religious differences
and unite against the common enemy,[61] to bar Catholics
from political office,[62] to stop Romish schools from
springing up over the land,[63] to change the immigration
laws and check the entrance of Catholic serfs,[64] and es-

59 - Ibid., p. 19; 41.
60 - Ibid., p. 42.
61 - Ibid., pp. 64-68.
62 - Ibid., p. 74; 112-113.
63 - Ibid., p. 106.
64 - Ibid., pp. 71-73.

pecially to change the naturalization laws so that the servants of despotism would no longer have the power of the ballot box.[65] "We must first stop this leak in the ship," he wrote, "through which the muddy waters from without threaten to sink us."[66]

But especially did Samuel Morse in his _Foreign Conspiracy_ plead for immediate action from his countrymen. "Must we wait for a formal declaration of war?" he asked. "The serpent has already commenced his coil about our limbs, and the lethargy of his poison is creeping over us; shall we be more sensible of the torpor that has fastened upon our vitals?...Because no foe is on the sea, no hostile armies on our plains, may we sleep securely? Shall we watch only on the outer walls, while the sappers and miners of foreign despots are at work under our feet and steadily advancing beneath the very citadel?"[67] With this impassioned plea Morse rested his case.

The reception given the _Foreign Conspiracy_ was greater than the most optimistic anticipation of the author. The _Downfall of Babylon_ sang its praises and asked the readers if they were prepared to stand "like

65 - _Ibid._, p. 143.
66 - _Ibid._, p. 143.
67 - _Ibid._, pp. 99-100.

sheep pent up in a corner by ravenous wolves and wait to be devoured?"[68] Even the ambitious task of reproducing the whole book in serial form was begun by this paper.[69] The Christian Spectator also reprinted much of the book, and praised it for "awakening the minds of home born Americans to some of the evils resulting from the increase of foreign immigration among us."[70] The Protestant Magazine hailed the work with enthusiasm and began reprinting it for its own readers.[71] A number of "Patriotic Associations" in the West paid to have extracts inserted in a Western religious publication, the Valley of the Mississippi.[72] A group of Boston ministers urged its reproduction in Zion's Herald,[73] and the Boston Recorder hoped that it would be "widely circulated and attentively read."[74] The first part of this wish was certainly fulfilled, for a second edition was announced only a short while after the first had left the presses[75] and a new edition was required annually for sometime.[76] Refutations by Catholics, includ-

---

68 - Downfall of Babylon, March 7, 1835.
69 - Ibid., May 30, 1835 and ff.
70 - Christian Spectator, June, 1835.
71 - Protestant Magazine, July, 1834.
72 - Morse, Foreign Conspiracy, p. i (preface)
73 - Ibid., p. i.
74 - Ibid., p. ii.
75 - New York Observer, April 11, 1835.
76 - A fifth edition appeared in 1841.

ing an address before the Georgia convention by Bishop
John England in which he denied the existence of such
a plot went unheeded,[77] and the second edition of the
Foreign Conspiracy appeared with the proud boast that
the operations of the Leopold Foundation had not been
denied and therefore must be considered as true.[78]

Such popularity made it inevitable that the
Foreign Conspiracy should not be the last of Morse's
nativistic works. Before the second edition had been
issued, he had rushed a new series of letters into being,
a series that was printed in the New York Journal of Commerce during 1835 under the imposing title, "Imminent
Dangers to the Free Institutions of the United States
through Foreign Immigration," and appeared in book form
immediately afterward.[79] If Imminent Dangers added little
to the outline of the Romish conspiracy which Morse had
already set forth, it served to clarify and point out how
this conspiracy was to be carried to completion. America
was pictured by the despotic nations of Europe as "the
poison fountain whence flow all the deadly evils which

77 - Guilday, Life and Times of John England, vol. ii,
pp. 209-210.
78 - Morse, Foreign Conspiracy, p. 12. The Preface to
the second edition is also reprinted in the fifth
edition.
79 - Morse, Samuel F. B., Imminent Dangers to the Free
Institutions of the United States through Foreign
Immigration (New York, 1835)

threatened their existence."[80] To stop this, he stated,
Catholic immigrants were being sent to America under
the control of Jesuit priests.[81] Austria needed only
to place these Popish puppets in control of the government and her victory would be won, for Romanism and liberty were at opposite poles and never could be reconciled.
'If she succeeds in fastening upon us the chains of papal
bondage," Morse warned, "she has a people as fit for any
yoke she pleases to grace our necks withal as any slaves
over whom she now holds her despotic rod."[82] And he
painted a dismal picture which showed that Austria had
chosen just the proper instrument to overthrow American
liberty, for armies and navies could avail her nothing
against the strength of the Western World.[83]

The conclusion of _Imminent Dangers_ summed up
the entire story of the plot which Morse had conceived
in one last outburst of eloquence: "They have already
sent their chains, and oh! to our shame be it spoken,
are fastening them upon a sleeping victim. Americans,
you are marked for their prey not by foreign bayonets,
but by weapons surer of effecting the conquest of liberty, than all the munitions of physical combat in the

80 - _Ibid._, p. 8.
81 - _Ibid._, pp. 9-17.
82 - _Ibid._, p. 29.
83 - _Ibid._, pp. 29-30.

military or naval storehouses of Europe. Will you not awake to the apprehension of the reality and extent of your danger? Will you be longer deceived by the pensioned Jesuits, who having surrounded your press, are now using it all over the country to stifle the cries of danger, and lull your fears by attributing your alarm to a false cause? Up! Up! I beseech you. Awake! To your posts! Let the tocsin sound from Maine to Louisiana. Fly to protect the vulnerable places in your constitution and laws. Place your guards; you will need them, and quickly too. And first shut your gates."[84]

While the Imminent Dangers was not as successful as Morse's first publication, not having reached a second edition until 1854,[85] these two ventures had convinced their author of the worth of nativistic propaganda. He had expounded his original thesis as thoroughly as was possible and so he cast about for a new topic. Aid in this quest came from an unexpected quarter. In the autumn of 1835 Morse was startled to have a young man call at his home and ask if he were addressing the author of the Foreign Conspiracy. After Morse had assured

84 - Ibid., p. 25.
85 - Morse, Samuel F. B., Imminent Dangers to the Free Institutions of the United States through Foreign Immigration (New York, 1854)

him that he was the same, the young man then introduced himself as Lewis Clausing, and stated that he
had written an exposé of the Jesuits which he wanted
Morse to read. Haste was imperative, said Mr. Clausing,
for the Jesuits were pursuing him, and any day they
might capture and kill him.[86] Morse, of course, agreed
to read the treatise and found it excellent. Clausing
told him a fantastic story, of student life in Germany,
of a murder which he had committed in a duel, of how
he had fled the country with the Jesuits following
him and of how the Jesuits had pursued him ever since.[87]
Even Morse was forced to admit that the young man was
suffering from illusions, but he insisted that they
were caused by the way the Jesuits had treated him in
his early life.[88] The Jesuit hallucination continued
to persecute Clausing, despite his friendship with such
a champion of Protestantism as Morse, and in July, 1836,
he was finally driven to suicide on the streets of New
York City.[89]

86 - Morse, Samuel F. B., The Proscribed German Student,
     being a Sketch of some Interesting Incidents in the
     Life and Death of Lewis Clausing; to which is added;
     A Treatise on the Jesuits, a Posthumous Work of
     Lewis Clausing. (New York, 1836) pp. 7-9.
87 - Ibid., pp. 9-50.
88 - Ibid., p. 55.
89 - New York Observer, July 23, 1836; Downfall of Babylon,
     July 23, 1836.

With Clausing dead, Morse hurried to take
advantage of the publicity surrounding his death and
rushed from the presses not only a story of Clausing's
life but also his treatise of the Jesuits, a work which
appeared under the title, The Proscribed German Student,
being a Sketch of Some Interesting Incidents in the Life
and Death of Lewis Clausing; to which is added: A Treatise on the Jesuits, a Posthumous Work of Lewis Clausing.[90]
Devoted largely to Clausing's "Treatise," the work offered
an interesting example of its author's diseased mind and
at the same time added another biting bit of propaganda
to the increasing list. Clausing was bitter in his statements; he reiterated Morse's warnings of a plot by European despots to take over the United States and insisted
that the Jesuits were the spies sent out by this organization to prepare the way.[91] He described how they operated
in disguise in private families and through the confessional,[92] and he grew frantic in regard to the way in
which the members of the Society of Jesus were securing
control of the educational systems of the nation.[93] "In-

90 - Published in New York in the fall of 1836.
91 - Morse, The Proscribed German Student, pp. 189-190;
     233-236.
92 - Ibid., pp. 202-217.
93 - Ibid., pp. 132-134.

numerable bayonets wait for occupation," Clausing
warned, "Now they have time, and tremble freemen
of America! They know perfectly well how to use
it."[94]

While Morse was adding this book to his
already mounting library of nativistic writings,
Maria Monk's opus had been given to the world and
was causing its flare of excitement in New York.
The next book that Morse produced shows how well he
had learned the lesson taught by the popularity of
the Awful Disclosures. It was well enough to expose
great plots, but for really large sales and many converts, a pornographic accent was necessary. It is
not surprising that his next work, appearing in 1837,
was entitled, Confessions of a French Priest, to which
are added Warnings to the People of the United States.[95]

Actually these Confessions were a little disappointing. The French priest remains quietly in the
background. Nowhere in the book is his name mentioned
and Morse hints in a preface that this is necessary,
since the author might come to an untimely end at the

94 - Ibid., pp. 188-189.
95 - Morse, Samuel F. B., Confessions of a French Priest,
     to which are added Warnings to the People of the
     United States (New York, 1837)

hands of the Jesuits should his identity be discovered.[96] This anonymous prelate tells his life
story and the story of priestly iniquity. The first
few pages describe the methods used by priests in
seducing young girls in the confessional; in training them from childhood for the sacrifice by words
and actions.[97] Having thus assured himself of an
attentive audience, the author tells the story of
his life; of his entrance into the priesthood in
France, his undergoing all the torments attendant
upon the rule of celibacy and the scoffing attitude
of other priests when his flesh refused to weaken.[98]
He tells of a love affair which drove him to drinking
poison, studying Greek and finally entering a LaTrappe
monastry. The failure of these palliatives in the relief of his spirit, and of the final decision through
a study of the Bible that celibacy was wrong and that
he could marry the girl after all concludes this episode.[99] Having finished the autobiography the author
evidently found himself with only one hundred and two
pages filled and the necessity of more stuffing. A

96 - Ibid., pp. v-vii.
97 - Ibid., pp. 2-6.
98 - Ibid., pp. 7-24.
99 - Ibid., pp. 25-102.

rambling account of Catholic cermonies and creeds
was added, giving some entertaining sidelights on
the moral qualities of French priests. The process
of seduction through the confessional was described
at some length although with a disappointing lack of
detail.[100] So, too, was the practice of priests keeping regular mistresses under the guise of cousins.[101]
But too much could not be expected from a work super-
vised by Samuel Morse. His Puritan upbringing would
not allow him to become a vender of obscenity comparable
to Maria Monk.

The Confessions of a French Priest was the
last of Morse's nativistic publications. While not as
popular as his Foreign Conspiracy it was well received,
and widely reprinted.[102] He remained an ardent nativist
for many years, although his later day bigotry was to
find expression in political nativism rather than in
the production of propaganda.[103]

100 - Ibid., pp. 103-111.
101 - Ibid., pp. 115-143.
102 - New York Observer, October 7, 1837.
103 - As late as 1854 Morse, as Democratic candidate
      for Congress, stated that his views on immigra-
      tion and Catholicism were expressed in his Foreign
      Conspiracy. Morse, Samuel F. B. Morse, vol. ii,
      p. 332. For a study of these political activities
      of Morse, as well as his nativistic writings, see
      Conners, Francis John, "Samuel Finley Breese Morse
      and the anti-Catholic Political Movements in the
      United States," Illinois Catholic Historical Re-
      view, vol. x, (October, 1927), pp. 83-122.

But while his pen no longer flowed, the
stream of propaganda which he had started swelled
to new proportions. His ideas proved popular; the
threatened Catholic plot to stamp out the United
States and destroy liberty was a thing which touched
the average American in a vital spot. Writers, realizing this, leaped to continue the legend which
Morse had introduced and to enlarge upon it to a
considerable extent in succeeding years.

Foremost among the group which realized the
effectiveness of this type of propaganda was the Reverend Lyman Beecher, whose pulpit shouts had aided
in the destruction of the Charlestown convent. Dr.
Beecher had been interested in the West for some time.
As early as the summer of 1830 he had written of the
importance of the Mississippi Valley in the religious
life of the country. "The moral destiny of our nation,"
he said, "and all our institutions and hopes, and the
world's hopes, turn on the character of the West, and
the competition is now for that of preoccupancy in the
education of the rising generation, in which Catholics
and infidels have got the start on us."[104] Beecher

104 - Beecher to his daughter Catherine, July 8, 1830.
    Beecher, Autobiography, vol. ii, p. 224.

felt so strongly on the matter at that time that he
was seriously contemplating moving to Cincinnati to
throw his weight on the side of Protestantism.[105] His
wishes were destined to immediate fulfillment. Before
the year was out he had received a call to become president of Lane Theological Seminary at Cincinnati, and
with this opportunity before him he packed his bags
and departed to battle the Pope for possession of this
garden spot of the world.[106]

Four years at Cincinnati only served to convince Beecher that his preconceived notions were correct
and that Protestants must put up a valiant battle to
protect the West from the minions of Rome. In 1835 he
gave those conclusions to the world in a much read volume entitled A Plea for the West.[107]

This nativistic outburst by Beecher took up
the Morse tradition and enlarged upon it in magnificent
fashion. Agreeing with Morse that the Catholic church
was dying out in Europe and must transfer its dominions
to the United States in order to survive,[108] he warned
that a direct declaration of war by Austria could have
made her design upon America no more apparent.[109] This

---

105 - Ibid., vol. ii, p. 225.
106 - Ibid., vol. ii, p. 249.
107 - Beecher, Lyman, A Plea for the West (Cincinnati,
1835)
108 - Ibid., pp. 52-53; 117.
109 - Ibid., p. 130.

design, said Beecher, was clearly demonstrated by the
rapid growth of Catholicism,[110] by European capitalists
transferring their funds to American lands,[111] and by
the great flood of Popish immigrants swarming into the
country.[112] "Clouds like the locuts of Egypt are rising
from the hills and plains of Europe," he said, "and on
the wings of every wind, are coming over to settle down
upon your fair fields."[113] This was all part of a great
designing scheme in the eyes of Dr. Beecher, for in this
belief the entire Mississippi Valley had been mapped and
plotted in the Vatican itself.[114] And the stream of
immigrants he saw only as "trains of powder between the
enemies' camp and our own magazine, which, though laid
by accident, may not be expected long to escape obser-
vation and use."[115]

In these arguments Beecher was furrowing soil
already well plowed by Morse, whom he quoted as basis
for many statements.[116] Beecher was an educator, and
it was natural that he should see in Catholic schools
a grave menace to the liberties of the United States.

110 - Ibid., pp. 125-126.
111 - Ibid., p. 73.
112 - Ibid., p. 55.
113 - Ibid., pp. 72-73.
114 - Ibid., pp. 55-56.
115 - Ibid., p. 115.
116 - Ibid., pp. 153-159.

Here, in his eyes, was the method by which Rome was
attempting to subvert America. Priests were establishing schools throughout the West to attract Protestant
children and convert them to the errors of Popery. Do
the priests, he asked, "tax their own people and suppli-
cate the royal munificence of Catholic Europe to rear
schools and colleges for the cheap and even gratuitous
education of Protestant children, high and low, - while
thousands of Catholic children are utterly neglected
and uncared for, and abandoned to ignorance and vice?
And is all this without design?"[117] To Beecher, of
course, the design was obvious, and he insisted that
Protestant children though not converted could not come
in contact with Catholic teachers without being corrupted.[118] Alleged statements of priests that this
was actually the design of the Catholic church were
cited with glee,[119] and Beecher ended with a passion-
ate plea that Protestant schools in the West be supported rather than allow the nation to fall into the
hands of the Pope through the inroads of immigration
and education.[120]

117 - Ibid., p. 99.
118 - Ibid., p. 98.
119 - Ibid., p. 107; 120.
120 - Ibid., p. 182.

The Plea for the West was hailed with enthusiasm by most of the religious papers and magazines
in America as soon as it appeared, reviews in the Christian Review,[121] the Christian Spectator,[122] the New York
Observer[123] and other prominent journals praised it
highly. The editor of the Western Monthly Magazine,
published in Cincinnati, attempted to defend the Catholic point of view and to refute Beecher's arguments,
but this stand aroused so much opposition from subscribers that he was forced to resign his post.[124]

Such reception convinced other authors that
Popish schools were worthy of investigation and there
followed a deluge of revelations in religious papers
exposing conversions that had resulted from the operations of Catholic schools in the West. The St. Louis
Observer was more outspoken than Beecher in its denunciation[125] and even such a secular paper as the Cincinnati
Journal listed Catholic schools throughout the West and
claimed that their true purpose was to gain converts.[126]
The New York Observer added its enthusiastic voice to

121 - Christian Review, June, 1836.
122 - Christian Spectator, 1835, pp. 481-503.
123 - New York Observer, June 20, 1835.
124 - Mott, History of American Magazines, p. 597.
125 - Quoted in New York Observer, July 26, 1834.
126 - Quoted in New York Observer, March 14, 1835.

these warnings.[127] The Downfall of Babylon enlarged
upon the plot by insisting that all tuition money paid
to Romish schools went to buy church land in the Mississippi Valley, and that in a short time Catholics would
own two-thirds of America, just as they possessed two-
thirds of Italy.[128]

With the suppression of the Jesuits in Spain
in 1835, new evidence was given the propagandists of a
Popish plot afoot. News of the suppression was widely
published in America[129] and a burst of alarm flared as
a result. "Whither can they fly?" asked the editors
of the Downfall of Babylon, "Whither but to our own
devoted country?"[130] The danger thus sounded was re-
echoed throughout the land and only increased the agitation.[131] The New York Observer added to its reputation by securing and publishing annual reports of the
Leopold Foundation exposing its sinister purposes.[132]

127 - Ibid., February 28, 1835; November 25, 1837.
128 - Downfall of Babylon, March 28, 1835.
129 - New York Observer, September 19, 1835.
130 - Downfall of Babylon, September 26, 1835.
131 - New York Observer, September 20, 1834; January
      23, 1836.
132 - Ibid., April 15, 1837; November 25, 1837; December
      2, 1837. The Downfall of Babylon expressed the
      belief that the New York Observer had done limit-
      less good to the United States by these exposures.
      Downfall of Babylon, August 29, 1835.

The press as a whole bristled with statistics re-
citing the threatening growth of Catholicism and the
rapid influx of Catholic immigrants,[133] the whole
movement being linked with the Leopold Foundation
by many of the editors.[134] While some effort was
made to call attention to the Association for the
Propagation of the Faith,[135] the precedent established
by Morse which placed all blame on the Austrian society
still remained the keynote of nativistic disturbance.

The writers who were thus pouring out warnings did not lessen their hold on the pen. They added
tales of the dread consequences to the people of the
United States should Popery extend its foul sway to
American shores. Romanism, they said, had ever been
hostile to Republicanism,[136] and principles of mon-

133 - American Quarterly Register, quoted in New York
Observer, September 20, 1834; Connecticut Observer, quoted in Ibid., June 29, 1833; National Intelligencer, March 21, 1835; New York
Journal of Commerce, quoted in Downfall of
Babylon, August 8, 1835; Downfall of Babylon,
January 3, 1835; July 4, 1835.
134 - Downfall of Babylon, July 23, 1836; Supplement
to Six Months in a Convent, pp. 200-201.
135 - Downfall of Babylon, February 20, 1836.
136 - Protestant Vindicator, November 4, 1835; Downfall of Babylon, October 20, 1834; February 7,
1835; August 27, 1835; Supplement to Six Months
in a Convent, pp. 11-13; Schmucker, S. S., Discourses in Commemoration of the Glorious Reformation of the Sixteenth Century (3d edition,
New York, 1838), pp. 123-124.

archy would be enforced even among liberty loving
Americans.[137] What matter that high churchmen disavowed any such intention? They had been trained
to keep no faith with heretics.[138] The ordinary
Catholics disavowed any plot because they had not
been told its secrets,[139] but when the time was ripe
the Pope could release them from their oath of allegiance and send them to carry the torch of Romanism
and despotism among Protestants.[140] Labored arguments
by many writers showed that this was inevitable; that
the Pope claimed temporal power and always had claimed
temporal power; that he would exert it over the new
world as soon as he had the power to strike.[141]

And when this time came, these authors shouted,
the Inquisition would be established on American shores
and converts to Popery made by flame and sword.[142] Already

137 - Spirit of '76, September 9, 1835.
138 - Schmucker, Discourse in Commemoration of the Glo-
      rious Reformation, pp. 126-128.
139 - Ibid., p. 125.
140 - Protestant Vindicator, October 21, 1835.
141 - New York Observer, November 1, 1835; Schmucker,
      Discourse in Commemoration of the Glorious Refor-
      mation, pp. 115-117; pp. 99-101; pp. 101-109;
      White, Practical and Internal Evidence, pp. 37-
      63; pp. 74-78; Danunou, Pierre, C. F., Outlines
      of a History of the Court of Rome and of the
      Temporal Power of the Popes (Philadelphia, 1837),
      pp. iii-iv; pp. ix-xi.
142 - Ellis, D. F., A History of the Romish Inquisition
      Compiled from Various Authors (Hanover, Indiana,
      1835), pp. 1-12. Having stated the dire consequences
      of Rome's conquest of America, the author stresses
      his argument by giving examples of the work of the
      Inquisition in other countries, pp. 13-120.

Catholics were preparing for this day, preparing by
attacking Protestants in the West[143] and in driving
Protestant missionaries away from Indiana.[144] Even
the slaves were being lured to the side of Catholicism, Americans were warned, to be used when the
time came to overthrow the country.[145] Tangible
evidence of such a plot was produced when Bishop
John England established a school for slaves in
Charleston. Newspapers voiced their anger,[146] and
sentiment was so strong that the school was ultimately closed.[147] Even more startling evidence, in
the minds of editors of religious papers, came in the
organization of Irish military companies in 1835.
It was charged that the bishops were sponsoring their
work,[148] that the foreigners intended to march on the
ballot boxes to secure their ends[149] and that American
liberties were being flaunted.[150] The Downfall of
Babylon prophesied that the crisis had arrived and
that unless these armed Papists were disbanded at

143 - Downfall of Babylon, August 14, 1834.
144 - Ibid., March 5, 1836.
145 - New York Observer, December 27, 1834; February
28, 1835.
146 - Ibid., April 11, 1835.
147 - Guilday, Life and Times of John England, vol. ii,
pp. 151-156.
148 - Mason, Cyrus, A History of the Holy Catholic Inquisition, (Philadelphia, 1835), pp. vii-viii.
149 - Spirit of '76, September 8, 1835.
150 - Ibid., September 5, 1835; September 10, 1835.

once there would soon be one hundred thousand of them
in the country, enough to use in securing its conquest .
for the Pope.[151]

But it was the immigrant who was objected to
most of all, and it was the constant stream of immigration which proved the greatest problem to nativistic agitators. Even the Protestant aliens were pictured as Jesuits in disguise,[152] and the foreign criminals who, it was charged, were being sent by European
nations were only dispatched to weaken America and make
the conquest easier.[153] The New York Observer by 1839
had lost all doubt that these immigrants were sent by
organized design[154] and the Protestant Vindicator ad-
monished its readers that such Papal serfs, even in
this country, could never be free for:

> Rome's true minions chain them down,
> In ignorance from heel to crown;
> In hopes, perchance, that when the Pope,
> Is forced from Europe to elope,
> He here may find a sovereign throne;
> And ready serfs to bend and groan.[155]

The editor of the Downfall of Babylon, Samuel

151 - Downfall of Babylon, September 19, 1835.
152 - Spirit of '76, August 4, 1835.
153 - Downfall of Babylon, June 11, 1836.
154 - New York Observer, September 14, 1839.
155 - Protestant Vindicator, January 20, 1841.

FLIGHT of POPERY from ROME to the WEST.

B. Smith, was among the most outspoken in his denunciation of this Catholic plot. Throughout 1835 his paper
was devoted to new exposures,[156] and by the end of the
year he was ready to capitalize on the excitement which
he had helped create. The remuneration took the form of
a booklet bearing the imposing title, The Flight of Popery
from Rome to the West,[157] and was published in part in
the Downfall of Babylon late in 1835 and separately the
next year.[158] It consisted largely of an elaborate drawing
depicting the Pope with all his cardinals sailing majes-
tically across the Atlantic, together with a few pages
of foreboding.[159] This little book was widely circulated
and important in influence. Smith saw only the most
dire consequences of the Catholic plot. "Beloved fellow
citizens," he warned, "listen to the voice of prudence,
ere the shrieks of freedom strike upon your ear. Every
Romish temple that rises in the West, will swell the
Jubilee of Popish triumph, till the day rolls on, when
the distant Valley of the West will toll the death of
our Republic."[160]

This agitation on the part of Morse and his

156 - Downfall of Babylon, May 9, 1835.
157 - Smith, Samuel B., The Flight of Popery from Rome
to the West (New York, 1836)
158 - Downfall of Babylon, December 12, 1835 and ff.
159 - Smith, Flight of Popery, p. 3.
160 - Ibid., p. 3.

followers naturally brought the problem of Catholicism
in the West to the organization that had the most concern with that region, the American Home Missionary
Society. Increased interest in the activity of this
society in the period when anti-Catholic propaganda
of this nature was being circulated is well reflected
in the increase in donations to its coffers, leaping
from $18,140 in 1827 to $101,565 in 1836, an effect
caused in part at least by fear of Popery in the
Mississippi Valley.[161] Agents of the society in the
West kept the matter before its members constantly,
frequently referring to Catholic activities in the
building of new schools and churches and convents.[162]
Especially were members of the society alarmed at the
increase in Catholic schools in the West. "Foreign
Papists," the Board of Directors reported, "are planting our fairest territories thick with their schools.
Colony after colony of men of a strange tongue and
stranger associations are possessing themselves of
our soil and gathering around our ballot boxes."[163]
This rapid migration was seen as "baneful to the civil

161 - Davis, The Half Century, p. 319.
162 - Goodykoontz, The Home Missionary Movement, p. 295.
163 - American Home Missionary Society, Annual Report
        for 1842.

freedom and religious well being of unnumbered thousands"[164] and while the society welcomed the Catholic
immigrants that it might convert them[165] it was on
the whole doubtful of the value of such conversions.[166]
The publication of the society, The Home Missionary devoted much space to the danger of Popery, giving detailed
statements on Catholic schools in the Mississippi Valley[167]
and on immigration as it developed.[168] "The Apocalptic
Beast," it warned, "is watching with intense anxiety, and
straining his eyeballs for a favorable moment to spring
in upon us with one immense bound and make us his prey.
Rome has more men, more money, more cunning and more per-
severance than we have. Rome never stops short of universal victory or universal defeat."[169]

Organizations similar to the American Home Missionary Society, formed throughout the eastern part of
the United States to care for religious needs in the West,
also gave much of their attention to the menace of Romanism. The Ladies Society for the Promotion of Education
at the West, looked with dread upon convent schools and

164 - Ibid., Annual Report for 1842.
165 - Ibid., Annual Report for 1842.
166 - Ibid., Annual Report for 1842.
167 - The Home Missionary, April, 1842.
168 - Ibid., July, 1842.
169 - Ibid., June, 1844.

applauded the Reverend Lyman Beecher with enthusiasm
when he sketched for their benefit the result of such
educational systems.[170] The Boston Ladies Society for
Evangelizing the West expressed grave fears in its
annual reports should the Catholic Germans in the Mississippi Valley remain unconverted to "Christianity."[171]
The Reverend Leonard Bacon voiced the point of view of
the members of the Society for the Promotion of Collegiate and Theological Education at the West when he pictured the Jesuit educator as "gliding with sinuous motion
to what he with the wisdom of the serpent, recognized as
the true seat of power in such a country," the schools.[172]
Thus was every organization which concerned itself with
the future of the interior valley, firmly convinced that
Catholicism must be battled in the West to save the whole
United States from Papal control.

The seeds of propaganda sown by writers, clergy,
newspapers and societies found a fertile field in the minds
of the American people. The works of Samuel Morse and his
disciples were believed and little or no doubt was cast on

170 - History of the Formation of the Ladies Society for
the Promotion of Education at the West; with Two
Addresses, delivered at its Organization, by the
Rev. Edward Beecher, D. D., and the Rev. E. N.
Kirk (Boston, 1846), p. 7.
171 - Boston Ladies Association for Evangelizing the
West, Annual Report for 1844, (Boston, 1844)
pp. 10 ff.
172 - Society for the Promotion of Collegiate and Theological Education at the West, Annual Report for 1845,
(New York, 1845), p. 23.

their authenticity. Americans of this period felt due
cause for alarm. In looking about them they found evidence of the plot Morse had outlined. About them they
saw a fast mounting flood of immigration pouring into
the country and disrupting all the old forms of life
to which they had been accustomed. That immigration,
combined with the agitation of the nativistic writers,
was destined to provoke the first political outburst
of No Popery in the latter years of the 1830's.

Immigration had been increasing steadily in
the years after 1830. Official census returns showed
that 84,066 aliens had landed upon American shores in
1840 in marked contrast to the 23,322 who had come ten
years earlier.[173] More than half a million foreigners
had come in that decade[174] and while this number constituted only about three per cent of the total population
in 1840[175] it was generally recognized both at the time
and since that the immigration figures were nearly fifty
per cent below the actual number of arrivals.[176]

This condition, alarming enough as it seemed,
was made doubly important when the Panic of 1837 swept

173 - Kennedy, Preliminary Report on the Eighth Census,
      pp. 13-14.
174 - Ibid., p. 14; Bromwell, History of Immigration,
      p. 16.
175 - DeBow's Compendium of the Seventh Census, p. 49.
176 - Ibid., p. 122; Condon, Irish Immigration to the
      United States, p. 82.

over the country. Prosperity vanished, and Americans
were made acutely conscious of the burdens placed upon
them by this alien influx. The competition between
immigrant and native American labor was strangely neglected at the time. Nativistic literature, objecting
to the alien on nearly every other score, failed to
mention this phase of the immigration problem. With
such unbounded resources and so vast an amount of internal improvements needed even the most ardent opponents of the alien failed to picture him as a dangerous
competitor for the American workman.[177] The colossal
task of bridging the American continent with roads and
canals afforded ample work for all comers.[178]

But on this score alone the foreigner escaped.
The panic of 1837 did serve to make Americans acutely
conscious of the burden of pauper support placed upon
their shoulders by the alien invasion. On this economic

177 - A single exception to this is an article in the
New York Observer, January 31, 1835, complaining
that Catholics purchased marble for their cathe-
drals from Italy when American marble should be
used to keep American workmen employed.
178 - A student of the economic effects of immigration
has come to the conclusion that there was no serious competition between native and immigrant
workmen before 1870. The natives controlled the
economic resources of the country and were in a
position to assign to the immigrant laborers
the work that they did not want to do. Page,
Thomas W., "Some Economic Aspects of Immigration
before 1870," Journal of Political Economy, vol.
xxi (January, 1913), p. 53.

phase were the cries of nativistic writers centered,
and with poverty stalking the land in the wake of
the financial crash, they found enthusiastic listeners.

There was some justification for the chorus
of objection that arose. The English Poor Law of 1834
empowered owners and rate payers to raise money on the
security of the poor rates to aid emigration, a law
that was extended to Ireland four years later.[179] While
the law specified that paupers assisted in this way
should be sent to British colonies, the majority of
them going to Canada eventually found their way to the
United States, not only because the social Irish nature desired more companionship than the wilds of Canada afforded, but because a heavy head money tax was exacted in that colony.[180] The natural migration streams
toward New England continued to flow with increasing
rapidity through the operation of the New Brunswick
lumber trade which grew in volume at this time[181] as
well as by direct contact with England and Ireland.
Most of the immigrants of that section came from these

179 - Hall, Prescott F., Immigration (New York, 1907),
      p. 29; Hitchins, Colonial Land and Emigration
      Commission, pp. 14-15; Smith, R. Mayo, Emigra-
      tion and Immigration (New York, 1895), p. 173.
180 - Haynes, G. H., "The Causes of Know Nothing Suc-
      cess in Massachusetts," American Historical Re-
      view, vol. iii, (October, 1897), p. 70.
181 - Abbott, Immigration, p. 25.

countries, as New England had no direct ship connec-
tions with Germany.[182]

      With the coming of these immigrants, many
of them destitute or so broken with disease on the
poorly kept lumber ships[183] that they were unable
to care for themselves, a heavy burden was placed
on the pauper relief facilities of New England and
the middle states. In 1832 there were 613 immigrants
and only 340 natives in the South Boston almshouse[184]
Three years later a survey conducted by the city
government of Boston showed 4,786 native paupers and
5,303 foreign paupers in the almshouses of New York,
Philadelphia, Boston and Baltimore.[185] The Massachusetts legislature was so alarmed at this situation
that it considered establishing separate workhouses
for aliens, but such a bill was not enacted at that
time.[186] New York City was forced to spend $279,999
in 1837 to support its poor, and three-fifths of those
receiving aid were of foreign birth.[187] There were in
the country as a whole at this time 105,000 paupers,

182 - Haynes, Causes of Know Nothing Success, p. 71.
183 - Abbott, Immigration, p. 25. Conditions on these
     ships are vividly described in Niles Register,
     September 27, 1834.
184 - Adams, James T., New England in the Republic,
     (Boston, 1927), p. 334.
185 - New York Observer, October 3, 1835.
186 - Ibid., March 28, 1835.
187 - Ibid., March 3, 1838.

more than half of whom were immigrants. It was estimated that each pauper required $42 from the public
funds for his support, a situation that meant that
American taxpayers were paying nearly $4,400,000
each year for this purpose.[188] There is little wonder that nativistically inclined citizens, with tax
rates rising to support Europe's poor and with in-
comes dwindling before the onslaught of the depression, shouted against the immigrant with renewed
vigor.

Especially did agitation mount when rumor
spread that many European countries were disregarding
international comity and shipping their paupers to
America in an effort to escape the burden of their
support. There seems to be little doubt that while
most of the countries of the world frowned on such
a practice, individual towns and parishes did not
hesitate to relieve themselves of their poor whenever possible. Newspapers had occasionally reported
the arrival of paupers[189] and criminals[190] that had

[188] - House of Representatives, Reports of Committees,
25th Cong., 2nd Sess., No. 1040, p. 3.
[189] - Niles Register, January 19, 1839; New York Observer, January 19, 1839. The paupers were
reported as still wearing their workhouse uni-
forms when they landed at New York, New York
Observer, March 1, 1834.
[190] - New York Observer, June 2, 1838; House Reports
of Committees, 25th Congress, 2nd Sess., No.
1040, p. 51.

been sent in this way and when American consuls abroad investigated the situation they found a surprising large number of towns and parishes engaging in the practice. In the British possession of Jamaica a law passed in 1831 required that every ship stopping there should carry away a number of paupers, a law that was only repealed after vigorous objections by the American consul.[191] The consul at London reported that immigrants sent out under the Poor Law of 1834 frequently were sent to the United States, 191 going there in the past year in addition to the thousands who were landed in Canada and immediately crossed the border.[192] Criminals were reported as being sent from Hesse Cassel, and the American representative at Liverpool stated that ninety per cent of the paupers who left there were sent to the United States.[193] Most of the American agents in Germany stated that while few paupers were actually sent out, nearly all of those leaving had so little money that they were paupers when they arrived.[194] The consul at Leipsic, however, had a

191 - Ibid., No. 1040, pp. 41-48.
192 - Senate Documents, 24th Cong., 2nd Sess., No. 5, p. 20.
193 - Ibid., No. 5, pp. 1-13.
194 - House Reports of Committees, 25th Cong., 2nd Sess., No. 1040, pp. 51-52.

different story to tell. He found a great organization was being built up among the smaller states of
Germany to ship all of their paupers and criminals
to the United States, agents being paid $75 for the
transportation of each immigrant. All towns in that
vicinity had made a regular practice of sending their
poor to America, he said, and he could do nothing.[195]
A committee of Congress named to investigate the situation added to the alarm when it reported in 1836 that
England had sent 320 paupers to the United States under
its Poor Law of 1834. These, the committee reported,
came from only 19 parishes, the remaining 15,616 had
yet to act and should they send out their poor in the
same proportion a flood of 41,000 paupers each year
would sweep over America.[196]

While the eastern states were affected principally by this onslaught of foreign poor, the south
was faced with problems almost as serious. The development of the cotton trade between southern ports and German cities had started migration flowing into the south
which was rapidly assuming larger proportions. New
Orleans was the most popular port of entry; the immi-

195 - Ibid., No. 1040, pp. 52-54.
196 - House Executive Documents, 24th Cong., 1st Sess.,
       No. 219, pp. 1-3.

grants bent on the fertile plains of the upper Mississippi Valley as their ultimate destination. The poorer
and less ambitious among them never progressed beyond
New Orleans or some other sea-board town, and these
cities were faced with a pauper problem almost as great
as that of New York and Boston.[197]

With such conditions rampant, there is little
wonder that nativistic writers turned their attention
to the pauper immigrant. Citizens were asked if America "must become the receptacle of all the cast off
population of Europe"[198] and editors insisted that
while the United States should be the haven of the
oppressed it "was not ambitious to become the asylum
for paupers and criminals from all parts of the world."[199]
Southerners were as indignant as easterners at this
seeming insult to America,[200] and papers throughout
the country took delight in reporting the flotsam of
foreign criminals and paupers washed up on our shores.[201]
Whenever a pauper was found who did have money his case

197 - Cole, Arthur C., "Nativism in the Lower Mississippi
       Valley," Mississippi Valley Historical Association
       Proceedings, vol. vi (1912-1913), p. 259.
198 - Downfall of Babylon, January 17, 1835.
199 - Massachusetts Yeoman, July 9, 1831.
200 - Niles Register, vol. xlix, p. 62.
201 - Downfall of Babylon, June 11, 1836; Spirit of '76,
       October 1, 1835; Baltimore Literary and Religious
       Magazine, September, 1838; Morse, Foreign Conspi-
       racy, pp. 141-142.

was heralded as typical of foreign intrigue.[202] Most
nativists viewed the action of European governments
in sending their paupers as part of the plot to destroy America and stamp out liberty and republicanism.
America would be weakened by such an influx[203] and in
addition it would be ready prey for the priests.[204]
The fact that that unpopular traveler, Mrs. Trollope,
scoffed at these reports only added to their prestige?[205]

     But the foreigner was objected to, not only
because of the additional burden that his coming placed
on the supporters of the poor, but for a variety of
other reasons as well. Stern New Englanders, brought
up to venerate the Puritan Sabbath, grew in wrath as
they saw that time honored institution sway before the
impiety of foreigner and Catholic.[206] The Irish were
accused of keeping in their own groups and refusing to
be assimilated,[207] a charge that was undoubtedly true
although they may have been driven to this attitude by

202 - New York Observer, April 18, 1835; Downfall of
      Babylon, June 27, 1835.
203 - Beecher, A Plea for the West, p. 54.
204 - New York Observer, December 7, 1839.
205 - Trollope, T. A., Domestic Manners of the Americans
      (London, 1832) vol. i, p. 121.
206 - New York Observer, August 30, 1828; The Protestant
      December 18, 1830; Downfall of Babylon, December
      27, 1834; January 3, 1835; January 17, 1835; Feb-
      ruary 14, 1835; July 11, 1835; March 5, 1836.
207 - Scisco, L. D., Political Nativism in New York State
      (Columbia Studies in History, Economics and Public
      Law, New York, 1901), pp. 26-27. Channing, History
      of the United States, vol. vi, p. 128.

the open hostility surrounding them.[208] The same
clannish ideas of the Germans aroused even more resentment[209] and with some justification. Many German
immigrants who arrived at this time thought only of
love of Fatherland and organized societies to perpetuate this ideal. Typical was the Deutsche Gessellschaft,
formed at Cincinnati in 1834 with the avowed object:
"Damit wir als Burger der Vereinigten Staaten denjenigen
Antheil an der Volksherrschaft nehmen knonnen, den uns
Pflicht und Recht gebieten."[210] Similar societies formed
in other cities and German festival days rather than
American were celebrated.[211]

As German migration grew many of the immigrants
had visions of new German states in the West. A society,
the Giessener Auswanderungs Gessellschaft, was formed in
Germany in 1833 to send Germans to fill the state of
Missouri, but the scheme failed. A society of the same
name was formed in Philadelphia in 1836 with the object:
"Einigung dur Deutschen in Nord-Amerika und dadurch Be-
grundung eines neuen deutschen Vaterlandes."[212] This
organization bought land in Missouri and actually en-

208 - Desmond, The Know Nothing Party, p. 9 note.
209 - Spirit of '76, September 26, 1835; New York Ob-
       server, August 3, 1839.
210 - Baker, Thomas S., Leneau and Young Germany in
       America (Philadelphia, 1897), p. 54.
211 - Ibid., p. 55.
212 - Ibid., pp. 61-63.

tered upon its schemes before it was disbanded. Similar
activities were carried on by the Germania Society of
New York and the Adelsverein in Texas.[213] Here was a
new and serious menace to American plans. The whole
future of the democratic experiment depended on the
ability of this country to assimilate the migratory
streams of the old. These German attempts to maintain
the old within the new must be checked or the country
would fail, and with it the light of republicanism.
There is little wonder that nativistic writers grew
excited; little wonder that thousands of converts were
won over to their cause.

Not only was the presence of the foreigner
considered a political and economic menace to American
institutions, but it was freely believed that the moral
tone of the community suffered with his coming. The
activities of the temperance societies brought them
into direct contact with the well known devotion of
the Irish to their whiskey and the Germans for their
beer. Nativistic papers complained that Irish in
particular kept grog shops[214] and that their priests
refused to give the temperance cause any aid.[215] The

213 - Ibid., pp. 68-69; Tiling, Moritz, The German
       Element in Texas, 1820-1850 (Houston, Texas 1913)
214 - Downfall of Babylon, June 25, 1836.
215 - Protestant Magazine, May, 1834.

New York Temperance Society after futile attempts
to bring reform to the immigrant groups, reported
in 1838 that efforts in that direction seemed well
nigh hopeless,[216] and a little later spoke of how
"this refuse of European population has been one of
the most formidable obstructions to this cause."[217]
As late as 1842 this same society was forced to admit
that it had convinced only 1300 Germans that they should
take the pledge, from among the thousands of immigrants
in the city.[218]

It was natural, in the eyes of native Americans,
that such a morally dissolute crew should indulge in all
manner of lawless practices. The coming of the Irish
had resulted in an increase in lawlessness and disorder,
growing from a natural proclivity of members of that
group to continue the feuds of the old country on the
soil of the new. "From New York," wrote a contemporary
observer," "they go in swarms to the railroads and canals
and public works where they perform the labor which the
Americans are not inclined to do; now and then they get
up a fight among themselves in the style of the ould
Ireland, and perhaps kill one another, expressing great

216 - New York Observer, May 19, 1838.
217 - Ibid., May 8, 1841.
218 - Ibid., June 11, 1842.

indignation and surprise when they find they must
answer for it, though they are in a free country."[219]
To the sober citizen of the period, these battles
reeked of riot and anarchy; they foretold the overthrow of American civilization unless they could be
checked.

Some of the brawls and bloodshed which followed in the path of the Irish were gruesome affairs,
and sufficient to cause alarm among even the most
hardy of the pre-Civil war population. The spring
election of 1834 in New York City ushered in a period
of unprecedented mob violence. Gangs of Irishmen armed
with stones and cudgels attacked the Whig committee,
put the mayor, sheriff and a posse to flight, and
terrorized the city. In Philadelphia at the same time
rioting among Irishmen assumed serious proportions when
shots were exchanged.[220] In the same year several employees of the Baltimore and Ohio Railroad were murdered by gangs of laborers, precipitating a period of
armed warfare in Maryland which was not ended until
troops had been sent from Washington to stop the fight-

219 - Latrobe, C., The Rambler in NorthAmerica in 1832-
      1833 (New York, 1835), vol. ii, pp. 222-223.
220 - McMaster, History of the People of the United
      States, vol. vi, p. 227.

ing.[221] Peace was only made after the citizens of
Ann Arundel and Prince George counties had met in
indignation, accused the rioters of being Irish Catholics, and a "gang of ruffians and murderers, combined together with the most solemn ties, to carry
into effect such hellish designs as their passions
or prejudices may prompt them to commit."[222]

In the spring of 1835 a riot which took on
even more grave an aspect broke out in New York City.
Rioting started on June 21, when a drunken Irishman
badly injured a small boy by beating him. Mobs began
to form but no action was taken until the next day when
several hundred people gathered and began attacking
Irish homes. The Common Council was hurried into session on June 23 to consider means of checking the disorder. While they were meeting news came of rioting
started in the Five Points region. Police, rushed to
the scene, were driven back by an Irish mob.[223] Meanwhile one American was killed, and many were hurt[224]
and although the mayor offered a large reward for the
originators of the plot[225] no one was apprehended.

221 - Ibid., vol. vi, p. 232; New York Observer, December
       6, 1834.
222 - Downfall of Babylon, December 27, 1834; New York
       Observer, December 6, 1834.
223 - New York Observer, June 27, 1835.
224 - Downfall of Babylon, July 4, 1835.
225 - Ibid., July 11, 1835.

Only a few months later mob unrest broke out in the
Bowery when an Irishman tried to take a horse from
two small boys. Supporters of both Irish and natives
rallied and the two gangs fought for some time.[226] In
the next year a pitched battle developed between the
Irish and a group styling themselves native Americans
who tried to demolish Irish grog shops in Central Park.
This fracas led to a two day interval of racial fighting.[227]   The serious flour riots in New York in 1837
were also considered the work of foreigners, probably
with justification, as they were the poorest element
in the population and the most susceptible to words of
agitators.[228]

   Meanwhile news was pouring in of bloodshed and
trouble all over the country. In Orono, Maine, a quarrel
between an Irishman and a Yankee sent a mob of armed incendiaries against the Irish section of the city.[229]   In
Detroit a group of Irish having imbibed too deeply of
patriotism and whiskey on July 4, 1835, attacked citizens on the principal street of the city until they were
disbanded by mobs of natives.[230]   Later in that year la-

226 - Spirit of '76, September 25, 1835.
227 - New York Observer, July 9, 1836.
228 - Headley, The Great Riots of New York, pp. 97-110.
229 - Spirit of '76, September 15, 1835.
230 - New York Observer, July 25, 1835; Downfall of
      Babylon, August 1, 1835.

borers on a canal in Indiana threw that state into a
furor of excitement.[231] A similar riot alarmed the
people of Florida.[232] In Albany small boys parading
through the streets with an effigy of Saint Patrick
launched a minor war which raged for a day between
natives and aliens.[233] Boston staged its Broad
Street riot in 1837.[234] In 1839 German laborers on
the Chesapeake and Ohio canal were attacked and their
homes destroyed by Irish competitors.[235] Troops were
called in and had to shoot down ten Irish leaders before the rioting could be stopped.[236] The harsh sen-
tences given to many of the participants failed to
quiet the fears of the people of Maryland where it
had been staged.[237]

If people were alarmed by the actual rioting
between Irish and natives, they had still greater cause
for worry through the words of warning from the pens of
nativistic writers. Propagandists seized upon these
disorders as a new source of anti-alien material. They
painted a dismal picture of the results of foreign Cath-

231 - New York Observer, September 5, 1835.
232 - Ibid., January 23, 1836.
233 - Ibid., March 25, 1837.
234 - Ibid., June 17, 1837.
235 - Ibid., August 31, 1839.
236 - Ibid., September 7, 1839.
237 - Ibid., November 2, 1839.

olic immigration; before had been peace and prosperity,
now only mob rule and violence. "How is it possible,"
they asked, "that foreign turbulence imported by ship
loads, that riot and ignorance in hundreds of thousands
of human priest-controlled machines, should suddenly be
thrown into our society and not produce here turbulence
and excess? Can one throw mud into pure water and not
disturb its clearness?"[238] The New York Observer bemoaned this new period of mob rule and blamed it entirely on slavery and Popery,[239] the Baltimore Literary
and Religious Magazine echoed its cry and prophesied
that as long as foreigners remained..."terror and crime
in all directions," would remain with them.[240] Especially were nativistic agitators alarmed when on one
occasion the police having failed to put down Irish
rioters, priests were called in and succeeded. It was
loudly asserted that priests stirred up trouble so that
they could increase their power by stopping it.[241]The
New York Observer warned solemnly that the government
was being surrounded by Popish priests who alone could
keep order among the riotous papists overrunning the

238 - Morse, Imminent Dangers, preface.
239 - New York Observer, August 15, 1835.
240 - Baltimore Literary and Religious Magazine, Novem-
       ber, 1839.
241 - Beecher, A Plea for the West, p. 93.

country,[242] and the Downfall of Babylon saw in the
rioting another evidence of the Catholic plot to
weaken the United States and so make it easier to
conquer when the moment came.[243]

This fear of foreign influence engendered
by rioting and disorder was given tangible basis in
the minds of many Americans by the part that immigrants were playing in the nation's politics, especially in eastern cities. Immigrants usually voting
in a body were attracted to the Democratic party by
its name, and aroused bitter antagonism in the hearts
of Whig politicians who saw their power dwindling.
This clannish method of voting gave rise, naturally,
to the charge that foreigners cast their ballots as
they were told to, and the belief was general that
Catholic priests had assumed dictatorial powers.[244]
Here then was a new danger, the conquest of the country
by Rome was made more of a reality by this unified vote.

Nativistic writers sensed this situation and
dealt with it at length. "Already," Americans were
warned, "does this Republic embrace thousands who are

242 - New York Observer, December 27, 1834.
243 - Downfall of Babylon, October 20, 1834.
244 - At least one modern investigator of the subject
       believes that these charges were true, and that
       the foreigners, long used to political control by
       priests in the old world, continued under their
       sway in the new. Cross, Ira, "The Origin, His-
       tory and Principles of the American Party,"
       Iowa Journal of History and Politics, vol. iv
       (1906), p. 527.

wholly under the influence of a venal priesthood, and
who, in unbroken ranks, go to our polls and vote as
they are commanded.   Already Roman priests have become
the most powerful politicans in our country."[245] Newspapers claimed that the people were prevented from en-
acting just laws because of the "ignorant interference
of foreign serfs."[246] The national government was
criticized for placing foreign born citizens in office.[247]
Editors insisted that the danger was made greater because of the even division existing between older par-
tics, giving the foreign vote a power far out of proportion to its numbers.[248] They insisted too that even
though priests did not control aliens, they were the
ready tools for unscrupulous politicnas,[249] a charge
undoubtedly founded on fact. Agitation against such
foreign influence in politics was given new weight
when a newspaper was established in Baltimore with the
avowed purpose of removing the danger of the foreign
born in politics.   It was called the Baltimore Pilot
and Transcript and was edited by General Duff Green.[250]

245 - Protestant Magazine, December, 1833.
246 - Spirit of '76, July 29, 1835.
247 - New York Observer, November 12, 1836.
248 - Spirit of '76, October 6, 1835.
249 - New York Observer, December 13, 1834.
250 - Protestant Vindicator, December 23, 1840.

Even the poet succumbed to the danger and asked:

> Have we not seen a Popish bishop leave
> His zealous care of souls, to stand in front
> Of our own free ballot box and strongly tell
> His followers not to vote but as he bids,
> And then 'approves,' and then holds up his card!
> See how they throng around and loud applaud
> His wily purpose, then depart to lend
> Their noisy clamour and their fiercest threats
> Against the friends of Liberty and Right;
> And taught by high example then depart
> To stifle free discussion by a mob.[251]

There was only one way to offset this foreign control of the ballot box, in the eyes of nativistic writers, and that was to forsake old party lines. The old parties were evenly balanced and willing to bargain with aliens to secure their votes. A new party must be formed, one which could be dependent entirely on native support and which could throw its entire weight against the Papists and their immigrant adherents.[252] Unlike many reforms, this met with enthusiastic response and thus the work of the propagandists was at last to bear fruit. Alarmed by supposed foreign aggression which became real with the panic of 1837, a new party was formed to usher nativism into the political field.

At first the political manifestations of na-

---

251 - Protestant Vindicator, January 12, 1841.
252 - Spirit of '76, July 29, 1835; Downfall of Babylon, July 4, 1835.

tivism were sporadic and local. Two weeks after the
Broadway Hall meeting of the New York Protestant Association had been broken up by Irish,[253] the first signs
of the new political interest began to appear in New York.
Ward meetings were held on March 27, 1835, by native American citizens to nominate nativistic tickets, but the
strength of the movement remained untested when these
tickets were promptly absorbed by the Whigs.[254] A more
serious effort, started in June, 1835, resulted in the
formation of the Native American Democratic Association.
James Watson Webb, editor of the New York Courier and
Enquirer served as the guiding light in this organization. It was launched with the issuing of a declaration
of purposes and the founding of an official newspaper,
the Spirit of '76. The platform pledged opposition to
foreigners in office, to pauper and criminal immigration,
and to the Catholic church.[255] The path of this new
association was not an easy one; in September a schism
occurred when one group, wanting to direct all its ire
against Catholics rather than foreigners, broke away.[256]
Nor would they return when their official paper warned

253 - See above, pp. 197-199.
254 - Scisco, Political Nativism in New York State,
       pp. 23-25.
255 - Ibid., pp. 25-27.
256 - Spirit of '76, September 15, 1835.

them if Protestant foreigners were admitted into the
country, Jesuits would disguise themselves as Protestants and attack the government in that way.[257] Despite this difference of opinion, similar native American associations had been formed in Brooklyn, New York,
Patterson, New Jersey and New Orleans by September, and
one was to be started in Cincinnati.[258] In New York its
success was unusual and although a nativistic party could
not carry the fall elections in 1835, the vote was so
menacing that the local Democratic party cast off its
foreign supporters.[259]

Thus encouraged, New York nativists prepared
for the spring elections of 1836. They made the mistake
of nominating for mayor for this contest Samuel F. B.
Morse. Although an outstanding nativist, Morse was also
a dyed in the wool Democrat, and lacking Whig support he
polled less than 2,000 votes, allowing the Democratic
party to carry the day.[260] Such a disastrous defeat
meant that the native American strength was lessened,
and it was not until the next year that it revived.

The Panic of 1837; however, meant that nativis-

257 - Ibid., September 16, 1835.
258 - Ibid., September 4, 1835.
259 - Scisco, Political Nativism in New York State,
       pp. 27-28.
260 - Ibid., pp. 28-30.

tic movements would receive support hitherto unknown.
Alarmed now at poverty stricken paupers and the need
of supporting them, the people of eastern cities flocked
to the standard of the parties which pledged themselves
to check or to end foreign immigration. Nativists in
New York nominated Aaron Clark for the mayoralty, and
with the support of Whigs, carried him into office, together with a complete common council.[261] A meeting of
citizens at Germantown, Pennsylvania formed a Native
American Assocation and drew up a constitution declaring against foreign office holders and voters.[262] It
was from this organization that the powerful national
party of the 1840's was to spring according to contemporary historians of the movement.[263] In Washington
seven hundred persons attended a mass meeting held in
July, 1837, and formed the Native American Association
of the United States, with similar demands.[264] In New
Orleans the "Louisiana Native American Association,"
which had been formed in 1835,[265] added new members

261 - Ibid., pp. 30-31.
262 - Lee, John Hancock, The Origin and Progress of the
      American Party in Politics (Philadelphia, 1855)
      p. 16.
263 - Ibid., pp. 15-16.
264 - McMaster, History of the People of the United States
      vol. vi, p. 428.
265 - Spirit of '76, August 24, 1835.

and issued an address deploring the addition to America of "the outcast and offal of society, the vagrant and the convict - transported in myriads to our shores, reeking with the accumulated crimes of the whole civilized world."[266] Similar associations were formed all over the United States, in a burst of antipathy against the foreigner and the Catholic.[267]

Nativists who were thus affiliated into political organizations and in a position to voice their demands, had two principal grievances. They objected to the political power of the foreigner gained through the franchise, and they objected to the pauper and criminal floods which came in the wake of the immigrant. For both of these seeming injustices they sought relief. Control of the franchise was purely a matter for the federal government to regulate. Nativists as a result began to deluge Congress with petitions as soon as their political associations had been formed.

The Native American Association of Washington was the first to realize this mode of attack. On January 15, 1838 it presented a memorial to Congress, signed by nearly a thousand members, and praying for the repeal of existing naturalization acts to stop foreigners from vo-

266 - Address of the Louisiana Native American Association (New Orleans, 1839)
267 - McMaster, History of the People of the United States vol. vii, pp. 369-370.

ting.[268] The memorial pointed out that the framers
of the Constitution never intended that a horde of
foreigners, ignorant of American language and institutions, should control the government. Five years was
all too short a time for proper citizenship training,
the memorialists insisted, especially in the face of
the position of power assumed by the immigrants in controlling the balance between the political parties.[269]
A month later citizens of Washington County, New York,
added a vehement approval to this memorial by a similar
petition, more outspoken in tone, and aimed principally
at the Catholic church. "Your memorialists earnestly
petition your honorable body," they said, "to inquire
whether the principles of the Roman Catholics, as held
at present as well as formerly, are not political and
hostile to civil and religious liberty? and whether their
religion is not essentially political, requiring the
union of church and state, and the subjection of the
latter to the former? and whether it does not require
allegiance to the Pope of Rome, holding the obligation
to obey him as paramount to all other authority, and

268 - Congressional Globe, 25th Cong. 2nd Sess.,
       pp. 100-101.
269 - House Executive Documents, 25th Cong. 2nd Sess.,
       No. 08., pp. 1-7.

his subjects not bound even by an oath, when he re-
quires the breach of it for the sake of his religion?
and whether it does not justify and imperiously require, legislative defense against this influence in
our government? and further whether there be not a
plan in operation, powerful and dangerous, under the
management of the Leopold Foundation, for the subversion of our civil and religious liberties, to be affected by the emigration of Roman Catholics from Europe,
and by their admission to the right of suffrage with us
in our political institutions."[270]

Both of these petitions were referred to a
select committee, rather than to the Committee of the
Judiciary, by action of the House of Representatives,[271]
although the House instructed the Judiciary Committee
to look into the matter as well.[272] The report of the
Select Committee, laid before members of the House on
July 2, 1838, reflected well the bigotry of the memorials which had been submitted to it. After citing
numerous cases of naturalization frauds and the dangers
growing from them[273] the report launched into a violent

270 - Ibid., 25th Congr., 2nd Sess., No. 154.
271 - Congressional Globe, 25th Cong., 2nd Sess., p. 101.
272 - Ibid., 25th Cong., 2nd Sess., p. 187.
273 - House Reports of Committees, 25th Cong., 2nd Sess.,
      No. 1040, pp. 106-108; 113-116.

denunciation of immigration and Catholicism. The despots
of Europe, it said, wanted to stamp out republicanism,
and had hit upon the device of sending immigrants to
America to accomplish this foul end. They might eventually be made Americans after a long period of education
but this could not be accomplished in five years, and
the committee ended with a recommendation that the probationary period of the naturalization law be extended
indefinitely, leaving the exact time to the discretion
of Congress.[274]

Members of the House refused to allow such a
nativistic point of view to go by without protest. William
Beatty of Pennsylvania immediately denounced the report
by asserting its doctrines were those of 1798, and asked
time to submit a counter report. Despite these objections,
the bill was read twice and committed after some debate,
although it was not brought before the house again until
several years later when nativistic excitement had reached
a new level.[275]   In the meantime, new petitions had been
flooded upon Congress, praying for a change in the naturalization laws in the same manner which had been recommended
by the Select Committee.[276]   They too were forced to wait

274 - Ibid., 25th Cong., 2nd Sess., No. 1040, pp. 12-16.
275 - Congressional Globe, 25th Cong., 2nd Sess., p. 489.
276 - Ibid., 25th Cong., 3rd Sess., p. 168; Executive
      Documents, 25th Cong., 3rd Sess., No. 162, pp.1-2;
      Senate Documents, 25th Cong., 3rd Sess., No. 246;
      Senate Documents, 26th Cong., 1st Sess., No. 43.

action until a later date.

Meanwhile nativists had turned their attention to the other grievance that they sought to remedy, legislation to prohibit the importation of foreign paupers and criminals. Several of the states had passed laws at an earlier period designed to afford such protection by requiring bonds from ship captains importing persons likely to become a public charge. Despite the earlier failure of these laws to operate successfully,[277] several states in the flare of nativistic excitement created by propaganda and mounting taxes, passed new laws of this nature, or made existing laws more stringent. A Maryland act of 1833 provided that captains must pay $1.50 for each passenger landed and that they might be required to post bond of $150 for any immigrant likely to become a public charge.[278] Massachusetts, in a similar act passed in 1837, placed the bond which might be required of captains importing indigent or infirm aliens at $1,000.[279]

These laws had scarcely been put into operation when their effectiveness was removed. In 1837 the Supreme Court, acting upon a similar New York law in operation since 1824, held that the state had no right to collect bonds on

277 - See above, pp. 293-295.
278 - Abbott, Immigration, pp. 109-110.
279 - Fairchild, Immigration, pp. 81-82.

immigrants, for such collection constituted an attempt to regulate trade and commerce.[280] The Massachusetts act of 1837 was specifically held to be unconstitutional on similar grounds a few years later.[281] The last vestiges of state power were taken away when the court held that they had no right to levy even a minimum tax on immigrants to be used to support a marine hospital for their benefit.[282]

Unable to solve the problem of removing the burden of pauper support by recourse to the states, nativists turned to the national government for relief. The power of the federal government to restrict immigration was unquestioned, and it seemed natural that aid should come

280 - City of New York vs. George Milne (January, 1837) 11, Peters, 102. The case arose when the corporation of New York City instituted action for debt against George Milne, consignee of the ship Emily, charging it had arrived in 1829 with 100 passengers and that the captain had not made the report required under the statute of 1824. The city claimed $15,000 as penalty for breaking the law. The defendant demurred to the declaration, the question reaching the Supreme Court on Constitutional grounds.

281 - James Norris vs. City of Boston (December, 1848) 48 U.S. 282. The case arose when Norris arrived as commander of a schooner from New Brunswick carrying nineteen immigrants. He paid the $38. required under the law of 1837 under protest and brought suit to recover, the case reaching the supreme court on a writ of error.

282 - George Smith vs. Turner (December, 1848) 48 U.S. 282. Smith, master of a British ship, landed a cargo of immigrants at New York and payed the health fee of one dollar for each under protest, bringing suit to recover on the basis of the unconstitutionality of the New York act. This and the above case are referred to as The Passenger Cases.

from this direction. As early as April 18, 1836, a petition from the Massachusetts legislature asking for national legislation to prevent the importation of foreign paupers had been introduced into the House of Representatives.[283] A day later the House acted upon a resolution requesting the Secretary of State to lay information on the matter before them, a request which elicited the response that such statistics were not available.[284] In May of this same year Senator Davis of Massachusetts introduced similar resolutions from the state legislature,[285] and after supporting them with an impassioned description of the difficulty of maintaining foreign paupers,[286] secured the passage of a resolution calling on the Secretary of the Treasury to furnish for the next legislature a report on foreign paupers in the United States.[287]

The Treasury Department was able to furnish more complete information than the State Department. In a report submitted on December 7, 1836, the whole question

---

283 - Congressional Globe, 24th Cong., 1st Sess., p. 373. The petition is printed in House Executive Documents 24th Cong. 1st Sess., No. 219, pp. 103.

284 - House Executive Documents, 25th Cong., 2nd Sess., No. 346.

285 - Senate Documents, 24th Cong., 1st Sess., No. 342.

286 - Congressional Globe, 24th Cong., 1st Sess., vol. ii, p. 414.

287 - Ibid., 24th Cong., 1st Sess., vol. ii, p. 614.

of foreign pauper immigration was thoroughly investigated. American consuls abroad looked into the situation, many of them finding that European governments were making this country a dumping ground for their undesirable population.[288] Customs House officials in the United States added testimony to the effect that while they did not believe that foreign governments deliberately dumped their pauper population in the United States, many of the immigrants arriving were unable to support themselves.[289]

Despite the evidence in this report of the presence of foreign paupers and the need for curbing their admission, Congress took no action. More petitions from citizens of Massachusetts [290] and New York,[291] presented in 1838 and stressing not only the burden upon the taxpayers through the support of alien poor but in addition the presence of a foreign conspiracy to weaken the country for papal conquest, finally stirred the legislators into action. A Select Committee on the question was named, instructed not only to investigate the whole subject but in addition to make recommendations for legislation.[292]

288 - Senate Documents, 24th Cong., 2nd Sess., vol. i, No. 5, pp. 1-13; 20.
289 - Ibid., 24th Cong., 2nd Sess., vol. i, Nov. 5, pp. 13-16.
290 - House Executive Documents, 25th Cong., 2nd Sess., No. 70.
291 - Ibid., 25th Cong., 2nd Sess., No. 313.
292 - Congressional Globe, 25th Cong., 2nd Sess., p. 101. The House Judiciary Committee was also instructed by resolution to consider the subject Congressional Globe, 25th Cong., 2nd Sess., p. 187.

The report of this committee, laid before members of
the House of Representatives on July 2, 1838, provided
nativists with arguments for years to come.[293] The
sympathies of the committee were clearly disclosed
when it solicited information on the question not only
from the mayors of Boston, New York, Philadelphia,
Charleston and New Orleans, but also from the Native
American Associations of New York and Washington.[294]
The report which they presented was naturally a damning
invective of pauper immigration in particular and of
all foreign immigration in general. Native American
Associations presented long and bitter accounts which
were included among the 116 pages[295] of the report.
Foreign consuls were again solicited and again stated
the prevalence of aided emigration of the poor.[296]
Statistics were presented showing the increase of pauperism in eastern cities and claiming that most paupers
were aliens.[297] Individual comments, all abhorring immigration, were included.[298] "One fact is unquestion-
able," the committee concluded, "that large numbers of

293 - Reports of Committees, 25th Cong., 2nd Sess.,
      No. 1040.
294 - Ibid., 25th Cong., 2nd Sess., No. 1040, pp. 2-3.
295 - Ibid., 25th Cong., 2nd Sess., No. 1040, pp.63-95.
296 - Ibid., 25th Cong., 2nd Sess., No. 1040, pp.41-48;
      51-55.
297 - Ibid., 25th Cong., 2nd Sess., No. 1040, pp. 3-4.
298 - Ibid., 25th Cong., 2nd Sess., No. 1040, pp. 51;
      55-58; 61; 95-103.

foreigners are annually brought to our country by
the authority, and at the expense of, foreign governments, and landed on our shores in a state of absolute destitution and dependence; many of them of the
most idle and vicious class; in their personal appearance the most offensive and loathsome, and their
numbers increasing with such rapidity by emigration
as to become burdensome to the American people; our
own citizens being obliged to contribute largely from
their own earnings to support them in idleness."[299]
Legislation should be passed, the committee believed,
to stop pauper immigration entirely.[300]

Despite this earnest recommendation, the report of the committee was allowed to lie neglected as
Congress turned to more urgent matters. A member of
the next Congress tried to revive the matter and secure action on the bill which had been introduced by
the committee, but objections were made and the appeal rejected.[301] There the matter rested as far as
the legislators were concerned.

But a step had been taken which was to provide able precedent for the future. Nativism had risen
from the fantasies of propagandists' pens to an impor-

299 - Ibid., 25th Cong., 2nd Sess., No. 1040, p. 9.
300 - Ibid., 25th Cong., 2nd Sess., No. 1040, p. 10.
301 - Congressional Globe, 25th Cong., 3d Sess., p. 159.

tant place in the sun of American political life.
Samuel Morse's attempt to save the West from Rome
had met with success beyond his fondest dreams. Already its effect was nation wide and everywhere the
bitter fruit of his pen ripened and scattered its own
seeds of personal bigotry and legislative intolerance.

VI

SAVING THE CHILDREN FOR PROTESTANTISM,
1840 - 1844.

Throughout the early years of its growth,
nativistic sentiment suffered under one grave handicap. Its appeal was largely to the lower classes.
Writers of propaganda found most of their converts
among a group which could appreciate the frank pornography of the Awful Disclosures and the Confessions of
a French Priest. The effectiveness of this appeal was
measured in mob rule, convent burning and riot. It
was not sufficient to influence the mass of middle
class voters in the 1830's when nativism barely missed
political success.

With the realization that greater numbers
alone could save America from the toils of Romish tyranny and the ascending tide of immigration, nativist
leaders turned their attention to the large body of
church going people for support. Heretofore this group
had subscribed to religious periodicals but save for
the withdrawing of their children from Catholic schools
after the Ursuline scare, they had otherwise gone about
their everyday affairs more or less indifferent to na-

tivism.

From the first, propaganda writers and those
sincere in their belief that Catholicism was a menace
to America, had made half hearted attempts to appeal
to the religious natures of these people. In such attempts they found one vulnerable spot; to the good Protestant of the day, unversed in Catholic beliefs, there
was only one true version of the Bible, the King James
version, which they all read. Propagandists seized upon
this as an opportune means of attracting their attention.
They stated that the condemnation of the Protestant Bible
by the hierarchy of Rome damned all Scriptures and denied
to its worshippers the true word of God.

This cry was echoed throughout the country early
in the 1830's and in the following decade it was expanded
and enlarged upon. The Catholic church, writers agreed,
had always opposed the reading of the Bible, just as it
did today.[1] They insisted that such a course was necessary for Rome; should worshippers before the Papal
throne read the true word of God they would discover
that their religion was false.[2] Propagandists went further and claimed that even priests were denied the Sacred

1 - McGavin, The Protestant, vol. i, pp. 231-293; Ricci,
    Secrets of Nunneries, pp. xv-xvi; Schumucker, Dis-
    course in Commemoration of the Glorious Reformation,
    pp. 26-27.
2 - The Protestant, March 31, 1832; Downfall of Babylon,
    November 7, 1835; McGavin, The Protestant, vol.i, p.571.

Book.[3] Religious newspapers throughout the 1830's printed
repeated letters from Catholic countries, recounting the
methods by which the Bible was kept from the people.[4] The
New York Observer had the grace to admit that a Douay version of the Scriptures did exist, but such admission was
used only as an excuse for a dull series of articles exposing its manifest falsehoods.[5] So firm was the belief
in Catholic hostility to the Bible that when, in 1836, a
Scriptural publishing house in New York burned down, Catholics were held responsible by the Downfall of Babylon[6] and
the Protestant Vindicator bemoaned the situation in typical
verse:

> See where the Bible is restrained
> From deathless souls who need its light,
> And priestly robes with blood are stained
> In leading souls to endless night;
> See where God's book is thought unfit
> For use by those whom he endowed
> With reasoning powers - whose path is lit
> By no bright pillar - by no cloud.[7]

Interest in the Catholic attitude toward the
Bible was naturally high among members of Bible societies.
Rome's complete denial of the Scriptures seemed assured
in their minds, when efforts in Boston[8] and Cincinnati[9]

3 - Downfall of Babylon, June 27, 1835.
4 - New York Observer, February 26, 1831; May 28, 1831;
June 8, 1833; February 25, 1837; January 26, 1839;
Downfall of Babylon, January 23, 1836.
5 - New York Observer, August 31, 1833 and ff.
6 - Downfall of Babylon, July 23, 1836.
7 - Protestant Vindicator, January 12, 1842.
8 - New York Observer, May 23, 1835.
9 - Shea, History of the Catholic Church, vol. iii, p.623.

to distribute Bibles among poor Catholic families were frustrated by their clergy. Checked in what they termed their Christian duty, local societies publicly announced that Catholics were opposed to the Scriptures in all forms. They further strengthened their claims by bringing to light old Papal decrees in which were found instances where the Bible had been condemned.[10]

This natural conflict between the Bible societies and the Catholic church would not have reached such large proportions had not the societies attempted to enlarge the scope of their service. In December, 1838, the Maryland Bible Society adopted a series of resolutions deploring the fact that while they had been sending God's word to the heathen abroad they had neglected to see that the Scriptures were read in the schools of their own state. This petition, calling upon the mayor of Baltimore and the governor for cooperation,[11] set an example which was to be followed all over the country. Members of the American Bible Society were quick to sense the importance of this new field for their activity. At their annual meeting in 1839 they listened to an impassioned appeal from the Reverend Robert J. Breckinridge urging nation wide

10 - Downfall of Babylon, May 23, 1835; New York Observer, July 21, 1838.
11 - Baltimore Literary and Religious Magazine, December, 1838.

efforts to place the Bible in the schools.[12] Indifferent
to his warning that a great struggle would ensue before
the Catholics would tolerate such a move the Society adopted resolutions committing itself to a program by which
it would urge Bible reading in the schools of the entire
nation.[13] Similar resolutions were adopted again a year
later[14] after the Methodist church had acted officially
to approve such a step.[15] The religious press gave unqualified approval to such action insisting that only
Catholics and infidels were opposed and that such a combination of Herod and Pilate should be ignored.[16]

Such activity on the part of the Bible Societies
led inevitably to conflict. Catholics were unwilling to
allow their children to attend public schools where part
of the program of instruction consisted of the reading of
an unauthorized version of the Scriptures. Throughout the
country a storm of Catholic protest arose, answered with
vigor by defenders of Protestantism. But it was in New

12 - Watchman of the South, July 18, 1839.
13 - Baltimore Literary and Religious Magazine, July, 1839.
14 - New York Observer, May 23, 1840.
15 - Journals of the General Conference of the Methodist
     Episcopal Church, vol. iii, p. 172. A resolution ad-
     opted by the General Conference in May, 1840, read as
     follows: "Resolved, That we highly approve of the use
     of the Bible as a class book in schools and seminaries
     of learning and will use our efforts for its introduc-
     tion into such schools and seminaries."
16 - New York Observer, September 5, 1840.

York City that this contest over Bible reading in the schools took on its most dramatic form.

The New York controversy was intensified by the nature of the public school system of that city in 1840 when Catholic citizens first began their complaints. New York schools at this time were under the control of the Public School Society, a benevolent association which had been formed in 1805 to care for the instruction of children financially unable to attend religious or private schools.[17]   Its founders had obtained a charter from the state legislature[18] and in their first appeal for funds, had stated that it would be a primary object of the society "without observing the peculiar forms of any religious society, to inculcate the sublime truths of religion and morality contained in the Holy Scripture."[19]   When the first school was opened a year later instruction in the Bible was given a prominent part in the curriculum.[20]

Although the Public School Society had been formed as a small organization designed to operate only one school it grew rapidly through gifts and grants from

17 - Palmer, A. Emerson, The New York Public School (New York, 1905), pp. 19-20.
18 - Bourne, William O., History of the Public School Society of the City of New York (New York, 1873), p. 4.
19 - Ibid., p. 7.
20 - Ibid., p. 26.

the state legislature.[21] At first these legislative
grants were sporadic, but a state act creating a common
school fund passed in 1805[22] was made to apply to the
city in 1813,[23] and the school society received and administered a considerable sum yearly under its terms. By
1822 the society was beginning to claim a monopoly upon
the education of the poorer children of the city,[24] a
position which it was forced to take by demands of the
Bethel Baptist church and other religious bodies which
clamored to share in the state school fund.[25] Alarmed
by this squabbling, the New York legislature, in 1824,
placed the administration of the share of the school
fund going to New York City in the hands of the Common
Council, that body being given the sole power to determine what organizations should share in it.[26]The Public

21 - Palmer, The New York Public School, p. 30. The name
     of the society was changed for a brief period to the
     Free School Society, but the original name was fi-
     nally restored.
22 - Laws of the State of New York, vol. iv. Containing
     all the Acts Passed at the 28th and 29th Sessions
     of the Legislature 1804 and 1805 and 1806 (Albany,
     1806), p. 126.
23 - Laws of the State of New York, Passed at the 36th,
     37th and 38th Sessions of the Legislature Commencing
     November, 1812 and Ending April, 1815.(Albany, 1815)
     vol. iii, pp. 38-39.
24 - Minutes of the Free School Society, March 13, 1822.
25 - 37th Annual Report of the Trustees of the Public
     School Society of New York, with a Sketch of the
     Rise and Progress of the Society (New York, 1842)
26 - Palmer, The New York Public School, p. 54.

School Society benefited greatly by the new arrangement,
as it did by a legislative act in 1826 allowing them to
charge tuition fees, thus vastly enlarging the scope of
their work,[27] although the fee system never operated
successfully.[28]

   The first conflict between this rapidly growing
society and the Catholic church came in 1831. In that
year the Common Council granted a share of the city proceeds from the common school fund to the Protestant Orphan Society.[29] The Roman Catholic Benevolent Society
immediately petitioned for a like share,[30] a petition
which the Public School Society, visioning a lessening
of its own funds, resisted vigorously.[31] When the Common Council decided in favor of Catholic claims feeling
was intensified among the Protestant groups.[32]

---

27 - Day, Mahlon, On the Establishment of Public Schools
  in the City of New York (New York, 1825), p. 4. New
  York Laws of 1826, p. 19. In 1829 the legislature,
  in response to petitions from the society, granted
  it an annual levy of one eighth of one per cent of
  certain taxes collected in New York City. Assembly Documents of the State of New York No. 296(1841),
  p. 6. This same session of the legislature authorized the society to mortgage its real estate.
  Palmer, The New York Public School, p. 73.
28 - Annual Report of the Public School Society for 1829.
29 - Palmer, The New York Public School, p. 80.
30 - Bourne, The Public School Society, p.124.
31 - Palmer, The New York Public School, p. 80.
32 - Ibid., p. 82.

The slight diversion of the common school fund
made necessary by this decision of the Common Council,
did not handicap the growth of the Public School Society
however. By 1840 it held a virtual monopoly over the
primary educational facilities of New York City, operating
nearly a hundred schools and distributing annually approximately $150,000, partly from the state common school fund
and partly from its own collections.[33]

Such power gave Catholic citizens of New York increasing cause for complaint, for while the society was avowedly non-sectarian, the Protestant version of the Scriptures
was read in all of the schools which it operated. As early
as 1838 an attempt on the part of Catholics to secure aid
from the legislature in stopping praying, singing and Bible
reading in schools receiving aid from the public treasury
had met with failure.[34] It was obvious that this objectionable practice would go on unless other means of relief were
found. Equally distasteful to Catholics were many of the
text books used in schools under the society's supervision.
There was considerable justification in charges that these

33 - Hassard, Life of John Hughes, pp. 141-142.
34 - William D. Griffith and others presented a memorial
   to the state legislature praying the enactment of a
   law prohibiting Bible reading, prayers and all other
   religious exercises in schools receiving aid from
   the state treasury. The memorial was not granted.
   New York Journal of Commerce, January 31, 1838.

books were biased in their treatment of the Catholic role in history and literature.

This anti-Catholic prejudice had found its way into both books of history and reading used in the New York schools. Catholics could hardly find the description of Luther in a Sequel to the English Reader to their liking when it declared: "Having lived to be witness of his own amazing success; to see a great part of Europe embracing his doctrines and shaking the foundation of the Papal throne, before which the mightiest monarchs had trembled, he discovered on many occasions, symptoms of vanity and self applause. He must have been more than man, if, upon contemplating all that he actually accomplished he had never felt any sentiment of this kind rising in his breast."[35] In this same work the description given of Cranmer's death,[36] the speech of Chatham against employing Indians[37] together with passages from Goldsmith's works[38] were capable of causing offense. Other historical works represented Catholics as deceitful. "John Huss," said one, "A zealous reformer from Popery who lived in Bohemia towards the close of the fourteenth and the beginning of the fif-

35 - Murray, Linday, Sequel to the English Reader (Burlington, Vermont, 1821), pp. 63-65.
36 - Ibid., p. 74.
37 - Ibid., p. 106.
38 - Ibid., p. 234.

teenth centuries, was bold and perservering; but at length, trusting himself to the deceitful Catholics, he was by them brought to trial, condemned as a heretic, and burnt at the stake."[39]   Even books on American history dwelt unduly upon Catholic perseuction.[40]

Some passages, typical of those sprinkled throughout books used by the Society, might have been passed over, but others were openly disrespectful. A "Dialogue between Fernando Cortez and William Penn" was too pointedly anti-Catholic to be excused in any way:

> Penn: Though what thou sayest should be true, it does not come well from thy mouth. A Papist talk of reason! Go to the inquisition and tell them of reason and the great laws of nature. They will broil thee as thy soldiers broiled the unhappy Guatimozin. Why dost thou turn pale? Is it in the name of the Inquisition or of Guatimozin? Tremble and shake when thou thinkest that every murder the inquisitors have committed, every torture they have inflicted on the innocent Indians is originally owing to thee.[41]

Almost equally objectionable was an ecclesiastical history which took every opportunity to em-

39 - Putnam, Samuel, Sequel to the Analytical Reader (Boston, 1831), p. 296.
40 - Wallis, H. H., History of the United States from the First Settlements as Colonies to the Close of the War with Great Britain in 1815 (New York, 1827), p. 11.
41 - Wood, Samuel, New York Reader, Number Three, Selections in Prose and Poetry from the Best Writers Designed for the Use of Schools (New York, 1819), p. 205.

phasize the corruption of Catholicism, charging that
Romish missions were mere schemes of ecclesiastical
ambition,[42] and referring to Biblical prophecy in forecasting the overthrow of the "Mother of Iniquity, the
Man of Sin, the Son of Perdition, the Mother of Harlots."[43] Another Ecclesiastical history circulated
at the same time devoted the first of its three volumes entirely to exposing the rise of Popery and its
many errors.[44] The presence of such books in a public
school system receiving support from the state certainly
gave Catholics every right to demand more just treatment.[45]

Unsatisfactory as the situation was, it might
have gone on unchanged for some time had not Governor
William Seward of New York precipitated the whole matter.
Although a Whig, Governor Seward had throughout his political life shown a marked tendency to favor the alien
and the foreign born. A journey through Ireland some
years before had convinced him that the miserable condition of the people there was due in part to their lack
of education,[46] and that if the poorer immigrants in

42 - Goodrich, C. A., Outlines of Ecclesiastical History
     on a New Plan, Designed for Academies and Schools
     (Hartford, 1830), p. 160.
43 - Ibid., pp. 157-158.
44 - New York Observer, April 12, 1834.
45 - Catholics did object to these passages during the
     controversy in New York, Protestant Vindicator,
     February 23, 1842.
46 - Seward, William H., Works (New York, 1853-1861),
     vol. iii, pp. 526-542. The formation of this
     attitude of sympathy is readily traceable in this
     series of letters, written from Ireland at the time.

America were to be assimilated, they must be given proper schooling.[47] With these beliefs, it was inevitable that, as governor, he should turn his attention to the situation in New York. His annual message to the people of the state, delivered on January 10, 1840, served to bring the whole matter before the public:

> The children of foreigners [he said] found in great numbers in our populous cities and towns are too often deprived of the advantages of our system of public education in consequence of prejudices arising from difference of language or religion...I do not hesitate, therefore, to recommend the establishment of schools in which they may be instructed by teachers speaking in the same language with themselves and professing the same faith. There would be no inequality in such a measure since it happens from the force of circumstances, if not from choice, that the responsibilities of education are in most instances confided by us to native citizens and occasions seldom offer for a trial of our magnanimity by committing that trust to persons differing from ourselves in language or religion.[48]

Encouraged by such an attitude, a group of Catholic churches in New York City which operated free parochial schools, immediately petitioned the Common Council, asking for a share of the state school fund which that body administered.[49] These petitioners

47 - Ibid., vol. i, pp. xlii-xliii.
48 - Ibid., vol. ii, pp. 215-216.
49 - Shea, History of the Catholic Church, vol. iii, p. 526.

charged that it was impossible for Catholic children
to obtain proper education in schools conducted by
the Public School Society, insisting that "its schools
were practically sectarian, and that its books and instruction had so strong a bias in favor of Protestanism
that Roman Catholics" were forced to provide their own
educational facilities.[50] The only method in which
they could obtain relief, the petitioners stated, was
to receive a share of the school fund to administer
their own private schools.

The Common Council had scarcely received this
document when members of the Public School Society, answered with two petitions of their own, one from the
executive committee, and the other from a special committee. These petitions presented an elaborate review of
the entire history of the school question, insisting
that each of the acts of the legislature and the Common
Council had made it clear that money raised by general
taxation was not to be used for sectarian teaching. If
money were diverted from the supply received by the Pub-
blic School Society to Catholic schools, the petitioners
stated, the society would be unable to continue its extensive operations. Other sects would demand their

50 - Annual Report of the Board of Education (New York,
       1853), p. 38.

share, and within a short time the entire school fund
would be dissipated among small religious schools,
giving not a general education, but sectarian instruction. Catholics only objected to the present system,
according to the Society, because their tenets were
not taught in the public schools.[51]

Less than a month after the presentation of
these petitions, the Common Council voted unanimously
against granting a share of the school fund to Catholics. Not only had they lost the first tilt of the
contest, but the committee report denying them their
claims was filled with bitter arguments against Rome
and widely circulated.[52]

The issue, however, was far from settled.
Leaders in the Catholic cause were convinced of the
justice of their claims and continued active. A newspaper, the Freeman's Journal, was established to voice
their claims when the older New York Catholic paper,
the Truth Teller refused to agitate the matter.[53] Meetings were held where speakers could urge upon Catholics
the necessity of concentrated action. Meanwhile the
Protestants rallied to the clarion call of the New York

51 - Both petitions were dated February 29, 1840. They
     were printed in full in the New York Observer,
     March 21, 1840.
52 - Ibid., May 2, 1840. The Council acted on the re-
     port on April 27.
53 - Ibid., August 1, 1840.

Observer: "The wiles of Jesuitism are too subtle to be
detected by the careless eye, and the progress of Popery
may be so slow and insidious that, before we are aware
of it, the throne of the Beast may be planted on the
shores of America and the religion of the anti-Christ
be the religion established by law."[54]

      The alarm of the editors of the Observer had
some justification. On July 18, 1840, Bishop John
Hughes had returned to New York and the Catholic effort was given the impetus which it needed.[55] Bishop
Hughes was well qualified to carry the standard of his
faith. A vigorous, stormy individual, powerful in leadership and indefatigable in contest, he had been chosen
bishop of the New York diocese in 1838[56] after a career
in Philadelphia which was distinguished by his defense
of Catholicism against the thrusts of its enemies. Two
days after he reached New York he attended a meeting of
members of his sect and read a carefully prepared address
which summed up the Catholic position clearly. The Public School Society, he charged, was filling the minds of
children with errors of fact which would excite them
against the religion of their parents. The school books

54 - Ibid., August 1, 1840.
55 - Shea, History of the Catholic Church, vol. iii,
     p. 526.
56 - Hassard, Life of John Hughes, p. 185.

used were not considered sectarian, he said, "as they
had been selected as mere reading lessons, and were not
in favor of any particular sect, but merely against the
Catholics."[57] In the following weeks Hughes held frequent meetings where the same arguments were stressed
and pressed upon his followers.[58]

Having thus prepared the way, Hughes super-
vised the drafting of a new petition. Charges of sectarian teaching by the Public School Society were repeated,
the petitioners insisting that the society trustees were
"deeply impressed with the importance of imbuing the
youthful mind with religious impressions; and that they
had endeavored to attain this object as far as the nature of the schools would admit."[59] They asked that
the Catholic schools be given a share of the school
money, saying that they would even accept supervision
by members of the society if necessary.[60]

Both the Public School Society and the New
York Methodist churches replied to this new demand.
The Trustees of the Society insisted once more that
their teachings were non-sectarian[61] and the Methodist

57 - New York Journal of Commerce, August 14, 1840.
58 - Ibid., August 21, 1840; August 26, 1840.
59 - Bourne, The Public School Society, pp. 189-191.
60 - Ibid., p. 194.
61 - Ibid., p. 196.

clergy used the excuse to attack the Catholic version
of the Scriptures as upholding the murdering of heretics and unqualified submission to papal authority in
all matters of conscience.[62] With both these petitions
widely circulated and public opinion rapidly shaping
itself on both sides,[63] the Common Council decided to
hold a public hearing where Catholics and representatives of the School Society could state their views.
On October 29, 1840, this debate began.[64]

Bishop Hughes stood alone for the Catholics,
while arrayed against him was a whole field of talent
gathered from among the legal profession and the Protestant clergy, ever anxious to hurl new bombs at Romanism. Representing the Public School Society were
Theodore Sedgwick, a lawyer and the Reverend Hiram
Ketchum; backing them in their arguments were the
Reverend Doctors Bond, Reese and Bangs of the Methodist church, the Reverend Spring of the Presbyterian
church and the Reverend Knox of the Dutch Reformed
church.[65] Bishop Hughes opened the public hearing

62 - Ibid., pp. 196-197.
63 - New York Observer, September 26, 1840. The re-
       monstrance by the Society stated that Catholics
       had been offered the right to censure all books
       used in the schools, but that they had refused,
       fearing that this would handicap their chances
       of securing a share of the school fund. This
       showed clearly, the remonstrance stated, that
       they were after money alone, and the Jesuitism
       of the whole movement was thus exposed.
64 - Bourne, The Public School Society, p. 202.
65 - Shea, History of the Catholic Church in the United
       States, vol. xxiii, p. 528.

before a crowded hall with a speech which lasted for
three hours.[66] He explained the Catholic petition and
the necessity for the relief before launching into an
attack on the Methodist claims, and ended by offering
to bet, a thousand dollars, that the Catholic Bible did
not sanction the burning of the heretics.[67] Effective
as this may have been, religious papers expressed their
horror and reminded the Bishop of a Common Council law
against betting.[68]

The first speaker for the Public School Society,
Theodore Sedgwick, gave a mild and somewhat labored defense of the policy of the society,[69] but this cautious
tone was not typical of the proceedings that followed.
Hiram Ketchum forgot sober argument and entered into a
biting attack on Popery, shouting that the Bible was
necessary to liberty and light and that he for one would
not have the Pope, a foreigner, dictate what should be
read in American schools.[70] The crowd cheered at Hughes'

66 - Hughes' biographer is responsible for the statement
     that his speech lasted three hours. Hassard, Life
     of John Hughes, p. 235. The reporter of the New
     York Observer recorded only a two hour speech.
     New York Observer, September 21, 1840. The follow-
     ing account of the meeting is drawn from the New
     York Observer, the New York Journal of Commerce,
     and Bourne, The Public School Society, pp. 202
     ff. The account given by Bourne is especially
     valuable as it is drawn entirely from the files
     of the Catholic paper, the Freeman's Journal.
67 - New York Observer, November 7, 1840.
68 - Ibid., November 7, 1840.
69 - Bourne, The Public School Society, pp. 230-236.
70 - Ibid., pp. 239-242.

discomfort when he attempted a reply and was bested in a brief argument.[71]   These lengthy harangues consumed the first day of the debate and when it was resumed the next morning the clergy took the floor and all facts and arguments were forgotten as they launched attack after attack on Catholicism. Dr. Bond devoted his whole speech to a theological treatise proving that the Rhemish Testament did sanction the murder of heretics;[72] Dr. Knox spent many words in proving that the New York schools were really Protestant institutions;[73] Dr. Spring ended an impassioned oration by shouting that Catholicism bred infidels. "I do say," he told the crowded galleries, "that if the fearful dilemma were forced upon me of becoming an infidel or a Roman Catholic, according to the entire system of Popery, with all its idolatry, superstition and violent opposition to the Holy Bible, I would rather be an infidel than a Papist."[74]

71- New York Observer, November 7, 1840.
72- Bourne, The Public School Society, pp. 255-259.
73- Ibid., pp. 270-273.
74- Protestant Vindicator, November 11, 1840. The proceedings of this debate, consisting largely of the anti-Catholic speeches of the clergymen attending, were published under the title, The Important and Interesting Debate on the Claims of the Catholics to a Portion of the Common School Fund; with the Arguments of Counsel before the Board of Aldermen of the City of New York, on Thursday and Friday, the 29th and 30th of October, 1840(New York, 1840)

The course of this debate had pointed the
way to the decision which would follow. Only one
speaker in the Protestant camp had attempted to stress
the real question at issue, the others had only taken
the opportunity to vent anti-Catholic sentiments. It
was evident that the decision of the Common Council
would be along the same lines; that the whole question
would be settled by prejudice rather than reason. However, the Council appointed a committee to investigate
the schools operated by the society[75] and listened to
a mild argument between Hughes and the trustees about
Catholic censorship of school books.[76] There was discussion, too, when the Catholics claimed the copyright
on speeches delivered at the public hearing and sought
to restrain newspapers from publishing them, especially
when investigation showed no such copyright to exist.[77]
Finally, on January 11, 1841, the Common Council acted.
A committee recommended that the Catholic petition be
refused, and by a vote of fifteen to one, the Council
accepted the report.[78] Once again Bishop Hughes and

75 - New York Journal of Commerce, November 7, 1840.
76 - Ibid., November 7, 1840.
77 - New York Observer, December 12, 1840.
78 - Ibid., January 16, 1841. The committee of the
     Common Council investigating the matter rec-
     ommended that school books in communities where
     Catholics were numerous should be remedied so
     that they would no longer give offense. Only
     few Catholic children were in the schools, the
     committee members discovered, and they expressed
     the hope that when the books had been expurgated,
     the number of Catholics attending would increase.

his followers had met defeat.

While the failure of the Catholics to secure
a share of the school fund had little permanent effect,
the activity to which their demands had stirred the
nativistic press was to hound them for many years. Almost as soon as the first petition had been circulated,
a volley of invective began to pour upon the Church and
its cause. Early in May, 1840, religious papers were
charging that Romanists refused to send their children
to the public schools only because they objected to
Bible reading. "What better evidence," they asked,
"can be given than that this church seeks to shut out
the light of divine revelation from the minds of its
members?"[79] Especially was it charged that this attack
upon the School Society was designed to hinder all education, a design of the Catholic church, for only when
its worshippers were ignorant could it keep their faith.[80]

With the return of Hughes to New York in July
the criticism became increasingly bitter. He had lately
come from the teachings of O'Connell, the editors of the
Protestant Vindicator claimed, to "demand that Protestants
collect funds to nurse Popery, bigotry and image worship.

79 - Ibid., May 2, 1840.
80 - Protestant Vindicator, October 28, 1840; February
     23, 1842; December 29, 1841.

They demand of Republicans to give them funds to train
up their children to worship a ghostly monarchy of
vicars, bishops, archbishops, cardinals and Popes. They
demand of us to take away our children's funds and bes-
tow them on the subjects of Rome, the creatures of a
foreign hierarchy!"[81] The Reverend W. C. Brownlee began a series of letters to Hughes attacking the Catholic
stand in this same paper,[82] stressing the fact that Romanists wanted a share of the school fund only to spread
their own religion.[83] Lengthy statistical arguments were
produced, showing that the small number of Catholics in
the city paid far less in taxes than they were demanding
from the school fund as their share.[84] Only the Popish
teachings giving them the right to keep no faith with
heretics allowed the priests to take the stand that they
had, if editors of the time may be believed.[85]

In December, 1840, matters were made worse by
a new burst of rioting and disorder. A meeting of sympathizers with the Protestant cause was called for December 8. The large number of "foreign Papists" in the

81 - Ibid., August 5, 1840.
82 - Ibid., November 3, 1841, and ff.
83 - Ibid., November 17, 1841.
84 - New York Observer, December 19, 1840; Protestant
     Vindicator, October 14, 1840; December 23, 1840.

crowd that gathered kept the speakers from mounting
the platform. After shouting against schools and the
School Society, they finally carried the day when the
meeting was adjourned in great disorder.[86] A few months
later Dr. Brownlee met with a similar reception when
he tried to reply to Hughes' statements in a public
meeting. Irish Catholics in the crowd called the
speaker a liar, finally causing the abrupt termination
of the lecture.[87] These incidents, magnified by the
nativistic press, attracted new interest to the struggle. James Gordon Bennett threw his powerful New York
Herald into the contest on the side of the School Society,
to be joined there later by the New York Commercial Advertiser, edited by William L. Stone.[88] While Stone had
oeen responsible for the exposure of Maria Monk, his attacks on Catholicism now made up for the harm which he
had done the nativistic cause. The New York Journal of

86 - New York Observer, December 11, 1841. The meeting
     was held in Sackett's Drill room, on Division street.
     The Observer called the attack "the greatest outrage
     upon the peaceful rights of American citizens that
     had ever disgraced our city or country."
87 - The meeting was held on July 8, 1841. Protestant
     Vindicator, July 28, 1841.
88 - Hughes wrote a letter to the New York Courier
     and Enquirer May 17, 1844, reviewing the whole
     school fund question and naming these two papers
     as most troublesome and important throughout its
     course. Hassard, Life of John Hughes, p. 279.

Commerce adopted a similar policy and announced from
the first that it would refuse to allow Catholics to
be singled out "for special privileges, as a reward
for their bigotry and exclusiveness."[89] With interest
thus growing, religious papers reported joyfully that
thousands of persons were being convinced daily that
the Romish religion was harmful to the United States
and should be wiped out.[90] The first victory was
celebrated by the Protestant Vindicator in one of
its bursts of verse:

> Our public schools have vexed the Pope;
> They seemed like ruin to his hope,
> To fix in time in our free home,
> The throne and golden calf of Rome!
> Because in them the Papist youth,
> Learned to distinguish lies from truth;
> Learned to become a thinking thing!
> Which Rome hates more than scorpion's sting!
> And hence the bull came thundering o'er
> We heard so late with savage roar;
> His warrant, all the schools to crush;
> Or failing there - (blush, Papists, blush)
> To expell the Romish youth, which heed
> Lest they, alas! should learn to read
> Christ's promises to sinners made,
> Without the Pope's paternal aid!
> That bull still roars - but all in vain;
> Columbia spurns the Papal chain;
> And hence, 'twill shortly come to pass,
> That bull shall find himself an ass.[91]

The defeat of the Catholic claim by the Common

89 - New York Journal of Commerce, February 26, 1840.
90 - New York Observer, November 14, 1840.
91 - Protestant Vindicator, January 20, 1841.

Council in January, 1841, was not accepted by nativistic
papers as the end of the battle. They warned that while
victory had been won, there were still left leaders of
the papal forces who had designs on the United States.
The school question had not known the last of Rome's
scheming and Protestants were cautioned to be ever on
the alert.[92] Nor were they amiss in their fears. Just
one month after the Common Council had announced its
decision, on February 11, 1841, Bishop Hughes called a
Catholic meeting at Washington Hall, organized a "Central Executive Committee on Common Schools," and urged
a petition to the state legislature which called for a
change in the whole administration, in order to do away
with sectarian influences in school instruction.[93] Opposed as he was to Godless schools, Hughes nevertheless
gave the measure his support.[94] The petition prepared
as the result of these suggestions was presented to the
legislature as a request from "Citizens of New York,"
with an attempt being made to keep the religious issue
in the background.[95] After some debate, the petition
was referred to a select committee of the assembly, and

[92] - New York Observer, January 16, 1841; Protestant
Vindicator, January 20, 1841.
[93] - Bourne, The Public School Society, pp. 350-351.
[94] - Hassard, Life of John Hughes, pp. 239-243.
[95] - Bourne, The Public School Society, p. 351.

there matters rested when the spring elections rolled
around.[96]

With the attempt to convert the state legislature to the Catholic stand, the school question had
definitely entered politics. Here was dangerous ground
for Bishop Hughes and members of his clergy. Certainly
his objections to the school system were legitimate and
justified, but he realized that it would be unwise to
launch his church into the political arena. Such a course
would give rise to untold criticism and offer the nativists an admirable opportunity to revive the old cry of
the contemplated union of church and state. There is
little doubt that Bishop Hughes, as a result, took no
part in political agitation, but religion did enter
into the elections, nevertheless. Handbills were distributed in Catholic sections of the city, appealing
to the religion of the voters in pleas for candidates
who favored their stand on the school question.[97]

96 - Ibid., p. 352.
97 - Such handbills were printed in the New York Observer
May 1, 1841; New York Journal of Commerce, March 18,
1841 and the Protestant Vindicator, March 31, 1841.
Typical of these is the handbill printed in the New
York Observer: "Catholics Arouse! To the Rescue!
Irishmen to your Post!! The friends of an equal distribution of the School Fund are called upon to ral-
ly! Come early to the polls and deposit your vote
for Daniel C. Plentz, the friend of the Catholics;
he openly proclaims that he is in favor of an equal
distribution of the School Fund. Daniel C. Plentz
was the only member of the Common Council who dared
proclaim to the world that he was willing we should
have a share of the School Fund. Irishmen, if you
would have your children educated, come and vote
for Daniel C. Plentz."

The sentiment of the voters upon this question was clearly expressed. The one member of the Common Council who had voted for the Catholic claim was defeated, even though members of his party were carried into office.[98] The press accepted this as a proper rebuke for Catholic interference in political matters[99] and faced the coming contest over the school fund in the legislature with considerable confidence.

More than confidence was needed to carry Protestant demands through the New York legislature however. Governor Seward had little sympathy with the protests of the Public School Society; throughout his political career he had expressed himself again and again as opposed to that form of education which discriminated against sect or creed.[100] Seward's attitude was based entirely upon his conception of justice and the needs of the state. "I desire to see the children of Catholics educated as well as the children of Protestants," he wrote to a friend, "not because

98 - New York Observer, April 17, 1841.
99 - Ibid., April 24, 1841.
100- This attitude was clearly expressed in a number of letters written by Seward at this time. See: Address to the Irishmen of Albany on St. Patricks Day, March 17, 1840, Seward, Works, vol. iii, p. 221; Seward to "B.S.," New York, November 12, 1840, Ibid., vol. iii, pp. 386-388; Seward to "B.S.," New York, November 15, 1840, Ibid., vol. iii, p. 389; Seward to Bishop John Hughes, May 18, 1841, Ibid., vol. iii, pp. 482-484; Seward to Benjamin Birdsall, June 30, 1841, Ibid., vol. iii, pp. 488-489.

I want them Catholics, but because I want them to become good citizens."[101] Unfortunately, this enlightened point of view led him to embrace the Catholic cause in the school funds controversy. He failed to see the errors of their demand; the fact that it would lead to a rapid dissemination of the state education fund among various sects until broad education along secular lines was impossible. His annual message in January, 1841, as a result, served as a plea for the Catholic cause. He pointed out the presence of more than twenty thousand children in New York City who were kept from schools because of the intolerant instruction vended by the Public School Society, and he urged upon the legislature the necessity of change. "I seek the education of those whom I have brought before you," he wrote, "not to perpetuate any prejudices or distinctions, which deprive them of instruction, but in disregard of all such distinctions and prejudices. I solicit their education, less from sympathy, than because the welfare of the state demands it, and cannot dispense with it."[102]

It was with this message ringing in their ears that members of the state senate turned to a consideration of the Catholic petition. Taken from the select committee,

101 - Seward to William Palmer, December 17, 1840, *Ibid.*, vol. iii, p. 480.
102 - *Ibid.*, vol. ii, pp. 279-280.

their demands were referred to the Secretary of State, John C. Spencer, who was also superintendent of common schools.[103] Spencer, despite influence brought to bear upon him,[104] prepared an able and impartial report designed to settle the whole troublesome question. Under his recommendations, the general school laws of the state of New York were to be extended to New York City. The Public School Society was to be done away with, in its place a school commissioner was to be elected in each ward to administer funds and regulate public instruction. In this way sectarian instruction in any ward would be impossible, for by their vote, Catholics could exert a powerful influence over the commissioners.[105]

The publication of this report immediately aroused a storm of protest. Trustees of the Public School Society insisted that educational unity would be sacrificed and that every election of a new commissioner would mean an outbreak of political opposition between Catholics and Protestants.[106] The religious press characterized the entire report as typical of

103 - Bourne, The Public School Society, p. 356.
104 - Bishop Hughes to John C. Spencer. "Letter to Archbishop Hughes on the School Question, 1841," American Catholic Historical Researches, n.s., vol. i, No. 3 (July, 1905), p. 263.
105 - Randall, History of the Common School System, pp. 123-132; New York Journal of Commerce, April 29, 1841. The report was read on April 26, 1841.
106 - Bourne, The Public School Society, pp. 373-381.

Jesuit intrigue, and spent columns of space demonstrating
methods by which Catholics would profit from the new arrangement should it be adopted.[107]

The Freeman's Journal expressed the Catholic
point of view when it gave its unqualified support to
Spencer's recommendation,[108] but this approval was hardly
sufficient to carry the measure through the legislature.
Nativistic agitators, recognizing the justice of the
proposals and fearing for the worst, resorted to a slightly unusual method of arousing Protestant fears. The New
York Journal of Commerce on May 20, 1841 had printed a
violent anti-Catholic article, built around the alleged
bull of excommunication launched against William Hogan
in Philadelphia several decades before.[109] On the morning when the measure was to be considered, copies of the
paper bearing this oath reached Albany. Each senator
when he reached his desk found a copy of this paper spread
before him, opened so that his eyes would fall on this
violent denunciation of Catholicism.[110] This timely use
of propaganda was effective. The senate voted to postpone consideration of the entire matter until January,

107 - New York Observer, June 10, 1841; June 12, 1841.
108 - Quoted in New York Journal of Commerce, May 4, 1841.
109 - New York Journal of Commerce, May 4, 1841.
110 - Ibid., June 12, 1841.

1842.[111]   Keenly disappointed, the Catholics insisted
that the article from the New York Journal of Commerce
had been entirely responsible for the outcome of the
vote[112] and charged with truth that the oath of excommunication had been taken bodily from the novel,
Tristam Shandy.[113]

That this single article, even effectively
used, was entirely responsible for the outcome of the
matter before the senate may well be doubted. Far
greater in importance, in the minds of members of the
legislature, was the realization that the entire school
question was pressing and troublesome. They were willing to postpone final consideration until after the fall
elections of 1841 to allow the people to express their
views and point the proper way to solution. In the November elections New York City would choose two state
senators and thirteen assemblymen, and the fate of the
Catholic requests would in large measure rest with these
men.[114]

---

111 - Ibid., June 12, 1841. The same devise was used at
      this time to force a postponement of consideration
      by the assembly of the report of the select com-
      mittee that had been appointed by that body. This
      committee had recommended changes almost as radi-
      cal as those proposed in the Senate. See Assembly
      Documents of the State of New York, No. 296, 1841,
      pp. 1-29.
112 - New York Journal of Commerce, June 12, 1841.
113 - Sterne, Lawrence, The Life and Opinions of Tristram
      Shandy (New York, 1813), vol. i, pp. 196-204.
114 - Scisco, Political Nativism in New York State, p. 34.

There is little wonder as a result, that
the November elections aroused intense excitement
among the nativists. Papers warned that the Catholics had not been idle, that they had been holding
meetings to prepare for the fray, and that Protestants
must flock to the polls to offset their insidious designs.[115] The clergy were equally active, and pulpits
throughout the city resounded with their exhortations
pleading defeat of the Catholic cause.[116] This rabid
expression of sentiment was enough to warn both the
Whigs and Democrats in New York City that the Protestant vote would be united against them should they accept Catholic claims. The Whigs as a result nominated
a ticket pledged against any change in the school system[117] and wrote into their local platform a declaration against sectarian schools.[118] The Democrats naturally less nativistic, attempted to avoid the issue
although a majority of the candidates which they nominated for the state assembly were pledged against
change, as were their two candidates for the senate.[119]

It was obvious that the Catholic cause would

---

115 - New York Observer, October 9, 1841; October 30,
    1841; New York Journal of Commerce, July 1, 1841;
    July 27, 1841; Baltimore Literary and Religious
    Magazine, November, 1840.
116 - Hassard, Life of John Hughes, pp. 243-248.
117 - New York Journal of Commerce, October 25, 1841;
    October 30, 1841.
118 - Scisco, Political Nativism in New York State, p. 35.
119 - New York Journal of Commerce, October 25, 1841.

receive little support from either of these major
parties. In this situation with defeat staring him
in the face, Bishop Hughes played a bold card. Catholic voters were called together at a meeting in Carroll Hall on October 30, four days before the election. There Hughes addressed them, telling them that
both parties had refused them satisfaction, and that
the only alternative was to put a ticket into the
field made up of independent candidates pledged to
support the Catholics on the school question. A ticket had been drafted, he told those gathered, and during
the course of the meeting the names of candidates for
whom they were to vote was read.[120]

If Hughes believed that he could win the Democrats to his side by the threat of an independent stand,
he was sadly mistaken. A day after the Carroll Hall
meeting the New York papers carried a card from the
Democratic candidates stating that they were now universally agreed against any change in the school system
to devote state money for secular purposes.[121] This

120 - New York Observer, November 6, 1841. The Observer
quoted Bishop Hughes as saying in regard to the
proposed Catholic party, "of that ticket I have
approved." There is ever reason to believe that
he may have used some such words, but the further
assertion of the Observer and other Whig papers
that Hughes told his listeners that it would be
a sin not to vote as he directed cannot be so
readily believed.
121 - New York Observer, November 6, 1841.

action by the Democrats forced Hughes to carry his
ticket through the election, even though he detested
a separate Catholic party[122] and believed that all
political action should be through regular party
channels.[123] He was far from dissatisfied with the
turn of events however. Hughes realized as did other
political leaders of the day, that the diversion of
Catholic support from the Democratic party would vastly weaken its strength. In this way Democrats could
not only be rebuked for deserting their foreign born
supporters, but it would be demonstrated that such
support was necessary in the future.

In this expectation Hughes was perfectly correct. Despite the formation of a Union Ticket just before
the election, based upon anti-Catholic principles and designed to balance the Catholic ticket,[124] the loss of Catholic
votes proved disastrous to the Democrats. The Whigs swept

122 - Ibid., December 11, 1841. Hughes maintained that
there was but one "escape from the circle of fire
which the political intrigues of both parties operated on by the sectarian spirit of the Public
School Society had well nigh closed around them.
This was to throw away their votes on fictitious
candidates and leave their adversaries of both
parties to fight out their own battles."
123 - Hughes to Governor Seward, March 22, 1842. Records of the American Catholic Historical Society
of Philadelphia, vol. xxiii, no. i (March, 1912),
p. 36.
124 - New York Journal of Commerce, November 3, 1841.
This ticket was announced on November 1, 1841,
two days before the election.

the polls, going into office with a majority of 290
votes over their opponents. If the 2,200 voters
who voted the Catholic ticket had given the Democrats
their support that party would have won, for the
Union ticket polled only a few votes, most of the
nativists voting for the Whigs.[125] Hughes had demonstrated without reasonable doubt that the Democrats
could not afford to cast off their Catholic supporters
if they wanted success.

But while this feature of the Carroll Hall
ticket had been a success, the entrance of Hughes and
the Catholics into the political arena was the signal
for a new burst of agitation against Rome. Here was
bait for nativistic papers which they snapped at eagerly.
They feared that the Catholics were entering politics
and would soon control the political life of the nation;
that union of church and state was inevitable. The New
York Observer shouted that the Bishop had torn off his
mask and was dictating politics in New York City.[126] The
New York Journal of Commerce gave enthusiastic response

125 - New York Tribune, November 12, 1841. The complete
       vote was as follows:
              Whig party   15,980 votes
              Democratic party   15,690   "
              Catholic movement   2,200   "
              Anti-Catholic movement   470   "
126 - New York Observer, November 6, 1841.

to this cry.[127] The editors of the <u>Protestant Vindica-</u>
<u>tor</u> charged that Hughes had never been naturalized.
"Now what right," they asked, "has a <u>foreigner</u> to
regulate our elections, to preside in political meetings, and to dictate a ticket to be voted for and declare his decision final?"[128] Newspapers that had
until this time refrained from abuse of Catholics
joined the chorus. The <u>New York Commercial Advertiser</u>
insisted that the act of the Bishop was an attempt to
break down the school system and force Americans to
support Romish seminaries.[129] The <u>New York Evangelist</u>
repeated the same warning.[130] The <u>Hartford Times</u> approved the stand taken by the Democrats in opposition
to Catholic claims[131] and the <u>New York Standard</u> bemoaned the working of "crafty priests."[132] When the
election was over the <u>New York Evening Post</u> rejoiced
in the fact that the attempt to unite crosier and politics had been defeated by the people.[133] According

---

127 - <u>New York Journal of Commerce</u>, November 6, 1841.
128 - <u>Protestant Vindicator</u>, November 17, 1841.
129 - <u>New York Commercial Advertiser</u>, October 30, 1841.
     Quoted in <u>New York Observer</u>, November 20, 1841.
130 - <u>New York Evangelist</u>, November 6, 1841. Quoted in
     <u>Ibid</u>., November 20, 1841.
131 - <u>Hartford Times</u>, November 2, 1841. Quoted in <u>Ibid</u>.,
     November 20, 1841.
132 - <u>New York Standard</u>, Quoted in <u>Ibid</u>., November 20,
     1841.
133 - <u>New York Evening Post</u>, Quoted in <u>Ibid</u>., November
     20, 1841.

to the other papers the whole Catholic effort was only part of a general plot to subvert the United States by obtaining control of its educational facilities.[134] When Bishop Hughes attempted to defend his stand[135] the New York Herald tore his statement to shreds and shouted that the venerable Bishop was lying boldly and treacherously.[136]

It was with this chorus of invective about their ears that the legislature assembled in January, 1842, to decide the whole troublesome question. The message read to them by Governor Seward made their task easier. He opened his discussion of the school question by bemoaning again the condition of the twenty thousand children of New York City kept from school because of religious and racial prejudices, comparing this with the tolerant educational system which covered the rest of the state. The Public School Society, he charged, had been given a fair trial and had failed to gain the broad confidence necessary for general educa-

134 - New York Observer, November 27, 1841.
135 - Hughes' statement was reprinted in the New York Observer, December 11, 1841. He charged that the New York Observer and the New York Journal of Commerce had taken sides with the Public School Society, and that every pulpit in the city had resounded with invective against Catholics. They had sought justice, he said, not as Catholics, but as citizens, until these papers and the press had introduced the religious issue.
136 - New York Herald, Quoted in New York Observer, June 1, 1844.

tion. As a result he recommended that the education of their children be restored to the people of New York City. This could be done by vesting the control of the common schools in a board of commissioners, selected by the people, which could appropriate the school money among all the schools, which should be organized and regulated in conformity with the general practice throughout the state.[137]

This broad and tolerant suggestion met with the usual protest from nativistic papers. The New York Observer condemned it as the most illogical statement ever printed, insisted that the people of the city itself should be allowed to decide whether or not a change was necessary, and expressed the belief that the Governor's suggestion "was a natural offspring of politics and popery."[138] The New York Journal of Commerce, only slightly less outspoken, charged the governor with perverting figures and facts in order to favor the Romanists.[139] But despite this criticism the legislature went ahead along lines suggested by Seward.[140] A bill, known after the

137 - Seward, Works, vol. ii, pp. 306-308.
138 - New York Observer, January 15, 1842.
139 - New York Journal of Commerce, January 7, 1842.
140 - While the Whigs had carried New York City, they had lost throughout the state and a Democratic majority controlled the legislature. This party was naturally more inclined against the Public School Society than their opponents and would be willing to favor a change.. New York Observer, November 13, 1841.

legislator who introduced it into the assembly as the
Maclay Bill, was submitted to both houses of the legislature soon after it convened.[141] Carrying out the suggestions made by Seward in his annual address, the measure
extended the state educational system over New York City.
Elective commissioners for each ward were to supervise
schools under them and together constitute a board of education to control the entire educational system of the
city.[142]

There was a chorus of objection from the nativistic press when the Maclay Bill was introduced. The
New York Observer insisted that Protestants would be unable to pay taxes should it be passed, for by paying them
they would be aiding the advance of Popery.[143] Hughes
was accused of being the author of the measure and acting for its passage,[144] a charge that was given weight
when a petition "half a mile long" and bearing the names
of 13,000 Catholics was submitted to the legislature,
asking that the bill be given favorable treatment.[145]
Extracts from Catholic school books were printed, and
the people warned that their children would be reading
similar glorifications of the Virgin Mary unless they

141 - New York Journal of Commerce, February 27, 1842.
142 - New York Observer, April 16, 1842.
143 - Ibid., February 5, 1842.
144 - New York Journal of Commerce, April 4, 1842.
145 - New York Observer, February 5, 1842.

brought pressure to have the measure defeated.[146] The

entire newspaper press of New York City, with the excep-

tion of the Sunday Times and the few Catholic papers,

opposed passage of the Maclay Bill.[147] When a vote was

near on the measure, friends of the Public School Society

called a meeting in front of the New York City hall that

was attended by more than twenty thousand enthusiastic

enemies of Catholicism.[148] A committee was named to

journey to Albany to present their views to the legisla-

ture.[149]

This agitation had little effect upon the legis-

lators. The Maclay Bill was passed by the assembly as

soon as it was introduced, with a majority of sixty-five

votes in its favor.[150] In the senate more delay was ex-

perienced, when the measure was referred to the appro-

priate committee,[151] allowing the Whigs a chance to ex-

146 - Watchman of the South, in Ibid., February 19, 1842.
147 - New York Observer, February 26, 1842. The Observer
      used the opportunity to charge that only Catholics
      and infidels who would publish a paper upon the
      Sabbath would favor such a measure.
148 - The meeting was held on March 16. New York Journal
      of Commerce, March 17, 1842.
149 - New York Observer, March 19, 1842. Opposition papers
      charged that the meeting was a failure. This the
      Observer denied, but admitted that towards its close
      the friends of the Public School Society had been
      disturbed by "a number of the Bishop's flock." Ibid.,
      March 26, 1842.
150 - New York Journal of Commerce, March 24, 1842.
151 - Ibid., March 24, 1842.

press hopes that it would fail to pass.[152]   These hopes
proved to be ill founded.   On April 8, 1842 a discussion
of the question was begun, attempts at delay were over-
ridden and the bill was passed and sent to Seward for
his signature.   This was forthcoming immediately and the
Maclay Bill became a law.[153]

The New York Observer printed a sorrowful editorial entitled "Triumph of the Roman Catholics," "The dark
hour is at hand," it said.   "People must only trust in God
to be saved from the Beast."[154]   The Protestant Vindicator
gave over two issues to forecasting the dire results which
would follow with Popery thus encouraged.[155]   Enraged by
the conduct of their governor, Whigs of New York City officially declared their opposition to the provisions of the
Maclay Bill.[156]   While the Democrats gave no such open

152 - The New York Journal of Commerce rejoiced to learn
      that "the Jesuitry of Bishop Hughes ... was likely
      to fail its object, for the delegation in the sen-
      ate from this district were unanimous and firm
      against destroying the public schools ... and
      while they stood so, the mischief could not be
      accomplished. " April 1, 1842.
153 - Ibid., April 12, 1842.
154 - New York Observer, April 16, 1842.
155 - Protestant Vindicator, April 20, 1842; May 4, 1842.
156 - New York Commercial Advertiser, April 11, 1842. The
      Whig General Committee adopted a resolution stating
      that it would be dangerous to place any man in the
      city councils whose sentiments on the school ques-
      tion were not clearly avowed and in favor of the
      old system. New York Journal of Commerce, April
      12, 1842. They also talked of repealing the bill
      that had been inflicted on them by Bishop Hughes,
      blaming its passage on two Whigs who had been ab-
      sent from the Senate when the vote was taken. Ibid.,
      April 14, 1842.

manifestation of nativistic feelings, the party split
into two factions in several wards, one dominated by
Irish Catholics, the other by native born voters.[157]
On the night that the bill was passed, the New York
streets were filled with shouting mobs which drove
the hated Irish before them and stoned the windows
of Bishop Hughes' home.[158] So turbulent were the
feelings of the people that the militia was called
out to guard Catholic churches.[159]

But this gloom and disorder availed little.
The Maclay Bill had been passed, the Public School
Society had been pushed from the picture. Sectarian
teaching, in theory at least, was destined to speedy
extermination. In practice, however, the Catholics
were doomed to still further disappointments. The
new measure placed the New York City schools under
the nominal supervision of the state education system,
and even before its passage the state Superintendent of
Common Schools had recommended a daily reading from the
Bible by teachers under his charge.[160] The Whigs, not
content even with such control, had begun to agitate

157 - New York Herald, April 14, 1842.
158 - New York Commercial Advertiser, April 13, 1842.
159 - Ibid., April 13, 1842.
160 - New York Observer, March 12, 1842. The Superin-
      tendent at this time was Samuel Young, who also
      held office as Secretary of State. His recommen-
      dation was dated, February 15, 1842.

soon after the passage of the bill, urging the election of trustees of the Public School Society as the educational commissioners for which it provided.[161] A continuous stream of such propaganda, carried on until the June elections, was effective. When election day came the opponents of Catholicism united into Union tickets in every ward, regardless of party,[162] and swept all before them, emerging with complete control of the school board.[163] To make matters worse, the new state Superintendent of Common Schools named in July was William L. Stone, exposer of Maria Monk, but long a prominent nativist.[164] The public school Bible was firmly entrenched while his regime lasted.

Thus Bishop Hughes emerged from his first contest with a victory that was hollow and worthless. Sectarian teaching, overthrown in theory, still endured in practice. The struggle had cost Governor Seward his office,

161 - New York Journal of Commerce, May 5, 1842; June 1, 1842; June 7, 1842.
162 - Scisco, Political Nativism in New York State, p. 37.
163 - New York Journal of Commerce, June 8, 1842.
164 - New York Observer, July 30, 1842. The Observer rejoiced at the appointment and commented on the extreme disappointment of the Papists.

when nativistic voters massed against him,[165] and it had made the Catholics realize that justice could not be expected from the people of New York. From that time on Hughes concentrated his efforts in building parochial schools for the education of Catholic children, so that they could be withdrawn from the public schools.[166]

But while Bishop Hughes was willing to admit defeat, others of his faith displayed a more pugnacious spirit. The Maclay Bill had specifically forbidden sectarian teaching in any school in the state sharing in the public funds, and it naturally seemed to many Catholics that this provision should be used to stop the reading of the Protestant Bible to Catholic children.

[165] - One of Seward's biographers maintains that the school funds controversy cost him 2,000 votes in the contest for the governorship, enough to cause his defeat. Seward, Works, vol. i, p. xliii. This same controversy was to bob up again in 1860. One reason why Seward was not nominated for the presidency by the Republicans at that time was because that party needed to absorb all the Know Nothing vote in Pennsylvania and Indiana, and it was feared that his earlier attitude would be held against him. Desmond, The Know Nothing Party, pp. 123-124. Seward remained a constant friend of the foreigner and the immigrant despite this. See Seward, Works, vol. iii, p. 258.

[166] - Hassard, Life of John Hughes, p. 251; Shea, History of the Catholic Church in the United States, vol. iv, pp. 108-109.

Despite the fact that the school board elections in June,
1843, went overwhelmingly in favor of nativistic candidates[167] the first of the petitions designed to prohibit
Bible reading was presented to the Board of Education
only a month later. Trustees of the Fourth Ward, where
Catholic numbers and sentiment were strong, presented the
petition, insisting that Bible reading was sectarian, and
should be forbidden.[168] Not until October 11 did the
School Board return its decision on the request; when
it did the answer was the only one which could be expected
from such a nativistically inclined group. The Bible without note or comment, the Board found, was not a sectarian
book, and reading from it could not be prohibited under
the Maclay Bill.[169]

Despite this obviously partisan decision, Catholics were able to find some relief. The elective trustees
who had charge of education in each ward had the right to
determine the books which could be read in the schools directly under their supervision. In wards where the popula-

167 - Scisco, Political Nativism in New York State, p. 37.
168 - New York Observer, July 23, 1843. The Observer be-
      moaned the fact that the Catholics had gained strength
      through an alliance with infidels and Jews in attempt-
      ing to secure favorable action on their petition.
169 - Ibid., October 14, 1843.

tion was preponderantly Catholic, as a result, Bible
reading was forbidden and the type of education desired by the backers of the Maclay Bill was more closely followed. In 1844 Bible reading had been abandoned
in thirty-one of the city schools.[170]

These successful efforts by Catholics were a
source of never ending alarm to nativistic editors who
did their best, by a constant stream of editorial comment, to warn the people of this Popish aggression.
"This is the work," they said, "of foreign sectarian-
ism, planting itself in our midst, forming political
alliances, and attaching itself to the fortunes of a
party that seeks to perpetuate its power even at the
expense of everything else."[171] Seward heard the charge
hurled against him that he had sold Christianity to a
foreign despot in return for foreign votes.[172] Editors
pointed out the confusion which would result should Catholic demands be acceded to: every child would have his
own religious instruction and schools would be given
over to courses in the Talmud, The Koran, the Douay
Bible and, for infidels, Robert Taylor's _Dioegesis_ "or
some other ritual of blasphemy."[173] When Hughes tried

170 - _The National Protestant_, December, 1844.
171 - _Ibid._, December, 1844.
172 - _Native American_ (Philadelphia), April 13, 1844.
173 - _New York American Republican_, May 23, 1844.

to defend himself against the charge that he was a
"papal panderer" who had carried religion into politics[174] he brought down a storm of ridicule and abuse
upon his head.[175] A prominent nativistic clergyman,
the Reverend Hiram Ketchum, traveled about New York
City throughout 1844 addressing large and enthusiastic
audiences upon the danger of Catholic aggression typified in their demands upon the schools.[176] When one
paper, the Albany Evening Journal endeavored to justify
the Catholic stand its subscription list dropped so
rapidly that the editor was forced to resign.[177] Each
new election was a signal for a new outburst of editorial comment and excitement.[178] Before the spring
election in 1844 processions marched through the city
streets carrying banners proclaiming "No Mutilated
School Books," and "The Book of Liberty! It Shall
Not be Excluded from our Schools."[179] Tension was
increased when handbills were distributed to ladies

174 - Philadelphia Sun, quoted in Ibid., May 6, 1844.
175 - Ibid., May 22, 1844. Hughes' defense was in
the form of an open letter to the mayor, printed
in the New York Courier and Enquirer, denying
that he had any political interests or that he
had worked for any party. His statement that
no party had approached him for support in the
last election was immediately twisted by the
editor of the New York American Republican to
mean that Hughes had approached a party.
176 - New York Observer, October 26, 1844. The meetings
were held in the Tabernacle to accomodate the
crowds.
177 - New York American Republican, May 25, 1844.
178 - New York Observer, August 24, 1844; New York American Republican, May 28, 1844; June 1, 1844.
179 - New York Observer, April 13, 1844.

showing that the Bible was unfit for school use by
printing passages which could be taken in a base
way by evil minded persons, a handbill that was
branded as so disgusting that it could be published only by a Jesuit.[180] This same election
brought into the field of controversy not only Bishop Hughes but also William Stone, Superintendent
of Common Schools for the state.[181] In spite of
this agitation and excitement, the Catholic cause
made some gains. When a resolution was introduced
before the Board of Education in December, 1844, to
the effect that the exclusion of the Scriptures from
the schools was in violation of the law, it was defeated by the members.[182] It was evident that these
determined advocates of nativism were beginning to

180 - New York American Republican, June 8, 1844.
181 - Native American (Philadelphia,) June 11, 1844
      and ff.
182 - New York Observer, December 28, 1844. The
      resolution was defeated by a vote of twenty
      to fourteen.

weaken in their stand.[183]

While this contest was raging in New York,
new fuel was added to the flames in other cities throughout the land. In January 1843, the Catholics of Philadelphia began to demand that the Protestant Scriptures
should no longer be read in the public schools,[184] a
demand which was to lead to bloodshed only a year and
a half later.[185] In September, 1843 similar efforts
were made by the Catholics of Newark, New Jersey, only

183 - The legal status of Bible reading in state sup-
      ported schools was not settled until many years
      later. In 1890 the Wisconsin courts gave the
      first expression to a liberal sentiment in the
      case of Weiss et al vs. the District Board of
      School District No. 8 of the City of Egerton,
      referred to as the Egerton Bible Case. The Su-
      perior Court held that Bible reading in the pub-
      lic schools was sectarian instruction and hence
      unconstitutional. Dohan, Our State Constitutions,
      p. 306; Cornelison, Relation of Religion to Civil
      Government, pp. 272-278. This decision applied
      only in Wisconsin, however, and other states lag-
      ged behind in a similar expression. In 1898 a
      Michigan court in the case of Pfeiffer vs. the
      Board of Education held that the reading of the
      Scriptures, without note or comment from the
      teacher, was not in violation of the clause of
      the state constitution forbidding sectarian in-
      struction. Dohan, Our State Constitutions, p.
      303. A similar view was upheld for Kentucky in
      Hackett vs. the Brooksville School District (1905)
      and for Massachusetts in Spiller vs. the Inhabi-
      tants of Woburn (1866) Ibid., p. 306. In Illi-
      nois Bible reading was forbidden in 1910 in the
      case of People vs. The Board of Education, where
      the court held that "the free enjoyment of relig-
      ious worship includes freedom not to worship."
      Ibid., p. 305.
184 - New York Observer, January 28, 1843.
185 - Catholic demands for exclusion of the Bible from
      the Philadelphia schools led directly to the Phila-
      delphia riots in 1844. See above, Chapter X.

to meet defeat at the hands of the Common Council.[186]
Less than a year later Protestant agitators tried to
introduce Bible reading into the Detroit schools, but
their efforts were useless before the overwhelming
Catholic population of that city.[187] While these instances were far from universal, the impression was
given that all over the country a united Catholic
movement to gain control of the education facilities
of the nation was going on. To firm nativistic believers, this seemed only part of the plot outlined
by Morse and his disciples, whereby the Pope was to
take over the United States. A foreign traveler in
America at the time reflected the current feeling
when he commented on the injustice done Catholics
who were forced to support public schools by taxation yet were unable to send their children to them.
"This heavy burden," he wrote, "will be borne only
until the Catholics in any State have numbers and
political power sufficient to compel a division of
the school fund, and the devotion of a fair proportion to their separate use...That day, in several
states, cannot be very distant, and is looked for-

---

186 - New York Observer, October 7, 1843.
187 - Shea, History of the Catholic Church in the
      United States, vol. iv, pp. 208-209.

ward to with dread by many Protestant Americans."[188]

This Protestant dread found expression, not in gloomy contemplation of the inevitable, but in a burst of propaganda against Catholicism and Catholic claims which was extremely effective. In the eyes of these agitators, Romish efforts were designed to accomplish one of two ends; to secure control of the educational facilities of the nation, or to drive the Bible from state supported public schools. The first of these charges was not a new one, for several years propaganda writers had been shouting the evil of Popish schools. They charged that such schools gave extremely poor training,[189] that pupils were taught only "Sabbath breaking, uncleanness and deception."[190] They insisted that Jesuits went so far as to disguise themselves as Protestants to obtain teaching positions,[191] not only in public schools but also as tutors in southern homes.[192] They shouted that efforts were made to attract Protestants to Catholic schools by giving the teachers the

188 - Nichols, Forty Years of American Life, vol.ii, p.84.
189 - Supplement to Six Months in a Convent, p. 46; Protestant Vindicator, November 4, 1835; October 28, 1840.
190 - Protestant Vindicator, October 28, 1835.
191 - Secret Instructions to the Jesuits; Faithfully Translated from the Latin of an Old Genuine London Copy, Edited by W. C. Brownlee (New York, 1841), Introduction, pp. 13-14.
192 - Morse, The Proscribed German Student, pp. 133-137.

learned title of professor and by charging less
tuition.[193] All these efforts, the propagandists
agreed, were for the sole purpose of luring Protestant children into their schools in order that
they might be converted to Popery.[194] There is

193 - Norton, Herman, Startling Facts for American
Protestants! Progress of Romanism since the
Revolutionary War; its Present Position and
Future Prospects. (New York, 1844),pp. 10-11.
194 - New York Observer, January 3, 1835; December 2,
1837; February 11, 1843; August 24, 1844;Beecher,
L., A Plea for the West, p. 102; Supplement to
Six Months in a Convent, pp. 55-56; The Episcopal
Bishop of Maryland spoke before a convention of
members of that church in 1841 praising the Protestant schools that had been established in the
state and glorying in the fact that now children
would not have to be sent to Catholic schools to
have "their souls endangered by the fascinations
of that corrupt and ensnaring oohism." Protestant
Vindicator, August 11, 1840. Several books were
published at the time devoted entirely to exposing the evils of Catholic education, notably,
Roman Catholic Female Schools (New York, 1837);
and Education in Romish Seminaries. A Letter in
Answer to Certain Inquiries respecting the Propriety of Selecting, as Places of Education, Seminaries Professedly under the Control of Religious
Societies of the Court of Rome. (New York, 1845).
It is interesting to note that these fears were
not entirely groundless. The Bishop of Cincinnati,
in appealing for funds from Europe in 1843, boasted
of the fact that more than half the students in his
Catholic schools were Protestants, stating that the
Jesuits who conducted them never forgot that their
teaching was an apostleship, that their first duty
was to train up these young hearts to piety. Annals
de l' Association de la Propagation de la Foi, vol.
xv, p. 366. See also, for a similar sentiment,
Brownson, H. F., The Life of O. A. Brownson (Detroit,
1898-1900), vol. ii, p. 201.

little wonder, as a result, that objection arose over
Catholic demands for a share of the school fund in
various states. Were Protestants to be taxed to build
Catholic schools that would convert the youth of the
land to Popery and hurry the day when the invasion of
that dread Monarch would take place?

The effectiveness of such propaganda cannot
be doubted, but its importance is dimmed when compared
to the excitement created by the Catholic demand that
the Bible be removed from public schools. Propaganda
writers leaped upon this new grievance with the enthusiasm that it deserved. The hated Papists had actually
dared attack the very bulwark of American Protestantism,
the Holy Scriptures. Nativists realized that here was
a cry which could be agitated among the sober, middle
class Christians who had been left unmoved by the ribald
phrase and libidinous tale of Maria Monk and her followers.

To such a Protestant, Rome's attack upon Bible
reading could mean only one thing. The Papists were opposed to the Bible; they were joining with infidels to
drive that sacred book from America. Writers turned
their efforts to tracing this opposition and learned
accounts were written to show that from the time of
the Council of Milan in the year 390, Catholics had

been forbidden the Scriptures and the "skulls, teeth,
shoulder-bones and petrified breath of saints began
to be the school books of the clergy and the common
people."[195] It was pointed out that in 1929 at the
Council of Toulouse definite action had been taken
to forbid the Scriptures to the common people, and
traditions of the church were given equal weight with
the divine words.[196] Reasons for this were not hard
to find for the propaganda writers. They asserted that
the Roman hiererachy had to forbid the Bible to members
of their faith, for the Scriptures exposed the errors
of Rome. Should the people read God's true word they
would rise in their wrath and throw off the Papal chains
to which they were bound.[197] No wonder, then, that Rome
was an enemy of the Bible. This cry was shouted from
the pulpit of nearly every Protestant church in New York
by the Reverend George B. Cheever during a series of lec-

195 - Cheever, George B., The Hierarchical Despotism;
     Lectures on the Mixture of Civil and Ecclesiasti-
     cal Power In the Governments In the Middle Ages
     in Illustration of the Nature and Progress of the
     Romish Church (New York, 1844), pp. 122-127.
196 - Ibid., pp. 128-131.
197 - New York Observer, July 30, 1842; Protestant Vin-
     dicator, October 20, 1841; Cheever, The Hierarch-
     ical Despotism, pp. 131-137; The Crisis, an Ap-
     peal to our Countrymen on the Subject of Foreign
     Influence in the United States (New York, 1844),
     p. 68.

tures given throughout 1843.[198] Members of the American
Institute of Education, gathered for their annual convention in 1844, heard the same shout reechoed by another
speaker.[199] The New York Observer[200] printed a series of
articles which also bore the same burden and books expanding upon the theme were poured from the presses.[201]

It was only natural, amid such a volley of
invective, that the Bible societies should be drawn into the fray. The American Bible Society, at its annual
meeting in New York in 1844, listened to an inspired address by the Reverend Hiram Ketchum, in which he recounted
the history of the school controversy in New York and
shouted that America was and always had been a Protestant country where the Protestant scriptures should be
venerated. Moved by his words, the Society adopted a

198 - New York Observer, June 30, 1843. The Observer
      reported that all of the lectures had been well
      attended and urged its readers to hear his true
      words.
199 - New York American Republican, May 4, 1844. The
      speaker was Professor Humphrey.
200 - New York Observer, July 30, 1842 and ff.
201 - Typical of the books published on the subject:
      Political Popery, or, Bibles and Schools, with
      the Condition, Progress and Ulterior Objects
      of Romanists in the United States (New York,
      1844); Crowell, John, Republics Established
      and Thrones overturned by the Bible (Phila-
      delphia, 1849); Watson, R., An Apology for
      the Bible (New York, 1835); Milan, Caeser,
      Can I Join the Church of Rome while my Rule
      of Faith is in the Bible? An Inquiry Presented
      to the Conscience of the Christian Reader (New
      York, 1844); Borrow, George, The Bible in Spain
      (New York, 1847); Rome's Policy Toward the Bible,
      (Philadelphia, 1844)

resolution, stating that "the Bible, from its origin, purity and simplicity of its style, is a book peculiarly appropriate for use in the common schools, and cannot be excluded from them without hazard both to our civil and religious liberties."[202] Especially did the American Bible Society and its defenders among the ranks of the public press express horror when, on May 8, 1844, the Pope issued a decree against societies distributing the unauthorized version of the Scriptures in Italy.[203] Here was proof of Rome's opposition to the Bible, coming at a singularly opportune time.

Effective as this may have been, far more impressive was a startling manifestation of Popish feelings in the United States itself. In 1842 and 1843 a story grew of a great meeting in New York State where the hated Romanists had piled hundreds of Bibles upon a fire and burned them to ashes. According to these tales, priests in the vicinity of Carbeau, New York, began to hold meetings during October, 1842, in which Catholics were instructed to assemble all the Bibles which had been given them by agents of Protestant Societies. On October 27

202 - New York Observer, May 18, 1844.
203 - New York Observer, July 27, 1844; Native American (Philadelphia), July 20, 1844; New York American Republican, July 19, 1844; September 18, 1844.

several hundred copies of the Holy Scriptures which had
been collected in this way were piled high upon the
ground and ignited, a priest kindling the fire. Despite protests of agents of Bible societies who were
present, the Scriptures were burned to ashes.[204]

It is probable that this "Champlain Bible
Burning," as it was promptly labeled, had some basis
in fact, although it was extremely unlikely that stories of it which circulated during the following years
can be accepted as completely true. Bishop Hughes insisted that the whole story was a humbug, and that the
burning had never taken place.[205] But regardless of
its truth or falsity, the effect was the same. A storm
of indignation greeted the news. Public meetings were
held in counties near the scene of the supposed outrage
to express Protestant indignation[206] and editors of nativistic prints outdid themselves in condemning the
priests who would thus attack the Word of God. "It
may be," said one, "that the embers of the late Bible
conflagration in Carbeau may kindle a flame that shall
consume the last vestige of Popery in this land of ours."[207]

204 - The account is drawn from narratives printed in the
      New York Observer, December 10, 1842; January 14,
      1843; American Protestant Magazine, September, 1845.
205 - New York Observer, January 14, 1843.
206 - Ibid., December 10, 1842.
207 - Ibid., January 14, 1843.

Another shouted the the "27th of October, 1842, will
be remembered in the United States as long as the Gunpowder plot of the 5th of November, 1605, will be remembered in England."[208] Two books were hurried from
the press to kindle Protestant bigotry and acquaint
all men with the true nature of Romanism which had
thus been exposed.[209] The Reverend George B. Cheever
not only flayed the burning in print as typical of the
auto da fe in Spain[210] but traveled about the eastern
section of the country delivering an address exposing
the horrors of the act.[211] While excitement was still
intense, news reached New York of another Catholic attempt to burn Bibles near Pittsburg.[212] Here was final
proof. People by this time were willing to believe that
even the burning of an anti-Catholic book store in Baltimore was part of a great Popish plot.[213]

208 - American Protestant Magazine, September, 1845.
209 - Dowling, John, The Burning of the Bibles, (Philadel-
      phia, 1843); and The Burning of the Bible; being a
      Defense of the Protestant Version of the Scriptures
      against the Attacks of Popish Apologists for the
      Champlain Bible Burners (New York, 1845)
210 - Cheever, Hierarchical Despotism, p. 144.
211 - New York Observer, February 11, 1843. The Observer
      reports the address before the New England Society.
212 - New York American Republican, September 7, 1844.
213 - Protestant Vindicator, May 12, 1841. The book store
      was operated by David Owen. Over it were the of-
      fices of an anti-Catholic newspaper, the Saturday
      Visitor.

Thus did the school controversy in New York bear its fruit. A flood of propaganda had covered the country by 1844, convincing the nativistically inclined that the real aim of the Romanists had been to drive the Bible from the schools in order to perpetuate opposition to God's word which had endured from early times. The propagandists had played well upon Protestant sympathy, and were being rewarded by new outbursts of nativists who insisted on expanding the three R's to include "Reading, 'riting, rithmatic" and religion.[214] Here was a new form of appeal powerful in its effects. Because of this agitation, the thousands of church members throughout the land had been reached. The Bible was the basis of their religion and their life. The Romanists were attacking the Bible. To defend the Word of God against Rome required strength in numbers and thousands of new comers to the ranks of nativism were willing to add their clamor to the growing cry against Popery.

214 - Cheever, Hierarchical Despotism, pp. 147-149. Several books were published, demanding the return of the Bible to the schools despite Catholic demands. Among these were: Defense of the Use of the Bible in the Schools (New York, 1830); Grimke, Thomas S., Address on the Expediency and Duty of Adopting the Bible as a Class Book in Every Scheme of Education, from the Primary School to the University, Delivered at Columbia, South Carolina, in the Presbyterian Church, on Friday Evening, 4th of December, 1829, before the Richland School (Charleston, 1830); Henry, James, Education and the Common Schools (New York, 1844).

VII

THE PROTESTANT ORGANIZATION IS STRENGTHENED
1840 - 1844

With the New York school controversy fresh
in the minds of the people, the nativistic societies
which had been sowing anti-Catholic sentiment with
increasing success since the middle 1830's foresaw
great crops of converts to their cause. Horrors of
the inquisition and convent had nurtured the seeds
of bigotry and intolerance to some extent but the
thinking, church going, middle class as a whole had
read such propaganda with skepticism. When the New
York Catholic vote not only violated political precedent, but went so far as to eject the Word of God
from the class room, thousands of men and women for
the first time began to consider Rome and her tenets
as an immediate and real menace. Alert nativists renewed their efforts to stamp out Popery, confident
that their cause would find favor with even greater
numbers in future years.

Especially active in this concentrated drive
against Catholicism were members of the Protestant Reformation Society. Headed by the eminent nativist, the

Reverend William C. Brownlee, the society gradually
expanded its membership and widened its field of interest.[1] An agent was sent to England to keep Americans
in touch with the English anti-Catholic societies and
the English No-Popery press.[2] Stress upon the religious
aspect of the cause brought a new influx of lay and clergymen into membership, many of the latter accepting a
life membership as gifts from their congregations.[3] Thus
by the end of 1840, the decade of continued success presaged a rosy future.

1 - In 1840 the officers of the society were: the Reverend W. C. Brownlee, president, James G. Eadis,
Treasurer; the Reverend C. C. VanArsdale, corresponding secretary; the Reverend Octavius Winslow,
foreign secretary; and Charles K. Moore, recording
secretary. Protestant Vindicator, June 24, 1840.
A year later, the same officers were reelected at
the tenth annual meeting of the society, held in
New York, with a few exceptions. Two vice-presidents were added at that time, Duncan Dunbar and
D. R. Downer, and D. A. H. Jackson was named corresponding secretary. Ibid., November 17, 1841.
Dr. Brownlee remained president from the time of
the organization of the society until his death
in 1843.
2 - Protestant Vindicator, June 23, 1841. This agent
was in close touch with the British Reformation
Society and the London Protestant Association.
He was responsible for the sending of many anti-
Catholic accounts taken from the Dublin Warder
and the London Protestant.
3 - Ibid., February 17, 1841. The Protestant Vindicator throughout this period prints frequent acknowl-
edgments from members of the clergy, thanking their
congregations for making them life members in the
society.

Encouraged by this new following, officers
of the Protestant Reformation Society entered upon a
unique scheme. A few years before the anti-Catholic
newspapers had introduced the lecturing agent system,
which had operated with considerable success. In 1840
a similar organization was launched by the officers of
the society, and by June, 1841, seven clergymen were
employed to travel constantly over the entire country,
speaking in each city and town upon the horrors of
Popery, and incidentally securing members for the
society and subscriptions for its official organ, the
Protestant Vindicator.[4] Both rural hamlet and metrop-
olis knew their invective, no audience was too large
or too small to allow them to pass before they had delivered their message of hate.[5] Even the colleges were
not immune to their influence, Princeton[6] and Harvard[7]
students assembling to hear violent exposures of Romanism. The success of these itinerant lecturers is at-

4 - Ibid., January 20, 1841. Agents listed operated
    over most of New England and the middle states.
5 - Ibid., January 20, 1841.
6 - Ibid., January 20, 1841. The paper printed a mo-
    tion adopted by the students of the Princeton The-
    ological Seminary thanking the Reverend Charles
    Sparry for his address, and promising to spread
    his doctrines from that time on.
7 - The National Protestant, November, 1845.

tested by the constant flow of contributions from listeners into the coffers of the organization which hired them.[8] Meanwhile enthusiastic converts to the No Popery cause were left in their wake.[9]

While the hinterland was thus being saved from the inroads of Romanism by the Protestant Reformation Society, the home field was not being neglected. Each winter the society sponsored a series of lectures in New York City, usually lasting over a period of many weeks. In 1840, the President, Dr. Brownlee, undertook the entire burden of this course, giving a series of twelve lectures from the pulpit of the Dutch Reformed Church.[10] So enthusiastic was the response that the society was forced to enlarge the scope of its lectures in 1841 by securing the Broadway Tabernacle and the services of nine clergymen speakers. In this year twenty-six lectures were given throughout the winter months.[11] Rabid and biting in their attacks, these ministers at-

8 - Protestant Vindicator, January 20, 1841; September 16, 1840. Reports of Lecturers printed show that contributions from each lecture ranged from $30. and $10., depending upon the size of the city.
9 - Ibid., May 26, 1841. A letter is printed from a citizen of Washington who was so stirred by the agent of the society that he proposes forming a similar society in that city.
10- New York Observer, March 7, 1840; February 22, 1840.
11- Protestant Vindicator, December 1, 1841.

tracted large audiences anxious to hear the worst about
the dread menace of Catholicism. That they were not
disappointed is deduced from the subject of a typical
lecture of the series:

> No. 16 - Celibacy of the Priests and Nuns;
> History of this modern innovation by ghostly
> tyranny; - its atrocious consequences. It con-
> verts monastaries, nunneries and nations into
> one vast brothel. Proof: historical facts.[12]

In 1842 a similar series of lectures was given
at the Sunday night services of many churches throughout the city. Officers of the society believed that in
this way a larger number of people could be reached than
through centrally located speakers.[13] It was this method
of attack which was to be used in the winter series from
that time until the close of the society's existence.[14]

Not only were these speakers active in winning
converts and spreading wide and far the doctrines of No-
Popery, but in addition they played a further part in
the anti-Catholic crusade. When the lecturing system
was inaugurated by the Protestant Reformation Society,
it was decided that all proceeds derived from the agents
should be used to publish tracts against Romanism.[15] This

12 - Ibid., December 1, 1841.
13 - Ibid., February 9, 1842.
14 - New York Observer, January 20, 1844. The Reverend
Herman Norton was the principal lecturer in the
series given in 1843-1844.
15 - Protestant Vindicator, June 23, 1841.

resulted in the release of a steady flood of written
denunications, which were spread throughout the land.
Nearly every phase of Catholic worship was treated in
the two series of tracts published in 1840 and 1841,
Romish image worship,[16] celibacy,[17] unity,[18] and fanaticism[19] were flayed in bitter language. Other tracts
presented statements gathered from the writers of the
past against Romanism,[20] urged Catholics to leave their
church to embrace the Protestant cause[21] and flaunted
again the alleged Bull of Excommunication against William
Hogan which had played its part in the School Funds controversy.[22]

Not only was the Protestant Reformation Society
stirred to further activity by the renewed interest in
anti-Catholicism that came with the New York controversy, but a similar rejuvenation was marked in minor societies throughout the land. While the Protestant Reformation Society was organized on a national scale, its headquarters were in New York and the feeling was prevalent
that similar societies could be supported in other cities.

16 - Tract No. 16, published in the Protestant Vindicator,
     April 6, 1842, Tract No. 14, in Ibid.,August 5, 1840.
17 - Tract No. 15, Ibid., November 11, 1840.
18 - Tract No. 5, Ibid., October 28, 1840.
19 - Tract No. 10, Ibid., July 22, 1840.
20 - Tract No. 16, First Series, Ibid., September 30, 1840.
21 - Tract No. 12, Ibid., June 24, 1840.
22 - Tract No. 17, Ibid., December 9, 1840.

All over the country these local organizations flourished, many of them affiliating with the parent society in New York. In Reading, Massachusetts, the Female Protestant Association was formed to sponsor sermons on Popery and circulate free tracts exhibiting its errors.[23] In Washington a similar society operated along the same lines, and staged debates on Catholicism.[24] Protestants of Philadelphia had organized no less than three separate anti-Catholic societies by the summer of 1842.[25] The Society of Inquiry of the Princeton Theological Seminary appointed a "Committee on the Romish Church, Public Morals and Infidelity," which undertook the task of instructing fellow students and townspeople into the errors of Romanism.[26] In the middle west the Louisville Protestant League spread its influence over Kentucky and neighboring states.[27]

23 - Protestant Vindicator, December 23, 1840. The society cooperated closely with the Protestant Reformation Society, circulating its tracts, and making the leading clergymen of Reading its life members.
24 - Ibid., June 9, 1841.
25 - Ibid., May 18, 1842.
26 - Ibid., May 18, 1842. The committee requested the Reverend Robert J. Breckinridge to supply a list of books which would combat the errors of Romanism. Breckinridge's reply, printed in this issue of the Protestant Vindicator, recommends the Bible as the most effective work, especially when compared to the decrees of the Council of Trent.
27 - Jenkins, T. J., "Know Nothingism in Kentucky and its Destroyer," Catholic World, vol. lvii (July, 1893), p. 513.

This emphasis upon local societies to carry
on the anti-Catholic crusade found expression even in
New York City. The Protestant Reformation Society
might be effective, but its efforts were scattered
over the nation. It was felt that the danger of Popery
in New York required more concentrated efforts and from
this belief grew the American Protestant Union, formed
in May, 1841. Headed by Samuel F. B. Morse as its first
president, the society announced itself as opposed to
"the subjugation of our country to the control of the
Pope of Rome and his adherents, and for the preservation of our civil and religious institutions." Its
purpose, according to the constitution adopted, was
"to preserve for ourselves and secure to posterity,
the religious, civil and political principles of our
country, according to the spirit of our ancestors, as
embodied and set forth in the Declaration of Independence and the Federal Constitution."[28] Alike in purpose
was the Orange Society, formed in New York in 1841, with

28 - The meeting for organization was held on May 30,
1841, at the Methodist church on Green Street,
with Samuel F. B. Morse in the chair. The society was formed as a "national defense society."
New York Observer, June 12, 1841.

branches in Baltimore and Philadelphia.[29]

This burst of activity among the openly anti-Catholic societies was paralleled by a similar stir of interest among religious societies the nation over. Aware that the New York controversy had created sentiment against Romanism in the minds of many of their members. These religious organizations turned more and more to exposing the errors of Popery and checking its spread. The powerful American Education Society for the first time felt this antipathy when they secured the Reverend Lyman Beecher as speaker at their annual meeting in 1843 and listened to him portray Popery as the greatest danger faced by the country, greater even than slavery or intemperance. "We must establish schools better than Popish schools if we are to save ourselves," he told his audience, "for Irish and Germans will send their children to Popish schools if Protestant schools are not available."[30]

---

29 - The Protestant Vindicator hailed the proposal for such a society, united against Popery yet including Protestant foreigners in its ranks, when it was proposed during the summer of 1841. Protestant Vindicator, August 11, 1841. The society was actually formed a few months later. Ibid., September 22, 1841. Catholic historians are inclined to place the entire blame for nativistic outbursts at this time on these Orange societies. See Guilday, Life and Times of John England, vol. ii, p. 379.

30 - New York Observer, May 30, 1841. The meeting was held in New York on May 11, 1841.

Equally interested in the cause of educating Catholic children to Protestantism was the American Tract Society. Its members were warned in 1842 that Romish teachers were fast securing a hold on the Mississippi Valley and that only through renewed efforts could the country be saved.[31] In the same year a new and effective means of combating this danger was devised. The society adopted a system of colportage, whereby missionary agents worked among the foreign and Catholic population, distributing tracts and endeavoring in every way to secure conversions to Protestantism.[32] The new system was successful from the first. By 1843 the society could look with pleasure on the work which its colporteurs had done among the Romanists,[33] and include in its annual report a long list of conversions to the true faith for which they had been responsible.[34] The hundreds of agents thus

31 - The Reverend Edward N. Kirk addressed the society on May 25. American Tract Society, Twenty-Eighth Annual Report (1842), pp. 10-12.
32 - American Tract Society, Twenty-Ninth Annual Report (1843), p. 4.
33 - Ibid., p. 47. The nature and purpose of the colportage system can be seen when it is realized that the first agent appointed was a converted Romanist. The Society boasted that after a year their colporteurs had accomplished a Reformation on a small scale.
34 - Ibid., pp. 48-51.

loosed by the Tract Society to scour the land, each

adding his voice to the popular clamor against Popery,

proved a powerful and effective instrument in further-

ing Protestant demands.[35] It was inevitable with this

new interest among its members, that the society should

increase the spread of its anti-Catholic publications

throughout the land.[36]

The American Bible Society displayed an even

greater interest in Catholicism which grew naturally

from Romish attacks on the Scriptures during the New

35 - The success of the system was reiterated at the
annual meeting in 1844 when a resolution was adopted praising it as "an important means of
evangelization...for the large and increasing
immigrant German and Roman Catholic population."
American Tract Society, Thirtieth Annual Report,
(1844), p. 4.
36 - Among the books and tracts published by the society
at this period are the following: On Purgatory and
Infallibility (New York, 1839); False Claims of the
Pope (New York, 1842); Dickinson, Austin, Thoughts
for Catholics and Their Friends (New York, 1844);
Destruction of the Inquisition at Madrid (New York,
1844); D' Aubigne, Merle, History of the Great Reformation, 3 vols. (New York, 1844); Dickinson,
Mrs. Austin, The Mother of Saint Augustine (New
York, 1845); Orchard, Isaac, Friendly Suggestions
to an Emigrant by an Emigrant (New York, 1845);
The Conversion of Luther (In German, New York,
1845); The Reformation in Europe (New York, 1845);
The Spirit of Popery (New York, 1845). American
Tract Society, Annual Reports, 1839-1842. The
Society also recommended a model Christian Library
that should be used in every school, including such
anti-Catholic works as Nevins, William, Thoughts
on Popery (New York, 1838), New York Observer,
May 23, 1840.

York controversy. Proceedings of the annual meeting of members of the society in 1843 were given over nearly entirely to a denunciation of Papal claims and ambitions. Impassioned speeches were followed by the adoption of equally heated resolutions which called on all members to spread the Bible in order to check the advance of the Beast.[37] Three years later a similar procedure was thought necessary.[38]

But with all this activity, enthusiastic Protestants still remained discontented. It was well enough to attack Romanism in America: to expose its errors and convert its disciples to true Christianity. That was necessary and important. Yet the feeling grew that something more was needed. Rome was sending its minions to America, steeped in the evils of her vile system. Why should some effort not be made to stop this migration at its source? Why should Americans not undertake the stupendous task of converting Italy and Rome itself to Protestantism? Then and then alone would the United States be saved, for then and then alone would the evil stream polluting its fair soil be checked at its fountain head.

37 - The meeting was held on May 11, 1843 in the Broadway Tabernacle. Resolutions were offered and speeches delivered by the Reverend V. D. Johns of Baltimore, the Reverend George B. Cheever and the Reverend L. N. Green. New York Observer, May 20, 1843.
38 - Ibid., May 23, 1846.

No sooner was this need felt than two missionary societies were formed to carry out the conversion of
Italy through distribution of the Protestant Bible.   The
first in the field was the Philo-Italian Society, formed
in New York in December, 1842.[39]   This addition to the
ranks of the anti-Catholic groups was hailed by the religious press, and ministers were urged to support its
objects.   "What champions," editors asked, "will not be
required by another generation to defend the ark of God
in America, if the impudence of Popery, with its insidious wiles, be not checked by some speedy and well directed blow? And what master stroke could be devised
better adapted to the end and the time than that which
is proposed by the new society?"[40]

Only a few months after this organization had
been launched, another society was formed with a similar
purpose. The Christian Alliance, with the declared purpose of diffusing "useful and religious knowledge among
the natives of Italy, and other Papal countries,"[41] en-

39 - The society was formed in New York on December 12,
     1842. New York Observer, January 21, 1843.
40 - Ibid., February 11, 1843.
41 - Address of the Reverend Leonard Bacon and the Rev-
     erend E. N. Kirk at the Annual Meeting of the
     Christian Alliance held in New York, May 8, 1845,
     with the Address of the Society and the Bull of
     the Pope against it. (New York, 1845), pp. 7-9.
     The constitution of the society is printed in
     this pamphlet. It was organized during the sum-
     mer of 1843.

joyed a greater popularity than the Philo-Italian
Society, due largely to its president, the Reverend
Lyman Beecher, long famed for his war against Romanism.[42]
While this new society had as its object the conversion
of all Papists to Protestantism, the members decided at
this first meeting that immediate efforts should be concentrated on Italy.[43] In this they enjoyed singular success, not in the number of converts gained, but in spreading word of the horrors of Popery among their fellow Christians in America.[44] Especially was the fame of the society
assured when Pope Gregory XVI issued an Encyclical letter
against Bible societies in Italy, naming the Christian Alliance as particularly troublesome.[45] While good members
stormed and raved,[46] the religious press seized upon the
letter as typical of the Pope's attitude toward Bibles,
Protestant or Catholic.[47] Aided by this effective pub-

42 - Ibid., p. 9.
43 - Resolutions to this effect adopted by the society
     at its annual meeting in New York in April, 1844
     are in the New York Observer, April 13, 1844.
44 - Reports of the annual meetings held in New York
     bristle with speeches and resolutions attacking
     Catholicism in the most violent terms. New York
     Observer, May 17, 1845; May 16, 1846.
45 - Addresses of the Reverend Leonard Bacon and the
     Reverend E. N. Kirk at the Annual Meeting of the
     Christian Alliance, pp. 38-39. The letter stated:
     "Against the plots and designs of the members of
     the Christian Alliance, we require a peculiar and
     most lively vigilance from those of your order."
46 - Ibid., pp. 39-46.
47 - Native American, July 20, 1844; New York Observer,
     July 27, 1844; New York American Republican, July
     19, 1844; September 18, 1844.

licity, the Christian Alliance marched on to continued
success, with the only objections coming from the more
violent of the nativistic agitators who felt the societies methods were too pacific and that the Papists should
be driven from the soil of America by force.[48]

The rapid growth of these anti-Catholic societies in the period just following the New York school controversy meant that the number of Protestants interested
in the crusade against Popery was increasing by leaps and
bounds. As the total of sympathizers mounted the group
in the country willing to read and support nativistic
newspapers and magazines grew in proportion. Quick to
realize this were the editors and publishers of these
journals, with the result that this period saw a great
flurry of activity in anti-Catholic publications.

Some of the papers which attained prominence
in the early 1840's were not new, having carried on successful operations for some years before. Foremost among
these was the Protestant Vindicator, official organ of
the Protestant Reformation Society, which continued to
send out its bi-monthly attacks on Romanism under the

48 - Hogan, William, Auricular Confession and Popish
     Nunneries, (Boston, 1845), pp. 194-196. Hogan
     maintained that the theory behind the Christian
     Alliance was wrong, and that Popery should be
     driven from America and all other fertile coun-
     tries. Then, he insisted, it would die of its
     own accord in barren Italy.

able direction of the Reverend W. C. Brownlee. Even
this violent opponent of Rome made some effort to appeal to the new church going class of No-Popery advocates attracted to the cause by the New York controversy. Catholics, it began to insist, should be saved
rather than exterminated. "Yes," wrote the editor, "I
do persecute Papists in the same manner as I would persecute my neighbor, who is fast asleep in his bed, and
his house on fire. I persecute him by rushing in through
the flames, and dragging him and his wife and little ones
out of doors, to a place of safety."[49]

This benevolent attitude was not ascribed to by
the Reverend Charles Sparry, one of the lecturing agents
whom the Protestant Vindicator employed. His violent denunciations of Romanism in Philadelphia brought about an
attack upon a church in which he was speaking. Windows
were broken and Sparry was forced to make an undignified
exit to the tune of the mob shouting that they should
have his life if he continued speaking against Catholicism.[50] The episode gave the editors of the paper an
opportunity to write columns about this latest outburst

49 - Protestant Vindicator, July 28, 1841.
50 - New York Observer, February 20, 1841. The Observer
     devoted its leading editorial to the matter, using
     it as a basis for the usual attack on Catholicism.

of Romish intolerance.[51]

Another of the journals to weather the stormy
years of the 1830's was the Baltimore Literary and Religious Magazine, edited by the Reverend Robert J. Breckinridge and the Reverend Andrew B. Cross, two men who
contributed constantly to the No-Popery cause. Their
magazine, devoted largely to learned arguments against
Romanism and designed to appeal to the clerical profession, never prospered, and finally suspended publication
in December, 1841, using as an excuse the forced retirement of Cross as an editor.[52] Its place was taken by a
new magazine, similar in every respect to the old, and
edited by Breckinridge. The first issue of this new venture, appearing in January, 1842, bore the title, The

51 - Protestant Vindicator, February 17, 1841; March 3,
1841. The editor hotly stated: "There may perhaps
be places in Europe where such outrages can be per-
petrated and sustained, but Romanists grossly mistake if they suppose they can do such things here
with impunity." Ibid., March 3, 1841.
52 - Spirit of the XIX Century, January, 1842. Perhaps
the true reason for the change of titles can be
found in another statement in this same magazine.
Breckinridge states that the Baltimore Literary
and Religious Magazine had lost money constantly,
due largely to unpaid subscriptions, amounting at
the time it ceased publication to approximately
$2,000. The accounts had been placed with a com-
mercial house to aid in the collection. It is
probable that this collection could be made easier by the suspension of the publication and the
erection of a new one in its place.

Spirit of the XIX Century. The change of title did
not serve to increase the subscription list, but at
the end of a year of publication the editor expressed
himself as satisfied. He had, he said, circulated
five and a half million pages during the eight years
in which he had been connected with the publication,
and while the number of subscribers had never been
large, they had been made up of the leading religious
men of the country.[53]

This proud boast was not enough to keep the
Spirit of the XIX Century alive. Its final issue appeared in December, 1843, bearing a "Farewell Address"
by the editor. His venture in the field of publication
had never been financially successful, he reported, for
the thousand copies of each issue sold did not pay for
the cost of printing and circulating the magazines. Despite this, he was willing to go on, but he felt that his
work was no longer necessary. New magazines had risen
to display the errors of Popery, and his own efforts
could rest.[54]

While financial matters may have had more to

53 - Ibid., December, 1842. The editor believed that
the reason the circulation had never increased
was because agents had never been employed to
popularize the publication.
54 - Ibid., December, 1843.

do with Breckinridge's decision than he was willing to
admit, his assertion that new publications had made
his own unnecessary was certainly true. All over the
country anti-Catholic magazines and newspapers were
springing into being in a flurry of publishing activity. In Baltimore, the Pilot and Transcript which had
been established to portray the danger of Catholics
in politics,[55] was joined in 1841 by the Saturday
Visitor, a violent paper attacking Popery in all its
forms.[56] Philadelphia joined the cities supporting
an anti-Catholic press when the Protestant Banner, a
bi-monthly paper, was founded in 1842.[57] A Presbyterian minister, the Reverend A. A. Campbell, established the Jackson Protestant in Jackson, Tennessee,
and circulated it throughout the southwest until his
death in 1846.[58] Far to the south, the New Orleans
Protestant began a successful career in 1844. In
Albany, New York, a monthly publication entitled The
Reformation Defended Against the Errors of the Times
was founded in the same year. More influential was
The American Protestant, published in New York and

55 - Protestant Vindicator, December 23, 1840. The
     editor was General Duff Green.
56 - Ibid., May 12, 1841.
57 - Ibid., May 18, 1842. The paper was established
     as one of the official organs of the American
     Protestant Association. See below, p. 434-441.
58 - American Protestant Magazine, August, 1846. No
     record has been found of the date on which pub-
     lication was begun.

circulating monthly copies throughout the country between 1845 and 1849.[59]   The West was given a new incentive to bigotry with the establishment of a newspaper
bearing the same name, The American Protestant at Cincinnati in 1845.   Edited by two able Presbyterian clergymen, this weekly publication played a large part in
the development of anti-Catholic sentiment throughout
that region, not only through its own columns but also
through its itinerant lecturers.[60]

     While all of these magazines and newspapers
enjoyed success, it remained for a monthly publication
founded in New York to attain the greatest popularity.
The Reverend Charles Sparry had been employed for many
years as lecturing agent for other papers[61] and it was
only natural, as a result, that he should enter the
field of publication himself.   In November, 1844, the
first issue of his magazine, The National Protestant,
appeared.   It was a success from the start.   By the
time that the second number came from the press the
subscription list had mounted to three thousand subscribers and it continued to increase from that time

59 - Information on many of the above publications has
    been secured from Gregory, Winifred (compiler)
    Union List of Serials in Libraries of the United
    States and Canada (New York, 1927)
60 - New York Observer, August 30, 1845.   The paper was
    established through the united efforts of the Prot-
    estant ministers of Cincinnati.   Its first editors
    were the Reverend N. L. Rice and the Reverend Booth.
61 - The Downfall of Babylon and the Protestant Vindicator.

on.[62]

The enthusiasm which greeted Sparry's effort demonstrates the fact that there still existed a reading public in America which scorned religious sentiments and tolerance and wanted only the worst about Popery. The National Protestant had as its motto "No Peace with Rome"[63] and lived up to this caption admirably. The editor was frank as to his purposes. He wanted, he said, "to develop the pestilential attributes and fearful consequences of Romanism, wherever it either sways or is tolerated - and to sound the alarm to Protestants, so that they may be on their guard against the wiles of Jesuitism, and the snares of the Devil, under the name of Popery."[64]

Conversion of Catholics "to Christianity" was not Sparry's purpose; most of them could not read, he believed, and any efforts in that direction would be worthless.[65] His interest was in exposure of Romanism alone, and the outspoken articles and gruesome pictures of Catholic persecution which sprinkled the pages of the publication attest his success.

62 - The National Protestant, December, 1844.
63 - The motto was printed on the cover of each issue.
64 - Ibid., April, 1845.
65 - Ibid., April, 1845.

Such tactics met with constant approbation
from the public. Before a year was out the editor
had employed no less than thirty-three ministers as
lecturing agents who spoke regularly over most of
the country, and concluded their impassioned sermons
on Popery with an appeal for new subscriptions. In
addition to these clerical representatives, the magazine employed sixty-one traveling agents to spread
its doctrines and increase its revenue.[66] By the
spring of 1845 the magazine was enlarged and improved,
and the editor stated that these changes were possible
because of steadily increasing patronage.[67]

But such tranquillity and peace only presaged
the storm. In May, 1845, the Reverend Sparry sold half
of his interest in the publication to another nativistically inclined clergyman, the Reverend H. Righter.
Righter found the financial affairs in a sorry state,
and the better to settle them, bought out Sparry's
interest entirely. In selling his control, Sparry
agreed that he would not start any similar magazine
in the future.[68] But while he was a gentleman of the

66 - Ibid., April, 1845.
67 - Ibid., May, 1845. The editor laid the gain in
     circulation to the rapidly growing interest in
     the struggle between Popery and Protestantism,
     believing that it was becoming the most talked
     of and most absorbing question of the day.
68 - This whole episode is told with considerable de-
     tail by Righter in Ibid., August, 1845. Righter
     stated that he was a country parson and so un-
     used to such scandalous tactics as those employed
     by Sparry.

cloth, Sparry also had a love for gain. As a result
he violated his agreement, and when the May issue of
The National Protestant appeared, readers were amazed
to find two magazines where one had been before. For
Sparry had secured copies of the plates for the number
before he left the organization, and could not resist
the temptation to publish them under his own name, at
the same time that the new editor was presenting them
to the world.[69] Righter expressed his stern disapproval
and sorrow at such tactics.[70] However, he was able to
weather the storm and build up such circulation as may
have been lost in the exchange.

But the experience had convinced Righter that
he was not endowed with proper attributes to be a business man. On the first opportunity he sold his magazines to a new editor, the Reverend D. Mead who changed
its name to The National Protestant Magazine or the
Anti-Jesuit, but continued it under the same policy.[71]
By the time that he was ready to give up the helm in
October, 1846, the subscription list had mounted to

69 - The American Antiquarian Society has two copies of
the magazine for this month, identical in every
respect but that one bears Sparry's name as editor,
and the other Righter's.
70 - Ibid., August, 1845. Righter bought a half interest
in the magazine for $500, paying a like sum for com-
plete control.
71 - The change was made with the January, 1846 issue.
The National Protestant Magazine or the Anti-Jesuit,
February, 1846.

more than five thousand. Its lecturing agents were so
successful that it was advertising for twenty more to
work on a salary basis, and it could boast that it was
the best established and most popular of the anti-Catholic magazines of the time.[72]

Sparry was naturally envious of the success
of this thriving publication which he had relinquished
and as a result he brought out a new magazine of his
own, The North American Protestant Magazine, or the
Anti-Jesuit. The first issue, appearing in April, 1846
indicated that Sparry still held to his old views of
violently denouncing Popery. Slightly smaller than the
National Protestant,[73] it made up for its size in its
extreme invective.[74] Both this magazine and the National Protestant enjoyed success until 1847, when they
were merged into another anti-Catholic publication, the

72 - Ibid., October, 1846. The change of editors and
publishers was made at this time. Mead sold his
interest to C. Billings Smith. The new editor
announced that in the past the publication had
done nothing but expose errors of Popery; in the
future it would continue to do this but would,
in addition, stress Protestant principles, thus
having a positive as well as a negative side.
73 - The National Protestant averaged about 25 pages
each issue. This publication had only 16 pages.
74 - The North American Protestant Magazine, or the
Anti-Jesuit, April, 1846. The frontipiece of
this first issue illustrates a Protestant clergyman being torn to pieces by dogs sicked on by
priests - a picture typical of the rest of the
contents.

American Protestant Magazine.[75]

      The increase in No-Popery agitation not only
brought these new openly anti-Catholic magazines into
the field early in the 1840's; it served also to create
a demand for literature against Romanism as was supplied
by the regular religious papers. The New York Observer
began a regular practice of printing two or three articles daily attacking Catholicism. The Christian Intelligencer joined in the chorus with enthusiasm.[76] The New
Englander, gave almost half its space to Rome from the
time of its founding in 1843.[77] Other religious magazines the country over followed the same practice, joining with enthusiasm in the cry against Popery.

75 - American Protestant Magazine, March, 1847. It was
announced that the National Protestant had been acquired some months before, the North American Protestant or the Anti-Jesuit, just completing the arrangements for amalgamation. For origins of the
American Protestant Magazine, see below, p. 452-454.

76 - Typical of the attitude of this paper was an article
printed in the Protestant Vindicator, September 2, 1840,
declaring that "to classify Papists among religious
denominations is just as absurd as to call asafoetida
a rose!"

77 - A typical volume of the New Englander, that for the
year 1844, included the following anti-Catholic articles: "Western Colleges and Theological Seminaries",
pp. 58-65; "The Protestant Principle," pp. 66-80; "Review of the Errors of the Times," pp. 143-174: "Miracles," pp. 208-221; "What are the Ministers to do
in the Great Controversy of the Age," pp. 222-232;
"Romanists and the Roman Catholic Controversy," pp.
233-255; "Apostolic Succession," pp. 273-296; "The
Roman Catholic Faith," pp. 414-419; "The Philadelphia
Riots," pp. 470-483, 624-630; "Review of Dr. Stone's
Mysteries Opened," pp. 510-527; "The Roman Catholic
Faith," pp. 568-588.

Into the attitude of intolerance created by
this flood of publication came new influences from
abroad destined to add thousands to the ranks of No-
Popery in America. The British Reformation Society
continued its operations[78] and was joined by a similar
organization, the Protestant Association.[79] In 1841
their efforts were aided with the founding of the Parker
Society in London, formed to republish the works of leaders of the English Reformation as a means of combating
Popery.[80] News of the activities of these societies was
heralded in America, nativistic papers here applauding
their success and reprinting articles from the publications which they sponsored.[81] Efforts of these English
organizations were directed against the Maynooth College
grant; a proposal before Parliament to aid a Catholic
university in Ireland by means of funds from the public
treasury. American nativistic publications grew wrath-
ful along with their English counterparts in insisting
that Popery should not be encouraged[82] and linked the

---

78 - New York Observer, June 19, 1841.
79 - Ibid., June 18, 1842.
80 - Protestant Vindicator, March 31, 1841.
81 - Ibid., June 24, 1840; July 8, 1840; September 2,
     1840; June 23, 1841.
82 - Baltimore Literary and Religious Magazine, October,
     1838; Protestant Vindicator, August 19, 1840; Amer-
     ican Protestant Magazine, June, 1845; Hogan, William,
     Synopsis of Popery as it Was and as it Is. (Hertford,
     1845), pp. 181-183.

Maynooth grant with the demand of Catholics in New York
for a share of the school fund, ascribing both to a great
Popish plot to secure control of the educational facilities of the world.[83]

Important as was the Maynooth controversy in
arousing anti-Catholic sentiment in England, it paled
before another great movement which was sweeping over
that country and sending nativistic agitators into new
heights of eloquence. The Oxford Movement, reaching its
culmination in the early years of the 1840's, provided
a basis for No-Popery shouts not only in Britain but in
America. The sermon preached by John Keble in 1833 has
been designated as the official beginning of the movement, but not until the early years of the 1840's did
it assume large enough proportions to attract attention
in the United States. In 1841 Newman's Tract XC appeared
among the Tracts for the Times, at about the same time
republication of these Oxford publications began in
America. Two years later Dr. E. B. Pusey preached his
famous sermon upholding transubstantiation; by 1845 Newman had accepted conversion to the Catholic faith and the
movement could come to an official close.[84]

83 - Protestant Vindicator, August 19, 1840.
84 - This brief account of the Oxford Movement in England
     is drawn from Ollard, S. L., A Short History of the
     Oxford Movement (London, 1915)

The reaction of the Oxford Movement in
America was instantaneous and violent. Religious
papers first became aware of this new movement in
1839. Their reaction was the only one that could
be expected from a press already steeped in anti-
Catholic prejudice. The first accounts of the movement branded it as a Popish aggression, designed only
to win converts to Rome and directed from the Vatican
itself.[85] From that time on Newman and Pusey were held
up for continuous scorn,[86] conversions of Protestants
to Catholicism through their influence were announced
with horror[87] and every effort was made to prove that
all of the Oxford Reformers were merely Papists in disguise.[88] When Catholic journals hailed the movement

85 - Watchman of the South, July 11, 1839; New York Observer, December 28, 1839.
86 - New York Observer, March 27, 1841; July 15, 1843.
   The Observer had been running a series of articles
   entitled "Puseyism," but changed them on July 15,
   1843, calling them "Newmania," and insisting that
   Newman was the real author of this Popish plot.
87 - Ibid., February 27, 1841 for a typical account.
88 - Protestant Vindicator, April 28, 1841; Baltimore
   Literary and Religious Magazine, May, 1841; New
   York Observer, June 26, 1841; April 2, 1842; The
   New Englander, 1844, pp. 143-147; The New York
   Observer during 1841 and 1842 published a daily
   article attacking the Oxford Movement as a Catholic effort. A number of books with the same purpose appeared. Typical of these were: Smyth,Thomas,
   The Prelatical Doctrine of Apostolic Succession Examined, and the Protestant Ministry Defended against
   the Assumptions of Popery and High Churchism (Boston
   1841), Anthon, Henry, The True Churchman Warned
   against the Errors of the Time (New York, 1843) and
   Smyth, Thomas, Ecclesiastical Republicanism; or the
   Republicanism, Liberality and Catholicity of Presbytery, in Contrast with Prelacy and Popery (New York,
   1843)

with delight,[89] Protestant alarm was only intensified.[90]

The effect of the Oxford Reforms was especially great in America due to the condition of the Episcopalian Church at the time. As early as 1835 a line of cleavage had been run through the church, separating its members into two radically opposed parties, the high churchmen on the one hand and the low churchmen or evangelicals, on the other. The high church party had adopted the name "Anglo-Catholic" and stood for authority of the church as opposed to the right of individual judgment. This branch of the church, under the able leadership of Bishop John Henry Hobart, had been making rapid headway for a number of years, much to the alarm of many who could not distinguish it clearly from Catholicism.[91]

The impact of the teachings of the Oxford Reformers upon such a divided church was certain to cause serious dissention. Low churchmen, linking the opposing party now with Newman and Pusey, hurled the charge of Popery through press and book. When the Catholic Bishop Francis Patrick Campbell of Philadelphia addressed an open letter to Bishops of the American Episcopal Church

89 - Brownson's Review, in Brownson, O. A., Works (Detroit, 1882-1887), vol. vi, pp. 568 ff.
90 - New York Observer, April 4, 1840.
91 - Sweet, Story of Religions in America, pp. 383-385.

asking them to return to the fold from which they had
strayed, these charges seemed to bear some truth.[92]
The Virginia convention of the Episcopal Church, meeting in the summer of 1841, heard the venerable Bishop
Richard Channing Moore denounce such an invitation. "I
beseech you as my sons," he told the assembled clergymen and laymen, "I call upon you as brethren, ... to
hold fast the great principles of the Protestant Reformation ... and to give no place nor countenance, no,
not for an hour, to these abominations of Popery issuing
from Oxford."[93] Swayed by his words, the convention went
on record as denouncing the Oxford Tracts as "Popery in
disguise."[94]

All over the country clergymen high in the
councils of the Episcopal organization echoed the cry
of Bishop Moore. Bishop Thomas C. Brownell of the
Connecticut Diocese charged his clergy to avoid Romanism and the Oxford teachings which approached it.[95]

92 - New York Observer, July 24, 1841. The letter is
     printed in the Spirit of the XIX Century, November,
     1842. The Observer insisted that this showed the
     Catholic desire to take over all other denomina-
     tions and that Protestants must unite for their
     own protection.
93 - Protestant Vindicator, June 23, 1841.
94 - New York Observer, June 12, 1841; Protestant Vindi-
     cator, June 23, 1841.
95 - Brownell, Thomas C., Errors of the Times, A Charge
     Delivered to the Clergy of the Diocese of Connect-
     icut at the Annual Convention holden in Christ
     Church, in the City of Hartford, June 13, 1843
     (Hartford, 1843).

Bishop John Henry Hopkins of Vermont was responsible
for repeated volumes attacking Catholicism and high
church principles in most outspoken terms.[96]   Bishop
Alexander Griswold of the Eastern Diocese, venerated
as one of the leading spirits of the establishment of
his church in the United States, expressed his fears
of Popery in a bitterly worded book,[97] in which he attempted to show the vast gulf that separated true Christianity from Romanism.[98]   The Reverend H. A. Boardman
attempted a similar publication, charging Oxfordism with
being Popery, thus drawing one of the few prominent defenders of Newman and Pusey into the field, Bishop George
W. Doane of New Jersey.[99]

> This flood of publication, bitter against Cath-

96 - Hopkins, J. H., The Novelties Which Disturb our
     Peace: Four Letters Addressed to the Bishops, Cler-
     gy and Laity of the Protestant Episcopal Church in
     the United States (Philadelphia, 1844); Hopkins,
     J.H., Lectures on the British Reformation (Boston,
     1844); Hopkins, J. H., An Humble Address to the
     Bishops, Clergy and Laity of the Protestant Episco-
     pal Church in the United States, on Tolerating
     Among our Ministry of the Doctrines of the Church
     of Rome (   ).
97 - Griswold, Alexander, The Reformation; a Brief Ex-
     position of some of the Errors and Corruptions of
     the Church of Rome (Boston, 1843).
98 - Ibid., pp. 6-7.
99 - New York Observer, March 27, 1841. Boardman's ac-
     cusation of the Popery of Oxfordism, together with
     Doane's reply, were published together in pamphlet
     form. Doane also set forth his views in another
     pamphlet, entitled Puseyism, No Popery (Boston,
     1843).

olicism, was an effective instrument in converting
thousands to the No-Popery cause. Clergymen and laymen in the Episcopal church were forced to accept no
compromise - they could no longer remain indifferent.
They could believe the impassioned words of the enemies of the Oxford Movement and anti-Catholic propagandists, or they could accept high church principles. There
was no other alternative. Such a situation was dangerous
to the extreme, as far as the Episcopal church was concerned. An open split was narrowly averted in 1843 when
two clergymen left the ordination of a new minister in
indignation, having convinced themselves that he was a
Romanist.[100] Only through the efforts of William A.
Muhlenberg, who called himself an Evangelical Catholic
and who strove constantly for reconciliation of the conflicting views, was an open break averted.[101] But the
pamphlet warfare continued until the 1850's,[102] providing a constant source of anti-Catholic sentiment.

The Oxford Movement had driven a great mass
of the members of the Episcopal church into the fray
against Romanism, but such an incentive had been lack-

100 - New York Observer, July 15, 1843. The two clergymen rose during a public ordination at St. Stephen's
Church, in New York, being conducted by Bishop
Onderdonk, and after denouncing the proceedings
and Romanism, left the building.
101 - Sweet, Story of Religions in America, p. 385.
102 - Ibid., p. 385.

ing for other denominations. Without this inducement,
the churches had, for the most part, sought to avoid
active participation in the anti-Catholic crusade. The
fanatical nature of the movement, the obscenity of the
propaganda writers and the bitter bigotry everywhere
manifest had tended to force them to shy away and watch
the struggle from aside. But with the New York school
controversy a change came. Catholics had attacked the
Bible; no Protestant denomination in America could stand
quietly by before such an assault. From 1840 there was
a growing movement among religious bodies toward participation in the fray; a movement which gradually placed the
Protestant churches of America among the most bitter opponents of Romanism.

Throughout the early 1840's a constant agitation
was carried on by outspoken clergymen and editors of religious publications designed to enlist churches and ministers in the Protestant cause. Clergymen were warned that
unless they awoke "from their dreamy confidence and false
charity, and roused their energies to a universal and perservering opposition to that artful, insinuating and
dangerous traitor, the Popist Priesthood; ere long we may
realize the terrors, cruelties, tortures and massacres
which our ancestors endured."103 They were told that

103 - American Text Book of Popery, p. 371.

Luther had not hesitated in taking sides, and told
that if he had, all the world might yet be in the
"spiritual gloom of the miserable, servile superstition crushed beggars of Naples and Rome."[104] They
were assured that they must take one side or the other;
that a great controversy between the true and false
religion was inevitable.[105] "It may be, in a degree,"
wrote one editor, "the battle of the Reformation over
again. For the prince of the power of the air has long
chafed under his defeat and the loss of his dominion
in that contest, nor will he rest until he has made one
mighty effort to recover his lost possessions."[106]

Nearly all of the Protestant denominations in
the United States responded to this appeal but by far
the most enthusiastic were the Presbyterians. Members
of this sect had not waited for the New York controversy
to throw anti-Catholicism into religious circles; from
the time that No-Popery had first been shouted in America they had given hearty approval to its cause.

The first official action of the Presbyterian

104 - Abbott, John S. C., Sermon on the Duties and Dangers of the Clergy and the Church (Boston, 1842) p. 13.
105 - New Englander, April, 1844; Protestant Vindicator. March 3, 1841; Addresses of the Reverend L. Bacon and the Reverend E. N. Kirk at the Annual Meeting of the Christian Alliance, pp. 12-13; The National Protestants, February, 1845; Ibid., April, 1845; Elizabeth, Charlotte, Falsehood and Truth, (New York, 1842), pp. viii-ix.
106 - The National Protestant, January, 1845.

church on Catholicism was taken in 1835, when the forces
against Romanism were just gathering their strength. The
General Assembly, meeting that year in Pittsburg, listened to a report from the Board of Education of the
church devoted almost entirely to Popery and its evils.
The report showed that members of the Board had imbibed
deeply of the propaganda being circulated by Morse and
his contemporaries. It warned that Romanism constituted
the greatest danger faced by the United States and that
the Pope was sending thousands of ignorant foreigners
and hundreds of corrupt priests to take possession of
the West. These slaves of Rome proposed to carry out
their base object by securing possession of the educational facilities of the nation and thus winning Prot-
ostant converts. "Viewing the influence they had already
secured," the report stated, "the immense population of
priests and laity they are annually receiving from abroad,
the interest and ardor of foreign despots in their service, and the free use of foreign gold; the base court
played to them by designing men and unprincipled politicians; the restraints they have already put upon the
periodical press, in many parts of the land; the un-
evangelized condition of large masses of our population,
and the destitution of our new settlements of religious
instruction and general knowledge; viewing all these

facts with the eyes of reflecting, patriotic and Christian men, who will longer slumber in a security so full
of danger? Shall our ministers refuse to be faithful?
Shall we not train our candidates with peculiar reference, both in their acquirements and destination, to
meet and discomfit in the field of argument ... this
ever growing and ever to be dreaded system?"[107]

Discussion of this report was entered upon with
enthusiasm by members of the Assembly. One criticism became apparent from the start of debate; the report had
not been violent enough in its denunciation of Popery.
Speakers dwelt upon the dangers and horrors of Romanism
and a new committee, on the "Prevelance of Popery in the
West" was named to bring in recommendations.[108] Critics
who had denounced the mildness of the previous report
were satisfied when this new committee brought in its
resolutions. The Pope was denounced as the anti-Christ,
the "Man of Sin and the Son of Perdition," the Catholic
church was declared to be not a church of Christ but an
apostate from God, corrupted by "various profane exor-

107 - New York Observer, May 30, 1835. The report of
       the committee was presented on May 22. Full re-
       ports of the proceedings of the General Assem-
       blies are given in the New York Observer.
108 - Ibid., June 13, 1835. The debate was staged on
       June 2, 1835.

cisms, idolatrous incantations and unauthorized addi-
tions, mutilations and ceremonies;" all Christians were
called upon to put down "so insidious, alarming and
ever growing an evil," and seminaries under Presbyterian control were urged to train all candidates for
the ministry on the Catholic controversy that they
might meet and discomfit the priesthood of Rome.[109]

Debate on these resolutions centered largely
upon their violence. They were defended by the Reverend Robert J. Breckinridge, chairman of the committee which had brought in the report, who insisted that
such violence was necessary to combat the evils of Rome.
Despite his arguments, the resolutions were laid on the
table by the Assembly after considerable debate, and it
was not until several days later that new resolutions
were introduced which could be acted upon. These new
recommendations were scarcely less outspoken than the
originals:

> Resolved, That it is the deliberate
> and decided judgment of this General Assem-
> bly, that the Roman Catholic church has es-
> sentially apostatized from the religion of
> our Lord and Savior Jesus Christ, and there-
> fore cannot be recognized as a Christian
> Church.

109 - The committee reported on June 6, under the chair-
manship of the Reverend Robert J. Breckinridge,
long famed in anti-Catholic controversies. New
York Observer, June 20, 1835.

> Resolved, That it be recommended to
> all in our communion to endeavor by the
> diffusion of light, by the pulpit, the
> press and all other Christian means, to
> resist the extension of Romanism, and lead
> its subjects to the knowledge of the truth,
> as it is taught in the Word of God.
> Resolved, That it is utterly inconsis-
> tent with the strongest obligations of Chris-
> tian parents to place their children for edu-
> cation in Roman Catholic Seminaries.[110]

That the Presbyterian church, thus early in the controversy, could place itself on record in such violent terms against Catholicism and send its ministry forth to spread these doctrines through the land forboded even more outspoken action for the future. But leaders in the anti-Catholic crusade, expecting aid from this quarter, were destined to disappointment. When members of the church came together the General Assembly in 1836 the seeds of controversy that were to flower in the great schism of the following year had already been sown. In 1837 that body was in the midst of controversy, only culminating when four synods professing more liberal doctrines than the church as a whole, were read out the Presbyterian organization.[111] Within a short time this expelled group, composing nearly 100,000 members of the church,

110 - Ibid., June 20, 1835. The resolutions were also
      printed in the Downfall of Babylon, July 4, 1835.
111 - Sweet, Story of Religions in America, pp. 375-
      378.

organized themselves into the New School Presbyterians
and began their separate existence.[112] And not until
this internal strife abated could No-Popery again assume
important proportions. The greater problems demanding
settlement allowed minister and layman alike to forget
the evils of Rome; even though Breckinridge and other
clergymen tried to affect a conciliation in order to
allow the church to present a united front against Catholicism.[113] These efforts were without avail, and for
several years the only action against Romanism by Presbyterians came through individual synods.[114]

Although the schism was not to be healed until
1869 the first heat of controversy was soon stilled and
by 1841 the church was again ready to turn its attention
to this pressing problem. The General Assembly of the
Old School Presbyterians had by that time felt the in-

112 - Ibid., pp. 378-379.
113 - Bishop Hughes, in a letter to Bishop Purcell,
      January 2, 1837, reported that Breckinridge was
      busy at Princeton trying to effect a reconcilia-
      tion for this purpose. Hughes commented on the
      fact that while the Presbyterians were thus en-
      gaged, the discussion over the Catholic religion
      had died down to a considerable extent. Hassard,
      Life of John Hughes, pp. 172-173.
114 - Typical of action by individual synods was that of
      the Synod of Philadelphia at its annual meeting in
      Baltimore in 1837. Members listened to a sermon
      on "The Dangers of Education in Roman Catholic
      Seminaries," in which old charges of Catholic ag-
      gression on the United States through control of
      the schools were revived in strong terms. Balti-
      more Literary and Religious Magazine, May, 1838.

fluence of the New York controversy, and stirred by
this latest aggression of Popery, turned to the old
question with new enthusiasm. Clergy and laity gathered at Philadelphia listened to two violent denunciations of Romanism,[115] and thus inspired, adopted a
series of resolutions which were to be far reaching
in effect:

> Resolved, That a preacher be appointed
> to deliver a discourse before the next Assem-
> bly on some general topic connected with the
> controversy between Romanists and Protestants.
> Resolved, That this Assembly most earnest-
> ly recommends to the Bishops of the several con-
> gregations under our care, both from the pulpit
> and through the press, boldly though temperately,
> to explain and defend the doctrines and princi-
> ples of the Reformation, and to point out and
> expose the errors and superstitions of Popery.
> Resolved, That this Assembly solemnly and
> affectionately warn all our people of the danger
> and impropriety of patronizing, or in any manner,
> directly or indirectly, supporting or encouraging
> Popish schools and seminaries.
> Resolved, That this Assembly recommend to
> the special attention of all our people the works
> on the Reformation which have been already, and
> may be still further issued by our Board of Pub-
> lication.
> Resolved, That the delegates of the several
> presbyteries be called on at the next meeting of
> the Assembly to report what has been done in com-
> pliance with these resolutions.[116]

115 - The two speeches were delivered by the Reverend
Boardman and the Reverend Robert J. Breckinridge.
Both spoke seriously of the menace of Popery, and
according to the reporter for the New York Observer, were listened to "with breathless attention."
New York Observer, June 12, 1841.
116 - New York Observer, June 12, 1841.

Having appointed a speaker for the next
Assembly who would devote the annual sermon to Popery
as was called for in these resolutions,[117] the members
adjourned, well satisfied that they had dealt a decisive blow at the dread Beast. Nativistic editors commented joyfully on this "mighty machine" which had been
set in operation and speculated on the effect that eleven
hundred ministers, all pledged to give sermons against
Romanism, would have.[118]

This action by the Presbyterian church had
fairly launched it into the campaign against Rome. In
the next year, members at the General Assembly listened
to an impassioned sermon on Popery by Breckinridge,[119]
and after hearing reports from the various presbyteries
as to the work that they had accomplished against Popery
during the year, expressed themselves as satisfied that
sufficient progress was being made.[120] While the resolutions adopted in 1841 had provided only for a sermon on
Popery the following year, the sermon was repeated yearly

117 - The Reverend Robert J. Breckinridge was named
      speaker and his sermon was to be on "What is
      the Rule of Faith." New York Observer, June
      5, 1841.
118 - Protestant Vindicator, June 9, 1841.
119 - New York Observer, May 28, 1642. The sermon is
      printed in full in the Spirit of the XIX Century,
      July, 1842.
120 - New York Observer, May 28, 1842.

and became an accepted part of the proceedings of the church.[121] In 1845 members of the Old School Assembly had a further opportunity to express their feelings on Catholicism when the question of the validity of Romish baptism was introduced into the session. The debate resolved itself largely into attacks on Catholicism, opponents of the measure insisting that the baptism had no validity inasmuch as the Romish church was not Christian but anti-Christian. Even its defenders prefaced their remarks with the statement that they did not want to be considered friends of Popery. The overwhelming sentiment of the members was seen when the Assembly refused to accept the validity of Catholic baptism by a vote of one hundred and sixty-nine to eight.[122]

The Methodist church was less violent in its reaction to Catholicism than the Presbyterian. Some feeling against Rome was manifest as early as 1836 when members of the General Conference thought it necessary to define the words "Catholic Church" used in the Apos-

121 - Ibid., June 3, 1843. Usually an active anti-Catholic agitator was chosen to give the sermon. This year it was delivered by the Reverend N. L. Rice.
122 - Ibid., May 31, 1845. The Observer praised the decision which, it said, "placed the Romish church where it beyond a question belongs, out of the pale of Christian churches, and stamps it as the anti-Christ of this day." Ibid., June 7, 1845.

tles Creed as "the Church of God in General."[123]   Four
years later a committee of the Conference urged the
establishment of religious magazines in the West to
offset the powerful Roman Catholic influence there.[124]
But it was not until 1844 when the New York controversy
and the propaganda resulting from it had played its part,
that the Methodists were ready to take united and vigorous
action.   In that year the Address of the Bishops to the
Conference was devoted largely to a denunciation of Popery
and an exposition of its schemes.   "These last few years,"
the bishops told the clergy and laity, "have been marked
with a renewed and simultaneous and mighty movement of
Papal Rome to recover that domination and influence that
she so reluctantly yielded to the champions of Scriptural
truth ... The establishment of schools and colleges, literary and theological, with a design to wield the mighty
engine of education to mould the minds of the rising generation in conformity with the doctrine of their creed,

123 - At first an effort was made to change the word
"Catholic" entirely so that it could be felt from
the creed.   Journals of the General Conference
of the Methodist Episcopal Church, vol. i, p. 434.
This plan was changed, and the Committee on Revisal instructed on May 16, 1836, to add an explanatory note to the words "Catholic Church." Ibid.,
vol. i, p. 450.   The committee reported on May 25,
recommending that the explanatory words: "By Holy
Catholic Church, is meant the Church of God in
General," be added.   This report was accepted.
Ibid., vol. i, p. 479.
124 - The report was adopted.   Ibid., vol. ii, pp. 53-54.

and the forms of their worship is no unimportant or
inefficient part of that extensive system of policy
that is now in operation. ... Romanism is now laboring, not only to recover what it lost of its former
supremacy in the Reformation, but also to assert and
establish its monsterous pretensions in countries never
subject either to its civil or ecclestiastical authority. With these weapons the Papal power has invaded
Protestant communities with such success as should awak-
en and unite the energies of the evangelical churches of
Christ in every part of the world."[125]

Brought face to face with the problem by this
address from their Bishops, members of the Conference
showed real concern about Catholicism. In their address
to the Wesley Methodist Conference in England they spoke
with resolute joy of the coming conflict with Popery,[126]
and urged fellow members of the Evangelical Association
to join in combating Romanism and in converting German
Catholic immigrants to Protestantism.[127]

125 - Ibid., vol. ii, pp. 167-169.
126 - Ibid., vol. ii, p. 175.
127 - Ibid., vol. ii, pp. 181-184. The great success of
   the Methodists in obtaining converts from among German Catholics is explained in part by the complaint
   voiced by the German Catholic paper, the Wahrheitsfreund, published in Cincinnati in 1839. The editors insisted that Methodists lured ignorant German
   immigrants into their churches by telling them that
   they were Catholic Churches, and that religious customs differed in America. Then, having secured them,
   they forced the immigrants to continue in membership.
   Quoted in Thie, "German Catholic Activity in the United States Seventy Years Ago," pp. 94-95.

But no sooner had members of the Methodist
church begun to interest themselves in the Catholic
problem than their attention was diverted to graver
matters.   In the same year that the Bishops made
their recommendations, the church was faced with
the question of slavery, and the General Conference,
instead of dealing with Romanism as did the Presbyterians, began the discussion that brought disunion
of its north and south branches.[128]   After 1844 their
attention was absorbed in this schism and efforts at
reconciliation;   Catholicism and the menace of the
Catholic in America was forgotten.

The Congregational church was faced with no
such schism as that which shook the Methodist structure
and the attention that it could pay to the problem of
Popery was proportionately greater.   Members of the
church were first made aware of the danger from Romanism
in 1835 when a deputation from the Congregational Union
of England visited America and left with a grave warning
to members of their sect that Popery must be exterminated
or it would triumph.   Congregationalists were warned that
they "had to do with a foe who rests his cause on time
and perserverance; whose hand seeks to undermine rather

128 - Sweet, Story of Religions in America, pp. 436-437.

than to storm; who can smile at a defeat if it puts
his opponents off his guard; and who, like the tiger
cat, can spring on his prey when he seems to be moving
away."129

Thus warned, the General Association of Massachusetts at its annual meeting in 1843 named a "Committee on Popery" to investigate the matter and report at
the next meeting.130 The report presented in 1844, shows
clearly the depth of feeling among New Englanders. It
warned that not since Luther had a time required greater
interest in the perils of Popery than the present.131 "At
the present day," it warned, "there is a growing danger
that the persecuting arm of the apostate church, which
has been weakened ever since the Reformation by Luther,
will be invigorated and will again send the sword and
the fagot where they have long been unknown."132 Members of the church were told of the Leopold Association
and the Catholic plot to stamp out republicanism by destroying the United States.133 They were told too that

___

129 - Reed, Andrew, and James Matherson, A Narrative of
the Visit to the American Churches by the Deputation from the Congregational Union of England and
Wales (London, 1835), vol. ii, pp. 77-80.
130 - Allen, William, Report on Popery Accepted by the
General Association of Massachusetts, June, 1844.
(Boston, 1844), Introduction. The committee named
consisted of William Allen, George Allen, and B.B.
Edwards, all clergymen.
131 - Ibid., pp. 5-6.
132 - Ibid., p. 10.
133 - Ibid., pp. 26-28.

the Romish church was the "Babylon the Great, the Woman drunk with the blood of the saints, and with the blood of the martyrs of Jesus."[134] They were informed that the Bible was opposed to Catholicism, and the committee gave a long and labored proof of this assertion.[135] "In view of these things," the report concluded, can there be any doubt that it is the duty of Protestant ministers to instruct the people of their charge concerning the character of the Catholic church, and to warn them against the sophistry, and the arts, and the efforts of Antichrist?"[136] With the acceptance of these recommendations, and strengthened by a similar decision of the Western Convention of the Congregationalist church made in the same year,[137] a new group of biogted clergy was released to lead their flocks in the ways of brotherly hatred.[150]

Only slightly less active against Catholicism were the smaller churches. The General Synod of the Dutch Reformed church in 1837 listened to a sermon on Popery by that master of invective, the Reverend William C. Brownlee, and recorded its sentiments as in tune with his.[139]

134 - Ibid., p. 9.
135 - Ibid., pp. 7-27.
136 - Ibid., p. 28.
137 - New York Observer, July 6, 1844.
138 - Ibid., July 6, 1844.
139 - Ibid., June 24, 1837.

In the same year the Lutheran Synod of South Carolina agreed with an address by the Reverend John Bachman based on opposition to Romish doctrines[140] and in 1838 the Synod of West Pennsylvania adopted a resolution calling for an annual sermon extoling the virtues of the Reformation.[141] The first of these sermons, delivered in 1838 by the Reverend S. S. Schmucker, was a violent denunciation of Catholicism.[142] By 1840, the Lutheran Church had decided to publish a _Protestant Almanac_ devoted to an exposition of the errors of Romanism[143] and four years later the official _Lutheran Observer_ announced its determination to join the anti-Catholic ranks.[144]

While this sporadic action against Romanism was sending thousands of ministers into their pulpits

140 - England, _The Works of John England_, vol. 1, pp. 58-79. Bachman's sermon was answered by Bishop England through the columns of the _United States Catholic Miscellany_. His answer is in _Ibid._, vol. 1, pp. 79-228.

141 - Schmucker, _Discourse in Commemoration of the Glorious Reformation_, p. iii. The resolution adopted by the Synod recommended that "a discourse of the Reformation be annually delivered by each member of the Synod before the people of his charge, and that one should annually be delivered before the Synod on the same topic."

142 - Schumucker's sermon was printed in book form under the title: _Discourse in Commemoration of the Glorious Reformation of the Sixteenth Century_.

143 - _Protestant Vindicator_, June 24, 1840.

144 - _Lutheran Observer_, quoted in _The National Protestant_, February, 1845. The editor stated that if any subscribers objected he would lay down his pen, for he felt it his duty to battle the Old Man of Sin.

to spread the gospel of intolerance through the land, there were still many defenders of Protestantism who were not satisfied. Catholicism was a great and powerful system, these agitators believed, and if it was to be vanquished, more concentrated efforts were required. As a result they began to demand a closer cooperation of the various Protestant churches, and the formation of a Protestant Alliance to offer a united front against the aggressions of Popery.[145] Protestants were asked whether they should "enter upon protracted discussions about the means to be employed, or the manner of going forth to meet the millions of Romanists, who are arriving upon our shores?"[146] and they were warned that such methods might prove fatal. One outgrowth of this effort to unite all evangelical sects came in a great Protestant Convention, held in London in the summer of 1846 "to increase and to establish the love and the faith of the Church of Christ throughout the world, and to present an unbroken

145 - Hogan, Auricular Confession and Popish Nunneries, pp. 199-200.
146 - American Protestant Magazine, September, 1845.

front against Popery and infidelity of every form."[147]
Another and more important outgrowth came in the formation of several national religious societies, designed
to unite the Protestant clergy of America against their
common foe.

The first of these societies in the field had
its origin in Philadelphia. Early in November, 1842, a
group of twenty-six Protestant clergymen, deciding that
time was ripe for action, united in addressing a letter
to all ministers in the city. They were, they stated,
deeply impressed with the blessings to mankind resulting
from the Reformation. They were alarmed at the constant
efforts being made to "delude Protestants with the vain
idea that the character and tendencies of the Great Apostacy, which for many centuries had blinded and oppressed a
large portion of mankind, have been essentially changed,
and believing that watchfulness and exertion are necessary

147 - Ibid., August, 1846. The convention and its work were
      lauded by nativistic publications of the time. The
      suggestion for such a convention came from the United
      States and met with popular response in an England
      still stirred by excitement centered about the Ox-
      ford Movement. Ibid., December, 1845. Representa-
      tives were sent from the national church organiza-
      tions of America, as well as from synods and smaller
      units. The National Protestant, December, 1845.
      When the convention was over, American Protestants
      tookparticular pride in contrasting its orderly and
      efficient work in contrast to "the confusion and up-
      roar and vituperation in the Council of Trent."
      American Protestant Magazine, November, 1846.

... and that the cause of truth and godliness may be strengthened and advanced by united council and effort among true Protestants," they urged all clergymen who shared their views to join with them in a meeting to be held on November 8th. [148]

This call was greeted with enthusiasm throughout the ministerial circles of Philadelphia. Sixty-one of the Protestant clergy responded, representing the New and Old School Presbyterians, the Baptists, Methodists, Episcopalians, the Associated Presbyterians, the Protestant Episcopalians, the German Reformed and the Congregationalists, with the Presbyterians and the Methodists supplying the largest number.[149] This group of enthusiasts were unanimous in agreeing on the "importance of united action for the protection and defense of the rights and privileges which distinguish the Protestant churches from the threatening assaults of Romanism."[150] To do this

---

148 - Address of the Board of Managers of the American Protestant Association, with the Constitution and Organization of the Association (Philadelphia, 1843), p. 5. The letter was dated November 2, and signed by twenty-six clergymen, headed by the Reverend C. C. Cuyler and the Reverend H. A. Boardman. The meeting was to be held at the church of one of the signers.

149 - Ibid., p. 6. Of the thirty-six ministers who responded in addition to the twenty-six signers of the original letter, nine were Methodists, seven were Old School Presbyterians, seven New School Presbyterians, and the remainder divided among other sects.

150 - Ibid., p. 6.

most effectively, they decided, they should form an American Protestant Association. Having taken this step, the clergy present named a committee to draw up a constitution and adjourned to await developments.[151]

This same group, with the addition of twenty-two more ministers who had heeded the summons,[152] assembled again two weeks later. After some discussion they adopted the constitution recommended by the committee named at the last meeting and formally organized themselves into the American Protestant Association electing E. E. Backus their first president.[153]

151 - The committee was composed of one member from each denomination present. The meeting was adjourned until November 22. Ibid., p. 6.
152 - Of these twenty-two new converts to the cause, seven were Methodists, five old School Presbyterians, five Baptists, three Protestant Episcopalians, and the remainder from smaller sects. These numbers cannot be taken as authentic, however, for ninety-four ministers present at this meeting signed the constitution that was adopted. Ibid., pp. 6-7.
153 - The meeting was held on November 22. Other officers elected were: Vice-presidents, the Reverends Stephen H. Tyng, John Kennaday and George B. Ide; Corresponding secretary, the Reverend Henry Boardman; Recording secretary, the Reverend William W. Spear, and Treasurer, A. H. Julian. Twelve churches were represented, Old School Presbyterian, New School Presbyterian, Protestant Episcopal, Associated Presbyterian, Methodist Episcopal, German Reformed, Associate Reformed, Baptists, Reformed Presbyterian, Independent, Lutheran and Methodist Protestant. Ibid., pp. 7-11.

The constitution adopted by this representative group of clergy typified their aims.[154] They asserted their belief that "Popery, was in its principles and tendencies, subversive to civil and religious liberty, and destructive to the spiritual welfare of men." They insisted that only through their unity could the United States be saved from the ravages of this foreign-directed system of tyranny. To combat this giant evil they agreed to encourage Protestant ministers "to give to their several congregations instruction on the differences between Protestantism and Popery," to insist on a further circulation of the Bible and books against Catholicism, and "to awaken the attention of the community to the dangers which ... threaten these United States from the assaults of Romanism."[155] The constitution further provided that similar associations should be formed in every city of the land, thus building up a great national organization of clergymen to combat Rome.[156]

The first step of this new organization was

154 - For the full constitution of the Association, see Appendix A.
155 - Ibid., pp. 7-8.
156 - Ibid., pp. 7-8. Sections of the constitution were also printed in the New York Observer, January 21, 1843.

to issue a lengthy Address to the people of the United
States, urging their support. This little circular was
in itself a bitter denunciation of Popery, insisting
that Catholicism still held to the bloody tenets it had
expressed centuries before,[157] that the Pope claimed
temporal powers and would use them to subdue the United
States within a short time,[158] and that when that day
arrived all religious and civil liberty would be stamped
from existence.[159] To combat this evil, the society believed, was the legitimate duty of every pastor in the
land[160] and the circular ended with a plea to all clergymen to unite in forming similar Protestant Associations
to be affiliated in some way with the Philadelphia group.[161]

　　　　This call met an immediate response. In the
same month that the Address was issued a Cincinnati Prot-

157 - Ibid., pp. 19-23.
158 - Ibid., p. 34.
159 - Ibid., pp. 25-26.
160 - Ibid., pp. 39-40.
161 - Ibid., p. 42. The members stated that while they
　　　had given their organization a national designation,
　　　they did not insist on being considered the parent
　　　body, but would be willing to cooperate with other
　　　societies on terms of full equality. This Address
　　　was printed in full in the New York Observer, March
　　　11, 1843 and March 18, 1843. The first edition of
　　　15,000 copies was soon exhausted, and it was nec-
　　　essary to print a second edition. First Annual
　　　Report of the American Protestant Association, to-
　　　gether with a Sketch of the Addresses at the First
　　　Anniversary, November, 18, 1843 (Philadelphia, 1844),
　　　pp. 4-5.

estant Association was formed under the guiding genius

of the Reverend Lyman Beecher.[162]   Before the parent

society was a year old, similar associations had been

formed in Albany, Baltimore and Pittsburgh, and others

were being projected in cities all over the country.[163]

The work accomplished by these groups of clergymen was

similar to that being carried on in Philadelphia.   There

a monthly course of lectures on Popery was instituted,

but proved so popular that the officers of the associa-

tion were forced to provide weekly speakers.[164]   They

thought it unnecessary to add to the growing number of

tracts on the evils of Romanism however, reporting that

independent publishers were carrying on this great work

in proper manner and that more books on Catholicism were

being sold than ever before.[165]   Well could the members

assembling for their first annual meeting in 1843 ex-

press jubilant pride in their accomplishments.[166]

162 - New York Observer, March 11, 1843. A similar or-
      ganization, the Protestant Association of New York,
      had been launched a short time before, but evidently
      had no connection with the Philadelphia group. Prot-
      estant Vindicator, June 11, 1842.
163 - First Annual Report of the American Protestant Asso-
      ciation, pp. 9-10.
164 - Ibid., pp. 5-6. The association did not consider it
      expedient to send out traveling lecturers thus early
      in its career.
165 - Ibid., pp. 7-8.
166 - The first annual meeting was held in Philadelphia on
      November 18, 1843. Fiery resolutions against Romanism
      were adopted denouncing that religion as anti-Chris-
      tian, and opposed to republicanism, and urging Prot-
      estants to refuse to send their children to "Papal
      schools." Speeches were delivered by the Reverends
      Colton, Chambers, Newton, Berg and Gillette. Ibid.,
      pp. 21-23.

During the second year of its existence, the association expanded these activities. The lecture series was continued[167] and in addition an official publication was launched.[168] This new addition to the list of anti-Catholic periodicals, The Quarterly Review of the American Protestant Association, made its bow on January, 1844. It was a learned and ponderous publication and devoted largely to theological arguments against Catholicism. This new nativistic organ typified well the audience to which it was to make its appeal. The first issue contained a plea to the clergy of the country to join in the No-Popery crusade,[169] and it continued throughout its long career[170] to fill its pages with materials

167 - Quarterly Review of the American Protestant Association, January, 1845. The entire annual report of the association is printed in this issue of the magazine.

168 - Ibid., January, 1845. The decision to start publication was reached by the Board of Managers only a month after the first annual meeting.

169 - Ibid., January, 1844. The first editor of this new magazine was the Reverend Rufus W. Griswold. New York Observer, May 11, 1844.

170 - In October, 1845, Herman Hooker who had published the Quarterly Review up to that time, transferred his interests to William S. Young who continued the publication. Quarterly Review of the American Protestant Association, October, 1845. Young transferred his interests almost immediately to the American Protestant Magazine, and the two publications were merged, being published after October, 1845, as the American Protestant Magazine.

which could be used by Protestant pastors as a basis
for sermons against Romanism.[171]

  With the successful launching of this publication, the American Protestant Association had
demonstrated its stability and marked its destiny as
one of continued prosperity. It was only natural,
as a result, that immitators should enter the field.
A society based directly on the Philadelphia association yet claiming no connection with it was the Society of the Friends of the Reformation, centered in
Baltimore. More than fifty ministers of that city
determined to form this society in March, 1843, and
inspired by that prominent No-Popery campaigner, the
Reverend Robert J. Breckinridge, perfected an organization and adopted a constitution at their first meeting.
Their purpose, this constitution declared, was "to maintain, defend and promote among the several denominations
of Christians to which the members belong the principles

171 - Typical of the contents are the articles in the
  first issue: "The Bible in Public Schools."
  "Romanism in Europe," "The Miracles and Lying
  Wonders of Rome," "Tillotson on Transubstantiation," "On the Progress of Popery and the Duties
  of the Church," "The Truth Necessarily Protestant," "Testimony of the Reformers Against Popery
  as Anti-Christ," "The Romish System of Persecution," and "The Worship of the Virgin and of the
  Popes of Rome." Each member of the magazine contained approximately 108 pages. Ibid., January,
  1844.

of the Reformation and of civil and religious liberty,
against all encroachments and errors whatever."[172]

The plan of operation adopted by this society
was similar to the one used by the Philadelphia association. Public meetings in various churches were relied
on to a large measure in spreading the gospel against
Popery; eight such meetings being held in the two months
after its organization in which ten thousand persons
heard Rome attacked with bitter invective.[173] With the
large funds collected at these gatherings tracts and
books against Romanism were published.[174]

There was one group of anti-Catholic agitators
which watched the growing success of these new associations with envy and a touch of malice. Members of the
Protestant Reformation Society were beginning to realize
that they were being outdistanced in this campaign whose

172 - Spirit of the XIX Century, May, 1843. The pre-
        amble of the constitution adopted stated: "Where-
        as, we are fully convinced that the principles of
        the Reformation are essential to the welfare of
        spiritual religion and civil and religious liber-
        ty; and that the time has come when it behooves
        the friends of the Reformation to unite in ef-
        forts to defend, maintain and promote those prin-
        ciples in our common country against all encroach-
        ments and errors from whatever source arising, and
        to act in concert on certain great Scriptural prin-
        ciples for the protection and perpetuation of the
        interests of the Protestant faith; we hereby or-
        ganize ourselves into an Association, the name and
        general objects of which are set forth in the fol-
        lowing Constitution."
173 - Ibid., May, 1843. These first lectures were held
        between March 21 and April 16. A large number of
        converts to the society were won through them.
174 - Ibid., May, 1843.

infancy they had nurtured. Their society was con-
tinuing to operate and even expanding slowly, but
members were flocking far more rapidly into the
American Protestant Association and similar bodies.
In such a situation it was natural for leaders of the
Protestant Reformation Society to indulge in a bit of
Calvinistic self-scrutiny in an effort to understand
these new developments.

Such introspection revealed the cause of the
declining interest in their society. The Protestant
Reformation Society had failed to meet the new conditions created by the New York controversy. Its methods
were still the methods of the 1830's; it still shouted
rabid invective and dwelt upon the lust and bloodshed
of Romanism. As church members attracted by the struggle over the Bible in the schools drifted into No-Popery
circles they naturally turned away from such tactics and
toward the societies which offered war upon Catholicism
combined with the solace of conservative Protestant principles. In this situation the American Protestant Association had prospered; the Protestant Reformation Society had declined.

A typical criticism of methods employed by the
Reformation Society was voiced in a book popular at the

time, <u>Humbugs of New York</u>, by David M. Reese.[175] Reese
devotes one chapter of his volume to "Ultra-Protestantism," classing it with the anti-slavery and anti-drink-
ing campaigns. "This," he wrote, "is the third of the
'Antis," yclept Anti-Popery in common parlance, which
we claim among the humbugs of the times, for the obvious
reason that both Popery and anti-Popery are impostures
upon the public."[176] The author made it clear from the
start that he had no sympathy with Romanism, and that
he viewed the "whole system of Popery to be corrupt,
demoralizing, infamous and false."[177] But he did object, he said, to the unchristian manner by which attacks on Catholicism were made, and to the demoralizing
influence of most of the publications of No Popery writers. "Tales of lust and blood and murder," Reese wrote,
"such as those with which the ultra-Protestant press is
teeming, in all the loathsome and disgusting details in
which they are recited; and especially when they are
represented as transpiring under the cloak of religion,
and the criminals occupying and disgracing the holy
office of the ministry, are adapted in the very nature

175 - Reese, David M., <u>Humbugs of New York, being a
Remonstrance Against Popular Delusion, whether
in Science, Philosophy or Relgion</u> (New York,
1838).
176 - <u>Ibid</u>., pp. 210-211.
177 - <u>Ibid</u>., pp. 211-212. Having finished his discussion of "Ultra-Protestantism," the author returns at the end of the chapter to emphasize
further the true nature of Popery. <u>Ibid</u>., pp.
229-232.

of things to strengthen the hands of infidelity and
irreligion."[178]

It was this criticism, typical of the belief
of thousands of church going men and women, which was
to spell the doom of the Protestant Reformation Society
and its rabid methods of attack. Members of the society saw that a change must be made if they were to continue their campaign with success. Opportunity for
that change came in 1843 when the guiding light of the
old organization, the Reverend William C. Brownlee, retired from active labors.[179] The work of reorganizing
the society was begun immediately, and in January, 1844,
the change was completed. The Protestant Reformation
Society passed from existence; in its place was born
the American Protestant Society.[180]

The constitution adopted by this new organization illustrates the change in its methods.[181] It was
still definitely an anti-Catholic society, bemoaning
"the influence of Romanism rapidly extending over this

178 - Ibid., p. 217.
179 - Circular Issued by the American Protestant Society, December, 1847 (New York, 1847), pp. 3-5;
Memorial of the Reverend W. C. Brownlee, D. D.
(New York, 1860), pp. 64-66. Brownlee lived
until 1860, when he died at the age of 77.
180 - Circular Issued by the American Protestant Society, December, 1847, p. 5.
181 - The constitution of this society is in Appendix A.

Republic endangering the freedom and institutions of
our country."[182]   It still spoke of Popish "superstition" and the "spiritual darkness" of Catholicism.
But the new spirit of toleration and Christianity was
apparent when the constitution described the methods
through which the society would carry on its work:

> Believing coercion in religious opin-
> ions, and the spirit of denunciation, to be
> inconsistent with the spirit of Christianity,
> the means to be employed to secure the ob-
> jects of the Society are light and love; in
> the use of these means, the Society will aim
> to enlighten Protestants concerning the nature,
> operations and influence of Romanism, as well
> as to guard against its encroachments upon our
> civil and religious institutions, and to awaken
> Christian feelings and Christian action for the
> salvation of Romanists, by the employment of
> the press, Lecturing Agents, Missionaries, and
> Colporteurs to circulate Bibles, Tracts and
> Books upon the subject - looking unto God for
> success in this work.[183]

Particularly was this new spirit exemplified
when the society launched its operations. Four lecturing agents who had been storming about the country ex-
horting against the Pope and Rome were inherited from

182 - The constitution is printed in each of the annual
reports of the American Protestant Society. The
copy used as a basis for this discussion is from
the Second Annual Report of the American Protestant Society, (New York, 1845), pp. 27-28. The
statements here quoted are in the preamble of
the constitution.
183 - Ibid., p. 27. The section quoted is Article III
of the constitution.

the Protestant Reformation Society, but officers of
the new organization found them so violently opposed to
the Catholic church that they were dismissed.[184] New
lecturing agents were procured, an effort being made
to select only converted Romanists who, understanding
the evils of Popery, could better explain those evils
to their audiences.[185] During the first year of its
existence the new society spent more than three thousand dollars in employing these agents;[186] two years
later this sum had grown to more than eleven thousand
dollars,[187] and in 1848 it reached nearly twenty thousand dollars.[188]

These agents carried out their labors well
within the spirit of the society which employed them.
Religious papers commented with pleasure on the Christian benevolence displayed by one of the leading speakers of the Society, the Reverend Herman Norton:

184 - Circular Issued by the American Protestant Society,
      December, 1847, pp. 8-9.
185 - Second Annual Report of the American Protestant
      Society, p. 10.
186 - Ibid., p. 28. The amount expended on lecturing
      agents in the first year was $3,701.61.
187 - Fourth Annual Report of the American Protestant
      Society (New York, 1847), p. 40. In this year
      $11,998.50 was used in this way.
188 - Fifth Annual Report of the American Protestant
      Society (New York, 1848), p. 27. The amount ex-
      pended was $19,975.80.

> We have had so many fiery spirits among
> us, and so much mischief has been done by
> fierce denunciation, that it was no easy task
> for Mr. Norton to overcome the prejudice which
> was arrayed against him. But the thing has
> been done in a most surprising manner. Bap-
> tist and Methodist and Presbyterian and Dutch
> and German Reformed churches are open to a
> hearing of the claims which he urges.[189]

Not only were these lecturing agents instructed
to inform Protestants of the evils of Popery; they were
told too to labor among the downtrodden Romanists of the
land and convert them to the true religion of the Gospel.[190]
In the first year of its organization missionary agents
of this nature were sent among the Portugese fishermen
on the New England coast[191] and the French inhabitants
of the northeast,[192] as well as among the Germans of the
West. While officers of the society warned that this
work would be slow and difficult to accomplish[193] the
annual reports to members were filled with pages glorify-
ing the conquests which had been made.[194] Most of these

189 - New York Evangelist, quoted in American Protestant
      Magazine, December, 1845.
190 - Second Annual Report of the American Protestant
      Society, p. 9. The society made an effort to
      secure its lecturing agents from among representa-
      tives of all denominations, specifying only that
      most of them should be converts from Catholicism.
191 - Ibid., pp. 14-16. Missionary agents were chosen
      able to speak the language of the group in which
      they were to work.
192 - Ibid., p. 17.
193 - Ibid., pp. 3-4.
194 - Ibid., pp. 11-26.

efforts were confined to the United States, although
funds were solicited to aid in the Waldenses by a
series of No-Popery lectures in 1845.[195]

Action such as this was certain to appeal to
the churches of the United States. A generation which
had given birth to the American Board of Commissioners
for Foreign Missions[196] warmed naturally to similar
missionary activities among the Papists of America.
In 1845 the society was able to report with joy that
many churches were aiding its efforts and that more
than one hundred ministers had endorsed its program
by subscribing to life membership.[197] Aware of the
strength to be gained by such support, the American
Protestant Society introduced a new feature into their
crusade. Lecturing agents were sent to church conventions, both national and local, all over the land. There,
before the gathered clergy, the purposes of the society

195 - New York Observer, May 31, 1845. The lectures were
delivered by the Reverend George B. Cheever, and
realized a profit of $1,005.87.
196 - Sweet, Story of Religions in America. The American
Board was launched in 1810 and from that time until
the Civil War American churches were extremely active in aiding missionary activities.
197 - Second Annual Report of the American Protestant
Society, p. 11. Many of the ministers had the fee
for life membership paid by their congregations or
by local groups. Thus in Ann Arbor, Michigan, The
Young Ladies Sewing Society paid life membership
fees for the Baptist, Methodist and Presbyterian
ministers of that town. American Protestant Magazine, December, 1845.

were explained and the ministers were urged to give their support to the campaign against Romanism.[198] This innovation, destined to become one of the most important instruments in the hands of the nativists, increased the popularity of the society and in addition spread far and wide the doctrines and hate which it preached.

Not only was the newly formed American Protestant Society active in sponsoring lecturing agents, but it embarked upon a program of publication unrivaled before by nativistic societies. During the first year of its existence it circulated more than 160,000 pages of tracts against Popery in addition to many books;[199]

198 - Reports of speeches given before church conventions by lecturing agents were published in the American Protestant Magazine, together with resolutions passed by each of the conventions praising the work of the society and endorsing its principles. Speeches thus reported were: the Reverend Burnham before the Columbia Presbytery, June 3, 1845, American Protestant Magazine, July, 1845; The Reverend Herman Norton before the Third Presbytery of Philadelphia, October 14, 1845, Ibid., November, 1845; the Reverend J. P. Burnham before the Montgomery Classes of the Dutch Reformed Church, October, 1845, Ibid., November, 1845; the Reverend H. Norton before the Baptists State Convention of Pennsylvania, November, 1845. Ibid., December, 1845; the Reverend H. Norton before the Synod of Philadelphia, November, 1845, Ibid., December, 1845. This practice of lectures before church organizations had been attempted once, in 1842, by the Protestant Reformation Society. See Protestant Vindicator, April 6, 1842.
199 - Circular Issued by the American Protestant Society, December, 1847, pp. 9-10.

a year later this number had grown to more than 180,000
pages and amibitious plans were laid for the future.[200]

200 - Second Annual Report of the American Protestant
Society, p. 10. Two years later the number of
pages of literature circulated free of charge
had mounted to 774,400. Fourth Annual Report of
the American Protestant Society, pp. 27-28. Typical of the books published by the society, in
addition to these tracts, was the list that appeared in 1844-1845: Book of Tracts on Romanism,
containing the Origin and Progress, Cruelties,
Frauds, Superstitions, Miracles, Ceremonies, etc.
of the Church of Rome (New York, 1844); Norton,
Herman, Startling Facts for American Protestants;
Progress of Romanism in the United States since
the Revolutionary War; its Present Position and
Future Prospects (New York, 1844); The Book of
Martyrs (New York, 1844); The Conversion and Sufferings of Sarah Doherty; Illustrative of Popery
in Ireland (New York, 1844); The Protestant Exiles
of Zillerthal; their Persecutions and Expatriation
on Separating from the Church of Rome and embracing
the Reformed Faith (New York, 1844); Morse, Samuel
F. B., Foreign Conspiracy against the Liberties of
the United States, 6th edition (New York, 1844);
Romanism Incompatible with Republican Principles
(New York, 1844); Our Country; Its Dangers and Duty
(New York, 1844); Norton, Herman, Signs of Danger
and of Promise; Duties of Protestants at the Pres-
ent Crisis (New York, 1844); American Protestant
Society Tracts on Romanism (New York, 1844); Canons
and Decrees of the Council of Trent, faithfully
Translated from the first Edition of 1564 (New York,
1844); History of the Western Apostolic Churches
from which the Roman Church Apostatized, and the
Immortal Saint Patrick Vindicated from the False
Charge of being a Roman Catholic (New York, 1844);
Secret Instructions to the Jesuits (New York, 1844);
Brownlee, W. C., The Roman Catholic Religion Viewed
in the Light of Prophecy and History; its Final
Downfall and the Triumph of the Church of Christ.
(New York, 1845)

At the same time new interest in the No-Popery cause was created by prizes offered for the best books on the evils of Romanism.[201]

Not only did the new society publish books and tracts to further its cause but in addition it entered the lists as sponsor of an anti-Catholic magazine. When the Reverend W. C. Brownlee retired from active labor in 1843 his paper, the Protestant Vindicator, ended its long and vigorous career as an exposer of Popery. This paper had served as official organ for the Protestant Reformation Society, it was natural that that society's successor should found and establish a paper to continue the tradition. Such a paper, the American Protestant, appeared in January, 1844, a bi-monthly publication similar to the Protestant Vindicator.[202] A year later it was converted into a monthly magazine, the American Protestant Magazine[203] and began a career which marked it as the most successful of the anti-Catholic publications.

201 - Second Annual Report of the American Protestant Society, p. 10. The first award was given for a book entitled, Romanism Incompatible with Republican Principles (New York, 1844). The premium was 100. Second prize of $25. was granted to, Our Country, Its Dangers and Its Duty (New York, 1844).
202 - Ibid., p. 11.
203 - New York Observer, June 14, 1845. The new magazine had 24 pages in each issue and sold for one dollar a year.

That this new publication reflected the
tolerant spirit of the organization which sponsored
it was apparent from the pronouncement of policy
which was promised by the editors in the first issue:

> It is our purpose in this work to make
> prominent our relations and duties to the
> Roman Catholic population of the United
> States. This will be done not in a con-
> troversial manner. During the heat and
> hurry of controversy, we fear that many
> have lost sight of their true position with
> respect to the Romanists among us. This we
> wish to present by statements of facts and
> the true grounds of obligation, rather than
> by the denunciation of ignorant men, who may
> be walking in the light with which they are
> favored. The Protestant community must be
> made to feel that they are called to labor
> for the best welfare of the papal population,
> not merely by the American Protestant Socie-
> ty, or by any other society, but the Prov-
> idence of God summons them and the authority
> of his word calls them into this vineyard.[204]

The success of this policy was attested by the
prosperity enjoyed by the American Protestant Magazine.
Only a few months after it started publication it was
able to absorb the Quarterly Review of the American Protestant Association and a few years later added the National Protestant and the North American Protestant, or
the Anti-Jesuit.[205]   By this time the circulation had
grown to more than 12,000 copies each issue and was mount-

204 - American Protestant Magazine, June, 1845.
205 - Ibid., March, 1847. See above, pp.404-409 for the
      earlier career of these magazines.

ing rapidly.[206]

       The success of this magazine was paralleled
by that of the society which sponsored its publication.
The plea of love and toleration had been successful;
membership grew beyond even the expectation of the
founders. Only a year after its founding three hundred and fifty life members had been enrolled in addition to several thousand regular members;[207] two years
later that number had been more than doubled.[208] Eqally
encouraging was the financial response of nativistically
inclined enthusiasts. During the first year the society's income was well over $6,000,[209] a year later that
amount had grown to nearly $7,000,[210] and members were
boasting that the proceeds of the American Board of Commissioners for Foreign Missions had been even less when
that organization was only two years old.[211] By 1847
the receipts had mounted to more than $19,000,[212] con-
siderably more than the American Bible Society had been
able to muster at its fourth meeting,[213] and a year later

206 - New York Observer, May 27, 1848.
207 - Second Annual Report of the American Protestant
     Society, pp. 30-32.
208 - Fourth Annual Report of the American Protestant
     Society, pp. 33-36.
209 - The treasurer reported receipts of $6,502.55. New
     York Observer, May 4, 1844.
210 - Second Annual Report of the American Protestant
     Society, p. 28. The amount taken in was $7,072.97.
211 - New York Observer, May 24, 1845. The boast was.
     made at the annual meeting of the society by the
     Reverend Gridley of Vermont.
212 - The receipts amounted to $19,709.13. Fourth Annual
     Report of the American Protestant Society, p. 40.
213 - Ibid., pp. 27-28.

nearly $30,000 was subscribed.[214] If financial response
is indicative of popularity, the American Protestant Society had taken its place beside the other great religious
societies of the day, and seemed destined to a career of
continued prosperity in its campaign against Rome.[215]

The American Protestant Society had been borne
to this fabulous success on the crest of an anti-Catholic
wave of sentiment which was sweeping over the country,
urged on by pulpit and press and organizations. In vain
did the Catholic Bishops at the Fifth Provincial Council
in Baltimore implore members of their faith to refute "all
those atrocious calumnies which deluded men ... constantly
circulate by every possible means against our holy religion."[216] Protestant Americans had imbibed deeply of the
intoxicating words of nativistic agitators; they had embraced the cause of No-Popery with an enthusiasm which
inspired wonder even among the more violent crusaders
against Rome. "Truly a great revolution in public sentiment is already accomplished," wrote an editor of an anti-

214 - Fifth Annual Report of the American Protestant Society (1848), p. 27. The exact amount was $28,494.43.
215 - The American Protestant Society continued in existence until 1849, when it was combined with the
Christian Alliance and other missionary societies
operating in the foreign field among Catholics, to
make a new nativistic society, the American and
Foreign Christian Union.
216 - The Fifth Provincial Council met in 1843. Quoted
in O'Gorman, History of the Roman Catholic Church,
p. 344.

Catholic journal in 1843, "when in the same city, the
same cause which in 1832 endangered a man's life, in
1835 jeoparded his character, and as late as 1840 exposed him to indictment, fine and imprisonment - in
1843 looms gloriously up on the top of a general movement of the piety of the community, and becomes the
very center of Christian unity."[217] Truly the New York
school controversy and the religious interest which it
had stimulated had borne their fruit.

[217] - Spirit of XIX Century, May, 1843.

VIII

THE PROPAGANDA OF ANTI-CATHOLICISM
1834 - 1844.

An understanding of the wave of anti-Catholic sentiment which swept over the United States in the early years of the nineteenth century is impossible without proper consideration of the mass of calumny being loosed at the same time by a legion of No-Popery writers. Conflicts over trusteeism within the Catholic church, Irish rioting, lawlessness and disorder, panics and pauperism, school controversies and political Popery; all these things were important in fomenting the spirit of intolerance growing steadily among the people. But had not a great army of writers seized upon this growing sentiment to flood the country with a constant stream of propaganda literature against Rome, that cry against the church could never have attained the heights that it did.

The array of No-Popery enthusiasts who penned their invective in the period before 1845 copied not only the enthusiasm but the vindictiveness of the first successful propagandists, Maria Monk and Samuel F. B. Morse. The mass of literature which flowed from their pens dealt with Rome in terms of uncontrolled bigotry and harshness.

Christian charity and tolerance were unknown; the writer
who fostered the most bitter attack secured not only the
greatest moral satisfaction but flattering material success from royalties as well. Men and women throughout
the United States who had supported the crusade against
Rome found in such outspoken words a vicarious vent for
their personal antipathies and purchased volume after
volume. As early as 1838 an impartial observer was complaining that books on the subject had become so numerous
that it was impossible to read them all.[1] By 1841 the
demand for these bitter attacks was so great that at
least one volume directed against Popery was appearing
every week[2] and separate bookstores dealing only in anti-
Catholic literature were being established in the larger
cities.[3]

     No minute feature of the Catholic church was
spared the written abuse of the authors who responded to
this demand. Books by the score appeared, running the
gamut between dull theological arguments to prove Popery
the anti-Christ of Scripture to the more enlivening erot-
ica of convent life and its alleged exposure. It was in
attacking the latter that the propaganda writer found his

1 - Reese, Humbugs of New York, pp. 226-227.
2 - New York Observer, May 8, 1841.
3 - Protestant Vindicator, May 12, 1841; December 16, 1835.

his true field; for in the gross accusations against
the morality of priest and nun the art of invective won
its greatest response.

There was no doubt in the minds of such writers
that the Church, by its very nature, bred immorality, and
that sin strewed its every path.[4] The doctrine that lying and perjury were justified in defense of faith, they
said, reached back so early into the history of the church
that even the works of the Fathers, steeped in Popery as
they were, could not be believed.[5] They insisted that
this same doctrine persisted, that Romanists were taught
to keep no faith with heretics,[6] and that hence their
oaths and testimony were worthless.[7] Books were written

4 - Hogan, William, Auricular Confession and Popish Nun-
neries (Boston, 1845); p. 101; Cheever, Hierarchical
Despotism, pp. 116-119; Emerlina, G. D., Frauds of
Papal Ecclesiastics; to which are added Illustrative
Notes from Letters by Gilbert Burnet and Gavin's
Master Key to Popery (New York, 1835), p. 39; Sch-
mucker, Discourse in Commemoration of the Glorious
Reformation, pp. 48-49; Protestant Vindicator, Octo-
ber, 21, 1835.
5 - Cheever, Hierarchical Despotism, pp. 42-56; National
Protestant, August, 1845.
6 - Smith, Samuel B., Synopsis of the Moral Theology of
the Church of Rome from the Works of Saint Ligori
(New York, 1836), p. 160; Schmucker, Discourse in
Commemoration of the Glorious Reformation, pp. 111-
112 note; Protestant Vindicator, September 30, 1840;
National Protestant, April, 1845; Berg, Joseph Fred-
erick, A Synopsis of the Moral Philosophy of Peter
Dens as Prepared for the Use of Romish Seminaries
and Students of Theology (New York, 1841).
7 - Elizabeth, Charlotte, Second Causes, or Up and Be
Doing (New York, 1843), pp. 191-193; Protestant
Vindicator, July 8, 1840; National Protestant,
May, 1845; Ibid., July, 1845.

to show that the Jesuits especially had imbibed deeply
of these tenets[8] and believed only in "impiety, immorality, falsehood, frauds in business, perjury, theft,
murder, infanticide and regicide."[9]

That such beliefs bred immorality and crime
was made even more inevitable by the system of indulgences introduced in the twelfth century and giving to
the "papal world a tariff of human crimes."[10] The use
of this system, the propagandists believed, made it the
interest of pope and priest that men should commit crimes
frequently and continually. The more vicious and corrupt
the people, the greater the profits of the priests."[11]
They revived ancient tables of indulgences[12] in which
murder and sexual crimes were taxed a smaller sum than

8 - Lester, Charles E., The Jesuits (New York, 1845);
    Michelet, M., The Jesuits (New York, 1845).
9 - The American Text Book of Popery: Being an Authentic
    Compend of the Bulls, Canons and Decretals of the
    Roman Hierarchy (New York, 1844), pp. 359-370.
10- Schmucker, Discourse in Commemoration of the Glorious
    Reformation, p. 40.
11- Ibid., p. 41.
12- One of the books cited by nativistic authors was an
    early English No-Popery work: Taxes of the Apostolic
    Chancery; or, the Book of Rates, now used in the Sin
    Custom House of the Church and Court of Rome: Con-
    taining the Bulls, Dispensations and Pardons for
    all Manner of Villanies and Wickedness with the
    Several Sums of Moneys Given and to be Paid for
    Them (London, 1674).

that exacted for eating flesh on fast days[13] and they
proclaimed loudly that those same tables were still in
force.[14] Catholic insistence that the indulgence system
had been abolished centuries before went unheeded; a
nativistic writer who boasted that he had been "late a
Popish priest" testified that he had sold them himself.[15]

Having constructed the plausibility for greater
crime among adherents to the faith of Rome, propagandists
found little exaggeration in tales which they told of
priestly plot and intrigue. Murders in France and other

13 - A typical list published at the time:

	L	s.	d.
For a layman murdering a layman	0	7	6
For him who has killed his father	0	10	6
For him who has killed his mother	0	10	6
Priest keeping a concubine	0	10	6
A man to change his vow	0	15	0
Eating flesh on fast days	0	10	6
For violating a maid	0	9	0
For incest with sister of mother	0	7	6

From the National Protestant, July, 1845. Similar
lists were published in Pond, Enoch, No Fellowship
with Romanism (Boston, 1843), pp. 135-136; Quarterly
Review of the American Protestant Association, January, 1845; Ibid., July, 1845.

14 - American Protestant Magazine, August, 1844; New
York Observer, December 25, 1830; Schmucker, Discourse in Commemoration of the Glorious Reformation,
pp. 41-42; Sinclair, Catherine, Shetland and the
Shetlanders; or, the Northern Circuit (New York,
1840), p. 35; Mendham, Joseph, The Venal Indulgences and Pardons of the Church of Rome, Exemplified in a Summary of an Indulgence of Sixtus IV
(London, 1845)

15 - Hogan, William, Synopsis of Popery, as it Was and
as it Is (Hartford, 1845), pp. 173-176.

Catholic countries were ascribed to priests[16] and it
was freely asserted that members of the Romish clergy
used poison frequently to remove obnoxious persons.[17]
Such crimes were further encouraged, nativists believed, because the church gave sanctuary to all criminals who respected its faith.[18] Writers drew dismal
pictures of European churches where outcasts flocked
to escape the law and where violence reigned.[19]

Any discussion of crime was certain to lead
the propagandists into a consideration of the confessional. All of them agreed that while the system of
indulgences and the very nature of Popery led naturally
to sin and lawlessness, it was to the confessors box
that much of the guilt of the church could be traced.
They pointed out that through the confessional the
priest had absolute control over his subjects, and
could command them to sin in any way.[20] Writers pictured Jesuit spies in every family where Catholic servants were employed, faithfully transcribing for their

16 - New York Observer, December 5, 1840; Protestant
     Vindicator, January 6, 1841; Ibid., July 28, 1841.
17 - Hogan, Auricular Confession and Popish Nunneries,
     pp. 55-57.
18 - Pond, No Fellowship with Romanism, pp. 147-149;
     Downfall of Babylon, April 18, 1835.
19 - Ricci, Scipio de, Secrets of Nunneries Disclosed
     (New York, 1834), p. 67.
20 - Hogan, Auricular Confession and Popish Nunneries,
     p. 168; Cheever, Hierarchical Despotism, p. 189.

confessors details of the family life.[21] But above all
else the confession gave criminals an opportunity of
having their sins forgiven that they might go forth to
sin again.[22] Under such a system, the propagandists
agreed, there was little wonder that crime flourished
almost unchecked.

Maria Monk and her backers had demonstrated
the profit to be gained from libidinous tales and it
was only natural that exposers of the confessional should
turn to the moral aspects of this institution. By the
early 1840's whole books were appearing devoted to this
fascinating theme and bearing such outspoken titles as
Auricular Confession and Popish Nunneries[23] and The Con-

21 - National Protestant, April, 1845; Hogan, Auricular
     Confession, p. 129.
22 - Protestant Vindicator, December 15, 1841; Ibid.,
     April 14, 1841; National Protestant or the Anti-
     Jesuit, April, 1845; Downfall of Babylon, April
     2, 1836; Hogan, Auricular Confession and Popish
     Nunneries, pp. 184-185. One author, who pro-
     fessed to have been a mistress of a priest in
     Cuba, described the joy of priests whenever a
     crime was committed, for it gave them an oppor-
     tunity to levy heavy fines from the penitent in
     the confessional box. Culbertson, Rosamond,
     Rosamond, or a Narrative of the Captivity and
     Sufferings of an American Female, under the
     Popish Priests in the Island of Cuba, with a
     Disclosure of her Manners and Customs, written
     by Herself. (New York, 1836), quoted in Down-
     fall of Babylon, April 2, 1836.
23 - Hogan, William, Auricular Confession and Popish
     Nunneries (Boston, 1845).

fessional, or an Exposition of the Doctrine of Auricular
Confession as Taught in the Standards of the Roman Church.[24]
Few nativistic writers could resist the temptation to add
to the large stock of knowledge that every American reader
of their products already had.

There was little doubt in the minds of these
propagandists as to the nature of the immorality. "Persuade a woman that if she sin, you can forgive her as
thoroughly and effectually as Almighty God can forgive
her," wrote one, "And you take away every check from
vice."[25] It was in this position assumed by the priest
that the writers saw the gravest danger. He lost his
character as a man and became a God, all women being
forced to obey him.[26] "Nothing," declared one expounder
of such doctrine, "then, is easier, if he has the least
desire for the penitent, than to persaude her that he is
divinely commissioned to -------."[27] The meaning of
that intriguing blank space was more easily understood

24 - Berg, Joseph F., The confessional, or an Exposition
     of the Doctrine of Auricular Confession, as Taught
     in the Standards of the Roman Church (3d edition,
     New York, 1841). A similar book published at the
     time was: Michelet, M., Spiritual Direction and
     Auricular Confession (Philadelphia, 1845). Popery
     Exposed: or, The Secrets and Privacy of the Con-
     fessional Unmasked (New York, 1845)
25 - Hogan, Auricular Confession and Popish Nunneries,
     p. 67.
26 - Protestant Vindicator, September 16, 1840; Supple-
     ment to Six Months in a Convent, p. 212.
27 - Hogan, Auricular Confession and Popish Nunneries,
     pp. 64-65.

by readers of the day when they were informed that whenever possible, both in Popish countries and America,
women were confessed entirely in the priests bedrooms,
confessional boxes being maintained only as a sham and
as a means of throwing jealous husbands off the scent.[28]

Especially was all doubt removed when writers
spread before them questions put to women in the confessional. Some writers, impressed with the moral nature
of their audience, refused to go into lurid detail,[29]
and even the most hardened expositors of Romanism shrank,
they said, from complete revelation.[30] The scenes that
they did depict between fair lady and confessor went far
to satisfy the curiosity of their readers. A typical
description which was, the author explained, "as fair a
sketch as I can, with due regard to decency, give," follows:

> But first let the reader figure to himself,
> or herself, a young lady, between the ages of
> twelve to twenty, on her knees, with her lips
> nearly close pressed to the cheeks of the priest,
> who, in all probability, is not over twenty-five
> or thirty years old...When priest and penitent

28 - Downfall of Babylon, April 4, 1835; Ibid., April
11, 1835; National Protestant Magazine or the
Anti-Jesuit, April, 1845.
29 - Emerlina, Frauds of Papal Ecclesiastics, p. 139;
Pond, No Fellowship with Romanism, pp. 132-133.
30 - Hogan, Auricular Confession and Popish Nunneries,
p. 35. Hogan states that all the questions can
be found in Antoine's Moral Theology and in Dens
De Peccatis, both books which he was forced to
study when in training for the priesthood at Maynooth College.

are placed in the above attitude, let us
suppose the following conversation taking
place between them, and unless my readers
are more dull of apprehension than I am
willing to believe, they will have some
ideas of the <u>beauties of Popery</u>.

Confessor: "What sins have you committed?"
Penitent: "I don't know any sir."
Con: "Are you sure you did nothing wrong? Ex-
     amine yourself well."
Pen: "Yes, I do recollect that I did wrong. I
     made faces at school at Lucy A."
Con: "Nothing else?"
Pen: "Yes, I told mother I hated Lucy A., and
     that she was an ugly thing."
Con: (scarcely able to suppress a smile at find-
     ing the girl perfectly innocent) "Have you
     had any immodest thoughts?"
Pen: "What is that, sir?"
Con: "Have you not been thinking about men?"
Pen: "Why, yes sir."
Con: "Are you fond of any of them?"
Pen: "Why yes, I like Cousin A. or R. greatly."
Con: "Did you ever like to sleep with him?"
Pen: "Oh no."
Con: "How long did these thoughts about men con-
     tinue?"
Pen: "Not very long."
Con: "Had you these thoughts by day or by night?"
Pen: "By ------."

     In this strain does this reptile confessor
proceed until his now half gained prey is filled
with ideas and thoughts to which she has been
hitherto a stranger. He tells her that she must
come tomorrow again. She accordingly comes, and
he gives another twist to the screw, which he has
now firmly fixed upon the soul and body of his
penitent. Day after day, week after week, and
month after month does this hopeless girl come
to confession until this wretch has worked up
her passions to a tension almost snapping and
then becomes his easy prey.[31]

31 - Hogan, <u>Auricular Confession and Popish Nunneries</u>,
     pp. 33-34.

This and similar revelations[32] never reached
the point of actual pornography, but they hinted at much.
An effective form of propaganda, they were widely used,
not only in publication, but in debate. Thus in Norwich,
New York, a Protestant clergyman published a pamphlet re-
citing confessional questions in Latin, and issued a public challenge to any priest to translate it into English
or to allow him to read it to a male Catholic congregation. Needless to say, his challenge went unheeded[33] but
Catholic refusal was taken by nativsts only as confession
of guilt. The absurdity of most of these charges would
have removed their sting had not nativistic enthusiasts
carried their prejudices into action. On two separate
occasions priests were arrested charged with seduction
of girls through the confessional, once in Philadelphia[34]

32 - Similar accounts of questions asked at confession
are in, Ibid., pp. 36-38; American Text Book of
Popery, pp. 330-336; Schmucker, Discourse in
Commemoration of the Glorious Reformation, pp.
60-62; Supplement to Six Months in a Convent,
pp. 236-237.
33 - Protestant Vindicator, March 31, 1841.
34 - Ibid., July 28, 1841; September 8, 1841. The accounts printed were taken from the Philadelphia
Ledger, with editorial comment by the Protestant
Vindicator. The process of seduction was described
in some detail: "He perseveringly pursued his object, and after repeated repulses, he at length,
under his own roof, and while clothed in the vest-
ments of his holy calling, accomplished his hellish
design, and the innocent pure minded girl - lay before him the ruined and polluted victim of his dev-
ilish arts and unholy passions." Ibid., September
8, 1841. The Vindicator reported that the priest,
John McNulty, was forced to pay his victim $2,500
by the jury.

and again in Evansville, Indiana.[35] The anti-Catholic
press reported the incidents with enthusiasm, and told
in each crimson detail how the priest in Evansville had
dragged his penitent from the confessional box to the
floor of the sanctuary to carry out his "hellist deed."

Discussion of the immorality of the confessional
naturally led propagandists into a consideration of the
entire moral structure of the Catholic church. They saw
celibacy unsanctioned by Christ[37] or the early church
fathers[38] as the basis of the universal corruption which
they maintained had existed for centuries. Sufferings of
early Catholic saints in an effort to preserve their purity were paraded before readers; how Saint Francis and Saint
Ulric had spent their days in icy waters to cool turbulent
flesh, how Saint Benedict had rolled in nettles, and how

35 - New York Observer, May 28, 1842; Shea, History of the
Catholic Church in the United States, vol. iii, p. 654.
Shea states that the priest, the Reverend Roman Wein-
zoepflen, was convicted of rape, but released a short
time later when the feelings of the citizens had died
down, insisting that the whole arrest was a trumped
up plot on the part of nativists. The New York Observer has a different story, stating that he escaped during the trial when an argument developed
between Irish and German Catholics in the court room.
36 - Protestant Vindicator, June 1, 1842.
37 - American Text Book of Popery, p. 180; Baltimore Literary and Religious Magazine, April, 1838.
38 - National Protestant, May, 1845; Baltimore Literary
and Religious Magazine, June, 1838.

an Irish priest, tempted by a beautiful girl, had seized
a knife and amputated the parts causing sensuality.[39]
The whole history of the church was bared to expose
the lax moral character of the Popes and their clergy,
and it was openly charged that throughout the years since
celibacy was forced on the clergy, houses of prostitution
had been sanctioned in Rome by the Church.[40]

That such a condition of immorality still followed in the wake of Catholicism and its priests the
propagandists did not question. The tale was often told
of how thirty notaries required sixty days to take down
all the testimony of the women of Seville against the dissolute habits of their spiritual advisers.[41] The testimony of prostitutes in Rome was produced to show that their
best customers were the priests,[42] one asserting that a

39 - Downfall of Babylon, December 20, 1834; National Prot-
     estant, July, 1845.
40 - Schmucker, Discourse in Commemoration of the Glorious
     Reformation, p. 37; American Text Book of Popery, pp.
     300-307; Giustiniani, L., Papal Rome as it is by a
     Roman, (2nd edition, Baltimore, 1843), pp. 185-194;
     Downfall of Babylon, April 16, 1836; New York Ob-
     server, May 25, 1844. Historical works dwelling on
     the immorality of the clergy in the past were popu-
     lar. Typical was, Pope Alexander VI and his Son,
     Caeser Borgia (Philadelphia, 1844), recording, ac-
     cording to the New York Observer, "the foulest chap-
     ter in the annals of human villainy." New York Ob-
     server, February 3, 1844.
41 - Hogan, Auricular Confession and Popish Nunneries,
     pp. 59-60; National Protestant, May, 1845.
42 - Emerlina, Frauds of Papal Ecclesiastics, pp. 138,
     140, 146.

holy father had "not only ravished her daughter, but also
abused one of her boys, in the most abominable manner possible."[43] Throughout the rest of the world priests employed
a "niece" or "cousin," writers insisted, to satisfy their
passions,[44] this violation of the moral code being approved
by the people as it kept the clergy from attacking innocent
wives and daughters.[45] "Licentiousness takes the lead of
the vices among these ungodly priests," one propagandist
declared. "They obtain constant access to the nunneries.
Their appetites and passions are without restraint. Their
unbridled lust stalks forth in broad daylight; and deeds
of iniquity are daily committed by them, which are enough
to make the savage of the wilderness blush."[46]

That this corruption of the clergy was confined to
Europe or Catholic countries was vigorously denied. Even
in America celibacy was taking its toll, writers warned,[47]
and this explained why priests never preached against immorality, for such tactics might injure the opportunities
for conquest.[48] Propagandists who claimed to be former
"Popish priests," described their experiences among the
American hierarchy; telling that seven out of every eight

43 - Ibid., pp. 145-146.
44 - White, Practical and Internal Evidence, pp. 106-111;
     Downfall of Babylon, March 21, 1845.
45 - Hogan, Auricular Confession and Popish Nunneries,
     pp. 48-49.
46 - Downfall of Babylon, March 5, 1836.
47 - Ibid., May 14, 1836; December 13, 1834.
48 - Emerlina, Frauds of Papal Ecclesiastics, p. 139.

priests were guilty of seduction through the confessional[49]
and describing three priests in one western convent who
were the fathers of more than one hundred children.[50]
Priests in our own country, cried a nativist, "are deeply
implicated in crime - so deeply as to proclaim in tones
that should reach every parent's heart, that as long as
celibacy forms a feature of Catholic policy, the priesthood is never to be trusted."[51]

      Closely linked with charges of immorality hurled
against the priesthood were accusations as to the avari-
cious characteristics of this same class. Writers insisted that vows of poverty received as little regard as
vows of chastity,[52] that priests in every country were
building up vast accumulations of wealth and that the
purses of the poor were wrung dry to satisfy their lust-
ful desires.[53] Only barren fields were left in the wake
of Catholicism, a thing which propagandists demonstrated

49 - Downfall of Babylon, October 24, 1835.
50 - Hogan, Auricular Confession and Popish Nunneries,
     pp. 46-47.
51 - National Protestant, May, 1845. Books published at
     the time insisted that the only way to bring morality
     to the country was to force the abandonment of this
     system. See : Feijo, Diego Antonio, Demonstration
     of the Necessity of Abolishing a Constrained Cleri-
     cal Celibacy; Exhibiting the Evils of the Institu-
     tion, and the Remedy (Philadelphia, 1844).
52 - Emerlina, Frauds of Papal Ecclesiastics, pp. 143-144;
     Downfall of Babylon, June 6, 1835.
53 - Protestant Vindicator, October 28, 1840; Priestcraft
     Exposed, October 1, 1834; Emerlina, Frauds of Papal
     Ecclesiastics, pp. 92, 136-138, 150-154.

by comparing the fertility of Protestant America with
Catholic Italy.[54] They agreed that the popes were justified in calling themselves Successors of the Fisherman,
as they for centuries[55] had fished for all the money
they could lay their hands on.

While the clergy were being charged with immorality and avarice, the convent system both in the
United States and Europe was not suffered to pass un-
noticed. Books poured from the anti-Catholic press
charging anew the depravity of these "slave factories"[56]
and bore such intriguing titles as Priests Prisons for
Women[57] and Open Convents, or Nunneries and Popish
Seminaries Dangerous to the Morals and Degrading to
the Character of a Republican Community.[58] Many of
these revelations laid bare the convent system in Europe. It was charged that in Catholic countries abroad
every convent had a lying in hospital adjoining, to care

---

54 - Ricci, Secrets of Nunneries, p. xvii; Hogan, Synop-
     sis of Popery, pp. 62-63.
55 - Downfall of Babylon, May 16, 1835.
56 - Baltimore Literary and Religious Magazine, October,
     1839.
57 - Cross, Andrew B., Priests Prisons for Women (Balti-
     more,------).
58 - Dwight, Theodore, Open Convents, or Nunneries and
     Popish Seminaries Dangerous to the Morals and De-
     grading to the Character of a Republican Community
     (New York, 1836). Other books devoted to exposing
     the monastic life were: Day, Samuel P., Monastic
     Institutions; their Origin, Progress, Nature and
     Tendency (Dublin, 1844); Mahoney, S. I., Six Years
     in the Monastaries of Italy (Boston, 1845)

for the infants born there,[59] and repeated tales were told of excavations in abandoned convent grounds where the bones of murdered children were found.[60] Propagandists paraded stories of nuns in Venice who received all visitors with bared breasts,[61] of nuns of Dijon who poisoned an abbot when he tried to stop their immorality,[62] of nuns of Brescia who constructed a special gate to allow pregnant members of the order to leave,[63] of nuns of Lerma who pretended to be delivered of miraculous stones when they were actually giving birth to babies destined for strangulation.[64] No wonder, writers agreed, that sisters who break convent rules are not dismissed from their orders; should they be loosed into the world they would reveal the true nature of convent life and this Popery dreads above all else.[65]

But if these descriptions of European conditions were ferreted out, the propagandists outdid themselves in obtaining information regarding the American convents. "No tongue can express so much iniquity as can be found and

59 - Hogan, Auricular Confession and Popish Nunneries, p.61.
60 - Spirit of '76, August 4, 1855; Protestant Vindicator, April 28, 1841.
61 - Emerlina, Frauds of Papal Eccleciastics, p. 149.
62 - Ibid., p. 12.
63 - Ibid., p. 149.
64 - Hogan, Auricular Confession and Popish Nunneries, pp. 62-63.
65 - Smith, Synopsis of the Moral Theology of Saint Ligori, pp. 231-232; Schumucker, Discourse in Commemoration of the Glorious Reformation, p. 53.

has been and now is practiced in these Romish brothels,"
wrote one enthusiast, "Noble and virtuous girls who pi-
ously seclude themselves from the world are seduced and
made the miserable victims of the lust of priests. Children are born and slaughtered by these devotees of wickedness. Not one, not ten, not twenty, nor fifty - not an
hundred, nor yet a thousand, but more than ten times that
number are born but to die with a few moments of life."[66]
Writers had the grace to admit that American convents did
not have lying in hospitals adjoining where the nuns could
be delivered of the fruits of their illicit love with
priests, but they saw in this only cause for additional
alarm. For without these hospitals, abortions had to be
resorted to:[67]

> It is not generally known to Americans
> that the crime of procuring abortion, a crime
> which our laws pronounce to be a felony, is a
> common every day crime in Popish nunneries. It
> is not known to Americans ... that strangling
> and putting to death infants, is common in
> nunneries throughout this country. It is not
> known that it is done systematically and method-
> ically, according to Popish instructions ...The
> Holy Church, not caring much how the aforesaid

66 - McMurray, A., Awful Disclosures! Murders Exposed!
Downfall of Popery! Death Bed Confession; Death
Bed Confession and Renunciation of the Right Reverend Bishop Mc Murray, Bishop of the Saint Mary's
Roman Catholic Church, Montreal, Canada (Buffalo,
1845), p. 27.
67 - Hogan, Auricular Confession and Popish Nunneries,
p. 61.

MOTHER ABBESS STRANGLING THE INFANT [illegible]

Mother Abbess Strangling an Infant

infants may come into this world, but anxious
that they should go from it according to the
ritual of the church, insists that the infant
should be baptized. This being done....the
mother abbess generally takes between her holy
fingers the nostril of the infant, and in the
name of the infallible church, consigns it to
the care of the Almighty; and I beg here to
state ... that the father is, in nearly all
cases, the individual who baptizes it."[68]

It was these practices that Americans were warned
against by the legion of anti-Catholic propagandists who
found in convent revelations a ready means of sale for
their products. American convents were generally referred
to as "Popish brothels"[69] or priests' harems[70] and pictured as always containing at least one nun who was "writh-
ing in the agonies of childbirth."[71] Newspapers published
accounts of fathers who had placed a daughter in a convent
and returned to find her pregnant.[72] Especially did the
propagandists insist that the whole nunnery system was out
of keeping with American freedom, and that only through
its abolition by law could the purity of the American
woman and the sanctity of the American state be pre-
served.[73]

68 - Ibid., pp. 61-62.
69 - Spirit of '76, August 4, 1835; Hogan, Auricular Con-
     fession and Popish Nunneries, p. 24; New York Ob-
     server, November 26, 1836.
70 - New York Observer, November 26, 1836, quoting the
     Religious Magazine.
71 - Hogan, Auricular Confession and Popish Nunneries,
     p. 59.
72 - Spirit of '76, August 4, 1835.
73 - Baltimore Literary and Religious Magazine, October,
     1839; December, 1839; Hogan, Auricular Confession
     and Popish Nunneries, p. 42.

Amidst such a chorus of revelation, it is only surprising that more "escaped nuns" did not appear upon the scene to add their testimony to the rising voice against Rome and her convents. Lacking the appeal of an actual nun who sought sanctuary as had Maria Monk and her imitators, the nativistic editors were forced to fall back on most intangible material. At first they launched inquiries as to the whereabouts of the nun Elizabeth Harrison who had been in the Ursuline convent at Charlestown, and spread vague rumors that she had been carried away to Canada.[74] When these rumors aroused only feeble interest they pounced upon the story of a young lady named Milly McPherson who was reputed to have fled from a convent in Bardstown, Kentucky, to escape the attentions of a priest.[75] Stories of this flight were magnified by the editors of the Western Protestant, their enthusiasm carrying them away to a point in which they named the priest who had attempted to seduce Miss McPherson,[76] and charged him with her abduction when she later disappeared.[77] This indiscrete step brought a libel suit against the editors of the paper

74 - Downfall of Babylon, May 2, 1835.
75 - New York Observer, June 11, 1836.
76 - Western Protestant, May 21, 1836, quoted in Downfall of Babylon, July 9, 1836.
77 - New York Observer, July 15, 1837.

which was finally settled when the priest was awarded
damages of one cent.[78] A similar tale imported from
England told of a nun who had refused to bow to the
lust of a priest, and after being kept seven years in
a cell, managed to escape.[79]

More important and effective than these stories was an incident occurring in Baltimore in 1838.
The efforts of the Reverend Robert J. Breckinridge
through the pulpit and the Baltimore Literary and Religious Magazine had been stirring up anti-Catholic
feeling in that city, a feeling which was directed especially against a Carmelite Convent located nearby.
Stories were told by Breckinridge of a painter who
heard mysterious and horrifying screams coming from
the dark interior[80] and a group of ladies also swore
that cries of "help, help, oh Lord, help" had emerged
from the building as they were passing.[81] More and more
were the suspicious eyes of Protestants of Baltimore fastened on this convent, until, in 1838, an event occurred
which seemed to confirm their worst fears. On a Sunday

78 - Ibid., July 15, 1837.
79 - Protestant Vindicator, November 11, 1835.
80 - Baltimore Literary and Religious Magazine, January,
     1840.
81 - Schmucker, Discourse in Commemoration of the Glorious
     Reformation, pp. 119-121.

afternoon in August one of the nuns, Olivia Neal, burst
from the building and rushed into the house of a neighboring Protestant, telling an incoherent tale of hardships
and attempts to escape.[82] The city flamed with excitement immediately. A mob gathered bent on burning the
convent to the ground, and Breckinridge was hastily
summoned. He talked with the escaped nun, and promised
her protection from the priests who might try to return
her to the reputed evil den.[83]

Protection which Breckinridge could offer meant
little however. The girl was carried away to a hospital
by the mayor of the city, and there pronounced insane by
a group of doctors.[84] Breckinridge hailed this verdict
as part of a popish plot[85] and used every excuse to stir
up feelings against the convent, charging that a whole
carriage load of women were carried away the night after
Sister Neal's escape from the institution; undoubtedly
to remove pregnant members of the group before searching
parties appeared.[86] For some time thereafter he harped
upon the incident, and his repeated queries as to the

82 - Baltimore Literary and Religious Magazine, September,
     1839.
83 - Breckinridge, Robert J., Papism in the United States
     in the Nineteenth Century (Baltimore, 184-), pp. 240
     ff.
84 - Baltimore Literary and Religious Magazine, October,
     1839.
85 - Ibid., October, 1839.
86 - Breckinridge, Papism in the United States, p. 225.

whereabouts of Miss Neal assumed the form of open charges
that she had been abducted and killed by the Papists.[87]

Satisfactory as these few escaped nuns may have
been to propagandists, they lacked the enthusiastic backing given to Maria Monk and others of the fence climbing
sisterhood who produced memoirs of their adventures. To
offset this handicap, nativistic writers cast about for
other means of setting forth the lurid immorality of Popery
under the guise of religious inquiry. One of these writers,
Samuel B. Smith, hit upon the fortunate scheme of producing
the revelations of a girl who had been a mistress to a priest.
By the close of 1835 he was hinting in the paper which he edited, the Downfall of Babylon, that important disclosures
of Romanism were about to be made and that the public should
be prepared for a tremendous shock;[88] early in 1836 Rosamond
Culbertson's Rosamond, or a Narrative of the Captivity and
Sufferings of an American Female under the Popish Priests
in the Island of Cuba, with a Full Disclosure of their
Manners and Customs written by Herself[89] made its bow.

87 - Baltimore Literary and Religious Magazine, July, 1840;
     Ibid., August, 1840; Protestant Vindicator, July 22,
     1840. The incident is described by Shea, History of
     the Catholic Church in the United States, vol. iii,
     pp. 448-450 and in Thie, "German Catholic Activity
     in the United States Seventy Years Ago," p. 91. Shea
     states that the mob raged about the convent for three
     days before turbulent feelings were quieted.
88 - Downfall of Babylon, June 27, 1835; November 24, 1835;
     December 19, 1835.
89 - Published in New York in 1836.

Smith's expectations as to its popularity were justified.
.. few months after its publication a second edition was
necessary to meet the demand.[90]

The book which attained such immediate notori-
ety was as vulgar as its title indicated. The author
tells of her life; how she married and lived happily
until the death of her husband, how, poverty stricken,
she was forced to live with a priest for five years of
continual horror.[91] She tells of an attempt upon her
life by an assassin hired by another lover of her priest;[92]
of how she was forced to watch her paramour seduce a fourteen year old girl in confession[93] and of numerous other
amatory adventures in which she played a part. Priests
in Cuba, she informers her readers, kept alcowaters in
every monastary, and adds with refreshing frankness, "In
this country we call them pimps."[95] The climax of her
revelations came in her exposure of a great plot among
the priests to capture little negro boys and grind them
up into sausage meat.[96] The popularity of Rosamond's

90 - Downfall of Babylon, June 11, 1836.
91 - Ibid., April 18, 1835. Nearly the entire book was
     published in this paper during 1835 and 1836 and it
     is from this source that the account of it is drawn.
92 - Ibid., June 27, 1835.
93 - Ibid., April 16, 1836.
94 - Ibid., April 2, 1836; January 2, 1836; June 11, 1836;
     January 23, 1836.
95 - Ibid., April 16, 1836.
96 - Ibid., April 2, 1836. The story is told by Smith
     also in his Decisive Confirmation, pp. 12-13. It
     was confirmed, according to Smith, by a New York
     doctor who was in Cuba at the time. Downfall of
     Babylon, January 2, 1836.

tale can be understood by the human touch with which she embellishes this tale. "Those who bought and eat these sausages," she wrote, "said they were the best sausages they ever eat."[97]

Smith's success in this venture inspired him to further efforts. Later in 1836 he scored a second success with a daring volume, The Wonderful Adventures of a Lady of the French Nobility, and the Intrigues of a Romish Priest, her Confessor, to Seduce and Murder Her.[98] The author was unable to publish this work as an autobiographical account, but he insisted it was a true tale, and there is little doubt that it was just as true as the adventures of Rosamond. The story itself concerns a pleasant little adventure that befell a lady of France whose husband left for the wars after he had placed her under the care of two priests. The priests take her into the woods to ravish and murder her, thus securing her money. The lady, faced with this untimely end, falls on her knees and baring her breast, begs them to plunge a sword therein that she may be spared the dishonor of their attack. Both priests are so aroused by this sight that they fall to fighting between themselves to decide

97 - Downfall of Babylon, April 2, 1836.
98 - Smith, Samuel B., The Wonderful Adventures of a Lady of the French Nobility, and the Intrigues of a Romish Priest, her Confessor, to Seduce and Murder Her (New York, 1836)

which shall have her first, and both are killed.[99]

Smith himself was so impressed with this fanciful tale that he extolled it in verse in his newspaper, telling of how the wife poured out her heart

> In gratitude and love to Him who saved
> From priestly lust, from infamy and death.[100]

The extravagance of the story goes far to illustrate the fanatical nature of the moral attacks produced by propagandists of this period, and to explain the hesitancy of the church going masses to accept the anti-Catholic crusade when it depended on such methods.

Almost as fanatical were the attempts of these writers to portray the despotic and persecuting nature of Catholicism. They outlined for their readers a great Papal system, controlled by the Pope and willing to do his bidding. The basis of this system, the propagandists stated, was idolatry, for Romanists were taught to worship idols only that they could worship the Pope himself.[101] In this way the head of the Catholic church has elevated himself above all men, until he considers himself stronger

---

99 - Ibid., This account is a summary of the book.
100- Downfall of Babylon, July 23, 1836.
101- Allen, Report on Popery, p. 13; New York Observer, December 19, 1840; Downfall of Babylon, September 26, 1835.

First Persecutions of the Waldenses in the Valleys of Piedmont

Catholic Persecution

than God.[102] That power, having no basis in history and acquired through fraud,[103] had been used only for purposes of evil throughout the ages, according to these propagandists. Upon it the Popes had based their right of censorship over all reform, science and literature;[104] an attack which had kept freedom of press and speech from Popish countries and kept them backward and enthralled in ignorance.[105]

102 - McGavin, The Protestant, vol. i, p. 83; Shobere, Frederic, Persecutions of Popery: Historical Narratives of the Most Remarkable Persecutions Occasioned by the Intolerance of the Church of Rome (New York, 1844), p. 179. Shobere demonstrates by syllogistic method that the true God of the Romanist is not God at all, but the Pope:

> All men are fallible.
> The Pope is not fallible.
> Ergo, The Pope is not man.

and;

> God alone is infallible.
> The Pope is infallible.
> Ergo, The Pope is God.

103 - Cheever, Hierarchical Despotism, pp. 15-19; 69-89. Cheever presents a profound and profusely documented argument to demonstrate how each Pope throughout the early years of the Church accumulated power by false and corrupt means.

104 - Schmucker, Discourse in Commemoration of the Glorious Reformation, pp. 97-98; White, Practical and Internal Evidence, pp. 117-125.

105 - Downfall of Babylon, August 29, 1835; June 25, 1836; Schmucker, Discourse in Commemoration of the Glorious Reformation, p. 70; Mendham, Joseph, The Literary Policy of the Church of Rome, Exhibited in an Account of her Damnatory Catalogues, or Indexes, both Prohibitory and Expurgatory (New York, 1835)

Upon that supreme authority claimed by the Pope rested too, the propagandists asserted, his assertion of temporal power. They searched the pages of history to flaunt instances when such power had been exerted over kings and peoples[106] and they shouted loudly that the Popes still claimed that dread right.[107] Propagandists averred that not only had this Papal claim brought into the modern world the antiquated system of a united church and state with all its insidious features,[108] but in addition it offered a direct menace to the government of the United States and other nations.[109] Books, bearing such titles as The Jesuit

106 - The Crisis - An Appeal to our Countrymen on the Subject of Foreign Influence in the United States (New York, 1844), p. 74; National Protestant, December, 1844.
107 - American Text Book of Popery, pp. 166-178; The Crisis, pp. 74-75; Pond, No Fellowship with Romanism, pp. 154-164; Books written to demonstrate this claim included: False Claims of the Pope (New York, 1842); Daunau, Pierre C. F., Outline of a History of the Court of Rome and of the Temporal Power of the Popes (Philadelphia, 1837); Barrow, Isaac, The Pope's Supremacy(New York, 1845)
108 - Cheever, Hierarchical Despotism, pp. 179-180;Waterous, Timothy, Timothy Waterous, Jr., and Zachariah Waterous The Battle Axe and Weapons of War, Discovered by the Morning Light: Aimed for the Final Destruction of Priestcraft. Being a Treatise Fitted to the Present Day, Calculated to Detect Hypocrisy Wheresoever it may be Found, without Respect to Persons (New London, 1841, 2nd edition), p. 36.
109 - American Text Book of Popery, p. 349; The Crisis, p. 73.

as Master; Premier as Slaves,[110] were
written expounding the dread consequences should that
temporal power ever be used. Writers warned that Romanism was "an artful contrivance to tyrannize over
all mankind, under the mask, and with the hallowed
and attractive title of the Redeemer of the World."[111]

Especially did propagandists see in this absolute power of the Pope a danger when it was used to
inflict the Romish religion on all the world. Papists
have decreed, they asserted, that all persons not of
the true faith should be killed.[112] In support of this

110 - Fulton, Justin D., The Jesuit as Master; President
and Premier as Slaves (Boston, -----). Other books
of a similar nature were: Brownlee, W. C., Popery
and Enemy to Civil and Religious Liberty; and
Dangerous to our Republic (4th edition, New York,
1840); Boardman, H. A., The Intolerance of the
Church of Rome (Philadelphia, 1845); Our Liberties
Defended; the Question Discusses, is the Protes-
tant or Papal System most Favorable to Civil and
Religious Liberty? (New York, 1841); Schmucker,
S. S., The Papal Hierarchy (-----,1845); Powell,
Thomas, An Essay on Apostolic Succession; being
a Defense of a Genuine Protestant Ministry against
the Exclusive and Intolerant Schemes of Papists and
High Churchmen; and supplying a General Antidote to
Popery (New York, 1842); Balch, William S., Romanism
and Republicanism Incompatible (-------); Romanism
Incompatible with Republican Institutions (New York,
1844.)
111 - American Text Book of Popery, p. 436.
112 - The Crisis, p. 75; Schmucker, Discourse in Commemoration of the Glorious Reformation, pp. 78-79; American
Text Book of Popery, p. 8; New York Observer, January
16, 1841; Protestant Vindicator, March 9, 1842.

startling statement they produced an alleged Jesuit oath declaring that "heretics, apostates, and even the schismatics, can be compelled, even by corporal punishment, to return to the Catholic faith."[113] Here, they shouted, was proof. Americans must drive Catholics from their midst or suffer death in return. When a number of the anti-Catholic leaders including the Reverend Robert J. Breckinridge, the Reverend W. C. Brownlee and the Reverend B. Kurtz produced threatening letters which they had received from Catholics the existence of Popish designs seemed certain.[114]

It was to the past that writers turned to find instances where Romanism had used its mighty power to slaughter Protestants who refused to accept its dictates. They searched Catholic theologians and the notes of the Rhemish testament to show that Popery had always favored such persecution; that its very creed called for the most sanguinary of practices.[115] "It is vain to deny," wrote one propagandist, "that Popery has been the cause

113 - Downfall of Babylon, November 14, 1835; St. Louis Observer, quoted in New York Observer, October 25, 1834; New Orleans Weekly Native American, quoted in Protestant Vindicator, September 16, 1840.
114 - Schmucker, Discourse in Commemoration of the Glorious Reformation, pp. 78-79.
115 - Cheever, Hierarchical Despotism, pp. 108, 112-115; New York Observer, February 11, 1832; February 4, 1837; February 11, 1837; Downfall of Babylon, February 14, 1835; February 21, 1835; March 7, 1835; March 14, 1835.

of the most bloody wars and the most cruel persecutions,
so that millions have been the victims of this perversion of the gospel and antichristian system of religion.[116]
Nor would these writers allow Catholics to deny their
statements. By book and article they recited for Protestant readers the dread history of Papal persecution,[117]
of famous martyrs who had suffered,[118] and of whole
peoples who had been slaughtered by the sword of Rome.[119]
Saint Bartholomew's Day and other major events in the
tyrannical history of Popery were dwelt upon and described in gruesome terms.[120] One nativistic editor,

116 - Allen, Report on Popery, pp. 24-25.
117 - McGavin, The Protestant, vol. i, pp. 114-137; A
History of Popery; to Which is Added an Examination of the Present State of the Romish Church
in Ireland and Specimens of Monkish Legends (London, 1838), pp. 277-336; Chobere, Persecutions
of Popery, pp. 19-179; Giustiniani, Papal Rome
as it Is, pp. 145-156; Pond, No Fellowship with
Romanism, pp. 165-196; American Text Book of
Popery, pp. 372-432; Cheever, Hierarchical Despotism, pp. 90-99.
118 - Quarterly Review of the American Protestant Association, January, 1844; Elizabeth, Charlotte, The
English Martyrology, Abridged from Fox (Philadelphia, 1843); Elizabeth, Charlotte, Ridley, Latimer,
Cranmer and Other English Martyrs (New York, 1844)
119 - Schmucker, Discourse in Commemoration of the Glorious Reformation, pp. 88-96; Quarterly Review of
the American Protestant Association, April, 1844;
New York Observer, April 13, 1839; Watchman of the
South, July 4, 1839; Browning, W. S., A History of
the Huguenots (Philadelphia, 1845); Elizabeth,
Charlotte, Wars with the Saints; or, the Persecutions of the Vaudois under Pope Innocent III (New
York, 1848).
120 - Morse, Proscribed German Student, pp. 85-86; Protestant Vindicator, September 22, 1841; March 23,
1842; New York Observer, July 3, 1841.

carried away by enthusiasm, estimated that more than
fifty million Protestants had been murdered by the
Catholic church, this number not including fifteen
million Indians in South America, two million Moors
and a million and a half Jews.[121] If these blood-
thirsty editors can be believed, it is difficult to
account for the survival of the human race.

One feature of the Catholic church which
lent itself well to the purposes of these writers
was the Inquisition. Articles and books streamed
from the press to describe the origin of this organized persecution and its introduction into various
countries.[122] Others dwelt upon the tortures used by
the inquisitors, describing at great length the process of slow roasting and other devices employed.[123]

121 - Protestant Vindicator, January 6, 1841.
122 - Emerlina, Frauds of Papal Ecclesiastics, p.45;
       History of Popery, pp. 188-189; Mason, Cyrus,
       A History of the Holy Catholic Inquisition
       (Philadelphia, 1835), pp. 13-119; McGavin,
       The Protestant, vol. ii, pp. 126-17; Prot-
       estant Magazine, November, 1833; Watchman of
       the South, September 19, 1839; The Story of
       the Inquisition (Boston, 184-); Ellis, B. E.,
       A History of the Romish Inquisition Compiled
       from Various Authors (Hanover, Indian, 1835);
       Berg, Joseph F., Mysteries of the Inquisition
       (----,1846); The Destruction of the Inquisition
       at Madrid (New York, 1844).
123 - Protestant Magazine, April, 1834; Schmucker,
       Discourse In Commemoration of the Glorious Ref-
       ormation, pp. 80-89; Emerlina, Frauds of Papal
       Ecclesiastics, pp. 41-43; Mason, History of the
       Holy Catholic Inquisition, pp. 151-175.

One writer compared the oft described Virgin's Kiss with Catholicism itself, telling of its outwardly beautiful form with the hidden daggers beneath. "It extends its arms," the account read, "with great deliberation and apparent affection, and, with a smiling face, presses its deluded victim to its heart - and the pressure is, wounds and death."[124] An enterprising showman in New York capitalized on the popular interest in these instruments of torture by exhibiting a model of one of the Inquisition buildings and urging all Protestants to view it to understand how Popery was kept alive in Europe.[125]

To all Catholic claims that the Inquisition was a thing belonging to antiquity and that persecutions had been abandoned years before, the No-Popery agitators answered only in derision. They shouted that the Inquisition building in Madrid had been in use in 1820,[126] that British soldiers in Malta were persecuted because they would not embrace the Romish cause,[127] that Protestants and Protestant missionaries in Ireland were mistreated and killed by priests and their followers.[128]

124 - New York Observer, July 13, 1833.
125 - Ibid., December 10, 1842.
126 - Protestant Vindicator, November 25, 1840.
127 - New York Observer, May 6, 1843.
128 - Ibid., August 9, 1834; November 7, 1835; November 12, 1842.

Whole books were written to prove that the persecuting
spirit still endured when Catholics dealt with Protestant groups in Italy[129] and especially on the island of
Madeira, where Protestants had been jailed for reading
the Bible.[130] To these propagandists Popery was still
ready and anxious to strike any cruel blow for its religion which expediency demanded.

The weakest point in this tale of terror which
writers sought to spin for their American readers was
the singular lack of a taste for blood displayed by Catholics in the United States. It was difficult for imbibers
of No-Popery literature to shudder at the Inquisition and
the threats of its revival when all about them were obviously peaceful and quiet followers of the Pope, bent
on no more dangerous a pursuit than supporting themselves
and their families. If Americans were to be aroused, they
must be convinced that the Inquisitors were at their very
doors, a gigantic task but one which the propagandists did
not shirk.

129 - National Protestant, December, 1844; New York Observer, February 20, 1830; Rhinewold, Dr., The
Protestant Exiles of Zillerthal; their Persecutions and Expatriation from the Tyrol on Separating from the Church of Rome (New York, 1842);
The Protestant Exiles of Zillerthal; their Persecutions and Expatriation on Separating from
the Church of Rome and Embracing the Reformed
Faith (New York, 1844)
130 - Quarterly Review of the American Protestant Association, April, 1845; Kalley, Robert R., Persecution in Madeira in The Nineteenth Century, being
an Exposition of Facts (New York, 1845); Gonzalves,
M. J., Persecutions in Madeira in the Nineteenth
Century (New York, 1845)

At first these efforts took the form of tales
of dread deeds practiced by Papists upon Protestants;
here a servant girl about to be converted from Romanism
had been beaten;[131] here a Catholic Bishop had read the
Bible and was being hurried away to the Inquisition at
Rome,[132] here a minister who had preached a sermon against
Catholics was attacked near his home.[133] Vague rumors calculated to spread apprehension were freely circulated.
Nativists were not ready to admit that an Inquisitor had
been appointed for America or that the Inquisition was
about to start its persecutions here.[134] But they did
insist that Rome was preparing for the day when such a
step would be possible. They pointed out that under
each Catholic cathedral great vaults had been built.
The clergy might insist that these were to hold the
remains of dead priests, but such insistence meant little. The propagandists knew that these were only waiting to be converted into Inquisition chambers when the
church felt that the time of its power was at hand.[135]

This insistence that persecution was destined

131 - New York Observer, August 27, 1836; March 12, 1842;
      Baltimore Literary and Religious Magazine, February
      1840.
132 - Baltimore Literary and Religious Magazine, August,
      1841.
133 - Downfall of Babylon, March 14, 1835.
134 - Ibid., June 13, 1835.
135 - Schmucker, Discourse in Commemoration of the Glo-
      rious Reformation, pp. 88-89; New York Observer,
      December 27, 1834; March 7, 1840; Downfall of
      Babylon, January 2, 1836.

in time to find its way to the United States allowed
writers to re-echo again the old cry of Rome's designs
upon the Mississippi Valley.[136] Nativistic newspapers
recorded the amount spent by Catholic missionary societies,[137] and warned that Protestant efforts in the West
were far less effective.[138] Nativistic writers bemoaned
the fact that the press was controlled by Jesuits and
could not sound the alarm.[139] They saw in every priest
a potential menace to all that liberty loving Americans
held dear.[140] "The confessor is a _spy_ in every house!"
wrote one editor, "the spy of an Italian despot, from the
splendid mansion to the rural cottage."[141] Even Jesuit
missionaries came under suspicion in these new attacks
when it was charged that they wished the friendship of

136 - Giustiniani, _Papal Rome as It Is_, pp. 225-226;
      The Crisis, p. 77; _New York Observer_, December
      10, 1842; _Protestant Vindicator_, June 24, 1840;
      September 22, 1841.
137 - _Home Missionary_, February, 1843; _National Protes-
      tant_, December, 1844; _New York Observer_, November
      7, 1840; _Protestant Vindicator_, June 24, 1840;
      June 23, 1841; October 20, 1841; Norton, _Startling
      Facts for American Protestants_, pp. 5-7.
138 - _The Native American_, August 1, 1844.
139 - _New York American Republican_, May 24, 1844; _The
      Trial of the Pope of Rome, the Anti-Christ or Man
      of Sin Described in the Bible, for High Treason
      against the Son of God, tried at the Sessions
      House of Truth before the Right Hon. Divine
      Revelation, the Hon. Justice Reason and the Hon.
      Justice History, taken in Shorthand by a Friend
      to St. Peter_ (2nd American edition, Boston, 1844),
      p. 158.
140 - _The Crisis_, p. 74; _Review of the Lady Superior's
      Reply_, p. 50; _Protestant Vindicator_, March 31, 1841.
141 - _Protestant Vindicator_, September 16, 1840.

the Indians simply to use them against Protestants
when the great contest between Romanism and the Reformed religion developed.[142]

 Tangible basis for these vague fears was
given by the Home Missionary, a magazine much interested in Catholic designs upon the West. In November, 1842, this publication contained the startling
plan of an Irish society recently launched to send
Catholic immigrants to the Mississippi Valley.[143] Actually this society was an innocent attempt by a group
of London capitalists to make a tidy profit and at the
same time increase the market for their manufactured
goods,[144] but, magnified as it was by the Home Missionary
and other propaganda agencies which took up the cry,[145]
it assumed the proportions of a great organization bent
on the destruction of America. To nativistic writers,
exposure of this plot came as a fitting climax to the
efforts of Samuel Morse.

 Such were the dire schemes by which Popery with
all its iniquity and anti-Scriptural doctrines was to be
forced upon the people of the United States. But writers

142 - Norton, Startling Facts for American Protestants,
  pp. 20-21.
143 - Home Missionary, November, 1842.
144 - The object of the society was set forth by its
  backers in a pamphlet issued at the time, Proposed
  New Plan of a General Emigration Society (London,
  1842)
145 - Trial of the Pope of Rome, pp. 160-161; Norton,
  Startling Facts for American Protestants, pp.14-20.

against the church did not stop here. They dwelt at
length upon those doctrines in order to convince enthusiastic Protestants of the religious gulf which
separated them from the followers of Rome. In their
theological attacks upon Catholicism, the propaganda
writers expended untold eloquence and reached heights
of vindictiveness paralleled only by their denunciation
of the moral depravity of priests and the confessional.
Here was a field of argument designed to appeal to the
religious nature of the American of that day, and writers
hunted through the Bible and history to find fuel for
their invective.

By far the most influential opponent of Rome
in this war of theological arguments was an obscure minister in New York, the Reverend William Nevins. Nevins
contributed a series of letters to the New York Observer
through 1833 and 1834, which created a mild stir among
readers of that influential paper. When those letters
were published in book form in 1836, sponsored by the
American Tract Society and bearing the title, Thoughts
on Popery they entered upon a triumphent career of spreading the No-Popery cry throughout the land. The editors
of the Observer believed that nothing had ever been
written to portray in clearer light the errors of Romanism[146] and the American Tract Society agreed when it

146 - New York Observer, April 2, 1836.

declared that "nothing has yet been issued which so
lays open the deformities of Popery to common minds
or is so admirably adapted to save our country from
its wiles, and to guard the souls of men from its
fatal snares."[147] That these estimates were shared
by the public was attested by the book's popularity.
One enterprising book seller in New York even went so
far as to advertise that he had been converted from
Popery through reading the work, and increased his
sales tremendously by this simple ruse.[148]

The popularity of Thoughts on Popery is easily explained. Most of the theological attacks upon
Catholicism appearing before or at this same time had
been dull and ponderous. They had been designed largely
to appeal to clergymen rather than to the man of the
street. Nevins transformed such effusions into a vigorous and easily understandable prose. The whole vista
of theological attack on Rome was suddenly opened to the
ordinary follower of the No-Popery cause. Thus did Nev-
in's opus wield a mighty influence; thus too did its popularity exceed that of other theological works, even including those from the pen of another renowned defender
of Protestantism, the Reverend Joseph Frederick Berg,
pastor of the Second Reformed Protestant Church of Phil-

147 - Twenty-Second Annual Report of the American Tract
    Society, (New York, 1836), p. 105.
148 - New York Observer, June 30, 1838.

adelphia.[149]

    The task which Nevins and Berg, together with a legion of other writers, had outlined for themselves was no simple one. They aimed to prove that the Bible and history sanctioned Protestantism alone; that Romanism was an anti-Scriptural heresy. At the very outset they faced an almost unsurmountable task, for Catholics could point to the venerable antiquity of their own church; they could show that Catholicism alone was descended from Biblical days, that the Protestant sects had been added only centuries later. A church built directly upon the labors of Christ, Catholic theologians insisted, must be the true church.

    Undaunted the propagandists plunged bravely into their task. They immediately refuted the charge that Catholicism was older than Protestantism. Protestantism,

149 - Berg was responsible for the authorship of a number of outspoken books, largely theological in their attack. They included: Lectures on Romanism (Philadelphia, 1844); The Confessional; or, an Exposition of the Doctrine of Auricular Confession as Taught in the Standards of the Roman Church (3rd edition, New York, 1841); The Great Apostacy Identified with Papal Rome; or, an Exposition of the Mystery of Iniquity and the Marks and Doom of Anti-Christ (Philadelphia, 1847); Mysteries of the Inquisition, (------, 1846); Oral Controversy with a Catholic Priest (-------, 1843); A Synopsis of the Moral Philosophy of Peter Dens as Prepared for the Use of Romish Seminaries and Students of Theology (New York, 1841).

they insisted, dated back to the time of Christ and
had endured constantly since that day; it had simply
been obscured by the blackness of Popery for a few
centuries before the Reformation.[150] They pictured
Christianity as a stream of purest thought flowing
through the ages, gradually losing its purity as the
muddy brooks of Romanism emptied into the original
stream,[151] and as a flower held in the dead grasp of
Popery until "God's gardner, Luther, transplanted it
to the soil of Ridley and Latimer; until he took it
from the superstition of the dead and the grasp of
the apostate, and by God's blessing, it has sprung

150 - National Protestant, April, 1845; October, 1845;
American Text Book of Popery, pp. 61-126; Horne,
Thomas H., A Protestant Memorial (New York, 1844),
pp. 49-78; Downfall of Babylon, February 21, 1835;
Protestant Vindicator, April 28, 1841; Griswold,
Alexander, The Reformation; a Brief Exposition of
some of the Errors and Corruptions of the Church
of Rome; (Boston, 1843); Hopkins, John H., The
Church of Rome in Her Primitive Purity Compared
with the Church of Rome at the Present Day (New
York, 1835); Horner, J., Popery Stripped of its
Garb (New York, 1836); Moore, Charles K., (editor)
Book of Tracts on Romanism: Containing the Origin
and Progress Cruelties, Frauds, Superstitions,
Miracles and Ceremonies of the Church of Rome
(New York, 1844); Odenheimer, William H., The
True Catholic No Romanist (New York, 1842); Ogilby,
John D., Lectures on the Catholic Church in England
and America (New York, 1844); Sprague, William B.,
Contrast Between True and False Religions (New York,
1837); Stanley J., Dialogues on Popery (New York,
1843); Brownlee, William C., Sketch of the History
of the Western Apostolic Churches from which the
Roman Church Apostatized (New York, 184-); Bennett,
William J. E., Lecture Sermons on the Distinctive
Errors of Romanism (London, 1842).
151 - Cheever, Hierarchical Despotism, pp. 5-7.

up into that noble church under which it is our happy
blessing to live."[152]   Elaborate tables were printed
to demonstrate the gradual addition through the early
centuries, of Popish corruptions to the original pure
stream of Christianity, corruptions only to be shaken
off by the reformers.[153]   Even Saint Patrick and other
saints of his time were hailed as Protestants with the
assertion that they lived before Romish iniguity had
created a Catholic church.[154]

The various papal practices which had been
added, one by one, throughout the ages, were not only
attacked for themselves but because of their origin.
For each of the distinctive errors of Romanism had
been copied directly from heathen religions. Writers
dwelt upon the horror of a Christian church built upon
paganism, and cited instance after instance where a
practice of Rome was patterned directly after those

---

152 - Watchman of the South, September 19, 1839.
153 - New York Observer, October 22, 1842; American
      Text Book of Popery, pp. 106-124.
154 - Protestant Vindicator, March 17, 1841; January
      26, 1842; Brownlee, William C., The Religion
      of the Ancient Irish and Britons not Roman
      Catholic, and the Immortal Saint Patrick Vin-
      dicated from the False Charge of Being a Papist
      (2nd edition, New York, 1841)

of one or another heathen religion.[155] Even the chair
supposedly used by Peter had, they claimed, the words
"There is one God, and Mohammet is his Prophet" en-
graved upon it.[156]

Upon these pagan practices propagandists based
the Papal claim of infallibility in spiritual affairs.[157]
The Pope had not the "shadow of a shade"[158] to assert
any control over the religious affairs of the world,
they insisted, for the Bible failed to give any such
sanction[159] and Romish claims that Peter had been at
Rome and declared that there his church should be centered were mere inventions and forgeries.[160] Moreover
the whole course of history had demonstrated that the
Pope was fallible, and writers cited arguments of the
Fathers over transubstantiation[161] and demanded to know

155 - The Protestant, March 31, 1832; New York Observer,
      May 25, 1833; Protestant Vindicator, March 3, 1841;
      National Protestant, January, 1835; November, 1845;
      Cheever, Hierarchical Despotism, pp. 34-41; Giustini-
      ana, Papal Rome as it Is, pp. 59-90; American Text
      Book of Popery, pp. 27-35; Poynder, John, Popery in
      Alliance with Heathenism; Letters Proving the Con-
      formity which Subsists between the Romish Religion
      and the Religion of the Ancient Heathens (London,
      1835); Whatley, Richard, Essays on the Errors of
      Romanism having Their Origin in Human Nature (Lon-
      don, 1837)
156 - Protestant Vindicator, May 4, 1842.
157 - Cheever, Hierarchical Despotism, pp. 20-24, 28-34.
158 - McGavin, The Protestant, vol. i, p. 687; vol. ii, p. 28.
159 - Protestant Vindicator, January 26, 1842; Cheever,
      Hierarchical Despotism, pp. 10-14; McGavin, The Prot-
      estant, vol. i, p. 687.
160 - Pond, No Fellowship with Romanism, pp. 125-126; McGavin,
      The Protestant, vol. i, pp. 87-95.
161 - Nevins, Thoughts on Popery, pp. 40-43; Protestant
      Episcopalian and Church Register, February, 1831.

how unity and infallibility could endure during the various schisms.[162]   Popery knew no unity, despite its claims, they concluded, in marked contrast to the unity which Protestantism enjoyed through its dependence on the Scriptures.[163]

Having thus devastated the Catholic claim to unity and infallibility, propagandists turned to various features of worship to find further fuel for their incendiarism. One of their blasts was released against the doctrine of transubstantiation. In accepting the words of Christ, "this is my Body," Catholics were guilty of a grave mistake, writers insisted. Christ had spoken figuratively, and they cited numerous examples of other figurative statements in the Bible.[164] That Romanists had accepted those words in a literal sense aroused their scorn; that priests could convert bread and wine into body and blood stirred their indignation.[165]

162 - Downfall of Babylon, August 1, 1835; September 12, 1835; New York Observer, November 14, 1840; Protestant Vindicator, January 20, 1841; Protestant Episcopalian and Church Register, November, 1832; March, 1833; April, 1833; Horne, Protestant Memorial, pp. 85-93; Beecher, Plea for the West, pp. 168-169.
163 - White, Practical and Internal Evidence, pp. 83-97; Allen, Report on Popery, pp. 20-21; Protestant Vindicator, January 6, 1841.
164 - Allen, Report on Popery, pp. 15-16; McGavin, The Protestant, vol. i, pp. 406-488; Nevins, Thoughts on Popery, pp. 103-105; Quarterly Review of the American Protestant Association, April, 1844; New York Observer, August 24, 1833; Baltimore Literary and Religious Magazine, October, 1838.
165 - Protestant Episcopalian and Church Register, August 1833; October, 1833; Protestant Vindicator, December 15, 1841.

"What are your Eastern fire eaters, sword swallowers
and dervishes?" asked one writer, "to a Popish priest?
Why, it would be easier to swallow a rapier ten feet
long, or a ball of fire as large as the mountain of
Orizaha, than to metamorphose flour and water into the
great and holy God, who created the heavens and the
earth and all that is therein."[166] And regardless of
the magical properties of the priest, it was certain
that Catholics in worshipping the host were guilty of
the worst form of idolatry, the idolatry common to all
who worship matter.[167]

166 - Hogan, Synopsis of Popery, pp. 160-161.
167 - Allen, Report on Popery, p. 17. Other doctrines of
      the church were also objected to. Catholic belief
      in purgatory was scorned as anti-Scriptural and
      instituted only for gain. Nevins, Thoughts on
      Popery, pp. 152-158; Quarterly Review of the Amer-
      ican Protestant Association, July, 1845; New York
      Observer, December 18, 1830; January 1, 1831;
      August 21, 1833; August 29, 1840; History of
      Popery, pp. 221-236; Allen, Report on Popery, p.
      25; McGavin, The Protestant, vol. i, pp. 532-570.
      Protestant Vindicator, July 22, 1840. Priests
      were criticised especially for refusing to re-
      lease from purgatory souls of poor men whose
      friends were unable to pay for masses. Protes-
      tant Vindicator, July 22, 1840; On Purgatory and
      Infallibility (New York, 1839). The doctrine of
      Extreme Unction was also branded as an unscrip-
      tural instrument devised to secure money for the
      clergy. Nevins, Thoughts on Popery, pp. 109-112;
      Quarterly Review of the American Protestant Asso-
      ciation, October, 1845; McGavin, The Protestant,
      vol. ii, pp. 204-217; Protestant Vindicator,
      September 2, 1840. One writer believed that
      this doctrine typified the craft of Catholicism,
      for, unable to secure converts among "men in the
      vigor of their intellect, she assails them at a
      time where their minds are enfeebled by pain and
      sickness." Protestant Vindicator, July 22, 1840.

Not content to expose the moral corruption of the confessional, propagandists turned their ire upon its spiritual features and shouted that here too Rome erred. They employed the usual Biblical arguments to show that the doctrine had no basis in God's words,[168] and they proclaimed joyfully that only one person was recorded in the Bible as confessing to priests - Judas.[169] Against this practice of confession to a priest, writers arrayed the Protestant belief in confession only to Christ. The Catholic belief, they said, "sends us to a brother as deep in offense as we, to confess to him, that we have sinned against our Father, when that Father is nearby, and when, moreover, he says, 'Come to Me.'"[170] And they expressed their outraged feelings in verse which proclaimed:

> 'Twere worse than madness to believe
> Man can his brother worm forgive,
> Or Yield unto the contrite one
> That peace which comes from Heaven alone.[171]

Not only was the confessional unscriptural and

168 - American Text Book of Popery, pp. 219-255; Nevins, Thoughts on Popery, pp. 51-56; Downfall of Babylon, December 26, 1835; New York Observer, February 19, 1831; September 21, 1833.

169 - Nevins, Thoughts on Popery, p. 151; New York Observer, February 22, 1834.

170 - Nevins, Thoughts on Popery, p. 149. See also, Schmucker, Discourse in Commemoration of the Glorious Reformation, p. 10; New York Observer, May 1, 1824.

171 - Protestant Magazine, November, 1833.

improper, then, but it led to the practices of penances
which spread only infidelity and disbelief. Writers
shuddered over penances which forced Catholic sinners
to repeat the Lord's Prayer to atone for their mis-
deeds.[172] Physical penances practied in Ireland[173]
and other Popish countries[174] they scoffed at; charging that such practices only bred sin and corruption,
and that from them grew the miserable conditions among
Romanists everywhere. That the whole penance system
was anti-Scriptural, the propagandists accepted without question, stating that the Catholic version of the
Bible erred in translating "repent" into "de penance."[175]

Especially did writers denounce these doctrines
of Catholicism as typical of the mercenary nature of the
Romish church. They gloated when they found inscribed
a Catholic church in New York, "My House Shall be called
the House of Prayer," and reminded their readers that the
Biblical passage continued: "but ye have made it a den of
thieves."[176] This belief nearly resulted in diaster for
the New York Journal of Commerce. In an editorial comment during the early months of 1841 the editor referred

172 - New York Observer, January 8, 1831.
173 - Protestant Vindicator, October 28, 1840; Hardy,
       Philip D., The Holy Wells of Ireland (London, 1841)
174 - Downfall of Babylon, September 19, 1835; April 2,
       1836.
175 - Nevins, Thoughts on Popery, pp. 112-116; National
       Protestant, September, 1845; Protestant Vindicator,
       March 3, 1841.
176 - Downfall of Babylon, January 3, 1835.

to priests "who will hardly afford the most mierable of
the people under them, even the consolations of religion
in the severist of afflictions without a fee,"[177] Catholics voiced strenuous objections to such a statement
and at a large meeting in Washington Hall, called on
the editor to prove his allegation or suffer a libel
suit.[178] A series of affidavits collected by the editor
and signed by Catholics who testified that they had been
forced to pay for different services satisfied the indignant citizenry and secured a suspension of the libel
charges, but gave nativistic papers a chance to shout
that Papists had been forced to admit the mercenary practices of their church.[179]

While the propagandists devoted some attention
to Biblical arguments to show that celibacy of the priesthood should be frowned upon[180] and even that the priesthood itself should be abolished[181] they turned with more
enthusiasm to the ceremonies and miracles of Catholicism

177 - Protestant Vindicator, November 17, 1841.
178 - New York Observer, December 4, 1841.
179 - Protestant Vindicator, November 17, 1841; New York
      Observer, December 4, 1841.
180 - Nevins, Thoughts on Popery, pp. 144-148; 204-207;
      Horne, Protestant Memorial, pp. 135-138; Schmucker,
      Discourse in Commemoration of the Glorious Reforma-
      tion, pp. 44-47; Ricci, Secrets of Nunneries, pp.
      xi-xii; Downfall of Babylon, December 20, 1834;
      October 17, 1835; Protestant Vindicator,, October
      21, 1835; New York Observer, August 31, 1833.
181 - Allen, Report on Popery, p. 23; Stratton, Book of
      the Priesthood, pp. 4-6, 11-16; 18-65.

as fit subjects for their ire. The Bible, they said,
had warned against praying to more than one Lord[182]
and vain repetitions[183] and bowing down to graven im-
ages.[184] Yet Romanists had erected idols for themselves in statues and relics of saints and the Virgin
Mary, and these they worshipped rather than God or His
Son.[185] Superstition had secured such a hold upon Catholicism, as a result, that bits of wood supposedly from
the cross were venerated far more than the spirit of
Christ,[186] and offerings before the bones of supposed
saints far outbalanced those dedicated to the Lord.[187]
"If in the next village to ours," declared one enemy of
Rome, "in enlightened New England, the inhabitants were
all pagans, and bowed down daily in a temple of Jupiter
or Venus, we are persuaded the holy majesty of Heaven
would be less insulted and less offended, than He is by

182 - Downfall of Babylon, February 7, 1835.
183 - National Protestant or the Anti-Jesuit, October,
      1845.
184 - Protestant Vindicator, July 8, 1840; Allen, Re-
      port on Popery, pp. 17-18.
185 - Nevins, Thoughts on Popery, pp. 65-69, 95-100;
      History of Popery, pp. 236-276; McGavin, The Prot-
      estant, vol. i, pp. 293-380; Allen, Report on
      Popery, pp. 18-19; New York Observer, January 30,
      1830; October 2, 1830; April 20, 1833; Downfall
      of Babylon, October 3, 1835; Protestant Vindica-
      tor, June 23, 1841; Quarterly Review of the Amer-
      ican Protestant Association, January, 1844.
      Protestant Association, January, 1844.
186 - Protestant Episcopalian and Church Register, Octo-
      ber, 1833.
187 - Pond, No Fellowship with Romanism, pp. 138-139.

the actual worship of Mary and the saints by a multitude among us who bear the name of Christians; for with the Bible in their hands, they substitute the creature in the place of the God head, and set up other mediators besides Him, who is 'the only mediator between God and man.'"[188]

It was this worship of saint and Virgin which made the No-Popery crusaders frown upon the sacrifice of the mass, where these idolatrous practices were carried out.[189] And viewing this ceremony with suspicion they turned only naturally to others of the Catholic Church,[190] commenting in horrified terms upon the Feast of the Ass,[191] the Blessing of Bells[192] and the blessing of animals in Rome.[193] "Can the annals of folly and extravagance, impiety and delusion," they asked, "furnish a parallel to such a display of fanaticism?"[194]

---

188 - Allen, Report on Popery, p. 20.
189 - Nevins, Thoughts on Popery, pp. 125-140; Giustini-
       ana, Papal Rome as it Is, pp. 30-51; Horne, Protes-
       tant Memorial, pp. 109-111; New York Observer,
       March 27, 1830; Cotter, J. R., The Mass and Ru-
       brics of the Roman Catholic Church Translated in-
       to English (New York, 1845); Hogan, William, High
       and Low Mass in the Catholic Church, with Comments
       (Boston, 1846)
190 - Emerlina, Frauds of Papal Ecclesiastics, pp. 120-
       135; The Ceremonies of the Holy Week in the Papal
       Chapel of the Vatican (-----, 1839)
191 - National Protestant, July, 1845; Downfall of Babylon,
       December 27, 1834; Emerlina, Frauds of Papal Ecclesi-
       astics, pp. 135-136.
192 - National Protestant, December, 1844.
193 - Ibid., January, 1845.
194 - Ibid., July, 1845.

The propagandists might have answered their own question by pointing to the miracles of which the Catholic church boasted. But miracles they considered not typical of Popish fanaticism, but rather an excellent example of the fraud practiced by the priests upon their people. Writers never grew tired of parading miracles of the past or present before their readers and explaining in elaborate detail the mechanical rather than the spiritual cause of the result attained.[195] The Virgin's house at Loretto was described with profound scorn.[196] A statue of Mary in Portugal which bowed when pleased by an offering was disclosed as a hoax concealing a small boy responsible for its actions.[197] Travelers told of still born babies restored to life long enough to be baptized in Dijon, and announced that priests jolted the table on which the infants lay to make them appear to move.[198] Often told was a tale of the clotted blood of Saint Januarius at Naples, which melted each year unless the priests willed otherwise. When Napoleon approached the city, these propagandists wrote, the blood

195 - Protestant Episcopalian and Church Register, September, 1830; Hogan, Synopsis of Popery, pp. 161-166; National Protestant, October, 1845; Emerlina, Frauds of Papal Ecclesiastics, pp. 5-7; New York Observer, September, 5, 1840.
196 - Emerlina, Frauds of Papal Ecclesiastics, pp. 59-63.
197 - New York Observer, January 25, 1854; Protestant Episcopalian and Church Register, August, 1833.
198 - Emerlina, Frauds of Papal Ecclesiastics, p. 9.

did not melt and the people rose in wrath against the
French. Napoleon, hearing of this, sent words to the
priests that unless the blood melted immediately he
would fire on the cathedral. But a few moments later
the blood was in liquid form and the people were satisfied.[199] A similar story was told of a weeping Virgin
at Naples, made to perform its miracles under Napoloen's
supervision.[200]

Venders of these tales were given an excellent
opportunity to pursue their trade in 1844. In that year
the Holy Coat of Treves, a coat supposedly worn by Christ,
was exhibited. It was visited by more than a million pil-
grims and performed countless miracles. Nativists gave
unqualified disapproval of this "disgusting blasphemy and
trickery"[201] and books and articles bemoaned the presence
of such superstition in the nineteenth century.[202] Science,
they warned, will die if such beliefs are fostered,[203] and
ignorance reign again as it did in the dark ages.[204] "We
have often said," wrote one propagandist," ... that the man

---

199 - Giustiniani, Papal Rome as it Is, pp. 250-262; Balti-
      more Literary and Religious Magazine, August, 1839;
      Downfall of Babylon, March 19, 1836.
200 - National Protestant, April, 1845.
201 - New York American Republican, August 30, 1844.
202 - Quarterly Review of the American Protestant Associa-
      tion, April, 1845; John Ronge, the Holy Coat of Treves,
      and the New German Church (New York, 1845); Marx, J.,
      History of the Robe of Jesus Christ, Preserved in
      the Cathedral at Treves (New York, 1845)
203 - Mason, History of the Holy Catholic Inquisition, p. 186.
204 - New York Observer, July 16, 1836.

who can bolt such a monstrous lump of superstition as
Popery itself, could swallow anything - nay, if he has
been able to take it down, with all its legends, fables
and absurdities, it is only wonderful that he can find
room for anything more." 205

To all these writers, there was only one encouraging thing about the whole corrupt Catholic Church.
Iniquitous and powerful as it was, it was destined not
to endure.   God, they said, had predicted the rise of
Popery as the "Man of Sin," the "Scarlet Colored Woman,"
the "Son of Perdition," "the Whore of Babylon," the "Beast
which sitteth on seven mountains." For the Bible had told
of the coming of a "Wicked One," "whose coming is after
the working of Satan, with all power and signs and lying
wonders, and with all deceivableness of unrightousness
in them that perish; because they received not the love
of the truth that they might be saved." To the nativist,
"lying wonders" meant only miracles; Romanism was being
referred to.[206] The Bible had told of a Babylon on seven
mountains; what could be clearer than that these were the
seven hills of Rome?[207] The Bible had prophesied a "Beast"

205 - Protestant Vindicator, June 24, 1840.
206 - Downfall of Babylon, November 29, 1834; Allen, Report
      on Popery, p. 7.
207 - Downfall of Babylon, October 17, 1835.

with seven heads and ten horns; again the seven hills
of Rome and the ten kingdoms of the Roman Empire.[208]
The Bible had warned of a "Man of Sin, the Son of Perdition, who opposeth and exalteth himself above all
that is called God;" and had not the Pope assumed power
greater even than that of the Creator?[209] The number
of the "Beast" had been foretold in the Scriptures as
"666;" nativistic writers showed that to Popery alone
did this dread number apply.[210] For did not the Latin
name assumed by the Pope, "Vicar General of God upon
Earth," produce that very prophetic number!

V I C A R I V S G E N E R A L I S D E I I N T E R R I S
5 1 100 - - 1 5 - - - - - - - 50 1 - 500 - 1 1 - - - - - 1 -

Formidable as was such proof to the propagandists, the Catholic church had provided them with even

208 - The Two Apololyptic Beasts in St. John's Revelation
Fully Explained and with an Accurate Engraving
(New York, 1842)
209 - Allen, Report on Popery, pp. 6-7.
210 - Baltimore Literary and Religious Magazine, October,
1839. The illustrations here given of this numerical method of computing the nature of Catholicism
are from a lengthy article in this publication.
One whole book, written in England in 1701 and devoted entirely to similar numerical computations,
was republished at the time, Fleming, Robert, An
Extraordinary Discourse on the Rise and Fall of
Papacy; or, the Pouring out of the Vials in the
Revelation of St. John, Chapter xvi, containing
Predictions Respecting the Revolutions of France,
the Fate of its Monarch; the Decline of Papal
Power, (New York, 1848)

more. For the "Man of Sin," said the Scriptures, "Causeth
all, both small and great, rich and poor, free and bond,
to receive a mark on the right hand, and on their forehead." And were not Romanists marked on the forehead
on Ash Wednesday,[211] and did not the priests receive a
mark on the hand and forehead when they were ordained?[212]
Thus was the coming of Popery forecast in the Scriptures,
and writers produced books[213] and articles[214] by the score
to convince all that the prophecy of the anti-Christ had

211 - Protestant Magazine, December, 1833; Downfall of
Babylon, June 6, 1835; Protestant Vindicator,
February 23, 1842.
212 - Downfall of Babylon, June 6, 1835; Protestant
Magazine, December, 1833.
213 - Campbell, J. N., Papal Rome Identified with the
Great Apostacy Predicted in the Scriptures. The
Substance of Three Discourses Addressed to the
First Presbyterian Church in Albany (Albany,
1838); Brownlee, W. C., The Roman Catholic Re-
ligion, Viewed in the Light of Prophecy and
History; its Final Downfall and the Triumph of
the Church of Christ (New York, 1844); Berg,
J. F., The Great Apostacy Identified with Papal
Rome: or, an Exposition of the Mystery of Iniquity, and the Marks and Doom of Anti-Christ (Philadelphia, 1847); Barnett, D., Truth and Error
Contrasted, Wherein the Great Apostacy as Prefigured in Cain, Baloom and Korah is Pointed Out
(Dublin, 1836); Junkin, George, The Great Apostacy: A Sermon on Romanism (Philadelphia, ------).
214 - American Text Book of Popery, pp. 36-41; History
of Popery, pp. 404-410; Elizabeth, Ridley and
Latimer, pp. x-xi; Allen, Report on Popery, pp.
6-9; Downfall of Babylon, August 8, 1835; Protestant Vindicator, March 31, 1841; New York Observer, December 18, 1830; January 10, 1835;
October 10, 1840; Quarterly Review of the American Protestant Association, April, 1844.

been fulfilled. While this great Apostacy might at
this time move forward in power and might, its doom
had been foretold. The Bible had stated that after
1,260 years Babylon would be destroyed[215] and enemies
of Rome saw in the future at least culmination of their
desires. Was there reason to be amazed, they asked,
that the Scriptures were denied to Catholic people when
such dire truths were foretold?[216]

With a ready sale awaiting any form of vindictive expose of the Catholic church propagandists cast
about for a greater means of profit and prejudice. In
search of this medium they hit upon the possibility of
pure fiction. The financial and influential success
of an earlier novel, Father Clement[217] assured nativistic writers that the reading public paid out its dollars
as freely for admitted fiction as attested memoir, and
it was no mere accident that whole streams of literary

215 - Protestant Vindicator, February 3, 1841.
216 - Schmucker, Discourse in Commemoration of the Great
    Reformation, pp. 30-31; McGavin, The Protestant,
    vol. i, pp. 570-579; Cheever, Hierarchical Des-
    potism, p. 145; Pond, No Fellowship with Romanism,
    pp. 197-221; Protestant Magazine, March, 1834;
    New York Observer, January 2, 1830; August 17,
    1833; Protestant Vindicator, August 19, 1840.
217 - A new edition was required in 1843, published in
    Baltimore in that year. Both the Reverend Robert
    J. Breckinridge and L. Giustiniani testified that
    they had been converted to the anti-Catholic cru-
    sade by reading the book. Baltimore Literary and
    Religious Magazine, July, 1843.

effort flowed from the presses in the years before 1844.

Many of these lurid bits of fiction portrayed
convent life in gruesome detail and more than made up for
the dearth of escaped nun's memoirs.[218] Others, less
specific in purpose, gave their pens to wholesale attacks
on Catholicism, a process usually resulting in long and
dull books in which the plot suffered while stilted Protestants and wily Jesuits argued at length over Biblical
texts.[219] Still others exposed the evils of Romanism by
lengthy descriptions of the martyrd sufferings of the
hero and heroine before the cruelty of the Popish Inquisitors.[220] All in all the fare placed before the No-
Popery enthusiast by these novelists was received with
as voracious an appetite as were the works of the earlier nativistic propagandist.

One phase of literary endeavor attracted much
attention from these writers of fiction. If the world
were to be saved from Romanism, the rising generation

218 - McCrindell, R., The English Governess (New York,
      1844); Hazel, Harry, The Nun of Saint Ursula;
      or, the Burning of the Convent, a Romance of
      Mount Benedict (Boston, 1845); Campbell, James
      M., The Protestant Girl in a French Nunnery, or
      the School Girl in France (New York, 1845).
219 - Andrew Dunn, (New York, 1835); Baird, Robert,
      The Life of Ramon Monsalvatge, a Converted
      Spanish Monk of the Order of the Capuchins
      (New York, 1845).
220 - Brownlee, W. C., The Whigs of Scotland (New York,
      1839); Meeks, J. C., Pierre and his Family; or, a
      Story of the Waldenses (New York, 1841)

must be acquainted with Popish errors and trained to
carry forward the struggle for Protestantism. Dull
theological arguments would not attract children; outspoken denunciations of Catholic immorality might but
were considered scarcely fit subjects for infant ears.
Upon the shoulders of fiction writers fell the important task of providing stories for the young which would,
to quote the New York Observer, "infuse into the youthful mind the proper sentiments that ought to be entertained respecting Jesuitical craftiness and deception."[221]

  First in this profitable field was Miss S.
Sherwood, whose children's novel, Edwin and Alicia, or
the Infant Martyrs,[222] aroused praise from critics for
its "moral and anti-Popish tone."[223] But Miss Sherwood
was destined to have the mantle of leadership removed
almost before it had been assumed. For in the late 1830's
there rose to fame as a purveyor of juvenile propaganda
a young English woman, Charlotte Elizabeth Tonna, whose
pen name, "Charlotte Elizabeth" was to grace no less than

221 - New York Observer, April 25, 1835.
222 - Sherwood, S., Edwin and Alicia, or the Infant
  Martyrs (New York, 1835)
223 - Downfall of Babylon, April 25, 1835.

nine books published in America between 1841 and 1845.[224]

Charlotte Elizabeth had a training and upbringing proper to fit her for her station in life. Her home
in Norwich, England, was situated but a short distance
away from the prisons where Protestant Martyrs suffered
under Bloody Mary. Throughout her infant years she used
to sit in contemplation of these grim structures and
imagine the horrors of the Popish system which had
caused these noble men suffering and death.[225] At the
age of five, her father gave her Foxe's Book of Martyrs,
and she read it as though absorbed. When she had finished
she sought out her father and with burning cheeks looked
up at him and said:

"'Papa, may I be a martyr?'

"'What do you mean, child?'

"'I mean, papa, may I be burned to death for
my religion, as these were? I want to be a martyr!

"He smiled, and made me this answer, which I

224 - Her books included, Alice Benden, or the Bowed
       Shilling and Other Tales (New York, 1841); The
       Church Visible in All Ages (New York, 1845);
       Falsehood and Truth (New York, 1842); Dangers
       and Duties (New York, 1841); Glimpses of the
       Past, or the Museum (New York, 1841); The Happy
       Mute (Boston, 1842); The Seige of Derry, or Suf-
       ferings of the Protestants, a Tale of the Revolu-
       tion (New York, 1844); Second Causes, or Up and
       Be Doing (New York, 1843); Personal Recollections
       (New York, 1843). In addition she published other
       books of travel and books designed for adult readers
       describing the persecution nature of Popery. She
       contributed short stories to American nativistic
       publications as well. See New York Observer,
       April 24, 1841; Protestant Vindicator, May 26, 1841.
225 - Elizabeth, Personal Recollections, p. 13.

have never forgotten, 'Why Charlotte, if the government
ever gives power to the Papists again, as they talk of
doing, you may probably live to be a martyr.'"[226]

With such an upbringing there is little wonder
that Miss Tonna devoted herself to the anti-Catholic
crusade. Her decision to do so, however, was not reached
until after she had been married and gone to live in Ireland where she could see Popery at its worst.[227] While
there some one gave her a copy of a great pro-Catholic
argumentative work, and as she read, she "semmed to be
holding communion with Satan himself, robed as an angel
of light, the transparent drapery revealing his hideous
form, but baffling my endeavors to send it away." Unable
to answer the arguments in favor of Catholicism, she burst
into tears and then and there decided to devote herself to
exposing the evils of that great system.[228] From that time
on she studied diligently, and the more she learned, the
greater was her abhorrence "to that gigantic lie and the
yearnings of compassion over its unhappy slaves."[229] Her
first actual efforts were directed against the Catholic
Emancipation Bill in 1829; she distributed tracts, sent
petitions to Parliament, and made speeches, but all to

226 - Ibid., p. 21.
227 - Ibid., pp. 100-140.
228 - Ibid., pp. 145-147.
229 - Ibid., p. 165.

no avail. The bill passed; she announced sadly that the
work of the Reformation and the Revolution had been un-
done,[230] and turned to the new field of endeavor which
was to be her life's work.

It was only natural that Charlotte Elizabeth
should give her attention to children. She believed that
they suffered grave danger in England and America from
the Romish schools which served as a constant lure, and
that if their souls and her country were to be saved,
this influence must be offset.[231] The novels from her
pen appear today as dull, pious, argumentative works,
little adapted to attract children or anyone else. The
popularity that they attained, however, shows that she
gauged her audience well, and their influence is not to
be questioned.

A survey of one of Charlotte Elizabeth's children's books will portray the nature of all of them, for
they bore startling elements of similarity. Falsehood
and Truth begins in rather dull fashion, with a discussion between a mother and her children, in which they talk
at length about the Bible and Elijah's sacrifice.[232] Finally their conversation drifts into the subject of idola-

230 - Ibid., pp. 266-283.
231 - Elizabeth, Falsehood and Truth, pp. viii-ix.
232 - Ibid., pp. 1-54.

try, and the mother makes the startling statement that there are idolaters among them even today. Little Sarah rises to the occasion and remarks, "Mamma is thinking of the poor Romanists, who worship their little imagines, and pray to saints and the Virgin Mary, and put their trust in what a man can do to save their souls."[233]

Up to this point the discussion has been carried on with unanimity and good feeling, but one of the older girls suddenly announces that the Catholics do not worship idols. All are aghast at this startling statement, and the girl's mother, realizing that she has been visiting friends near a large "Popish establishment," shuddered at a grave fear which suddenly gripped her soul.[234] That fear seems confirmed when the children tell her later in the day that their older sister has been praising priests and "the bad religion,"[235] and that she had actually been talking with Romish clergymen while away.[236] Little Sarah, who is rapidly rising to the position of prigish heroine, suggests that "when Papa comes home, perhaps we shall all have one of our nice little talks about the whole matter, and dear Sister will soon be convinced and set right again."[237]

233 - Ibid., p. 55.
234 - Ibid., pp. 55-59.
235 - Ibid., pp. 66-68.
236 - Ibid., pp. 69-71.
237 - Ibid., p. 74.

This pleasant little assembly takes place
the next evening, and consists largely of a lengthy
monologue by the father of the family on the horrors
of Romanism, plentifully sprinkled with Biblical references. By the time that it is over the erring sister has been beaten into submission by his torrent of
words, and admits her mistake, swearing that she will
never leave the true Protestantism again.[238] Encouraged
by this victory, the father journeys away to visit the
friends where his daughter first imbibed the evils of
Popery, where another well earned conquest to Presbyterianism results.[239] On his return he finds that his
daughters have partaken so deeply of his sentiments that
they have cut the pictures out of their Bibles, considering them Popish because they interferred with pious
thoughts.[240] With this action winning hearty approval
from the father, and another long lecture on Romanism
and all its errors the story comes to its close.[241]

Charlotte Elizabeth did not confine her efforts
entirely to children's tales, however. In 1841 she pub-

238 - Ibid., pp. 78-121.
239 - Ibid., pp. 125-169.
240 - Ibid., pp. 185-187.
241 - Ibid., pp. 188-209.

lished one of the many annuals, which at that time were
riding the tide of popularity along with gift books.[242]
Others followed her into this profitable field, and within a short time the country was being flooded with these
annual volumes, bearing such titles as The Protestant
Keepsake[243] and The Native American; a Gift for the People.[244]
Filled with story, verse and argument against Catholicism,
these books added force to the rising tide of propaganda,
and gold to the pockets of their compilers.

From other sources too, came new and unexpected
aid. Books describing travel in foreign climes devoted
more and more space to a discussion of Papal countries
and the horrors bred there by the corrupt religious system.[245]
Writers of history were turning their prejudiced eyes toward the Reformation, and not only extoling the virtues of
that movement which gave Protestantism to the world, but
exposing all of the real and imaginary errors of Rome's

242 - Elizabeth, Charlotte, The Protestant Annual (London,
      1841)
243 - The Protestant Keepsake, (London, 1840)
244 - Orr, Hector, The Native American; a Gift for the
      People (Philadelphia, 1845) Other gift books and
      almanacs published at this time included, The Prot-
      estant Almanac for 1841 (Baltimore, 1841); Kurtz,
      B., and J. C. Morris, The Year Book of the Reforma-
      tion (New York, 1844); The American Keepsake or
      Book for Every American (Boston, 1845); Horne,
      Thomas H., A Protestant Memorial (New York, 1844)
245 - Headley, Joel T., Letters from Italy (New York,
      1845); Sinclair, Catherine, Shetland and the Shet-
      landers (New York, 1840); Elizabeth, Charlotte,
      Letters rom Ireland (New York, 1843)

past.[246]   Deservedly the most popular of these studies
was a <u>History of the Great Reformation in the Sixteenth
Century</u>, a well written four volume work from the pen of
J. H. Merle D'Aubigne.[247]   Widely circulated and often
reprinted,[248] the bitter attack on Rome which characterized its pages was given considerable weight.   Even the
poet was swayed from his worship of the muse to give
vent to verse of little merit exposing the errors of
Popery, verse which was published widely in magazine,
newspaper and book.[249]

Thus were the forces of No-Popery agitation
gathered from among the writers of all types at home and
abroad.   By 1844 they were distributing their invective
from biased pens into novels, theological attacks, moral
exposures and horrified tales of the Inquisition.   Upon
this rising tide of literature the forces of the anti-
Catholic crusade were to be swept onward into national
political organization.

246 - <u>The Reformation in Europe</u> (New York, 1845); Lath-
       bury, Thomas, <u>The State of Popery and Jesuitism
       in England from the Reformation to the Period of
       the Roman Catholic Relief Bill in 1829</u> (London,
       1841); Dowling, John, <u>The History of Romanism</u>
       (-------); <u>A History of Popery, to which is Added
       an Examination of the Present State of the Romish
       Church in Ireland and Specimens of Monkish Legends</u>
       (London, 1838)
247 - D! Aubigne, J. H. Merle, <u>History of the Great Ref-
       ormation in the Sixteenth Century</u> (New York, 1846)
       Individual volumes had been published before 1846.
248 - <u>New York Observer</u>, January 7, 1837; February 24,
       1838; <u>Protestant Vindicator</u>, June 24, 1840.
249 - Extracts from the verse of the period are in Appen-
       dix B.

IX

NO-POPERY ENTERS NATIONAL POLITICS
1840 - 1844.

It was inevitable that the great mass of anti-Catholic propaganda of the years between 1834 and 1844 should bear fruit. The thousands who read of the menace which these venders of prejudice peddled from pulpit and press, were stirred to action; not only to strike a telling blow at Rome, but to protect their own country as well. Driven to the ballot box to defend themselves against the specter, countless voters banded together to form a national nativistic party bent on carrying the cry of No-Popery to the doors of the White House.

The causes motivating the growth of this new organization were similar to those which had inspired political nativism in the 1830's. The meagre success enjoyed by the earlier parties had not hindered the influx of immigrants during the 1840's. Goaded by increasingly unsatisfactory economic conditions in Germany and Ireland[1] and aided by improved methods of ocean transpor-

1 - Morehouse, Frances, "The Irish Migration of the Forties," American Historical Review, vol. xxxiii (April 1928), pp. 579-592; Hansen, Marcus L., "The Revolutions of 1848 and German Emigration," Journal of Economic and Business History, vol. ii, pp. 630-644; Smith, Immigration and Emigration, p. 42.

tation[2] the number of foreigners entering the United States passed the hundred thousand mark in 1842[3] and continued to mount with such rapidity that it had more than doubled five years later.[4]

Nativistic agitators of the preceding decade had seized upon the alien inflow as a pretext for bitter propaganda. Now with immigrants increasing so rapidly, this propaganda burst out in a new torrent. Arguments of ten years before were recast and sounded anew with

2 - Baker, Lenau and Young Germany in America, p. 9; Page, "The Transportation of Immigrants," pp. 737-738. By 1840 the cost of passage between Bremen and New York had fallen to below $15., including food, although five years later a $20. carrying fee was being charged, probably due to increased demands for transportation. Niles Register, vol. lxviii, p. 289. An especially prominent factor in encouraging emigration from Germany were the ship agents, offering fabulous tales of wealth and prosperity in America to the peasants.

3 - The arrivals for each year from 1840-1845 were as follows:

	1840	84,066
	1841	80,289
	1842	104,565
First three		
quarters of		
	1843	52,496
	1844	78,615
	1845	114,371

Kennedy, Preliminary Report of the Eighth Census, pp. 13-14.

4 - In 1847 the number of arrivals was 234,968. Ibid., pp. 13-14. According to these figures, the immigrant stream between 1830 and 1840 amounted to only about 3 percent of the total population of the United States, while between 1840 and 1850 it amounted to about 7 per cent. Desmond, The Know Nothing Party, p. 13. These figures were especially alarming when it was realized at the time that official estimates were approximately 50 per cent below the actual number of arrivals. DeBow's, Compendium of the Seventh Census, p. 122.

additional vigor; to them were added greater calumny
than ever before.

In the revival of the cry against the foreign
pauper, propagandists found one of their strongest appeals. Economic difficulties in the old world were such
that men had been rendered destitute of all but the most
slender resources; these they utilized to pay for transportation, being left little with which to face life in
America. Moreover, as competition between carriers for
the immigrant trade brought lowered rates of passage,
conditions on the ships became so deplorable that they
bred disease among thousands.[5]   Attempts by the govern-

5 - Conditions on immigrant ships of this day were al-
    most unbelievably bad. Owners sold their excess
    ship space to agents whose only interest was to
    fill it with as many passengers as possible. Usual-
    ly each persons was alloted ten or twelve square
    feet of deck space in a dark and unsanitary hold,
    seldom only five feet high. Ventilation was only
    through hatches, and these were closed in bad
    weather. To make matters worse, the immigrants
    were required to cook their own food in these nar-
    row quarters. Kapp, Immigration and the Commis-
    sioners of Immigration, pp. 19-25. British ships
    were most poorly cared for, partly because of poor
    supervision and partly because they carried the
    Irish. It was not uncommon to find six families
    in one of these vessels living on one life boat.
    Page, "Transportation of Immigrants," pp. 738-739.
    When it is considered that the immigrants were
    banded together under these conditions for voyages
    lasting six weeks or more, there is little wonder
    that illness and disease raged almost unchecked on
    the ships. Ibid., p. 737. Well could a saddened
    observer of these ships write: "If crosses and
    tombstones could be erected on the water....the
    whole route of the emigrant vessel from Europe
    would long since have assumed the appearance of
    crowded cemeteries." Kapp, Immigration and the
    Commissioners of Immigration, p. 43.

ments of the United States and European countries[6]
to regulate overcrowding proved abortive, and aliens
by the score arrived so ravaged by pestilence that
they were unable to care for themselves and became
objects of public charity immediately.[7] Nativistic
writers spread before their readers voluminous statistics reiterating that two-thirds of all paupers in
the public almshouses were foreign born[8] and that
those who were not supported from public taxation
made their living by begging in the streets.[9] "The
evil," they warned, "fungus like, is rapidly growing by what it feeds upon; and it has now so fastened
itself upon the whole body of the American people
that it hangs a loathsome mass upon every community
and corporation throughout our once pure and health-

6 - England was the first country to try to regulate
the conditions on immigrant ships, an act passed
in 1803 provided that only three passengers could
be carried for every five tons burden of the vessel. Page, "Transportation of Immigrants," pp.
741-743. The American act of 1819 restricted
American vessels to two immigrants to every five
tons burden. Bromwell, History of Immigration,
pp. 208-209. Neither of these countries made any
attempt to enforce these regulations however, Germany after 1830 alone keeping its immigrant ships
under close supervision. Page, "Transportation
of Immigrants," p. 742.
7 - Brewer, Daniel C., The Conquest of New England by
the Immigrant (New York, 1926), pp. 89-90.
8 - New York Observer, November 27, 1841; October 29,
1842; The Crisis, pp. 25-29; New York American
Republican, July 23, 1844; July 26, 1844; Native
American, April 26, 1844.
9 - The Crisis, p. 30.

ful community. Three fourths of this pauperism is
the result of intemperance, moral depravity and sheer
idleness."[10]

The 1840's witnessed not only a revival of
propaganda dealing with the economic effects of pauper
immigration, but a re-echoed cry that most of the foreign poor were dumped upon American shores by European
countries anxious to be rid of their refuse.[11] That
this was done with the avowed object of wiping out the
republicanism of the United States and establishing an
old world despotism was nowhere doubted.[12] European
monarchs, it was averred, "perceive that, like the Rod
of Aaron, Republicanism is destined to swallow the whole
serpent brood of monarchies unless it receives its death
sting here. War has been tried, and as it failed when
the giant was an infant, it would be worse than a for-
lorn hope now."[13] Even President Tyler's expressed fears
that the United States must annex Texas in order to pre-

10 - Ibid., p. 31.
11 - Native American, November 14, 1844: National Prot-
     estant, February, 1845; New York Observer, January
     4, 1845; The Crisis, pp. 6, 24, 32, 34, 44.
12 - New York American Republican, June 25, 1844; New
     Orleans Native American, quoted in Ibid., October
     3, 1844; Native Eagle, December 3, 1845; Native
     American, April 24, 1844; August 3, 1844; August
     9, 1844; August 13, 1844; October 29, 1844; The
     Crisis, pp. 3-4, 15.
13 - New York American Republican, May 31, 1844.

vent English domination there were scorned, writers
insisting that he should concern himself with the
graver danger faced by America itself.[14]

With immigrants sent from the old world with
the purpose of effecting the ruin of the United States,
nativists saw little cause for wonder in the fact that
many were numbered among the criminal and lawless strata
of society.[15] It was estimated that more than twenty
thousand professed criminals entered New York alone each
year[16] and writers warned that this number would increase
annually as the efficiency of the police systems in London and Paris was improved.[17] That intemperance and moral
laxity should follow caused no surprise.[18] But nativistic
editors were frankly perturbed at the operations of Father
Mathew, a Catholic priest who devoted himself to the cause
of temperance reform in the early 1840's, both in Ireland
and in America. Every editor was faced with a painful decision in regard to this cleric; he was a Romanist and
must be condemned, yet he was carrying on an admittedly
valuable work in checking excessive drinking among his
people. Some editors forgot their prejudice and wel-

14 - Ibid., June 1, 1844.
15 - Protestant Vindicator, December 1, 1841; New York
     Observer, January 25, 1845; The Crisis, pp. 17,
     32-33.
16 - National Protestant, February, 1845.
17 - The Crisis, p. 43.
18 - Native American, August 22, 1844.

comed Father Mathew to America, announcing that he had
more chance of getting into Heaven than the Pope and
all his cardinals.[19] Others saw in his efforts only
another Popish plot to collect money for the advancement of Catholicism[20] and to unite all members of this
faith in a great organization to conquer the world.[21]
Superstition offered no substitute for intemperance,[22]
they warned and announced with seeming joy that drinking in Ireland was increasing despite his efforts.[23]
Editors who were themselves active in the temperance
movement could not hold such views of a comrade at
arms without indicating the general feeling against
Catholicism and the immigrant.

Increased rioting and group enmity among German and Irish immigrants was pointed to by nativists as
sufficient evidence of the fact that in no wise could
these turbulent groups be assimilated. Old world feuds
were fought on city streets and rural hamlets; native
citizens began to hear of Orangemen and Ribbonmen and
Corkonians.[24] "Who are the political, street, canal
and railroad rioters?" cried one editor, "Foreigners!

19 - New York American Republican, May 27, 1844.
20 - Baltimore Literary and Religious Magazine, May,1841;
     Protestant Vindicator, November 11, 1840.
21 - Baltimore Literary and Religious Magazine, December
     1840.
22 - Protestant Vindicator, March 31, 1841.
23 - Spirit of the XIX Century, May, 1842.
24 - McMaster, With the Fathers, p. 95.

Men always ready and prepared to enter into any fray,
whose object may be to resist the authorities."[25] Even
a wit of the period remarked that while Saint Patrick
was the name of an order, Saint Patrick's day, "particularly in the morning, is more associated with the idea
of disorder than order."[26]

Agitators had considerable basis for their
claims. Rioting covered the country in the wake of
the immigrant stream. In New York the spring elections in 1842 brought pitched street fighting between
Irish and Orangemen aided by native Americans.[27] Two
years later a street brawl was precipitated when officers tried to capture pigs running loose on the city
streets, only to face determined resistance from a mob
of Irish owners.[38] Pitched battles were frequent among
foreign laborers on a canal near New Haven, Connecticut,
throughout the period.[29] In Pottsville, Pennsylvania a
Lutheran church was sacked by a crowd of drunken Irish
laborers.[30] Bloodshed followed a parade of German military companies in Cincinnati in 1842 when one of the of-

25 - Native American, September 27, 1844.
26 - a'Beckett, George A., The Comic Blackstone (Philadelphia, 1844)
27 - McMaster, History of the People of the United States,
vol. vii, p. 373; The Crisis, pp. 55-56.
28 - New York American Republican, September 4, 1844.
29 - Native American, September 30, 1844.
30 - Ibid., August 27, 1844.

ficers of the company killed a small boy who had been annoying them, an act which led to an uproar of feeling among nativists.[31] Louisville had its taste of turmoil when a German paper there, the _Blotbachter_ warned immigrants to go armed to the polls in order to protect themselves in an election in 1844. The warning, printed in other papers, aroused such a strong sentiment that the editor was forced to leave town to protect his life.[32] Rioting in St. Louis during 1840 was responsible for the death of one German[33] and that city[34] as well as Canton, Ohio,[35] witnessed rioting when anti-Catholic lecturers were attacked by foreign mobs.

Nativists might shout against the turbulent immigrant and find ready listeners, but an argument gaining effectiveness through its originality played an even greater part in directing sentiment against the foreigner. America, with work enough for all, had found no fault with foreign labor up to 1840. With the country still suffering from the effects of the Panic of 1837, agitators took the opportunity to excite

---

31 - New York Observer, August 20, 1842.
32 - Cole, "Nativism in the Lower Mississippi Valley,"
    p. 265.
33 - New York Observer, October 3, 1840.
34 - Native Eagle, April 14, 1846.
35 - Native American, April 11, 1844.

native workmen against the immigrant competitor. As
early as 1841 writers were beginning to point out that
American laborers were deprived of their occupations
by cheap foreign hirelings;[36] by 1844 that cry had
swelled to a chorus of complaint.[37] Propagandists
insisted that the United States had been peopled so
well that more workers were unnecessary,[38] that associations of foreigners had been formed to deprive Americans of opportunity[39] and that even the mercantile
business had passed almost entirely into the control
of aliens.[40] "Our laboring men," they insisted," are
met at every turn and every avenue of employment with
recently imported workmen from the low wage countries
of the old world. Our public improvements, railroads
and canals are thronged with foreigners. They fill our
large cities, reduce the wages of labor, and increase
the hardships of the old settlers."[41] With these beliefs freely circulated there is little cause for wonder that New England, where a change from agriculture
to manufacturing intensified depression, should be the
most enthusiastic section in its nativistic sentiment

36 - North American Review, January, 1841, quoted in
     Fairchild, Immigration, pp. 73-74.
37 - The Crisis, pp. 18, 68; Native American, June 21,
     1844.
38 - Native American, June 4, 1844; November 13, 1844.
39 - The Crisis, pp. 54-55, 56; Native American, June
     24, 1844.
40 - The Crisis, pp. 21-22.
41 - Native American, November 29, 1844.

a few years later.[42]

Important as may have been this agitation
against the alien laborer, it paled into insignificance
when compared with the propaganda released against the
alien voter. Here was a shout which had been raised
before, and writers were assured of a ready reception
for their words. As a result, they besieged their
readers with statistics on the growth of Catholic and
foreign influence upon the ballot[43] and they shouted
against ecclesiastical control of aliens in American
elections.[44] Both the Democratic and Whig parties were

42 - The New England states were undergoing a transfor-
mation from an agricultural to an industrial society
in these years, with the accompanying rural decay of
that section. Between 1820 and 1850 the amount of
manufacturing in the single state of Massachusetts
increased six fold. With the painful readjustments
necessary from such a change made more intense by
the alien problem the intensely nativistic sentiment of these states during the Know Nothing period
can be understood. See, Chickering, Statistical
View of the Population of Massachusetts, p. 42;
Haynes, "Causes of Know Nothing Success in Massachusetts," p. 72; DeBow's Compendium of the Seventh Census, p. 129.
43 - Native American, April 15, 1844; Native Eagle, December 18, 1845; The Crisis, pp. 16, 43. Despite
the great alarm expressed by nativists at the size
of the Catholic vote, it was estimated at the time
that there were only about 1,150,000 Catholics in
all the United States. Guilday, Life and Times of
John England, vol. ii, p. 382.
44 - New York American Republican, April 25, 1844; May
2, 1844; Native American, May 22, 1844; October 21,
1844; New York Observer, January 16, 1841; October
16, 1841; February 11, 1843; April 27, 1844; The
Crisis, p. 13; The Trial of the Pope of Rome, p.
164. Despite frequent claims by nativists that
Bishop Hughes of New York played a prominent part
in politics throughout this period, Hughes himself
vigorously denied any such interference. Hassard,
Life of John Hughes, pp. 378-379.

denounced for their efforts in attempting to secure the votes of naturalized aliens by granting them privileges[45] and appointing those of foreign birth to political office.[46] "The Republican principle is reversed," cried the editor of the Native American, "instead of office holders being the servants of the people, they actually hold it over their masters and dictate to them as imperiously as would the autocrat of all the Russias to his serf-born subjects."[47]

Nativists saw laxity in enforcement of the naturalization laws as a basis for most of the foreign political activity. There seemed to be only one way out of this difficulty: the five year period of probation fixed by federal statute as a prelude to naturalization[48] was, they argued, far too short a time. It had been fixed by the framers of the government only as a means of pleasing the French and Irish who had aided America during the Revolution; it was not intended to be

45 - Native Eagle, December 19, 1846; Native American, May 18, 1844; May 24, 1844; October 3, 1844; The Crisis, pp. 9, 12, 24.
46 - Native Eagle, December 20, 1845; April 14, 1846; The Crisis, pp. 67-68.
47 - Native American, August 19, 1844.
48 - The five year period was established through acts in 1802 and 1813. Printed in Bromwell, History of Immigration, pp. 190-193; 195.

permanent.[49] Ignorant Irish and Germans were unable
to comprehend the complicated American political system
in such a short period;[50] they became voters with little
understanding of what they should do.[51] To such inbred
ideas of despotism and might as were theirs, freedom
was a concept beyond realization. "It would be necessary to un-educate them," one writer said, "and then
to re-educate them before they could be fitted intellec-
tually and morally to perform the solemn and responsible
duties which devolve upon an American citizen."[52] Even
Daniel Webster imbibed sufficiently of these sentiments
to deliver an impassioned oration at Faneuil Hall in
Boston and call for a reformation of the naturalization
laws.[53]

Such an adjustment was necessary, nativists believed, not only to prepare the foreigner better for the
duties of citizenship, but to stop the fraud engendered

49 - Native American, July 9, 1844.
50 - The Crisis, pp. 35-37,
51 - Native American, July 17, 1844; July 29, 1844; The
     Crisis, pp. 7-8, 14.
52 - New York American Republican, April 26, 1844.
53 - The speech was delivered on November 8, 1844, and
     was inspired by the defeat of the Whigs in the elec-
     tions of that year, a defeat laid at the door of the
     foreign vote by Webster, Native American, November
     12, 1844. Webster was answered by a Catholic cham-
     pion, Brownson. Brownson, Works, vol. x, pp. 17 ff.

by the existing system. They charged that political
parties, anxious for foreign votes, used their influence
in securing improper naturalization[54] and even marched
aliens from the jails and pauper houses to the polls on
election day.[55] A joke popular at the time typified the
situation:

"Have you been naturalized?" inquired a chal-
lenger of a foreigner not long since.

54 - Nativists reproduced a number of advertisements
which they charged were circulated about New York
City by Democratic party leaders, offering to secure the naturalization of any foreigner in return
for his vote. A typical advertisement follows:
"Those desiring to become American citizens
are invited to call on the Democratic Republican Naturalization Committee of the Ward in
which they reside, or on the general Naturalization Committee of the party at Tammany Hall."
The Crisis, p. 41. Similar advertisements were reproduced in the Native American, April 11, 1844.
55 - Native American, April 17, 1844; New York American
Republican, May 3, 1844; The Crisis, pp. 15, 44.
That there was some basis for these charges was
shown by the impeachment proceedings against Judge
B. C. Elliott, of the city court of Lafayette, in
Louisiana. He was found guilty of accepting regular
fees from the Democratic committee of the state to
issue naturalization papers to all foreigners that
they recommended. Senate Documents, 25th Cong.
2nd Sess., No. 173. He was removed from office in
1844 but the many foreigners he had fraudulently
naturalized were allowed to continue voting. Niles
Register, vol. lxvii, p. 384. Conditions in New York
state were so bad that Governor Seward devoted a special message to the legislature to naturalization
frauds in 1841. Seward, Works, vol. ii, pp. 395-404.

"Yes."

"Where were you naturalized?"

"In Montreal."[56]

It was inevitable that from such a situation
a new nativistic political party should come into being.
Democrats had bartered their birthright for the alien
vote; Whigs were but little better. With relief from
immigrant laborers and paupers and change in the naturalization laws unavailable from these two older parties, nativists were driven to the formation of their
own organization to secure their ends. As early as
1839 a Native American Association had been formed in
New Orleans,[57] which, two years later, issued a call
for similar organizations in every city of the United
States.[58] In response to this, nativistic political
parties were formed in St. Louis and in Lexington, Kentucky,[59] and people in eastern cities started agitation
to revive the organizations which had attempted action
a decade before.

The movement for the establishment of this new
nativistic party was not to get fairly under way until

56 - The Crisis, p. 43.
57 - Address of the Louisiana Native American Associa-
     tion (New Orleans, 1839)
58 - Desmond, The Know Nothing Party, pp. 27-28; McMaster,
     With the Fathers, pp. 94-95.
59 - McMaster, With the Fathers, p. 95.

New York enthusiasts gave it their support. By 1843
the Democratic party, in control of the city, had so
aroused native citizens through concessions to foreign
born voters[60] that a group of disgruntled natives organized a crude party of their own.[61] A few months
later their efforts found followers in every ward and
it was possible to call a city wide convention which
drafted a constitution and adopted the name of the American Republican Party.[62] Members agreed to work to secure a law requiring twenty-one years residence for voters, to repeal the New York school law, to oppose selection of foreigners for office and to accept no nomination
from any other party.[63] In October, 1843, this group
took over a newly established nativistic newspaper, the
American Citizen as its official organ,[64] and in the fall
elections of that year astounded all observers by polling

60 - New York Journal of Commerce, October 23, 1843.
     Democratic favor was expressed in granting market
     licenses and petty offices to foreigners.
61 - Carroll, Anna E., The Great American Battle, or the
     Contest between Christianity and Political Romanism
     (New York, 1856), p. 264. According to the story
     told by Miss Carroll, a group of sympathizers with
     nativism, happening to meet in a blacksmith's shop,
     decided to form the party. The first body to be
     formed was in the eleventh ward, on June 13, 1843.
     Scisco, Political Nativism in New York State, p. 39.
62 - New York American Republican, July 11, 1844.
63 - New York Journal of Commerce, November 4, 1843.
64 - Ibid., November 3, 1843.

8,690 votes, less than 6,000 votes behind the Whigs[65]
In five months time the new party built up an organization capable of showing the power and enthusiasm with
which New Yorkers were willing to welcome any nativistic
movement.

The success of this attempt in New York prompted
imitation elsewhere. A few months after the fall elections a similar group of American Republicans had launched
themselves in Philadelphia,[66] finding ready support among
those antagonistic toward the political activity of the
Irish of that city during the preceding years.[67] Only
through some singular success, however, could this new
organization attain its ambition. Opportunity for this
success came with the spring elections of 1844 in New
York City. Nominating for mayor a prominent citizen,

65 - Ibid., November 22, 1843. The complete vote in
     the election was as follows:
Democratic party	14,410 votes
Whigs Party	14,000 votes
Nativist movement	8,690 votes
Walsh Democrats	320 votes
Anti-Slavery Movement	70 votes
66 - Native American, April 25, 1844. The Philadelphia
     group issued a proclamation of their purposes at
     this time, but they probably had been organized
     for several weeks.
67 - McMaster, History of the People of the United States,
     vol. vii, pp. 374-375. The Irish voters had attemp-
     ted to rebuff the Philadelphia Democrats by desert-
     ing them in 1842 and returning in 1843. This demon-
     stration of the strength of the Irish vote, causing
     defeat for the Democrats when they left the party,
     caused considerable nativistic excitement.

James Harper of the firm of publishers bearing his
name,[68] the American Republicans were carried into
office by a substantial majority over their Democratic rivals.[69] Jubilant members of the party in
Philadelphia staged a victory mass meeting to celebrate the success of their New York brethren,[70] and
the future seemed bright to members of this political
group.

Victory in the New York election was especially important to the American Republican party through the
impetus thus given for further expansion. By March, 1844,
branches had been established in every county of New York
state and New Jersey[71] and three months later a state
convention for New York was being considered.[72] A southern wing of the party was launched at Charleston, South
Carolina, in May;[73] two months later Boston received the
organization with open arms,[74] after No-Popery sermons

68 - Desmond, The Know Nothing Party, p. 36.
69 - New York American Republican, April 26, 1844. The
     following vote shows the results of the election:
            Nativist movement   24,510 votes
            Democratic party   20,540 votes
            Whig party   5,300 votes
70 - Native American, April 16, 1844.
71 - New York American Republican, June 26, 1844.
72 - Ibid., June 22, 1844.
73 - Ibid., June 7, 1844.
74 - Ibid., July 13, 1844.

from nearly every Protestant pulpit in the city had aroused its people.[75] By the autumn of 1844 thriving branches of the party were operating in Buffalo, Rochester, Utica and Albany, and had also been established in all of the leading cities in Virginia, Maryland, Georgia and Mississippi.[76] Pittsburgh, too, was a center of activity by this time[77] and traveling agents were covering the entire country, establishing new local units.[78] A headquarters had been set up in Washington, and this lusty nativistic infant was fast assuming Gargantuan proportions.[79]

New York members of the party took the lead in forming a state organization. Delegates from local groups assembled at a state convention in Utica in September, 1844[80] but failed to agree on methods to be used in state politics and adjourned without definite action. In other states the party was not sufficiently advanced to attempt state organization, and

75 - New York Observer, February 8, 1845. A letter is printed describing in detail the factors stirring up nativistic excitement in Boston as a prelude to the formation of the party there.
76 - New York American Republican, October 9, 1844.
77 - The National Protestant, December, 1844.
78 - New York American Republican, October 9, 1844.
79 - Native American, August 24, 1844.
80 - The convention assembled on September 10, later adjourning to New York where it met on September 23, 1844. New York American Republican, September 24, 1844.

the American Republicans faced the presidential election
of 1844 still as a series of local entities. Nativism
was given some national recognition however, through the
tacit support given its principles by the Whig party.
Whigs drifted naturally toward a nativistic point of view,
they represented the aristocratic elements of society and
looked with disfavor upon the poorer groups of immigrants.[81]
The party standard bearer in 1844, Henry Clay, had unquestioned sympathies in this direction and his vice-presiden-
tial candidate Frelinghuysen had been so long connected
with evangelical organizations that he was considered an
out and out No-Popery enthusiast.[82] With other Whig leaders sharing in these views,[83] there was little doubt but
that votes of the American Republicans should be cast for
Clay in 1844. Editors of that party freely admitted their
Whig sympathies, and insisted that the party was absorbing
the Whigs, just as it would the Democrats within a few
years.[84]

  While Seward, the most prominent Whig of New York
state, was an avowed enemy of all nativism, other members

---

81 - Cole, "Nativism in the Lower Mississippi Valley,"p.262.
82 - Stephenson, History of Immigration, p. 119.
83 - Cole, op. cit., pp. 264-265; Niles Register, vol. lxvi,
  pp. 232-234; American Catholic Historical Researches,
  vol. vii (January, 1911), p. 10.
84 - New York American Republican, September 2, 1844; October 14, 1844.

of the party there realized the value of votes which
might be secured from the American Republicans.[85]   An
understanding was reached between the two parties there,
through which Whig support was promised the American
Republicans in the local elections in return for their
support of Henry Clay in the national canvass.[86]   As the
election approached, the nativists entered upon this arrangement with enthusiasm; giant mass meetings with twenty
thousand and more in attendance listened to impassioned
orations against the foreigner and the Catholic.[87]   In
Philadelphia feeling ran equally high and mass meetings
held there rivaled those of New York;[88] placards covered
the city calling on the Protestant churches to array themselves against Popery.[89]   The results of the election gave
cause for new celebrations by the American Republicans.
While their political allies, the Whigs, had failed to
carry the country, they had emerged triumphant in the two
local elections where their strength had been concentrated.
In New York city the nativist ticket was completely vic-

85 - Millard Fillmore Papers (Publications of the Buffalo
     Historical Society, vols. X and XI, Buffalo, 1907),
     vol. ii, pp. 253-255.
86 - Scisco, Political Nativism in New York State, p. 49.
87 - New York American Republican, October 5, 1844; Octo-
     ber 14, 1844.
88 - Native American, October 1, 1844; New York American
     Republican, September 26, 1844; October 2, 1844.
89 - Native American, October 8, 1844.

torious, sending four members to Congress as well as filling local offices,[90] and in Philadelphia three of the four congressmen chosen were advocates of America for Americans.[91] "At the two points where our principles are understood," boasted an official organ of the party, "we have triumphed by overwhelming majorities. Let us regenerate perfectly the city and country, and then each become a missionary for the next four years to redeem his country from foreign influence."[92]

The strength of the American Republican party made it apparent to leaders of that organization that dependence on Whig support was no longer necessary. As a result the Whig alliance in New York was cast off[93] and the party here faced a separate existence with confidence and high hope. If it was to continue extensive operations in the future however, a national organization must be effected. Suggestion for a convention to perfect a national American Republican party was made first by delegates at a state convention of the party held in Harrisburg, Pennsylvania, in February, 1845.[94]

90 - Scisco, Political Nativism in New York State, pp. 50-51.
91 - Native American, October 9, 1844.
92 - Ibid., November 4, 1844.
93 - Scisco, Political Nativism in New York State, p. 52.
94 - Proceedings of the Native American State Convention held at Harrisburg, February 22, 1845 (Philadelphia, p. 3.

The suggestion met a ready response, and on July 4, of
that same year, one hundred and forty-two delegates
representing every section of the union assembled at
Philadelphia for a three day meeting.[95] After changing
the party name to Native American, adopting bitter resolutions against the foreigner and the Catholic and issuing an Address to the people of the United States calling upon them for aid,[96] the delegates adjourned, to meet
again in the second national convention of the party in
1847. As was the case before, this meeting was held at
Philadelphia. Resolutions similar to those passed two
years before were again placed before the people, and
Zachary Taylor was endorsed as the proper presidential
candidate. It is dubious whether or not nativistic support helped him to secure election in the following year,[97]
for by this time the life of the Native American Party was
rapidly drawing to a close.

The principles of this party, advocated with such
enthusiasm during its brief career, demonstrate clearly how
thoroughly its members had imbibed sentiments against the

95 - Address of the Delegates of the Native American National Convention, Assembled at Philadelphia, July
4, 1845, to the Citizens of the United States
(Philadelphia, 1845).
96 - Ibid.,
97 - Brand, Carl F.,"History of the Know Nothing Party in
Indiana," Indiana Magazine of History, vol. xviii
(1922), pp. 49-50; Desmond, Know Nothing Party,
p. 46.

Catholic and the immigrant from propagandists. In its
public documents, the Native American party stated three
principal objects: to change the naturalization laws
in order to force foreigners to reside in the United
States twenty-one years before becoming citizens, to
restrict the authority of naturalization to the Federal
Courts, and to reform the gross abuses arising from party corruption.[98]   In addition to these three aims, a
number of minor reforms were agitated: a restriction of
office holding to natives, a continuation of the Bible
as a school book, a prevention of all union between
church and state, a lessening of the number of street
riots and election troubles.[99]

It was upon the first of those major reforms
that the members of the American Republican party showed
the most complete agreement. They pointed out, in party
addresses and official publications, that Americans themselves were forced to live in the United States twenty-one

98 - Address of the Executive Committee of the American
Republicans of Boston to the People of Massachusetts
(Boston, 1845), p. 12; Address to the People of the
State of New York by the General Executive Committee
of the American Republican Party of the City of New
York (New York, 1844), p. 3; Address of the American
Republicans of the City of Philadelphia to the Native
and Naturalized Citizens of the United States (Phil-
adelphia, 1844)
99 - The Crisis, p. 8.

years before exercising the franchise[100] and they insisted
that an equal time should be required of the foreigner.[101]
Party leaders asked how foreigners, steeped in the ignorance and despotism of Europe, could master the complicated American political organization in less than twenty-
one years.[102] "At this moment," the leaders of the American Republicans in New York wrote, "there exists on the
continent of Europe, in the heart of its most despotic
government, a society protected by the crown of Austria,
patronized by the most unflinching supporters of civil
and religious despotism ... for the express purpose of
exporting to this country (free America) the abject
slaves of their country, who, bound in fetters of civil
and religious serfdom, would be incapable in twice twenty-
one years, of understanding the principles of civil and
religious freedom which alone fits a man to become an
American citizen."[103]

100 - Address to the People of the State of New York, pp.
3-4; Address of the American Republicans of Charleston, South Carolina, printed in the New York American Republican, September 24, 1844; Address of the
Delegates of the Native American National Convention;
New York American Republican, April 25, 1844; September 6, 1844.
101 - Address to the People of the State of New York, p.5.
102 - Address of the Executive Committee of the American
Republican Party of Boston, p. 13; Address to the
People of the State of New York, p. 4.
103 - Address of the Executive Committee of New York City,
printed in New York American Republican, April 26,
1844. Sentiments against the foreign immigrant
similar to those expressed years before by Samuel
F. B. Morse filled many of the publications of the
party. See especially, Address of the Executive
Committee of the American Republican Party of Boston, pp. 3-5, 7-8, 14; Address of the Delegates of
the Native American National Convention.

Almost equal unanimity existed on the need of
placing only Americans in office[104] and the necessity of
restricting naturalization to the courts of the United
States.[105] Members of the party agreed too, in public
at least, that they held no brief against the immigrants
and were willing to welcome all if they would confine
themselves to their own activities and not disrupt American political life.[106] That most of the individual members of the party shared in this sentiment may well be
doubted. Certainly, both as individuals and collectively,
they gave themselves up to enthusiastic denunciation of
the Catholic church.

Acting as a party, the American Republicans were
forced to proceed with caution in this attack on Romanism,
that enemies might have no opportunity of hurling the
charge of proscription at them.[107] There is little wonder that in official party pronouncements references to
Catholicism were couched in more polite phrase than was
usual to the nativist of the day. But despite these well

104- Address to the People of the State of New York, pp.
6-7; New York American Republican, August 6, 1844.
105- Address of the Executive Committee of the American
Republican Party of Boston, p. 14.
106- Address of the Louisiana State Native American Convention, printed in the National Protestant, January,
1845; Address of the Delegates of the Native American
National Convention; Address of the Executive Committee of the American Republicans of Boston, p.9,pp.12-13.
107- New York American Republican, September 11, 1844; The
Crisis, pp. 46-47.

chosen words, the sentiment of the party on this great
issue was clearly expressed. The Romish church, it believed, was spreading grasping hands over America. Papal
priests had used their political influence to control
elections in an effort to weaken the position of natives.
If America were to be ruled by Americans rather than by
the Pope, definite action in the form of a political combination was necessary to oppose this great religious
power.[108] Even the first national convention of the party gave up much of its report to a spirited denunciation
of the Church, leaving no doubt as to its meaning although
nowhere mentioning Catholicism by name.[109]

While the official publications of the American
Republicans were hampered in their outspokenness by political propriety, the party ward meetings felt no such handicap. Here individual members, gave proper vent to their
bigotry; here the work of the propagandists found true expression. Ward meetings in Philadelphia and New York
passed violent resolutions deploring the exclusion of
the Bible from the schools by Papists and condemning Popery as a religion of force and despotism which must be

108 - Proceedings of the Native American State Convention
Held at Harrisburg, pp. 11-13; Address to the People
of the State of New York, pp. 5-6; Address of the
Executive Committee of the American Republicans of
Boston, pp. 10-11.
109 - Address of the Delegates of the Native American National Convention.

driven from America.[110] Nativistic newspapers, depending for support upon these same members of the party,
were equally strong in their invective against Romanism.[111]
So universal was this feeling among members of the American Republican party that one of the leading Catholics
of the day, was firm in his conviction that the whole
movement was aimed entirely at Catholicism, and that Protestant foreigners were actually welcomed into the party.[112]

Violent as were these demands and aims of the
American Republican party, it was inevitable that the
leaders should attempt to force them upon the various
states and the nation as a whole. In both New York and
Pennsylvania, the two states where the party was centered, constitutional conventions were held during the
early 1840's to draft new constitutions. Nativistic
sentiment cropped up in the Pennsylvania convention with
a proposal to insert a constitutional clause forbidding
foreign born office holders;[113] that same sentiment caused

110 - New York Observer, April 13, 1844; August 24, 1844;
      New York American Republican, June 1, 1844; Septem-
      ber 6, 1844.
111 - Native American, May 1, 1844; August 7, 1844; New
      York American Republican, April 24, 1844; Native
      Eagle, December 9, 1845; July 15, 1846.
112 - Brownson, Life of O. A. Brownson, vol. ii, p. 107.
113 - McMaster, History of the People of the United States,
      vol. vii, p. 370. The Pennsylvania constitutional
      convention was held in 1841.

the introduction of a provision into the New York convention to confine the governorship of the state to a
native born citizen.[114] While both of these proposals
failed, they typify the activity of this new and vigorous party.

Demands of the American Republicans in New
York were partially responsible for a change in the immigration laws of that state, finally perfected in 1847,
which were designed to restrict the importation of pauper
immigrants.[115] Fear of aliens dispatched to the United
by European countries was also stirred in Congress by
the activity of members of the party, with the result
that in 1844 the Secretary of State was called on to lay
evidence of such a practice in his possession before the

114 - Native Eagle, July 22, 1846.
115 - Change in the New York law resulted from an investi-
       gation begun in 1842, disclosing frequent abuse and
       fraud in the administration of the system then in
       operation. Kapp, Immigration and the Commissioners
       of Immigration, pp. 59-60. The new law provided
       that ship captains must pay one dollar for each
       alien brought into the country, and in addition
       post a $300 bond for every immigrant likely to be-
       come a public charge. The Immigration Commission
       of the state was also created by this act to sup-
       ervise immigration. Fairchild, Immigration, pp.
       80-81. Popular sentiment in favor of such an act
       had been expressed in a large mass meeting held
       in New York City. Abbott, Immigration, p. 139.
       Despite this, the act was held unconstitutional
       in the Passenger Cases, in 1849. Fairchild, Im-
       migration, p. 81.

Senate.[116] Subsequent investigation by a committee
named for the purpose disclosed that both criminals[117]
and paupers[118] were being sent to America by many countries of the old world, a fact confirmed by the Secretary of State in a lengthy report made early in 1845.[119]
But while these reports offered nativistic publications
excellent material for propaganda purposes, Congress
made no attempt to meet the situation, and no measures
to effect a change were considered.

But if members of the American Republican party
could sit quietly by while foreign paupers overran America, their feelings were far different on the question
of the naturalization of aliens. As nativistic sentiment
swept the country in the early 1840's, and as this nativistic party sent its representatives to the halls of Congress, the naturalization laws and the naturalization machinery were subjected to an ever intensifying wave of
abuse. American Republicans had pledged themselves to

116 - Congressional Globe, 28th Cong., 1st Sess., p. 62.
The resolution was introduced by Senator Berrien
of Georgia, for the Judiciary Committee.
117 - Senate Documents,28th Cong., 2nd Sess., No. 173,
pp. 106, 109, 112, 124, 175, 140-141, 142. Evidence was presented by many witnesses in official
positions.
118 - Ibid., pp. 7, 12, 16, 19, 22, 23, 25, 27, 29, 31,
32, 112, 113, 118, 120, 127, 175.
119 - Senate Documents, 28th Cong., 2nd Sess., No. 42.
Evidence presented by the Secretary of State disclosed that many of the American consuls in Europe,
particularly in Germany, testified that paupers and
criminals were still being dumped on American soil,
pp. 6-7.

labor for a twenty-one year probationary period for
naturalization and as they carried this project onward Congress was forced to endure heated debate on
this question.

First interest in the naturalization laws
was aroused not by the native Americans, but by enemies of any extension of the existing naturalization
period. Early in 1842 the legislature of Missouri,
realizing the strength of the German vote in that
state, urged Congress to "resist all measures designed
to cause further delay or difficulty in the attainment
of citizenship."[120] Before the year had passed friends
of the alien carried their principle even further in an
attempt to reduce the probationary period from five to
two years. Senator Robert J. Walker of Mississippi who
introduced the measure, insisted that such a step was
necessary to return to the true stand of Washington and
the members of the first government, and that only in
this way could proper government be secured for western
states where aliens outnumbered the native born population.[121] Walker's motion was laid on the table by the
Senate before any definite action could be taken on it,

120 - House Executive Documents, 27th Cong., 2nd Sess.,
       No. 37.
121 - Congressional Globe, 27th Cong., 2nd Sess., p. 817.

but its introduction did serve to bring forward the
first Congressional friend of nativism, Senator William
S. Archer of Virginia. In an impassioned appeal against
Walker's measure,[122] Archer forecast for members of the
Senate the part he was to play in furthering nativist
agitation in the halls of Congress in future years.

Opportunity for the display of this leadership
came early in 1844, and grew directly from the growing
sentiment in favor of the American Republican party in
that year. On May 31 John Quincy Adams of Massachusetts
presented to the House of Representatives a petition
from citizens of Philadelphia praying for a change in
the laws to secure a twenty-one year period of probation
before the naturalization of aliens. Adams insisted in
presenting the measure that it did not represent his own
principles, and moved immediately that it be referred to
the Judiciary Committee. Such a step would in time have
brought the whole question before Congress for debate and
many members were opposed to this procedure. A counter
motion to lay the memorial on the table immediately was
passed with only twenty-six votes recorded against it,
and there the matter rested.[123]

122 - Ibid., 27th Cong., 2nd Sess., p. 817. Archer was
responsible for the motion to lay the measure on
the table, and after his speech, the motion was
agreed to, 21 to 18.
123 - Ibid., 28th Cong., 1st Sess., p. 674. The motion
to lay the memorial on the table was introduced by
William H. Hammett, and was carried by a vote of
128 to 26.

A torrent of protest from the Philadelphia nativistic press greeted this action. Citizens were called upon to redress this mighty wrong[124] and a great mass meeting attended by 15,000 cheering natives heard speakers urge that the Congressmen who had kicked out the memorial should be kicked out themselves.[125] High praise was sung for the twenty-six members of the House who had voted against laying the memorial on the table. They, one editor cried, "were found possessed of some slight recollections of those principles for which our fathers bled - the good old principles of Saxon liberty - the principles which cost to John, his power - to James, his throne - to Charles, his head - to George, his provinces: principles which are destined to supply for both the vitiated factions which disturb the last hope of the free their grave and epitaph."[126]

Not only had Congress stirred a hornets nest of opposition from the American Republicans about its ears; it had, in addition, inspired them to the production of still more memorials. In the few months after Adam's

124 - Native American, June 6, 1844.
125 - Ibid., June 8, 1844. The mass meeting was held in front of the State House in Philadelphia on the night of June 7. Resolutions were adopted in which the natives present pledged themselves not to vote for any of the members of the House from Pennsylvania who had voted in favor of laying the measure on the table.
126 - Ibid., June 13, 1844.

petition was laid on the table, the House of Representatives and the Senate were besieged with dozens of pleas, all urging the same general action; all insisting that a twenty-one year probationary period for naturalization was necessary to protect the safety and the prosperity of America. In dealing with these new petitions, Congress made no mistake. As each was presented it was referred to the Judiciary Committee of the House or the Senate, usually with a speech by the legislator presenting it expressing his own disapproval of its objects.[127] Only Senator Archer was firm in his ex-

127 - On June 1, 1844, Senator James Buchanan introduced a petition from citizens of Philadelphia, Congressional Globe, 28th Cong., 1st Sess., pp. 675-676; on June 3 he presented a similar petition, Ibid., 28th Cong., 1st Sess., p. 677; on June 5 E. J. Morris of Pennsylvania presented eight petitions in the House, Ibid., 28th Cong., 1st Sess., p. 690; on June 6 Senator D. W. Sturgeon of Pennsylvania presented a memorial from citizens of that state, Ibid., 28th Cong., 1st Sess., p. 690; and on June 7 offered another similar petition, Ibid., 28th Cong., 1st Sess., p. 694; on June 8 Senator Buchanan presented five more, all from Philadelphia, Ibid., 28th Cong., 1st Sess., p. 697; on June 13 Senator Rufus Choate of Massachusetts presented three memorials from Pennsylvania citizens, Ibid., 28th Cong., 1st Sess., p. 718; on June 14 similar memorials were introduced by Senator Thomas Benton of Missouri and Senator Buchanan, Ibid., 28th Cong., 1st Sess., p. 727; on June 15 Senator E. H. Foster of Tennessee presented one memorial and Senator Archer of Virginia three more, all from Pennsylvania, Ibid., 28th Cong., 1st Sess., p. 736; on the same day a similar memorial was offered in the House, Ibid., 28th Cong., 1st Sess., p. 742; on December 10, J.R. Ingersoll of Pennsylvania presented a petition from his native state and asked that it be referred to a select committee of nine, a request that was refused by the House, the memorial going instead to the Judiciary committee, Ibid., 28th Cong., 2nd Sess., p. 18.

pression of favor for the petitions which he presented,
and urged upon Congress the necessity of immediate action
to check fraudulent voting and open contempt of existing
laws.[128]

Throughout 1844 these memorials accumulated in
the hands of the Judiciary committees of the House and
Senate. It was becoming increasingly obvious, as the
months passed and the flood of memorials did not diminish,
that some action on them would be necessary. A growing
mass of people, particularly in the eastern states, were
beginning to demand that delay be ended and the members
of Congress expose their views on this whole great question. In December, 1844, this action came. Senator Henry
Johnson of Louisiana submitted a resolution calling on the
Judiciary committee to "inquire into the expediency of mod-
ifying the naturalization laws of the United States, so as
to extend the time allowed to enable foreigners to become

128 - On June 7, 1844, Archer presented a memorial from
       citizens of Philadelphia, and not only spoke in
       favor of the measure, but advocated immediate ac-
       tion by the Senate. Congressional Globe, 28th Cong.
       1st Sess., p. 694. On June 11 Archer introduced
       eleven more petitions and his speech in favor of
       them drew into the fray Senator Buchanan and Sena-
       tor William Allen of Ohio. At the same time simi-
       lar memorial were presented by Senators George
       Evans of Maine, William C. Rives of Virginia and
       Thomas Benton of Missouri. Ibid., 28th Cong.,
       1st Sess., pp. 704-705.

citizens; to require greater guard against fraud in the
steps to be taken in procuring naturalization papers; and
to prevent, as far as is practicable, fraud and violence
at elections."[129] This sweeping motion was introduced on
December 11, five days later debate in the Senate was begun, after Johnson had amended his own bill to add the
words, "and to prohibit the introduction of foreign convicts into the United States."[130]

All of the pent up feelings of nativists, long
curbed in the legislative halls of their country, were
loosed in this debate on Johnson's motion. Johnson himself opened the discussion with a lengthy plea for a change
in the existing system of naturalization, insisting that
fraud and corruption had crept into the government through
its operation, and that "most of the foreigners, ignorant
of the nature of our government and its political institu-
tionswere mere instruments in the hands of designing men,
to be used at elections for the most corrupt purposes."
The present naturalization policy, he said, had been introduced when the United States needed immigrant laborers;
now that need was no longer felt. It was not necessary,
then, to attract aliens by offering them political induce-
ments; it would be well to bar from citizenship these law-

129 - Ibid., 28th Cong., 2nd Sess., p. 19.
130 - Ibid., 28th Cong., 2nd Sess., p. 32.

less, turbulent groups who were unfit for its res-
ponsibilities. "This question soars far above party considerations," he said. "It is a question upon
which depends, not only the purity of our political
institutions, but the preservation of our government
itself. All parties ... are equally interested in
guarding against a repitition of the abuses complained
of, which, if not prevented in the future, may ultimately destroy our government."[131]

The glove thus thrown down by Senator Johnson
was taken up with enthusiasm by his fellow senators.
William S. Archer of Virginia echoed his words and
urged immediate action.[132] Archer's fellow senator
from Virginia, William C. Rives, agreed with what Johnson had said, and painted a dismal picture of the fraud
attendant upon naturalization as it was then carried out.
"Immigrants are marched in," he told the Senate, "by pla-
toons, or companies, of twenty, thirty or fifty; they are
carried up to the desk of the clerk of the court, without
attracting the cognizance of the judge; and then a mummery
of words is pronounced, and a pantomimic exhibition on the
part of the foreigner, who, in all probability, understands
nothing that is going on - in ignorance of our language -

131 - Ibid., 28th Cong., 2nd Sess., p. 32.
132 - Ibid., 28th Cong., 2nd Sess., p. 33.

and then forthwith he is adopted an American citizen
and goes forth to exercise all the privileges."[133] Even
opponents of the Johnson resolution caught the spirit
of these enthusiasts and urged immediate action to settle the question, an action required by the growing demands of the people of the country.[134] It was inevitable, in view of this debate, that the resolution would
be accepted by the Senate. There was little opposition
when the vote was finally taken, and the Judiciary Committee was thus launched upon an inquiry which was to
probe the whole naturalization system.[135]

The debate on Johnson's measure had disclosed
the form that the investigation of the Judiciary Committee would take. Most of the speakers had stressed the
fact that fraud was a product of the existing system, in
their reiteration of this charge they had found excuse
for advocacy of a twenty-one year period of probation
for citizenship. Subsequent resolutions passed by the
Senate impressed on the committee the necessity of a
thorough investigation of this phase of the matter[136]

133 - Ibid., 28th Cong., 2nd Sess., p. 33.
134 - Ibid., 28th Cong., 2nd Sess., p. 33.
135 - Ibid., 28th Cong., 2nd Sess., p. 33.
136 - Ibid., 28th Cong., 2nd Sess., p. 38. The resolu-
       tion, submitted by Senator Alexander Barrow of
       Louisiana, instructed the Judiciary Committee to
       enquire specifically whether fraud had existed
       in federal courts in naturalization proceedings
       and whether a law should be passed to recall the
       citizenship papers of any aliens naturalized
       through corrupt means. It was passed on Decem-
       ber 17, 1844.

and empowered it to take rigorous action in this survey.[137] By the early months of 1845 considerable progress had been made,[138] encouraged by a continued barrage
of petitions from groups of citizens in Pennsylvania and
Missouri.[139] On March 3, 1845, they were ready to lay
their report before the Senate. The report offered a
damning criticism of the whole naturalization process
then in operation. Witnesses who had been examined in
four large ports of entry, New York, Philadelphia, Baltimore and New Orleans, testified that the whole system
was honeycombed with abuse. Fraudulent citizenship
papers were obtained through party manipulation,[140]
they testified, and judges and court officials swore
they were kept busy during the period before each elec-

137 - Ibid., 28th Cong., 2nd Sess., p. 67. A resolution
      adopted by the Senate on December 26, 1844 auth-
      orized the Judiciary Committee to take testimony
      by commissioners in carrying on its investigation.
138 - On February 18, 1845, Senator John M. Berrien for
      the Judiciary Committee reported that agents had
      been sent to New York, Philadelphia, Baltimore and
      New Orleans to investigate, and that while the
      agent in New Orleans had not yet reported, those
      in the eastern cities had completed their labors.
      The report, he said, would be ready within a short
      time. Ibid., 28th Cong., 2nd Sess., p. 303.
139 - Senator Buchanan of Pennsylvania presented a peti-
      tion from Philadelphia citizens on December 17,
      1844, Ibid., 28th Cong. 2nd Sess., p. 37; Archer
      of Virginia presented a similar petition from Penn-
      sylvania citizens on the same day, Ibid., 28th Cong.
      2nd Sess., p. 38; on December 23, 1844, he presented
      a similar petition from Pennsylvania, Ibid., 28th
      Cong., 2nd Sess., p. 62; and on February 18, 1845,
      one from citizens of St. Louis, Ibid., 28th Cong.,
      2nd Sess., p. 303.
140 - Senate Documents, 28th Cong., 2nd Sess., No. 173,
      pp. 82, 84, 89, 91, 92, 95, 96, 138, 139, 186,
      187, 189.

tion caring for these party aliens.[141] Moreover
professional witnesses were employed by foreigners
to swear that they had been in the country the necessary five year period, witnesses who sometimes testified for a dozen or more aliens in one day.[142] It
was a usual practice, too, for court clerks to issue
naturalization papers with judges not even in atten-
dance,[143] and testimony was given to show that foreign
paupers were marched from the almshouses to the polls
by party henchmen in order to secure their votes.[144]
In Louisiana, agents found, conditions were particularly
bad, with foreigners controlling the voting places, and
refusing to allow native citizens to cast their ballots.[145]

In the face of such evident fraud, the Judiciary Committee felt it necessary to offer a bill which
would bring relief. The measure presented with the report and immediately passed to its second reading by the
Senate embodied many of the changes insisted on by the
American Republicans. Their demand that a twenty-one
year probationary period should be added was not acceded

141 - Ibid., 28th Cong., 2nd Sess., No. 173, pp. 10, 13,
      14, 16, 17, 23, 25, 30, 41.
142 - Ibid., 28th Cong., 2nd Sess., No. 173, pp. 18, 20,
      28, 53, 56, 64, 74, 75, 139, 142, 143.
143 - Ibid., 28th Cong., 2nd Sess., No. 173, pp. 107, 147.
144 - Ibid., 28th Cong., 2nd Sess., No. 173, p. 90.
145 - Ibid., 28th Cong., 2nd Sess., No. 173, pp. 144-197.

to, but elaborate provisions to prevent evasions of
the naturalization law were agreed upon. The new law
provided that collectors of customs were to keep records of all aliens entering the country, with a thorough
description of the alien, and that each immigrant should
be given a copy of this registration. When an alien had
been in residence three years he should present this registration as a proof and make his first application for
citizenship. After two more years, he could be made a
citizen, but only by federal courts.[146] Admirably suited
as was this law to stop existing fraud, it was allowed to
die in the Senate without further action.

For while this measure was traversing the way-
ward legislative channels of the upper branch of the legislature, the scene of nativistic interest had shifted to
the House of Representatives. The whole matter of naturalization and demands of the American Republicans was
precipitated there by the introduction of a supposedly
harmless petition from the citizens of Massachusetts asking for a change in the naturalization laws. This memorial, submitted on December 15, 1845, by Robert C. Win-

146 - Ibid., 28th Cong., 2nd Sess., No. 173, pp. 198-202.
The Native Eagle praised this report of the Judiciary Committee in highest terms and deplored the
manner in which its startling revelations had been
neglected by the press. December 12, 1845.

throp of Massachusetts, would normally have followed
the usual path to extinction through the Judiciary
Committee.[147] But a new champion of nativism had arrived in the House. Lewis C. Levin, a representative
from Pennsylvania, objected to such a procedure immediately. So important a measure should be debated, he
insisted, and the House was forced to accede to his
wishes.[148]

    Two days later, on December 17, 1845, a de-
bate began that was to rage until December 30 with

147 - In January, 1845, the Judiciary Committee of the
House of Representatives had acted on petitions
presented to it, reporting adversely on demands
for a twenty-one year probationary period. Reports of Committees, 28th Cong. 2nd Sess., No.
87, pp. 1-6. The committee had reported out a
bill similar to the Senate measure designed to
restrict fraud in naturalization, which was read
twice and then referred. Congressional Globe,
28th Cong., 2nd Sess., p. 224. For a full report of the speeches for this measure and the
measure itself see, Congressional Globe, 28th
Cong., 2nd Sess., Appendix, pp. 192-231.
148 - Congressional Globe, 29th Cong., 1st Sess., p. 52.
The resolutions, read to the House two days later
when debate began, read as follows:
    "Resolved, that the rights, interests and
morals of the people demand an immediate
and thorough revision of the naturalization laws; and we regard it as the imperative duty of Congress so to amend these
laws, that, while a liberal and just policy shall be adopted to such foreigners as
are or may come among us, the rights and
privileges of our countrymen shall be kept
inviolate, and the ballot box permanently
guarded against every improper influence.
    "Resolved, that our Senators and Representa-
tives in Congress are hereby especially requested to use their utmost exertions forthwith to procure such amendments in the naturalization laws as shall carry out and perpetuate, as far as possible, the principles
indicated in the foregoing resolve."
Ibid., 29th Cong., 1st Sess., p. 67.

almost uninterrupted fury. As far as the legal status
of the matter was concerned, this weighty argument was
simply over the question of referring the Massachusetts
memorial to the Judiciary Committee or to a select committee named for the purpose. Nativistic enthusiasts
insisted upon the select committee, thus insuring a report and final settlement of the whole matter. Actually
this debate amounted to more than mere verbiage over the
choice of committees; it represented the final effort of
the American Republicans to popularize their views and
force them upon the legislative branch of the government.

That this was their purpose cannot be doubted
when the debate itself is considered. The speeches of
the first day were opened by the new found champion of
the nativists, Lewis C. Levin[149] who stated frankly that
he represented the Native Americans in desiring a change
in the naturalization laws, and that this party, soon to
number a million voters in its ranks, wanted only to have
the question in the open where opinions could be expressed,
rather than buried in a committee.[150] His words were

149 - Levin was a representative in Congress from the First
Pennsylvania district. He was a native of South Carolina, a man of stout build and florid eloquence. Desmond, The Know Nothing Party, p. 42. It is interesting to note that despite his enthusiasm for the
cause of nativism, his wife was converted to Catholicism ten years before her death in 1881 and his son
also became a Catholic. At least a priest who aided
in preparing Mrs. Levin for her death so testified.
This priest was the Reverend D. A. Merrick, S. J. His
recollections are printed in the American Catholic
Historical Researches, vol. vii (April, 1911), p.189.
150 - Ibid., 29th Cong., 1st Sess., p. 68.

echoed by other nativists and by honest believers that
change was necessary,[151] and were answered with enthusiasm by Democrats and Whigs alike.[152] With a pattern
of invective thus set, Levin took the floor again to
sum up in a ponderous argument all the nativist's claims
and demands in a mighty burst of eloquence.

Levin's first insistence was that the party which
he represented was a permanent party, certain to rise to
new and greater glories.[153] "It is identified with\the
birth of the Republic," he told his fellow representatives,
"the day-flash of our liberty, the maturity of our independence, and the establishment of our glorious constitution ...The farmer at the plow feels its warmth in his
heart. The boy at school, as his peach blossom cheek

151 - Speakers in favor of a change in the naturalization
laws were Robert C. Winthrop of Massachusetts,
William Campbell of New York, Thomas M. Woodruff
of New York, William Yancey of Alabama, and Robert
Dale Owen of Indiana. Ibid., 29th Cong., 1st Sess.,
pp. 69-74.
152 - Opponents of the measure advocating placing the resolution in the hands of the Judiciary committee were
Richard Bradhead of Pennsylvania, William B. Maclay
of New York, Cornelius Dorough of Pennsylvania,
William W. Payne of Alabama, and Leonard H. Simms
of Missouri. Many of the speeches by these men were
obviously designed to appeal to the aliens among
their own constituents, the speech of Simms in
particular being devoted to a long eulogy of the
foreign born and the valuable part that they had
played in the development of the country. Ibid.,
29th Cong., 1st Sess., pp. 69-74.
153 - Levin's speech is printed in full in Congressional
Globe, 29th Cong., 1st Sess., Appendix, pp. 46-50.

flushes with pride, shoots a brighter glance from his eye
at the thought of the name, that is itself that principle,
and which equally defies slander, repels calumny, con-
quers argument and soars above scorn, contempt and hatred."[154]
What if that party did have only one idea, he asked? "If
one idea can disenthrall this great country from the vassa-
lage in which the foreign vote binds it to Europe, it will
do more than all the myriads of ideas engendered by our opponents."[155]

To Levin, this foreign vote constituted a real
and serious danger. He sketched for the benefit of his
listeners European despots, attacking the United States
not by force, for this means was barred to them; attacking instead by means of the alien vote, a thing far more
dangerous than armies.[156] To save itself from this designing influence and to build up a great American nation[157]
the ballot box had to be taken from those untrained and unversed in the governmental systems of their adopted country.[158] Congress alone could do this, for the constitution had granted solely to this body the right to deal
with the alien. In addition the states, which were powerless to cope with the situation depended upon Congress for

154 - Ibid., 29th Cong., 1st Sess., Appendix, p. 47.
155 - Ibid., 29th Cong., 1st Sess., Appendix, p. 48.
156 - Ibid., 29th Cong., 1st Sess., Appendix, p. 47.
157 - Ibid., 29th Cong., 1st Sess., Appendix, p. 50.
158 - Ibid., 29th Cong., 1st Sess., Appendix, p. 50.

protection.[159]

Levin's powerful arguments called for an answer.
This answer was delivered the following day when the debate raged throughout the House, with Levin himself providing most of the nativistic arguments.[160] A day later
the debate was checked to allow other business to continue[161] but was resumed again on December 29. For two
more days the arguments raged, bringing forth no less
a champion than Stephen A. Douglas as an opponent of
nativism.[162] Finally, in the closing moments of December 30, 1845, the vote was taken. Despite the oratorical
outbursts of Native American speakers, the House was in
no wise moved and it agreed without serious division to
refer the Massachusetts memorial to the Judiciary committee.[163] The Native American party had lost a major vic-

159 - _Ibid._, 29th Cong., 1st Sess., Appendix, p. 48.
160 - _Congressional Globe_, 29th Cong., 1st Sess., pp. 77-82.
161 - _Ibid._, 29th Cong., 1st Sess., p. 63.
162 - Douglas delivered his speech, largely on the constitutional aspects of naturalization, on December 30.
Ibid., 29th Cong., 1st Sess., pp. 113-114. Other
speakers who favored the Native American cause during
the final two days of argument were Washington Hunt
of New York, and Robert J. Ingersoll of Pennsylvania.
Ibid., 29th Cong., 1st Sess., pp. 105-107; p. 118.
The many speakers opposed to the change included
Henry Bedinger of Virginia, Alexander B. Sims of
South Carolina, James Dixon of Connecticut. _Ibid._,
29th Cong., 1st Sess., pp. 114-118.
163 - _Ibid._, 29th Cong., 1st Sess., p. 118. No vote on
the question was recorded.

tory by so large a margin that not even a roll call was necessary. The nativistic press might claim that the "gag rule" was being revived and applied by Congress,[164] but such insinuation did little good. Congress had expressed itself, and there was no doubt now of its attitude.

With such a clear manifestation of sentiment voiced by the House of Representatives, it was inevitable that the Judiciary Committee, after finally receiving the Massachusetts resolution, should act unfavorably upon it. On February 10, 1846, its report was given, reviewing the whole question of naturalization[165] and deciding that "no alteration of the naturalization laws is necessary for the preservation of the rights, interests and morals of the people, or for the guarding of the ballot box against every 'improper influence.'"[166] Native American newspapers branded the report as breathing the spirit of Benedict Arnold[167] and a "servile, truckling, pope's-toe-kissing resolution"[168] but the die had been cast. Until the Know Nothing agitation was to bring a revival a few years later, nativism and the twenty-one year naturalization period were dead issues in the legislative halls of the

164 - Native Eagle, January 1, 1846.
165 - Reports of Committees, 29th Cong., 1st Sess., pp. 1-5.
166 - Congressional Globe, 29th Cong., 1st Sess., p. 353.
167 - Native Eagle, February 16, 1846.
168 - Ibid., March 2, 1846.

nation.[169]

Unfruitful as had been the legislative efforts
of the American Republicans, the part which they played
in creating a spirit of nativism throughout the land was
far from insignificant. Filled with violent invective
against the immigrant their petitions and speeches in
Congress had been re-echoed throughout the nation. Even
more important were the efforts launched by the party to
increase its own supporters through the press and the lecture platform. In that day of political journalism, it
was inevitable that the party leaders should turn their
efforts to the newspaper field almost as soon as the first
local organization of the nativists had been launched; it
was inevitable too that those efforts should result in a
journalistic tirade against the foreigner and the Catholic.

Most influential among the many newspapers founded
to support the American Republican party were those in New
York and Philadelphia where the organization had its greatest strength. A small newspaper, the American Citizen had

169 - Native American congressmen made infrequent attempts
to express their views in minor issues, but with no
important results. Thus Levin tried to secure an
act restricting enlistment in a regiment of rifle-
men being raised in 1846 to native born Americans,
giving a long speech in favor of his proposal. Congressional Globe, 29th Cong., 1st Sess., pp. 605-
609. His suggestion was rejected by a vote taken
on April 10, three days after it was introduced.
Ibid., 29th Cong., 1st Sess., p. 655. See also
Ibid., 29th Cong., 1st Sess., p. 832.

been established as the organ of the party in New York
with its first inception[170] but before a year was out
this first publication had given way to a lusty rival,
the New York American Republican. A large daily newspaper, filled with news of the party which it represented
and with propaganda against Catholic and immigrant alike,
this new publication forged ahead rapidly, until by the
summer of 1844 it boasted a circulation of more than
15,000 copies daily and was second only to the New York
Sun in the amount of patronage received.[171] So great
was the demand that its publishers felt justified in
establishing a Weekly American Republican to appeal to
an even larger audience.

Such a successful example in New York City led
to an immediate imitation in Philadelphia. On February
22, 1844, the prospectus of a new newspaper the Native
American appeared,[172] and on April 11 the first issue
made its bow. The principles of this newest addition
to the nativistic papers typified its spirit:

> The principles of this Paper are - That
> Native-born Americans are competent to make
> and administer their own laws.
> That, in framing their institutions, they
> are not bound to consult the judgment or feel-
> ings of the inhabitants of any other portion
> of the globe.

170 - New York Journal of Commerce, November 4, 1843.
171 - New York American Republican, August 19, 1844.
172 - Native American, August 19, 1844. February
22 was chosen because of the patriotic enthusiasm always aroused among native Americans by
Washington's birthday.

The EVILS we complain of are --
That the cheap rate at which American
privileges are granted has invited to this
country the less worthy part of the population of the Old World - and that this population has been used by political demagogues
to their own benefit and the detriment of
the country.
The REMEDIES we propose are -
To extend the Period of Naturalization.
To elect none but natives to office.
To reject foreign interference from all
our institutions, social, religious and political.[173]

While the Native American had thus devoted it-

self primarily to the principles which marked the Amer-

ican Republican party, it shared, as did members of that

party, in the violent feeling against Catholics. Articles

exposing Popery found frequent place in its pages,[174] a

policy which seemed to please subscribers for by Septem-

ber, 1844, the publishers felt encouraged to launch a

second nativistic paper, the National American, a semi-

weekly publication.[175]

This successful enterprise brought a rival paper

into the Philadelphia field late in 1845, another daily

publication, bearing the title: The Native Eagle and Amer-

ican Advocate. Unlike its predecessor, the Native Eagle

173 - Ibid., April 11, 1844.
174 - As typical examples see Ibid., June 22, 1844 and ff.
      and September 11, 1844 and ff.
175 - Ibid., September 19, 1844. The editor of the new
      publication was Hector Orr, a well known figure in
      nativistic circles.

devoted itself largely to the working class, and demanded
as first among its claims "protection of American labor
by protecting the American laborer."[176]   The ease of
naturalization, its editors insisted, had brought thousands of foreign workers to America to compete with American industry; naturalization laws must be changed so that
this lure would no longer exist.[177]

    With the spread of the American Republican Party
this localization of its press in New York and Philadelphia
could cease.   Throughout 1844 and 1845 similar newspapers
were founded in cities all over the country.   Most of these
new publications were definitely anti-alien papers,[178] in

176 - Native Eagle, December 1, 1845.
177 - Ibid., December 1, 1845.
178 - Among the definitely native American papers established at this time are the following: The American
Ensign (Philadelphia); The Weekly American Ensign
(Philadelphia); The American Republican (Boston);
The Daily American (Jeffersonville, Indiana); The
Lancaster American Republican (Lancaster, Pennsyl-
vania); The Native (Harrisburg, Pennsylvania); and
The Penant and Native American (St. Louis), all
founded in 1844.   In the next year the following
papers were added: The Weekly Eagle and Advocate
(Philadelphia); The American (New York); The New
York American Sentinel (New York); The Pittsburg
American Eagle (Pittsburg);The American Citizen
(Cincinnati); The American (Poughkeepsie New York);
and the Harrisburg Statesman and Native American
Advocate (Harrisburg, Pennsylvania).   In 1846 new
papers founded were: The American Press and Repub-
lican (Lancaster, Pennsylvania); The Ann Arbor Amer-
ican (Ann Arbor, Michigan); The American Vineyard
(Detroit, Michigan); The Worcester Native American
(Worcester, Massachusetts); and the Baltimore American Republican (Baltimore).   The above list has
been secured from notices in the following papers
and publications: Native American, July 10, 1844,
August 14, 1844; August 27, 1844; November 2, 1844;
November 14, 1844; Native Eagle, December 1, 1845;
December 20, 1845; December 8, 1846; Proceedings
of the Native American Convention at Harrisburg,p.5.

name and principle, others had been established before
and simply embraced the aims of this rising political
party.[179] But in either case the result was the same.
They gave themselves up to an enthusiastic editorial
policy of denouncing the Catholic and the immigrant.
Thus were the forces of the propagandists bolstered
in a powerful way from a new source.

It was not to newspapers alone that backers
of this party devoted their attention. Monthly magazines
were also established, boasting a national circulation,
and not only supplying their readers with news of the
American Republicans, but bemoaning in the usual way the
foreign influence on American shores. Most prominent

179 - Papers embracing the American Republican cause
included: The New Haven Courier (New Haven,
Connecticut); The Baltimore Clipper (Baltimore);
Windsor Journal (Windsor, Vermont); Daily Mer-
cury (Bangor, Maine); Charlotte Journal (Char-
lotte, North Carolina); Newark American Citizen
(Newark, New Jersey); Lexington Inquirer (Lex-
ington, Kentucky); China Republican (China, New
York); Shelby News (Shelby, Kentucky); Lancaster
Union and Sentinel (Lancaster, Pennsylvania)
Norfolk American (Norfolk, Virginia); New Orleans Topic (New Orleans); The American Flag
(Trenton, New Jersey); Bunker Hill Aurora (Boston); Morning Courier (Louisville, Kentucky);
Public Index, (Portsmouth, Virginia). The above
list has been taken from references in the following periodicals: Native American, November 7, 1844;
November 13, 1844; November 20, 1844; National Protestant, December, 1844; Tuska, Benjamin, Know Nothingism in Baltimore (New York, 1925), p. 4.

among these publications were the Metropolitan Magazine
and Republican Review and the American Republican Magazine [180] both established in New York in 1844. Even the
device of lecturing agents, found so succesful by the
anti-Catholic societies, was resorted to, speakers touring the eastern states.[181]

  Thus were forces of nativism mustered throughout the nation by 1844. Speakers and writers of this new
party were adding their lusty voices to the cry of the
propagandists against Rome. The American Republicans,
trembling on the brink of success in that same year, were
destined to a brief and unsuccessful career. But the work
which they had done lived after them. Prejudice, sown by
their organs of propaganda, created so strong a feeling
against the Catholic and the immigrant that mob force
and riot was about to take its bloody toll.

180 - The first issue of the American Republican Magazine
contained patriotic stories and verse, as well as
news of the party and such articles as "The Inso-
lence of Foreigners," and "The Constitution."
American Republican Magazine, October, 1844.
181 - Proceedings of the Native American State Convention
at Harrisburg, p. 9.

X

THE PHILADELPHIA RIOTS OF 1844

By the middle of the year 1844, anti-Catholic agitators could look back upon their work with a feeling of quiet satisfaction. The ill-advised efforts of Bishop Hughes in the New York school controversy had been put to good use by propagandists' pens. Religious interest, centered about Catholic attacks on the Protestant Bible, had attracted nativistic sympathizers and encouraged clergymen and itinerant lecturers to mount the rostrum and rant against the evils of Rome. Anti-Catholic societies had been placed upon a sound basis, and the American Protestant Society was entering upon a career which seemed to glow with promise. Magazines and newspapers bent on exposing Popery were circulating in ever increasing volume. A political party had been cast which was to train its force upon Rome by aiming straight at the nation's capitol. Agitators who could look back to a time less than two decades before when anti-Catholicism was only a latent force could feel a justifiable pride in their own accomplishments through this brief span.

That such forces of intolerance could stalk

through the land without disaster was impossible. Prejudice against Popery, stirred to fever heat, must inevitably burst its bonds. Such was the case in the summer of 1844 when No-Popery enthusiasts in the city of Philadelphia cast aside all restraint and for weeks turned this haven of brotherly love into a chaos of hatred, persecution and bloodshed. Later when their passions had been spent, a calm was to ensue for several years. The physical blows at Rome had rebounded to stun No-Popery into a coma which lasted into the 1850's.

The city of Philadelphia had a heritage that fitted it well for violence and mob rule. Rioting had been common there all through the age of the enforcement of the rule of the "divine right of the majority." Several years before, Pennsylvania Hall had been burned and the city had swarmed with abolitionists' riots. The taste for disorder thus engendered had been satisified in the next years with frequent pitched battles between fire companies, and had culminated in the railroad and weaver riots in Kensington, when native and alien laborers had battled in open combat.[1] Elections had been constant scenes of disorder and reached a climax in the

1- The history of these disturbances is traced in the
   Native American, July 16, 1844.

March balloting of 1844 when Irish and Americans had
fought openly in the streets of one of the suburbs.[2]

In such an atmosphere of conflict, cries of
the No-Popery enthusiasts would find ready ears, and by
1844 they resounded throughout the city. The American
Protestant Association, which included most of the Protestant clergymen of Philadelphia, had been formed and
had sent its clerical members forth to their pulpits to
shout against the dread "Beast." A local tract society
was boasting of distributing two million pages of leaf-
lets a year, most of them aimed at Catholicism.[3] Speakers
were being imported from other cities to lift their voices
against Rome.[4] Debating societies were holding prolonged
arguments upon the effect of Popery on free institutions.[5]
Lusty orators for the city branch of the American Republican party were indulging in frequent tirades against
Catholicism. In such an atmosphere, any suspected Catholic aggression would inevitably spell trouble.

On November 14, 1842 Bishop Francis Patrick Kenrick of the Philadelphia diocese addressed a letter to the
Board of Controllers of the public schools complaining that

2- Ibid., May 29, 1844. The election was held on March
  15, 1844, and the rioting was centered in Spring
  Garden.
3- Foik, "Anti-Catholic Parties," p. 58. The society
  was the Philadelphia Tract Society.
4- New York Observer, January 21, 1843. The Reverend
  George B. Cheever was particularly active in delivering lectures.
5- McMaster, History of the People of the United States,
  vol. vii, p. 375.

the Protestant version of the Scriptures was being read
in the schools of the city, and that the exercises each
day were opened with prayers and the singing of hymns.
He asked respectfully that the Catholic children be allowed to use their own version of the Bible and excused
from other religious exercises.[6] In January, 1843, the
school board agreed that the request was perfectly proper,
and passed resolutions stating that no pupil was required
to attend any Bible reading if his parents were opposed
and that children whose parents preferred any one version
of the Scriptures could be allowed to read from that.[7]

There can be little doubt that Bishop Kenrick's
action had been prompted by the efforts of Bishop Hughes
in New York a year before. But if Bishop Kenrick believed
that he could secure his end without a torrent of protest
comparable to that which had descended about the head of

6 - The letter is printed in the New York Observer, January
    28, 1843, and the First Annual Report of the American
    Protestant Association, pp. 24-25. As early as 1834
    Catholic complaints against sectarian instruction in
    the Philadelphia schools had been received by the
    Board of Controllers. At that time schools had been
    specifically forbidden books of a sectarian nature or
    any form of religious instruction. There is every
    reason to believe that these instructions had not
    been lived up to by the teachers, and that little
    effort was made to enforce them. McMaster, History
    of the People of the United States, vol. vii, p. 376.
7 - New York Observer, January 28, 1843. The Controllers
    stated that they took no action in regard to hymn
    singing and religious instruction because those
    things had been specifically forbidden by the law
    of 1834.

the New York diocese he was sadly mistaken. The cry
that Kenrick was driving the Bible from the schools
was raised immediately. A bitter pamphlet, A Reply
to the Allegations and Complaints Contained in Bishop
Kenrick's Letter to the Board of Controllers of the
Public Schools was hurried from the press and broadcast wholesale over the city.[8] "The interference of
foreign prelates," said the author, "and of a foreign
ecclesiastical power, should perish at our threshold.
Let a grave be sunk, then, over which even the great
Papal hierarch himself cannot step."[9] Enthusiastic
chorus to these violent words was given by the American Protestant Association[10] and its clerical members
shouted loud amens from their pulpits. In Kensington
a member of the school Board who tried to stop Bible
reading in a local school caused such excitement that
a giant mass meeting was held to demand his resignation.[11]

8 - Colton, Walter, A Reply to the Allegations and Com-
    plaints Contained in Bishop Kenrick's Letter to the
    Board of Controllers of the Public Schools. (Phil-
    adelphia, 1844).
9 - Colton's entire work was published in the Quarterly
    Review of the American Protestant Association, Jan-
    uary, 1844. The accompanying extract is from this
    source, pp. 21-22.
10- First Annual Report of the American Protestant Asso-
    ciation, p. 7.
11- McMaster, History of the People of the United States,
    vol. vii, pp. 376-377. McMaster's account is drawn
    from the Philadelphia Public Ledger. The mass meet-
    ing was held late in February, 1844, and drew such
    crowds that they were unable to enter the Odd Fellows
    Hall, where the meeting had been scheduled, but were
    forced to move to the Methodist church nearby.

Catching the spirit of the occasion, anti-Catholic
leaders staged a similar public gathering in Independence Square, Philadelphia on March 11, 1844, and
after listening to fiery speeches, adopted resolutions
stating:

> That the present crisis demands that
> without distinction of party, sect, or
> profession, every man who loves his coun-
> try, his Bible and his God, is bound by
> all lawful and honorable means to resist
> every attempt to banish the Bible from our
> public institutions.[12]

In vain did Bishop Kenrick publish a second letter to
the Controllers of the schools on the following day,
stating that he "did not object to the use of the Bible,
providing Catholic children be allowed to use their own
version."[13] The day had passed when such a pallative
could quiet Protestant fears. Resentment throughout
Philadelphia and its suburbs continued to grow.

Amid such controversy the growing American
Republican party in Philadelphia thrived with new vigor.
Adopting the cry of the nativists with enthusiasm, they
carried into their political meetings demands that the
Bible be restored to the schools and that the Papists
be punished for their bold attack on the Word of God.

12 - New York Observer, March 16, 1844.
13 - New Englander, 1844, pp. 472-473.

Public meetings where such sentiments were expressed
by rabid masters of invective naturally aroused a
lusty resentment among the foreign elements of the
city. Mutterings of reprisal were heard all over
Philadelphia as the days passed and antipathies increased, particularly in the suburb of Kensington,
an industrial section where Irish laborers were concentrated in large numbers.

On April 25, 1844, these threats of violence
were translated into action. A Native American meeting
had been scheduled for the third ward of that city.
Bolder spirits among the Irish openly threatened to
burn down the house in which the meeting was to be
held, and the American Republicans, believing in discretion as the better part of valor, had changed their
plans and held their meeting elsewhere.[14] Trouble was
avoided for only a few days.

The storm broke a little more than a week
later when the Kensington members of the Native American
party, flying in the face of earlier threats, decided
to hold another meeting in the third ward. Members had
scarcely assembled at this meeting on the night of Friday, May 3, when a mob of Irish swept down upon them and

14 - Native American, April 26, 1844.

and forced them to take to their heels with more speed
than dignity.[15]   Driven from their place of meeting,
the remnants of the nativists gathered immediately
afterward at the George Fox Temperance Hall and passed
a series of fiery resolutions:

> That we, the citizens of Kensington, in
> mass meeting assembled, do solemnly protest
> against this flagrant violation of the rights
> of American citizens, and call upon our fellow
> citizens at large, to visit with their indigna-
> tion and reproach, this outbreak of a vindic-
> tive, anti-Republican spirit, manifested by a
> portion of the alien population of Third Ward,
> Kensington.
> Resolved, that in view of the above trans-
> action, we invite our fellow citizens at large
> to attend the next meeting to sustain us in the
> expression of our opinions.
> Resolved, that when we adjourn we adjourn
> to meet in mass meeting on Monday afternoon at
> four o'clock, at the corner of Second and Mas-
> ter streets.[16]

Such resolutions meant that bloodshed was openly welcomed.   In calling on their fellow citizens for
support at a second mass meeting, the Native Americans
were throwing the gauntlet at the feet of Irishmen never
reluctant to retrieve it.   This dangerous situation was
made even more tense by the attitude of the nativistic
press.   The Native American, in describing the meeting
in Kensington, hinted darkly that a "Popish priest" had
been seen nearby just before the riot started,[17] and

15 - New York Observer, May 11, 1844; Native American,
     May 4, 1844.
16 - Ibid., May 4, 1844.
17 - Ibid., May 4, 1844.

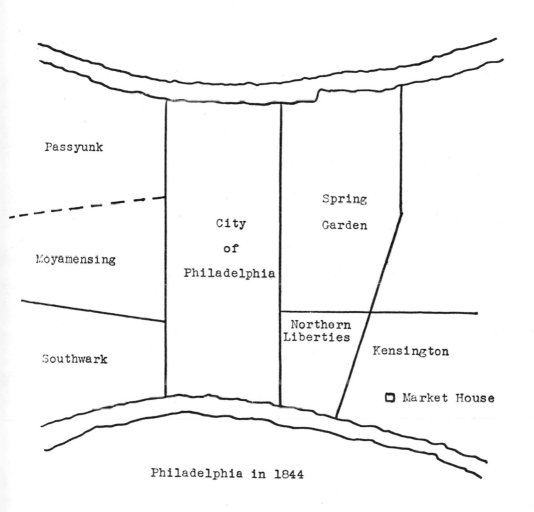

Passyunk

Moyamensing

Southwark

City
of
Philadelphia

Spring
Garden

Northern
Liberties

Kensington

□ Market House

Philadelphia in 1844

laid all the blame for the turmoil to "political demagogues and the Catholic clergy."[18] "It has indeed,"
the editor wrote, "come to a high pass, when the native born citizens of a country, dare not assemble in
town meeting, without being prepared to resist the
assaults of these foreign bullies. It reminds us of
the time when the farmer carried with him to the field,
his rifle, to defend himself from the assaults of out-
lying Indians. We are the friends of peace. We would
do everything right to preserve it, but if we are to be
assaulted by a horde of foreigners, when assembled for
peaceful purposes, why let them find that blows can be
given as well as taken."[19]

Even such ill advised recommendations were not
sufficient to calm the ruffled spirit of this vindictive
editor. On the morning of Monday, May 6, the day upon
which the postponed meeting was to be held, his newspaper appeared with a flaming notice spread upon the front
page:

Native Americans

The American Republicans of the City and
County of Philadelphia, who are determined to
support the Native Americans in their Constitutional Rights of peaceably assembling to
express their opinions on any question of public policy, and to sustain them against the

18- Ibid., May 6, 1844.
19- Ibid., May 6, 1844.

assaults of aliens and foreigners are requested to assemble on this afternoon, May
6, 1844, at four o'clock, at the corner of
Master and Second Streets, Kensington, to
express their indignation at the outrage of
Friday evening last, and to take the necessary steps to prevent a repetition of it.
Natives be punctual, and resolved to sustain your rights as Americans, firmly but
moderately.[20]

The type of men who responded to such an

appeal naturally expected trouble, nor were they to

be disappointed. Several thousand strong they had

scarcely gathered at their appointed meeting place

when a cloud burst deluged their ranks and drove

them in a bedraggled procession through the streets

of the Irish section of Kensington to the Market

House. Just as they were entering this building

several shots rang out, fired from the windows of

the Hibernia Hose house, an Irish fire company, and

from Irish homes near the building. The meeting was

thrown into a turmoil immediately. One of the march-

ers, a young man named George Shiffler, had been struck

and mortally wounded. He was carried from the meeting

by four men who shouted, "American citizens, arise.

Defend yourselves. One of your number has been wounded.

Shot down in the street." A grey haired man managed to

make himself heard above the shouting and cried, "On,

20 - Ibid., May 6, 1844.

on Americans. Liberty or death." Amid this excitement
a band of Irish laborers stormed the building. The natives lost courage and made a hasty retreat for the second time.[21]

This retreat was only to gather scattered forces,
however. Before night had fallen the natives again assembled, laid elaborate plans for the funeral of Shiffler
and others who had been killed in the fighting, and
marched in a body to the scene of the afternoon's rioting. Several Irish homes were attacked before the militia arrived on the scene at eleven o'clock and drove
the rioters before them. "When the natives had got their
blood up," one nativistic newspaper remarked with some
bitterness, "and were fast gaining the ascendancy, the
peace officers thought it high time to interpose the
authority of the law."[22]

The dawn of a new day found the whole city
in the grip of intense excitement. Great crowds were

21 - The account of this rioting is drawn from the New
York Observer, May 11, 1844; Native American,
May 7, 1844; New York American Republican, May
10, 1844; The New Englander, 1844, pp. 475-479.
Catholic hostorians who had described the Philadelphia outbreak have done so in a prejudiced
manner. All base their accounts on Shea, History of the Catholic Church in the United States,
vol. iv, pp. 46-55. Shea refuses to admit that
Irish struck the first blow, and states that native Americans marched directly from a meeting
being held to uphold Bible reading in the schools
to attack Irish homes and churches. See also,
O'Gorman, History of the Roman Catholic Church,
pp. 356-360; Catholic Encyclopedia, vol. viii, p. 678.
22 - New York Observer, May 11, 1844; Native American,
May 7, 1844; May 8, 1844.

gathered on every corner, listening to speakers shout against Catholicism. A procession was hastily formed and marched through the streets bearing a torn American flag on which was painted: "This is the flag that was trampled under foot by the Irish Papists." Bishop Kenrick issued a proclamation deploring the Catholic participation in the disorder, but when those proclamations were posted over the city they were torn down and made into cockade hats for the natives.[23] The Native American appeared with its columns shrouded in black,[24] a device adopted by the New York American Republican when it published an account of the rioting.[25] Two Irishmen recognized as among the leaders in the attack the night before were captured by a group of natives and taken to the home of an alderman while a mob followed and shouted, "Kill them. Kill them. Blood for Blood."[26]

With feeling running high throughout the city, the editor of the Native American completely lost his sense of balance. His paper, snatched from hand to hand by the milling thousands in the city that Tuesday morning, called for mob action and bloodshed:

23 - New York American Republican, May 9, 1844.
24 - Native American, May 7, 1844.
25 - New York American Republican, May 10, 1844.
26 - Ibid., May 8, 1844. The two men were arrested by the aldermen and held under bail of $1,000.

Heretofore we have been among those who have entered our solemn protest against any observations that would bear the slightest semblance of making the Native cause a religious one, or charging upon our adopted fellow citizens any other feeling than that of a mistaken opinion as to our views and their own rights. We hold back no longer. We are now free to declare that no terms whatever are to be held with those people.

Another St. Bartholomew's day is begun on the streets of Philadelphia. The bloody hand of the Pope has stretched itself forth for our destruction. We now call on our fellow citizens, who regard free institutions, whether they be native or adopted, to arm. Our liberties are now to be fought for, let us not be slack in our preparations.[27]

With these sentiments burning in their minds, native Americans assembled that afternoon in the State House yard. Orators tried to warn them against bloodshed and cautioned them to keep the peace, but their words were answered by cries of "No, No," from the crowd. A series of fiery resolutions were passed, asserting the right of peaceful assembly and charging the Papists with attempts to drive the Bible from the schools.[28]

Immediately following the meeting the natives banded together and marched through the streets to the scene of the first trouble in Kensington. Traversing the Irish section shouting insults against the Catholic and foreigner alike, the marchers met with gun fire from

27 - Ibid., May 7, 1844.
28 - Ibid., May 8, 1844.

one of the neighboring houses. One native was shot
dead by this first volley where upon the vengeance of
the mob knew no bounds. The Hibernia Hose house was
stormed and demolished; before midnight more than thirty houses belonging to Irishmen had been burned to the
ground. The tardy arrival of the military forces brought
the scene of carnage to a close.[29]

     The third day of rioting witnessed a culmina-
tion of all the feelings of hate which had been bred in
the prolonged period of disorder. Groups gathered on
the streets of Kensington early in the afternoon, shouting against the Pope, and demanding vengeance for the
natives who had been killed. They had organized into
well knit bands for the express purpose of demolishing
Irish homes. Whole rows of houses went up in flames.
The militia appeared but proved powerless to stop the
pillage. All over Kensington Protestant Irish and native Americans hurried to protect themselves from the
incendiaries by hanging large banners from their homes
with "Native American" painted thereon. Lacking these,
they hastily fastened a copy of the newspaper of that
name to their doors. The mob always stopped before such
a display to cheer.[30]

29 - New York Observer, May 11, 1844; Native American,
    May 8, 1844.
30 - Native American, May 9, 1844.

Progressing through the streets of Kensington and leaving a path of desolation behind them, the rioters finally came to Saint Michael's Catholic church. The rumor had spread through the crowd that the Catholics had concealed weapons within the walls of this building, and that suspicion was enough. While the presiding priest fled in disguise to protect his life[31] the mob attacked. Again the militia stood helplessly by while the faggot was applied and flames consumed the church and the seminary adjoining it.[32]

With their taste whetted, the rioters turned toward Saint Augustine's Church. A hurry call was dispatched for the mayor of the city, who had been neglecting his duties to celebrate the birthday of his daughter.[33] Arriving just in time, the mayor tried to quiet the milling mob, assuring them that the church contained no arms and that he himself had the key.[34] His words had an opposite effect from that intended. Confident now that

31 - "The Very Reverend T. J. Donaghoe," Records of the American Catholic Historical Society of Philadelphia, vol. xxiii, No. 2 (June, 1912), pp. 75-77. Donaghoe was pastor of the church at the time and only managed to escape after the mob had gathered about the building.
32 - Native American, May 9, 1844; New York Observer, May 11, 1844.
33 - "The Anti-Catholic Riots in Philadelphia in 1844," American Catholic Historical Researches, vol. xiii, No. 2 (April, 1896), p. 53. An account of the riots by a Catholic eye witness.
34 - Ibid., pp. 53-54.

the building was defenseless, the rioters brushed
past the mayor and the few militia-men who were
available, burst open its doors, and applied the
torch.[35] By ten o'clock that night another charred
and smoking ruin offered mute evidence of unbridled
hatred. Throughout the city priests and nuns trembled in fear of their lives and property[36] and Kensington was fast assuming the aspect of a war-torn
town as Irish refugees fled with their belongings.[37]

The burning of Saint Augustine's church
marked the peak of mob rule. Philadelphia awakened
on the morning of Thursday, May 9, sobered by a chorus of criticism resounding throughout the nation.
"We would give worlds," wrote the editor of the Spirit
of the Times, "to wipe off the foul blot from the dis-
graced name of our city."[38] Even the Native American
appeared in chastened form, declaring: "No terms that
we can use are able to express the deep reprobation
that we feel for this iniquitous proceeding, this wan-

35 - Native American, May 9, 1844.
36 - A letter written by Sister M. Gonzoga, a nun at a
Catholic orphan asylum in Philadelphia, at midnight on May 9, describes the tense situation
among the sisters and members of the clergy. It
is printed in the American Catholic Historical
Researches, vol. viii, No. 2 (April, 1891), pp.
89-90.
37 - "The Anti-Catholic Riots in Philadelphia in 1844,"
p. 52.
38 - "The Philadelphia Anti-Catholic Riots of 1844,"
American Catholic Historical Researches, n.s.,
vol. vii (July, 1911), pp. 231-233.

ton and uncalled for desecration of the Christian altar.[39]
On that afternoon thousands of citizens assembled in the
State House yard at the request of the mayor to consider
means of stopping the reign of terror. Resolutions were
adopted calling for the appointment of special peace officers in each ward, to patrol the streets armed and with
conspicuous badges in their hats. Sworn in immediately,
these men patrolled the streets all that night; although
in Kensington they were virtually deserted because thousands of Irish families had left the city in order to protect their lives and property.[40] Quiet thus descended
upon a mollified and suffering city.

　　　But feeling ran high in isolated instances.
On May 10 a group of natives were caught destroying tomb-
stones in a Catholic cemetery.[41] The following Sunday
all Catholic churches in the city remained closed at the
orders of the Bishop who feared further violence.[42] A
few days later most of the citizens were thrown into a
turmoil of excitement when mysterious signs were posted
over the city proclaiming: "Fortunio and his Seven Gifted
Servants." These dread words, taken to be a secret message from the Bishop to the Catholics telling them to arm

39 - Native American, May 9, 1844.
40 - Ibid., May 10, 1844.
41 - Ibid., May 11, 1844.
42 - "The Philadelphia Anti-Catholic Riots of 1844,"
　　　p. 231.

themselves and incite further bloodshed, were soon explained as the advertisements of a new drama being performed at the National theater.[43] Before this flurry abated an Irishman was seen purchasing a dray load of muskets, and clamorous natives stormed at the Mayor's door until the Irishman was hurried before the police and made to explain that his purchase was simply part of a commercial transaction.[44]

In this tense situation, more trouble was brewing. Members of the American Republican party might be ashamed of the church burning which had marked their sally into lawlessness, but the fact that the Kensington meeting had been fired on by Irish was a thing they could not forget. Party leaders in Philadelphia issued a lengthy address in which they set forth their stand. "The murderous assault on American citizens, the trampling under foot and tearing into shreds the American flag ... is the cause, the origin, of the whole trouble. Disgraceful as is the burning of the churches, fearful and appalling as is the act ... is it an outrage of a greater character than that which sends the souls of men without a moment's time for preparation to the bar of God's judgment? Let not the atrocity of the latter be forgotten in that of

43 - New York American Republican, May 13, 1844.
44 - Ibid., June 15, 1844.

the former, awful as it is."[45]

The party itself, and the press which supported it, worked constantly to bring this view before the people. A clamor was raised demanding that authorities investigate where Irish secured the guns they had used, and the rumor circulated that more were concealed in Catholic churches ready for another assault on the natives.[46] A concert artist was imported to give a series of performances for the benefit of the Kensington sufferers.[47] A ship was launched, built by American laborers in Kensington to commemorate the eight natives killed during the rioting.[48] The climax to these endeavors came on July 4, 1844, when a giant celebration was staged in the city. Seventy thousand persons took part in a procession in which were drawn carriages containing the widows and orphans of the natives who had fallen in the rioting.[49] As the parade passed through the streets it was showered with floral wreaths with sentiments attached, of which the following is typical:

45 - Native American, May 15, 1844.
46 - Ibid., May 28, 1844.
47 - Ibid., July 3, 1844. The concert singer was loudly advertised as an American born citizen and the editor of the Native American said of his efforts: "Had he been a foreigner, with a voice and style of singing he possesses, his fortune would have been made; but being a native he has spent his time singing his countrymen into office."
48 - Ibid., August 8, 1844. While the ship was launched at this time it had been built and exhibited more than a month before.
49 - Ibid., July 6, 1844.

With this wreath my most fervent wishes are given,
That you may be happy on earth and in heaven;
Then let me indulge in the delightful hope
That you will protect me from the rule of the Pope.[50]

Stirred by such activities, natives soon forgot the torrent of objection which their church burning had aroused, and again turned suspicious eyes upon the Irish. These apprehensions flared anew only a day after the Fourth of July celebration. On the morning of July 5 a group of Irish laborers attacked and demolished a number of tents erected by the Native Americans as accommodations for their celebration of the day before. Immediately new rumors spread over the city. One told of how these Irish had burned an American flag. Another, far more serious in its consequences, charged that Catholics had been seen carrying large quantities of arms and ammunition into the Church of Saint Philip de Neri in Southwark.[51]

Such a tale was sufficient to stir Philadelphia into action. By nightfall on July 5 a crowd had gathered before the church and it seemed that another flaming sacrifice would be added to the disgraceful total. The sheriff was hurriedly sent for; when he arrived the crowd demanded that he search the church for arms. Entering with a group

50 - Ibid., July 8, 1844.
51 - New York Observer, July 13, 1844; Native American, July 6, 1844.

of police, the sheriff returned a short time later with twelve muskets which he exhibited to the mob. A chorus of satisfaction went up, but still the rioters were not appeased. They had seen, they insisted, more arms than those carried into the church, and they demanded that a new searching party of twenty citizens be dispatched. Such a group was formed, and accompanied by the sheriff, made a thorough tour of the building. There they found seventy-five more muskets, together with a quantity of ammunition, supplies probably stored there by an ill advised pastor as a precautionary measure during the earlier church burnings. Wise counsel prevailed among the leaders of the searching party and they kept all knowledge of their find to themselves, fearing violence should the mob learn of the presence of the munitions. Disgruntled, the crowd about the church finally dispersed near midnight when the military forces arrived.[52]

By the following morning, news of the committee's find had leaked out and at nine o'clock a crowd gathered about the church. All that day they milled about, checked from violent action only by the presence of large forces of the militia who were ranged before

52 - The account of the riot is drawn from the New York Observer, July 13, 1844; New York American Republican, July 8, 1844; Native American, July 8, 1844; The New Englander, 1844, pp. 624-631.

the church doors. By night the mob had increased to
such an extent that the militiamen were ordered to fire
into them to prevent an attack. A prominent citizen,
Charles Naylor, protested this order before a volley
could be fired, and for his pains was promptly arrested
and clapped into the church, there to be held under the
guard of an Irish military company, the Hibernian Greens,
which had been assembled. Angry as was the mob at this
action, the order to fire had had its effect, and the
crowd broke up without further delay.[53]

Before leaving the scene, however, leaders of
the rioters issued an ultimatum that unless Naylor was
released by noon of the following day he would be taken
by force. When crowds began assembling on the next
morning, Sunday, July 7, they had prepared themselves
to carry out their threat. Two cannon were procured
from ships at the wharves, and at twelve o'clock these
were hauled before the doors of the church. Only wet
powder prevented their being fired. With the artillery
useless, the mob secured a log, and using this as a
battering ram broke down the doors of the church and
emerged in triumph with Naylor. But the presence of
the Hibernian Greens had been discovered and the rioters

53 - New York Observer, July 13, 1844; Native American,
     July 8, 1844.

now issued a new demand that unless that foreign military company were removed the church would be burned. Leaders of the forces for law and order realized the futility of combating such mob violence, and the military company was marched into the street. There it was attacked by the crowd, at least one member being killed.[54]

Returning to the church after this foray, the mob listened to speeches by Native American leaders pleading with them to disperse, but all to no avail. A side door was broken down and the rioters poured into the building, but they were prevented from doing serious damage by a large force of members of the American Republican party who had been placed there to guard it. Still not discouraged, the participants continued their stand and serious danger threatened as nightfall approached. A hurried call brought more military companies to the scene. These established themselves in full fashion with cannon trained on the principal avenues of approach.

While the church was thus being guarded, another military company on the way to the scene of the disorder ran afoul of a crowd of agitators. In the scuffle

54 - New York Observer, July 13, 1844; Native American, July 8, 1844.

that ensued the soldiers were ordered to fire; a volley
from their muskets broke up the mob but left seven citizens dead on the streets. When word of this spread
over the city, new crowds poured into the vicinity of
Saint Phillip de Neri's church, intent on revenge. A
cannon was procured, and fired point blank into the soldiers about the door, together with a volley of musket
fire. The military answered, and firing on both sides
continued for several hours. Not until another company
had been called out to capture the rioter's cannon was
peace restored in the war torn city.[55]

Sensing the hostility which had been aroused
against the military companies by the night's activity,
the mayor ordered them withdrawn early on the following
morning. While gangs raged through the streets of the
city all during the day no damage was done;[56] meanwhile
Catholic families were still leaving the city by the
thousand to escape mob fury.[57] The arrival of the governor of the state to plead for peace brought some order, but for days the streets were crowded with excited
men and women.[58] When Philadelphia took stock of its

55 - Native American, July 8, 1844; New York Observer,
     July 13, 1844.
56 - New York Observer, July 13, 1844.
57 - Native American, July 9, 1844.
58 - Ibid., July 9, 1844.

vindictive venture it found that thirteen citizens
had been killed and more than fifty wounded in the
three days of fighting.[59] It was a sober and chastened city which turned to the awful duty of burying
the victims of this lawless interlude.

But while Philadelphia publicly mourned
its dead and made open expiation for the fury of the
mob, beneath the surface the great mass of the citizens were secretly exultant. Another blow had been
struck at Popery, churches had been burned and Catholics driven from their homes. Substantial Quaker
merchants who spoke of the outrage in horrified words
in public, returned to their shops to express the pious
belief that "the Papists deserve all this and much more,"
and, "it were well if every Popish church in the world
were leveled with the ground."[60] Official inquiries
reflected this same spirit of intolerance. A committee
of investigation laid the blame for the riots entirely
on the Irish, who had broken up a peaceful meeting of
American citizens.[61] The Grand Jury's presentment,
brought in after the close of the first period of riot-

59 - Ibid., July 10, 1844.
60 - A Catholic working in Philadelphia at the time is
     responsible for this statement, having observed
     his Quaker employers, all substantial merchants,
     speak against the rioting in public and utter the
     quoted sentiments in private. "The Anti-Catholic
     Riots in Philadelphia in 1844," p. 51.
61 - New York American Republican, May 13, 1844.

ing, was even more outspoken. Entire blame for the
rioting, it found, rested upon "the efforts of a portion of the community to exclude the Bible from our
public schools. The Jury are of the opinion that these
efforts in some measure gave rise to the formation of
a new party, which called and held public meetings in
the district of Kensington, in the peaceful exercise of
the sacred rights and privileges guaranteed to every
citizen by the constitution and laws of our State and
Country. These meetings were rudely disturbed and fired
upon by a band of lawless, irresponsible men, some of
whom had resided in our country only for a short period.
This outrage caused the death of a number of our unoffend-
ing citizens, led to immediate retaliation, and was followed up by subsequent acts of aggression in violation
and open defiance of all law."[62]

A second Grand Jury reporting on the July riots
was just as outspoken in its harsh condemnation of the
Irish and its vindication of the native Americans. It
spoke of the earlier Kensington attack as a "murderous
outrage upon the constitutional rights of citizens;" of
how revenge was naturally sought after such foreign interference; of how the excuse for that blow came when
the Church of Saint Phillip de Neri was armed by the

62 - The presentment is printed in the Native American,
   June 17, 1844, and the New York American Republican,
   June 17, 1844.

priests.[63] Equal resentment resulted from efforts of
the city to pay for the churches which had been destroyed, a duty that should obviously be assumed under
the laws of the state.[64] All the chicanery of the law
was resorted to by stubborn nativists, and it was not
until many years later that Saint Augustine's church
was restored with public funds; Saint Michael's church,
lying beyond the official jurisdiction of the city, was
never paid for.[65] Aside from a permanent military force
stationed in the city,[66] Philadelphia gave no indication
of altering its anti-Catholic views in the future.

Meanwhile the excitement engendered by events
in the City of Brotherly Love had spread to other sections of the country. New York, where the American Republicans boasted even greater strength than in Philadelphia, became another hot bed of intolerance once the
example had been set by her sister city. Native Americans in New York were particularly ripe for trouble,
for one of their processions in Brooklyn had been at-

63 - Native American, August 5, 1844.
64 - Shea, History of the Catholic Church in the United
     States, vol. iv, p. 59.
65 - "The Anti-Catholic Riots in Philadelphia in 1844,"
     p. 64.
66 - New York Observer, July 20, 1844. The Philadelphia
     Common Council passed an ordinance for the organiza-
     tion of a permanent military force to be stationed
     in the city, to consist of one regiment of infan-
     try, one batallion of artillery and one or more
     troops of cavalry.

tacked by an Irish mob only a few days before fighting broke forth in Philadelphia.[67] When news of events in Kensington were hurled into this tense atmosphere by the New York American Republican under headlines which proclaimed, "The Voice of Blood,"[68] riot even more serious than that in Philadelphia might reasonably have been expected.

That New York remained outwardly calm during the period of strife can be ascribed to the vigorous efforts of Bishop John Hughes and to the quieting effect of the New York American Republican, whose editors cried constantly for peace.[69] Hughes took a firm attitude from the very start. He publicly declared that if "a single Catholic Church were burned in New York, the city would

---

67 - Native American, April 11, 1844. A Native American meeting in Brooklyn was attacked on April 9, with Irish throwing stones at the speakers. When the meeting adjourned the members marched away and past a Catholic church. Just as they had passed a mob of Irish rushed from the church and attacked the rear of the procession. The fight that followed lasted several hours although there was no serious bloodshed. The Irish attack was caused by the spread of a rumor that the Native Americans were going to burn the church.

68 - New York American Republican, May 9, 1844. The editor commented editorially on the riots: "Dependent and degraded FOREIGNERS who are not capable of appreciating the blessings they enjoy in a free country, have risen in arms against the native citizens. They have commenced the war of blood. Thank God, they are not yet strong enough to overcome us with brute force. There is yet time to stay the bloody hand of tyranny. A revolution has begun, 'Blood will have Blood.' It cannot sink into the earth and be forgotten. The gory vision will rise like the ghost of Banquo and call for revenge."

69 - Ibid., May 9, 1844; May 10, 1844.

become a second Moscow."[70] Upon the Catholics of Philadelphia he placed the blame for the trouble which had
ensued there. "They should have defended their churches,"
he wrote, "since the authorities could not or would not do
it for them. We might forbear from harming the intruder
in our house until the last, but his first violence to
our church should be promptly and decisively repelled."[71]
Such an attitude, belligerent as it was, was needed. Only
through open threat could bloodshed be averted in New York
in those troubled days.

As soon as news of the first assault on the Native American meeting in Kensington reached New York, members of that party there moved into action. A large meeting was held on the night of May 7, where those attending
listened to spirited speeches against Catholic aggressions
and passed resolutions appropriating awards for the conviction of the Irish rioters and determining to attend the
funerals of the American victims.[72] When the meeting adjourned it did so only after calling a great mass meeting
of all citizens of New York, to meet on the night of May 9
in Central Park, to consider any further action that should
be taken.

70 - Hassard, Life of John Hughes, p. 276.
71 - Ibid., p. 276.
72 - New York American Republican, May 8, 1844.

Bishop Hughes realized well the danger which might ensue from such an assembly. A delegation of Native Americans from Philadelphia was to arrive and be present, bearing the national flag which they alleged had been torn and trampled by the Irish at Kensington. Excitement stirred by this exhibition might very probably lead to rioting and possibly church burning in New York city. Hughes immediately sought out legal talent and inquired as to whether property destroyed by such a mob would be paid for by the state under New York law. He was told that no compensation was possible.[73] It was obvious to Hughes that Catholics must defend their own church property to save it from destruction. He rallied the members of his sect and stationed between one and two thousand men, armed as well as possible, about each church.[74] And he hurried from the press an extra edition of the Freeman's Journal to warn the city of his action and to place Catholic citizens on their guard. They were urged to defend their property at all costs, but to keep peace until the first blow had been struck. Especially were they told to stay away from the Central Park mass meeting or any other native meetings which

73 - Shea, History of the Catholic Church in the United States, vol. iv, p. 106.
74 - Hassard, Life of John Hughes, p. 276.

might be called.[75]

The American Republicans watched these preparations with resentment and fear. When Hughes had made his purpose clear a delegation from the party sought out Robert H. Morris, mayor of New York, and asked his advice and protection from the menacing foreigners. Morris agreed with them that only in one way could bloodshed be averted. On the afternoon of May 9, just before the meeting was to assemble, placards were posted over all the city announcing that it had been postponed.[76] Native Americans immediately issued statements explaining that due to the universal excitement among the people postponement was necessary in order to prevent rioting.[77] But to Bishop Hughes should go the well deserved credit for this truce.[78] Had the mass meeting been held and the turbulent feelings of New York Americans whipped to fever heat, bloodshed would most certainly have ensued. Hughes stated that the Irish had determined to set fire to the whole city if the natives attacked them, and they would probably have car-

75 - Ibid., pp. 277-278; Shea, History of the Catholic Church in the United States, vol. iv, p. 106.
76 - Shea, History of the Catholic Church in the United States, vol. iv, p. 106.
77 - New York American Republican, May 10, 1844.
78 - Hassard, Life of John Hughes, p. 278.

ried out their threat.[79]

Excitement brought on by the Philadelphia riots had not been confined to New York alone. In St. Louis news of the mob rule fanned Protestant passions until bloodshed was narrowly averted. Prejudice in St. Louis was centered against a Jesuit college and medical school operated there. Due to gross negligence, students and faculty members of the medical school had left several sections of human bodies lying about the college grounds. A crowd collected immediately, ready to believe the worst about Catholicism after the Philadelphia episode. Rumors spread that the Jesuits had established a branch of the

79 - Shea, History of the Catholic Church in the United States, vol. iv, p. 106. Catholic feelings were undoubtedly stirred to a high pitch by the prejudiced accounts of the Philadelphia rioting printed in the Freeman's Journal. A typical account, probably accurately quoted, in the Native American, shows the attitude: "The natives mustered in overwhelming force, and the Irishmen, now a mere handful, and worn out by the fatigues of the previous two days, offered no resistance but were shot down without mercy. Here and there someone with the courage of despair made a stand, but he too, after a little, was shot down; and it is sickening to read how such and such an Irishman, one named Rice for instance, after keeping a mob of his cowardly assailants at bay for nearly an hour, was finally shot through the back of the head by a native who stole around from the rear. One thing is now plain - that the promises of the authorities to protect the property of the Catholics is all moonshine! On such promises the Catholics of Philadelphia relied, and their churches and their houses were cooly destroyed without let or hinderance. The inference is clear. Let every man be prepared to defend himself and his property." Quoted in Native American, May 17, 1844.

Inquisition in St. Louis; that men and women were being
tortured and put to death, and that these remains represented the bloody products of their work. With this cry
raised about the city a mob was formed which rushed upon
the collge bent on burning it to the ground. Only an
armed force of Irish and sober minded Protestants who
surrounded the buildings for several hours, checked the
rioters and prevented the destruction of the school.[80]

But while the Philadelphia outburst had stirred
up interested in nativism, it had done little good and
untold harm to its cause. Bloodshed and rioting had followed in the wake of the American Republicans and their
cohorts; respectable citizens the country over shied from
a party which sanctioned mob rule. Nativists defended
their violence with enthusiasm. The first blow, they
averred, had not been struck by members of their own
ranks, but by Irish Papists. Americans had assembled
at Kensington only to feel the wrath of foreign blows.[81]

80 - O'Hanlon, Life and Scenery in Missouri, pp. 92-93.
     O'Hanlon was a priest in St. Louis at the time and
     an eye witness.
81 - New York American Republican, May 13, 1844; July 4,
     1844; July 16, 1844; New York Observer, July 20,
     1844; Native American, May 14, 1844; Proceedings
     of the Native American State Convention at Harris-
     burg, pp. 16-24; Pittsburg Chronicle, May 10, 1844,
     quoted in Native American, May 14, 1844. Accord-
     ing to the New York American Republican, May 13,
     1844, all New York papers with the exception of
     the Plebian, the Tribune, the Sun and the Freeman's
     Journal took the attitude that rioting had been
     caused by foreigners rather than native Americans.

"We love not riots," wrote one editor, "we abhor bloodshed, but it is idle to suppose that Americans can be
shot down on their own soil, under their own flag, while
in the quiet exercise of their constitutional privileges,
without a fearful retribution being exacted."[82]   Not only
had Catholics attacked natives at Kensington; they had
precipitated the later riots by arming their churches.
Nativistic publications recited the number of guns and
the amount of ammunition found in the Church of Saint
Phillip de Neri[83] and clamored before the governor of
Pennsylvania to investigate the source of these supplies.[84]   They stressed repeatedly that the entire trouble had been caused by a premeditated Irish attack, determined on years before when anti-Catholic activities
were begun, and designed to restore to Popery in America all the iniquity which it enjoyed in Europe.[85] Even

82 - New York American Republican, May 8, 1844.
83 - New York Observer, July 13, 1844; New York Journal
     of Commerce, quoted in Ibid., July 13, 1844.
84 - Native American, July 31, 1844. It was charged that
     the priest in charge of the church, the Reverend
     William H. Dunn, had organized an armed force to
     protect the Catholic property and had secured a
     permit from the governor of the state to purchase
     the arms found. The governor, David R. Porter, de-
     nied giving the permit, but a letter was produced
     by the priest in the governor's handwriting, which
     settled the blame on the executive in the eyes of
     the editors of the Native American at least.
85 - New York Observer, May 25, 1844; New York American
     Republican, May 8, 1844.

the halls of Congress were forced to listen to such
accusations when the spokesman of the American Republicans there, Lewis C. Levin, described the riots and
their causes before the nation. "Drilled bands of
foreign robbers," he shouted, "rushed with impetuous
fury upon native born Americans who carried no weapons
but what equal rights had given them. In the majesty
of freemen, they stood, armed only with moral power.
The element opposing them was physical force. It was
an imported element - an European weapon - one peculiar
only to the feudal institutions of the old world."[86]

Especially did members of the American Republican party insist that they had had no part in the
church burning and the property destruction which marked
the latter part of the mob rule on Philadelphia. They
had, they said, deplored such action from the start, and
they recounted tales of party members who stood within
the churches to battle the rioters who entered, striving
always to check bloodshed and pillage.[87] Taking this
attitude, the party tried constantly to keep alive the
memory of Kensington and to impress upon Americans that
fellow citizens had been shot down by the bullets of

86 - Congressional Globe, 29th Cong., 1st Sess., Appendix,
p. 49.
87 - New York American Republican, May 11, 1844; The New
Englander, 1844, p. 474.

foreign Papists. Shiffler, the first native to fall,
became a glorious martyr in their eyes, and litho-
graphs of his death were displayed in most of their
homes.[88] In 1845 and 1846 the anniversary of the Kensington riot was celebrated with elaborate ceremonies
in the very Market house where the first shots were
fired and before thousands who looked on and approved.[89]
"While this Republic retains a place among the nations
of the earth," declared a nativistic paper on May 6,
1846, "this day will remain enshrined in the hearts of
native Americans."[90]

        But such vain hopes were devoid of realization.
Americans remembered May 6, 1844, as a day to be torn
from their chronicles rather than venerated in song and
story. In vain did Native American's cry that the Philadelphia incident was another Papal plot to bring discredit upon the foes of Rome.[91] In vain Protestant societies insisted that their activities had had nothing
to do with the bloodshed and pillage.[92] Upon all of

88 - Native Eagle, November 3, 1846.
89 - Ibid., April 6, 1846.
90 - Ibid., May 6, 1846.
91 - Native American, May 15, 1844; New York American
     Republican, May 9, 1844; The Crisis, p. 76.
92 - Quarterly Review of the American Protestant Asso-
     ciation, January, 1845.

nativism had been fixed the stigma of mob rule; upon all
the forces of No-Popery lay the curse of popular disapproval.

The Philadelphia riots brought about a decline
in American nativism. Church members who had rushed to
the crusade throughout the early 1840's as suddenly deserted as they had enlisted. They were willing to bemoan
the presence of an anti-Christ among them, but like the
respectable citizens they were, they shied from mob rule
and civil bloodshed.

Meanwhile new forces had come into being which
were to eclipse the importance of Catholic aggression and
immigrant invasion in the minds of nativists. Manifest
destiny had created a crisis which was to supercede all
local ills. Only a few months after the mobs of Philadelphia had wrought their havoc Polk was carried into office with his cry for the "reannexation" of Texas and
Oregon. With Texas added to the Union, war with Mexico
was precipitated; a war from which the United States
emerged with more territory and a renewed problem of
slavery. For four years nativists sublimated their zeal
against Rome in sectional conflict. Not until the compromise of 1850 had settled for a time the burning issue
of slavery could nativism rise from its lethargy and enter national politics on the advancing wave of Know-

Nothingism.   Until that day the No-Popery crusade must

lapse.   Until that day nativism was a dormant force,

its strength expended, its cause forgotten.

APPENDIX A.

Constitutions of anti-Catholic Societies

Constitution of the American Society
for Promoting the
Principles of the Protestant Reformation[1]

Whereas, the principles of the court of Rome are totally irreconcilable with the Gospel of Christ; liberty of conscience; the rights of man; and with the constitution and laws of the United States of America, and whereas, the influence of Romanism is rapidly extending throughout this Republic, endangering the peace and freedom of our country, - therefore, being anxious to preserve the ascendancy of 'pure religion and undefiled' and to maintain and perpetuate the genuine truths of Protestantism unadulterated; with devout confidence in the sanction of the Great Head of the Church to aid our efforts in withstanding the 'power and great authority of the Beast, and the strong delusion of the False Prophet,' we do hereby agree to be governed by the following constitution:

I   This Society shall be called the American Society for Promoting the Principles of the Protestant Reformation.

II To act as a Home Missionary society - to diffuse correct information concerning the distinctions between

1 - From The Protestant Vindicator, June 24, 1840.

Protestantism and Popery - to arouse Protestants to a
proper sense of their duty in reference to the Romanists -
and to use all evangelical methods to convert the Papists
to Christianity by Lectures, and the dissemination of
suitable tracts and standard books upon the Romish controversy.

III Any person who subscribes to the principles of
this constitution, and who contributes in any way to the
funds of this Society, may be a member, and shall be entitled to vote at all public meetings.

IV The officers of this Society shall be a President,
Vice-President, a Treasurer, a Foreign Secretary, a Corresponding and a Recording Secretary, - all to be elected by
members of this Society.

V This Society shall annually elect an Executive
Committee of twenty gentlemen residing in New York City
and its vicinity, five of whom shall be a quorum to do
business, providing the President, or some one of the
officers be one of them present. They shall enact their
own by-laws, fill vacancies in their body, employ agents,
and fix their compensations, appropriate the funds, call
special meetings of the Society, and zealously endeavor
to accomplish the object of the institution.

VI Any Society or Association formed on the same
principle may become auxiliary to this Society; and the

officers of each auxiliary Association shall, <u>ex-officio</u>, be entitled to deliberate at all meetings of the Society, for the transaction of its affairs.

VII This constitution may be amended by a vote of two-thirds of all the members present at an Annual Meeting of the Society, which shall be held on the second Tuesday of May, and should it be prevented from taking place at that time, all the officers elected at the former meeting shall hold over until such meeting shall be duly called and held.

VIII Any person contributing the sum of twenty dollars, or more, to the funds of the Society, shall be constituted a Life Member; and those who have made donations or otherwise rendered imminent service to the cause, shall bo ontitled to honorary membership."

Constitution of the American Protestant Association[2]

Whereas, we believe the system of Popery to be, in its principles and tendency, subversive of civil and religious liberty and destructive to the spiritual welfare of men, we unite for the purpose of defending our Protestant interests against the great exertions now making to propagate that system in the United States; and adopt the follow-

2 - <u>Address of the Board of Managers of the American Protestant Association, with the Constitution and Organization of the Association</u>, pp. 7-8.

ing constitution: --

Article I. This Society shall be called the American Protestant Association.

Article II. The objects of its formation, and for the attainment of which its efforts shall be directed, are --

1. The Union and encouragement of Protestant ministers of the gospel, to give to their several congregations instruction on the differences between Protestism and Popery.

2. To call attention to the necessity of a more extensive distribution and thorough study of the Holy Scriptures.

3. The circulation of books and tracts adapted to give information on the various errors of Popery in their history, tendency and design.

4. To awaken the attention of the community to the dangers which threaten the liberties, and the public and domestic institutions, of these United States from the assaults of Romanism.

Article III. This Association shall be composed of all such persons as agree in adopting the purposes and principles of this constitution, and contribute to the funds by which it is supported.

Article IV. The officers of the Association shall be a President, three Vice-Presidents, a treasurer, a

corresponding secretary, a recording secretary, and
two lay directors from each denomination represented
in the Association, to be elected annually; together
with all the ministers belonging to it; who shall form
a Board for the transaction of business of whom any sev-
en, at a meeting duly convened, shall be a quorum, the
stated meetings of the Board to be quarterly.

Article V. The Board of Managers shall, at the first
meeting after their election, appoint an executive committee, consisting of a minister and a layman from each denomination represented in the Association, of which the secretaries and treasurer shall be ex-officio members. This
committee to meet as often as they may find necessary for
the transaction of the business committed to them, and to
report quarterly to the Board of Managers.

Article VI. The duties of the Board shall be, to carry
out in every way most expedient in their view, the ends and
purposes for which this Association was organized; and to
aid and encourage the formation of similar Associations in
the various parts of the United States; and to render an
annual report of their proceedings to the Association at
their annual meeting on the second Tuesday of November.

Article VII. The Board of Managers shall have power
to enact such by-laws as may not be inconsistent with this
constitution, and to fill all vacancies that may occur between the annual meetings.

Article VIII. This constitution shall be subject to amendments only at the annual meetings of the Association, by the vote of two thirds of the members present at such meeting.

Constitution of the American Protestant Society[3]

Whereas, the influence of Romanism is rapidly extending over this Republic, endangering the freedom and institutions of our country, by withholding the 'Word of God' from large masses of men, leaving them in ignorance and under the influence of superstition; and whereas we desire to secure the permanency of our free institutions, and through them the liberty of conscience, to maintain and perpetuate 'pure religion and undefiled,' and also to rescue from error and from sin those who are in spiritual darkness, we adopt the following

Constitution

Article I

As this society is of a national character, it shall be called 'The American Protestant Society.'

Article II

The object of this society is to diffuse throughout the United States the principles of the Protestant relig-

3 - From the Second Annual Report of the American Protestant Society, pp. 27-28.

ion, for the purposes of enlightening the minds of both
Protestants and Romanists respecting the doctrines and
duties revealed in the Word of God, and to diffuse correct information concerning the distinctions between Protestantism and Romanism.

Article III

Believing coercion in religious opinions, and the
spirit of enunciation, to be inconsistent with the spirit
of Christianity, the means to be employed to secure the
objects of the Society, are Light and Love; in the use
of these means the Society will aim to enlighten Protestants concerning the nature, operations and influence
of Romanism as well to guard against its encroachments
upon our civil and religious institutions, as to awaken
Christian feelings and Christian action for the salvation
of Romanists, by the employment of the press, lecturing
agents, missionaries and colporteurs, to circulate Bibles,
tracts and books upon the subject, - looking unto God for
success in this work.

Article IV

As it is a prominent object of this Society to diffuse correct information on the subject of Protestantism
and Romanism, the Society will moreover appoint a committee of literary gentlemen, who will receive donations of
books, and money for the purchase of books, in order that

a library may be collected, that shall embrace the standard works on these subjects that have been published by Protestant and Roman Catholic writers; which library shall be kept in connection with the depository of the Society, and be under the control of the executive committee, for the use of Protestant ministers of all denominations, and of literary gentlemen, who may desire to resort to it for purposes of reference.

Article V

The officers of the Society will be a President, Vice Presidents, Recording Secretary, a Corresponding and Foreign Secretaries and a Treasurer.

Article VI

The Society will annually elect an Executive Committee, to consist of at least twelve gentlemen, residing in New York, five of whom shall be a quorum for the transaction of business. The officers of the Society are ex-officio members of the Executive Committee. The Committee shall have power to fill their own vacacies, and to enact their own by-laws.

Article VII

The Executive Committee shall appoint the editor of the American Protestant; also committees on agencies, on the printing department, and on the various business of the Society.

Article VIII

Any Society or Association formed on the same principles, in any part of the United States, may become auxiliary to this Society.

Article IX

Any person who subscribes to this Constitution and contributes three dollars annually, may be a member of this Society, and be entitled to vote at all public meetings; a contribution of the sum of twenty-five dollars constitutes a life member, and fifty dollars a life director.

Article X

The annual meeting of the Society shall be the fourth Wednesday in April of each year, when this constitution may be altered by a vote of two-thirds of the members present.

APPENDIX B

Selections from Anti-Catholic Verse

Patrick's Purgatory[1]
or
Pope Leo in Search of the Undiscoverable

Pope Hannibal Jingo died the other day,

And the Mother of Harlots retains his clay,

But his soul, as the Popish legends tell,

Too bad for heaven and too good for hell,

Is raging about from story to story,

In search of a place called purgatory.

Now up and down, one way and another,

Like a sucking pig that has lost its mother;

He rambles and raves, and thrusts in his snout,

And cocks his dull ears with an air of doubt:

And is struck, as well he may, with surprise,

That he should not know where the region lies.

At length he met with a hovering ghost,

Tossed like himself from pillar to post,

For Erasmus, poor soul! when he left the light,

Being neither whole Papist nor Protestant quite,

By Papal Bull was condemned and driven,

To flit forever between hell and heaven.

Emerlina, Frauds of Papal Ecclesiastics, p. 98. The
same poem is also printed in the National Protestant
July, 1845.

Him did Pope Hannibal Leo accost,

Told him his mission and how he was crossed,

And begged if he knew, he would show him the way,

For it was most absurd for a Pope to stray;

"And if," quoth Infallible, "Entrance I win,

I'll reward your service by getting you in."

Erasmus replied that having no need,

He thanked him as much as if he did,

And said, "For two hundred and fifty years,

I have traveled the upper and lower spheres;

And have heard of no place that agrees with the story,

Excepting your old friend St. Patrick's Purgatory!"

"O Where," quoth the late Infallible, "Where,

Shall I find it, in earth, or heaven, or air?"

"In the Island of Saints, and the Land of Stingo,"

Said the Flying Dutchman to Pope Doctor Jingo.

So each made a bow and politely parted,

And Hannibal once more on his mission started.

Arrived at Lough Derg he looked round to discover,

Some waterman's shade to ferry him over,

But spying the ghost of the late Patrick McTool,

Confessed he was wandering like a ninny and fool,

And besought him as ever he hoped for glory,

To ferry him over to the Purgatory.

"In truth, Holy Father," said Pat, as low

He stooped to kiss the Infallible Toe,

"That's what I'm just groping about for myself;

For though it brought both of us in much pelf,

I'm afraid we know little or nothing about it,

And as for myself, I'm beginning to doubt it."

"Nay Nay," quoth Pope Leo, "That's heresay flat,"

"It would be on earth," replied Baltimore Pat;

"But here," and the Jesuit sighed as he spoke;

"We have got no tradition our falsehood to cloak;

Here truth appears truth, and without fear may be told;

For a lie has no credit - popes and priests no gold.

The Pilgrim's Legacy[2]

The Mayflower, on New England's coast, has furled her
                    tattered sail,

And through her chafed and moaning shrouds December
                    breezes wail,

Yet on that icy deck, Behold! A meek but dauntless band,

Who, for the right to worship God, have left their native
                    land;

And to a dreary wilderness, this glorious boon they bring,

A Church without a bishop, and a state without a king.

2 - From Cheever, Hierarchical Despotism, p. 64. This verse
     was set to music and was popular as a hymn sung at the
     opening of anti-Catholic lectures. It was also sold
     widely for use in churches and the home. New York Ob-
     server, February 17, 1844.

Then prince and prelate, hope no more to bend them to
        your sway,
Devotion's fire enflames their breasts, and freedom
        points the way,
And in their brave heart's estimate, 'twere better not
        to be,
Then quail beneath a despot where a soul cannot be free;
And therefore o'er the wintry wave, those exiles come to
        bring
A church without a bishop and a state without a king.

And still their spirit, in their sons, with freedom walks
        abroad,
The BIBLE is our only creed, our only monarch, God!
The hand is raised - the word is spoke - the solemn pledge
        is given
And boldly on our banner floats, in the free air of heaven,
The motto of our sainted sires, and loud we'll make it ring,
A church without a bishop and a state without a king.

        The Pope a Blasphemer[3]
      The Pope pretends to have the keys
      Of earth and hell and heaven:
      Affirms that power over these
      To him is amply given.

3 - From the Protestant Vindicator, April 14, 1841.

Power to rule - to damn - to save!

Three words being subject to one knave!

Oh! Pope! If ever blasphemy

Were found in man - 'Tis found in thee.

The Repenting Sinners Song to the Priest at the Discharge of his Duty[4]

Come all ye sons of men, a mystery behold;

Can worship of the eternal God be priced or bought with
> gold?

When worship doth approach, then lucre hath not ceased,

But money passeth round the room to the pocket of the
> priest.

In words he craves but small; in honor he is held;

Deceitful soul, we've found him out, he never can be
> filled.

And now, you holy priests, with all your sacred throng;

Come forth before the sinful world, that you may hear the
> song.

Can you go in the fold, by Christ, who is the door?

And preach to us God's sacred word and steal and play the
> whore?

I say, ye holy priests, can you such deeds maintain,

And preach the gospel of the world and sell the same for
> gain?

4 - Waterous, The Battle Axe or Weapons of War, p. 73.
The poem contains a number of verses in a similar
vein.

Ye're base, like Sodom's sons, whose luxury you require;

And shall you not be punished with that same eternal fire?

Your snare is laid so deep to catch the soul of man,

That none but God's eternal eye can see your horrid plan.

And none can make it known but God who dwells aloft;

He shall disclose your dismal snares and rend your fetters

off

Ye're snakes within the grass, the world shall see full

well,

When God shall break your covenant, with devils and with

hell.

Carrier's Poem of the
Protestant Vindicator[5]

If by the fruit we know the tree,

The curse of Rome we here may see;

Apart from all her monstrous tricks,

Her sin-compelling bits of sticks!

Her Savior murdered now afresh,

When sinners crave his blood and flesh!

Her incense smoke - and juggling bells;

Her nods and signs and miracles!

Her grim bastiles, her reeking shrines,

5 - From the Protestant Vindicator, January 20, 1841. A
lengthy "Carrier's Address" was printed at the start
of each year, usually devoted entirely to bitter words
against Catholicism.

Her nurseries for concubines!

Her purgatorial fires, so sure,

To save the rich - and burn the poor!

And all her other things of fame,

The Romish anti-Christ may claim.

We've Conquered America[6]

Lo! O'er America's beautiful soil

Is scattered the legion who gathers the spoil;

The scorned and degraded of Europe's high powers

Their land have deserted to desecrate ours.

They came o'er the foam of the wild sweeping sea,

To darken the land, the bright land of the free,

And with soul-galling shackles of bigotry bind

The noble, the God-like, the Glorious mind.

O Sons of America, list to the cry!

The loud fearful warning that rings in the sky;

Will ye bend to the yoke of bondage so vile?

Shall idols your altars most sacred defile?

Arouse ye, arouse ye, O men of the North!

Let the south send her champions fearlessly forth,

And the east and the west, let them gird on the sword,

And away to the strife in the might of the Lord.

6 - From the National Protestant, May, 1845.

The Priest Outwitted [7]

A parent asked a priest his child to bless,
The priest then told the child he must confess.
"Well," said the boy, "Suppose that I am willing,
What is your charge?" "To you 'tis but a shilling."
"Do all men pay and all men make confession?"
"Yes, every man of Catholic profession."
"To whom do you confess, sir?" "Why, the dean,
And pay him smartly, too; a whole thirteen."
"Do deans confess, sir priest?" "Yes boy, they do,
And pay the bishop dearly for it, too."
"Do bishops so confess? Well then, to whom?"
"Why, they confess and pay the church of Rome."
"Well," said the boy," all this is mighty odd,
And does the Pope confess?" "Ah yes, to God."
"And does God charge the Pope?" "No," quoth the priest,
"God charges nothing." "Why, then, God is best.
God can forgive, and he is always willing,
To him I will confess (through Christ) and save my
shilling."

---

7 - From the Christian Advocate and Journal of Commerce,
quoted in the Protestant Vindicator, August 19, 1840.

BIBLIOGRAPHY

Manuscript materials concerning the origins
of nativism in the United States in the period before
the Civil war was almost entirely lacking. Men carried
away to emotional enthusiasm against the Catholic or
immigrant usually regretted their intolerance in later
life and destroyed any written records which might con-
nect them with the nativistic movement. This factor,
combined with the brief life and transitory nature of
the anti-Catholic societies and parties, has resulted
in the dearth. Both the nativistic parties and societies can be known only from the published records that
they left behind them.

With such manuscript unavailable, principal
reliance in this study has been placed upon newspapers,
magazines and contemporary books and pamphlets. The
religious press has been of special value in tracing
the rise of nativism, for the interest in the anti-
Catholic movement manifest by the churches was reflected in their publications. Church newspapers and
magazines, as a result, devoted far more space to the
activities of anti-Catholic societies and agitators
than the secular press. Secular papers have also been
employed, however, in an effort to offset the over-en-

thusiasm of the religious newspapers.

Equally important in the growth of a nativistic spirit at that time were the propaganda
books against Catholicism. All of the books and
pamphlets of this nature known to have been published in the United States between 1800 and 1844
are listed in this biliography. Even more important in providing information about the whole movement were the avowedly anti-Catholic newspapers and
magazines, files having been used covering virtually
the entire period treated.

PRIMARY SOURCES

Reports of Societies

American Education Society, Annual Reports. Andover,
1816-1817; Boston, 1818-1845.

American Home Missionary Society, Reports ... Presented by the Executive Committee. New York,
1827-1845.

American Protestant Association, Address of the Board
of Managers of the American Protestant Association,
with the Constitution and Organization of the Association. Philadelphia, 1843.

American Protestant Association, First Annual Report of

the American Protestant Association, together with a Sketch of the Addresses at the First Anniversary, November 18, 1843. Philadelphia, 1844.

American Protestant Society, Annual Reports. New York, 1844-1849.

American Protestant Society, Circular Issued by the American Protestant Society, December, 1847. New York, 1847.

American Tract Society, Annual Reports. Boston, 1815-1845.

Annales de l'Association de la Propagation de la Foi, recueil Periodique des lettres des eveques et des missionaires des missions des deux mondes, et de tous les documens relatifs aux missions et a l'Association de la Propagation de la Foi. Paris et Lyons, 1827-1845.

Boston Ladies Association for Evangelizing the West, Annual Report for 1844. Boston, 1844.

Boston Society for the Prevention of Pauperism, Annual Reports. Boston, 1836-1844.

Society for the Promotion of Collegiate and Theological Education at the West, Annual Reports. New York, 1844-1845.

Ladies Society for the Promotion of Education at the West, History of the Formation of the Ladies Society for the Promotion of Education at the West; with Two

Addresses, Delivered at its Organization, by the
Rev. Edward Beecher, D. D., and the Rev. E. N.
Kirk. Boston, 1846.

Ladies Society for the Promotion of Education at the
West, Annual Reports. Boston, 1847-1851.

Trustees of the Public School Society of New York,
Annual Reports. New York, 1835-1842.

Newspapers

The Agis-Yeoman (Worcester, Massachusetts), April 24-
December 25, 1833.

The American Protestant Vindicator and Defender of Civil
and Religious Liberty against the Inroads of Popery
(New York, New York) October 14, 1835-January 5,
1836; June 24, 1840-June 1, 1842.

Boston Atlas (Boston, Massachusetts) January-June, 1831.

Boston Observer and Religious Intelligencer (Boston, Massachusetts) January 1-June 25, 1835.

Boston Courier (Boston, Massachusetts), 1831.

The Downfall of Babylon, or the Triumph of Truth over
Popery (Philadelphia and New York) August 14, 1834-
November 12, 1836. The paper was published between
August, 1834 and July, 1837.

The Jesuit (Boston, Massachusetts), September-December,
1829. One of the more violent Catholic newspapers.

<u>Massachusetts Spy</u> (Worcester, Massachusetts), 1820-1830, 1833, 1837.

<u>Massachusetts Yeoman</u> (Worcester, Massachusetts), September 1, 1824-August 24, 1835; 1826-1831.

<u>National Agis</u> (Worcester, Massachusetts), January, 1831-April, 1833.

<u>The Native American</u> (Philadelphia, Pennsylvania), April 11, 1844-November 30, 1844. A daily paper and organ of the American Republican party.

<u>The Native Eagle and American Advocate</u> (Philadelphia, Pennsylvania), December 1, 1845-December, 1846. A daily paper and organ of the Native American Party.

<u>The New York American Republican</u> (New York, New York), April 24, 1844-October 15, 1844. A daily newspaper published as the organ of the American Republican party.

<u>The New York Journal of Commerce</u> (New York, New York), January 1, 1835-December, 1845. A daily Whig paper showing strong nativistic leanings.

<u>The New York Observer</u> (New York, New York), 1823-1850. Rich in material.

<u>The New York Tribune</u> (New York, New York), April 10, 1841-January 5, 1842.

<u>Priestcraft Exposed</u> (Concord, New Hampshire), April 1, 1834-October 1, 1834. A small bi-monthly paper.

Priestcraft Unmasked (New York, New York), January 1,
    1830-November 15, 1830. Published bi-monthly.

The Protestant (New York, New York), December 18, 1830-
    March 31, 1832. First of the anti-Catholic news-
    papers. Publication was begun on January 2, 1830.

The Watchman of the South (Richmond, Virginia), January,
    1840-December, 1841. A weekly Presbyterian paper,
    violently nativistic.

The Weekly American Republican (New York, New York), 1844.
    The weekly edition of the New York American Republican.

The Spirit of '76 (New York, New York), July 29, 1835 -
    October 6, 1835. A daily paper, and the first of
    the nativistic political papers.

Magazines

The American Protestant Magazine (New York, New York), June,
    1845-December, 1849. A monthly magazine, official or-
    gan of the American Protestant Society.

American Quarterly Review (Philadelphia, Pennsylvania),
    1831-1835.

The American Republican Magazine (New York, New York), 1844.
    An organ of the American Republican Party. The first
    issue appeared in October, 1844.

The Baltimore Literary and Religious Magazine (Baltimore,
    Maryland), January, 1838-December, 1841. Filled with

bitter theological attacks on Catholicism.   The
first issue appeared in January, 1835.   Super-
ceded by Spirit of the XIX Century.

Biblical Repertory and Theological Review (New York,
New York), 1825-1840.

Brownson's Quarterly Review (Boston, Massachusetts),
1844-1845.   A Catholic quarterly.

The Christian Review (Boston, Massachusetts), 1836-1837.

The Christian Spectator (New York, New York), 1835.   A
quarterly publication.

Methodist Magazine and Quarterly Review (New York, New
York), 1830-1833.

The Home Missionary (New York, New York), 1828-1844.
Organ of the American Home Missionary Society.

The National Protestant (New York, New York), December,
1844-September, 1846).   The name was changed in
January, 1846, to The National Protestant Magazine
or the Anti-Jesuit.   One of the most violent anti-
Catholic publications.   Absorbed in 1847 by the
American Protestant Magazine.

The New England Magazine (Boston, Massachusetts), 1834-
1835.

The New Englander (New Haven, Connecticut), January,
1844-December, 1845.

Niles' Register (Philadelphia, Pennsylvania), September,

1819-December, 1845. Contains much information
on the more open phases of the anti-Catholic
movement.

The North American Protestant Magazine or the Anti-
Jesuit (New York, New York), April, 1846. The
magazine appeared as a monthly between April,
1846 and 1847 when it was absorbed by the American Protestant Magazine.

The Protestant Episcopalian and Church Register (Philadelphia, Pennsylvania), January, 1830-August,
1833. A monthly magazine containing many attacks
on Catholicism.

The Protestant Magazine (New York, New York), September,
1833-August, 1834. First of the anti-Catholic magazines in the United States.

The Quarterly Review of the American Protestant Associa-
tion (Philadelphia, Pennsylvania), January, 1844-
October, 1845. Organ of the American Protestant
Association. Absorbed in 1845 by the American
Protestant Magazine.

The Spirit of the XIX Century (Baltimore, Maryland),
January, 1842-December, 1843. Largely anti-Catholic in contents, devoting most of its space to
theological arguments. Failed in 1843.

Publications of Nativistic Parties

Address of the American Republicans of the City of
Philadelphia to the Native and Naturalized Citizens of the United States. Philadelphia, 1844.

Address of the Delegates of the Native American Na-
tional Convention assembled at Philadelphia,
July 4, 1845, to the Citizens of the United
States. Philadelphia, 1845.

Address of the Executive Committee of the American
Republicans of Boston to the People of Massachusetts. Boston, 1845.

Address of the Louisiana Native American Association.
New Orleans, 1839.

Address to the People of the State of New York by the
General Executive Committee of the American Re-
publican Party of the City of New York. New
York, 1844.

Proceedings of the Native American State Convention
Held at Harrisburg, February 22, 1845. Philadelphia, 1845.

Anti-Catholic Books

Abbott, John S. C., Sermon on the Duties and Dangers of
the Clergy and the Church. Boston, 1842. A sermon

by a Nantucket Congregationalist against Catholicism.

Bacon, T. S., <u>Both Sides of the Controversy Between the
Roman and the Reformed Church</u>. New York, ------.

Baird, Robert, <u>The Life of Ramon Monsalvatge, a Converted
Spanish Monk, of the Order of the Capuchins</u>. New
York, 1845. A romantic novel depicting Catholicism
in Spain.

Balch, William S., <u>Romanism and Republicanism Incompatible</u>.
----------.

Barnett, D., <u>Truth and Error Contrasted, Wherein the Great
Apostacy as Prefigured in Cain, Baloom and Korah is
Pointed Out</u>. Dublin, 1836. A theological argument
widely circulated in the United States.

Barrow, George, <u>The Bible in Spain</u>. New York, 1847. The
author was agent for the American Bible Society.

Barrow, Isaac, <u>The Pope's Supremacy</u>. New York, 1845.
A book of documents designed to show that the Popes
exercised temporal power all through the ages and
in the present.

Bassiere, Peter, <u>Conversion of Peter Bassiere from the
Romish Church to the Protestant Faith, in a Letter
to his Children</u>. New York, 1833.

Baxter, Richard, <u>Jesuit Juggling; or, Forty Popish Frauds
Detected and Disclosed</u>. New York, 1834.

Beecher, Lyman, <u>A Plea for the West</u>. Cincinnati, 1835.

A sermon given by Dr. Beecher all over the United States.

Bennett, William J. E., Lecture Sermons on the Distinctive Errors of Romanism. London, 1842. A collection of sermons against Catholicism preached at Portman chapel during 1842.

Berg, Joseph F., The Confessional; or, an Exposition of the Doctrine of Auricular Confession as Taught in the Standards of the Roman Church. 3d ed., New York, 1841.

----------------, The Great Apostacy Identified with Papal Rome; or, an Exposition of the Mystery of Iniquity and the Marks and Doom of Anti-Christ. Philadelphia, 1847.

----------------, Lectures on Romanism. Philadelphia, 1840. A series of sermons given at the author's church, the Second Reformed Protestant Church in Philadelphia.

----------------, Mysteries of the Inquisition. Philadelphia, 1846.

----------------, Oral Controversy with a Catholic Priest. Philadelphia, 1843.

----------------, A Synopsis of the Moral Philosophy of Peter Dens as Prepared for the Use of Romish Seminaries and Students of Theology. New York, 1841.

Breckinridge, Robert J., Papism in the United States in the Nineteenth Century. Baltimore, 184-.

Brownell, Thomas C., <u>Errors of the Times. A Charge
Delivered to the Clergy of the Diocese of Connecticut at the Annual Convention, holden in Christ
Church, in the city of Hartford, June 13, 1843.</u>
Hartford, 1843. A charge by the Bishop of the
diocese warning the clergy against Catholicism
and Oxfordism.

Browning, W. S., <u>A History of the Huguenots.</u> Philadelphia, 1845. A description of the cruelty and persecuting spirit of the Catholic church.

Brownlee, William Craig, <u>The Doctrinal Decrees and Canons
of the Council of Trent, Translated from an Edition
Printed at Rome in 1564.</u> New York, 1842. Contains
an introduction and notes by Dr. Brownlee.

---------------------, <u>Popery.</u> New York, 1836.

-----------------, <u>Popery an Enemy to Civil and Religious
Liberty and Dangerous to our Republic.</u> 4th ed.,
New York, 1840.

-----------------, <u>The Religion of the Ancient Irish and
Britons not Roman Catholic and the Immortal Saint
Patrick Vindicated from the False Charge of being a
Papist.</u> 2nd ed., New York, 1841.

-----------------, <u>The Roman Catholic Religion viewed in
the Light of Prophecy and History; its Final Downfall and the Triumph of the Church of Christ.</u> New
York, 1844.

--------------------, editor. <u>The Secret Instructions</u>
<u>of the Jesuits: Faithfully Translated from the</u>
<u>Latin of an old Genuine London Copy</u>. New York,
1841. Printed with the Latin and English in
parallel columns.

--------------------, <u>Sketch of the History of the West-</u>
<u>ern Apostolic Churches from which the Roman Church</u>
<u>Apostatized</u>. New York, 184-.

--------------------, <u>The Whigs of Scotland</u>. New York,
1839. A description of Catholic persecutions.

Campbell, J. N., <u>Papal Rome Identified with the Great</u>
<u>Apostacy Predicted in the Scriptures</u>. <u>The Sub-</u>
<u>stance of Three Discourses Addressed to the First</u>
<u>Presbyterian Church of Albany</u>. Albany, 1838.

Campbell, James M., <u>The Protestant Girl in a French</u>
<u>Nunnery; or, the School Girl in France</u>. New York,
1845. An anti-Catholic novel popular in England
and reprinted in the United States.

Carroll, Anna E., <u>The Great American Battle; or, the</u>
<u>Contest Between Christianity and Political Romanism</u>.
New York, 1856. A contemporary account giving something of the history of the nativistic parties, as
well as serving as an instrument of propaganda.

Carter, Thomas, <u>Sketches of Remarkable Conversions and</u>
<u>other Events among French Romanists in the City of</u>
<u>Detroit</u>. New York, -----.

Cheever, George B., The Hierarchical Despotism; Lectures on the Mixture of Civil and Ecclesiastical Power in the Governments of the Middle Ages in Illustration of the Nature and Progress of the Romish Church. New York, 1844. A learned work, written in answer to a sermon by Bishop Hughes of New York.

Chillingworth, W., The Works of W. Chillingworth, A. M., Containing his Book Entitled, The Religion of Protestants a Safe Way to Salvation, together with his Sermons, Letters, Discourses and Controversies. Philadelphia, 1840. The first American reprinting of a famous English anti-Catholic work.

Colton, Walter, A Reply to the Allegations and Complaints Contained in Bishop Kenrick's Letter to the Board of Controllers of the Public Schools. Philadelphia, 1844. An attack on Catholics for trying to prohibit Bible reading in the Philadelphia schools.

Connelly, Pierce, The Coming Struggle with Rome, not Religious but Political; or, Words of Warning to the English People. London, -----. One of the works inspired by the Catholic Emancipation bill.

----------------, Domestic Emancipation from Roman Rule. A Petition to the Honourable House of Commons, from the Reverend Pierce Connelly. London, -----.

Cotter, J. R., The Mass and Rubrics of the Roman Catholic Church Translated into English. New York, 1845. Designed to show the mass opposed to the will of God and the practices of the early church.

Coustos, John, The Mysteries of Popery Unveiled in the Unparalleled Sufferings of John Coustos, at the Inquisition of Lisbon, to which is Added, the Origin of the Inquisition and its Establishment in Various Countries; and the Master Key to Popery by Anthony Gavin. Hartford, 1821.

Cramp, J. M., A Text Book of Popery. New York, 1832.

Cross, Andrew B., Priest's Prisons for Women. Baltimore, -----.

Crowell, John, Republics Established and Thrones Overturned by the Bible. Philadelphia, 1849. Shows that Catholicism, by opposing the Bible, opposes republicanism.

Culbertson, Rosamond, Rosamond; or, a Narrative of the Captivity and Sufferings of an American Female under the Popish Priests in the Island of Cuba, with a Full Disclosure of their Manners and Customs, written by herself. New York, 1836.

D'Aubigne, J. H. Merle, History of the Great Reformation in the Sixteenth Century. 4 vols. New York, 1846. A bitterly anti-Catholic history which was widely read.

Daunou, Pierre C. F., <u>Outlines of a History of the Court</u>
<u>of Rome and of the Temporal Power of the Popes</u>.
Philadelphia, 1837. An argument based on history
and Scripture against all temporal power.

Day, Samuel P., <u>Monastic Institutions; their Origin,</u>
<u>Progress, Nature and Tendency</u>. Dublin, 1844. A
book written to expose the inquity of the Catholic
monastic orders.

Dowling, John, <u>The Burning of the Bibles</u>. Philadelphia,
1843. A description of the Champlain Bible burning
and an attack on Catholicism, with an introduction
by W. C. Brownlee.

Dowling, John, <u>The History of Romanism</u>, ----------. One
of the most quoted books of the period.

Dwight, Theodore, <u>Open Convents; or, Nunneries and Popish</u>
<u>Seminaries Dangerous to the Morals and Degrading to</u>
<u>the Character of a Republican Community</u>. New York,
1836.

Elizabeth, Charlotte, <u>Alice Benden; or, the Bowed Shilling</u>
<u>and other Tales</u>. New York, 1841. Author's real name
was Charlotte Elizabeth Tonna. This work dwells especially on Catholic persecution in England under
Queen Mary.

--------------------, <u>The Church Visible in all Ages</u>, New
York, 1845.

--------------------, <u>Dangers and Duties</u>. New York,1841.

--------------------, <u>The English Martyrology, Abridged</u>
<u>from Fox</u>. 2 vols., Philadelphia, 1843.

--------------------, <u>Falsehood and Truth</u>. New York,
1842. One of the author's usual novel's for children, filled with long Biblical arguments against
Catholicism.

--------------------, <u>Glimpses of the Past; or, the Museum</u>.
New York, 1841. A group of children visit a museum
and their mother entertains them with a comparison
of the idolatry of Indians with the idolatry of
Catholicism.

--------------------, <u>The Happy Mute</u>. Boston, 1842. The
author tells of her experience in converting a half
witted mute to Protestantism.

--------------------, <u>The Protestant Annual</u>. London, 1841.

--------------------, <u>Ridley, Latimer, Cranmer and Other</u>
<u>English Martyrs</u>. New York, 1844. A discussion of
Catholic persecution.

--------------------, <u>Second Causes; or, Up and be Doing</u>.
New York, 1843. A pious tract arguing that Christians should unite to drive Popery from the world.

--------------------, <u>The Siege of Derry; or, Sufferings</u>
<u>of the Protestants: A Tale of the Revolution</u>. New
York, 1844.

--------------------, War with the Saints; or, the Persecutions of the Vaudois under Pope Innocent III.
New York, 1848.

Ellis, B. F., A History of the Romish Inquisition Compiled from Various Authors. Hanover, Indiana, 1835.

Emerlina, G. D., Frauds of Papal Ecclesiastics; to which
are Added Illustrative Notes from Letters by Gilbert
Burnet and Gavin's Master Key to Popery. New York,
1835. Published first in 1691. Told in the form
of a journal of the author as a priest before he
left the church.

England, John and Richard Fuller, Letters Concerning the
Roman Chancery. Baltimore, 1836.

Feber, George S., The Difficulties of Romanism. New York,
1840.

Feijo, Diego Antonio, Demonstration of the Necessity of
Abolishing a Constrained Clerical Celibacy; Exhib-
iting the Evils of the Institution and the Remedy.
Philadelphia, 1844. The author was the Bishop of
Brazil.

Fleming, Robert, Extraordinary Discourse on the Rise and
Fall of the Papacy, Containing Predictions respecting
the Revolutions in France and the Fate of its Monarch.
New York, 1848. Originally printed in England in 1701.

Fulton, Justin D., The Jesuit as Master; President and Premier as Slaves. Boston, -----.

Gavin, Anthony, A Master Key to Popery. 3d ed., London, 1773. The author was a Spanish priest. His lurid account was to be reprinted frequently in the United States.

----------------------, A Master Key to Popery, Giving a Full Account of all the Customs of the Priests and Friars and the Rites and Ceremonies of the Popish Religion. New York, 1812.

----------------------, The Master Key to Popery: Customs of Priests and Friars and Rites and Ceremonies of the Popish Religion, Inquisition, etc. Cincinnati, 1834.

Giustiniani, L., Papal Rome as it is, by a Roman. 2nd ed., Baltimore, 1843. The author boasted of being "late a Popish priest," and had become a Lutheran minister. The book contains an introduction by W. C. Brownlee.

Gonzalves, M. J., Persecutions in Madeira in the Nineteenth Century. New York, 1845. A description of Catholic persecution on the island.

Griswald, Alexander, The Reformation; a Brief Exposition of some of the Errors and Corruptions of the Church of Rome. Boston, 1843. The author was Episcopalian bishop of the Eastern Diocese.

Hardy, Philip D., <u>The Holy Wells of Ireland</u>. London,
1841. An attack on Catholic penances in Ireland.

Hazel, Harry, <u>The Nun of Saint Ursula; or, the Burning
of the Convent: a Romance of Mount Benedict</u>.
Boston, 1845. An anti-Catholic novel built about
the Charlestown convent burning.

Hobart, John Henry, <u>The Principles of the Churchmen
Stated and Explained, in Distinction from the Corruptions of the Church of Rome, and from the Errors
of Certain Protestant Sects</u>. New York, 1837. The
author was the Episcopal Bishop of New York.

Hogan, William, <u>Auricular Confession and Popish Nunneries</u>.
Boston, 1845. Attacks all practices of Catholic
church but is largely concerned with the confessional.

———————————————, <u>High and Low Mass in the Catholic
Church, with Comments</u>. Boston, 1846. Presents
Latin and English copies of the mass with copious
critical notes.

———————————————, <u>Synopsis of Popery, as it Was and
as it Is</u>. Hartford, 1845.

Hopkins, John Henry, <u>The Church of Rome in her Primitive
Purity Compared with the Church of Rome of the Present Day</u>. New York, 1835. The author was the Episcopal Bishop of Vermont.

———————————————, <u>An Humble Address to the Bishops</u>,

Clergy and Laity of the Protestant Episcopal
Church in the United States on the Tolerating
among our Ministry of the Doctrines of the Church
of Rome. ----------. A book inspired by the Oxford movement.

------------------, The Novelties which Disturb our
Peace: Four Letters Addressed to the Bishops,
Clergy and Laity of the Protestant Episcopal
Church in the United States. Philadelphia, 1844.
Devoted to an attack on the Catholic doctrine
of the Eucharist and the attitude of the Oxford
Reformers to it.

Horne, Thomas, A Protestant Memorial. New York, 1844.
A theological attack on Catholic doctrines, reprinted from an English edition.

------------------, Romanism Contradictory to the Bible.
New York, 1833.

Horner, J., Popery Stripped of its Garb. New York, 1836.

Howitt, William, A History of Priestcraft in all Ages
and Nations. New York, 1833. An attack on all
priests, but particularly those of the Catholic
church.

Hughes, John and John Breckinridge, Controversy between
Rev. Messrs. Hughes and Breckinridge on the Subject:
Is the Protestant Religion the Religion of Christ?"

Philadelphia, 1833. A printed account of the discussion held by these two champions.

Hughes, John and John Breckinridge, A Discussion of the Question: Is the Roman Catholic Religion, in any or in all its Principles or Doctrines, Inimical to Civil or Religious Liberty? Philadelphia, 1836. A similar published account of a later discussion.

Janeway, J. J., Antidote to the Poison of Popery. New York, --------.

Junkin, George, The Great Apostacy; a Sermon on Romanism. Philadelphia, ----------.

Kalley, Robert R., Persecution in Madeira in the Nineteenth Century; Being an Exposition of Facts. New York, 1845. The author was a clergyman who wrote from first hand information.

Kurtz, B., and J. C. Morris, The Year Book of the Reformation. New York, 1844.

Lathbury, Thomas, The State of Popery and Jesuitism in England from the Reformation to the Period of the Roman Catholic Relief Bill in 1829. London, 1841.

Lester, Charles E., The Jesuits. New York, 1845. A book exposing the errors of this group by quotations from their works.

Mahoney, S. I., Six Years in the Monasteries of Italy. Boston, 1845.

Malan, Caeser, Can I Join the Church of Rome while
my Rule of Faith is in the Bible? An Inquiry
Presented to the Conscience of the Christian
Reader. New York, 1844.

Marx, J., History of the Rome of Jesus Christ, Pre-
served in the Cathedral at Treves. New York,
1845. An attack on Catholic miracles.

Mason, Cyrus, A History of the Holy Catholic Inquisition. Philadelphia, 1835. A history of the Inquisition and a warning that it may be established
in America.

McCrindell, R., The English Governess. New York, 1844.
A novel depicting affairs in Spain resulting from
Catholicism.

McGavin, William, The Protestant. Essays on the Prin-
cipal Points of Controversy between the Church of
Rome and the Reformed. 2 vols., Hartford, 1833.
A publication of this ponderous Scotch work, with
an American introduction by the Reverend George
Bourne.

Meeks, J. C., Pierre and his Family; or, a Story of the
Waldenses. New York, 1841. A story of Catholic
persecution.

Mendham, Joseph, The Literary Policy of the Church of
Rome, Exhibited in an Account of her Damnatory

Catalogues, or Indexes, both Prohibitory and Expurgatory. 2nd ed., New York, 1835.

--------------------, The Venal Indulgences and Pardons of the Church of Rome, Exemplified in a Summary of an Indulgence of Sixtus IV. London, 1845. Designed to show that indulgences were still employed by the Catholic church.

Michelet, M., The Jesuits. New York, 1845. A series of lectures showing the iniquity of the Jesuits through their history.

--------------------, Spiritual Direction and Auricular Confession. Philadelphia, 1845. Exposes confession as a power to further the will of the Catholic church.

Monk, Maria, Awful Disclosures of the Hotel Dieu Convent of Montreal or the Secrets of Black Nunnery Revealed. New York, 1836.

--------------------, Further Disclosures by Maria Monk, Concerning the Hotel Dieu Nunnery of Montreal; and also her Visit to Nun's Island and Disclosures Concerning that Secret Retreat. New York, 1837.

Moore, Charles K., editor, Book of Tracts on Romanism: Containing the Origin and Progress, Cruelties, Frauds, Superstitions, Miracles and Ceremonies of the Church of Rome. New York, 1844.

Morse, Samuel F. B., Confessions of a French Priest, to Which are Added Warnings to the People of the United States. New York, 1837.

----------------------, Foreign Conspiracy against the Liberties of the United States. 5th ed., New York, 1841.

----------------------, The Proscribed German Student; being a Sketch of some Interesting Incidents in the Life and Death of Lewis Clausing; to which is added: a Treatise on the Jesuits, a Posthumous Work of Lewis Clausing. New York, 1836.

Nevins, William, Thoughts on Popery. New York, 1836. One of the most important of the propaganda books because of its clear presentation of theological arguments against Catholicism.

Norton, Herman, Signs of Danger and of Promise; Duties of Protestants at the Present Crisis. New York, 1844. The crisis was created by the growth of Catholicism.

Odel, Jeremiah, Popery Unveiled; to which is Annexed a Short Recital of the Origin, Doctrines, Precepts and Examples of the Great Church Militant and Triumphant. Bennington, Vermont, 1821. Written especially to appeal to the poorer people; in poor English and bad grammar. A violent attack.

Odenheimer, William H., The True Catholic No Romanist.
New York, 1842.

Ogilby, John D., Letters on the Catholic Church in
England and America. New York, 1844.

Orr, Hector, The Native American; a Gift for the People.
Philadelphia, 1845. One of the first of the nativistic gift books.

Pond, Enoch, No Fellowship with Romanism. Boston, 1843.
Written especially to convince children of the errors of Catholicism.

Pope, Richard T. P., Roman Misquotation; or, Certain
Passages from the Fathers, adduced in a work entitled, "The Faith of Catholics," brought to the
test of the Originals and their Perverted Character Demonstrated. Dublin, 1841.

Powell, Thomas, An Essay on Apostolic Succession; being
a Defense of a Genuine Protestant Ministry against
the Exclusive and Intolerant Schemes of Papists and
High Churchmen; and Supplying a General Antidote to
Popery. New York, 1842.

Poynder, John, Popery in Alliance with Heathenism; Letters Proving the Conformity which Subsists between
the Romish Religion and the Religion of the Ancient
Heathens. London, 1835.

Reed, Rebecca Theresa, Six Months in a Convent. Boston,

1835. The first of the nun's revelations, and
one of the most popular.

Rhinewald, The Protestant Exiles of Zillerthal; their
Persecutions and Expatriation from the Tyrol on
Separating from the Church of Rome. New York,
1842.

Ricci, Scipio de, Secrets of Nunneries Disclosed. New
York, 1834. Compiled from the manuscript of Ricci,
who had been Catholic Bishop of Pistoia and Prato.

Richardson, James, The Roman Catholic Convicted upon his
Own Evidence of Hostility to the Protestant Churches
of Britain. New York, 1823.

Rogers, John, Anti-Popery; or, Popery Unreasonable, Unscriptural and Novel. New York. 1841. The author
was a prominent Quaker lawyer, and the book was
designed to win members of his sect to the anti-
Catholic causes.

Schmucker, S. S., Discourse in Commemoration of the Glorious Reformation of the Sixteenth Century. 3rd ed.
New York, 1838. Delivered before the Evangelical
Lutheran Synod of West Pennsylvania in 1837. One
of the most violent attacks on Catholicism.

--------------------, The Papal Hierarchy. -------, 1845.

Secker, T., Five Discourses Against Popery. Windsor,
Vermont, 1827. A theological attack on Catholicism.

Sherwood, Miss A., Edwin and Alicia; or, the Infant
Martyrs. New York, 1835. A novel for children
exposing the persecuting nature of Catholicism.

Shobere, Frederic, Persecutions of Popery: Historical Narratives of the Most Remarkable Persecutions Occasioned by the Intolerance of the Church
of Rome. New York, 1844. A history of the more
famous persecutions down to the beginning of the
nineteenth century.

Slocum, J. J., Reply to the Priest's Book, Denominated,
"Awful Exposure of an Atrocious Plot formed by
Certain Individuals Against the Clergy and Nuns
of Lower Canada, through the Intervention of Maria
Monk." New York, 1837. The author was the clergyman who was partially responsible for the publication of the Awful Disclosures.

Smith, Samuel B., Synopsis of the Moral Theology of the
Church of Rome, from the Works of St. Ligori. New
York, 1836. An attempt to depict the immorality
taught in Catholic schools.

------------------, The Wonderful Adventures of a Lady
of the French Nobility, and the Intrigues of a
Romish Priest, her Confessor, to Seduce and Murder
Her. New York, 1836.

Smyth, Thomas, Ecclesiastical Republicanism; or, the

Republicanism Liberality and Catholicity of Presbytery in Contrast with Prelacy and Popery. New York,
1843.

———————————————————, The Prelatical Doctrine of Apostolic Succession Examined and the Protestant Ministry
Defended against the Assumptions of Popery and High
Churchism. Boston, 1841. A series of twenty-one
lectures delivered by the author at his Presbyterian
church in Charleston, South Carolina.

Sprague, William B., Contrast Between True and False Religions. New York, 1837. Has a chapter contrasting
true Christianity with Romanism.

Stanley, J., Dialogues on Popery. New York, 1843.

Stratten, Thomas, The Book of the Priesthood: an Argument
in Three Parts. New York, 1831. A theological argument to demonstrate that original Christianity had no
priests.

Thornwell, James H., Arguments of Romanists Discussed and
Refuted. Charleston, 1845. An argument against the
divine inspiration of the Apocryphal books of the
Bible.

Waterous, Timothy, Timothy Waterous, Jr., and Zachariah
Waterous, The Battle Axe and Weapons of War, Dis-
covered by the Morning Light: Aimed for the Final
Destruction of Priestcraft. Being a Treatise

<u>Fitted to the Present Day, calculated to Detect
Hypocrisy wheresoever it may be found, without
Respect to Persons</u>. 2nd ed., New York, 1841.
A fanatical attack on the Catholic priesthood,
largely in verse.

Wharton, C. H., <u>Concise View of the Principal Points
of Controversy between the Protestant and Romish
Churches</u>. New York, 1817. A series of sermons
given in Saint Mary's church, Brooklyn, New York.

Whatley, Richard, <u>Essays on the Errors of Romanism
having their Origins in Human Nature</u>. 2nd ed.,
London, 1837.

White, J. Blanco, <u>Letters from Spain</u>. ------------.

--------------------, <u>Practical and Internal Evidence
against Catholicism, with Occasional Strictures
on Mr. Butler's Book of the Roman Catholic Church;
in Six Letters Addressed to the Impartial among
the Roman Catholics of Great Britain and Ireland</u>.
Boston, 1835. A theological attack prompted by
the Catholic Emancipation Bill.

--------------------, <u>The Poor Man's Preservative against
Popery</u>. New York, 1835.

Young, John, <u>Lectures on the Chief Points of Controversy
Between Protestants and Romanists</u>. London, 1845.

<u>American Keepsake or Book for Every American</u>. Boston, 1845.

A patriotic gift book inspired by the Native
American party.

The American Text Book of Popery: being an Authentic
Compend of the Bulls, Canons and Decretals of
the Roman Hierarchy. New York, 1844. Not a
compendium of Catholic works as the title indi-
cates, but a narrative argument against Catholicism.

The Burning of the Bible; being a Defense of the Protestant Version of the Scriptures against the Attacks of Popish Apologists for the Champlain
Bible Burners. New York, 1845.

The Conversion and Edifying Death of Andrew Dunn. Philadelphia, 182-. Another edition was printed in New
York, in 1835. An anti-Catholic novel long popular
in England.

Ellmer Castle. Boston, 1833. An English novel reprinted
in the United States, picturing Catholic intolerance
toward the Bible.

An Exposition of the Principles of the Roman Catholic Religion, with Remarks on its Influence in the United
States. Hartford, 1830.

Father Clement, A Roman Catholic Story. Boston, 1827.
An anti-Catholic novel, filled with theological arguments.

A History of Popery, including its Origin, Progress,

    Doctrines, Practice, Institutions and Fruits,

    to the Commencement of the Nineteenth Century.

    New York, 1834. Less than half the book is

    taken up with actual history, the remainder is

    a fanatical attack on the Catholic church.

A History of Popery, to Which is Added an Examination

    of the Present State of the Romish Church in Ire-

    land and Specimens of Monkish Legends. London,

    1838.

John Ronge, the Holy Coat of Treves and the New German

    Church. New York, 1845. Describes the miracles of

    the Holy Coat of Treves and the German movement away

    from Catholicism led by John Ronge.

Lorette, History of Louise, Daughter of a Canadian Nun.

    New York, 1834.

Narrative of Van Halen's Don Juan; Imprisonment in the

    Dungeons of the Inquisition at Madrid and his Es-

    cape in 1817 and 1818; to which are added his Jour-

    ney to Russia, his Campaign with the Army of the

    Caucasus, and his Return to Spain in 1821. New

    York, 1828.

Our Liberties Defended: the Question Discussed, is the

    Protestant or Papal System most favorable to Civil

    and Religious Liberty? By a Protestant, under the

<u>Signature of Obsta Principis, and a Catholic,</u>
<u>under the Signature of Catholicus.</u> New York,
1841. Articles appearing originally in the
<u>New York Journal of Commerce.</u>

<u>Pope Alexander VI and his Son Caeser Borgia.</u> Philadel-
phia, 1844. Written to show the iniquity of Catholicism in the past.

<u>Popery Exposed; or, the Secrets and Privacy of the Con-</u>
<u>fessional Unmasked.</u> New York, 1845.

<u>The Protestant Almanac for 1841.</u> Baltimore, 1841. Pub-
lished by the Lutheran church as an argument against
Catholicism.

<u>The Protestant Exiles of Zillerthal; their Persecutions</u>
<u>and Expatriation on Separating from the Church of</u>
<u>Rome and Embracing the Reformed Faith.</u> New York,
1844. Devoted largely to an attack on Catholic
persecution.

<u>The Protestant Keepsake.</u> London, 1840. A gift book
filled with anti-Catholic stories, verse and articles.

<u>The Reformation in Europe.</u> New York, 1845. First part
of book devoted to a discussion of the errors of
Catholicism; remainder with how Reformation did
away with those errors.

<u>The Secret Instructions to the Jesuits.</u> London, 1759.
One of the early editions of this bit of propaganda

that was so widely circulated in the United States.

Secret Instructions to the Jesuits. Princeton, New
    Jersey, 1831. Printed from a London copy of 1725.

The Spirit of Popery: an Exposure of its Origin, Char-
    acter and Results; in Letters from a Father to his
    Children. New York, 1844. Written for children.
    Each so called error of Catholicism is taken up
    and discussed in turn.

Supplement to Six Months in a Convent, Confirming the
    Narrative of Rebecca Theresa Reed, by the Testi-
    mony of more than 100 Witnesses, whose Statements
    have been given to the Committee, Containing a
    Minute Account of the Elopement of Miss Harrison,
    With Some Further Explanations of the Narrative
    by Miss Reed, and an Exposition of the System of
    Cloister Education, by the Committee of Publica-
    tion, with an Appendix. Boston, 1835.

Taxes of the Apostolic Chancery; or, the Book of Rates
    Now Used in the Sin Custom House of the Church and
    Court of Rome: Containing the Bulls, Dispensations
    and Pardons for all Manner of Villainies and Wicked-
    ness, with the Several Sums of Moneys given and to
    be Paid for Them. London, 1674. A book used and
    reprinted in America to show the use of a system
    of indulgences.

<u>Tracts on Romanism.</u> New York, 1836. A collection
of tracts issued by the American Tract Society.

<u>The Trial of the Pope of Rome, the Anti-Christ or</u>
<u>Man of Sin Described in the Bible, for High</u>
<u>Treason against the Son of God. Tried at the</u>
<u>Sessions House of Truth before the Right Hon.</u>
<u>Divine Revelation, the Hon. Justice Reason</u>
<u>and the Hon. Justice History.</u> Taken in Short-
<u>hand by a Friend to Saint Peter.</u> 2nd ed.,
A complete account of the trial of Catholicism,
with witnesses, speeches of lawyers and the like,
ending with the conviction of the Pope.

Anti-Catholic Pamphlets

Allen, William, <u>Report on Popery Accepted by the General</u>
<u>Association of Massachusetts, June, 1844.</u> Boston,
1844. An attack on Catholicism recommended to the
Congregationalist ministers of the state.

Alvord, Henry, <u>Romanism in Rome.</u> Boston, -------.

Anthon, Henry, <u>The True Churchman Warned against the</u>
<u>Errors of the Times.</u> New York, 1843. Published
to show the errors of the Oxford Reformers and
their efforts to establish Catholicism.

Boardman, H. A., <u>The Intolerance of the Church of Rome.</u>
Philadelphia, 1845.

Brainerd, Thomas, Our Country Safe from Romanism; a
Sermon Delivered at the Opening of the Third
Presbytery of Philadelphia at its Sessions in
the Western Presbyterian Church, Philadelphia,
1841. Philadelphia, 1843. A plea to Presbyterian ministers to preach against Catholicism.

Dickinson, Austin, The Mother of Saint Augustine.
New York, 1845.

Dickinson, Austin, Thoughts for Catholics and their
Friends. New York, 1844.

Grinke, Thomas S., Address on the Expediency and Duty
of Adopting the Bible as a Class Book, in Every
Scheme of Education, from the Primary School to
the University; Delivered at Columbia, South
Carolina, in the Presbyterian Church, on Friday
Evening, 4th of December, 1829, before the Richland School. Charleston, 1830.

Henry, James, Education and the Common School. New
York, 1844. A published address by the superin-
tendent of common schools of Herkimer county,
New York, against Catholic claims.

Ide, George B., The Ministry Demanded by the Present
Crisis. Philadelphia, 1845. Holds the present
crisis to be caused by the spread of infidelity
and Catholicism.

Jackson, Luther and Austin Dickinson, Thoughts for Catholics and their Friends. New York, 1843. Designed to show the necessity of keeping the Bible as a school book despite Catholic claims.

Marsh, George P., The Papists and Puritans; an Address before the New England Society of the City of New York. New York, 1845. Contrasts Catholicism and the spirit of the Reformation which brought the Puritans to America.

McMurray, Rev. Bishop A., Awful Disclosures! Murders Exposed! Downfall of Popery! Death Bed Confession! Death Bed Confession and Renunciation of the Right Rev. Bishop McMurray, Bishop of Saint Mary's Roman Catholic Church, Montreal, Canada. Buffalo, 1845. A rabid account of how the author was converted to Protestantism by reading history and the Bible.

Morse, Samuel F. B., Imminent Dangers to the Free Institutions of the United States through Foreign Immigration. New York, 1835. Letters originally published in the New York Journal of Commerce. A second edition appeared in 1854.

Norton, Herman, Startling Facts for American Protestants! Progress of Romanism since the Revolutionary War; its Present Position and Future

Prospects. New York, 1844. A disclosure of
how Catholics intend to conquer the United
States.

Orchard, Isaac, Friendly Suggestions to an Emigrant,
by an Emigrant. New York, 1845.

Smith, Samuel B., Decisive Confirmation of the Awful
Disclosures of Maria Monk, Proving her Residence
in the Hotel Dieu Nunnery and the Existence of
the Subterranean Passages. New York, 1836. A
refutation of the attack made on Maria Monk by
G. Vance.

--------------------, The Escape of Saint Francis Patrick,
Another Nun from the Hotel Dieu Nunnery of Montreal.
New York, 1836.

--------------------, The Flight of Popery from Rome to
the West. New York, 1836. An exposure of the Pope's
plan to move from the Vatican to the Mississippi
Valley.

--------------------, Renunciation of Popery. 6th ed.,
Philadelphia, 1833. A brief account of the author's
life and the reasons that led him to abandon Catholicism and become a Protestant.

Stevens, R. V. A., An Alarm to American Protestants. A
Sermon on the Political Tendencies of Popery, considered in Respect to the Institutions of the United

States, in the Church Street Church, Boston,
November 27, 1834. Being the Day of Annual
Thanksgiving. Boston, 1834.

Waddell, Thomas, Letters to the Editors of the
Catholic Miscellany: Illustrating the Papal
Doctrine of Intention: the Opus Operatum;
Roman Infallibility and the Knavery of Popish
Writers. New York, 1830.

Watson, R., An Apology for the Bible. New York, 1835.

An Awful Warning; or, the Massacre of Saint Bartholomew.
London, 1812. A history of the massacre, bitter
against Catholicism.

The Ceremonies of the Holy Week in the Papal Chapel of
the Vatican. ----, 1839. An account poking ridicule at the Catholic ceremonies.

The Crisis: an Appeal to our Countrymen on the Subject
of Foreign Influence in the United States. New
York, 1844. Directed largely against immigration;
only the last eight pages having to do with Catholicism.

Defense of the Use of the Bible in the Schools. New York,
1830.

The Destruction of the Inquisition at Madrid. New York,
1844. A much quoted account of the horrors discovered when the Inquisition buildings were opened

during the Napoleonic wars.

Dreadful Scenes in the Awful Disclosures of Maria Monk.
New York, 1836. A series of steel engravings depicting the events described by Maria Monk.

Education in Romish Seminaries. A Letter in Answer to
Certain Inquiries Respecting the Propriety of Selecting, as Places of Education, Seminaries Professedly under the Control of Religious Societies
of the Court of Rome. New York, 1845. Devoted
to proving that Protestants going to Catholic
schools are always converted.

Evidence Demonstrating the Falsehoods of William L.
Stone. New York, 1836. Designed to show that
Stone's report condemning Maria Monk was written
without a proper investigation of the Hotel Dieu
Convent.

False Claims of the Pope. New York, 1842. An attack
on the temporal power of the Pope.

Interview of Maria Monk with her Opponents, the Authors
of the Reply to her Awful Disclosures, now in Press,
held in this City on Wednesday, August 17, 1836.
New York, 1836. A detailed argument with the committee of Protestant clergymen who investigated the
Hotel Dieu convent and branded the Awful Disclosures as false.

On Purgatory and Infallibility. New York, 1839.

Our Country; its Dangers and its Duty. New York, 1844.
Winner of the second prize offered by the American
Protestant Society for the best attacks on Cathol-
isiom.

Political Popery; or, Bibles and Schools, with the Condition, Progress and Ulterior Objects of Romanists
in the United States. New York, 1844.

The Protestant Catechism, Showing the Principal Errors
of the Church of Rome. Charleston, 1828. Questions
and answers attacking Catholic beliefs.

A Review of the Lady Superior's Reply to "Six Months in a
Convent," being a Vindication of Miss Reed. Boston,
1835.

Roman Catholic Female Schools. New York, 1837. A warning to parents not to patronize Catholic schools.

Romanism Contradictory to the Bible. New York, 1832.

Romanism Incompatible with Republican Institutions. New
York, 1844. A work awarded first prize by the American Protestant Society.

Rome's Policy Toward the Bible. Philadelphia, 1844. Attempts to prove Catholics hostile to the Bible.

The Sanctity of the Church of Rome. New York, --------.
One of the tracts printed by the Protestant Reformation Society.

Seasonable Caveat Against Popery. New York, 1844.

The Story of the Inquisition. Boston, 184-. An
    account of a girl taken into the Inquisition as
    the mistress of the Inquisitor and of her expe-
    riences.

The Two Apocolyptic Beasts in St. John's Revelation
    Fully Explained and with an Accurate Engraving.
    New York, 1842. Designed to show that Cathol-
    icism was the "Man of Sin" and "Babylon" referred
    to.

                    Pro-Catholic Works

Baxter, Roger, The Most Important Tenets of the Roman
    Catholic Church Fully Explained. Washington, 1820.
    A short explanation and proofs of the principal
    Catholic beliefs.

Blyth, Stephen C., Narrative of the Conversion of Stephen
    C. Blyth to the Faith of the Catholic Apostolic and
    Roman Church, to which is Annexed a Brief Refutation
    of the Current Objections to many Articles of the
    Catholic Faith and Discipline. Montreal, 1822.

Carey, M., Letters on Religious Persecution, by a Catholic
    Layman. Philadelphia, 1827.

Cobbett, William, A History of the Protestant Reformation

in England and Ireland; Showing how that Event
has Impoverished and Degraded the Main Body of
the People in Those Countries. In a Series of
Letters Addressed to all Sensible and Just Englishmen. New York, 1832. An attack to answer
nativist's charges that the poor condition of
Ireland was due to Catholicism. Just as bitter
as the Protestant attacks.

Doane, George W., Puseyism, No Popery. Boston, 1843.
An argument to show that Oxford Reformers were
not leaning toward Catholicism.

Eckel, Mrs. L. St. John, Maria Monk's Daughter; an
Autobiography. New York, 1874. An argument in
favor of Catholicism written by a woman claiming
to be Maria Monk's daughter.

Hughes, John, The Conversion and Edifying Death of
Andrew Dunn. Philadelphia, 1828. A novel published by Hughes identical in name with an anti-
Catholic novel popular at the time; this work
depicting the conversion of the hero to Catholicism.

---------------, The Review of the Charge Delivered
May 22nd, 1833, by the Right Reverend Bishop
Onderdonk, on the Rule of Faith. Philadelphia,
1833. A work growing from the Hughes-Breckin-

ridge controversy on the Rule of Faith.

Saint George, Mary Edmund, <u>An Answer to Six Months in a</u>
<u>Convent Exposing its Falsehoods and Manifold Ab-</u>
<u>surdities</u>. Boston, 1835. Written by the Mother
Superior of the Ursuline Convent in Charlestown.

Sherwood, Reuben, <u>The Reviewer Reviewed; or Doctor Brown-</u>
<u>lee versus the Bible versus the Catholic Church ver-</u>
<u>sus the Fathers, ancient and modern, versus his own</u>
<u>Creed, versus Himself</u>. Poughkeepsie, 1840. An at-
tack on the anti-Catholic views of the Reverend W.C.
Brownlee.

Scank, Phileman, <u>A Few Chapters to Brother Jonathan Con-</u>
<u>cerning Infallibility etc.; or Strictures on Nathan</u>
<u>L. Rice's Defense of Protestantism</u>. Louisville,
1835. Prose and verse attacking Protestantism and
especially the Protestant minister, Nathan L. Rice.

Sleigh, W. W., <u>An Exposure of Maria Monk's Pretended Ab-</u>
<u>duction and Conveyance to the Catholic Asylum, Phil-</u>
<u>adelphia</u>. Philadelphia, 1837.

Smith, Samuel M., <u>To Every Sincere Inquirer after Truth</u>,
<u>with an Appendix Containing the Renunciation of</u>
<u>Popery</u>. New York, 1834. A pro-Catholic work evi-
dently designed to sell to Protestants who would
confuse the name of its author with Samuel B. Smith,
the anti-Catholic writer.

Stone, William L., Maria Monk and the Nunnery of the Hotel Dieu; Being an Account of a Visit to the Convents of Montreal and a Refutation of the Awful Disclosures. New York, 1836. The account of a minute investigation of the Hotel Dieu convent.

Vale, G., Review of the Awful Disclosures of Maria Monk, New York, 1836. An attack on their authenticity.

Address of the Catholic Lay Citizens of Philadelphia to their Fellow Citizens in Reply to the Presentment of the Grand Jury in Regard to the Causes of the Late Riots in Philadelphia, Philadelphia, 1844. The presentment was violently anti-Catholic in tone.

Awful Exposure of the Atrocious Plot formed by Certain Individuals against the Clergy and Nuns of Lower Canada through the Intervention of Maria Monk. New York, 1837. A detailed attack on the Awful Disclosures and on Maria Monk's character, together with hundreds of affidavits proving her statements to be false.

Catholicism Compatible with Republican Government and in Full Accordance with Popular Institutions; or, Reflections upon a Premium Tract issued by the American Protestant Society under the Signature of 'Civis.' New York, 1844. A Catholic defense on a subject often attacked by nativists.

Reflections on the Late Riots, by Candid Writers in
Poetry and Prose. Philadelphia, 1844. A pro-
Catholic account of the Philadelphia riots,
largely in verse.

Public Documents
Congressional Documents

Congressional Globe, 1833-1846. Washington, 1833-1846.

House Documents, 1833-1847. Washington, 1833-1847.

Reports of Committees, 1833-1847. Washington, 1833-1847.

Senate Documents, 1833-1847. Washington, 1833-1847.

Census Returns

DeBow, J. D. B., Statistical View of the United States,
Embracing its Territory, Population,- White, Colored and Slave- Moral and Social Conditions, Industry, Property and Revenue; the Detailed Statistics of Cities, Towns and Counties; Being a Compendium of the Seventh Census. Washington, 1854.

Kennedy, Joseph C. G., Preliminary Report on the Eighth
Census, 1860. Washington, 1862. Contains corrected
reports on immigration statistics for the entire
period.

Compendium of the Enumeration of the Inhabitants and Sta-

tistics of the United States, as Obtained at
the Department of State, from the Returns of
the Sixth Census, by Counties and Principal
Towns, Exhibiting the Population, Wealth and
Resources of the Country. Washington, 1841.
Little on immigration but valuable figures
showing population and industrial growth.

State Documents

"Bill more Effectively to Suppress Riots and to Indemni-
fy Persons for Injuries done Thereby," Commonwealth
of Massachusetts, Legislative Documents No. 17(1835),
pp. 1-5.

Laws of the State of New York Passed by the 39th and 40th
and 41st Sessions of the Legislature Commencing January, 1816 and ending April, 1818. Albany, 1818.

Laws of the State of New York Passed at the 47th Session
of the legislature Begun January 6, 1824. Albany,
1824.

"Memorial and Remonstrance of the Trustees of the Public
School Society of the City of New York," Senate
Documents of the State of New York, No. 97. Al-
bany, 1844.

Report of the Select Committee Consisting of the Delegation from the City of New York on the Bill Entitled,

'An Act to Improve and Extend the Benefits of Common School Education in the City of New York,' Assembly Documents of the State of New York, No. 296. Albany, 1841.

"Reports and Resolves Concerning the Destruction of the Convent on Mount Benedict," Commonwealth of Massachusetts Legislative Documents No. 37 (1835), pp. 1-24.

Travelers' Accounts, Journals and Memoirs

Barca, Calderon de la, Life in Mexico During a Residence of Two Years in that Country. London, 1843. Widely circulated in America as propaganda against Cathlic idolatry.

Beecher, Lyman, Autobiography and Correspondence, Charles Beecher, ed. 2 vols., New York, 1865.

Elizabeth, Charlotte, Letters from Ireland, New York, 1843. An attempt to show Irish ills due to Catholicism rather than British misrule.

Elizabeth, Charlotte, Personal Recollections. New York, 1843. An autobiography of the life of this prominent propagandists telling of her efforts and writings, and arguing constantly against Catholicism at the same time.

Finley, James B., Autobiography. Cincinnati, 1854. The

author was a revivalistic circuit rider who devoted much of his time to attempts to convert
Catholics to Protestantism.

Headley, Joel T., _Letters from Italy_. New York, 1845.
Describes the degraded condition of the people there,
and places the entire blame on Catholicism.

Kenrick, Francis Patrick, _Diary and Visitation Record
of the Rt. Rev. Francis Patrick Kenrick, Adminis-
trator and Bishop of Philadelphia, 1830-1851, later
Archbishop of Baltimore_. Lancaster, Pennsylvania,
1916. Gives the official Catholic point of view of
the Philadelphia riots of 1844.

Latrobe, C., _The Rambler in North America in 1832-1833_.
2 vols., New York, 1835. Contains excellent descriptions of Irish immigrants and their effect on
American life.

Lyell, C., _A Second Visit to the United States of Amer-
ica._ 3 vols., London, 1849.

Marryat, Fredrick, _A Diary in America_. 3 vols., London,
1839.

Martineau, Harriet, _Society in America_. 3 vols., London,
1837.
This and the three items above are excellent accounts of American life by British travelers. All
scoff at the nativistic agitation.

Morse, Samuel F. B., Samuel F. B. Morse, his Life and
Journals. Edward L. Morse, ed. 2 vols., Boston,
1914. Largely the author's journals, but poorly
edited.

Murray, Nicholas, Memoirs. New York, 1862. Extracts
from the author's diary, letters, etc. A good
picture of the life of a prominent anti-Catholic
agitator and propagandist.

Nichols, Thomas, Forty Years of American Life. 2 vols.
London, 1864. The best travel account by an English writer in describing American Catholicism
and immigration. Author is an excellent observer
but too outspoken in favor of Catholicism.

O'Hanlon, John, Life and Scenery in Missouri. Dublin,
1890. An autobiographical account of an Irish
priest who acted as Catholic missionary in the
Mississippi Valley between 1843 and 1860.

Reed, Andrew and James Matherson, A Narrative of the
Visit to the American Churches by the Deputation
from the Congregational Union of England and Wales.
2 vols., London, 1835. Much discussion of Catholicism and a warning to American Congregationalists
of its dangers.

Salzbacher, J., Meine Reise nach Nord-Amerika in Jahre
1842. Vienna, 1845. Contains a map showing lo-
cation of Catholic missions and a table at end of

volume on the growth of American Catholicism.

Sinclair, Catherine, Shetland and the Shetlanders; or, the Northern Circuit. New York, 1840. A book of travel warning against Catholicism.

Thaxter, Lucy W., An Account of Life in the Ursuline Convent at Mount Benedict, Charlestown. Manuscript in Treasure Room, Widener Library, Harvard. An account written in 1843 by one of the pupils in the convent at the time of the burning. Describes life in the convent and the mob attack.

Towle, George M., American Society. 2 vols., London, 1870. Written by an American; describes immigration and its effects on the United States.

Trollope, F. A., Domestic Manners of the Americans. 2 vols., London, 1832. Bitter in her attacks on nativism.

"Catholic Recollections of Samuel Breck," American Catholic Historical Researches, xii, No. 4 (October, 1895). Author born in Boston in 1771 and describes Pope's Day in Taunton in 1774; an evidence of a good memory if nothing else.

Ship and Shore: or, Leaves from the Journal of a Cruise to the Levant. New York, 1835. Describes the effects of Catholicism on the southern states of Europe.

Contemporary Writings

Beecher, Lyman, The Works of the Reverend Lyman Beecher
3 vols., Boston, 1852. Contain the anti-Catholic
sermons of Dr. Beecher.

Brownson, O. A., The Works of O. A. Brownson. 20 vols.,
Detroit, 1822-1887. Contain Brownson's Quarterly
Review and other writings of this prominent de-
fender of Catholicism.

England, John, The Works of the Right Reverend John England, First Bishop of Charleston. 5 vols. Baltimore, 1849.

---------------, The Works of the Right Reverend John
England, First Bishop of Charleston. Sebastian G.
Messmer, ed. 7 vols., Cleveland, 1908. A more val-
uable collection than the earlier edition of Bishop
England's works. Devoted largely to his defense of
Catholicism against Protestant attacks.

Millard Fillmore Papers. Publications of the Buffalo
Historical Society, vols. x and xi., Buffalo, 1907.
Most of the Fillmore correspondence was destroyed,
this remaining the best collection of his speeches
and letters.

Henni, John Martin, "Letters of the Right Reverend John
Martin Henni and the Reverend Anthony Urbanek,"
Wisconsin Magazine of History, vol. x (August,

1926). Reports of Henni, who was missionary agent in the Mississippi Valley in the 1840's, to the Leopoldine Association. Consists largely of extracts from the Berichte of the Leopoldine Association.

Hughes, John, The Complete Works of the Reverend John Hughes. Lawrence Kehoe, ed., 2 vols., New York, 1866.

Seward, William H., Works. George E. Baker, ed. 4 vols., New York, 1853-1861. Much material on the New York school controversy and on nativism in general.

Thie, Joseph A., "German Catholic Activity in the United States Seventy Years Ago," American Catholic Historical Society of Philadelphia, Records, vol. xx, No. 2 (June, 1909). Translated notes from the first German Catholic newspaper published in the United States, the Wahrheitsfreund, published at Cincinnati, 1839-1841.

Washington, George, The Writings of George Washington. Worthington C. Ford, ed., 14 vols., New York, 1889-1893.

"The Anti-Catholic Riots in Philadelphia in 1844," American Catholic Historical Researches, vol. xiii, No. 2 (April, 1896). An account of the riots by a Catholic eye witness.

"Archbishop Hughes to Governor Seward on the School Question," American Catholic Historical Society of Philadelphia, Records, vol. xxiii (March, 1912). Correspondence between the Governor and Bishop on Catholic claims for a share of the school fund.

"Correspondence between Bishop Conwell of Philadelphia and Bishop Lessis of Quebec, 1821-1825; Relating Principally to the Hogan Schism," American Catholic Historical Society of Philadelphia, Records, vol. xxii (December, 1911). One of the best accounts of the Philadelphia conflict over trusteeism told by Bishop Conwell.

"Letters Concerning some Missions to the Mississippi Valley, 1010-1027," American Catholic Historical Society of Philadelphia, Records, vol. xiv (March, 1903). A group of letters from Catholic missionaries describing their condition and needs, taken from the Annales de l'Association de la Propagation de la Foi.

"The Philadelphia Anti-Catholic Riots of 1844," American Catholic Historical Researches, n.s., vol. vii (July, 1911). A long editorial from the Philadelphia Spirit of the Times of May 12, 1844, deploring the rioting and the disgrace to the city.

Miscellaneous

a'Beckett, George A., The Comic Blackstone. Philadel-
      phia, 1844. A humorous work occasionally attack-
      ing immigration.

"Autodicus," The Critique of the Vision of Rubeta: a
      Dramatic Sketch in One Act. Philadelphia, 1838.
      A play defending the Critique, especially against
      charges of immorality, and evidently written by
      the author of the Critique himself, as the name
      "Autodicus" means "one who judges himself."

Burleigh, William Henry, Our Country; its Dangers and
      its Destiny: Being a Desultory Poem Pronounced
      before the Allegheny Literary Society at its
      Semi-Annual Celebration, September 2, 1841.
      Allegheny, 1841. A long poem praising the
      United States and mentioning Catholicism as
      among the evils that beset the country.

Carey, Mathew, Reflections on the Subject of Emigra-
      tion from Europe with a View to Settlement in
      the United States. 3d ed., Philadelphia, 1826.
      Written by an Irish immigrant to encourage immi-
      gration to America.

Chickering, Jesse, A Statistical View of the Popula-
      tion of Massachusetts from 1765 to 1840. Boston,
      1846. Valuable statistics on the growth of manu-

facturing and industry and the effect of this
on the people.

Curtis, George T., The Rights of Conscience and of
Property; or, the True Issue of the Convent
Question. Boston, 1842. Written by the chair
man of the Massachusetts legislative committee
considering paying the Ursuline order for the
destruction of the Charlestown convent. Argues
that payment should be made.

Day, Mahlon, On the Establishment of Public Schools
in the City of New York. New York, 1825.

Goodrich, C. A., Outlines of Ecclesiastical History
on a New Plan, Designed for Academies and Schools.
Hartford, 1830. One of the violently anti-Catholic school books of the day.

Moore, Justus E., The Warning of Thomas Jefferson; or,
a Brief Exposition of the Dangers to the Apprehended to our Civil and Religious Liberties from
Presbyterianism. Philadelphia, 1844. An attempt
to show that Presbyterians caused the formation
of the Native American party and the Philadelphia
riots; with a plea to vote against the Presbyterian, Freylinghuysen, Whig vice presidential
candidate in 1844.

Murray, Linday, Sequel to the English Reader; or, El-

egant Selections in Prose and Poetry. Windsor,
Vermont, 1821. One of the anti-Catholic school
books used in New York schools.

Putnam, Samuel, Sequel to the Analytical Reader in
which the Original Design is Extended so as to
Embrace an Explanation of Phrases and Figurative
Language. Boston, 1831. A New York school book,
objected to for its anti-Catholic nature.

Reese, David M., Humbugs of New York, being a Remonstrance against Popular Delusion, whether in
Science, Philosophy or Religion. New York, 1838.
Condemns "ultra-temperance," "ultra-abolitionism,"
and "ultra-Protestantism."

Sterne, Lawrence, The Life and Opinions of Tristram
Shandy. 2 vols., New York, 1813.

Stetson, Caleb, A Discourse on the Duty of Sustaining
the Laws, Occasioned by the Burning of the Ursuline
Convent. Boston, 1834. A sermon delivered at Bed-
ford, deploring the Charlestown mob violence.

Wallis, H., History of the United States from the First
Settlements as Colonies to the Close of the War
with Great Britain in 1815. New York, 1827. A
school book used in New York and objected to by
Catholics.

An Account of the Conflagration of the Ursuline Convent

by a Friend of Religious Toleration. Boston,
1834. A collection of newspaper extracts condemning the Charlestown convent burning and defending Catholicism.

Documents Relating to the Ursuline Convent in Charlestown. Boston, 1842. Contains reports of committees just after the convent burning deploring the
act, and of later committees urging payment of the
Ursulines.

The Important and Interesting Debate on the Claims of
the Catholics to a Portion of the Common School
Fund; with the Arguments of Counsel before the
Board of Aldermen of the City of New York, on
Thursday and Friday, the 29th and 30th of Octo-
ber, 1840. New York, 1840.

Journals of the General Conference of the Methodist
Episcopal Church, 1796-1856. 3 vols., New York,
1856.

Journals of the General Conventions of the Protestant
Episcopal Church in the United States, 1785-1835.
William S. Perry, ed. 3 vols., Claremont, New
Hampshire, 1874.

New York Reader Number One, Adapted to the Capacities
of the Younger Class of Learners: Being Selections
of Easy Lessons Calculated to Inculcate Morality
and Piety. New York, 1826.

New York Reader Number Two, Being Selections in Prose
and Poetry for the Use of the Schools. New York,
1812.

New York Reader Number Three, from the Best Writers Designed for the Use of Schools and Calculated to
Assist the Scholar in Acquiring the Art of Reading and at the Same Time to Fix his Principles
and Inspire him with a Love of Virtue. New York,
1819. This and the above books used in New York
schools and objected to because of their anti-
Catholic nature.

Proposed New Plan of a General Emigration Society; by
a Catholic Gentleman. London, 1842. A proposal
to send Irish Catholics to settle a part of the
Mississippi Valley by a group of London land
speculators.

Report of the Committee Relating to the Destruction of
the Ursuline Convent. Boston, 1834. The committee of the city of Boston deplored the mob violence and asked reimbursement for the Ursuline
order.

Trial of John R. Buzzell before the Supreme Judicial
Court of Massachusetts for Arson and Burglary in
the Ursuline Convent in Charlestown. Boston,
1834. The best account of the trial of the con-

vent burners, filling more than 100 pages, and
giving the speeches and testimony in full.

Trial of John R. Buzzell, the Leader of the Convent
Rioters, for Arson and Burglary committed on
the Night of the 11th of August, 1834, by the
Destruction of the Convent on Mount Benedict
in Charlestown, Massachusetts. Boston, 1834.
Violently anti-Catholic in tone.

The Trial of Persons charged with Burning the Convent
in the Town of Charlestown (Mass.) before the
Supreme Judicial Court Holden at East Cambridge
on Tuesday, December 2, 1834. Boston, 1834. A
brief account of the trial.

The Trial of the Convent Rioters. Cambridge, 1834.
A brief account compiled from newspaper reports.

The Vision of Rubeta; an Epic Story of the Island of
Manhattan. Boston, 1838. An attack on William
L. Stone's investigation of the Hotel Dieu Con-
vent in satiric verse.

SECONDARY WORKS

Books

Abbott, Edith, Historical Aspects of the Immigration
Problem: Select Documents. Chicago, 1926.

Adams, James T., The Founding of New England. Boston, 1921.

----------------, New England in the Republic. Boston, 1927.

Adams, William F., Ireland and Irish Emigration to the New World from 1815 to the Famine. New Haven, 1932.

Bagenal, Philip H., The American Irish and their Influence on Irish Politics. Boston, 1882.

Baker, Thomas S., Lenau and Young Germany in America. Philadelphia, 1897. An excellent description of the radical activities and societies of German immigrants before the Civil War.

Bancroft, George, History of the United States of America. 6 vols., Boston, 1876.

Benjamin, Gilbert G., The Germans in Texas. Philadelphia, 1909.

Boese, Thomas, Public Education in the City of New York: its History, Condition and Statistics. New York, 1869. Contains a discussion of the Public School controversy.

Bourne, William, History of the Public School Society of the City of New York. New York, 1873. A detailed account of the history of the society by one of its avowed friends.

Bowers, Claude G., Jefferson and Hamilton. Boston, 1925.

Brann, Henry A., John Hughes. New York, 1892. A
brief account of Hughes' life of little value.

Brewer, Daniel C., The Conquest of New England by
the Immigrant. New York, 1926.

Bromwell, W. J., History of Immigration to the United
States. New York, 1856. Compiled statistics
for the period 1819-1856 of greatest value.

Bronwson, H. F., The Life of O. A. Brownson. 3 vols.,
Detroit, 1898-1900. A life of the Catholic editor written by his son, and filled with reproduc-
tions of documents.

Burns, James A., The Catholic School System in the
United States. New York, 1908.

Byrne, William, A History of the Catholic Church in
New England. 2 vols., Boston, 1899.

Byrne, Stephen, Irish Emigration to the United States;
What it has been and what it Is. New York, 1873.

Channing, Edward, A History of the United States.
6 vols., New York, 1905.

Chickering, Jesse, Immigration into the United States.
Boston, 1848. A criticism of the accuracy of
census returns by an able statistician.

Cobb, Sanford H., The Rise of Religious Liberty in
America. New York, 1902. The most valuable book
for a survey of the anti-Catholic feeling of colonial days.

Cornelison, Isaac, The Relation of Religion to Civil Government in the United States of America. New York, 1895. Many extracts from court decisions and state constitutions on legal status of Catholics.

Cullen, James B., The Story of the Irish in Boston. Boston, 1899.

Darling, Arthur B., Political Changes in Massachusetts, 1824-1848. New Haven, 1925.

Davis, Emerson, The Half Century; or, a History of Changes that have Taken Place, and Events that have Transpired, chiefly in the United States between 1800 and 1850. Boston, 1851. A handy reference work on the religious societies of the day, but untrustworthy.

Desmond, Humphrey J., The Know Nothing Party. Washington, 1904. A moderate account by a Catholic. Unbiased except when treating attacks on the Catholic church.

Dorchester, D., Christianity in the United States. New York, 1889.

Dwight, Henry Otis, The Centennial History of the American Bible Society. 2 vols., New York, 1916.

Fairchild, H. P., Immigration; a World Movement and its American Significance. New York, 1925.

Faulkner, H. U., American Economic History. New York,
     1924.

Faust, Albert B., The German Element in the United
     States. 2 vols., New York, 1927.

Fiske, John, Old Virginia and her Neighbors. 2 vols.,
     Boston, 1899.

Flom, G. T., History of Norwegian Immigration to the
     United States to 1848. Iowa City, 1909.

Flynn, Joseph M., The Catholic Church in New Jersey.
     Morristown, New Jersey, 1904.

Franklin, Frank G., The Legislative History of Naturali-
     zation in the United States. New York, 1906.

Freri, Joseph, The Society for the Propagation of the
     Faith and Catholic Missions, 1822-1900. Baltimore,
     1902. A brief history of the society with statis-
     tics on its growth in the United States.

Goodykoontz, Colin B., The Home Missionary Movement and
     the West, 1798-1861. Unpublished doctoral disserta-
     tion, Harvard University, 1920.

Guilday, Peter, The Life and Times of John England, First
     Bishop of Charleston, 1786-1842. 2 vols., New York,
     1927. A scholarly account of the entire Catholic
     church in America during the years treated.

--------------, A History of the Councils of Baltimore.
     New York, 1932.

Hall, Arthur J., Religious Education in the Public Schools of the State and City of New York; a Historical Study. Chicago, 1914.

Hall, Prescott F., Immigration and its Effects upon the United States. New York, 1907.

Hassard, J. R. G., The Life of the Most Reverend John Hughes. New York, 1866. Contains a wealth of material on the anti-Catholic movement and the part Hughes played in combating it.

Hay, M. V., The Chain of Error in Scottish History. New York, 1927. Much information on the origins of anti-Catholic sentiment at the time of the Reformation.

Headley, Joseph T., The Great Riots of New York, 1712-1873. New York, 1873. Description of election riots between foreigners and native Americans.

Hickey, Edward J., The Society for the Propagation of the Faith: its Foundations, Organization and Success. Washington, 1922.

Hitchins, Fred D., The Colonial Land and Immigration Commission. Philadelphia, 1931.

Humphrey, Edward F., Nationalism and Religion in America, 1774-1789. Boston, 1924.

Jarvis, Edward, Immigration into the United States. Boston, 1872.

Johnson, Stanley C., A History of Emigration from the
    United Kingdom to North America, 1763-1912.
    London, 1913.

Kapp, Friedrick, Immigration and the Commissioners of
    Emigration of the State of New York. New York,
    1870. A good statistical study of immigration,
    especially with reference to New York.

Kirlin, Joseph L. G., A History of the Catholic Church
    in Philadelphia. Philadelphia, 1906.

Leahy, William, The Catholic Church in New England, 2
    vols., Boston, 1899.

Macy, Jesse, Political Parties, 1840-1860. New York,
    1900.

Maury, Reuben, The Wars of the Godly. New York, 1928.
    A popularly written account of the anti-Catholic
    movement in the United States from colonial times
    to 1928.

McCain, James R., Georgia as a Proprietory Province.
    Boston, 1917.

McCarthy, Charles, The Anti-Masonic Party: a study of
    Political Antimasonry in the United States, 1827-
    1840. Washington, 1903.

McCoy, John, A History of the Catholic Church in the
    Diocese of Springfield. Boston, 1900.

McCrady, Edward, The History of South Carolina under

the Proprietory Government, 1670-1719. New York, 1901.

McMaster, John Bach, A History of the People of the United States from the Revolution to the Civil War. 8 vols., New York, 1910.

----------------, With the Fathers. New York, 1896. Contains an essay on "The Riotous Career of the Know Nothings."

Mereness, Newton D., Maryland as a Proprietory Province. New York, 1901.

Mott, Frank L., A History of American Magazines, 1741-1850. New York, 1930.

Monroe, James F., The New England Conscience. Boston, 1915.

Nevins, Allan, The American States During and after the Revolution, 1775-1789. New York, 1927.

O'Daniel, V. F., The Right Reverend Edward Dominic Fenwick, O. P., Founder of the Dominicans in the United States. Washington, 1920. Fenwick was a priest in Ohio and the first bishop of Cincinnati.

O'Gorman, Thomas, History of the Roman Catholic Church in the United States. (American Church History Series, vol. ix) New York, 1895.

Ollard, S. L., A Short History of the Oxford Movement. London, 1915.

Osgood, Herbert L., The American Colonies in the Seventeenth Century. 3 vols., New York, 1907.

---------------, The American Colonies in the Eighteenth Century. 4 vols., New York, 1924.

Palmer, A. Emerson, The New York Public School being a History of Free Education in the City of New York. New York, 1905.

Purcell, Richard J., Connecticut in Transition, 1775-1818. Washington, 1918.

Randall, S. S., History of the Common School System of the State of New York from its Origin in 1795 to the Present Time. New York, 1871.

Raper, Charles L., North Carolina; a Study in English Colonial Government. New York, 1904.

Roberts, Edward F., Ireland in America. New York, 1931.

Schlegel, F., The Philosophy of History. 2 vols., London, 1835. Lectures forming the basis for many of Samuel F. B. Morse's attacks on Catholicism.

Scisco, L. D., Political Nativism in the State of New York. (Columbia University Studies in History, vol. xiii, No. 2). New York, 1901.

Shaughnessy, Gerald, Has the Immigrant Kept the Faith: A Study of Immigration and Catholic Growth in the United States, 1790-1920. New York, 1925.

Shea, John Gilmary, History of the Catholic Church in

the United States. 4 vols., New York, 1886-1892.
Still the standard work on the history of the
church.

Smith, James W., History of the Catholic Church in
Woonsocket. Woonsocket, 1903.

Smith, R. Mayo, Emigration and Immigration. New York,
1895.

Stephenson, George M., A History of American Immigration, 1820-1924. Boston, 1926.

Sweet, W. W., The Story of Religions in America. New
York, 1930.

Thurston, Herbert, No Popery; Chapters on Anti Papal
Prejudice. London, 1930. A study of the anti-
Catholic nature of early historians.

Tiling, Moritz, The German Element in Texas, 1820-1850.
Houston, Texas, 1913.

Trowbridge, John, Samuel Finley Breese Morse. Boston,
1901. A concise treatment of the life of the inventor, only mentioning his anti-Catholic activities.

Verwyst, D. C., Life and Labors of the Right Reverend
Frederick Boroga. Milwaukee, 1900.

Von Holst, Hermann, Constitutional and Political History
of the United States. 8 vols., Chicago, 1885.

Warne, F. L., The Tide of Immigration. New York, 1916.

Webb, B. S., The Centenary of Catholicism in Kentucky,
    Louisville, 1884.

Whipple, Leon, The Story of Civil Liberty in the United
    States. New York, 1927. A bitter attack on the
    anti-Catholic agitators and parties, based on the
    better known historians.

Whitney, Louisa, The Burning of the Convent. A Narra-
    tive of the Destruction by a Mob of the Ursuline
    School on Mount Benedict, Charlestown, as Remem-
    bered by one of the Pupils. Boston, 1877. An
    account, written from memory, of life at the con-
    vent and of the burning, from the point of view of
    a Protestant pupil.

Williams, Michael, The Shadow of the Pope. New York,
    1932. A popular account of the entire anti-Cath-
    olic movement in the United States, stressing most
    the political campaign of 1928.

Wright, Richardson, Forgotten Ladies. Philadelphia,
    1928. Contains a biographical sketch of Maria
    Monk, written in popular style.

A Brief Account of the Friendly Sons of Saint Patrick;
    with Biographical Notices of Some of the Members
    and Extracts from the Minutes. Philadelphia, 1844.

The Catholic Encyclopaedia. 15 vols., New York, 1910.
    Many articles under "Hughes," "Bible Reading" etc.

describing events of the period. Good bibliographies of Catholic publications.

The Charlestown Convent; its Destruction by a Mob on the Night of August 11, 1834; with a History of the Excitement before the Burning, and the Strange and Exaggerated Reports Relating thereto, the Feeling of Regret and Indignation afterwards; the Proceedings of Meetings, and Expressions of the Contemporary Press. Boston, 1870. A thorough history of the convent burning.

The Life of the Reverend Herman Norton. New York, 1853. A survey of the life of Norton, long active in the anti-Catholic movement before the Civil War.

Memorial of the Reverend W. C. Brownlee, D. D., New York, 1860.

Articles

Brand, Carl F., "History of the Know Knothing Party in Indiana," Indiana Magazine of History, vol. 18 (1922). Deals with the origins of the party before 1845, as well as the later period.

Cole, Arthur C., "Nativism in the Lower Mississippi Valley," Mississippi Valley Historical Association Proceedings, vol. vi (1912-1913). One of the few published studies of nativism recognizing the social ramifications of the movement.

Condon, Edward M., "Irish Immigration to the United States since 1790," Journal of the American Irish Historical Society, vol. iv (1904). A statistical discussion showing that Irish immigration before the Civil War was larger than shown in census figures.

Condon, Peter, "Constitutional Freedom of Religion and Revivals of Religious Intolerance," United States Catholic Historical Society Records and Studies, vol. iv (1906), and vol. v, p. 2 (1909).

Connors, Francis J., "Samuel Finley Breese Morse and the anti-Catholic Political Movements in the United States," Illinois Catholic Historical Review, vol. x (October, 1927).

Cross, Ira, "The Origin, Principles and History of the American Party," Iowa Journal of History and Politics, vol. iv (1906). A sketchy account drawn from secondary sources.

Dohan, James H., "Our State Constitutions and Religious Liberty," American Catholic Quarterly Review, vol. xl (April, 1915). Deals with the religious provisions in state constitutions, especially in reference to Catholics.

Farrand, Max, "Immigration in the Light of History," The New Republic, December 23-December 29, 1916. Statistics on immigration before 1820.

Fitzgerald, James, "The Causes that Led to Irish Emigration," Journal of the American Irish Historical Society, vol. x (1911).

Foik, Paul J., "Anti-Catholic Parties in American Politics, 1776-1860," American Catholic Historical
Society of Philadelphia Records, vol. xxxvi (March,
1925). A prejudiced and sketchy history of nativistic political movements.

Gladden, Washington, "The Anti-Catholic Crusade," Century Magazine, March, 1894. Only a brief treatment
of the period before the Civil War.

Graham, J. E., "Anti-Catholic Prejudice, Ancient and Modern," Ecclesiastical Review, vol. 53 (1915).

Griffin, Martin I.J. "The Church of the Holy Trinity, Phil-
adelphia ... the First Opposition to Ecclesiastical
Authority," American Catholic Historical Society of
Philadelphia Records, vol. xxi, No. 1 (March, 1910).
An account of the conflict over trusteeism in this
church.

Hansen, Marcus L., "The Revolutions of 1848 and German
Emigration," Journal of Economic and Business History, vol. ii (1929-1930).

Haynes, G. H., "The Causes of Know Nothing Success in
Massachusetts," American Historical Review, vol.

iii (October, 1897). An excellent study of economic and social conditions in the state leading to nativism.

Hughes, T., "An Alleged Popish Plot in Pennsylvania,
1756-1757," American Catholic Historical Society
of Philadelphia Records, vol. x (1899).

Jenkins, T. J., "Know Nothingism in Kentucky and its
Destroyer," Catholic World, vol. lvii (July, 1893).
Of little value, ascribing to one Catholic editor
all credit for the failure of nativism in Kentucky.

Kofoid, Carrie P., "Puritan Influences in the Formative
Years of Illinois History," Transactions of the Illinois State Historical Society for 1905. Discusses
the anti-Catholic spirit of the people as a Puritan
influence.

Meehan, Thomas F., "New York's First Irish Emigrant Society," United States Catholic Historical Society
Records and Studies, vol. vi, (1913). An account
of the Irish Emigrant Society formed in New York
in 1817 to encourage Irish emigration to the middle west.

Morehouse, Frances, "The Irish Migration of the Forties,"
American Historical Review, vol. xxxiii (1927-1928).

Page, Thomas W., "Some Economic Aspects of Immigration
before 1870," Journal of Political Economy, vol.

xxi (January, 1913). A study of the effect of
foreign competition on American labor.

---------------, "The Transportation of Immigrants and
Reception Arrangements in the Nineteenth Century,"
Journal of Political Economy, vol. xix (November,
1911). An excellent study of this phase of immigration.

Payne, Raymond, "Annals of the Leopoldine Association,"
Catholic Historical Review, vol. i. Extracts from
the Berichte der Leopoldinen-Stiftung in Kaiser-
thume Oesterreich with a full explanation and notes
on the origin of the Association.

Rider, S. S., "Inquiry Concerning the Origin of the Clause
Disfranchising Roman Catholics," Rhode Island Historical Tracts, Second Series, No. 1. Discusses
the 18th century Rhode Island law against Catholics
and whether or not it was enacted in the 17th century by Williams.

Shea, John G., "Pope Day in America," United States Catholic Historical Magazine, vol. ii (January, 1888).
A good description of this New England institution.

Stauffer, V., New England and the Bavarian Illuminati,
Columbia University Studies in History, Economics
and Public Law, vol. 82. New York, 1918. Tells
of the part played by the father of Samuel Morse
against this movement.

Stephenson, George M., "Nativism in the Forties and Fifties with Special Reference to the Mississippi Valley," Mississippi Valley Historical Review, vol.ix (December, 1922) Largely political in its discussion.

Thompson, Mary P., "Anti-Catholic Laws in New Hampshire," Catholic World, vol. li (April and May, 1890). Devoted entirely to the colonial period and to the early constitutions.

Tucker, Ephraim, "The Burning of the Ursuline Convent," Worcester Society of Antiquity Collections, vol. ix. (1890). A history of the entire episode, showing decided anti-Catholic leanings.

Vogel, E. V., "Ursuline Nuns in America," Records of the American Catholic Historical Society, vol. i. A history of the order in America.

Walsh, J. J., "Keeping Up the Protestant Tradition," Catholic World, vol. ci (June, 1915). An account of the part in the nativistic movement played by Maria Monk and Samuel Morse.

Walsh, James S., "Some Religious Discussions in Philadelphia Just after the Revolution," American Catholic Historical Society of Philadelphia Records, vol. xvii (March, 1906). Describes the efforts of a Catholic priest to defend his religion before verbal attacks.

American Catholic Historical Researches. Pittsburg, 1884-1886, Philadelphia, 1887-1912. Contain a large amount of material on the anti-Catholic movement.

"Anti-Catholic Movements in the United States," Catholic World, vol. xxii (March, 1876). Describes in prejudiced fashion the Ursuline convent burning, the Philadelphia riots, and the growth of the Know Nothing party.

"The Anti-Catholic Spirit of the Revolution," American Catholic Historical Researches, vol. vi (October, 1889). An account of the general feeling against Catholics in the colonies during the Revolutionary period.

"Change in the Sentiments of the Revolutionists toward 'Popery' after the French Alliance," American Catholic Historical Researches, n.s. vol. v (January, 1909). Shows growth of spirit of toleration as result of alliance with Catholic France.

"The Destruction of the Ursuline Convent at Charlestown, Massachusetts," United States Catholic Historical Society Records and Studies, vol. ix (1916).

"An Early Philadelphia Catholic Truth Society," American Catholic Historical Society of Philadelphia Records, vol. xxxviii (March, 1927). Tells of society formed in 1827, the Society for the Defense of the Cath-

olic Religion from Calumny and Abuse.

"Fear of Catholicism in Colonial Pennsylvania, 1755-

1756," American Catholic Historical Researches,

vol. xvii (April, 1900). A discussion of the fear

of Catholicism aroused by the Seven Years War.

"Leisler's No-Popery Revolt in New York, 1690," American

Catholic Historical Researches, vol. xiv (July, 1897)

"Letters of Roger Williams Referring to 'Romanists' and

the 'Popish Leviathan,'" American Catholic Historical

Researches, n. s., vol. v, (January, 1909).

"Obstructions to Irish Immigration to Pennsylvania, 1736,"

Pennsylvania Magazine of History and Biography, vol.

xxi, (1897).

"The Philadelphia Riots," The New Englander, vol. 11 (1844).

A violent anti-Catholic description of the rioting

"Pope Day in the Colonies," American Catholic Historical

Researches, n.s., vol. iii (April, 1907).

"Projected Settlement West of Pennsylvania from which the

'Church of Rome' would have to be Excluded, 1754-

1774," American Catholic Historical Researches, n.s.,

vol. v (January, 1909). Description of a scheme for

settlement outlined by Samuel Hazard.

"The Temperance Movement and Father Theobold Mathew's

Visit to the United States, 1840-1851," United States

Catholic Historical Society Records and Studies, vol. vi (1911).

"The True History of Maria Monk," Catholic Truth Society Publications, vol. xix (1894).

"The Truth about Maria Monk," Watson's Magazine, May, 1916.

"The Very Reverend T. J. Donaghoe," American Catholic Historical Society of Philadelphia Records, vol. xxiii (June, 1912). An account of the life of the priest who was in charge of one of the churches burned during the Philadelphia rioting in 1844.

Pamphlets

O'Dwyer, George F., The Irish Catholic Genesis of Lowell. Lowell, 1920.

Schade, Lewis, Immigration into the United States from a Statistical and National Point of View. Washington, 1856. A statistical argument favoring unrestricted immigration. Contains a description of the burning of the Ursuline convent.

Tusca, Benjamin, Know Nothingism in Baltimore, 1854-1860. New York, 1925. A sketchy study, treating briefly the earlier activities of the Native American party.

Politics and People

The Ordeal of Self-Government in America

An Arno Press Collection

Allen, Robert S., editor. **Our Fair City.** 1947

Belmont, Perry. **Return to Secret Party Funds:** Value of Reed Committee. 1927

Berge, George W. **The Free Pass Bribery System:** Showing How the Railroads, Through the Free Pass Bribery System, Procure the Government Away from the People. 1905

Billington, Ray Allen. **The Origins of Nativism in the United States, 1800-1844.** 1933

Black, Henry Campbell. **The Relation of the Executive Power to Legislation.** 1919

Boothe, Viva Belle. **The Political Party as a Social Process.** 1923

Breen, Matthew P. **Thirty Years of New York Politics, Up-to-Date.** 1899

Brooks, Robert C. **Corruption in American Politics and Life.** 1910

Brown, George Rothwell. **The Leadership of Congress.** 1922

Bryan, William Jennings. **A Tale of Two Conventions:** Being an Account of the Republican and Democratic National Conventions of June, 1912. 1912

The Caucus System in American Politics. 1974

Childs, Harwood Lawrence. **Labor and Capital in National Politics.** 1930

Clapper, Raymond. **Racketeering in Washington.** 1933

Crawford, Kenneth G. **The Pressure Boys:** The Inside Story of Lobbying in America. 1939

Dallinger, Frederick W. **Nominations for Elective Office in the United States.** 1897

Dunn, Arthur Wallace. **Gridiron Nights:** Humorous and Satirical Views of Politics and Statesmen as Presented by the Famous Dining Club. 1915

Ervin, Spencer. **Henry Ford vs. Truman H. Newberry:** The Famous Senate Election Contest. A Study in American Politics, Legislation and Justice. 1935

Ewing, Cortez A.M. and Royden J. Dangerfield. **Documentary Source Book in American Government and Politics.** 1931

Ford, Henry Jones. **The Cost of Our National Government:** A Study in Political Pathology. 1910

Foulke, William Dudley. **Fighting the Spoilsmen:** Reminiscences of the Civil Service Reform Movement. 1919

Fuller, Hubert Bruce. **The Speakers of the House.** 1909

Griffith, Elmer C. **The Rise and Development of the Gerrymander.** 1907

Hadley, Arthur Twining. **The Relations Between Freedom and Responsibility in the Evolution of Democratic Government.** 1903

Hart, Albert Bushnell. **Practical Essays on American Government.** 1893

Holcombe, Arthur N. **The Political Parties of To-Day:** A Study in Republican and Democratic Politics. 1924

Hughes, Charles Evans. **Conditions of Progress in Democratic Government.** 1910

Kales, Albert M. **Unpopular Government in the United States.** 1914

Kent, Frank R. **The Great Game of Politics.** 1930

Lynch, Denis Tilden. **"Boss" Tweed:** The Story of a Grim Generation. 1927

McCabe, James D., Jr. (Edward Winslow Martin, pseud.) **Behind the Scenes in Washington.** 1873

Macy, Jesse. **Party Organization and Machinery.** 1912

Macy, Jesse. **Political Parties in the United States, 1846-1861.** 1900

Moley, Raymond. **Politics and Criminal Prosecution.** 1929

Munro, William Bennett. **The Invisible Government** and **Personality in Politics:** A Study of Three Types in American Public Life. 1928/1934 Two volumes in one.

Myers, Gustavus. **History of Public Franchises in New York City,** Boroughs of Manhattan and the Bronx. (Reprinted from **Municipal Affairs,** March 1900) 1900

Odegard, Peter H. and E. Allen Helms. **American Politics:** A Study in Political Dynamics. 1938

Orth, Samuel P. **Five American Politicians:** A Study in the Evolution of American Politics. 1906

Ostrogorski, M[oisei I.] **Democracy and the Party System in the United States:** A Study in Extra-Constitutional Government. 1910

Overacker, Louise. **Money in Elections.** 1932

Overacker, Louise. **The Presidential Primary.** 1926

The Party Battle. 1974

Peel, Roy V. and Thomas C. Donnelly. **The 1928 Campaign:** An Analysis. 1931

Pepper, George Wharton. **In the Senate** and **Family Quarrels:** The President, The Senate, The House. 1930/1931. Two volumes in one

Platt, Thomas Collier. **The Autobiography of Thomas Collier Platt.** Compiled and edited by Louis J. Lang. 1910

Roosevelt, Theodore. **Social Justice and Popular Rule:** Essays, Addresses, and Public Statements Relating to the Progressive Movement, 1910-1916 (*The Works of Theodore Roosevelt,* Memorial Edition, Volume XIX) 1925

Root, Elihu. **The Citizen's Part in Government** and **Experiments in Government and the Essentials of the Constitution.** 1907/1913. Two volumes in one

Rosten, Leo C. **The Washington Correspondents.** 1937

Salter, J[ohn] T[homas]. **Boss Rule:** Portraits in City Politics. 1935

Schattschneider, E[lmer] E[ric]. **Politics, Pressures and the Tariff:** A Study of Free Private Enterprise in Pressure Politics, as Shown in the 1929-1930 Revision of the Tariff. 1935

Smith, T[homas] V. and Robert A. Taft. **Foundations of Democracy:** A Series of Debates. 1939

The Spoils System in New York. 1974

Stead, W[illiam] T. **Satan's Invisible World Displayed,** Or, Despairing Democracy. A Study of Greater New York (The Review of Reviews Annual) 1898

Van Devander, Charles W. **The Big Bosses.** 1944

Wallis, J[ames] H. **The Politician:** His Habits, Outcries and Protective Coloring. 1935

Werner, M[orris] R. **Privileged Characters.** 1935

White, William Allen. **Politics:** The Citizen's Business. 1924

Wooddy, Carroll Hill. **The Case of Frank L. Smith:** A Study in Representative Government. 1931

Wooddy, Carroll Hill. **The Chicago Primary of 1926:** A Study in Election Methods. 1926